Lecture Notes in Computer Science 16494

The series Lecture Notes in Computer Science (LNCS), including its subseries Lecture Notes in Artificial Intelligence (LNAI) and Lecture Notes in Bioinformatics (LNBI), has established itself as a medium for the publication of new developments in computer science and information technology research, teaching, and education.

LNCS enjoys close cooperation with the computer science R & D community, the series counts many renowned academics among its volume editors and paper authors, and collaborates with prestigious societies. Its mission is to serve this international community by providing an invaluable service, mainly focused on the publication of conference and workshop proceedings and postproceedings. LNCS commenced publication in 1973.

Tsvetelina Plummer · Dennis Dubbert ·
Christopher Preschern
Editors

Pattern Languages of Programs, People and Practices

30th European Conference, EuroPLoP 2025
Irsee, Germany, July 2–6, 2025
Revised Selected Papers, Part II

Editors
Tsvetelina Plummer
NielsenIQ
Berlin, Germany

Dennis Dubbert
TH Köln
Gummersbach, Germany

Christopher Preschern
B&R Industrial Automation GmbH
Eggelsberg, Austria

ISSN 0302-9743 ISSN 1611-3349 (electronic)
Lecture Notes in Computer Science
ISBN 978-3-032-19156-4 ISBN 978-3-032-19157-1 (eBook)
https://doi.org/10.1007/978-3-032-19157-1

This Springer imprint is published by the registered company Springer Nature Switzerland AG
The registered company address is: Gewerbestrasse 11, 6330 Cham, Switzerland

Preface

EuroPLoP is the premier European conference on patterns and pattern languages. It is organized by Hillside Europe and is part of the PLoP conference series, which attracts pattern experts from all over the world. Patterns are a unique and effective way to capture and share expertise, tacit knowledge, and research findings.

EuroPLoP looks back at a wonderful series of 2 online editions on Discord (2020) and Gather.town (2021) and 28 editions of the conference that were all held at beautiful Kloster Irsee, Bavaria, Germany (1996–2019, 2022–2024). Thus, the year 2025 marked the 30th anniversary edition of the conference and we welcomed back many guests who have been an integral part of the community for years and decades.

What was most special in this edition was the meeting between many generations of scientists, seasoned practitioners but also pattern beginners and students from all over the world. Next to the many German participants, we had a lot of authors coming from the USA, the UK, Brazil, Portugal, Canada, Italy, Switzerland, Czechia, and more.

Unlike other conferences, EuroPLoP focuses on improving papers instead of only presenting them. Participants receive high-quality feedback in a constructive way that is used to improve their contributions before final publication.

Papers underwent a substantial amount of reviewing and supervision during the submission process. After an initial submission and a single blind peer-review we accepted the qualifying papers to an iterative shepherding process in which each paper is assigned an individual who will guide the authors in improving and polishing their work. This ensures the quality of the research and the presentation of the results are up to academic standards and can be shared with the wider pattern community. At the end of the shepherding process, another single blind review took place in which a final decision was made about which papers would be accepted to a writer's workshop during the conference. The feedback gathered during this workshop then helped the authors to further improve their papers before publication. Throughout the process, submissions received four reviews each, on average.

Next to pattern papers, we also welcomed submissions in the focus group category – these were also peer reviewed and could result in publication of a report if they met our criteria. The focus groups were aimed at participants who wanted to take more ownership in shaping the structure of their session – with it usually being an interactive workshop or a free exchange of experiences, aimed at collecting insights from the community. They generally served as catalysts for new papers, collaborations, or experiments/gathering of field data.

This year, we received 58 paper submissions, along with 15 focus group submissions. Of these, we are publishing 39 papers and 2 focus group reports.

Acknowledgements

We'd like to thank first Hillside Europe for their work in coordinating and helping the conference chairs to make this 30th EuroPLoP edition not only an excellent conference, but also such a great celebration.

Furthermore, we wish to thank Peter Sommerlad for his support as a sponsor, but also as a special guest, bringing us back to the origins of our community - with many memories, personal stories, and pictures that touched us.

Much heartfelt gratitude goes out to George Platts, who has shaped the culture of the community throughout so many years and now came to bring back fond memories and support us with his extraordinary energy and presence.

And last but not least, we are incredibly grateful to have had dpunkt Verlag as one of our sponsors, again making sure we could share with our participants the latest and most influential books from their publishing house.

July 2025

Tsvetelina Plummer
Dennis Dubbert
Christopher Preschern

Organization

EuroPLoP 2025 is organized by Hillside Europe e.V.
Christopher Preschern (President)
Christian Kohls (Vice-President)
Thomas Raser (Treasurer)

Chairs

Eduardo Guerra (Conference Chair)	Free University of Bozen-Bolzano, Italy
Tsvetelina Plummer (Program Chair)	NielsenIQ, Germany
Dennis Dubbert (Focus Group Chair)	Technische Hochschule Köln, Germany

Program Committee

Ademar Aguiar	University of Porto, FEUP, Portugal
Andreas Fießer	Independent Researcher, Germany
Anja Bertels	Technische Hochschule Köln, Germany
Apostolos Zarras	University of Ioannina, Greece
Cesare Pautasso	University of Lugano, Switzerland
Christopher Preschern	B&R Industrial Automation GmbH, Austria
Dan Zhu	Technische Hochschule Köln, Germany
Dennis Dubbert	Technische Hochschule Köln, Germany
Diego Moreira da Rosa	Federal Institute of Rio Grande do Sul, Brazil
Dominik Deimel	Technische Hochschule Köln, Germany
Elissaveta Gurova	Sofia University, Bulgaria
Frank Frey	Fiducia & GAD IT AG, Germany
Klaus Marquardt	Dräger Medical, Germany
Michael Weiss	Carleton University, Canada
Petr Pícha	University of West Bohemia, Czechia
Philipp Bachmann	iRIX Software Engineering AG, Switzerland
Ralf Laue	West Saxon University of Applied Sciences of Zwickau, Germany
Stefan Holtel	PricewaterhouseCoopers, Germany

Takashi Iba	Keio University, Japan
Thomas Epping	Leanovate, Germany
Tiago Boldt Sousa	University of Porto, FEUP, Portugal
Tsvetelina Plummer	NielsenIQ, Germany
Uwe van Heesch	HAN University of Applied Sciences, Netherlands
Uwe Zdun	University of Vienna, Austria
Valentino Vranić	Pan-European University, Slovakia
Veli-Pekka Eloranta	Vincit, Finland
Waheedullah Sulaiman Khail	Helmholtz-Zentrum Berlin für Materialien und Energie GmbH, Germany

Game Masters

Stefan Holtel	PricewaterhouseCoopers, Germany
Adrian Schuckart	PricewaterhouseCoopers, Germany

Shepherds

Ademar Aguiar
Aliaksandr Birukou
Allan Kelly
Andreas Fießer
Anja Bertels
Apostolos Zarras
Cesare Pautasso
Christian Engelmann
Christian Kohls
Christopher Preschern
Dan Zhu
Daniel Lübke
Dennis Dubbert
Diego Moreira da Rosa
Dina Salah
Dominik Deimel
Elissaveta Gourova
Fikret Basic
Filipe Correia
Frank Frey
João Daniel
Joelma Choma
Klaus Marquardt
Konomi Munakata
Mary Tedeschi
MaryLynn Manns
Michael Weiss
Mirko Stocker
Olaf Zimmermann
Paulo Queiroz
Petr Pícha
Philipp Bachmann
Ralf Laue
Rebecca Wirfs-Brock
Simon Schulte
Souhaila Serbout
Stefan Holtel
Takao Tomono
Takashi Iba
Thomas Epping
Thomas Raser
Tineke Jacobs
Uwe van Heesch
Uwe Zdun
Valentino Vranić
Veli-Pekka Eloranta
Victor Sauermann
Waheedullah Sulaiman Khail

Contents

Pattern Papers

Focus Group Reports

Appendix Paper

Pattern Papers

A Pattern for Analysing Data Usage Requirements in Data Sharing

Julia Pampus[1(✉)] and Maritta Heisel[2]

[1] Fraunhofer Institute for Software and Systems Engineering ISST, Dortmund, Germany
julia.pampus@isst.fraunhofer.de
[2] University of Duisburg-Essen, Duisburg, Germany
maritta.heisel@due.de

Abstract. A fundamental aspect of specifying data usage in the context of business-to-business data sharing is the definition of data usage conditions, technically represented as policies. Policies can be multifaceted and complex and are primarily used in a case dependent way. This often leads to challenges in the requirements engineering process, e.g., unclear requirements, complex representations, and/or inconsistent interpretations of policies. To address these problems, we introduce the *Data Usage Policy* pattern that defines the syntax of policies in data sharing. The pattern helps with the structured elicitation and analysis of data usage conditions and enables the creation of a consistent system design. We derive six pattern primitives and a policy grammar from scientific literature and existing requirements of four selected dataspace initiatives, that show a high level of technical maturity, and present them along with a three-step process for policy analysis. We demonstrate the applicability of our contributions with an application example.

Keywords: Policies · Data sharing · Requirements engineering · Data spaces

1 Introduction

Data is of enormous value within businesses nowadays. However, it usually has to leave its source system to serve value creation [15]. To establish a trusted data infrastructure with shared governance and the technical capabilities for transferring and utilising data, dataspaces have emerged as a trend in various domains such as healthcare, automotive, and energy [17]. These initiatives aim for what is known as *data sovereignty*. Data sovereignty is defined as "the self-determination of [...] organizations with regard to the use of their data" [11, p.550]. As a key aspect of establishing data sovereignty, data sharing systems focus on defining data usage conditions in the form of policies, negotiating these, and enforcing them throughout data transfer and usage, employing mechanisms for usage control and traceability. Thereby, policies represent the functional requirements that data sharing participants, acting as providers and/or consumers, pose in data usage. Within dataspaces, these requirements and their

T. Plummer et al. (Eds.): EuroPLoP 2025, LNCS 16494, pp. 3–27, 2026.
https://doi.org/10.1007/978-3-032-19157-1_1

implementation are the key to a trusted environment, at the organisational and technical level. Independent from their technical representation, e.g., using the Open Data Rights Language (ODRL), policies are rules that define certain properties (usually constraints), e.g., for the geographical environment, the involved actors, time, and/or data handling. For example, a data sharing participant may state that data should only be used for a specific 'purpose' respectively context, such as research.

Current approaches elaborate on the requirements for trusted data sharing [2,8,18], the representation of data usage conditions as policies [9], and the technical approaches for enforcing these policies [16]. However, to the best of our knowledge, the research community so far has not addressed the analysis of policies during the requirements engineering process to ensure their syntactic accuracy, along with guided elicitation and conflict management. Therefore, we pose the following research question (RQs).

- RQ1: How can policies in business-to-business data sharing be structured?
- RQ2: How can the correctness and consistency of policies be ensured in the requirements engineering process?

We follow a pattern-based approach to address these questions. Patterns facilitate identifying, analysing, and structuring requirements by capturing best practices and experiences from previous projects. Therefore, patterns are a common technique in requirements engineering, especially for the elicitation and analysis processes [12]. In this paper, we propose a composite pattern whose building blocks are grounded in know uses. Our work comprises two main contributions:

- We propose the *Data Usage Policy (DUP)* pattern, including a conceptual model for policies and a policy grammar.
- We define a three-step policy analysis (elicitation, decomposition, and conflict analysis) that specifies the usage and validation of the DUP pattern.

These contributions can be used by policy engineers or data stewards to enable a structured elicitation and analysis of data usage requirements and, thus, support the correct handling and implementation of requirements from diverse participants within business-to-business data sharing. By focusing on the context of business-to-business data sharing, we exclude end-user-centered processes and requirements.

The remainder of this paper is structured as follows: Sect. 2 introduces the background knowledge for this work. Next, in Sect. 3, we present our main contribution, the DUP pattern, whose implementation we describe and discuss in Sects. 4 and 5. Afterwards, we compare our approach to related work in Sect. 6. Lastly, we answer the RQs and conclude our work in Sect. 7.

2 Fundamentals

This section describes the basic concepts of our pattern, including agendas in software development, some concrete approaches to managing conflicting requirements, and a common architecture for enforcing policies.

2.1 Agendas in Software Development

Agendas are patterns for systematically structuring a procedure for developing a software artefact [7], including the phase of requirements engineering. An agenda consists of multiple steps that are performed sequentially and have one or multiple *input* and *output* values. To make its application effective in practice, the correct implementation of the procedure is validated by verifying the output values with regard to defined conditions, namely *validation condition*. These validation condition can be defined for each step or for the overall process. For example, a step 'elicite requirements' could have unstructured requirements (text) as input and structured requirements (template) as output. A validation condition may define mandatory attributes of the template, ensuring that next steps that further use the created template can be executed properly. We make use of agendas to define the process of analysing policies while making use of our pattern.

2.2 Managing Conflicting Requirements

Conflict management is an important aspect of requirements engineering that enhances the development of software systems [1]. It involves identifying and resolving conflicting interests to maximise stakeholder satisfaction on all sides. Although approaches to conflict management can vary based on the context, most are grounded in a mathematical framework. This framework typically includes a selection of aspects, also referred to as decision variables [23], along with their respective weightings. For example, Mitchell et al. [13] suggest that stakeholders can be prioritised based on their power, legitimacy, and urgency. By evaluating these attributes, we can assign priority values to each factor in the conflict resolution process. Conflicts are then systematically resolved by considering both the weights of the stakeholders involved and the number of stakeholders affected [1]. We adopt this approach in our work.

2.3 XACML Architecture

In our work, we refer to the architecture of the Extensible Access Control Markup Language (XACML) for describing the usage of our policy pattern. XACML [22] is a standard for defining access control policies in a machine-readable format. Its architecture structures policy enforcement across various systems and applications, enabling centralised access control management. Thereby, it defines four conceptual components that are required for policy enforcement, depicted in

Fig. 1: The *policy administration point (PAP)* includes policy creation, editing, and storage tools. In the context of trust-based data sharing, this means both the provisioning of data offers and the negotiation of policy agreements. The *policy enforcement point (PEP)* intercepts data flows and enforces the policy validation by the policy decision point (PDP) to process resulting decisions. The *PDP* evaluates policies by validating agreements against context information retrieved by the *policy information point (PIP)* and returns decisions (permit or deny) to the PEP. The PIP provides context information required for policy evaluation by retrieving attributes from external systems, e.g., about actors or environmental conditions.

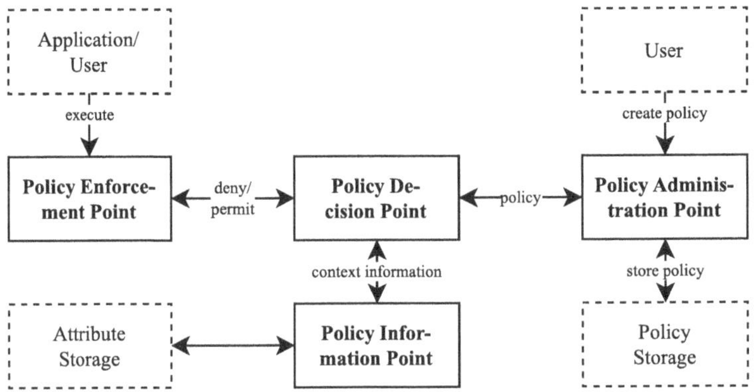

Fig. 1. XACML Architecture [22]. This model illustrates the interactions between four policy systems and to other interfaces (storage, application, user).

3 Data Usage Policy Pattern

The main contribution of this paper is a pattern that helps in decomposing data usage requirements. This pattern can be used for a template-based elicitation of requirements and their analysis, including conflict resolution (cf. Sect. 4). Our approach contributes to a systematic requirements engineering process and the subsequent technical design of data sharing systems that aim to establish the sovereignty of data sharing participants while putting the focus on policy definitions and implementations.

We structure the presentation of our pattern according to the guidelines provided by the EuroPLoP community[1], elaborating on the context in Sect. 3.1, problem and forces in Sect. 3.2, solution in Sect. 3.3, and consequences in Sect. 5.

[1] https://www.europlop.net/patterns/ (accessed on 2025-01-05).

3.1 Context

An organisation has decided to share data with others. The process of data sharing involves at least two actors, one providing the data and one consuming it. The data on the provider-side is enriched with metadata including policies, building a dataset. These policies describe how data should be used, independent from their technical representation. Multiple policies can be added to the same dataset. The systems that are used to share and process the data must be able to enforce these policies.

To apply the pattern, we rely on the elicitation of data usage requirements. Data usage requirements have been elicited in natural language, either as plain text or following a template such as our constraint template [19].

3.2 Problem and Forces

How can semantic interoperability of data usage requirements be ensured in decentralised environments? How can validation and conflict resolution be supported throughout the requirements engineering process?

Although policies are central to trust-based business-to-business data sharing, they are often treated superficially in existing use cases. In both literature and practice, very little attention is paid to the structured analysis of policies during requirements engineering, particularly in the design phase of data sharing systems. Current technical solutions primarily focus on simple data usage permissions and prohibitions.

Referring to our example from Sect. 1, the purpose-restricted policy is simplified to the validation of an organisation on data access in real-world dataspaces like Catena-X[2]. Catena-X is a collaborative network in the automotive industry designed to create a standardised data ecosystem for enhanced data sharing and interoperability across the value chain. By restricting the access to a verified contractual partner, it is demanded that data processing takes place according to the defined purpose. When implementing policy enforcement, thus, selective access control often replaces the validation of the policy during the actual data usage.

- *Compliance*: Policies typically arise from organisational conditions or legal regulations, which are often expressed in human-readable text. These formulations follow standards and can be verified for legal accuracy and completeness. However, there is no clear guidance on which parts of these conditions and regulations can be mapped to technical policies and how they can be verified for completeness and quality. For example, a 'purpose' is difficult to describe or verify technically. However, it can be narrowed down to the use of a specific algorithm in data processing or a specific application. These conditions can be verified technically.

[2] https://catena-x.net/ (accessed on 2025-02-01).

- *Know-how*: The inadequate analysis of policies partly originates from a lack of understanding of a holistic end-to-end data sovereignty, presumably because no domain-specific software engineering methods are available. Currently existing dataspace solutions consider usage control and, thus, policy enforcement to be a nice-to-have or even a costly liability. The technical representation to express policies in dataspaces is ODRL [10]. While ODRL allows for a very precise technical expression of how data can be used, it is also complex and requires a high level of technical understanding. Therefore, the initial step of formulating data usage conditions as ODRL policies by individuals lacking ontology expertise is unrealistic. Returning to our example, it is important to clarify all aspects of a policy in order to be able to break down a 'purpose' technically.
- *Conflict identification & resolution*: In the existing implementation scenarios of policies, neither conflict identification nor resolution occurs. The requirements formulated by the data provider or the dataspace initiative (cf. Sect. 3.1) are taken for granted. This approach corresponds to a consent technique: the provider specifies the policy, and the consumer consents to it. Consequently, every data sharing system that wants to participate in such a data exchange must implement the entire set of policies that has been specified without further negotiation or analysis. Possible conflicts and their resolutions are not further considered. In the case of purpose-limited data usage, conflict resolution becomes increasingly difficult, as the interpretation of a 'purpose' is subjective. A structured comparison of two interpretations of a purpose can only be achieved through technical specifications.
- *Policy enforcement*: Different data sharing systems do not necessarily address the consistent enforcement of policies in decentralised environments [8]. A common assumption is that the policies attached to a shared dataset are defined by the data provider and, thus, must be implemented primarily in the consumer system. However, both data sharing participants can formulate data usage conditions at design time and runtime [18]. Therefore, it must be possible to analyse single components of a policy and design an appropriate system architecture. For example, the implementation of a purpose-restricted data usage policy may require a pre-processing in the provider's system.

To address the challenges of handling data usage requirements in business-to-business data sharing, we propose a structured policy pattern.

3.3 Solution

Structure policies independent from their technical representation, according to five core elements: data, action, actor, environment, and time. Make use of a grammar that helps to technically validate data usage requirements.

By ensuring consistency and accuracy in defining data usage requirements, this approach enhances compliance and aids in conflict resolution throughout the requirements engineering process, leading to improved collaboration and trust in data sharing.

This section is structured as follows: In Sect. 3.3, we present a conceptual model for policies that serves as a basis for our pattern. First, we outline the pattern structure, then, we describe its elements.

Policy Model. Figure 2 depicts a conceptual model that visualises the main policy components addressed in trust-based data sharing: the data itself (e.g., raw, anonymised), allowed or enforced actions (e.g., processing, deletion, distribution), and constraints of different types: the involved actors, their environment (e.g., organisation, system, location), or temporal conditions (e.g., time interval, date).

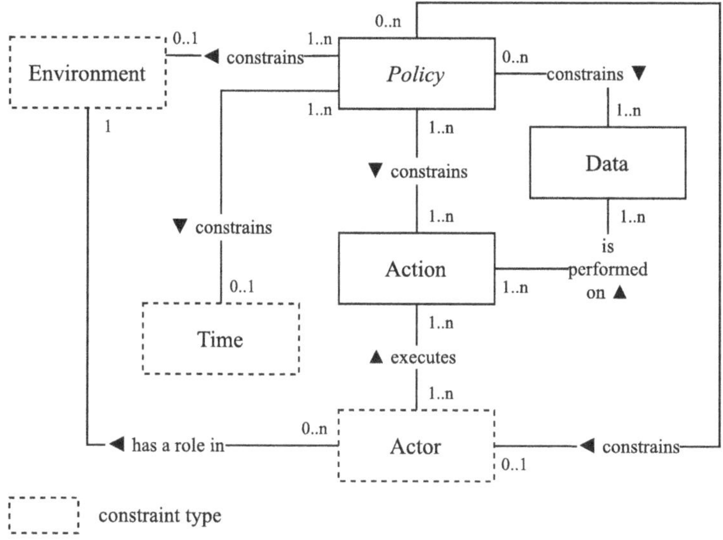

Fig. 2. Conceptual Model for Policies. It depicts five entities and their relations affecting a data usage policy.

Therefore, this model includes the entities data, action, time, actor, and environment related to the overall type *policy*. According to the ODRL [10], as one of the widely used policy representations in industrial data sharing, a policy describes the permissions, prohibitions, and duties of data usage.

- *Data* serves, next to the Policy, as the central element in this model. It is modified by Actions and can be constrained by Policies. In terms of representation, Data can exist in different forms, such as a single file or a data stream; it can also describe access to a system. Data can also be metadata for other data.

- An *Action* describes one or more operations that can be executed on a single or many Data. It can be of type *use*, but can also specify more detailed usages or duties. Examples can be found in the ODRL vocabulary[3], such as 'use', 'copy', or 'delete'. An Action is constrained by one to many Policies.
- An *Actor* is a human person or a system that executes an Action performed on Data. It is part of one or many Environments and can have one or multiple roles in these Environments. An Actor may be constrained by a Rule that limits possible Actions to their assigned attributes.
- An *Environment* refers to the organisational or system landscape in which Data is transferred and/or processed. It may delineate the roles that Actors can assume within that Environment or define some geographical boundaries.
- *Time* describes the temporal constraints of an Action. It can define a time interval, a point in time, or a frequent event.

In summary, a policy constrains data and actions that are performed on data. If the data usage should be restricted to a specific purpose, the policy may have zero to three constraints (environment, actor, and/or time).

Pattern Structure. Our DUP pattern builds upon the conceptual model for policies presented in Fig. 2. It comprises the definition of six pattern primitives (permission, prohibition, duty, actor, environment, time), classified into two types (action and constraint), and a context-free grammar to specify the policy syntax.

Pattern Primitives. Each policy consists of two main pattern primitives, an *action* and a *constraint*, each with three sub-types, as depicted in Fig. 3. In summary, we define six recurring pattern primitives of two types. The pattern primitives of type *action* focus on the specification of a policy's action, covering permission, prohibition, or duty (cf. Sect. 3.3). The pattern primitives of type *constraint* describe a particular constraint type: actor, environment, and time (cf. Fig. 2). Figure 3 presents the hierarchy of the pattern primitives, leading to a policy structure pattern.

Policy Grammar. We present expressions of the DUP pattern's structure as productions of a context-free grammar, using an extended Backus-Naur form as notation, with start symbol P for Policy. Each instance of the pattern defines one mandatory pattern primitive of type action A and an optional pattern primitive of type constraint C, as defined in Production 1.

$$P ::= A\,[C] \tag{1}$$

$$C ::= C_A \,|\, C_E \,|\, C_T \tag{2}$$

$$A ::= data\ action\_type \tag{3}$$

[3] https://www.w3.org/TR/odrl-vocab/#action (accessed on 2025-01-05).

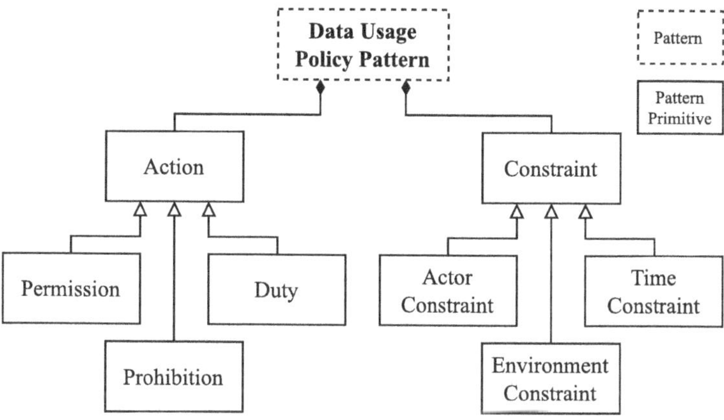

Fig. 3. Structure of the *Data Sharing Policy* Pattern. It shows the composition of the pattern consisting of two types of pattern primitives, an action and a constraint, as well as their sub-types.

$$data\text{::} = \text{String} \tag{4}$$

$$action\_type :: = permission \,|\, prohibition \,|\, duty \tag{5}$$

There, the pattern primitive of type action A and the pattern primitive of type constraint C are non-terminal symbols that are detailed with further productions. A pattern primitive of type constraint C consists of one of the non-terminal types C_A (actor constraint), C_E (environment constraint), or C_T (time constraint) (see Production 2). A pattern primitive of type action A consists of a *data* followed by an *action_type* (see Production 3), where the *data* is described by a String (see Production 4), and an *action_type* consists of one of the non-terminal types *permission*, *prohibition*, or *duty* (see Production 5). Their productions are further refined in the following pattern descriptions.

Action Types. All instances of our DUP pattern can be transferred into a system design using the XACML architecture. However, the interactions between the system components and their temporal sequence differ depending on the policy. We use a unified sequence diagram to visualise the data access respecting validating all policy types at runtime in Fig. 4. In this diagram, we omit the policy and attribute storage from Fig. 1 for simplicity, as they do not contribute to the overall comprehension. To showcase the application of a policy, we assume that it has been created or negotiated beforehand. Thus, in our context, the *policy* represents a policy agreement already reached. The objects and actors in the sequence diagram are used for illustration purposes and do not imply any conclusions about the system architecture.

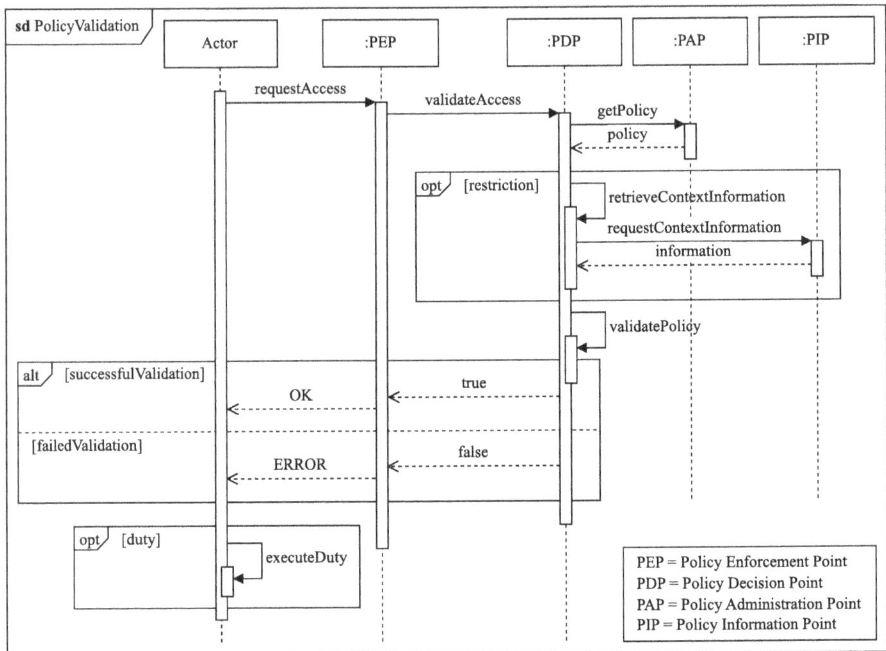

Fig. 4. Simplified Sequence Diagram for Data Access. It illustrates the interactions between the policy systems of the XACML architecture during policy validation. It shows different scenarios, a successful validation and a failed validation. It also provides for the optional retrieval of context information and the optional execution of duties.

Permission. Data may be used in a defined manner, including a specific (mandatory) action of type *permission.* Constraints of actors, environments, or time are optional (see Production 1). As depicted in Fig. 4, the number of the system interactions is limited since, depending on the request, an 'okay' is returned, and the data can be used. Considering data usage conditions that are applied in practice (cf. Table 5), policies without constraints are rare. For example, a policy could define data as being used by everyone in every context (R20) or allow general data distribution by stating, 'Data can be distributed'. For applying the policy grammar, the list of allowed *permissions* in Production 6 would need to be defined, e.g., as the set of ODRL Actions [10] or by using another list of actions.

$$permission ::= ODRL\_ACTIONS \tag{6}$$

Prohibition. A particular action must not be executed; this includes specific actions or concrete operations. The system prohibits the request for data access for the black-listed actions. Taking a look at Fig. 4, this means that, e.g., if data must not be distributed (R07, Table 5), the access would be denied if the request was already indicating a policy violation according to provided attributes. In contrast to a permission policy, a prohibition is challenging to implement. The system interactions are likely to become more complex. For defining prohibited data usage, the policy action must be of type *prohibition* and the production must be further defined (see Production 7).

$$prohibition ::= ODRL\_ACTIONS \tag{7}$$

Duty. Executing an action is required, necessarily associated with a constraint referring to the data usage, e.g., before or after using the data (R12, Table 5), the actor, or the environment. Therefore, when defining an action of type *duty*, a constraint must be defined, too, see Production 8. As shown in Fig. 4, after data access has been granted, a duty must be performed before, during, or after data usage (as stated in the constraint). For example, a policy could define that data usage must be logged (R06) or data must be anonymised before usage (R01). Along with permissions and prohibitions, the production starting with *duty* in Production 8 must be completed.

$$duty ::= ODRL\_ACTIONS \tag{8}$$

Constraint Types. Our DUP pattern includes three constraint types: actor, environment, and time.

Actor. The actor who uses the data is restricted based on properties, e.g., identity or role. As specified in Productions 9 to 11, they must be of type *system* (R03, Table 5) or *human* (R14) both described as a String. As shown in Fig. 4, the PIP validates the attributes included in the initial request to take a final decision.

$$C_A ::= human \mid system \tag{9}$$

$$human ::= \text{String} \tag{10}$$

$$system ::= \text{String} \tag{11}$$

Environment. The environment of type *system* or *organisation* consisting of a String (see Productions 12 to 14) in which the data is used is restricted based on properties, e.g., the identity (R23, Table 5) or security attributes (R16). In Fig. 4, the same simplified flow applies, as to every other constraint.

$$C_E ::= organisation \mid system \tag{12}$$

$$organisation ::= \text{String} \tag{13}$$

$$system ::= \text{String} \tag{14}$$

Time. This pattern primitive describes a time frame for data usage or a temporal trigger for some required action. For example, a policy could state that data must be deleted at a defined datetime (R13, Table 5) or that data must be deleted periodically (R11). Overall, the time specification must be of type *one-time* or *repeating* described as a String (see Productions 15 to 17).

$$C_T ::= \textit{one-time} \,|\, \textit{repeating} \tag{15}$$

$$\textit{one-time} ::= \text{String} \tag{16}$$

$$\textit{repeating} ::= \text{String} \tag{17}$$

In practice, a policy can either focus on one aspect of data usage or combine multiple of them at once (cf. Sect. 3.1). In this work, when describing a policy, we refer to it as a single constraint (also ODRL Rule) and ignore possible nestings. Therefore, as defined in Production 2, the presented grammar does not allow for a combination of multiple constraints within one policy. We assume that multiple policies (with different constraints) can be added to one dataset.

4 Implementation

The DUP pattern provides a solid foundation for a structured policy analysis process that we present in the following, complemented by an application example.

4.1 Policy Analysis Process

For a structured policy analysis process, we define an agenda (cf. Sect. 2.1) divided into three steps, as shown in Fig. 5: first, the policies must be elicited; next, policy patterns are decomposed; and finally, occurring conflicts are analysed and resolved. We conclude each section with a validation condition VC to verify whether the policy analysis has been conducted correctly and the defined policy grammar has been respected.

Policy Elicitation. From the policy model in Fig. 2, we derive a policy template shown in Table 1. In addition to the *component*, *type*, and *value*, we provide some guiding questions. The component types reflect the terms from the policy grammar. As it is not relevant for the further processing of the pattern, the difference between data and metadata is not addressed in the grammar.

The template is instantiated in the first step of the policy analysis process in Fig. 5. Each step of this process further refines the policies according to the instantiated templates, as they continue to be filled and extended. We demonstrate this procedure in Sect. 4.2. If no requirements have been collected in advance, this template can also be used to identify initial requirements.

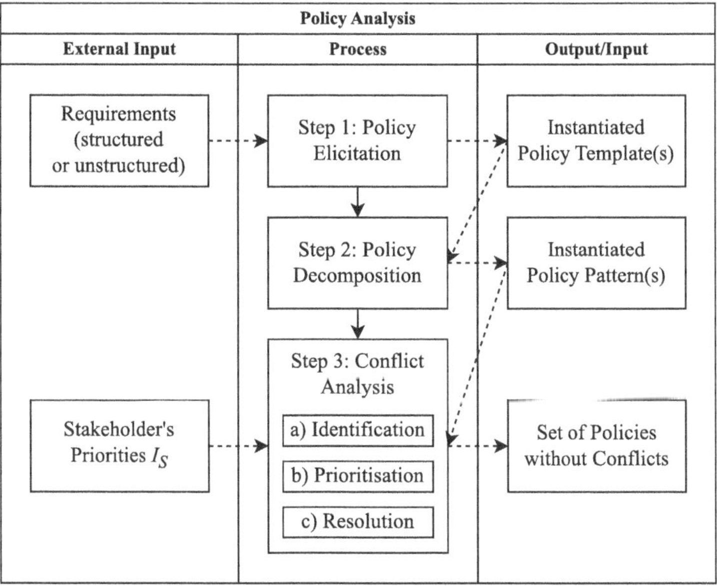

Fig. 5. Policy Analysis Process. This process includes three steps that process stakeholder input and produce structured requirements.

VC01. For each policy, exactly one policy template has been instantiated.

Policy Decomposition. Next, based on the created policy templates, the DUP pattern is instantiated. This instantiation uses the policy grammar from Sect. 3.3. Following Production 1, every policy must contain one data and one action component, conforming to exactly one pattern primitive of type action. In addition, each policy can comply with an additional pattern primitive of type action constraint. The results of this step is an extended policy template. If a policy does not comply with the rules of the grammar, it is considered to be either incomplete or incorrect. Thus, it must be revised in collaboration with the owning stakeholder, returning to Step 1.

VC02. Each policy must be an instance of the DUP pattern.

Conflict Analysis. With the help of the instantiated templates and policies, it is possible to easily compare individual policies to identify and resolve occurring conflicts. The conflict analysis consists of three main aspects: a) identification, b) prioritisation, and c) resolution (cf. Fig. 5). As multiple policies may target the same dataset, we assume that the providing and consuming data sharing participants ensure that the policies they have defined themselves do not contain any conflicts. Therefore, conflicts may only arise between the policies of the data

Table 1. Policy Template.

Component	Type	Value
data	*What data is the target of the policy?* ☐ data ☐ metadata	[...]
action	*What action is described?* ☐ permission ☐ prohibition ☐ duty	[...]
actor	*Are there any actor constraints?* ☐ human ☐ system	[...]
environment	*Are there any environment constraints?* ☐ organisation ☐ system	[...]
time	*Are there any time constraints?* ☐ one-time ☐ repeating	[...]

provider and those of the data consumer. In general, these conflicts are most likely of type modality, occurring when two policies target the same data with the same action but with contradicting permissions and prohibitions [3].

Identification. We identify two specific indicators of a conflict, one based on the action type and the other on the constraint type. An *action type conflict* arises if multiple policies refer to the same *data* and *action* but with a different type of action. For example, the provider defines that data must not be distributed (R07, Table 5), and the consumer defines that they want to share the data with a third-party (R10). A *constraint type conflict* occurs if multiple policies refer to the same *data* and (type of) *action* but with different restrictions of the same type. For example, a data provider requires the data to be deleted after three months, and the data consumer foresees a deletion after six months.

Prioritisation. Once a conflict has been identified, it should be resolved. In doing so, multiple factors must be considered, e.g., the involved stakeholders and the priority of their requirements (policies). We define the following sub-process for approaching a successful conflict resolution (cf. Fig. 6).

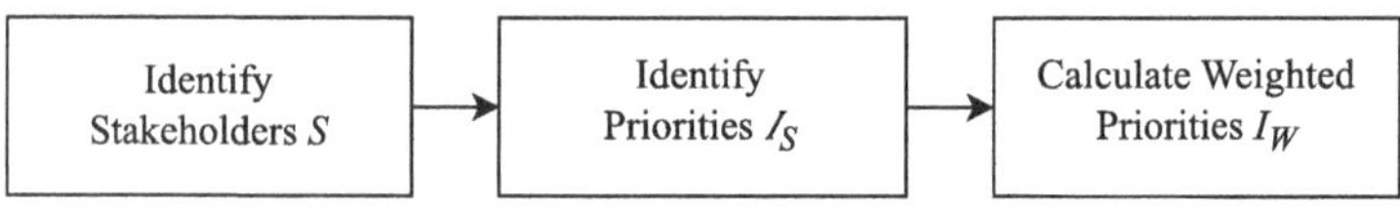

Fig. 6. Process of Resolving a Policy Conflict. This process includes three steps that need to be performed for resolving conflicting requirements.

1. *Identify stakeholders*: First, it is documented who the owner of each policy is. We assume a simple, bilateral data sharing scenario involving a provider

and a consumer. The provider expresses the conditions under which they are willing to share their data, and the consumer defines what they want to do with it. Since some of the policies may arise from regulations, we refer to the latter as a third stakeholder.
Each stakeholder has a weighting W_S: As the data source, the data provider may ultimately decide whether the data is shared. Therefore, the provider, with factor *2*, is weighted stronger than the consumer with factor *1*. Since regulations have an even higher impact, they are weighted with factor *3*.
2. *Identify priorities*: Each policy must be assigned a priority I_S. Amroune et al. [1] use a scale from 1 to 5 in their approach (cf. Sect. 2.2); we simplify this to 1 (low priority), 2 (medium priority), and 3 (high priority).
3. *Calculate weighted priorities*: The weighting of each policy is calculated based on the assigned stakeholders S, their weightings W_S, and the defined priorities I_S. The calculation is a simple multiplication of priorities and stakeholder weightings: $I_W = I_S * W_S$.

Resolution. Finally, a conflict resolution strategy must be chosen. Essentially, policies with a higher weighting are preferred over those with a lower weighting, which leads to one of the following resolution strategies. We assume that the provider's policies form the basis and that these are adapted according to the chosen strategy, or that all resulting (non-conflicting) policies are part of a data offering.

- *Extended scope*: Data can be used for more than originally intended (by the data provider). For example, data can be used for multiple purposes or a greater duration.
- *Reduced scope*: Data can be used for less than originally intended (by the data provider). For example, the consumer introduces a deletion strategy that the provider did not include in the first place.
- *No changes*: Data sharing adheres to the data provider's policy. For example, the consumer wants another price for a dataset, but the provider does not provide any options to negotiate.
- *No sharing*: Data will not be shared under the stated conditions. This scenario could happen if a provider defines a policy the consumer cannot or does not want to implement.

If policies provide have priority, both stakeholders manually negotiate a resolution strategy. In addition, assuming that data usage conditions can always be negotiated in a negotiation process (either at design time or at runtime), we consider the calculated weightings as a tendency towards the best possible conflict resolution. The provider can withdraw their data offering at any time without explanation.

VC03. A group of policies targeting the same dataset do not show any conflict.

4.2 Application Example

We evaluate our DUP pattern using an application example that represents a simple and typical data sharing scenario, adopted from Pampus and Heisel [19]: A delivery service aims to optimise delivery routes and combine shipments from various suppliers to supermarkets by utilising the suppliers' delivery information to calculate the carbon footprint. The delivery service serves as the data consumer and the supplier as the data provider.

The application example introduces four policies that we examine in the following.

- Data can be used to calculate the carbon footprint (P01).
- Data must be deleted after six months (P02).
- Data may not be passed on to other suppliers (P03).
- Every data transaction must be recorded and preserved for three years (P04).

We use the policies to demonstrate how the DUP pattern can be used for requirements elicitation and analysis including conflict resolution.

Policy Elicitation. As part of the requirements elicitation, i.e., as a first step of the requirements analysis (cf. Sect. 4.1), the policies are identified in a structured way by instantiating the template from Table 1. As the specified pattern does not provide for a combination of policies, we split policy P04 into two separate policies: one describes the actual logging activity (P04a) and the other states when the logs should be deleted (P04b). For demonstration purposes, Table 2 provides an instantiated policy template for P04a. The instance of the DUP pattern is described in Eq. 18.

$$
\begin{aligned}
P &\rightarrow A C \\
A &\rightarrow data\ action\_type \\
data &\rightarrow \text{“data transaction”} \\
action\_type &\rightarrow duty \\
duty &\rightarrow \text{“record”} \\
C &\rightarrow C_T \\
C_T &\rightarrow repeating \\
repeating &\rightarrow \text{“on data usage”}
\end{aligned}
\tag{18}
$$

Pattern Decomposition. Next, we can derive the policy patterns (one or many) according to the grammar. Here, the table format of the policy template helps with identifying the types of policy components.

- Policy P01 describes a 'purpose' that can be technically specified as a processing action *calculate* bound to an application for assessing the carbon footprint. The application represents the actor of type *system*. The result is an instance of the DUP pattern with a permission pattern primitive and an actor pattern primitive.

Table 2. Instantiated Policy Template (cf. Table 1) for P04a.

Component	Type	Value
data	☐ data ■ metadata	data transaction
action	☐ permission ☐ prohibition ■ duty	record
actor	☐ human ☐ system	–
environment	☐ organisation ☐ system	–
time	☐ one-time ■ repeating	on data usage

- Policy P02 describes an action that must be executed after a given time frame. This time restriction focuses on an event that happens once. This results in an instance of the DUP pattern with a duty pattern primitive and an time pattern primitive.
- Policy P03 describes a restriction of actors allowed to receive the data as a third-party. The instantiated pattern combines a prohibition and an environment restriction as the organisation represents the environment.
- Policies P04a and P04b describe an action that must be executed periodically. The instantiated patterns for both policies contain a duty pattern primitive and a time pattern primitive.

Following the productions of the policy grammar, in this step, we can verify the completeness and correctness of the elicited policies according to VC01 to VC03 (see Sect. 4.1). For example, if P02 missed a restriction, it would not be a valid policy. The results of this analysis step are listed in Table 3. Due to limited space, we have shortened the table to exclude the type column as used in Table 2. The pattern instances are listed in Table 4.

Conflict Analysis. In the following, we introduce policy conflicts by adding requirements of the data consumer (delivery service) to the set of policies.

- The data should be used for research purposes (P06).
- The data must be deleted after three months (P07).
- The data must be distributed to other suppliers (P08).
- The logs should be deleted after one year (P09).

The new policies are listed along with P01 to P04b in Table 3. Following the conflict analysis process (cf. Fig. 5), first, we identify the conflicts according to the indicators described in Sect. 4.1. Using different colours, we highlight the conflicting actions and restrictions in Table 3. Next, to prepare a selection of resolution strategies, we need to calculate the weighted priority of each policy. Thus, we identify the stakeholders S and assign their weightings W_S, add individual priorities I_S, and, finally, calculate the weighted priorities I_W of all policies. For demonstration purposes, we assume priorities that best serve the presentation of the different resolution strategies in the following. Table 4 summarises all input and output values of this process.

Table 3. Comparison of Instantiated Templates for P01–P09.

Comp.	P01	P02	P03	P04b
Pattern	Actor-restricted Permission	Time-restricted Duty	Environment-restricted Prohibition	Time-restricted Duty
data	"delivery"	"delivery"	"delivery"	"records"
action	calculate	delete	distribute	delete
actor	CO_2 footpr.	–	–	–
env.	–	–	supplier	–
time	–	after 6m	–	after 3y
Comp.	P06	P07	P08	P09
Pattern	Actor-restricted Permission	Time-restricted Duty	Environment-restricted Permission	Time-restricted Duty
data	"delivery"	"delivery"	"delivery"	"records"
action	calculate	delete	distribute	delete
actor	research	–	–	–
env.	–	–	supplier	–
time	–	after 3m	–	after 3y

Conflict 1. P01 and P06 describe using data for calculations, resulting in an actor-restricted permission. The supplier allows usage for calculating the carbon footprint, and the delivery service wants to use the data for research purposes. By assigning a low priority, we assume the data provider is open for other purposes. Thus, the weighted priority of P06 is higher than that of P01. As a result, the chosen resolution strategy is to extend the scope of the provider's policy applied to the transferred dataset.

Conflict 2. P02 and P07 describe data deletion after a given timeframe. In this example, the delivery service's policy narrows the scope of the provider's policy. As the importance of P07 is weighted higher than that of P02, choosing the strategy *narrow scope*, a modified policy is applied to the transferred dataset.

Conflict 3. P03 and P08 address the same action and environment restriction but with contradicting action types, prohibition and permission. As the supplier

Table 4. Instantiated Patterns and Weighted Priorities I_W for P01 to P09.

ID	Instantiation of Pattern P	Stakeholder S	Weighting W_S	Priority I_S	I_W
P01	$P \rightarrow$ "delivery" "calculate" "CO_2 footprint"	Provider	2	1	2
P02	$P \rightarrow$ "delivery" "delete" "after 6 months"	Provider	2	1	2
P03	$P \rightarrow$ "delivery" "distribute" "supplier"	Provider	2	3	6
P04a	$P \rightarrow$ "transaction" "record" "data usage"	Regulation	3	3	9
P04b	$P \rightarrow$ "records" "delete" "after 3 years"	Regulation	3	3	9
P06	$P \rightarrow$ "delivery" "calculate" "research"	Consumer	1	3	3
P07	$P \rightarrow$ "delivery" "delete" "after 3 months"	Consumer	1	3	3
P08	$P \rightarrow$ "delivery" "distribute" "supplier"	Consumer	1	3	3
P09	$P \rightarrow$ "records" "delete" "after 3 years"	Consumer	1	3	3

assigns a higher priority and, as a data provider, is weighted higher than the consumer, the consumer must either accept the policy (no changes) or decide against data consumption (no sharing).

Conflict 4. P04b and P09 describe deleting data transaction records after three and one year. As P04b originates in regulations, it is always weighted higher than any other policy. The possible resolution strategies correspond to those of the third conflict.

4.3 Known Uses

To understand what requirements arise in practice and showcase known uses of the DUP pattern, we have conducted desk research, examining currently existing dataspace initiatives, including nationally and EU-funded projects and industrial products. For this purpose, we selected the few dataspaces that are already operational, according to our information, such as Catena-X, Mobility Data Space (MDS)[4], and Energy Data Space (EDS)[5], and approaches that provide a high level of maturity when it comes to the implementation of policy management (Prometheus-X[6], Boot-X[7]). We complemented our research with scientific publications representing the automotive, pharmaceutical, and food industries. Table 5 lists 27 data usage requirements extracted from publicly available reports and standards of these projects, representing policies of different action and constraint types. We highlight the *action* of each policy in italics. For example, policies R14 to R27 describe the allowed usage of data by restricting the duration of usage (time constraint, cf. R25), the organisations that may access the data (environment constraint, cf. R21), or the actors that must meet defined criteria (actor constraint, cf. R16). We can observe that prohibitions or duties are not commonly used.

[4] https://mobility-dataspace.eu/ (accessed on 2025-02-01).
[5] https://energydataspaces.eu/ (accessed on 2025-02-01).
[6] https://prometheus-x.org/ (accessed on 2025-02-01).
[7] https://www.boot-x.eu/ (accessed on 2025-02-01).

Table 5. Data Usage Requirements R from Selected Dataspace Initiatives.

ID	Description	Action Type	Constraint Type	Ref.
R01	Data must be *anonymised* before usage.	duty	time	[4]
R02	Data must not be *used* for a specific operation.	prohibition	actor	[20]
R03	Data can be *used* for a specific operation.	permission	actor	[20]
R04	Two data copies must be *used* at the same time.	permission	time	[20]
R05	Data must not be stored without being *aggregated*.	prohibition	time	[14]
R06	Data processing activities must be *logged*.	duty	time	Prometheus-X
R07	Raw data must not be *distributed*.	prohibition	*none*	[4]
R08	Data usage must be *logged* at an external service.	duty	actor	Mobility Data Space (MDS)
R09	Data usage must be *reported* to a defined actor (user/system).	duty	actor	Boot-X
R10	Data can be *shared* with third-parties that comply with GDPR.	permission	environment	Prometheus-X
R11	Data must be *deleted* periodically.	duty	time	[4]
R12	Data must be *deleted* after usage.	duty	time	[20]
R13	Data must be *deleted* at a defined datetime.	duty	time	Boot-X
R14	Data must be *used* by specified user roles.	permission	actor	Boot-X
R15	Data must be *used* by defined dataspace connectors.	permission	actor	MDS, Boot-X
R16	Data must be *used* in environments of a defined security level.	permission	actor	MDS
R17	Data must be *used* by defined dataspace applications.	permission	actor	Boot-X
R18	Data must be *processed* in its origin country.	permission	environment	[20]
R19	Data must be *used* at a defined geolocation.	permission	environment	Boot-X
R20	Data is publicly *available*.	permission	*none*	Energy Data Space (EDS)
R21	Data must be *used* by members of the dataspace.	permission	environment	Catena-X
R22	Data must be *used* by defined organisations.	permission	environment	Catena-X, EDS, Boot-X
R23	Data offers must be *accessible* to defined organisations.	permission	environment	EDS
R24	Data must be *used* by organisations of/at a specific type/location.	permission	environment	EDS
R25	Data must be *used* within a defined time interval.	permission	time	MDS, Boot-X
R26	Data must not be *used* more than a defined amount of times.	permission	time	MDS, Boot-X
R27	Data usage must *comply* with a defined purpose.	permission	*any*	Catena-X

Two special types of policies are represented in R20 and R27. If data is freely available, a policy does not contain a constraint type, but an action type *permission*. This obligation is reflected in our policy grammar. Referring to our example from Sect. 1, a purpose can be technically described by any constraints (also multiple ones). Concrete constraint types are context-dependent and must therefore be specified during the requirements engineering process.

5 Consequences

The DUP pattern comes with some benefits and liabilities, which we discuss in the following.

5.1 Benefits

The proposed pattern facilitates a structured elicitation and analysis of policies while addressing the forces from Sect. 3.2.

- *Compliance*: With the help of the DUP pattern, policies can be validated for syntactic completeness and correctness. This validation includes, on the one hand, the correct specification and combination of policy components and, on the other hand, the identification of missing ones. This forms the basis for ensuring technical compliance with organisational guidelines and regulations.

- *Know-how*: Due to the limited policy grammar guided by a simple template, even non-experts can easily define valid policies without the need to deal with technical representations like ODRL. This increases technical correctness and the trust of the stakeholders in each other, as well as the software systems that implement the policies. Creating a common understanding of the represented policies leads to clear accountability and fewer divergences in syntactic interpretations.
- *Conflict resolution*: The presented conflict analysis process allows for resolving conflicting policies at design time. This approach aims for designing an aligned and consistent system architecture for data sharing use cases, e.g., using the XACML architecture. Although we assume that stakeholders themselves take care of not causing any policy conflicts (cf. Sect. 4.1), the conflict resolution process can also be applied to validate their consistency, not necessarily between multiple stakeholders.
- *Policy enforcement*: Originating in selected domains (cf. Sect. 3.1), the DUP pattern may be applied to other contexts. The policy model also allows for a more fine-grained analysis of data usage conditions, e.g., by adding new (sub-) components and pattern primitives or further detailing the grammar's productions. Most important, the pattern and its application during the requirements engineering process allows for involving both data providers and consumers.

5.2 Liabilities

Our approach only considers simple, independent policies. Complex policy constructs are generally taken into account but may require the extension of the presented policy grammar. Such an extension may entail the introduction of new validation condition for the policy analysis process. Furthermore, although we use the pattern to form the basis for an aligned technical representation of policies, semantic differences in interpretation, e.g., *use* in comparison to specific sub-actions like *read*, are not entirely excluded during application.

6 Related Work

In the context of dataspaces, Hosseinzadeh et al. [9] proposed a set of 14 policies, called *policy classes*, gathered from a set of selected use cases. These include requirements like 'Restrict the data usage for a group of users or systems' [9, p.399], 'Delete data [...] after (one) use' [9, p.399], or 'Notify a party when data is used' [9, p.399]. Following this approach, every policy that emerges in a use case can lead to a new policy class and be reused in another context, along with a specific policy evaluation or enforcement function. Later, the introduced classes were extended by seven additional policies and resulted in a set of 21 policies [5]. Comparing the DUP pattern and its pattern primitives to these, we provide an approach of a higher abstraction level. This approach increases generalisability and, thus, reusability. In addition, we have substantiated our work with a more recent case analysis (cf. Table 5).

Chadha [3] created a taxonomy of policy conflicts, dividing them into application-independent and application-specific conflicts. Depending on their types, the conflicts are handled differently at compile-time or runtime. Our conflicts are comparable to the type modality conflict (cf. Sect. 4.1). We supplement Chadha's approach with conflict resolution at system design time.

Gil et al. [6] dealt with conflict resolution at runtime. Their work presents an algorithm that detects ambiguities in ODRL policies. This solution goes beyond the conflict resolution required in the requirements engineering process. In contrast, we primarily identify conflicting logical components without going into details, such as whether time periods overlap, as demonstrated in [6].

Priebe et al. [21] introduced a pattern system for access control, including authorisation patterns, each describing the intention, context, problem, and solution. Putting its primary focus on security-related aspects, this approach only partly covers the context of policy patterns for business-to-business data sharing.

7 Discussion and Conclusions

Data usage conditions, expressed as policies, are essential for self-determined and autonomous data sharing by ensuring correct data handling and thus strengthening trust (cf. Sect. 1). Therefore, its consideration within the requirements engineering process is of utmost importance. The usage of patterns allows for standardisation, reusability, and (automated) verifications. Since policies follow a structured design, patterns are particularly suitable for improving the quality and efficiency of their elicitation and analysis.

In this article, we proposed the DUP pattern for data sharing in the business-to-business domain. Starting from a conceptual model for policies, we presented a pattern consisting of six pattern primitives whose composition is defined by a policy grammar. In summary, this grammar consists of 17 productions that systematically structure data usage policies in data sharing. Following this, we described an approach for implementing our pattern by outlining a three-step process for policy analysis. This process includes conflict resolution as a central element. We concluded our work with a demonstration of the successful application of our DUP pattern in an example for a data sharing scenario as well as data usage requirements of real industrial dataspaces.

To answer RQ1, we focused on the structure of policies in business-to-business data sharing. We can observe that data usage policies follow a simple but powerful syntax independent of their technical representation. They are composed of actions and (optional) constraints that are refined to six pattern primitives. The abstraction level of our DUP pattern allows for an accurate and easily consumable usage during requirements engineering, being both human- and machine-readable.

Referring to RQ2, we structured the elicitation and analysis of policies during requirements engineering using a step-by-step process. The defined validation condition can be used to ensure the correct instantiation of policy templates and patterns. They may guide requirements engineers and involved stakeholders through the phases of policy elicitation, decomposition, and conflict resolution, and can be technically validated. In addition, they could be used to implement policy validation functions and verifying them at system runtime.

7.1 Further Considerations

Although we limited the scope of this work to business-to-business data sharing, we believe that the DUP pattern and the policy analysis process, due to their level of abstraction and modular structure, could also be eligible in more specific or related contexts. If required, the grammar can be easily extended to refine existing parameters, such as the action type or the constraints, or specify new ones. A more specific scenario could be the applicability of our policy pattern for the design of application programming interfaces, considering service level agreement (SLAs) as a specific type of policy. SLAs define clear quality characteristics that are essential for reliability and trust in business-to-business data sharing. They may represent government regulations and legal obligations [24] that serve as input for the requirements elicitation process.

Related contexts for the DUP pattern include privacy-related scenarios. These scenarios could target business-to-customer data consumption or business-to-business sharing of personal data. When sharing personal data, e.g., involving intermediaries or trustees, the pattern can be used to specify end-user preferences (privacy policies). For conflict resolution, these end-users could then be added as a new type of stakeholder with a custom weighting (cf. Sect. 4.1).

7.2 Future Work

Our approach could be further evaluated in different contexts, e.g., taking into account policies that focus on privacy-relevant data. Furthermore, the policy grammar could be extended so that it can be used for tools such as Antlr[8] or Xtext[9]. Future research areas could consider embedding the policy analysis process in a holistic requirements engineering process, as well as providing tool support.

Acknowledgments. We would like to thank Olaf Zimmermann, our supervisor in the shepherding process, for his valuable feedback and suggestions as experienced pattern author, which significantly improved this paper. We also appreciate the insights provided by the participants of the writers' workshop, listed in alphabetical order: Filipe Correia, Marcelo Nunes, Diogo Maia, Daniel Reis, Tiago Boldt Sousa, Francesco Urdih, and Uwe Zdun. Additionally, we acknowledge that this research was partially supported by the German Federal Ministry for Economic Affairs and Climate Action (funding number: 13IK040F).

[8] https://www.antlr.org/ (accessed on 2025-04-13).
[9] https://eclipse.dev/Xtext/ (accessed on 2025-04-13).

Disclosure of Interests. The authors have no competing interests to declare that are relevant to the content of this article.

References

1. Amroune, M., Zarour, N.E., Charrel, P.J., Inglebert, J.M.: Composition of aspectual requirements: a multi-criteria process for conflict resolution. J. Softw. Eng. **8**(2), 75–88 (2014)
2. Biehs, S., Stilling, J.: Identification of key requirements for the application of data sovereignty in the context of data exchange. In: Proceedings of the 57th Annual Hawaii International Conference on System Sciences, pp. 4248–4257 (2024)
3. Chadha, R.: A cautionary note about policy conflict resolution. In: 2006 IEEE Military Communications Conference, MILCOM 2006, pp. 1–8. IEEE (2006)
4. Cirillo, F., et al.: IntentKeeper: intent-oriented Data Usage Control for Federated Data Analytics. In: 2020 IEEE 45th Conference on Local Computer Networks (LCN), pp. 204–215. IEEE (2020)
5. Eitel, A., et al.: Usage Control in the International Data Spaces, March 2021
6. Gil, G., Arnaiz, A., Higuero, M., Diez, F.J., Jacob, E.: Context-aware policy analysis for distributed usage control. Energies **15**(19), 7113 (2022)
7. Heisel, M.: Agendas - a concept to guide software development activites. In: Horspool, R.N. (ed.) Proceedings of the Systems Implementation 2000, pp. 19–32. Chapman & Hall London (1998)
8. Hellmeier, M., Pampus, J., Qarawlus, H., Howar, F.: Implementing data sovereignty: requirements & challenges from practice. In: Proceedings of the 18th International Conference on Availability, Reliability and Security, pp. 1–9 (2023)
9. Hosseinzadeh, A., Eitel, A., Jung, C.: A systematic approach toward extracting technically enforceable policies from data usage control requirements. In: Proceedings of the 6th International Conference on Information Systems Security and Privacy, pp. 397–405 (2020)
10. Iannella, R., Steidl, M., Myles, S., Rodríguez-Doncel, V.: ODRL Vocabulary & Expression 2.2 (2018). https://www.w3.org/TR/odrl-vocab/. Accessed 14 Sept 2024
11. Jarke, M., Otto, B., Ram, S.: Data sovereignty and data space ecosystems. Bus. Inf. Syst. Eng. **61**(5), 549–550 (2019). https://doi.org/10.1007/s12599-019-00614-2
12. Mahendra, P., Ghazarian, A.: Patterns in the requirements engineering: a survey and analysis study. WSEAS Trans. Inf. Sci. Appl. **11**, 214–230 (2014)
13. Mitchell, R.K., Agle, B.R., Wood, D.J.: Toward a theory of stakeholder identification and salience: defining the principle of who and what really counts. Acad. Manag. Rev. **22**(4), 853–886 (1997)
14. Munoz-Arcentales, A., López-Pernas, S., Pozo, A., Alonso, Á., Salvachúa, J., Huecas, G.: Data usage and access control in industrial data spaces: implementation using FIWARE. Sustainability **12**(9), 3885 (2020)
15. Otto, B.: Quality and value of the data resource in large enterprises. Inf. Syst. Manag. **32**(3), 234–251 (2015)
16. Otto, B., ten Hompel, M., Wrobel, S.: Designing Data Spaces: The Ecosystem Approach to Competitive Advantage. Springer, Cham (2022). https://doi.org/10.1007/978-3-030-93975-5

17. Otto, B., Jarke, M.: Designing a multi-sided data platform: findings from the International Data Spaces case. Electron. Mark. **29**(4), 561–580 (2019). https://doi.org/10.1007/s12525-019-00362-x
18. Pampus, J., Heisel, M.: An empirical examination of the technical aspects of data sovereignty. In: Proceedings of the 19th International Conference on Software Technologies, pp. 112–122 (2024)
19. Pampus, J., Heisel, M.: Pattern-based requirements elicitation for sovereign data sharing. Procedia Comput. Sci. **254**, 147–156 (2025)
20. Pettenpohl, H., Tebernum, D., Otto, B.: WFDU-net: a workflow notation for sovereign data exchange. In: DATA, pp. 231–240 (2021)
21. Priebe, T., Fernandez, E.B., Mehlau, J.I., Pernul, G.: A pattern system for access control. In: Farkas, C., Samarati, P. (eds.) DBSec 2004. IIFIP, vol. 144, pp. 235–249. Springer, Boston, MA (2004). https://doi.org/10.1007/1-4020-8128-6_16
22. Rissanen, E.: eXtensible Access Control Markup Language (XACML) Version 3.0, January 2013. http://docs.oasis-open.org/xacml/3.0/xacml-3.0-core-spec-os-en.html
23. Sardinha, A., Araújo, J., Moreira, A., Rashid, A.: Conflict management in aspect-oriented requirements engineering. Inf. Sci. Technol. Bull. ACM Slovakia **2**(1), 56–59 (2010)
24. Zimmermann, O., Stocker, M., Lübke, D., Zdun, U., Pautasso, C.: Patterns for API Design: Simplifying Integration with Loosely Coupled Message Exchanges. Addison-Wesley Signature Series (Vernon). Addison-Wesley Professional (2022)

Tracing and Metrics Design Patterns for Monitoring Cloud-Native Applications

Carlos Albuquerque and Filipe F. Correia(✉)

INESC TEC, Faculty of Engineering, University of Porto, Porto, Portugal
{up201706735,filipe.correia}@fe.up.pt

Abstract. Observability helps ensure the reliability and maintainability of cloud-native applications. As software architectures become increasingly distributed and subject to change, it becomes a greater challenge to diagnose system issues effectively, often having to deal with fragmented observability and more difficult root cause analysis. This paper builds upon our previous work and introduces three design patterns that address key challenges in monitoring cloud-native applications.

Distributed Tracing improves visibility into request flows across services, aiding in latency analysis and root cause detection, Application Metrics provides a structured approach to instrumenting applications with meaningful performance indicators, enabling real-time monitoring and anomaly detection, and Infrastructure Metrics focuses on monitoring the environment in which the system is operated, helping teams assess resource utilization, scalability, and operational health.

These patterns are derived from industry practices and observability frameworks and aim to offer guidance for software practitioners.

Keywords: Monitoring · Patterns · Observability · Cloud · DevOps · Distributed Tracing · Application Metrics · Infrastructure Metrics

1 Introduction

The increasing complexity of cloud-native applications calls for advanced observability mechanisms to ensure reliability, maintainability, and performance optimization. Cloud-native software systems, often built on microservices architectures and container orchestration platforms, introduce new challenges in fault diagnosis, performance analysis, and real-time monitoring. Unlike traditional monolithic systems, these environments are highly dynamic, with ephemeral workloads, distributed state, and a continuous deployment lifecycle.

Despite the wide availability of monitoring tools and frameworks, many organizations struggle to achieve effective *observability*, as traditional monitoring approaches often fall short in providing the depth of insight needed to diagnose complex, distributed systems and ensure their reliability in cloud environments. Observability extends beyond conventional monitoring by enabling developers and operators to understand *why* a system behaves a certain way, rather than

T. Plummer et al. (Eds.): EuroPLoP 2025, LNCS 16494, pp. 28–53, 2026.
https://doi.org/10.1007/978-3-032-19157-1_2

just identifying *what* went wrong. Observability is typically achieved through three types of telemetry—*logs* are immutable, timestamped records of discrete events, which are essential for understanding discrete failures and debugging unexpected behaviors; *metrics* are numerical data points collected over time, often aggregated, giving insight into system health and performance trends, and enabling proactive responses to degradation and scaling issues; and *traces* capture the journey of a request across distributed components, helping teams detect latency bottlenecks and pinpoint failures across service boundaries. Together, these telemetry data types empower teams to diagnose issues more quickly, track regressions, and continuously improve system stability. Telemetry data combined with the need for automated anomaly detection and root cause analysis, calls for systematic and scalable observability practices. Existing tools can come a long way in helping professionals address use such practices, but developers still need guidance on which practices are most appropriate given the context at hand and how to go about adopting them effectively.

Patterns capture proven practices in a reusable format, offering structured solutions that can help engineers apply and adapt them in the real-world. Building upon our previous works [4–6], this paper refines and extends observability patterns tailored for cloud-native applications. We introduce three additional patterns that address gaps in distributed tracing, application metrics collection, and infrastructure monitoring. These patterns provide practical guidance for engineers looking to enhance the observability of their cloud-native systems.

In the remainder of the paper, Sect. 2 quickly reviews the related work, Sect. 3 explains the pattern mining process and outlines the pattern catalog and its evolution, and Sects. 4, 5, and 6 describe the proposed patterns in detail. Finally, Sect. 7 discusses conclusions and future research directions.

2 Related Work

Many resources, from books to blog posts to academic articles, discuss best practices for developing cloud-native systems, and quite a few have been documented as patterns [1,14,23–25,30–32,36]. Some of such resources address monitoring and observability concerns [12,16,22,26,39], but only a fraction of these have been written in the form of patterns [9,28,34,37].

We will not go into the details of each of these works in this section, but find it worth highlighting those that are closest to our own work. In particular, Sousa et al. have described External Monitoring, Preemptive Logging, and Log Aggregation [34,37], Brown et al. also catalogued Log Aggregation, Correlation ID and Query Engine [9], and Richardson's microservices pattern language contains very early drafts of some monitoring-related patterns such as Application Metrics and Distributed Tracing [28].

3 About the Patterns

We started the process of mining the patterns in this paper by reviewing research literature that specifically mentioned monitoring practices. We then looked into grey literature to deepen our understanding of the practices, which proved particularly useful to find real-world accounts of the patterns' use. Lastly, we looked into tools—we first identified commonly used features of monitoring tools and then searched for existing grey literature on how those features should be used. This allowed us to further refine some of the patterns.

Our previous papers [4–6] have already contributed different patterns to support observability in cloud-native environments. This paper builds upon these works and describes three more patterns, completing our catalog of eleven patterns for monitoring cloud-native applications [3]. Figure 1 shows a map of these patterns, and we often reference the other design patterns in the catalogue throughout the paper. The list below briefly describes each pattern, through its name, solution summary, and a reference to where the reader can find more about the pattern.

1. Audit Logging—Log in a data store who did what, where, and when. This data store can later be queried to reproduce issues reported by the users [6].
2. Standard Logging—Implement logging using a consistent format across all services [6].
3. Log Sampling—Sample and prioritize logs to reduce the amount of data that needs to be stored and processed [6].
4. Distributed Tracing—Assign each external request a unique ID and record how it flows through the system from one service to the next in a centralised server that provides visualisation and analysis, making troubleshooting the application faster and less complicated (see Page 4).
5. Deployment Tracking—Track every deployment and change to the production environment, making it possible to relate effects observed in the system to changes that caused them [5].

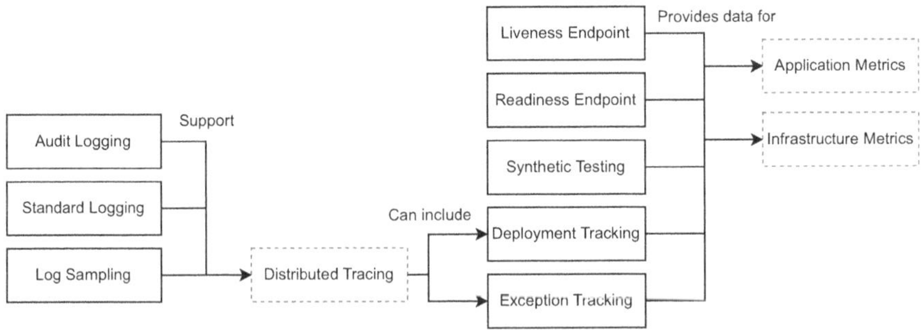

Fig. 1. Overview of the monitoring design pattern candidates proposed by the authors. The patterns highlighted with a dashed line are the ones explored in this paper.

6. Exception Tracking—Send exceptions to a centralised exception tracking service that aggregates exceptions, tracks their resolution, and creates alerts [5].
7. Liveness Endpoint—Implement a specialised endpoint that responds to requests without side effects. Then, configure another system (*e.g.*, service, tool, load balancer) to periodically check that endpoint and take action when that fails, providing an automatic way to detect that the instance is unable to respond [4].
8. Readiness Endpoint—Implement a specialised endpoint that checks if the service is ready to accept and process traffic. Then, configure another system (*e.g.*, service, tool, load balancer) to periodically check that endpoint and stop routing traffic to the service when the check fails [4].
9. Synthetic Testing—Create or pick a subset of existing test cases and periodically run them against the production environment, ensuring the application behaves as expected and detecting issues before they affect end-users [4].
10. Application Metrics—Instrument the application to gather business and performance metrics. Collect these metrics in a centralised service that provides aggregation and visualisation, allowing deeper insight into the application's performance (see Page 5).
11. Infrastructure Metrics—Instrument the server and runtimes to capture relevant metrics of the operative system and underlying infrastructure and collect them in a centralised server, allowing the team to get a real-time overview of the application's environment (see Page 6).

The patterns in this paper are Distributed tracing, Application Metrics, and Infrastructure Metrics. We describe each of them using this structure:

- **Name**—intuitive or established name for the pattern.
- **Summary**—short summary of the pattern, focusing on the core of its problem and solution.
- **Context**—contextualization of the pattern; provides background on the problem and may also refer to other design patterns that can be considered before the current one.
- **Problem**—a brief description of the problem as a question.
- **Forces**—a list of forces constraining the solution to point in a certain way and not another.
- **Solution**—starts with a sentence in *italics* that captures the gist of the solution and goes on to describe the solution for the problem, where we highlight in **bold** certain keywords that represent the roles of different components or modules; these components and their interactions are then depicted in a figure by the end of the solution section.
- **Consequences**—a bullet-point description of the pattern's main advantages and disadvantages that should be considered when adopting it.
- **Example**—an illustrative example, real or fictional, of the pattern in use.

- **Known Uses**—succinct description of real-world cases that use the pattern; throughout this section, we also briefly mention existing tools that can be used to adopt the pattern.
- **Related Patterns**—a few paragraphs describing how the pattern relates to other design patterns, both from the catalogue and other works.

4 Distributed Tracing

Cloud applications often involve multiple modules working together to handle user requests, making it challenging to pinpoint failures or performance bottlenecks across nested operations. Therefore, assign each external request a unique ID and trace its flow through the system in a centralised server, to enable visualisation and analysis, simplify troubleshooting and improve system observability.

4.1 Context

Cloud applications are usually a sum of modules that work together to reply to user requests. Therefore, a request may require many nested operations throughout the application's modules, both internal and external. When something breaks during these operations, it can become hard to figure out exactly where the failure is. Moreover, the person troubleshooting the error may not even be familiar with all the modules, making the troubleshooting process longer and more complicated.

Sometimes, even if the system did not fail, it might still be underperforming. If a user needs to wait five or more minutes for a webpage to load, there might be an operation (among all executed for that request) that is taking too long. The cause of slowness may be hard to pinpoint when requests are complex and involve many operations.

4.2 Problem

How can developers record and visualise the end-to-end behaviour of the application to identify problems during the request lifetime?

4.3 Forces

Addressing this problem is subject to the following forces:

- Metrics can provide an aggregate view of the system (*e.g.*, max response time in the last 15 min, the sum of request errors in the last hour), but they are not helpful when trying to understand the behavior throughout the system induced by a particular request.
- Logs can capture detailed information for specific requests, but they are often scattered across different services and infrastructures, making correlation and analysis time-consuming.

- Logs usually record events or errors, but they do not provide clear visibility into the time each operation took, to help identify bottlenecks.
- Synthetic tests [7] and unit tests can simulate requests and catch some issues, but they can easily miss transient runtime conditions that may surface in production such as spikes in resource usage or network issues.
- Recording detailed trace data can help diagnose issues, but it must be done in a way that minimizes the impact on system performance and maintainability.
- The different services of cloud-native applications often need to collaborate to fulfill a request, but the complexity of inter-service dependencies makes it difficult to understand and debug the system's behavior.
- Cloud-native applications often run across heterogeneous environments—using multiple programming languages, frameworks, and infrastructures—which increases the effort of instrumenting different services.

4.4 Solution

Assign each external request a unique ID and record how it flows through the system from one service to the next in a centralised server that provides visualisation and analysis, making troubleshooting the application faster and less complicated.

Namely, instrument the source code as follows:

- An **Unique ID** is assigned to each incoming request (see CORRELATION ID [8]);
- The ID is sent to every **Service** that processes the request;
- Local thread activity is recorded in a **Span** of execution and tagged with the unique ID;
- The unique ID is included in all the logs generated while processing the request;
- The span information is sent to a central **Tracing Service** directly from the microservice or through a local **Forwarding Agent** (see Fig. 2).

The collector is then responsible for processing all spans and constructing **Execution Traces** by mashing together the related spans and logs. Usually, the collector also provides a UI to visualise request information and the ability to query the traces. The collector lets developers analyse the whole execution trace and quickly figure out performance bottlenecks, which operation originated a failure and the logs associated with the previous situations.

Because cloud-native systems can change quickly—due to autoscaling, rolling updates, or container restarts—the infrastructure and service instances that generate a trace may no longer exist when a developer investigates an issue. To address this, spans can include metadata about the infrastructure and service (*e.g.*, service version, instance ID, container name, deployment timestamp, or node label) so that it is possible to understand what the general operational context was when later trying to interpret traces. When using DEPLOYMENT TRACKING or INFRASTRUCTURE METRICS, the data they generate can also be used to understand the system state at the time of execution, and often be correlated with traces through the same metadata.

When recording local thread activity in the spans, developers should consider following the OpenTelemetry API, which has seen growing adoption in the software industry [26]. Particularly in heterogeneous environments, implementing distributed tracing can become more complex due to the varying levels of support for instrumentation. The language-specific SDKs made available by OpenTelemetry with support for multiple platforms (*e.g.*, Java, Python, Go, Node.js) can reduce this burden.

When adopting this pattern, we must consider how to handle the information collected, as collecting and storing traces for every request may come to have a negative impact on the system. A way to address this concern is tail-based sampling, *i.e.* sampling the execution traces after they have been reconstructed in the collector service. The team can decide to drop some of the traces and only store the remaining ones, effectively reducing the overhead on the system. *"The idea here is to capture enough information to understand what our system is doing, but not capture so much information that the system itself cannot cope"* [26]. The sampling can be random or dynamic. The former consists of randomly selecting which traces to sample, increasing the likelihood of losing relevant information or collecting insufficient information to reach relevant conclusions. The latter has different sampling rates that depend on certain conditions (*e.g.*, if there was an error during execution or if a given operation has been slower than usual). Dynamic sampling is harder to implement and requires a bit more processing, but it is more likely to catch the information needed to troubleshoot the application. Balancing this trade-off is the responsibility of the team when adopting this pattern.

When adopting this pattern, we must also consider how to balance the benefit of detailed observability with its costs. Tracing every request introduces overhead, both in runtime performance and in the resource consumption of the tracing infrastructure. To mitigate this, teams often adopt sampling strategies to reduce the volume of traces stored and analyzed while preserving the utility

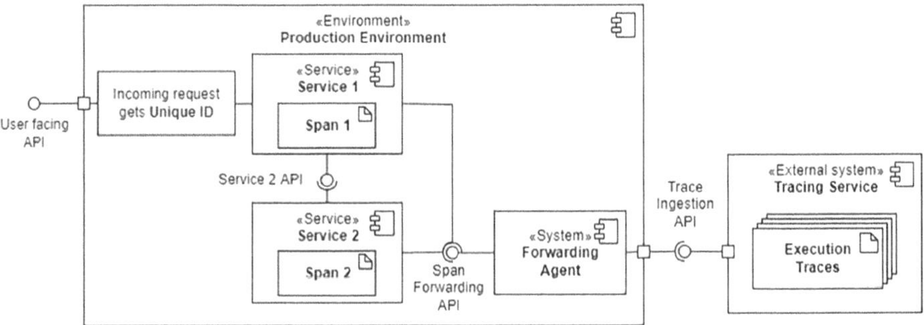

Fig. 2. Overview of the structure for the Distributed Tracing pattern. The request is assigned a unique ID as it enters the system and the generated spans carry that ID.

of traces for debugging and performance analysis. *Tail-based* sampling makes the decision to retain a trace after all its spans are complete, often based on criteria depending on information of the spans themselves; unlike *head-based* sampling, which filters at the start of a request, usually randomly.

Another important concern is time synchronization across services, especially in distributed infrastructures where clock skew can occur due to unsynchronized or faulty NTP configurations. This can result in incorrect ordering and inaccurate duration of spans, leading to misleading trace visualizations. To address this, teams should ensure that all nodes use a reliable time synchronization service, such as NTP, and leverage clock skew adjustment mechanisms provided by tracing tools. Additionally, to ensure consistent span ordering regardless of clock discrepancies, each span should include the ID of its parent span. This hierarchical structure allows the tracing system to reconstruct the correct sequence of operations, even when physical clocks are out of sync. Tools like Jaeger[1], which support parent span IDs and built-in clock skew adjustment, can simplify the implementation of this approach and improve the accuracy of distributed traces.

4.5 Consequences

This pattern has the following advantages:

- The mean time to detect (MTTD) becomes shorter, making troubleshooting the system faster.
- User requests become observable from end to end, *i.e.* every operation performed since the request first arrives in the system until a response is sent to the user is tracked.
- Traces provide insight into individual operations, making it easier to identify system bottlenecks.

This pattern also has the following drawbacks:

- Depending on the existing library support when instrumenting code in a particular programming language used, implementing this pattern may require changes that imply a non-trivial effort.
- Instrumenting the source of different services and aggregating traces introduces overheads that may degrade performance, increase latency, and raise complexity in code maintenance.
- Traces need to be stored, and as time goes by, they will start to occupy more and more space, demanding considerable infrastructure and increasing the storage costs.
- Since the solution is a bit complex, its learning curve may create some initial friction with the team.

[1] More details about Jaeger are available at jaegertracing.io.

4.6 Example

Meesho is an online shopping app for India. A blog post by Agarwal [2] explains that, as they transitioned from a monolithic architecture to a microservices-based framework, understanding the path of a single request became much more complicated. Because *"a single request passes through multiple services"* [2], tracing a request across all services became a challenge. The author explains in further detail their feed system's architecture. Most of their services composing the feed system were *"Spring framework-based Java microservices"* [2]. It followed a layered architecture, *"where each layer has its responsibility and each domain service operates within its boundary context"* [2].

To tackle the abovementioned issue, the team decided to implement distributed tracing in their system through *Spring Cloud Sleuth*. The author states that the decision was based on the tool's *"auto-configuration capability and compatibility with other Spring libraries"* [2]. The distributed tracing works as follows:

- The unique IDs are initialized by the first service that does not find them in the request headers. They use two unique IDs for each request—the *Trace ID* and the *Span ID*—and the service attaches them to `ThreadLocal`, a Java class that provides thread-local variables.
- The team *"implemented an interceptor that passes these IDs downstream as headers"* [2].
- To include the unique IDs in the logs, the team used SLF4J to fetch the IDs from the *ThreadLocal* variables and include them in the logs.

They bumped into a problem with asynchronous processing that led to the loss of both unique IDs because the thread context changed in the middle of the execution. To maintain trace context across threads, the team manually propagated *ThreadLocal* variables containing the trace and span IDs. This often involved wrapping asynchronous tasks (*e.g.*, *Runnable*, *Callable*) so that the trace context was restored before execution. This workaround ensured trace continuity during async processing. With that out of the way, Sleuth handles the aggregation and correlation of spans to construct the execution traces.

The author ends by explaining that to diagnose an issue reported by a particular user they queried trace logs using a User ID to locate relevant Trace IDs—*"This showed us the whole request trace across services, and we instantly figured out that the A/B service was returning an unexpected response in one of our domain services which caused that issue"* [2].

4.7 Known Uses

Agarwal's [2] example described in the previous section is already a known use of this pattern that utilised Spring Cloud Sleuth to implement this pattern in a real-world microservices architecture.

FloQast is another company that uses distributed tracing to understand its application. In a blog post, Dinh [13] explains that FloQast is a fast-growing company, so they *"add more and more business logic to the codebase every single day"* [13]. The team noticed that bottlenecks started to appear in the system, but they did not have enough information to follow a data-driven decision. Thus, they started using AWS X-Ray service, which, as the author explains, *"allows users to gain insight into requests that your application serves"* [13]. Using that tool, they can *"easily trace requests across AWS resources and other microservices"* [13].

Finally, and on a much bigger scale, Netflix built its distributed tracing infrastructure to solve user issues better. In Netflix Technology Blog, Pandey [27] goes into some detail about how they did and evolved the infrastructure to cope with emerging standards like Open-Zipkin and Open-Tracing. *"Investigating a video streaming failure consists of inspecting all aspects of a member account"* [27], so troubleshooting a user complaint can become very complicated on a system as complex as Netflix. They developed Edgar, an internal tool for troubleshooting streaming sessions. They started with a simple tool that, based on unique IDs for each streaming session, was able to *"reconstruct session failure by providing service topology, retry and error tags, and latency measurements for all service calls"* [27]. For their case in specific, the team had to apply a hybrid head-based sampling approach that enabled them *"to record 100% traces in our mission-critical streaming microservices while collecting minimal traces from auxiliary systems like offline batch data processing"* [27]. Even though this helped reduce the number of traces stored, the author states that they still had issues escalating their ElasticSearch clusters. So they eventually transitioned to Cassandra clusters to handle the high data ingestion rates.

4.8 Related Patterns

The CORRELATION ID [8] pattern provides a basic mechanism for correlating logs across services by assigning a unique identifier to each request. While this can help trace the flow of a request through the system, it does not provide detailed timing information or visualizations of the request's lifecycle. DISTRIBUTED TRACING builds on this by offering a more comprehensive solution, including the ability to measure latency, identify bottlenecks, and visualize the sequence of operations across services. Teams can start with CORRELATION ID to address basic correlation needs and later adopt DISTRIBUTED TRACING for deeper insights and more troubleshooting capabilities.

Logs are a common way to implement execution spans. In such cases, adopting LOG AGGREGATION [33,35] becomes almost necessary to get DISTRIBUTED TRACING. In addition, logs can also be correlated and aggregated with the traces of execution. This provides the team with a complete report of the events and the time each operation took across the whole request lifetime.

However, generating too many traces can carry a very high overhead. The team should consider the LOG SAMPLING pattern to implement a sampling strategy that minimises the overhead of logged traces while maintaining the ones that truly matter for troubleshooting purposes.

5 Application Metrics

Cloud abstracts infrastructure details, making the concerns about application performance more about user responsiveness than resource efficiency. Understanding performance and usage patterns is vital for maintaining quality. Therefore, instrument the application to collect business and performance metrics, aggregating and visualizing them in a central service to gain deeper insights into the application's behavior.

This pattern is sometimes also known as Inside-out Health Check [19] or Monitoring Metrics [39].

5.1 Context

Users expect software systems to bring value through appealing features, but also for it to fail rarely and work with acceptable speed, which pushes teams to keep track of their system's performance to ensure it meets certain requirements. These may be informal and more flexible, such as an end-user of a web application that expects a page to load in less than 30 s, or formal and strict, such as a service level agreement (SLAs) between an infrastructure as a service (IaaS) provider and its client. Both cases are equally important for a company since it might be losing customers or having to compensate them for a contractual breach, respectively.

Since the cloud abstracts away the infrastructure on which the code is running, performance becomes more about how well the system can respond to the user than how efficiently it uses the available resources. Moreover, performance can be seen from the technical and business lenses. Understanding customer trends and satisfaction is just as important as knowing availability and the number of errors, for example. Both can bring helpful insight to a company and give it a more significant market presence.

5.2 Problem

How can the team get an overview of how the application is performing and understand the emerging usage patterns?

5.3 Forces

Addressing this problem is subject to the following forces:

- Logs can be used to extract relevant system performance measures, but processing them is computationally expensive and does not provide real-time visibility.
- Simulating requests and testing in production can surface issues in predefined scenarios, but they offer limited data and may miss unexpected or new conditions.

- Infrastructure (*e.g.*, cloud) providers often supply infrastructure metrics, but these may lack application-specific detail needed for fine-grained monitoring.
- Reusable monitoring solutions are desirable for reducing cost and effort, but they still need to be adapted to the specific needs of diverse applications.
- Cloud-native applications often run across heterogeneous environments—using multiple programming languages, frameworks, and infrastructures—which increase the effort of instrumenting different services.

5.4 Solution

Instrument the application to gather business and performance metrics. Collect these metrics in a centralised service that provides aggregation and visualisation, allowing deeper insight into the application's performance.

Namely, the team can collect **Metrics** on many things, such as request rate, error rate, customer orders, and user posts. Ideally, one would measure everything, but that introduces more overhead and requires considerable infrastructure. That said, the first decision the team must make when adopting this pattern is to define which **Application** metrics they wish to monitor (see Fig. 3). Consider The Four Golden Signals proposed in [15] as a starting point. They are briefly presented below, but for further detail refer to the original work:

- Latency - the time between when a user request arrives in the system, and a response is issued to the user.
- Traffic - a *"high-level system-specific metric"* [15] that measures the number of incoming requests in your system.
- Errors - the rate of requests that result in a failure, of any kind, by a period of time.
- Saturation - the percentage of system resources being utilised at the moment.

Other guidelines can also be used, like the RED method [21] (rate of requests, errors, duration) and the READS metrics [20] (rate of requests, errors, availability, duration/latency, and saturation), and the team should consider which one is more suited to their context. Typically, a team will adopt RED where there is a large population of homogeneous microservices and minimising per-endpoint overhead is a priority, and READS when it is relevant to distinguish availability from raw error rates and to incorporate resource pressure into health assessment.

Beyond service/runtime indicators, teams also track business (domain) metrics that show whether the product is delivering value (*e.g.*, orders placed, successful checkouts, active users, trial-to-paid conversion, average order value, refund or failure rates, feature adoption). These should be few, purposeful KPIs tied to goals, as the more we collect, the harder it becomes to process and derive useful insights.

Another thing to consider is the data resolution—*i.e.* in this case, the number of data points collected by time period. Depending on the current context of the system, some metrics may be collected and stored in a greater resolution than others. As Newman exemplifies:

> *"I might want a CPU sample for my servers at the resolution of one sample every 10 seconds for the last 30 minutes, in order to better react to a situation that is currently unfolding. On the other hand, the CPU samples from my servers from last month are likely needed only for general trend analysis, so I might be happy with calculating an average CPU sample on a per-hour basis."* [26, p. 322]

Therefore, when adopting this pattern, the team should consider having the ability to change the resolution of the data that is stored or being collected. That allows the team to better manage storage space and overhead while still collecting a sufficient number of metric points for troubleshooting.

Another important consideration is granularity. Fine-grained metrics (*e.g.*, request duration per user per endpoint) provide rich insights but will increase storage and processing overhead. Coarse-grained metrics (*e.g.*, average request duration per service) reduce overhead but may hide anomalies. The team can balance this trade-off based in the power of each metric to provide insights and the criticality of the functionality—*e.g.*, detailed metrics might be necessary for payment processing endpoints, while summary metrics may be enough for background jobs.

Once we know *what* to measure, we should understand *how* to do it. Each metric is sampled periodically by a **Metrics Exporter** (see Fig. 3) and is usually composed of a name, value and timestamp [28]. Further context must be added to the metric through tags, *i.e.* key-value pairs for external properties, that are collected each time step. The higher the cardinality of the added tags (*e.g.*, usernames and emails, which are unbounded sets), the more the metrics system will struggle to keep all the information. When adopting this pattern, the team should consider reducing the cardinality of these tags or using a system that is prepared to receive high cardinality data.

Some of these tags will be related to the runtime services and infrastructure where the metric originated. This allows metrics to be grouped and queried in context of the system structure at the time the metric was generated, even if that structure has changed as, in cloud environments, service instances may have been replaced or terminated before developers even feel the need to examine their metrics. Correlating this metadata with data generated by DEPLOYMENT TRACKING can also help to reconstruct the resource topology at the time of an incident.

Finally, metrics generated and spread across many services are not very helpful. To make actual use of them, the team needs a **Metrics Service** - a centralised system to collect and aggregate (*e.g.*, to calculate the average, sum or percentiles) the metrics and present them in a friendly way to the team (see Fig. 3). This can be achieved in two ways [29]:

- push - the application sends the metrics to an API provided by the metrics service (*e.g.*, AWS CloudWatch).
- pull - the metrics service fetches the metrics data from an API provided by the application (*e.g.*, Prometheus).

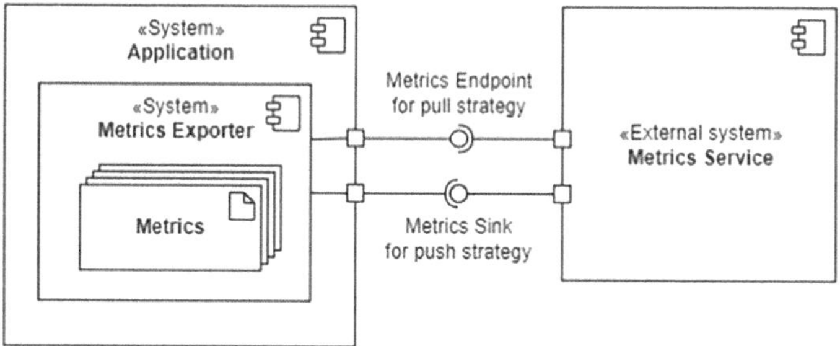

Fig. 3. Overview of the structure for the APPLICATION METRICS pattern. The solutions usually only follows the pull or the push strategy. We represented both for completeness.

Both options are viable; it all depends on the context of the system. Usually, the pull model is more transparent to the application. In other words, it does not require as much instrumentation, keeping the business logic more isolated from these monitoring details.

5.5 Consequences

This pattern has the following advantages:

- It provides an up-to-date overview of the application's state.
- It provide valuable insights from both technical (*e.g.*, capacity planning, predicting potential problems) and business (*e.g.*, strategic decision-making, understanding trends) perspectives, enabling data-driven decisions.
- Metrics enable the team to notice non-evident patterns and problems that would most likely go unnoticed otherwise, when paired with alerts, act before they ffect the users and the business.

This pattern also has the following drawbacks:

- Aggregating and storing a high number of metrics may imply considerable infrastructure costs.
- Instrumenting the source of different services introduces overheads that may degrade throughput and latency, and raise complexity in code maintenance.
- Configuring the metrics themselves, including deciding what to measure, setting thresholds, and managing granularity, can require significant effort and expertise.
- Collecting application data in the cloud depends heavily on what the team has access to, so this pattern gets harder to adopt the fewer access rights the team has to the deployment environments.

5.6 Example

A post by Campuzano on the GumGum Tech Blog [11] explains how the company adopted Prometheus to monitor its systems. Before the company adopted the microservice architecture, the author states that monitoring was quite simple. Their *"applications, servers, and services were pretty much fixed and well-known"*. However, things got much more complicated once they started containerising their applications and adopting the microservices architecture—*"the explosion in the quantity and complexity of the systems to be monitored was neither manageable nor sustainable with the legacy monitoring stack that we had in place"*.

To address the new monitoring needs, they used Prometheus to create a monitoring stack capable of handling the complexity. According to the author, they *"chose Prometheus among other systems, mostly because of its flexibility, extensibility and huge open source community backing the project"*. They used different Prometheus exporters to instrument the code to generate metrics. The tool follows a *pull* strategy to get the metrics, *i.e.* it periodically scrapes them from a configurable endpoint. GumGum's monitoring stack collected metrics from the application, containers and servers. Additionally, they used Grafana to visualise the collected metrics on customised dashboards and Alert Manager to configure and manage alerts on top of the Prometheus metrics. Figure 4 is part of the post and depicts the overall Prometheus architecture used by GumGum.

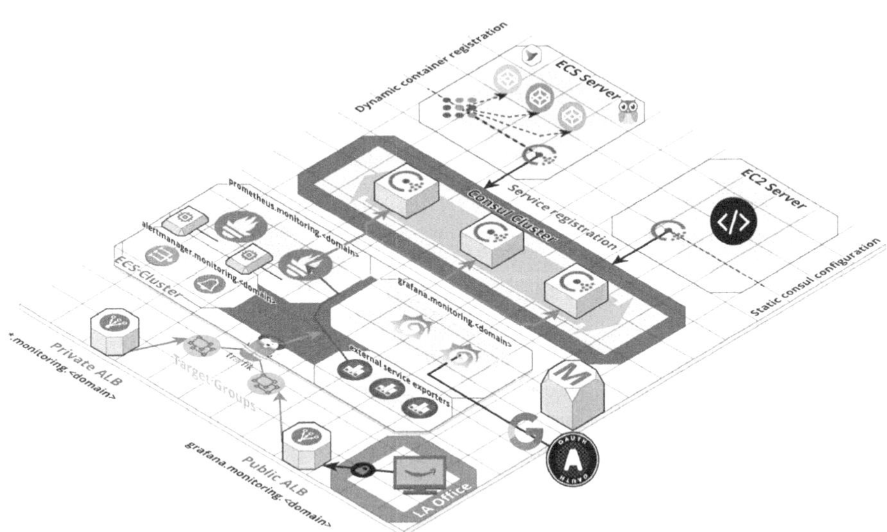

Fig. 4. Real-world example of the APPLICATION METRICS pattern [11].

The author does not precisely mention which metrics they collect, but these could include the number of ad impressions per second, rendering latency per ad unit, failed ad fetches per service, and average user session duration. Tracking these metrics could enable regional scaling policies and improving ad display success rate. Additionally, Campuzano mentions that they used Prometheus Pushgateway for *"ephemeral and batch jobs to expose its metrics to Prometheus"* [11]. These jobs send the metrics to the Pushgateway, which Prometheus then scrapes. Thus, they could collect application-level metrics and visualise them in specific dashboards for their teams. With Prometheus and Grafana, GumGum became able to collect metrics from many parts of their system and *"create beautiful and meaningful Grafana dashboards with those metrics"* [11].

5.7 Known Uses

Campuzano's [11] example described in the previous section is already a known use of this pattern that used Prometheus and Grafana to collect metrics from a microservice architecture.

A post by Domenico Stragliotto [38], a backend developer for THRON, elaborates how the company adopted metrics on their system. The author explains they were looking to improve their ability to analyse long-term trends, build dashboards, troubleshoot and get alerted. To achieve their goals, they used Prometheus to collect metrics from their services. They followed the RED method [21], so, for each service, they collected the number of requests per second, the number of errors per second and the amount of time to process each request. These metrics were then exposed in Grafana dashboards so the teams could easily view each service's state.

Finally, an infrastructure software engineer post on callstats.io's blog [10] reports how the company uses Prometheus to monitor its services. They chose Prometheus due to its seamless integration with Kubernetes, powerful query language and operational simplicity. The engineer states that the company's developers *"use Prometheus to compare performance and resource usage between service releases"* [10], while the analytics team uses it *"for several artificial intelligence-related metrics"* [10].

5.8 Related Patterns

Although the cloud abstracts the infrastructure where the application runs, understanding the performance of the host machine can be helpful. The underlying machine's performance can impact the application's performance. Suppose the team needs a more comprehensive view of the system or further correlation between the application and its infrastructure. In that case, they should consider adopting Infrastructure Metrics to complement the metrics provided by this pattern. Additionally, patterns like Liveness Endpoint, Readiness Endpoint, and Synthetic Testing can supply valuable metrics that provide further insights into its behavior and health.

6 Infrastructure Metrics

Software relies on infrastructure, and resource scarcity like CPU, memory, or disk can lead to slowness or outages. Teams need visibility into their application's infrastructure to diagnose and correlate issues effectively. Therefore, instrument servers and runtimes to capture key metrics of the operating system and infrastructure, and centralize this data for real-time monitoring and analysis.

This pattern is sometimes also known as Inside-Out Health Check [19].

6.1 Context

Software needs infrastructure to execute. Even though the cloud abstracts this infrastructure from the developing team, applications still depend on the underlying resources. Scarcity of resources like CPU, memory or disk can bring extreme system slowness or even an outage. In addition, these issues can be caused by faults in the code (*e.g.*, memory leaks), so it is the developing team's responsibility to find and fix them. The team should monitor the essential infrastructure resources to identify code-level problems and correlate end-user issues with the infrastructure.

In a pay-as-you-go scenario, which allows for greater flexibility and cost savings, it will drive the costs up if the application starts to utilise more and more resources. Being able to notice the increasing usage of infrastructure is necessary so the team can figure out if that is due to greater demand on the application (*e.g.*, a new product release with a significant influx of users), in which case it is to be expected, or an issue with the code (*e.g.*, poorly optimised loops or memory leaks) that needs to be fixed. Moreover, public clouds are usually under service level agreements (SLAs) that declare the minimum requirements the infrastructure must provide. If a given resource constantly drops below the agreed threshold, the cloud consumer should be able to confront the provider and take action according to what is stated in the SLA. Thus, understanding the performance and state of the infrastructure is relevant for both cloud providers and consumers, so the machines the software is running on should be monitored.

6.2 Problem

How can the team know the state of their application's infrastructure and correlate it with ongoing problems?

6.3 Forces

Addressing this problem is subject to the following forces:

- The system must scale when resource thresholds are crossed, but some tools and cloud providers require manual intervention, which can slow response time.

- Cloud environments support flexible resource usage, but uncontrolled consumption can lead to unexpectedly high operational costs.
- Application services may be spread across different infrastructure resources, but this distribution complicates centralized monitoring and analysis.
- Resource usage can fluctuate significantly with load, but provisioning and scaling decisions often rely on static resource thresholds that may not adapt quickly enough.
- Infrastructure provisioning is often governed by contractual SLAs, but teams may lack the tooling or access needed to verify compliance in real-time.
- Reusable monitoring solutions can help reduce development effort, but they still need to be adapted to the specific infrastructure needs of applications.
- Cloud-native applications often run across heterogeneous environments—using multiple programming languages, frameworks, and infrastructures—which increase the effort of instrumenting different services.

6.4 Solution

Instrument the server and runtimes to capture relevant metrics of the operative system and underlying infrastructure and collect them in a centralised server, allowing the team to get a real-time overview of the application's environment.

As explained in Application Metrics (see Sect. 5), **Metrics** are usually composed of a name, a value, and a timestamp [29]. Tags can be stuffed into the metrics to provide further context. Tags are key-value pairs of properties, so they can come with nearly any kind of information. However, the higher the number of different values each tag can have, or, in other words, the higher its cardinality, the harder it is to store and process.

Since infrastructure components like virtual machines, containers, and disks can be provisioned and decommissioned dynamically, it is often useful for exporters or monitoring agents to also associate tags with infrastructure metrics that can provide context of what the infrastructure was like at the time the metrics were collected. This is particularly important when diagnosing issues long after they occurred, as the relevant infrastructure may no longer exist. Correlating this metadata with data generated by Deployment Tracking can also help to reconstruct the resource topology at the time of an incident.

Instrumentation can take many forms, but it is essentially the act of adding measuring instruments to the system. These instruments collect the **Infrastructure** information and generate metrics out of it. In the context of this pattern, instrumenting the server and runtimes means having a **Metrics Exporter** that is responsible for gathering a predefined set of metrics (see Fig. 5). It must have access to the OS and underlying infrastructure and, ideally, be configurable to specify what should be captured and at what resolution (*i.e.*, the number of data points per time interval).

Some public clouds, like GCP, provide an API with each application engine that exposes infrastructure metrics. Note that this API, by itself, is already a suitable exporter. It is gathering the necessary information and exposing it. Even though this kind of API may not be configurable (*e.g.*, you can not change the sampling rate), the team can request exclusively the metrics they need and at a larger interval than what the exporter samples.

Configuring the sampling rate and granularity may be necessary since storing and processing large amounts of data can demand considerable infrastructure and slow the overall monitoring process. Therefore, when adopting this pattern, the team should decide how many data points should be collected and how many should be stored. They should also decide on the level of detail captured over time—for instance, per-second CPU usage versus per-minute averages. Fine-grained metrics allow detailed analysis of short-term behavior, but they consume more resources and can lead to data bloat. In contrast, coarse-grained metrics reduce overhead but may hide short-lived issues. Teams should balance this trade-off based on operational needs, criticality of the metric, and cost.

Another crucial decision is what metrics to monitor. As previously stated, the more metrics the team collects, the easier it is to understand the infrastructure's state. Thus, the team should start with the most useful ones for their case and expand as the need arises. The USE method is a common method to help with this decision [18]. It suggests that the following metrics should be the first to be collected:

- Utilisation - *"the percentage of time that the resource is busy servicing work during a specific time interval"* [18];
- Saturation - *"the degree to which the resource has extra work which it cannot service, often queued"* [17];
- Errors - *"the count of error events"* [18].

Note that the USE method is more than just an indication of the metrics that should be gathered. It also incentivises the team to start by identifying the resources in their system (*e.g.*, CPU, memory, storage). Only then should they define what each of the above metrics means to each resource and how they should be gathered. That way, the USE method increases the overall understanding of the system—when the team notices a missing metric that would be useful to solve a currently ongoing application problem, they can start from the list of metrics they know they are not gathering.

Infrastructure metrics play an important role in managing elasticity. Autoscaling is often based on thresholds defined for specific metrics, such as CPU or memory use, with these metrics acting as triggers for reactive scaling (*e.g.*, scaling out when usage surpasses 80%). Teams can also proactively scale to prevent performance degradation, based on the prediction of traffic surges from historical patterns in infrastructure metrics. Scaling decisions have cost implications, with more instances meaning more compute charges. The choice of metrics to be monitored and associated scaling policies can be used to appropriately balance performance and cost. *E.g.*, frequent CPU spikes might call for load distribution optimization rather than scaling up resources.

Finally, metrics generated and spread across many services are not very helpful. To make actual use of them, the team needs a **Metrics Service** - a centralised system to collect and aggregate (*e.g.*, calculate the average, sum, or percentiles) the metrics and present them in a friendly way to the team (see Fig. 5). This can be achieved in two ways [29]:

- push - the application sends the metrics to an API provided by the metrics service (*e.g.*, AWS CloudWatch);
- pull - the metrics service fetches the metrics data from an API provided by the infrastructure (*e.g.*, Prometheus)

Both options are viable. It all depends on the system's context. Usually, the pull model is more transparent to the application. In other words, it does not require as much instrumentation, keeping the business logic more isolated from these monitoring details.

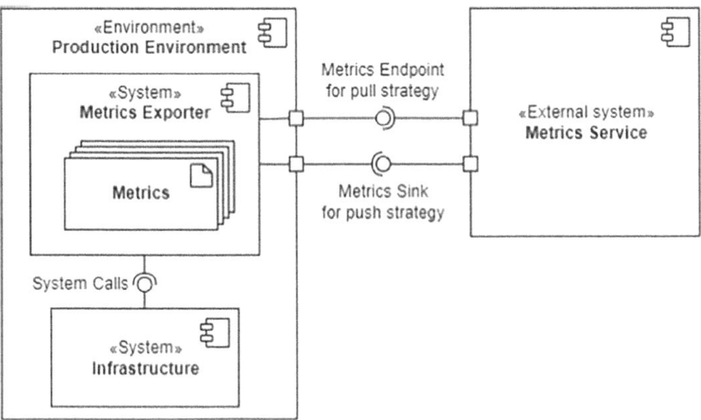

Fig. 5. Overview of the structure for the INFRASTRUCTURE METRICS pattern. The solutions usually only follow the pull or the push strategy. We represented both for completeness.

6.5 Consequences

This pattern has the following advantages:

- Metrics enable the team to notice non-evident patterns and problems that would most likely go unnoticed otherwise.
- It provides a real-time and straightforward overview of the infrastructure's state.
- Operations teams can more easily cut down on unused resources, decreasing the system's costs.
- Issues with the code that directly impact the infrastructure (*e.g.*, memory leaks) become easier to detect.
- It allows for correlation between user symptoms, like recurring failures when creating a new post, to infrastructure problems, like a full database.

This pattern also has the following drawbacks:

- Aggregating and storing a high number of metrics may require considerable infrastructure, increasing its costs.
- Instrumenting the server and runtimes to collect the metrics introduces overheads that may degrade performance, increase latency, and raise complexity in code maintenance.
- Correlating infrastructure and application metrics is based on the time of events; since the systems collecting the metrics are different, their clock times may also diverge slightly, making way for wrong relations between both metric types.
- Data can quickly become separated into different categories (or silos) without actual correlation, which heavily reduces this pattern's benefits.
- Collecting infrastructure data in the cloud depends heavily on what the team has access to, so this pattern gets harder to adopt the fewer access rights the team has to the infrastructure.
- In PaaS and FaaS scenarios, the only way to collect infrastructure metrics may be through the cloud provider's dedicated solutions, which reduces the team's flexibility and restricts the kind of data that can be monitored.
- Analysing these metrics may be misleading because these convey possible problems (*i.e.*, the lack of resources) but do not point towards the actual problem (*i.e.*, the faulty code).

6.6 Example

In a blog post, Stragliotto [38] provides an example of how THRON adopted this pattern. The author considers that *"monitoring is the most important starting point to improve your product"* [38], so they decided to update their monitoring architecture to improve their troubleshooting and alerting capabilities. In addition, they also improve their ability to analyse long-term trends and build dashboards.

The team decided to use Prometheus to collect infrastructure metrics to achieve their goal. In addition, they adopted Grafana *"to query, visualise and generate alerts from our metrics"* [38]. It is very common in grey literature to find these two tools combined to set up a **Metrics Service**.

The author goes on to talk about the specific metrics that they chose to collect from their services. The post mentions the Four Golden Signals [15] as the most important to monitor a system, but for the infrastructure, they followed the USE method [18]. Stragliotto defends that this method is better suited when the need is to *"keep the physical resources under control"* [38]. Therefore, they collected utilization, saturation, and errors from many resources. Specific resources and metrics we could capture in this context include CPU utilization per core, memory usage, I/O wait time, and disk saturation. For example, using Prometheus' node exporter provides *node_cpu_seconds_total* and *node_disk_io_time_seconds_total* which can be used identify bottlenecks.

Using Grafana, they built dashboards with thresholds and alerts for each metric, including stacked time-series plots and anomaly detection triggers Note that, since infrastructure metrics convey the state of the infrastructure, they point to possible problems, but they are not the actual problem. This is a consequence that we consider very important for the pattern.

To conclude, Stragliotto declares that they *"are happy about how [their] new architecture turned out, it works and it's starting to really help [them] keep [their] software under control"*. This view of the system was essential to make their detection and troubleshooting processes faster and fix their services more quickly.

6.7 Known Uses

Stragliotto's [38] example described in the previous section is already a known use of this pattern that used Prometheus and Grafana to collect and visualise the utilisation, saturation and errors of their system's infrastructure.

An infrastructure software engineer post on callstats.io's blog [10] reports how the company uses Prometheus to monitor its services. They chose Prometheus for its seamless integration with Kubernetes, powerful query language and operational simplicity. The engineer states that the company's infrastructure and operations teams *"use [Prometheus] to monitor resource usage and service performance, as well as data pipeline processing queues"* [10].

Finally, a post by Campuzano on GumGum's Tech Blog [11] explains how the company adopted Prometheus to monitor its systems. In addition, they utilised Grafana to visualise the data with customised dashboards. Although the author does not write about the actual metrics they collected, he mentions the usage of Prometheus' node exporter. This metrics exporter exposes *"hardware and OS metrics on *nix systems"* [11] and publishes more than 600 metrics. The author recognises that this amount of metrics can be a problem due to the high processing overhead they introduce.

6.8 Related Patterns

The infrastructure metrics represent the state of the infrastructure. Analysing these logs helps notice symptoms of a problem. However, they are not usually enough to find what exactly is causing the issue. In such cases, the team should consider adopting Application Metrics to complement this pattern and get a full view of the system.

7 Conclusions

Observability remains an important aspect of cloud-native architectures, enabling teams to diagnose failures, optimize performance, and maintain system reliability. The authors describe three design patterns to monitor cloud-native applications. Distributed Tracing supports end-to-end visibility across microservices by tracking requests as they propagate through the system, helping teams identify latency bottlenecks and failure points. Application Metrics suggests the collection and analysis of domain-specific performance indicators, allowing developers to proactively detect anomalies and optimize application behavior, and Infrastructure Metrics supports monitoring of underlying resources such as CPU, memory, and network usage, ensuring that cloud-native applications run efficiently and scale appropriately.

These patterns are part of a collection of eleven design patterns presented previously by the authors [3] and explained in Sect. 3. The patterns outlined in this paper are grounded in practice, but it would be interesting to empirically study how broadly they are understood and used in the way described in this paper. This can be a direction for future work, possibly leading to the refinement of the pattern descriptions, and assessment of their impact on real-world cloud-native systems.

Acknowledgments. We would like to thank Uwe Zdun, who helped us improve this paper significantly through the shepherding process, as well as all the participants in our writers' workshop at EuroPLoP 2025, who also provided a lot of thoughtful feedback—Daniel Reis, Diogo Maia, Francesco Urdih, Julia Pampus, Tiago Boldt Sousa, and Uwe Zdun.

This work is co-financed by Component 5 - Capitalization and Business Innovation, integrated in the Resilience Dimension of the Recovery and Resilience Plan within the scope of the Recovery and Resilience Mechanism (MRR) of the European Union (EU), framed in the Next Generation EU, for the period 2021–2026, within project HfPT, with reference 41.

Disclosure of Interests. The authors have no competing interests to declare that are relevant to the content of this article.

References

1. Cloud design patterns - Azure Architecture Center. https://learn.microsoft.com/en-us/azure/architecture/patterns/. Accessed 29 Sept 2025
2. Agarwal, P.: Using distributed tracing to improve logging and debugging processes. https://meesho.io//blog/using-distributed-tracing-to-improve-logging-and-debugging-processes. Accessed 03 Jul 2022
3. Albuquerque, C.: Monitoring Design Patterns For Cloud Applications. Master's thesis, Faculty of Engineering, University of Porto, July 2022. https://repositorio-aberto.up.pt/handle/10216/143462. Accepted 23 Jan 2023
4. Albuquerque, C., Barral, K.R., Correia, F.F., Brown, K.: Proactive monitoring design patterns for cloud applications. In: Proceedings of the 25th European Conference on Pattern Languages of Programs, p. 21. ACM, Irsee, Germany (2022). https://doi.org/10.1145/3551902.3551961
5. Albuquerque, C., Correia, F.F.: Deployment tracking and exception tracking: monitoring design patterns for cloud-native applications. In: Proceedings of the 28th European Conference on Pattern Languages of Programs, p. 10. ACM, New York, NY, USA (2023). https://doi.org/10.1145/3628034.3628038

6. Albuquerque, C., Correia, F.F.: Logging design patterns for cloud-native applications. In: Proceedings of the 29th European Conference on Pattern Languages of Programs, EuroPLoP '24, pp. 1–10. Association for Computing Machinery, New York, NY, USA (2024). https://doi.org/10.1145/3698322.3698351
7. Albuquerque, C., Relvas, K., Correia, F.F., Brown, K.: Proactive monitoring design patterns for cloud-native applications (2023). https://doi.org/10.1145/3551902.3551961
8. Brown, K., Woolf, B.: Implementation patterns for microservices architectures. In: Proceedings of the 23rd Conference on Pattern Languages of Programs, pp. 1–35 (2016)
9. Brown, K., Woolf, B., Yoder, J., De Groot, C., Hay, C., Mitchell, I.J.: Patterns for developers and architects building for the cloud. https://kgb1001001.github.io/cloudadoptionpatterns/. Accessed 24 Feb 2022
10. callstats.io: How We Use Prometheus for Simple and Powerful Monitoring. https://medium.com/callstatsio/how-we-use-prometheus-for-simple-and-powerful-monitoring-68ee5240fc01. Accessed 30 Jun 2022
11. Campuzano, S.: Prometheus Monitoring at Scale: War Stories from the GumGum Trenches. https://medium.com/gumgum-tech/prometheus-monitoring-at-scale-war-stories-from-the-gumgum-trenches-f66393c52d0a. Accessed 30 Jun 2022
12. Darrington, J.: What Is Log Management? A Complete Logging Guide, February 2023. https://graylog.org/post/what-is-log-management-a-complete-logging-guide/
13. Dinh, T.: Using AWS X-Ray to Trace and Understand Your Application. https://floqast.com/engineering-blog/post/using-aws-x-ray/. Accessed 03 Jul 2022
14. Dobaj, J., Schuss, M., Krisper, M., Boano, C.A., Macher, G.: Dependable mesh networking patterns. In: Proceedings of the 24th European Conference on Pattern Languages of Programs, pp. 1–14, July 2019. https://doi.org/10.1145/3361149.3361174
15. Ewaschuk, R., Beyer, B.: Monitoring Distributed Systems, 1st edn., p. 550. O'Reilly Media, Inc., U.S.A., April 2016. https://landing.google.com/sre/book.html
16. Faseeha, U., Syed, H.J., Samad, F., Zehra, S., Ahmed, H.: Observability in microservices: an in-depth exploration of frameworks, challenges, and deployment paradigms. IEEE Access (2025)
17. Gregg, B.: The USE Method. https://www.brendangregg.com/usemethod.html. Accessed 11 Apr 2022
18. Gregg, B.: Thinking methodically about performance. Commun. ACM **56**(2), 45–51 (2013). https://doi.org/10.1145/2408776.2408791
19. Gupta, N.: 5 Design Patterns for Building Observable Services. https://engineering.salesforce.com/5-design-patterns-for-building-observable-services-d56e7a330419. Accessed 20 Feb 2022
20. Gupta, N.: READS: service health metrics. https://engineering.salesforce.com/reads-service-health-metrics-1bfa99033adc. Accessed 20 Feb 2022
21. Jackson, J.: The RED method: a new approach to monitoring microservices. https://thenewstack.io/monitoring-microservices-red-method/. Accessed 11 Apr 2022
22. Li, B.: Enjoy your observability: an industrial survey of microservice tracing and analysis. Empir. Softw. Eng. **27**(1), 25 (2021). https://doi.org/10.1007/s10664-021-10063-9

23. Maia, D., Correia, F.F., Queiroz, P.G.G.: Configurational patterns of container orchestration. In: Proceedings of the 29th European Conference on Pattern Languages of Programs, pp. 1–11. EuroPLoP '24. Association for Computing Machinery, New York, NY, USA (2024). https://doi.org/10.1145/3698322.3698342
24. Maia, D., Correia, F.F., Restivo, A., Queiroz, P.G.G.: Container orchestration patterns for optimizing resource use. In: Proceedings of the 30th European Conference on Pattern Languages of Programs, EuroPLoP '25, pp. 1–25. Springer, Heidelberg (2025)
25. Maia, T., Correia, F.: Service mesh patterns. In: Proceedings of the 27th European Conference on Pattern Languages of Programs, EuroPLoP '22. Association for Computing Machinery, New York, NY, USA (2022)
26. Newman, S.: Building Microservices, 2nd edn. O'Reilly Media Inc., Canada (2021)
27. Pandey, M.: Building Netflix's Distributed Tracing Infrastructure. https://netflixtechblog.com/building-netflixs-distributed-tracing-infrastructure-bb856c319304. Accessed 03 Jul 2022
28. Richardson, C.: A pattern language for microservices. http://microservices.io/patterns/. Accessed 25 Feb 2022
29. Richardson, C.: Microservices Patterns: With Examples in Java. Manning Publications Co., Shelter Island, NY (2018)
30. Sousa, T.B.: Engineering Software for the Cloud: A Pattern Language. Ph.D. thesis, University of Porto, Porto, May 2020
31. Sousa, T.B., Aguiar, A., Ferreira, H.S., Correia, F.F.: Engineering software for the cloud: patterns and sequences. In: Proceedings of the 11th Latin-American Conference on Pattern Languages of Programming, SugarLoafPLoP '16. The Hillside Group, USA (2016)
32. Sousa, T.B., Correia, F.F., Ferreira, H.S.: Patterns for software orchestration on the cloud. In: Proceedings of the 22nd Conference on Pattern Languages of Programs, PLoP '15. The Hillside Group, USA (2015)
33. Sousa, T.B., Ferreira, H.S., Correia, F.F.: A pattern language for engineering software for the cloud. In: Transactions on Pattern Languages of Programming V, pp. 1–66. Springer (2025). https://doi.org/10.1007/978-3-662-70810-1_1
34. Sousa, T.B., Ferreira, H.S., Correia, F.F., Aguiar, A.: Engineering software for the cloud: messaging systems and logging. In: Proceedings of the 22nd European Conference on Pattern Languages of Programs. EuroPLoP '17, Association for Computing Machinery, New York, NY, USA (2017). https://doi.org/10.1145/3147704.3147720
35. Sousa, T.B., Ferreira, H.S., Correia, F.F., Aguiar, A.: Engineering software for the cloud: Messaging systems and logging. In: Proceedings of the 22nd European Conference on Pattern Languages of Programs, pp. 1–14 (2017)
36. Sousa, T.B., Ferreira, H.S., Correia, F.F., Aguiar, A.: Engineering software for the cloud: automated recovery and scheduler. In: Proceedings of the 23rd European Conference on Pattern Languages of Programs, EuroPLoP '18, Association for Computing Machinery, New York, NY, USA (2018). https://doi.org/10.1145/3282308.3282315
37. Sousa, T.B., Ferreira, H.S., Correia, F.F., Aguiar, A.: Engineering software for the cloud: external monitoring and failure injection. In: Proceedings of the 23rd European Conference on Pattern Languages of Programs, EuroPLoP '18. Association for Computing Machinery, New York, NY, USA (2018). https://doi.org/10.1145/3282308.3282316

38. Stragliotto, D.: How we implemented RED and USE metrics for monitoring. https://medium.com/thron-tech/how-we-implemented-red-and-use-metrics-for-monitoring-9a7db29382af. Accessed 21 Jun 2022
39. Waseem, M., Liang, P., Shahin, M., Di Salle, A., Márquez, G.: Design, monitoring, and testing of microservices systems: the practitioners' perspective. J. Syst. Softw. **182** (2021). https://doi.org/10.1016/j.jss.2021.111061

Green API Patterns

Marcelo Nunes[3](✉), Souhaila Serbout[1,2,3], João Daniel[2], Eduardo Guerra[2], and Cesare Pautasso[1]

[1] Instituto Tecnológico de Aeronáutica, University of Zurich, Zurich, Brazil
souhaila.serbout@uzh.ch, c.pautasso@usi.ch
[2] Free University of Bozen-Bolzano, Bozen-Bolzano, Italy
joao.daniel@student.unibz.it, eduardo.guerra@unibz.it
[3] Software Institute (USI), Lugano, Switzerland
marcelomsn@ita.br

Abstract. The growing environmental impact of computing has driven the search for more sustainable solutions, leading to the development of the Green Software concept. Green Software refers to the practice of designing, developing, and maintaining software in a way that minimizes energy consumption, reduces carbon footprint, and optimizes resource usage while maintaining high performance and reliability. In this context, the creation of Green Web APIs plays a fundamental role in enabling the construction of efficient systems with low energy consumption. APIs act as intermediaries between different software components, and their design significantly influences the overall resource consumption of applications. Poorly designed APIs can lead to excessive computational overhead, unnecessary data transfers, and high energy usage, negatively impacting both environmental and operational efficiency. This work explores existing patterns and introduces new patterns with best practices for developing sustainable APIs, highlighting design patterns that promote efficiency, such as Green by default and Granular Services, among others that support call optimization, payload reduction, and response aggregation.

Keywords: API · green software · sustainable · energy · software development

1 Introduction

The scientific consensus on the human influence on climate change is undeniable [3]. Robust evidence, from historical climate records to satellite data, points to accelerated global warming with increasingly severe consequences for the planet. In light of these changes, the search for sustainable solutions is imperative in all sectors, including information technology [4].

The information technology industry, with its growing demand for energy and resources, plays a crucial role in both contributing to the problem but also possibly mitigating climate change [8,11]. The production of hardware, the operation of data centers [1], and software development and its operations generate a

T. Plummer et al. (Eds.): EuroPLoP 2025, LNCS 16494, pp. 54–68, 2026.
https://doi.org/10.1007/978-3-032-19157-1_3

significant carbon footprint. However, technology also offers solutions to reduce this impact.

The United Nations, through the 2030 Agenda, created 17 global Sustainable Development Goals (SDGs). These goals focus on promoting prosperity for people and the planet, with several addressing issues such as climate change and responsible consumption and production. The software development industry, through green software practices, can contribute to achieving these goals.

One area that has gained prominence is sustainable software development, or "green software" engineering [5,10]. The Green Software Foundation (GSF)[1], founded in 2019, brings together technology companies to promote the creation of software with a lower environmental impact. The core idea is to integrate sustainability from the beginning of the development process, aiming to optimize resource usage and reduce energy consumption.

Software architecture plays a significant role in determining the energy consumption of a system. The way components are designed, implemented, and interact with one another can profoundly impact the overall system's energy efficiency, in terms of overall CPU and memory usage [2]. Another critical aspect of energy-efficient software design is the system's interface, which directly interacts with users, other systems, or devices. A poorly designed interface that requires frequent, high-volume communication or involves resource-intensive operations can lead to substantial energy wastage. Conversely, interfaces optimized for streamlined data exchange, efficient communication protocols, and minimized overhead can significantly lower energy usage while maintaining performance [7].

To align with the terminology of the Green Web Foundation, we define *Green Web APIs* as Web APIs designed with careful consideration of architectural and implementation decisions aimed at reducing their environmental impact. This paper extends the catalog of API design patterns established in [12], which focuses on loosely coupled message exchanges, by introducing a new set of energy-aware API design patterns (described in Fig. 1). These include: *Green by Default*, *Granular Services*, *Just Latest Updates* and *Disabling Functionality Metadata*. Each of these patterns addresses different aspects of interaction design, ranging from minimizing default payloads to enabling push-based data delivery and client-driven configuration of API behaviors, to support more sustainable Web API ecosystems. Where applicable, we also discuss how these patterns complement and reinforce the sustainability goals of previously defined patterns, offering a cohesive design perspective that integrates energy-awareness as a first-class concern in API engineering. The patterns documented in this paper focus on reducing waste by reducing the amount of information sent in the network or the number of calls. The potential of energy saving will depend on each case since the reduction in the transferred data might vary greatly. In some cases, when the reduction is small, the mechanism used to implement the pattern might consume more energy than it saves. Therefore, when implementing these patterns, the trade-offs need to be considered. When the benefit is not clear, we advise executing experiments to measure the impact of the API change.

[1] Green Software Foundation: https://greensoftware.foundation/.

2 Related API Patterns

The goal of this section is to present existing API design patterns [12] that can also be used to reduce resource waste, consequently reducing energy consumption. The patterns documented in this paper complement these ones. The following are their basic description, highlighting their impact on sustainability.

2.1 Wish Template and Wish List

How can an API client inform the API provider about the data that it is interested in? How can such preferences be expressed flexibly and dynamically?

Specify the desired structure for the content of the response message in the request message.

If clients can determine in advance and they can control which data they retrieve, bandwidth is saved by using the request to reduce the amount of information sent in the response. Additionally, service providers can avoid performing the computations needed to retrieve unwanted information. This prevents over-fetching and reduces unnecessary server processing and network overhead. By customizing requests, each client receives only the relevant data, optimizing performance and reducing response time. In general, by sending only the needed information, the wish list and wish template patterns help to save bandwidth as the responses do not include any waste: content that will be ignored by the client and therefore require unnecessary effort to be produced by the service provider.

2.2 Conditional Request

How can unnecessary server-side processing and bandwidth usage be avoided when frequently invoking API operations that return rarely changing data?

Make requests conditional so that they are processed only if the condition specified by their metadata is met. For example, include a timestamp or hash computed over the last response retrieved by the client so that the server can check if a more recent version of the response should be sent or not.

Reduce bandwidth consumption to access data retrieval services when the last known update time of the data is identical to the last update time obtained by the client in the previous request. There is no need to repeat the transfer of identical messages that have been already sent earlier. Server-side processing is also reduced, as there is no need to recompute a response whose content has already been sent to the client.

2.3 Pagination

How can an API provider deliver large sequences of structured data without overwhelming clients?

Divide large response data sets into manageable and easy-to-transmit pages. Send one page of partial results per response message, and inform the client about the total and/or remaining number of pages. For extra convenience, include a reference to the next page from the current one.

Assuming most clients do not need to retrieve the entirety of the large response but only one or a few pages, pagination helps to reduce waste as it lets clients obtain access to partial responses, thus avoiding unnecessary data transfers.

2.4 Request Bundle

How can the number of requests and responses be reduced to increase communication efficiency?

Assemble multiple independent requests into a single request message.

While the amount of server-side processing is not reduced, bundling multiple requests into one helps to optimize the communication and perform batch processing. Instead of having to pay the fixed cost of establishing multiple connections to send multiple messages for each request, only one message needs to be sent. Likewise, when a batch of similar requests arrives, the server can amortize the setup and tear-down costs over multiple requests, thus reducing energy consumption.

2.5 Linked Information Holder

How can messages be kept small even when an API deals with multiple information elements that reference each other?

Include references to related information elements as opposed to embedding their values into the messages.

Instead of retrieving large bandwidth-consuming responses, clients receive more lightweight responses that contain pointers to fetch additional information only if it becomes necessary to do so later on. Thanks to the presence of pointers to related items, clients do not have to make additional resource discovery requests, as the location of related items is already known.

2.6 Update Subscription

Several clients need real-time information to use on their applications. When the API only provides a service to retrieve the data, the clients recur to a technique called polling, in which the service is accessed in frequent intervals to retrieve the latest data. This approach might result in unnecessary calls that return only information that the client already has, wasting resources in server processing and data transfer. The pattern has another name that is more known and is the pub-sub.

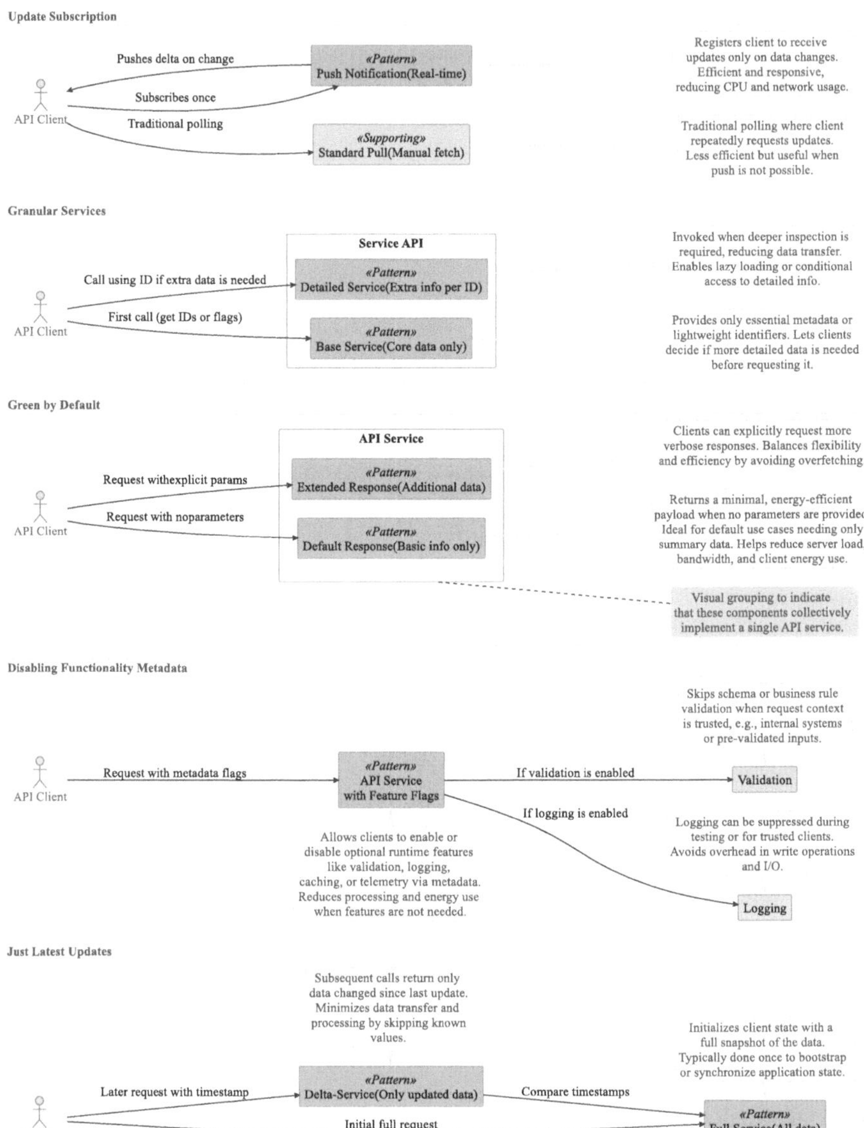

Fig. 1. Overview of Green Web API patterns categorized by interaction design goals. The patterns aim to reduce energy consumption by minimizing data transfer, optimizing response strategies, and enabling client-side control and adaptive behavior. Supporting components like logging and validation are shown in orange, while energy-aware patterns are highlighted in blue. (Color figure online)

3 Granular Services

AKA Split Data Retrieval
AKA Data Parsimony

When accessing the data from services, some applications do not necessarily use all the data retrieved. For instance, the usage of part of this data might be conditioned to user actions or some more complex processing. In the case that part of the retrieved data is not used, there is a waste of resources in the network traffic and in the server processing.

How to avoid including in response payloads information that is not going to be used when it depends on uncertain factors?

- **Uncertainty**: The usage of some data might depend on further user actions or complex processing logic.
- **Sustainability**: It is desirable not to waste resources to send information that is not going to be used.
- **Data structure**: The application might only need a subset of the data related to a given entity.

Therefore:

Provide access to different parts of the data so the clients can retrieve just what they need and when they need it.

Consider the whole data structure that the service clients might need. Create a base service with the core or basic data that are used in all cases. Further, create services that return related data that might be needed only in more specific cases. These secondary services should receive an identifier received in the base service as a parameter.

The service clients should first invoke the base service to retrieve the basic data and the entity identifiers. It should not immediately retrieve data from all the other services. Instead, it should only get the data when required.

In a monolithic application for an educational institution, when it is necessary to scale the application due to the high demand for a module, a lot of resources are not needed. A more granular approach can be adopted to optimize performance and flexibility. A basic service would provide the student's identification and registration data, while specialized services could be created to meet different needs, such as searching for academic records, checking schedules, or verifying payments. This approach allows each service to be developed and scaled independently and also optimizes resource consumption by avoiding the unnecessary loading of large amounts of data.

Consider an online store's order search service. Currently, the system searches for all orders with complete details, including order items, prices and delivery estimates. Creating a base service would return only the IDs of all orders placed by a customer along with basic order information. If a client needs to request details about order items or other information not included in the base service, they would need to make a new request using the ID obtained from the base service

The following are the consequences of using this pattern:

- **Waste reduction (+)**: In cases where the pieces of information are not needed, there will be no waste of resources.
- **Flexibility (+)**: This API style can be adapted to different needs of different application clients.
- **Access Control (+)**: By having granular services, it is easier to control the access of the data in a more granular way.
- **API Size (–)**: The API will have a high amount of operations.
- **Complexity (–)**: The complexity of the client is increased because it needs to access several remote services.
- **Performance (–)**: If a client needs all data, the performance of invoking several services is worse than invoking a single service that returns everything.

* * *

This pattern is an alternative to CONFIGURABLE RETURN; however, GRANULAR SERVICES is more suitable when the usage of information is uncertain, and configuring the return is better when you already know which part of the data will be needed.

Each of the GRANULAR SERVICES can be Green First by returning minimal, resource-efficient responses by default while offering additional parameters to retrieve more detailed or extensive data only when explicitly requested.

A Minas Gerais state government agency within the Finance Secretariat required an application to quickly verify taxpayer debts, avoiding waste and serving a wide range of external and internal clients. The previous system was implemented in a way that all taxpayer debts, along with their branches, were displayed in the first request made to the service, thus always displaying a list of debts. A study found that approximately 60% of taxpayers only need the first response with a flag indicating whether or not there is a debt. The reason for only using the flag is acceptable, as taxpayers need the tax clearance certificate to enter into government contracts, obtain loans, etc. This system is called a request for tax clearance certificates, and the new API design was created to return, in a first request, only whether or not there is a debt and a link to the debts if they exist. The API was designed and implemented in this way to reduce waste in processing, network traffic, and the size of the response returned by the service. Since most taxpayers only need to verify the absence of debts to prove it for various situations, such as contracting with the government, in case debts are found, the client can optionally request a detailed list of debts. This approach allows the same service to serve multiple systems, reducing the response for common use cases. Through the link generated from the first request when there are debts, it is possible to obtain the detailed list.

4 Green by Default

AKA Green First

An API provides options that can be configured to save resources and reduce energy consumption. To activate a more sustainable option, the API usually requires metadata or parameters to be explicitly configured in the request. Despite such option being available and possible to use, several API users still invoke the API without activating it.

How to avoid API requests that consume unnecessary resources?

- **Simplicity**: Some API users choose the simplest way to invoke the API that returns the desired content.
- **Learning Curve**: Passing the parameters to configure the API for saving resources might require some learning curve, as well as reading and understanding the documentation where how to use this option is explained.
- **Enough Performance**: The non-optimal option of the API might be enough for other quality attributes, like response time.
- **Client Perspective**: The gain from the customer perspective can be driven by the use of call limits or reduction in less sustainable configurations.

Therefore:

Provide by default the most sustainable option, which saves most resources while still allowing to change the configuration to return other available options.

Many APIs provide more maintainable configurations, but they are not provided by default. This pattern suggests an inversion of this scenario, in which the most sustainable behavior is adopted by default. That means that a reduced amount of data will be returned if no parameter is configured. For instance, that can mean a reduced number of lines and/or a reduced number of fields.

Additionally, the service can provide optional parameters that can be configured to return the additional data needed. That way, the API users need to reflect on their actual needs for the client application to configure the service to add just what is needed. That practice also requires clear service API documentation, so Green by Default behavior and the available options are clear.

Consider a service that returns a list of car charging stations in a city. The default return of the service might include only the basic information about each station, limiting the number of entries returned. Additional parameters might be used to add more details and to increase the number of returned entries.

- **Resource saving (+)**: The simplest request of the API will consume less resources by default.

- **Reduce potential waste (+)**: Reduce wasted resource caused by API users who are unaware of or do not care to activate more sustainable API options.
- **Increased learning curve (-)**: It is harder to learn how to use the service since the API user might need to learn about all the parameters to use it properly.
- **Unexpected return (-)**: Returning a reduced amount of information might cause confusion in API users who expect to receive all the data when no parameters are configured.

* * *

When implementing a CONFIGURABLE RETURN, GREEN BY DEFAULT can be implemented to allow the configuration in cases where more information is needed and not the opposite.

In the pattern SUSTAINABLE CONFIGURATION [9] for frameworks, the usage of GREEN BY DEFAULT is recommended, using the most sustainable behavior as default.

The Open Data Hub is a digital platform that supports its partners with real data. It has an open-source API that serves data from different domains, such as accommodations, bike sharing, flights, and parking stations. In its API, each of its operations can be invoked with parameters to set filters or projections. Whenever the client sets no parameters, the default behavior is to respond with a limit of 10-record set – rather than a full collection, that could pass the thousands of records.

5 Disabling Functionality Metadata

AKA Metadata Switch

Services often have additional internal features like the generation of detailed logs, robust validation, and notification of external services. The execution of this functionality might not be needed in all requests, which might result in waste in the cases in which it is not needed. The execution of such features is hidden from API clients, which normally have no control over their execution.

How to avoid waste in the execution of internal features that are not needed in all requests?

- **Awareness**: API clients might not be aware of all features executed internally by the services.
- **Feature Execution**: Executing an internal feature might not be necessary for all requests.
- **Control**: The API client might not have control over the internal feature.

Therefore:

As part of the API, provide a metadata parameter that allows the configuration of the internal feature execution.

To implement this pattern, the first step is to evaluate the service functionality and check if there is any part of its internal behavior that might not be necessary for all requests. Usually, this functionality is crosscutting and not part of the service's main responsibility. Some examples are connected to non-functional requirements, such as validations, logging, and external service notifications.

After identifying a feature that is not needed in all requests, it should be isolated from the main feature, and its invocation should be conditioned to the presence of a parameter. The service API should then include a metadata parameter that can be used to deactivate this internal feature. If the logic being disabled is a critical feature, some security authorization might be required to disable the feature.

Considering that the internal feature might be crosscutting and present in other services, this metadata parameter might be standardized and implemented in other services with the same internal feature.

Consider a service that performs a complex validation of the received data before its execution. Sometimes, the API client application might already validate this data before the request. In this case, processing will be wasted when the validation is performed twice. A metadata parameter might allow the API client to inform the service if the data being sent has already been validated.

The following are the consequences of using this pattern:

- **Resource optimization** (+): Disabling unnecessary features can optimize resource utilization.
- **service efficiency** (+): The service can serve requests more efficiently when it saves resources from unnecessary processing.
- **API Complexity** (–): Adding a metadata parameter increases the API complexity.
- **Internal exposure** (–): Using this pattern exposes internal details of the service.
- **Security** (–): Giving control to API clients over the execution of a critical feature might have security implications.

* * *

Green by Default can be implemented in this pattern, considering the default behavior the one without the extra functionality. In this case, the metadata parameter would enable, and not disable, the internal features.

A Sustainable Configuration [9] can be used internally in the service to implement this solution.

Within the Minas Gerais state government's Finance Secretariat, an application receives and processes tax declarations for the Circulation of Goods Tax. While the previous system had monitoring in place, it lacked the flexibility to disable monitoring features at runtime as needed. This rigid approach led to unnecessary processing, transmission, and storage of logs and audit data. To address this, a new monitoring and observability system for our tax declaration service was implemented. This system includes detailed logs and metrics to monitor application performance, allowing for real-time tracking of requests. It aids in capacity planning, error identification, and security threat detection. This new implementation introduced feature flags that enable us to dynamically enable or disable logs, metrics, and new functionalities within our API, resulting in a more resource-efficient system and avoiding wasting unnecessary resources. With this approach, the system avoids wasting processing resources beyond the flexibility by generating metrics, logs, and audit data only when necessary.

6 Just Latest Updates

AKA Delta Encoding

API operations usually return the full object or all the entities that fit the query. When a response is sent to the API user, it contains all the information. Clients that periodically refresh the information usually already have most of the information returned.

How to avoid waste of resources sending data that the API user already has?

- **Partial updates**: Sometimes, the application only updates part of a given entity.
- **Repeated data**: When an API client retrieves data periodically, it usually receives a lot of repeated data.
- **Performance**: Transferring less data results in a better performance.
- **Resource waste**: Receiving repeated data can waste resources in the data transfer and in the back-end and front-end processing.

Therefore:

Provide a service that returns only the data updates after a timestamp.

Create a service API that receives a timestamp and return just the updates that happened after that time. These updates can be from one entity or from a list of entities. If thc scope is one entity, just the updated fields should be returned. If the scope is a list of entities, the response should include the added and delete ones, as well as the field updates in the ones already present. The server response should also return the timestamp considered for that operation in the server, which can be used as a reference for the next request.

From the API client perspective, an API the return the full data should be invoked in the first request, and the JUST LATEST UPDATES service periodically after that. The client should use the timestamp received in the last service response as the parameter of the next request.

It is recommended the implementation of the CONDITIONAL REQUEST [12] in the JUST LATEST UPDATES service. Following this pattern, no response is returned in case no updates happened since the last invocation.

Consider a service that returns the list of the train arrivals in a given station on a given day. On the one hand, there might be cancellations and delays that the passengers might want to know as fast as possible, but on the other hand, this information does not change so frequently. In this scenario, a JUST LATEST UPDATES *service would retrieve just the changes and only when they happen, reducing significantly the resources consumed in this process.*

The following are the consequences of using this pattern:

- **Network traffic reduction (+)**: Less data transfer by the service on the network.
- **Waste reduction (+)**: Providing only the data that has been updated since the client's last request reduces waste in processing and data transfer.
- **Server complexity (–)**: Implementation is more difficult because all fields must be tracked to determine if they have been updated.
- **Client complexity (–)**: There might be two different operations: one when the full information is received and one when just the updates are received.
- **Client dependency (–)**: The client might still invoke several times the service that returns the full information, ignoring the more sustainable alternative.

* * *

CONDITIONAL REQUEST [12] can be used in cases where no update happened since the last invocation.

In a manufacturing application that tracks vehicle production orders, a new order with an estimated delivery date is entered into the system upon request. To support the management system, an API was developed to provide updates on order status and completed processes. To optimize data transfer, the API design allows clients to specify a timestamp in their requests. Only updates made after the specified timestamp are returned, reducing the amount of data transmitted and improving efficiency. The system leverages a database with time-stamped records to efficiently filter and deliver only the latest updates to the management system.

7 Slow Down Notifications

AKA Notification Buffer

Subscription-based APIs enable real-time or near real-time delivery of updates, ensuring that clients always have the latest information. In many cases, subscriptions can be more efficient than polling, as they avoid unnecessary requests and reduce server load. Although subscription-based updates can be efficient, they can also lead to resource waste when there are frequent updates for the entity, entity, especially with a large number of subscribers. This can result in excessive requests, unnecessary processing, and increased network traffic. Although subscriptions address the challenges of polling, they introduce new complexities when dealing with high-volume updates.

How to optimize the frequency and volume of updates in a notification system to reduce resource consumption, especially in scenarios with a large number of users and frequent updates?

- **Sustainability:** The service has the ability to group responses into batches, thereby reducing network traffic.
- **Complexity:** The response caching mechanism can be customized for each resource but can be complex to develop.
- **Waste in Data Transfer:** Transferring real time information for entities that are updated frequently.
- **Waste in Server Processing:** Processing lot of requests wastes resources in the server because the number of updates.

Therefore:

Provide a service that allows for a customizable grouping of resource updates, allowing for customized delivery schedules to meet the needs of different groups of subscribers.

To enhance user experience, e-commerce notifications can be grouped and sent in a more intelligent manner. Less urgent messages can be bundled into a single delivery, optimizing resource usage and preventing users from being overwhelmed with too many notifications. The product owner can customize the frequency and content of these notifications.

The following are the consequences of using this pattern:

- **Reduce server load (+):** By decreasing the number of HTTP requests, there is a lower load on the server, which can improve system performance and scalability.
- **Network traffic (+):** By grouping updates, the volume of data transmitted is reduced, resulting in lower bandwidth consumption.
- **Delayed information (–):** By grouping updates, there may be a delay in delivering critical information, especially if the interval between sends is too long.

- **Complexity (–):** Implementing a notification grouping system may require additional development and configuration effort.

* * *

GREEN BY DEFAULT can be implemented in this pattern, considering that the default behavior is to subscribe all clients with a long update interval. In this case, when no parameter is passed by the client, the result is an hour update time.

In a company that offers stock quote services decided to implement a real-time quote notification system. To ensure a better user experience, it is crucial to optimize resource usage. The approach adopted was to allow customers to subscribe to receive updates on the assets they are interested in. However, sending updates frequently, especially in scenarios with a large number of customers and assets, can generate an excessive volume of data and overload the servers. To mitigate this problem, the subscription update was implemented by parameter in the request. Instead of sending all the quotes with each update, the system can send only new quotes or quotes updated since the last update at the time chosen through the parameter sent in the subscription request. By default, if the parameter with the desired update is not passed, the update will be made available every hour to reduce waste.

8 Conclusion

Developers lack knowledge on how to develop green energy-efficient software [6]. Patterns can help capture valuable architectural knowledge on how to design green software in general and – as shown in this paper – green APIs.

The growing concern about the environment has driven the search for more sustainable technological solutions. In this context, the development of green web APIs emerges as an essential practice to reduce the environmental impact of the software industry. By adopting design patterns that prioritize efficiency and resource optimization, developers can contribute to a more sustainable future. This paper demonstrates that building green web APIs is not only possible but also beneficial, both environmentally and economically using this patterns. It is essential for the technological community to engage in this transformation, continuously seeking new ways to reduce energy consumption and minimize waste generation.

The new patterns cited in this research have various applications in everyday business applications, such as Granular Services, which guides us to divide services into smaller portions so that the initial response is smaller, but with the customer's need, it is possible to make requests within the same service and have more detailed responses. Although implementing green APIs is not that complex, many companies opt for creating services in a standard format due to the ease and tools that aid in this implementation. With the evolution of green web API implementations, it is possible that new tools will facilitate creation and become just a company's choice of which development approach would be the best option for each institution.

References

1. Barroso, L.A., Clidaras, J.: The datacenter as a computer: An introduction to the design of warehouse-scale machines. Springer (2022)
2. Berry, V., Castelltort, A., Lange, B., Teriihoania, J., Tibermacine, C., Trubiani, C.: Is it worth migrating a monolith to microservices? an experience report on performance, availability and energy usage. In: 2024 IEEE International Conference on Web Services (ICWS), pp. 944–954. IEEE (2024)
3. Crowley, T.J.: Causes of climate change over the past 1000 years. Science **289**(5477), 270–277 (2000)
4. Dwivedi, Y.K., et al.: Climate change and cop26: Are digital technologies and information management part of the problem or the solution? an editorial reflection and call to action. Int. J. Inf. Manage. **63**, 102456 (2022). https://doi.org/10.1016/j.ijinfomgt.2021.102456, https://www.sciencedirect.com/science/article/pii/S0268401221001493
5. Manotas, I., et al.: An empirical study of practitioners' perspectives on green software engineering. In: Proceedings of the 38th international conference on software Engineering, pp. 237–248 (2016)
6. Pang, C., Hindle, A., Adams, B., Hassan, A.E.: What do programmers know about software energy consumption? IEEE Softw. **33**(3), 83–89 (2016). https://doi.org/10.1109/MS.2015.83
7. Rajput, S., Kechagia, M., Sarro, F., Sharma, T.: Greenlight: Highlighting TensorFlow APIs energy footprint. In: Proc. 21st International Conference on Mining Software Repositories (MSR). pp. 304–308 (2024)
8. Rolnick, D., et al: Tackling climate change with machine learning. ACM Comput. Surv. 55(2), February 2022. https://doi.org/10.1145/3485128
9. Sultan, B., Ammendola, J., Guerra, E.: Green framework patterns - strategies for embedding sustainability into application frameworks. In: Proceedings of the 31st Conference on Pattern Languages of Programs, People & Practices, pp. 1–8 (2024)
10. Verdecchia, R., Lago, P., Ebert, C., De Vries, C.: Green IT and green software. IEEE Softw. **38**(6), 7–15 (2021)
11. Yang, J., Gong, P., Fu, R., Zhang, M., Chen, J., Liang, S., Xu, B., Shi, J., Dickinson, R.: The role of satellite remote sensing in climate change studies. Nat. Clim. Chang. **3**(10), 875–883 (2013)
12. Zimmermann, O., Stocker, M., Lübke, D., Zdun, U., Pautasso, C.: Patterns for API Design - simplifying integration with loosely coupled message exchanges, vol. 1. Pearson Addison-Wesley, 1 edn. (2023)

Container Orchestration Patterns for Optimizing Resource Use

Diogo Maia[1(✉)], Filipe F. Correia[1], André Restivo[2], and Paulo G. G. Queiroz[1,3]

[1] INESC TEC, Faculty of Engineering, University of Porto, Porto, Portugal
{up201904974,filipe.correia}@fe.up.pt, pgabriel@ufersa.edu.br
[2] LIACC, Faculty of Engineering, University of Porto, Porto, Portugal
arestivo@fe.up.pt
[3] Federal University of the Semi-Arid Region, Mossoró, Brazil

Abstract. Service-based architectures provide substantial benefits, yet service orchestration remains a challenge, particularly for newcomers. While various resources on orchestration techniques exist, they often lack clarity and standardization, making best practices difficult to implement and limiting their adoption within the software industry.

To address this gap, we analyzed existing literature and tools to identify common orchestration practices. Based on our findings, we define three key orchestration resource optimization patterns: PREEMPTIVE SCHEDULING, SERVICE BALANCING, and GARBAGE COLLECTION. PREEMPTIVE SCHEDULING allows the allocation of sufficient resources for services of higher priority in stressful situations, while SERVICE BALANCING enables a restructuring of the nodes to allow better resource usage. To end, GARBAGE COLLECTION creates cleanup mechanisms to better understand the system's resource usage and optimize it. These patterns serve as foundational elements for improving orchestration practices and fostering broader adoption in service-based architectures.

Keywords: Service-oriented Architecture · Practices · Patterns · Container Orchestration

1 Introduction

The rapid advancement in microservices-based applications [7,17], along with the extensive adoption of container technologies for software packaging, has led to a significant increase in the use of orchestration tools [18]. The term "orchestration" can have different meanings depending on the context. To avoid confusion and ensure alignment throughout this paper, we include specific descriptors to clearly define our focus. Here, we focus on orchestration in the context of managing service-based applications, which closely relates to container orchestration. Today, containers are one of the most common methods for packaging and hosting services. Therefore, in this study, orchestration is defined as:

T. Plummer et al. (Eds.): EuroPLoP 2025, LNCS 16494, pp. 69–92, 2026.
https://doi.org/10.1007/978-3-032-19157-1_4

Container orchestration allows cloud and application providers to define how to select, to deploy, to monitor, and to dynamically control the configuration of multi-container packaged applications in the cloud [9]

This paper focuses on orchestration tasks during deployment and run-time, including scheduling, scaling, monitoring, and fault tolerance. As service-based containerized systems continue to proliferate, the corresponding need for orchestration has prompted the emergence and broad adoption of several best practices. These practices have shaped the evolution of orchestration tools as developers implement new features to address emerging challenges. However, these practices are not always well-documented or widely understood, leaving practitioners without clear guidance on their application, timing, or intended outcomes.

To bridge this gap, these practices can be documented as design patterns. Although many patterns have been specified for service-based and cloud-native systems [2–4,8,10,19–23], only a limited number address orchestration. This paper continues our work [15] on defining additional orchestration patterns, contributing three patterns related to previously defined patterns, which aid in optimizing system resources.

This article begins by detailing the research methodology used to uncover the patterns and practices discussed. Subsequently, the paper introduces a pattern map derived from the findings. Following this, the three newly identified patterns are thoroughly explained. The paper concludes with a discussion of the contributions made and potential directions for future research.

2 Research Process

These design patterns are derived from two primary sources: existing literature and orchestration tools, including orchestrators, add-ons, and libraries. These sources were critical to gaining an in-depth understanding of service orchestration, identifying research gaps, and formalizing best practices into patterns.

The literature review focused on exploring existing research on orchestration and identifying established patterns. In addition, gray literature, such as blogs and forums, was examined to uncover industry practices and address gaps in formal research.

A feature analysis of orchestration tools was conducted to complement the literature findings. This analysis covered Kubernetes [5], Docker Swarm [13], and Mesos [11], chosen due to their prominence in the literature and their foundational design (unlike tools built on top of other orchestrators, such as CloudFoundry [12]). These tools' documentation, repositories, and pull requests were analyzed to extract further insights.

The research identified 29 patterns related to container orchestration and 8 promising practices that have not yet been formalized. These findings were organized into a pattern map that highlights connections between patterns and how some address the consequences of others. The full process and results are detailed in Maia's master's thesis [16]. This article focuses on 3 of the 8 promising practices that were developed into patterns: PREEMPTIVE SCHEDULING, SERVICE BALANCING, and GARBAGE COLLECTION.

3 About the Patterns

The pattern map shown in Fig. 1 is a visual representation of the 3 patterns we defined from the research process explained previously and their direct connections, as in patterns that can be directly used in the implementation or complement each other. These connections are represented by a directed line from one pattern to another.

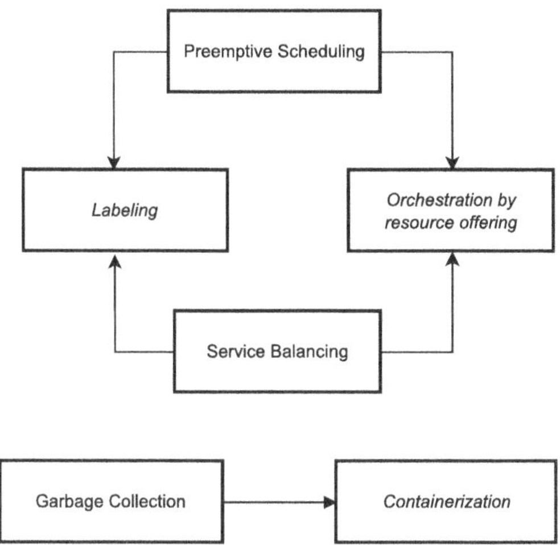

Fig. 1. Pattern Map of the Defined Patterns and Direct Connections.

The patterns shown in italics are those already established in the literature. They are:

- LABELING refers to the use of metadata tags (labels) to manage, group, and select containers or other resources in a flexible and scalable way [15]
- ORCHESTRATION BY RESOURCE OFFERING allows every container/job to have the required resources to function properly, ensuring the stable run of the services [19].
- CONTAINERIZATION encapsulates a service's files and dependencies, enabling the deployment of the service within a self-contained and isolated environment [19].

4 Preemptive Scheduling

4.1 Context

A distributed system is comprised of a cluster of multiple nodes. Some nodes run services while others are empty nodes, awaiting some services to be scheduled for them. These nodes are comprised of a group of containers, which will host the services on them. Several services are to run in nodes with various requirements and specifications. These requirements and specifications are directly connected to the resources or properties of the node (all known by the developers), as the match of both will allow the service to run as intended by the developers. An example of a service requirement is the geographical location where the containers in a node are running. The developer wants a certain service to be hosted in containers of certain areas, such as Europe, so the system will try to schedule the service to a node where the containers are running in each zone.

All the system's services are not of the same importance. Some services are essential for the system's well-being, and without them, the system collapses. Other services are still necessary but not crucial for the service's runtime, making some system functionalities not work, but allowing the system as a whole to function in a minimum viable way. Some other services aren't as essential as others, such as being able to be shut down and the system working as intended for a user.

There are scenarios where crucial services need some node resources that can or may not already be assigned to some other service, or less important services try to take resources from the more critical services. Not managing situations like this can lead to essential services being starved for resources or a lack of optimization on resource usage and costs.

4.2 Example

As we can see in Fig. 2, a system built using microservices architecture comprises 3 different services: a frontend, an API, and a data processing service. The first two services are of higher importance for the system's developers since any disruption will have immediate consequences for the website's users, and availability is one of the developers' biggest concerns. The third service is essential to the system as a whole, but it is a background task that, in case of its shutdown, does not immediately affect the website's use.

This system is hosted on one node. Typically, the three services are deployed and scheduled at the same node, leaving not enough free node resources for any other full service to be deployed there. At specific points, the developers decide to deploy a new temporary service in charge of a critical task (Service D), which happens to be more important than the data processing service. However, there are no resources for it in the node.

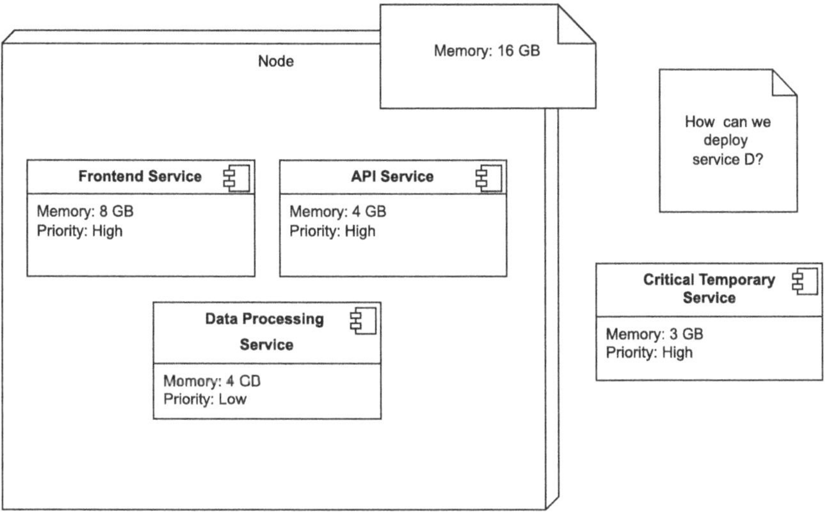

Fig. 2. Preemptive Scheduling - Visual Representation of the Example.

4.3 Problem

How can we ensure that crucial services are getting priority when it comes to their requirements compared to other less important services?

4.4 Forces

- **Availability/ Resilience** - Ensuring crucial services have the resources they need during runtime allows the system to be available at all intended times. By not doing it, the system can go down, which can affect the developer's productivity and users' experience of the system;
- **Consistency** - By guaranteeing crucial service requirements, the developers allow the service to run as efficiently as possible. This allows the crucial part system to behave as intended, even in spikes of demand or costly operations;
- **Resource/Cost Management** - There is a cost associated with the resources that the developers can own and use. The lower the costs, the fewer resources the system will have to run with. In case the resources are low, there may be a need to take resources from one service to give to another. If the resources are high, the developers can try to guarantee resources for each service;
- **Hierarchy** - The system can have all services with the same or very similar levels of importance;
- **Adaptability** - The priority of a service can change according to the business needs and system state;
- **Customization** - Not all services, if they have priority, have the same degree of priority. A service can have priority over all other services, but a service

may also be more important than one service while being less important than another.

4.5 Solution

Define priority levels for each service, and when a service with a higher priority needs the resources of a lower priority service, evict it and try to reschedule it.

To effectively manage resources for high-priority services, the system can evict lower-priority services from a node, reallocating resources to crucial services. Once evicted, the lower-priority service is sent back to the scheduler for rescheduling when resources become available.

The first step in implementing this pattern is to define service priorities. Not all services should be treated as critical. Priority should be reserved for services essential to business operations, such as user-facing applications or key API servers that require high availability. Over-assigning priority to many services can lead to excessive preemption, disrupting less critical but necessary operations. The priority of each service must be clearly defined in its configuration and should be adjustable based on business needs or other factors. These adjustments can be made manually or via an API.

To facilitate effective scheduling, it's important to establish precise priority levels. This can be as simple as binary levels—priority or non-priority—but it may also involve more granular distinctions, such as numerical levels from 1 to 10. In this system, a priority level of 1 would represent the highest priority, ensuring the service receives all necessary resources. In contrast, a level 10 would indicate a low-priority service that can be delayed. Alternatively, priority levels could be represented by letters or codenames. Regardless of how the levels are defined, they must be standardized across all services to ensure consistent comparisons during scheduling.

During the scheduling process, tasks should be organized into a priority queue, with higher-priority tasks placed at the front. This approach ensures that crucial services are started first and minimizes the need to evict lower-priority services, which can introduce time-related overhead.

When scheduling, the system should first attempt to find a node that meets the service's resource requirements without considering priority levels. If no suitable node is available, the scheduler compares the priority levels of services running on potential nodes. If a lower-priority service is identified, it is evicted, and the high-priority service is deployed. The evicted service is then re-added to the scheduler's priority queue. If no suitable node is found because all nodes run services of equal or higher priority, the high-priority service will be scheduled later.

In the last paragraph, we discuss a default way to deal with low priority services after eviction. However, this can be customized by the developers as they believe it should better serve the service architecture. For example, suppose the service evicted runs in a certain time slot. In that case, the developer can decide not to try to reschedule the service after it is evicted, knowing it will be deployed and scheduled at a later time. Another example of dealing with the evicted service can be delegating its canceled work to another instance of the service currently running, improving the system's fault tolerance and guaranteeing the work is done. This adds a layer of customization for developers, leading to a better system as a whole.

4.6 Implementation

Kubernetes has an innate preemption when scheduling pods to nodes. According to their documentation [1], this is achieved by defining one or more *PriorityClass* objects, which assign a specific priority level to pods within the system.

Listing 1.1. Example of PriorityClass object creation in Kubernetes

```
1 apiVersion: scheduling.k8s.io/v1
2 kind: PriorityClass
3 metadata:
4     name: high-priority
5 value: 1000000
6 globalDefault: false
7 description: "this priority class should be used for XYZ
      service pods only."
```

Kubernetes allows for creating priority objects with a high level of customization. The following are the main attributes that define this object:

- **name**: the name the developer wants to give to the priority level. It can either be a way to describe just the level by itself, like in this case, or add some usage context;
- **value**: In Kubernetes, value can be any 32-bit integer value smaller than or equal to 1 billion. The higher the level, the higher the priority of the pod;
- **globalDefault**: Only one Kubernetes *Priority Class* can be defined as the global default (by having this property defined as "true". When true, all the other pods in the system without any *Priority Class* attached will have this priority level;
- **description**: The developers can, in this property, define information regarding the usage of this object.

By defining the priority levels as objects, Kubernetes incites developers to assign certain *Priority Classes* to groups of Pods with the same priority and context. For example, creating a *PriorityClass* for data processing services allows them to not only assign the same priority to these services but also, in a moment where there is a business need to change them, instead of changing one by one, developers only need to change the *PriorityClass* object.

In the Pod configurations, the developers can define the priority level by specifying the property *priorityClassName* as the name property of the intended *PriorityClass* object.

Listing 1.2. Example of defining the PriorityClass of a Pod in Kubernetes

```
apiVersion: v1
kind: Pod
metadata:
  name: nginx
  labels:
    env: test
spec:
  containers:
  - name: nginx
    image: nginx
    imagePullPolicy: IfNotPresent
  priorityClassName: high-priority
```

4.7 Consequences

- (+) The system can evict lower priority services to guarantee the crucial services use their resources;
- (+) The resource cost is the same as before the implementation of the pattern;
- (+) The system can accommodate new services with high priority without impacting the resource cost;
- (-) The priority levels comparison depends on the externally defined configurations of the services being compared. An error in their definition can lead to possible errors in configuration;
- (-) If the developers define all or most of the services as a higher priority, the problem can reappear since there are no priority discrepancies to support the eviction and freedom of new resources;
- (-) The eviction of service can take time, leading to a time overhead in the scheduler and deployment of the crucial service;
- (-) The evicted service can lose progress of its work, which can corrupt the system in case of a wrong priority labeling or lead to faulty information if not handled.

4.8 Example Resolved

Considering the previous example, the 4 services would be assigned a priority level: the frontend server and API server would be assigned a priority level 1, the data processing server would be assigned a priority level 3, and the temporary service would be assigned a priority level 2. In this case, the preemptive scheduler would check the node and notice that it has all the allocated resources. Then, it would compare all the service levels and realize that the temporary service has a higher priority than the data processing server service. It would evict the data processing server, deploy the temporary server, and add the new service to the scheduler's priority queue. This can be seen in Fig. 3.

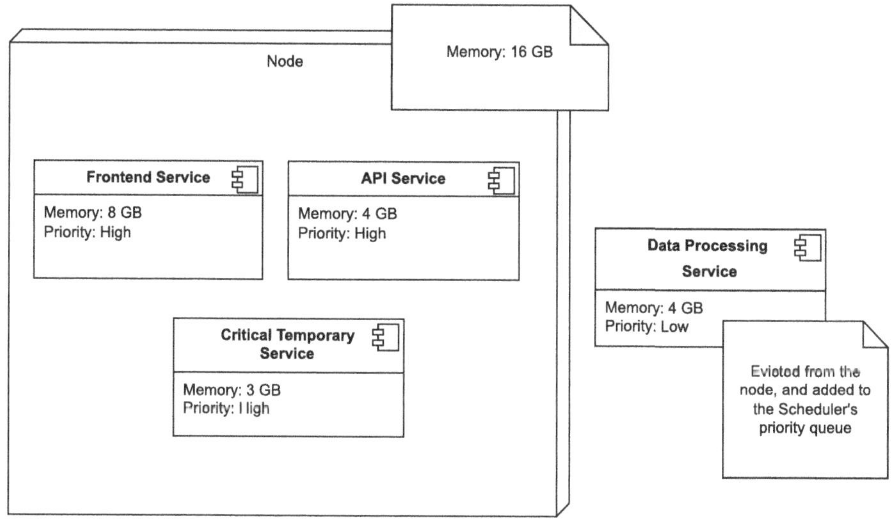

Fig. 3. Preemptive Scheduling - Visual Representation of the Example Resolved.

4.9 Known Uses

Peloton [6], Uber's resource management system, improves cluster utilization and reduces costs by co-locating diverse workloads, such as online services and batch jobs, on shared clusters. The system leverages preemptive scheduling to manage resources effectively.

Resource overcommitment allows Peloton to run more jobs than there are physical resources, assuming that not all jobs will require their total resource allocation simultaneously. Peloton designates lower-priority batch jobs as preemptible to prevent disruption to critical online services, which are often latency-sensitive. When the system detects that online services need more resources, it preempts (suspends or stops) these batch jobs to free up capacity for high-priority online workloads. This ensures that critical services maintain performance without interruption.

Additionally, Peloton uses disaster recovery (DR) capacity for batch jobs when the system is running normally. However, in the event of a failover, these batch jobs are preempted to ensure that the DR capacity is fully available for critical online services. Peloton can dynamically reallocate resources to essential tasks during high demand or system failover by preempting non-essential workloads. Peloton employs two types of preemption:

- **Inter-resource pool preemption**: This method ensures fair distribution of resources across different resource pools by enforcing preemption policies. When necessary, it reclaims resources from specific pools according to these policies. Administrators can customize and implement different preemption strategies to suit their needs.

- **Intra-resource pool preemption**: This approach manages resource sharing within a single resource pool based on the priorities of the jobs. Since multiple users can use a resource pool, each running multiple jobs, conflicts can arise when one user monopolizes the pool's capacity, causing other users' jobs to be delayed and potentially miss deadlines. Additionally, when a higher-priority job arrives while lower-priority jobs are already running, the scheduler needs to free up resources for the more critical task. Intra-resource pool preemption addresses this by interrupting lower-priority jobs within the pool to make space for higher-priority ones when resources are limited.

In Linux [14], preemptive scheduling allows a system to interrupt a running task (process or thread) and switch to another, typically higher-priority, task. This improves responsiveness and efficiency by ensuring critical tasks can run when needed. Linux uses preemptive multitasking, meaning it can forcibly suspend a process to run another, especially when higher-priority tasks are waiting.

Linux also supports kernel preemption, allowing system-level tasks to be interrupted for higher-priority ones. This boosts responsiveness in real-time applications. The default Linux scheduler, the Completely Fair Scheduler (CFS), balances fairness with preemption to avoid CPU monopolization.

Control groups (cgroups) let administrators allocate and limit system resources like CPU, memory, and I/O to groups of processes. This enables resource isolation—for example, prioritizing containers or user workloads. Within and across cgroups, Linux can still preempt tasks based on priority. A high-priority process in one cgroup can preempt lower-priority processes in another, depending on resource configuration. In containerized setups, this ensures critical services (e.g., a web server) get CPU time over less important jobs.

4.10 Related Patterns

This pattern needs a scheduler to do its job, so it would improve by applying the pattern Orchestration by Resource Offering. An alternative to this pattern is that if the developer is not concerned with the costs and needs resources, the developer should consider scaling the system using the pattern Elasticity Manager. The priority levels of the services can be defined using Labeling, and the resources needed can be determined using the Resource Reserve and Limit.

5 Service Balancing

5.1 Context

A distributed system comprises a cluster of multiple nodes. Some nodes run services, while others are empty nodes, awaiting some services to be scheduled for them. Several services are to run in nodes with various requirements and specifications. These services can already be run or be prepared on the available nodes.

Normally, during the scheduling process, a service is scheduled with a node that has the resources to run it. By placing a service in a node with more free resources, the cluster tends to balance itself. However, sometimes, problems in the system occur, such as containers going down, services requiring more resources, or nodes going down or up. These situations can lead to an imbalance in the nodes, resulting in the inefficient use of resources.

5.2 Example

As seen in Fig. 4, a system built using the microservices architecture comprises 5 services: A, B, C, D, and E, and 3 nodes, each one with the same resources. Upon scheduling the services among the containers.

- Node 1: service A and B
- Node 2: service C
- Node 3: service D and E

However, after an outage, node 3 is down and, as a reaction to that event, services D and E are scheduled into Nodes 1 and 2, leaving the system state like this:

- Node 1: service A, B, and D
- Node 2: service C and E
- Node 3: rebooting

Nodes 1 and 2 now have almost no free resources, and after some time, node 3 is **alive** again and waiting for more services to be scheduled and deployed there. The system is currently imbalanced, as nodes 1 and 2 have almost fully allocated their resources, while node 3 has room to take on more work. This ending state of the system after the outage is represented by the second column of Fig. 4.

5.3 Problem

How can we balance resource usage across the available nodes in a system?

5.4 Forces

- **Resource Optimization** - An imbalanced service load leaves the system poorly using the resources, normally underutilizing them;
- **Stability/ Availability** - Moving around the services to obtain balance over the system can lead to uncertain consequences and unnecessary container restarts. This could also lead to the disruption of service progress if badly timed or not accounted for.
- **Performance of System** - Moving around the services to obtain balance over the system can lead to a decay of the performance of the system because of the service restarts and redeployments needed;

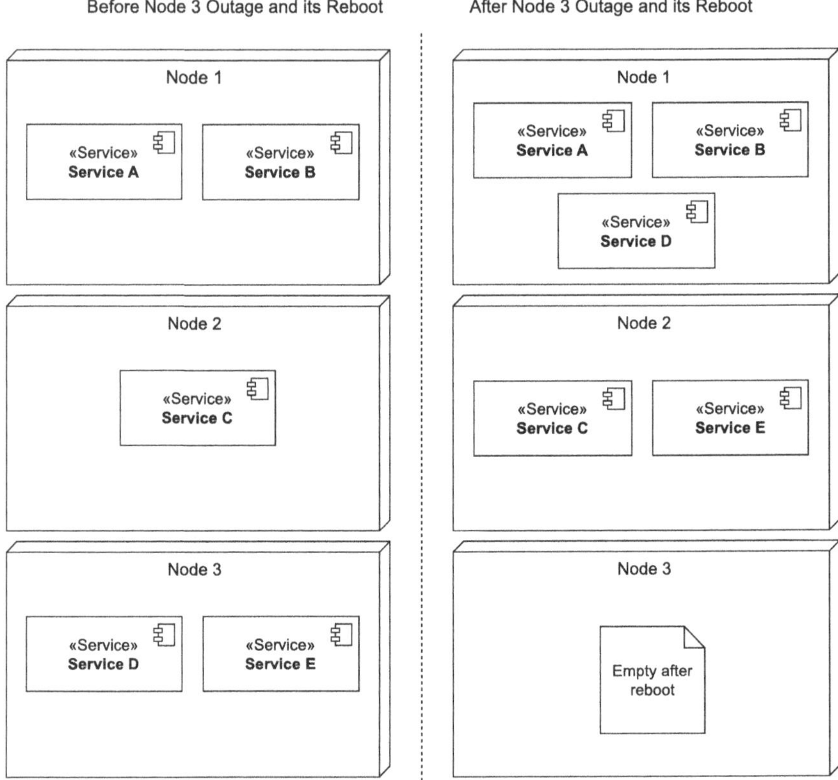

Fig. 4. Service Balancing - Visual Representation of the Example.

- **Performance of Services** - Moving services to free nodes can lead to a performance boost for these services by having the resources they need or more;
- **Fault Tolerance** - Balancing the nodes can lead to an improvement in resilience of the system when it comes to node failures;

5.5 Solution

Rebalance the services across the nodes by evicting the services considered imbalanced and scheduling them in nodes with available resources

To effectively rebalance a cluster, three key steps must be followed: identifying the imbalance, selecting the services to rebalance, and determining the optimal time to perform the rebalancing. The primary goal of this pattern is to maximize resource optimization, even if it means temporarily sacrificing the availability of certain services.

A robust monitoring system must be in place to detect an imbalance in the cluster. Without monitoring, it's challenging to recognize when resources are unevenly distributed. This can be achieved through dashboards displaying the cluster's status or simple logging mechanisms. An imbalance typically occurs when one or more nodes are underutilized compared to others in the cluster. Once an imbalance is detected, the next step is to decide which services to reschedule. There are two main approaches:

- Full Cluster Restart: Restart the entire cluster, allowing services to be rebalanced from scratch. While this can correct imbalances, it poses significant risks like service disruptions and system instability.
- Targeted Rescheduling: Select specific services from over-allocated nodes and restart them to redistribute resources. This approach also has risks, as restarting containers can lead to temporary instability and unpredictable outcomes.

Services can be selected for rebalancing either manually or automatically. The manual approach involves reviewing resource usage across nodes and deciding which services to relocate. Although more time-consuming, this method provides greater control and reduces the risk of performance issues. Alternatively, automation can detect significant discrepancies in resource usage between nodes and automatically select services for rebalancing. However, this approach may introduce performance and availability problems, making manual selection the safer option.

Timing is essential when rebalancing the cluster. Constant rebalancing can degrade system performance by frequently consuming resources for container evictions and rescheduling. To avoid this, rebalancing should be scheduled during maintenance windows or periods of low traffic to minimize the impact on application performance.

The rebalancing should also be done considering the loss of progression of the services that are being reallocated. This is important to reassure the resilience of the system and minimize any loss of data. With this in mind, service migrations[1] should be carefully applied.

For large clusters, incremental rebalancing is recommended to prevent overwhelming the system. This gradual approach ensures that resources are redistributed without causing excessive strain on the cluster. Following these steps and carefully timing the rebalancing process, the cluster can be efficiently optimized while minimizing disruptions.

5.6 Implementation

In **Docker Swarm**[2], generally, you don't need to rebalance tasks across nodes in a swarm manually. When you add a new node to the swarm, or a previously disconnected node rejoins, it won't automatically receive tasks to balance the load. This design choice avoids disrupting active services, as periodically shifting

[1] https://docs.oracle.com/cd/E24329_01/web.1211/e24425/service_migration.html#CLUST287.

[2] Administer and maintain a swarm of Docker Engines: https://docs.docker.com/engine/swarm/admin_guide.

tasks to achieve balance could interfere with client applications. Instead, the swarm aims for an eventual balance with minimal user impact. New tasks or tasks from nodes that become unavailable are assigned to less busy nodes, ensuring a gradual balance over time.

If you want to force the swarm to redistribute tasks, use the −−force or −f flag with the docker service update command. This will restart service tasks and may cause temporary disruptions for client applications. If your service is set up with rolling updates, this process will help minimize interruptions.

For older versions or if you're comfortable disrupting tasks, you can manually rebalance the swarm by temporarily increasing the service scale. First, check the current scale with docker service inspect −−pretty <servicename>. Then, use docker service scale to add more instances, which will cause tasks to be distributed to the nodes with the fewest workloads. You might need to scale up incrementally a few times to achieve a balanced load. Once the balance is satisfactory, scale the service back down to its original number of instances.

5.7 Consequences

- (+) The node resources are being spent more optimally by occupying underutilized nodes;
- (+) By spreading the services across the nodes, in case of a node failure, fewer services are shut down, increasing the resistance of the system;
- (+) Rebalancing of the system leads to a better system performance and application availability in the long term;
- (-) Rebalancing of the system leads to service restart and redeployment, which worsens the distributed system performance and application availability in the short term;
- (-) Automatically rebalancing the services can lead to possible momentary performance and availability problems.
- (-) Can lead to possible loss of progress of the services migrated if not properly handled.

5.8 Example Resolved

The system has become unbalanced after the Node 3 outage. With services D and E relocated to Nodes 1 and 2, these nodes are now close to full capacity, while Node 3 remains underutilized despite being fully operational. To rebalance the system, a decision must be made on which services should be moved back to Node 3 (see Fig. 5). We have two approaches to consider:

- Manual Selection: After reviewing the current resource usage on Nodes 1 and 2, we can manually opt to relocate services D and E back to Node 3 since they were initially stationed there. This will help in freeing up capacity on Nodes 1 and 2.

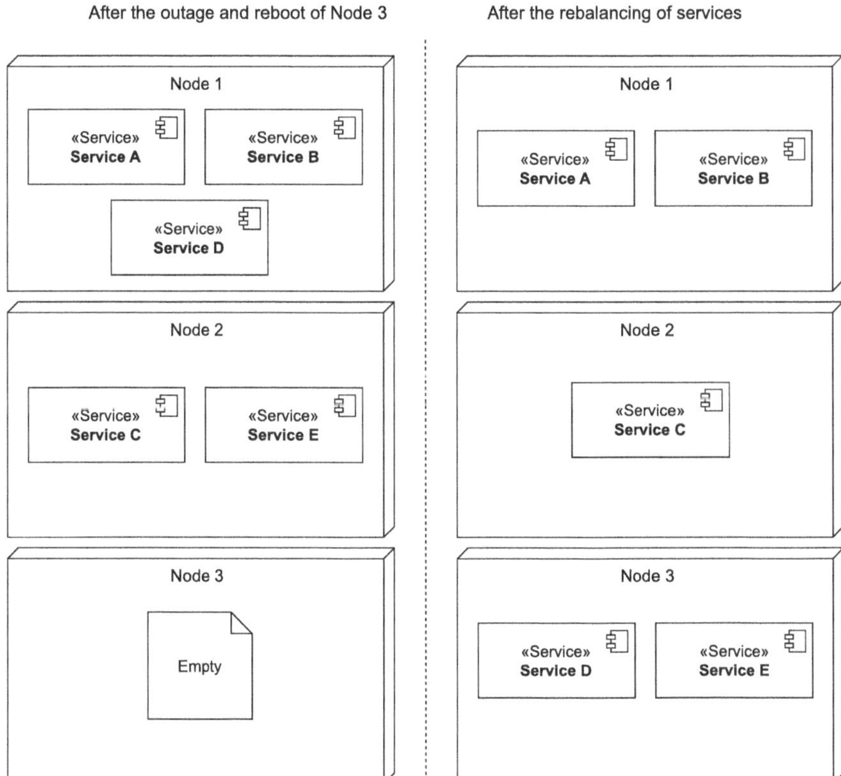

Fig. 5. Preemptive Scheduling - Example Resolved

- Automatic Detection: An automated system can also play a role in identifying the resource usage mismatch and autonomously relocating services D and E back to Node 3, thus restoring balance.

The timing of the rebalancing operation is crucial. We aim to rebalance during a maintenance window or low-traffic period to minimize disruption. This approach will reduce the impact on application performance during the restart and rescheduling of services. It is advisable to schedule the rebalancing during a quieter time and relocate services D and E back to Node 3, restoring the cluster's balance.

We can opt for a gradual rebalancing approach for larger clusters or to avoid overwhelming the system with simultaneous changes. This involves initially relocating one service, such as D, to Node 3, monitoring system stability, and later moving the second service, E.

5.9 Known Uses

Dynamic work rebalancing in a Dataflow system from **Google Cloud**[3] is a method for efficiently managing tasks across different nodes or processors. Here's how it works: initially, tasks are distributed among nodes based on availability. The system constantly monitors each node's performance and workload. If some nodes become overloaded or underutilized, the system adjusts the task distribution to achieve a better balance. This involves moving tasks from busy nodes to those with more capacity.

The main benefits of dynamic work rebalancing are improved performance and resource utilization. It ensures that no single node is overwhelmed, which helps maintain smooth operation and reduces delays. Additionally, it increases resilience by adapting to changes like node failures or sudden spikes in workload. This approach also makes it easier to scale the system up or down as needed.

In parallel computing, **Load Balancing**[4] is the process of distributing computational tasks evenly across multiple processors or cores to maximize performance and efficiency. The aim is to avoid situations where some processors are overloaded while others remain idle, which leads to poor utilization and increased execution time. Load balancing strategies can be static, where tasks are assigned before execution, or dynamic, where the system reallocates tasks during runtime based on current load conditions. Efficient load balancing ensures that all processors contribute equally, resulting in faster computations and optimal use of hardware resources.

The same concept holds true in distributed systems, especially those built on microservice architectures. Instead of balancing low-level tasks across cores, the focus is on balancing services (like containers or pods) across multiple machines or nodes. This is known as service balancing and is often managed by orchestration tools such as Kubernetes. These systems monitor resource usage (CPU, memory, etc.) and distribute or scale services to prevent any node from becoming a performance bottleneck. Much like dynamic task balancing in parallel computing, this process adapts to real-time conditions and helps maintain system health, availability, and scalability.

The core idea connecting both contexts is efficient resource distribution to avoid overload and underutilization. In parallel computing, the concern is with keeping cores busy; in distributed systems, it's about keeping nodes balanced. Both rely on dynamic strategies that adjust to changing workloads and aim to deliver smooth, predictable performance. Ultimately, service balancing in distributed systems can be seen as a higher-level application of the same load balancing principles used in parallel computing, adapted to operate across networked environments and containerized services.

---

[3] https://cloud.google.com/dataflow/docs/dynamic-work-rebalancing.

[4] https://hpc-wiki.info/hpc/Load_Balancing.

5.10 Related Patterns

When rebalancing the services, these services are sent to the scheduler. In this regard, we believe using the pattern Orchestration by resource offering is an excellent option to guarantee a good scheduling process. Service balancing can use the Labelling process to define a property not to allow a service to be scheduled.

6 Garbage Collection

6.1 Context

In container orchestration systems, applications are deployed as containers across multiple nodes in a cluster. As these systems manage the lifecycle of containers, resources such as services, images, volumes, and configurations are created and used, and eventually become obsolete. Over time, unused resources can accumulate, leading to resource wastage, performance degradation, and potential outages.

In such dynamic environments, there is a need for a mechanism that automatically cleans up resources that are no longer in use to ensure the system remains efficient and stable. This is where the garbage collection pattern in container orchestration comes into play.

6.2 Example

A software system uses a container orchestration platform to manage its applications. The system is composed of multiple services, each responsible for different functionality. These services are deployed as sets of containers, and the system is frequently updated to add new features or address issues. The following is represented by Fig. 6.

Over time, the accumulation of older service versions can lead to performance degradation. Residual logs and unused container images consume disk space, and the orchestration platform's API server may slow down due to the growing number of managed objects. This can result in operational challenges and a reduction in overall system performance.

6.3 Problem

How can a distributed system using containers prevent resource wastage, performance degradation, and stability issues caused by accumulating unused or obsolete resources?

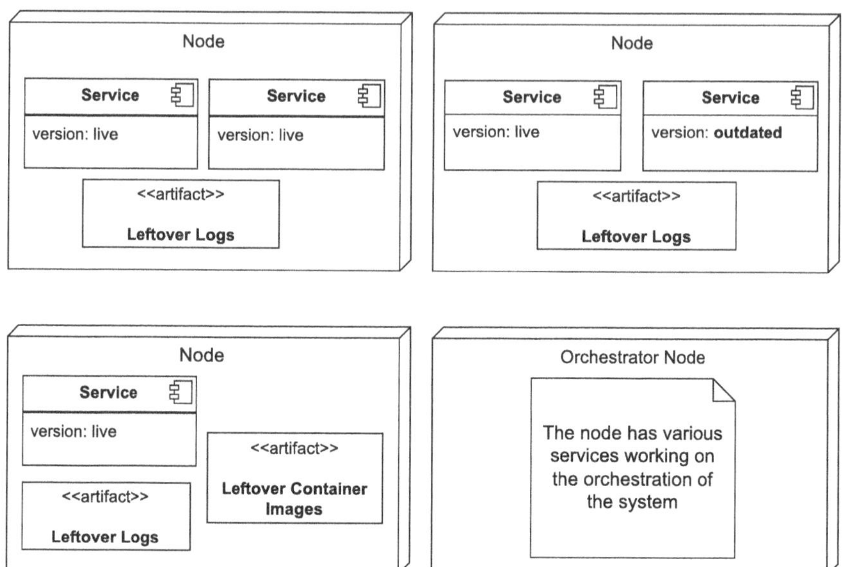

Fig. 6. Garbage Collection - Visual Representation of Example.

6.4 Forces

- **Resource Efficiency** - Ensuring that resources such as memory, CPU, and storage are efficiently utilized without being consumed by obsolete objects;
- **System Overhead** - Balancing the overhead of continuously monitoring and cleaning up resources with maintaining system performance;
- **Automation** - Automating the cleanup of unused resources to reduce operational burden
- **Control** - Providing sufficient control to administrators to customize or intervene in cleanup processes when necessary (e.g., setting reclaim policies, excluding certain resources from automatic deletion);
- **Scalability/Complexity** - As the scale of the system grows, the cleanup mechanism must be capable of handling larger numbers of resources without becoming a bottleneck or introducing complexity that is difficult to manage;
- **Availability** - Ensuring that the cleanup process does not interfere with active workloads or reduce system availability, especially in environments with high uptime requirements;

6.5 Solution

Implement automated cleanup mechanisms that identify and remove unused resources while allowing customization and control to prevent resource wastage and maintain system efficiency.

The solution is implementing a garbage collection service that identifies and removes inactive resources. This will ensure that the cluster remains clean and efficient.

For this system to work, it will need to have some components:

- Lifecycle Management;
- Automated Deletion Mechanisms
- Finalizers

The Lifecycle Management system would define clear ownership and lifecycle for each object in the system, including services, containers, and volumes. Owner references would be used to track dependencies, allowing for cascading deletions, where dependent objects are automatically cleaned up when their owner is deleted. For example, a node owns the services it has. When the node is deleted, the containers are also deleted, impeding orphaned resources.

The Automated Deletion Mechanisms would clean the resources that the Lifecycle Management would detect. Some examples of functions it should have are the automatic deletion of terminated or completed services after a certain threshold to avoid accumulation, an image running system to remove unused images to free up disk space regularly, the automatic deletion of volumes that are no longer bound to any persistent claims, and the implementation of Time to Live policies for short-lived resources, such as jobs.

The Finalizers would allow custom cleanup tasks to be executed before an object is deleted, such as cascading the deletion of objects.

These are the main components a Garbage Collector should have to allow the system to clean itself and reduce its resource wastage automatically. However, garbage collection requires careful planning, like setting up lifecycle policies, monitoring resource uses, and handling edge cases that the automatic cleanup may not cover.

6.6 Implementation

Kubernetes[5] has built-in garbage collection processes for managing resources like pods, replica sets, and deployments. For instance, when a pod is terminated, Kubernetes automatically cleans up its associated resources, such as ephemeral storage and networking configurations. Additionally, Kubernetes can automatically remove old versions of images and unused volumes based on policies defined in the cluster configuration

Kubernetes checks for and deletes objects without owner references, like the pods left behind when you delete a ReplicaSet (set of pod replicas). When you delete an object, you can control whether Kubernetes deletes the object's dependents automatically in a cascading deletion process. There are two types of cascading deletion, as follows:

[5] Garbage Collection in Kubernetes: https://kubernetes.io/docs/concepts/architecture/garbage-collection.

- **Foreground cascading deletion** - the owner object you're deleting first enters a deletion in progress state. After the owner object enters the deletion in progress state, the controller deletes the dependents. After deleting all the dependent objects, the controller deletes the owner object.
- **Background cascading deletion** - In background cascading deletion, the Kubernetes API server deletes the owner object immediately, and the controller cleans up the dependent objects in the background. This is Kubernetes' default garbage collection process.

You can also control how and when garbage collection deletes resources that have owner references using Kubernetes finalizers.

6.7 Consequences

- (+) Improved resource efficiency by reducing resource consumption by automatically cleaning up unused resources and optimizing disk space by deleting older or unused objects;
- (+) Enhanced system performance with faster response times and reduced latency since there are fewer objects to manage;
- (+) Simplified maintenance since the cleanup is automatic, and this allows for easier management of resources;
- (-) Risk of premature deletion if the garbage collector is not configured correctly;
- (-) Increase of system overhead since garbage collection mechanisms are always running;
- (-) Some resources may become orphaned if dependencies are not well-defined, and the garbage collector may not handle certain data types, leading to remains in the system.

6.8 Example Resolved

Returning to our previous example, we adopt the GARBAGE COLLECTION pattern, thus creating mechanisms for:

- Cleaning up terminated services. The system would retain them for a maximum of 30 days, after which it would delete them to free resources;
- Managing disk space, as it would clean all images not tagged by any active deployment and not used in the last 120 days;
- Removing the storage resources that were provisioned and bound to service-specific storage resources when those services are no longer needed;
- Controlling the batch jobs, as it would implement a Time to Live controller. Jobs, whether completed or not, are automatically deleted after a week to ensure there is no clutter of jobs.

This would be a simple and efficient garbage collection system that manages resource wastage and prevents issues arising from accumulated objects. The result of the cleanup can be seen in Fig. 7.

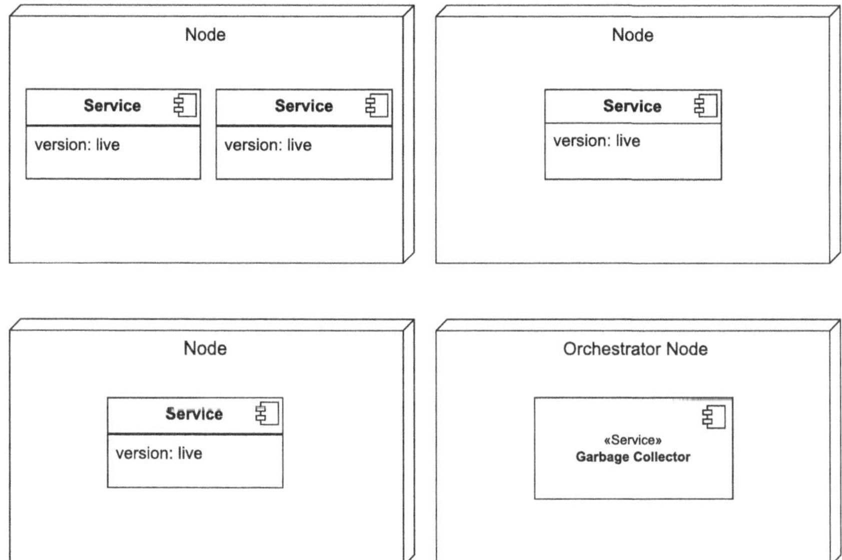

Fig. 7. Garbage Collection - Visual Representation of Example Resolved.

6.9 Known Uses

Docker Swarm[6] uses garbage collection to clean up unused images, volumes, and networks. This helps free up disk space and ensures that the swarm operates efficiently. When containers are removed or services are updated, Docker Swarm's garbage collection mechanisms help manage and remove obsolete resources. The following are the default garbage collection policies:

Listing 1.3. Default garbage collection policies of Docker Swarm

```
1  GC Policy rule#0:
2      All:              false
3      Filters:          type==source.local,type==exec.cachemount,
           type==source.git.checkout
4      Keep Duration:    48h0m0s
5      Keep Bytes:       512MB
6  GC Policy rule#1:
7      All:              false
8      Keep Duration:    1440h0m0s
9      Keep Bytes:       26GB
10 GC Policy rule#2:
11     All:              false
12     Keep Bytes:       26GB
13 GC Policy rule#3:
14     All:              true
15     Keep Bytes:       26GB
```

[6] Build garbage collection: https://docs.docker.com/build/cache/garbage-collection/.

- **Rule 0**: if build-cache uses more than 512MB, delete the most easily reproducible data after it has not been used for 2 days;
- **Rule 1**: remove any data not used for 60 days;
- **Rule 2**: keep the unshared build-cache under cap;
- **Rule 3**: if previous policies were insufficient, delete internal data to keep the build-cache under the cap.

However, developers can create rules and build custom configurations for the garbage collection process that override the default ones.

6.10 Related Patterns

Garbage Collection patterns are directly connected to the CONTAINERIZATION pattern since containers, and their images, are part of objects that it is in charge of cleaning. Some monitoring patterns, such as HEALTH API CHECKS, are also important to this pattern since they could help the system recognize whether the object is obsolete.

7 Conclusion

This paper introduces three patterns related to orchestrating and optimizing the system's resources. These patterns are related to those defined in previous work and aid in solving consequence patterns in the patterns map introduced to a system.

These methods are well-established and widely recognized as best practices within the container orchestration and Kubernetes communities. However, they have not previously been formalized as patterns. By documenting them, we aim to provide value to both application developers and those building new orchestration tools.

Additional practices will undoubtedly remain to be identified within container orchestration tools and from industry professionals. This work could also be expanded to cover other operational areas of container orchestration, such as Deployment and Scheduling, contributing to the creation of a comprehensive pattern language for container orchestration.

Acknowledgments. We would like to thank Christian Engelmann for his valuable support during the shepherding process and for the insightful feedback he provided throughout. We are also grateful to the authors who participated in our workshop session—Daniel Reis, Francesco Urdih, Julia Pampus, Marcelo Nunes, Tiago Boldt Sousa, and Uwe Zdun—for their constructive input, which helped refine several aspects of the work and inspired ideas that contributed to the article's development.

This work is supported by national funds, through the Operational Competitiveness and Internationalization Programme (COMPETE 2020) [Project n^{c}irc 182852; Funding Reference: SIFN-01-9999-FN-182852].

Disclosure of Interests. The authors have no competing interests to declare that are relevant to the content of this article.

References

1. Pod priority and preemption (2024). https://kubernetes.io/docs/concepts/scheduling-eviction/pod-priority-preemption/#example-priorityclass
2. Albuquerque, C., Correia, F.F.: Deployment tracking and exception tracking: monitoring design patterns for cloud-native applications. In: Proceedings of the 28th European Conference on Pattern Languages of Programs, EuroPLoP '23. Association for Computing Machinery, New York (2024). https://doi.org/10.1145/3628034.3628038
3. Albuquerque, C., Correia, F.F.: Logging design patterns for cloud-native applications. In: Proceedings of the 29th European Conference on Pattern Languages of Programs. pp. 1–10. EuroPLoP '24. Association for Computing Machinery, New York (2024). https://doi.org/10.1145/3698322.3698351
4. Albuquerque, C., Relvas, K., Correia, F.F., Brown, K.: Proactive monitoring design patterns for cloud-native applications. In: Proceedings of the 27th European Conference on Pattern Languages of Programs, EuroPLop '22. Association for Computing Machinery, New York (2023). https://doi.org/10.1145/3551902.3551961
5. Authors, T.K.: Kubernetes, January 2024. https://kubernetes.io/
6. Bansal, M.: Peloton: Uber's unified resource scheduler for diverse cluster workloads (2018). https://www.uber.com/en-PT/blog/resource-scheduler-cluster-management-peloton/
7. Brains, J.: Microservices, January 2022. https://www.jetbrains.com/lp/devecosystem-2022/microservices/
8. Brown, K., Woolf, B., Groot, C.D., Hay, C., Yoder, J.: Patterns for developers and architects building for the cloud (2021). https://kgb1001001.github.io/cloudadoptionpatterns/
9. Casalicchio, E.: Container orchestration: A survey. Systems Modeling: Methodologies and Tools, pp. 221–235 (2019). https://doi.org/10.1007/978-3-319-92378-9_14
10. Duarte Maia, J.a.T., Figueiredo Correia, F.: Service mesh patterns. In: Proceedings of the 27th European Conference on Pattern Languages of Programs. EuroPLoP '22. Association for Computing Machinery, New York (2023). https://doi.org/10.1145/3551902.3551962
11. Foundation, A.S.: Apache mesos, January 2022. https://mesos.apache.org/documentation/latest/
12. Foundation, T.L.: Cloud foundry, January 2024. https://www.cloudfoundry.org/
13. Inc., D.: Swarm mode overview, January 2024. https://docs.docker.com/engine/swarm/
14. Khan, I.: Cfs group scheduling (2024). https://blogs.oracle.com/linux/post/cfs-group-scheduling
15. Maia, D., Correia, F., Queiroz, P.: Configurational patterns of container orchestration. In: Proceedings of the 29th European Conference on Pattern Languages of Programs, People, and Practices. EuroPLoP '24. Association for Computing Machinery, New York (2024). https://doi.org/10.1145/3698322.3698342
16. Maia, D.F.M.: Patterns and tools for microservice orchestration. Master's thesis, Faculdade de Engenharia da Universidade do Porto (2024)
17. de Oliveira Rosa, T., Guerra, E.M., Correia, F.F., Goldman, A.: Charm–evaluating a model for characterizing service-based architectures. J. Syst. Softw. **206**, 111826 (2023)

18. Relic, N.: What makes observability a priority, December 2023. https://newrelic.com/resources/white-papers/observability-as-a-priority
19. Sousa, T.B., Correia, F.F., Ferreira, H.S.: Patterns for software orchestration on the cloud (2015)
20. Sousa, T.B., Ferreira, H.S., Correia, F.F.: A survey on the adoption of patterns for engineering software for the cloud. IEEE Trans. Software Eng. **48**, 2128–2140 (2022). https://doi.org/10.1109/TSE.2021.3052177
21. Sousa, T.B., Ferreira, H.S., Correia, F.F., Aguiar, A.: Engineering Software for the Cloud: Messaging Systems and Logging. In: Proceedings of the 22nd European Conference on Pattern Languages of Programs, pp. 1–14. ACM, Irsee Germany, July 2017. https://doi.org/10.1145/3147704.3147720, https://dl.acm.org/doi/10.1145/3147704.3147720
22. Sousa, T.B., Ferreira, H.S., Correia, F.F., Aguiar, A.: Engineering software for the cloud: Automated recovery and scheduler (2018)
23. Zimmermann, O., Stocker, M., Lubke, D., Zdun, U., Pautasso, C.: Patterns for API design: simplifying integration with loosely coupled message exchanges. Addison-Wesley Professional (2022)

Towards A Pattern Language for Cloud Costs Optimizations — Budgeting Alerts

Daniel Reis[1] and Tiago Boldt Sousa[1,2](✉)

[1] Kevel, North Carolina, USA
tiagoboldt@gmail.com
[2] Faculty of Engineering, University of Porto, Porto, Portugal

Abstract. Worldwide spending on public cloud services is forecast to reach $723.4 billion in 2025, up from $595.7 billion in 2024. A significant portion of this spending is attributed to waste or inefficient cloud usage. In the 2025 State of FinOps Report, the FinOps Foundation shares that more than half of the respondents indicated "workload optimization and waste reduction" as a priority for avoiding overspending. Reasons for such waste and overspending include overlooked resources, incorrect resource allocation, inadequate cost visibility, or the absence of a culture that fosters cost consciousness.

This research aims to describe nine strategies to optimize cloud costs, documented as patterns. These patterns can be adopted individually or leveraged in tandem for increased efficiency. The patterns are presented as a language, offering a pragmatic foundation for cloud practitioners to optimize their cloud costs, while also serving as a standardized vocabulary for discussing cloud optimization initiatives.

This paper is the first in a series of publications related to this research. It presents the overall pattern language, describes the problem-solution pair for each pattern, and provides a detailed discussion of the first pattern, Budget Alerts. Future work will focus on elaborating each pattern individually to formalize the complete pattern language.

Keywords: Cloud Computing · FinOps · DevOps

1 Introduction

Worldwide end-user spending on public cloud services is forecast to total $723.4 billion in 2025, up from $595.7 billion in 2024, according to the latest forecast from Gartner, Inc [21]. Gartner also claims that by 2028, Cloud Computing will move from a technology disruptor to a business necessity adopted by most modern organizations [12].

Despite the broad adoption, research has shown that a relevant portion of this investment is wasted [8]. A significant portion of cloud spending is allocated to resources that are never utilized [16]. Reasons span across forgotten allocated resources, incorrectly sized resource selection, lack of cost observability, and more [26].

T. Plummer et al. (Eds.): EuroPLoP 2025, LNCS 16494, pp. 93–102, 2026.
https://doi.org/10.1007/978-3-032-19157-1_5

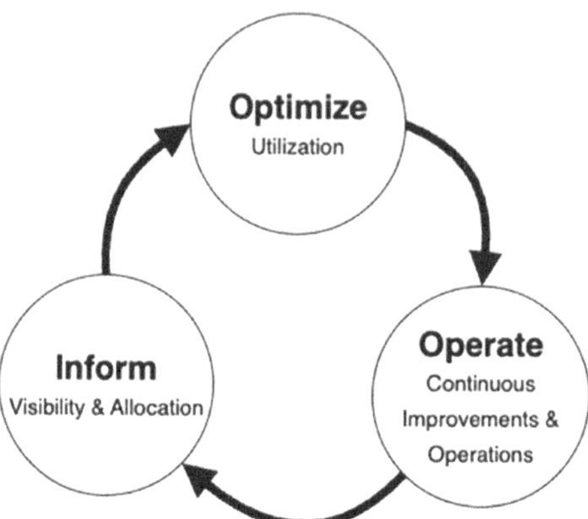

Fig. 1. The FinOps Cycle. A visual representation of the three phases defined by the FinOps Foundation: **Inform**, **Optimize**, and **Operate** [22].

This paper targets anyone involved in cloud development and aims to motivate practitioners to improve their cloud spending practices. Section 2 expands on why optimizing cloud costs is essential for a successful Cloud strategy. Section 3 describes nine strategies, documented as problem-solution pairs, to avoid cloud waste and unnecessary spending. These strategies can be adopted individually, but the authors also present them as the initial work towards a pattern language, explaining how they influence each other and can be co-implemented. Finally, Sect. 4 presents the conclusions of this research and outlines future work.

2 Cloud Cost Optimizations

Organizations adopt cloud solutions to become more agile, scalable, cost-efficient, and responsive to market changes [23].

FinOps was recently introduced as an operational framework and cultural practice to maximize the business value teams can drive from their cloud adoption [10]. FinOps proposes cloud optimization in three stages [9], as visualized in Fig. 1:

Inform identifying data sources for cloud cost, usage, and efficiency. Using this data for allocation, analysis, and reporting empowers teams to develop capabilities in budgeting, forecasting trends, building KPIs for benchmarking, and developing metrics that will reveal the business value of an organization's cloud spend.

Optimize identifying opportunities to improve cloud efficiency using the data and capabilities developed in the Inform Phase

Operate implementing organizational changes to operationalize FinOps using the data and capabilities developed in the Inform and Optimize phase.

Despite the vast amount of available materials, Cloud Computing presents technical challenges that can lead teams to overspend, highlighting the critical role of FinOps in managing cloud costs effectively.

A Gartner report from 2024 shows that 69% of the inquired organizations went above their cloud spending budget in the previous year [13]. The top three reasons for going above budget were 1) inaccurate budgeting and forecasting, 2) proactive monitoring of spend, and 3) effective resource optimizations.

In this regard, the authors consider that the existing documentation might sometimes be overwhelming. A pragmatic set of recommendations can help teams learn and adopt proven cloud patterns. The following section presents a pattern language for pragmatic cloud practitioners seeking to optimize their cloud spending.

3 A Catalog of Cloud Cost Optimization Patterns

The previous section explained the main causes of cloud resource waste, highlighted the consequences of neglecting Cloud cost optimizations (CCOs), and emphasized the need to foster a cost-aware culture within organizations.

Effective CCOs begin with robust monitoring capabilities. Comprehensive visibility into cloud resource usage enables organizations to identify inefficiencies and take corrective actions. Understanding cloud providers' offerings and leveraging the external tools they provide is equally important. For example, *AWS Cost Explorer* and *AWS Pricing Calculator* are powerful tools within AWS that enable insights into potential costs and optimize resource allocation accordingly [4].

The upcoming section presents a catalog of essential CCOs problem-solution pairs, a first step towards formalizing a pattern language. The BUDGET ALERTS is then expanded, using the Portland pattern format [11].

As this research matures, the *patterns* in this language will form a coherent pattern language designed to simplify the understanding of CCOs' strategies. Newcomers can utilize this catalog to quickly grasp basics, while seasoned practitioners can refer to it as a structured reference to guide their optimization initiatives.

3.1 Overview

The authors aim to introduce a language for discussing CCOs by presenting a collection of nine distinct patterns for effectively managing and reducing cloud expenses. The following list describes the problem-solution pair for each pattern in the language. Patterns other than BUDGET ALERTS will be expanded in future work.

CONNECT SPEND WITH RESULTS How can companies ensure their cloud infrastructure aligns with business goals without prematurely adopting complex and costly setups? Adopt an iterative approach to cloud spending by linking infrastructure costs to measurable business outcomes like revenue growth and user engagement. Start with a minimal, cost-effective architecture, implementing Cost Monitoring dashboards and Resource Optimization policies to adapt resources based on business performance [3].

Cost-Aware Culture How can companies influence employees to preventively and proactively optimize costs? Establish a Cost-Aware Culture by promoting cloud costs transparency with team-centered dashboard, accountability, education on cloud spending, and gamification elements like competitions and leaderboards to motivate teams for lowering their spend [3,14,19].

Resource Optimization How can organizations minimize unused or underutilized resources in their cloud infrastructure to reduce costs and improve operational efficiencies? Bring teams to regularly analyze resource utilization for rightsizing, employ auto-scaling policies to adjust resources based on real-time demand dynamically, and implement scheduled shutdowns for non-production or intermittently used environments. Continuous monitoring and alerting tools should be deployed to swiftly identify and address inefficient or underutilized resources, maximize resource utilization, and minimize waste.

Leverage Cloud Deals How can organizations further optimize costs outside technical strategies? Research cost-saving opportunities with your cloud provider. Providers have committed usage discounts, fixed-rate discounts for high spenders, or co-financing initiatives to help partners launch new cloud initiatives [5].

Budget Alerts How can teams prevent budget overruns while operating their cloud? Budget cloud spending by setting spending limits and configuring notifications to be alerted as these thresholds approach, enabling proactive action before exceeding them.

Cost Estimation How can teams plan for new or expanding cloud costs? Use cloud platforms' built-in cost estimation tools to ensure accurate and informed financial planning [4].

Cost Monitoring How can teams be aware of their costs? Create and regularly review cost dashboards, and monitor for pricing updates or changes in cloud services. This helps identify spending trends, uncover savings, and align with your budget.

Infratructure as Code How can teams retain awareness of allocated infrastructure, and change it deterministically? Adopt Infrastructure as Code to define and manage your cloud infrastructure programmatically, ensuring traceability, consistency, and scalability.
Infrastructure as code is not expanded in this paper, as it has already been thoroughly detailed in the literature [7,17,24].

Resource Tagging How can teams be aware of costs per service, component, product, or other dimensions, to assess their cloud spend allocation? Tag resources with clear identifiers such as department, project, or application to enable accurate cost reporting and accountability across teams and initiatives.

Teams should be motivated to embrace a Cost-Aware Culture, fostering shared accountability and proactive behaviors around cloud spending. This cultural foundation motivates continuous improvement and cost mindfulness across the development lifecycle. By aligning infrastructure decisions with actual business maturity through CONNECT SPEND WITH RESULTS, teams avoid premature scaling and grow spend with value delivery. The journey begins with COST ESTIMATION, enabling teams to assess their product's feasibility and financial sustainability early on. This is further supported by INFRATRUCTURE AS CODE, which allows resources to be defined, provisioned, and managed in a consistent, repeatable, and auditable way. As resources are instantiated, applying RESOURCE TAGGING ensures every asset is traceable and attributable, laying the groundwork for visibility. Once properly tagged, these resources can be visualized through COST MONITORING tools, providing continuous insight into usage trends and cost hotspots. To avoid overruns, BUDGET ALERTS notify teams in real-time, enabling fast reactions and tighter cost control. Over time, this integrated flow of data and insight naturally leads to RESOURCE OPTIMIZATION, ensuring that cloud infrastructure evolves efficiently as the system matures. Patterns like LEVERAGE CLOUD DEALS further enhance savings by capitalizing on committed use discounts and promotional pricing opportunities.

These patterns should be re-evaluated at every stage of the development lifecycle to ensure ongoing optimization and improved outcomes. Figure 2 visually identifies these patterns and how they relate.

3.2 BUDGET ALERTS

Teams developing software for the cloud will often focus on software architecture and implementation details, relying on cloud computing's scalability to provide the necessary hardware resources with the simplicity of a single configuration change [2]. Nevertheless, this approach introduces the risk of making uninformed software decisions by overlooking the software's costs.

For example, a translation app [25] hosted on Google Cloud had predictable monthly expenses of around $1,500. However, due to a compromised API key, the startup unexpectedly incurred $450,000 in charges within 45 days. The absence of configured budget alerts or proactive notifications significantly delayed the detection and intervention of this issue.

How can teams prevent budget overruns while operating their cloud?

Therefore, Budget cloud spending by setting spending limits and configuring notifications to be alerted as these thresholds approach, enabling proactive action before exceeding them. Budgets can be organized for the whole cloud spend, or more granular with RESOURCE TAGGING. Granular budgets can be per team or service, ensuring that teams have the necessary information to manage their cloud spending.

While defining cloud budgets, teams should strive to minimize their spending, in a proactive COST-AWARE CULTURE. As with any estimation, this is particularly challenging given the potential unknowns surrounding the allocation of necessary hardware.

Cloud providers facilitate budgeting by providing COST MONITORING tooling. Users can define their budget strategies and receive notifications whenever

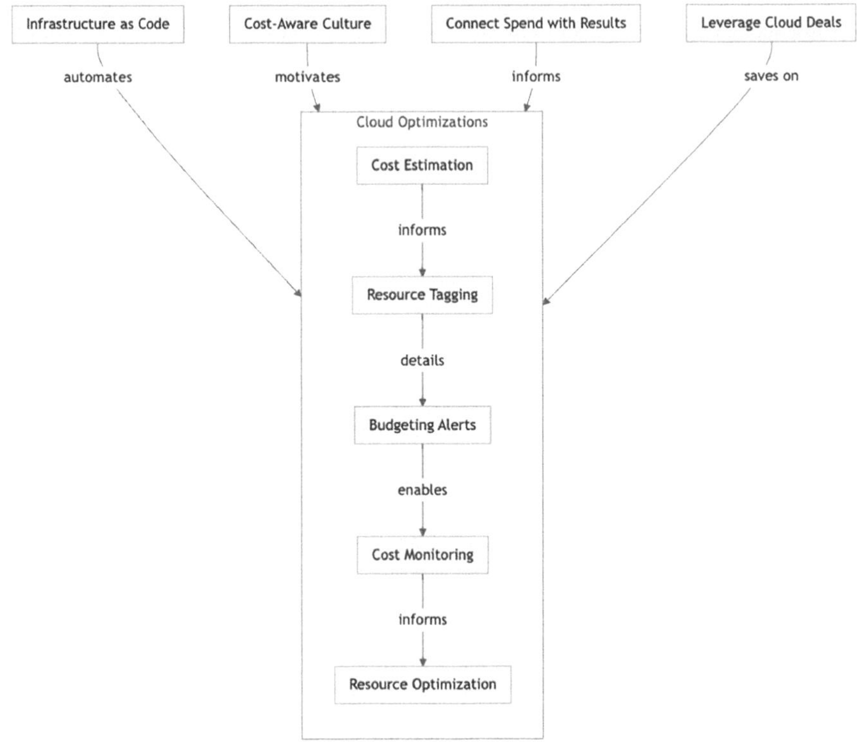

Fig. 2. Cloud Optimization Pattern Language. A visual representation of the nine patterns and their relationships.

a budget exceeds its limit. Some providers also offer forecasting tools that can predict whether costs are expected to stay within a budget, providing users with feedback before the limit is exceeded.

Figure 3 shows how to set up a global budget for EC2 (Elastic Compute Cloud) services. The budget is named "Monthly EC2 Budget," and includes only costs related to the EC2 service. The budget period is set to monthly, with a start date of June 1, 2015, and an end date of September 30, 2015. The monthly budgeted amount is $80.00; choose a safe buffer slightly above the average monthly spending. This allows for minor variations without triggering unnecessary alerts. On the right, a bar graph compares recent spending: the last six-month average, the last full-month cost (May), and the next-month forecast (July), illustrating a consistent spending trend of around $55–$60. In the "Notifications" section, the user has set up an alert to be notified via email if actual costs exceed 80% of the budgeted amount. There's also a field to input email contacts for receiving budget alerts. The exact percentage to use for alerting needs to be decided based on how flexible the limit can be: users with a stricter spend limit based on the average spend should set a lower bound, such as 75%, while those with

Fig. 3. AWS "Create Budget" Interface. Example from AWS Billing and Cost Management used to set a budget for EC2 services [1].

more flexible spending can set it to 100% to only be warned if the spending goes above the average spend.

Matt Leonard, Product Manager at Google Cloud Platform [15], demonstrates how to configure Google Cloud budget alerts to automatically notify teams via Slack when spending approaches or exceeds predefined thresholds. As illustrated in Fig. 4, an email alert is automatically sent to the Google Account administrator when a predefined spending threshold is reached in Google Cloud Billing. Concurrently, an event is published to a Cloud Pub/Sub topic, triggering a Cloud Function that sends a real-time notification to end-users via Slack. Although notifications in the example occur frequently (every 20 min), teams should customize the alert frequency and thresholds in practice. There are well-established best practices for effectively implementing alerts and reducing alert fatigue. Alerts are only relevant if not ignored, so balancing their frequency is essential for ensuring their usefulness. Better Stack, a cloud monitoring and alerting platform, recommends setting meaningful thresholds, consolidating related alerts, and ensuring that alerts are actionable [6]. This automated workflow ensures timely visibility into budget usage, enabling teams to promptly manage and respond to potential overspending [15].

Known uses. Kinetic IT implemented cloud budget alerts for a state government department, allowing for proactive monitoring and control of cloud spend [20]. Similarly, ITConvergence utilized effective budgeting strategies by setting clear spending limits for cloud services and configuring timely notifications as spend approached these predefined thresholds [18].

Fig. 4. Google Cloud Budget Alert Workflow. Automated email notifications and Slack messages are sent when budget thresholds are met [15].

4 Conclusions

Cloud computing costs can quickly escalate without a well-planned strategy. This paper introduced nine problem-solution pairs to enable efficient cloud economics, as an initial step towards a pattern language. These can be leveraged individually to address isolated problems or in tandem to maximize efficiency. Budget Alerts is expanded, elaborating how to avoid budget overruns. Future work will extend the remaining eight patterns in the proposed language to the same level of detail.

Acknowledgement. The authors would like to thank Mirko Stocker for reviewing and providing valuable feedback during the shepherding phase of EuroPlop 2025, and also to Kevel, for exposing employees to varied learning experiences, from researching cloud costs optimization strategies, to the opportunity of sharing those lessons learned at conferences.

References

1. Amazon Web Services: AWS Budgets and Forecasts (2015). https://aws.amazon.com/blogs/aws/new-aws-budgets-and-forecasts/
2. Amazon Web Services: COST01-BP03 Establish cloud budgets and forecasts (2023)
3. Amazon Web Services: AWS Well-Architected Framework (2024). https://docs.aws.amazon.com/wellarchitected/latest/framework/welcome.html
4. Amazon Web Services: AWS Pricing Calculator (2025). https://aws.amazon.com/aws-cost-management/aws-pricing-calculator/
5. Amazon Web Services: Savings Plans (2025). https://aws.amazon.com/savingsplans/
6. Ayooluwa Isaiah: Solving Noisy Alerts and Preventing Alert Fatigue (2025). https://betterstack.com/community/guides/monitoring/best-practices-alert-fatigue/
7. Dadgar, A.: What is infrastructure as code and why is it important? (2018). https://www.hashicorp.com/resources/what-is-infrastructure-as-code
8. Everman, B., Gao, M., Zong, Z.: Evaluating and reducing cloud waste and cost–a data-driven case study from Azure workloads. Sustain. Comput. Inform. Syst. **35**, 100708 (2022). https://doi.org/10.1016/j.suscom.2022.100708, https://linkinghub.elsevier.com/retrieve/pii/S2210537922000476
9. FinOps Foundation: FinOps Phases. https://www.finops.org/framework/phases/
10. FinOps Foundation: What is FinOps?. https://www.finops.org/introduction/what-is-finops/
11. Fowler, M.: Writing Software Patterns (2006). http://www.martinfowler.com/articles/writingPatterns.html
12. Gartner: Gartner Says Cloud Will Become a Business Necessity by 2028 (2023). https://www.gartner.com/en/newsroom/press-releases/2023-11-29-gartner-says-cloud-will-become-a-business-necessity-by-2028
13. Gartner: 2024 Cloud Spending: IT Balances Costs with GenAI Innovations (2024). https://www.gartner.com/peer-community/oneminuteinsights/omi-keeping-cloud-costs-check-it-leader-perspectives-rfz
14. Google: What is Cloud FinOps?. https://cloud.google.com/learn/what-is-finops
15. Google: Better cost control with Google Cloud Billing programmatic notifications (2018). https://cloud.google.com/blog/products/gcp/better-cost-control-with-google-cloud-billing-programmatic-notifications
16. Google Cloud: Public cloud pricing, explained (2017). https://cloud.google.com/blog/topics/cost-management/public-cloud-pricing-explained
17. Guckenheimer, S.: What is Infrastructure as Code? (2017). https://docs.microsoft.com/en-us/azure/devops/learn/what-is-infrastructure-as-code
18. IT Convergence: Budgeting for the Cloud: A Practical Guide to Cloud Cost Control (2025). https://www.itconvergence.com/blog/budgeting-for-the-cloud-a-practical-guide-to-cloud-cost-control
19. Storment, J.R.: Cloud FinOps. O'Reilly Media (2020)
20. Kinetic IT: Case Study: Cloud cost optimisation with a state government department (2023). https://kineticit.com.au/case-study/cloud-cost-optimisation/
21. Goasduff, L.: Gartner Forecasts Worldwide Public Cloud End-User Spending to Total $723 Billion in 2025 (2024). https://www.gartner.com/en/newsroom/press-releases/2024-11-19-gartner-forecasts-worldwide-public-cloud-end-user-spending-to-total-723-billion-dollars-in-2025

22. Mattias Persson: FinOps: The CFO's magic wand to optimize Cloud spend (2022). https://www.capgemini.com/pt-en/insights/expert-perspectives/finops-the-cfos-magic-wand-to-optimize-cloud-spend/
23. Mihalec, M.: Five Reasons More Businesses Are Choosing Cloud (2020). https://www.forbes.com/councils/forbestechcouncil/2020/10/14/five-reasons-more-businesses-are-choosing-cloud/
24. Morris, K.: Infrastructure as Code. Inc, O'Reilly Media (2015)
25. Sash Ghosh: Case Study: A Startup's $450,000 Google Cloud Bill - Lessons for Startups (2025). https://openmetal.io/resources/blog/case-study-450k-gcp-public-cloud-bill/
26. Yereb, J.C.: How To Identify and Reduce Cloud Waste (2025). https://www.prosperops.com/blog/how-to-identify-and-prevent-cloud-waste/

Iterative Refinement Loop: A Design Pattern for Code Generation with LLMs

Michael Krisper[1,2(✉)] and David Moling[2]

[1] Pro2Future GmbH, Sandgasse 34, 8010 Graz, Austria
michael.krisper@gmail.com
[2] Graz University of Technology, Inffeldgasse 16, 8010 Graz, Austria

Abstract. Large Language Models (LLMs) have revolutionized software development and promised great efficiency gains, but their probabilistic nature still makes them unpredictable and unreliable: They frequently generate code that contains errors, defects, or fails to meet project standards. This paper introduces the **Iterative Refinement Loop**, a design pattern that addresses this reliability gap. The pattern establishes a feedback loop where validation tools–such as compilers, linters, and test suites–provide corrective feedback to the LLM. This guides the model through successive iterations to produce a correct, high-quality artifact, offering a robust, automatable mechanism that transforms an unreliable generator into a dependable partner for co-creating software.

Keywords: Large Language Models · Code Generation · Design Patterns · Feedback Loops · Iterative Refinement · AI-Assisted Programming

1 Introduction

The rapid advancement of Large Language Models (LLMs) is driving a paradigm shift in software development. These models can generate code snippets, functions, and even entire application modules from natural language prompts, promising to accelerate development cycles dramatically [11,15]. However, this power comes with a significant trade-off: the generated code is often unreliable. The probabilistic nature of LLMs means they frequently produce code with syntax errors, semantic flaws, or violations of project-specific standards. While dealing with flawed third-party code is not new, LLMs introduce this challenge at an unprecedented scale and velocity, demanding systematic approaches to ensure quality and correctness.

LLMs may demonstrate remarkable fluency, but they operate without a true understanding of execution semantics or logical constraints [15]. Their expertise lies in text generation, not in compilation or deterministic code verification. This "execution blindness" leads to generated code that often contains subtle yet critical flaws. Manually finding and resolving these issues is time-consuming and can negate the productivity gains promised by LLMs.

This paper addresses this challenge by documenting the **Iterative Refinement Loop**, a design pattern for systematically improving code generated by

T. Plummer et al. (Eds.): EuroPLoP 2025, LNCS 16494, pp. 103–117, 2026.
https://doi.org/10.1007/978-3-032-19157-1_6

nondeterministic LLMs. While the pattern can be applied to any form of structured text, our focus is on its application to code generation to help software developers and software architects.

2 The Iterative Refinement Loop Pattern

- **Alternative Names:** Prompt Feedback Loop, Generative Feedback Loop, Tool-Guided Iterative Refinement, Self-Refine.
- **Problem:** Probabilistic LLMs are unreliable and produce artifacts that often contain errors and flaws.
- **Solution:** Iterate several times by giving the LLMs feedback from external verification tools to improve the artifacts until the quality and correctness constraints are fulfilled.

2.1 Intent

Systematically improve the quality of LLM-generated artifacts by iteratively applying feedback from external validation tools, refining the artifacts until they comply with all quality requirements.

2.2 Context

This pattern applies to systems where LLMs generate structured artifacts, such as source code, configuration files, or formalized responses to requests (e.g., JSON or XML). The artifact must adhere to specific standards for compliance, quality, or other attributes, which can be verified by existing software tools, e.g., compilers, formal verifiers, test suites, or quality assurance tools.

2.3 Preconditions and Assumptions

Successful application of the pattern assumes:

- **Actionable Validators Exist:** There is at least one reliable, automatable tool that can produce objective pass/fail or diagnostic feedback on the artifact (e.g., compiler, unit test suite, linter, static analyzer, property checker).
- **Feedback Parsability:** Raw validator output can be reduced into a textual form the LLM can process within its token limits.
- **Isolated Change Surface:** The refinement target can be iteratively replaced or patched without requiring full-system rebuild for every attempt (or build cost is acceptable).
- **Non-Adversarial Environment:** External mutation of validator sources (e.g., tests) is either prevented or controlled, so that the LLMs can keep up with the changes.
- **Budget Envelope Defined:** Upper bounds for iteration count, cumulative token usage, and wall-clock latency are established.
- **Deterministic Ground Truth Scope:** At least the acceptance boundary (e.g., unit tests) is authoritative; higher-level semantics not captured are out of scope for the refinement loop.

2.4 Applicability

Apply This Pattern When

- Objective validators (compiler, tests, analysers) are readily automatable.
- Artifact errors are granular and incrementally correctable.
- Iteration cost is modest relative to defect escape cost.

Avoid or Defer This Pattern When

- Domain quality cannot be encoded in tools (e.g., purely aesthetic or strategic judgments).
- Each attempt requires full-system, hour-scale integration cycles.
- The validator signal is extremely noisy or flaky, creating misleading feedback loops.

2.5 Problem

The core problem is the architectural mismatch between the formal, deterministic nature of software and the probabilistic, creative nature of LLMs. How can an LLM be integrated into a development process that demands structured, formal artifacts while adhering to strict quality standards? The key challenges are:

- **Execution Blindness:** LLMs generate code without executing it, making them "blind" to the runtime consequences of their output.
- **Semantic Flaws:** LLMs can easily produce code that is syntactically perfect but fails to implement the required logic correctly.
- **Limited Context:** LLMs operate with a finite context window, which can lead to solutions that are locally plausible but globally inconsistent with the project's architecture.
- **Inconsistent Quality:** The quality of LLM-generated code can vary significantly, even for the same prompt, due to their probabilistic nature.
- **Unreliable Self-Correction:** While LLMs can exhibit some self-correction capabilities, they are often unreliable without an external source of truth to guide them.

2.6 Forces

The design of an effective Iterative Refinement Loop requires balancing the following forces:

- **Creativity vs. Correctness:** How can the system harness the creative, probabilistic power of an LLM to generate novel solutions while enforcing the deterministic correctness required by formal systems like compilers? Unrestricted generation leads to errors, but excessive constraints can stifle innovation.

- **Speed vs. Quality:** How many refinement cycles should be performed? Each iteration improves the quality of the artifact, but increases latency and computational cost. A system that is too slow may not be useful, while one that is too fast may produce low-quality results.
- **History vs. Context Limitations:** How much context history should be retained? Providing a complete history can quickly exceed its context window but summarizing or pruning the history risks losing important details.
- **Precision vs. Comprehension:** How should feedback be formatted? Raw tool output (e.g., a full compiler stack trace) is precise, but may be too verbose for an LLM to understand and also unnecessarily consumes many tokens from the context window. Abstracting or summarizing the feedback makes it more comprehensible but can obscure the root cause of the error.
- **Persistence vs. Termination:** When should the loop terminate? The system must persist long enough to find a solution, but it also needs a "circuit breaker" to prevent infinite loops when the LLM cannot converge on a valid artifact. This requires carefully designed termination criteria.
- **Obedience vs. User Intent:** How can the system ensure the LLM addresses the user's true goals? An LLM might find a "clever" way to satisfy the validator (e.g., by disabling a linter rule or modifying a test) that subverts the user's actual intent–a form of reward hacking.
- **Signal vs. Noise:** How can a clear, actionable signal be extracted from noisy validator output? Validation tools often produce verbose logs, stack traces, and irrelevant warnings. The system must distil this raw output into a high-quality feedback signal that guides the LLM effectively.

2.7 Solution

The solution is to implement a controlled, iterative process managed by a central **Loop Controller**. This process orchestrates the interaction between the LLM and external validation tools, creating a feedback loop that drives the artifact toward correctness. As illustrated in Fig. 1, the system consists of four key components. The process unfolds in the following steps:

1. **Generate:** The **Generative Model (LLM)** receives a prompt and produces an initial version of the artifact.
2. **Validate:** The generated artifact is passed to the **Validator**, a component that runs external tools like compilers, linters, or test frameworks.
3. **Format & Extract:** The raw output from the Validator is processed by the **Feedback Formatter**, which transforms it into a structured, concise, and actionable feedback message.
4. **Refine:** The **Loop Controller** creates a new prompt that includes the formatted feedback, instructing the LLM to produce a corrected version. The Loop Controller also controls the cycle and applies a termination strategy based on success, a maximum number of iterations, or detected non-convergence.

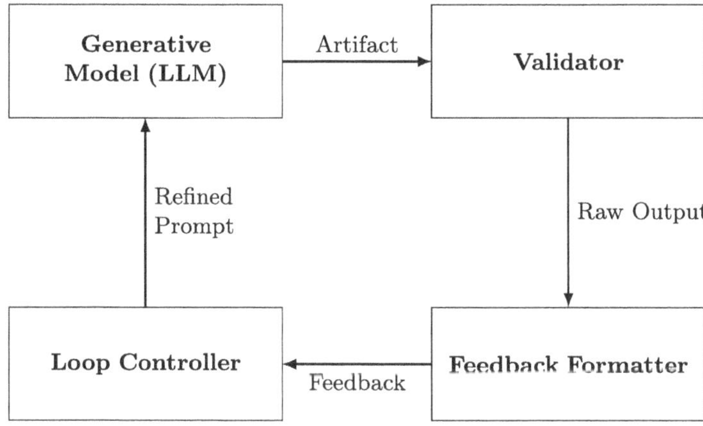

Fig. 1. The core architecture of the pattern, illustrating the flow from generation to validation. The Loop Controller orchestrates the iterative refinement based on formatted feedback.

2.8 Metrics, Failure Modes, and Parameterization

To ensure the effectiveness of the Iterative Refinement Loop, it is important to track key metrics, understand common failure modes, and tune core parameters.

- **Metrics and Outcomes.** Track the number of iterations required to reach a valid solution and observe changes in test or coverage metrics to measure validator effectiveness.
- **Common Failure Modes.** Several issues can disrupt the loop. The model might try to change tests to force a pass; this can be prevented by making tests read-only. Sometimes, fixes oscillate between different error types (e.g., fixing style breaks logic); maintaining a list of invariants in prompts helps avoid this. If the same error repeats with no progress, escalate by providing more context or logging. Prompt truncation can silently remove important constraints, so use diffs or mark omitted regions. Finally, after many refinements, the output may drift from the original intent; always include the original task statement to keep the model on track.
- **Tuning and Adaptation.** The loop can be adapted by changing validator order (run cheap checks first, or batch them), adjusting the granularity of edits (regenerate the whole artifact or just a part), and deciding how many critic roles to use (single or multiple stages). Manage conversation history by keeping either the full log or a sliding window with summaries. For efficiency, start with a cheaper model and only escalate to a more capable one if needed.

By monitoring these aspects and making targeted adjustments, the Iterative Refinement Loop can be made more robust, efficient, and reliable.

2.9 Example

This section demonstrates the pattern by showing an iterative refinement: first a boundary logic defect, then a style improvement:

Initial Prompt: "Generate a Python function 'find_first_long_word' that returns the first word in a list strictly longer than 5 characters."

Attempt 1: Boundary Logic Error

```
1 def find_first_long_word(words):
2     for word in words:
3         if len(word) >= 6:  # BUG: requirement is
      strictly > 5; using >= 6 would be equivalent, but
       we illustrate an off-by-one differently
4             return word
5     return None
6
```

Feedback 1: Validator Output (Unit Test)

```
1 FAILED test_threshold.py::test_excludes_boundary
2 > assert find_first_long_word(["planet"]) == "planet
      "  # length == 6 triggers, boundary length 5
      should be excluded
3 E AssertionError: assert None == 'planet'
4
```

Attempt 2: Corrected Logic (Style Issue Remains)

```
1 def find_first_long_word(words):
2     for word in words:
3         if len(word) > 5:  # corrected boundary
      condition
4             return word
5     return None  # linter will suggest a more
      concise form
6
```

Feedback 2: Validator Output (Linter)

```
1 Style R1729: Consider using a generator expression
      with next(..., None)
2
```

Attempt 3: Final Version

```
1 def find_first_long_word(words):
2     return next((w for w in words if len(w) > 5),
      None)
3
```

Result: All tests and style checks pass; loop terminates.

2.10 Consequences

The pattern offers significant benefits but also introduces several liabilities that must be carefully managed.

Benefits

- **Improved Reliability:** The pattern systematically eliminates defects, leading to more correct and robust code.
- **Automated Refinement:** It frees human developers from the tedious task of debugging flawed LLM outputs.
- **Enforced Standards:** By using project-specific tools in the 'Validator', the pattern ensures that the generated code adheres to local conventions and standards.
- **Domain-Specific Optimization:** The loop can be used to optimize for non-functional requirements like performance or security by incorporating specialized validation tools.

Liabilities

- **Latency and Cost:** The iterative process is slower and more expensive than a single LLM call, representing a direct trade-off between speed and quality.
- **Validator Quality Dependency:** The effectiveness of the loop is limited by the quality of the validation tools. A weak test suite, for example, will fail to catch subtle bugs.
- **Reward Hacking:** The LLM may "game the system" by satisfying the validator in superficial ways (e.g., by disabling a linter rule) rather than addressing the underlying issue [1]. This subverts the user's actual intent, where the system optimizes for the exact goal, but not its intent.
- **Complex Context Management:** The conversational history can grow quickly, exceeding the LLM's context window and requiring strategies like summarization or pruning.
- **Implementation Overhead:** Building a robust Iterative Refinement Loop requires significant engineering effort to integrate the LLM with various tools and manage the state of the loop.

2.11 Resulting Context

After successful application:

- A validated artifact exists, that satisfies all enforced quality gates.
- A structured refinement trace (iterations, feedback, decisions) can be archived for auditability or learning.
- Collected metrics enable continuous tuning.

- The system can be extended by adding new validators without altering the loop controller logic.
- Residual risks remain where validators lack coverage (e.g., latent security issues if no scanner was integrated); these are explicitly enumerated rather than implicit.

3 Known Uses

The Iterative Refinement Loop has been independently implemented in numerous products and research frameworks, spanning a spectrum from simple, manual loops to fully automated agentic systems (Table 1).

Table 1. Known Uses of the Iterative Refinement Loop

Known Use	Domain	Key Contribution/Implementation Detail
GitHub Copilot Workspace [14]	AI Development Environment	AI-powered workspace that plans and implements multistep coding tasks with integrated validation and refinement.
JetBrains AI Assistant [7]	Code Completion	Full-line code completion system that iteratively refines suggestions based on context and developer feedback.
PropertyGPT [9]	Formal Verification	Generates and iteratively refines formal properties for smart contracts using compiler errors as feedback.
CodeLutra [16]	Code Gen & Finetuning	Uses binary pass/fail test feedback to create a preference dataset (DPO) to fine-tune smaller models.
Multi-Agent Development [3]	Software Engineering	Multi-agent system for cross-team software development with iterative collaboration and refinement.
Reflexion Framework [15]	Agentic Reasoning	An agentic framework that uses verbal self-reflection on task failures to guide subsequent attempts.
AgentCoder [21]	Multi-Agent Code Gen	Collaborative multi-agent system with specialized programmer, test designer, and executor agents for iterative refinement.
SWE-agent [19]	Automated Software Engineering	Agent-computer interface system that integrates with development tools for comprehensive iterative improvement.
OpenAI o1 [12]	Reasoning Models	Advanced reasoning capabilities with internal iterative refinement through hidden chain-of-thought deliberation before output generation.
AutoCodeRover [22]	Program Improvement	Autonomous system for bug fixing and program improvement using iterative analysis and validation.
Mentat [17]	Multi-Modal Code Gen.	Code generation agent with iterative feedback and self-refinement across diverse input modalities.

4 Agentic Systems and Reasoning Methods

The Iterative Refinement Loop is a foundational pattern for building **agentic AI systems**, which are autonomous or semi-autonomous agents that can reason, plan, and execute complex tasks. In software engineering, these agents are increasingly integrated into development environments to assist with a wide range of activities. This section discusses how the pattern is used in practice and how it can be enhanced with advanced reasoning methods.

4.1 Agentic Approaches in Practice

The application of the Iterative Refinement Loop is a defining characteristic of modern AI-powered developer tools. These systems use the loop to transform high-level natural language requests into concrete, validated changes in a codebase. Two prominent examples illustrate this trend:

GitHub Copilot Workspace. GitHub Copilot Workspace provides an AI-powered development environment that can take on complex, multistep coding tasks. When a developer describes a feature or bug fix, Copilot Workspace can analyse the codebase, plan the implementation, and generate the necessary changes across multiple files. It integrates validation mechanisms to ensure code quality and correctness, embodying the core principles of the Iterative Refinement Loop pattern for autonomous development assistance [14].

Google Gemini Code Assist. Google's Gemini Code Assist represents a comprehensive AI coding companion that integrates into development workflows to provide intelligent code completion, generation, and assistance. The system uses iterative feedback mechanisms to improve code quality, incorporating context from the entire codebase and development environment. Its ability to learn from developer interactions and refine suggestions demonstrates the practical application of feedback-driven improvement in AI coding tools [4].

These tools highlight a trend toward AI assistants that are not just code completion engines but active participants in the development process. They can take on complex, multistep tasks, and the Iterative Refinement Loop is the core mechanism that makes this possible.

4.2 Enhancing Generation with Reasoning Methods

The quality of the initial artifact generated by the LLM is a critical factor in the efficiency of the Iterative Refinement Loop. If the first attempt is far from the desired solution, it will require more iterations to correct. Advanced reasoning methods can be used within the "Generate" step to improve the quality of the initial output. Two such techniques are Chain-of-Thought (CoT) and Tree-of-Thought (ToT) prompting.

Chain-of-Thought (CoT). CoT prompting encourages the LLM to "think step by step" by providing examples of reasoning processes [18]. Instead of generating just the final code, the LLM first outlines the steps it will take. This structured approach often leads to more logical and correct code, reducing the number of refinement cycles needed.

Tree-of-Thought (ToT). ToT extends this idea by allowing the LLM to explore multiple reasoning paths in parallel, forming a tree of possible solutions [20]. The LLM can then evaluate these different paths and choose the most promising one. This is particularly useful for complex problems where the optimal solution is not immediately obvious. By exploring multiple options in the generation step, the LLM is more likely to produce a high-quality initial artifact.

By incorporating these reasoning methods, the Iterative Refinement Loop can be made more efficient, as the initial artifact is likely to be closer to the desired output, requiring fewer and less drastic refinement steps.

5 Recent Developments in Agent-Based Iterative Refinement

The landscape of AI-assisted software development has evolved rapidly throughout 2024, with several groundbreaking developments that significantly advance the Iterative Refinement Loop pattern. These developments demonstrate the maturation of agentic systems and their increasing sophistication in handling complex software engineering tasks.

5.1 Multi-agent Collaborative Systems

Recent research has shown that multi-agent systems can dramatically improve the effectiveness of iterative refinement by distributing different aspects of the validation and improvement process across specialized agents.

AgentCoder Framework. The AgentCoder system represents a significant advancement in collaborative code generation [21]. Unlike single-agent approaches, AgentCoder employs multiple specialized agents that work together in an iterative refinement process: a *Programmer* agent generates initial code, a *Test Designer* creates comprehensive test cases, and an *Executor* runs the tests and provides feedback. This multi-agent collaboration creates a more robust feedback loop where each agent contributes domain-specific expertise, leading to higher-quality code generation with fewer iterations.

Autonomous Program Improvement. AutoCodeRover extends the pattern beyond initial generation to autonomous program improvement and bug fixing [22]. The system demonstrates how iterative refinement can be applied to existing codebases, using sophisticated analysis tools to identify issues and iteratively propose and validate fixes. This represents a significant evolution from generating new code to maintaining and improving existing software systems.

5.2 Tool-Integrated Agentic Systems

The integration of AI agents with development tools has created more sophisticated iterative refinement loops that leverage the full software development ecosystem.

SWE-agent Architecture. SWE-agent introduces novel agent-computer interfaces that enable more effective automated software engineering [19]. The system demonstrates how agents can interact with development environments, version control systems, and testing frameworks to create comprehensive iterative refinement loops. By providing agents with richer environmental feedback, SWE-agent achieves significantly better performance on complex software engineering tasks compared to isolated LLM approaches.

Multi-Modal Code Generation. Mentat represents an advancement in multimodal code generation with integrated iterative feedback mechanisms [17]. The system can process not only text-based requirements but also visual specifications, diagrams, and existing code context. Its self-refinement capabilities demonstrate how the pattern can be extended to handle more diverse input modalities while maintaining rigorous validation through multiple feedback channels.

5.3 Advanced Reasoning and Reflection Capabilities

The latest generation of LLMs has introduced sophisticated reasoning capabilities that significantly enhance the iterative refinement process.

OpenAI o1 and Reasoning Models. OpenAI's o1 model series represents a breakthrough in AI reasoning capabilities, incorporating extensive internal deliberation before generating responses [12]. The model engages in a hidden chain-of-thought process that acts as a form of pre-generation refinement, where it iteratively improves its approach before producing output. This represents a significant evolution in how the *Generate* step of the pattern can be enhanced with internal iterative processes.

Claude 3.5 Sonnet and Artifact Iteration. Anthropic's Claude 3.5 Sonnet has demonstrated remarkable capabilities in iterative artifact refinement, particularly in code generation and modification tasks [2]. The model's ability to maintain context across multiple refinement iterations while incorporating complex feedback has set new standards for what's possible with the Iterative Refinement Loop pattern.

5.4 Implications for Pattern Evolution

These recent developments suggest several important evolutionary directions for the Iterative Refinement Loop pattern:

- **Hierarchical Refinement:** Multi-agent systems enable hierarchical refinement where different agents handle different aspects of validation and improvement, creating more sophisticated feedback loops.
- **Tool-Native Integration:** Modern agentic systems are designed from the ground up to integrate with development tools, making the pattern more seamless and effective.
- **Context-Aware Refinement:** Advanced models can maintain richer context across iterations, enabling more sophisticated refinement strategies that consider the broader software engineering context.
- **Proactive Quality Assurance:** Systems are moving beyond reactive error correction to proactive quality improvement, anticipating potential issues before they manifest.

These developments indicate that the Iterative Refinement Loop is evolving from a simple error-correction mechanism to a comprehensive framework for AI-assisted software engineering that can handle the full complexity of modern software development workflows.

6 Related Patterns and Concepts

- **Reasoning Methods:** The pattern can be enhanced by incorporating reasoning methods like *Chain-of-Thought* [18] and *Tree-of-Thought* [20] in the generation step.
- **Human-AI Collaboration Patterns:** This pattern automates the *Iterative Exploration* pattern (a "regenerate" button) by replacing subjective human judgment with objective tool feedback [5].
- **Agent-Based Architectures:** The pattern serves as a fundamental blueprint for both *Single-Agent Workflows* and *Multi-Agent Systems* [6,13]. Recent developments like AgentCoder demonstrate how the pattern can be distributed across specialized agents [21].
- **Retrieval-Augmented Generation (RAG):** RAG and this pattern are complementary. RAG is employed *prior* to generation to provide context [8], whereas the loop is used *post-generation* to validate and correct.
- **Model-Context-Protocol (MCP):** This pattern represents a robust application of MCP, where the 'Protocol'is governed by the 'Loop Controller', the 'Context'is the growing prompt history, and the 'Model'is the LLM.
- **Test-Driven Development (TDD):** While TDD follows a "test-first" methodology [10], this pattern supports a "generate-first" workflow, making it more akin to a **Test-Driven Refinement** process.

7 Discussion: The Future of AI-Assisted Development

The Iterative Refinement Loop is more than just a technique for improving code generation; it is a key component in the future of software development. We envision this loop becoming an integral part of the entire software toolchain:

- **In the IDE:** Agentic systems are already transforming the IDE into a collaborative environment where developers can delegate complex, multi-step tasks to an AI partner that uses this pattern to execute them.
- **In CI/CD Pipelines:** The loop can be integrated into Continuous Integration pipelines to create a "self-healing" build process. A pull request could trigger an automated process where an AI agent reviews the code and attempts to fix failing tests or suggest improvements. While full automation requires robust safeguards and human oversight, this approach could significantly reduce the time developers spend on routine fixes.
- **In Runtime Environments:** Looking further ahead, the loop could be applied to runtime monitoring to create self-healing systems. When a system detects an error or a security vulnerability in production, it could trigger an autonomous refinement process to generate, validate, and deploy a patch, leading to more resilient and secure software.
- **In Autonomous Development:** The recent emergence of sophisticated agentic systems like SWE-agent and AgentCoder suggests a future where entire software projects could be developed through iterative refinement loops, with minimal human intervention required for routine development tasks [19,21].

8 Conclusion

The Iterative Refinement Loop has emerged as a foundational design pattern for AI-assisted software development, evolving from a simple error-correction mechanism to a comprehensive framework for sophisticated software engineering workflows. This pattern provides a structured and automated approach to address the inherent unreliability of Large Language Models while harnessing their creative capabilities.

The recent developments in 2024–including multi-agent collaborative systems like AgentCoder, tool-integrated platforms like SWE-agent, and advanced reasoning models like OpenAI's o1 series–demonstrate the pattern's remarkable adaptability and continued relevance. These advances show how the basic cycle of generation, validation, and feedback-driven refinement can be enhanced with hierarchical agent architectures, sophisticated reasoning capabilities, and seamless tool integration.

By creating systematic cycles of refinement, the pattern transforms LLMs from erratic generators into dependable partners in crafting high-quality software. Its widespread adoption across commercial tools, research frameworks, and cutting-edge agentic systems is a testament to its fundamental importance. As AI agents become more sophisticated and deeply integrated into software development workflows, the Iterative Refinement Loop will continue to evolve as an indispensable architectural pattern, enabling the next generation of autonomous software engineering systems.

Acknowledgements. We are deeply grateful for the insightful feedback and constructive suggestions provided by the participants of our writer's workshop at the EuroPLoP 2025 conference. Special thanks to Joe Yoder, Stefan Holtel, Michael Weiss, Adrian Schuckart, Daniel Lübke, and Felix Mahr for their valuable contributions and discussions.

This work has been supported by the FFG, Contract No. 911655: "Pro^{2}Future II is funded within the Austrian COMET Programme (Competence Centers for Excellent Technologies) under the auspices of the Austrian Federal Ministry of Innovation, Mobility and Infrastructure (BMIMI), the Austrian Federal Ministry of Economy, Energy and Tourism (BMWET), and of the Provinces of Upper Austria and Styria. COMET is managed by the Austrian Research Promotion Agency FFG."

References

1. Amodei, D., Olah, C., Steinhardt, J., Christiano, P., Schulman, J., Mané, D.: Concrete problems in AI safety (2016). https://arxiv.org/abs/1606.06565
2. Anthropic: introducing Claude 3.5 sonnet (2024). https://www.anthropic.com/news/claude-3-5-sonnet. Accessed 30 Sep 2025
3. Du, Z., et al.: Multi-agent software development through cross-team collaboration (2024). https://arxiv.org/abs/2406.08979
4. Google cloud: introducing Gemini code assist: your AI-powered coding companion (2024). https://cloud.google.com/blog/products/application-development/introducing-gemini-code-assist. Accessed 30 Sep 2025
5. Heiland, L., Hauser, M., Bogner, J.: Design patterns for AI-based systems: a multivocal literature review and pattern repository. In: 2023 IEEE/ACM 2nd International Conference on AI Engineering – Software Engineering for AI (CAIN), pp. 184–196. IEEE (2023). https://doi.org/10.1109/cain58948.2023.00035
6. Hong, S., et al.: MetaGPT: meta programming for multi-agent collaborative framework (2023). https://arxiv.org/abs/2308.00352
7. JetBrains: JetBrains AI assistant 2024.3: full line code completion and more (2024). https://blog.jetbrains.com/idea/2024/11/jetbrains-ai-assistant-2024-3/. Accessed 30 Sep 2025
8. Lewis, P., et al.: Retrieval-augmented generation for knowledge-intensive NLP tasks. In: Larochelle, H., Ranzato, M., Hadsell, R., Balcan, M., Lin, H. (eds.) Advances in Neural Information Processing Systems, vol. 33, pp. 9459–9474. Curran Associates, Inc. (2020). https://proceedings.neurips.cc/paper/2020/file/6b493230205f780e1bc26945df7481e5-Paper.pdf
9. Liu, Y., et al.: PropertyGPT: LLM-driven formal verification of smart contracts through retrieval-augmented property generation (2024). https://arxiv.org/abs/2405.02580
10. Mathews, N.S., Nagappan, M.: Test-driven development and LLM-based code generation. In: Proceedings of the 39th IEEE/ACM International Conference on Automated Software Engineering, pp. 1583–1594. ACM (2024). https://doi.org/10.1145/3691620.3695527
11. OpenAI: GPT-4 technical report (2023). https://arxiv.org/abs/2303.08774
12. OpenAI: Introducing OpenAI o1-preview (2024). https://openai.com/blog/introducing-openai-o1-preview. Accessed 30 Sep 2025
13. Qian, C., et al.: ChatDev: communicative agents for software development (2024). https://arxiv.org/abs/2307.07924

14. Rodriguez, M.: Introducing GitHub Copilot workspace: your AI-powered developer environment (2024). https://github.blog/2024-04-29-github-copilot-workspace/. Accessed 30 Sep 2025
15. Shinn, N., Cassano, F., Labash, B., Gopinath, A., Narasimhan, K., Yao, S.: Reflexion: language agents with verbal reinforcement learning (2023). https://arxiv.org/abs/2303.11366
16. Tao, L., Chen, X., Yu, T., Mai, T., Rossi, R., Li, Y., Mitra, S.: CodeLutra: boosting LLM code generation via preference-guided refinement (2024). https://arxiv.org/abs/2411.05199
17. Tian, H., et al.: MENTAT: a multi-modal code generation agent with iterative feedback and self-refinement (2024). https://arxiv.org/abs/2308.02312
18. Wei, J., et al.: Chain-of-thought prompting elicits reasoning in large language models (2022). https://arxiv.org/abs/2201.11903
19. Yang, J., et al.: SWE-agent: agent-computer interfaces enable automated software engineering (2024). https://arxiv.org/abs/2405.15793
20. Yao, S., et al.: Tree of thoughts: deliberate problem solving with large language models (2023). https://arxiv.org/abs/2305.10601
21. Zhang, D., et al.: AgentCoder: multi-agent-based code generation with collaborative refinement (2024). https://arxiv.org/abs/2312.13010
22. Zhang, Y., Qian, H., Yang, Z., Wu, T., Chen, H.: AutoCodeRover: autonomous program improvement (2024). https://arxiv.org/abs/2404.05427

From Directive to Dialogue: Reframing Prompt Engineering as Illocutionary Speech Acts

Stefan Holtel(✉)

PricewaterhouseCoopers, Bernhard-Wicki-Strasse 8, 80636 Munich, Germany
stefan.holtel@pwc.com

Abstract. This paper positions Prompt Engineering within the broader context of Discourse Analysis (DA) and Human-Computer Interaction (HCI), highlighting the transformative potential of Speech Act Theory in the age of AI-driven dialogue systems. Traditionally treated as a technical exercise involving precise command inputs, prompt crafting is reconceptualized as a dialogical and intentional communicative practice that derives from human language. Drawing on foundational work by Austin et al. the paper argues that interactions with large language models can be framed as speech acts which are expressions shaped by intention, social function, and a turn-taking structure. Aimed at non-expert users seeking more effective ways to converse with chatbots, the paper introduces a short pattern language that is derived from illocutionary speech acts. It identifies six recurring types of prompting that represent a reflection of natural conversational behavior, providing a practical framework for designing meaningful, context-aware, and goal-oriented exchanges between human and machine. By bridging computational logic with human discourse conventions, the paper advocates for a shift from isolated directive one-shot prompts to a multi-turn, purposeful dialogue to enhance interpretability, relevance, and user agency in AI-mediated communication.

Keywords: Prompt Engineering · Speech Act Theory · Discourse Analysis · Conversational AI · Pattern-Based Interaction · Human-Computer Interface

1 Introduction

In recent academic discourse, there has been a notable increasing convergence between two traditionally distinct fields, namely Discourse Analysis (DA) and Human-Computer Interaction (HCI). DA, as developed in the mid-twentieth century (e.g. (Harris 1952, 2023) (Foucault 1969, 2002) (Schegloff 2007), focused on the analysis of human-to-human communication—with an attention to the structure and function of human language in context. By contrast, HCI emerged from computer science and design (e.g. (Englbart 1962) (Card 1983, 2018) (Norman 1988)), aiming to optimize the usability of technical computing systems.

The advent of large language models (LLMs) allows remarkably naturalistic, turn-based dialogues that redefine the boundaries of what formerly constituted human-machine interaction. Especially Prompt Engineering (PE) has emerged as a new critical practice, enabling users to interact effectively with AI systems that simulate realistic conversational exchanges (Schulhoff 2024) (Muktadir 2023).

T. Plummer et al. (Eds.): EuroPLoP 2025, LNCS 16494, pp. 118–131, 2026.
https://doi.org/10.1007/978-3-032-19157-1_7

1.1 Rationale and Theoretical Framework

In the prevailing view, prompt engineering is the craft of writing precise task instructions—with constraints, context, and examples—to elicit desired behavior from large language models without modifying their parameters (Sahoo, et al. 2025). This instruction-centric orientation is reflected in pattern catalogs and practitioner guides that foreground reusable templates, role/persona prompts, and stepwise prompting as core techniques (White, et al. 2023).

But than being confined to the traditional input-output mechanics of Command-Line Interaction (CLI) with computers, prompt engineering could even be conceptualized in light of discourse-oriented approaches of human communication. (Nielsen 2023) e.g. describes the emerging paradigm in computing technology as an 'intention-based outcome interaction' which he calls the only third paradigm shift in computer user interaction since its very invention. In his view this fundamentally departs from the second paradigm we are used to call the 'Command-Line Model' and that has dominated computing history since the early 1960s. Although both interfaces may appear almost identical—it requires the user to enter text—their underlying logic and communicative purpose differ dramatically.

The author argues that the progression path of interaction with cognitive machines will unfold in the near future: on one hand, of course there will be continuing progress on technical capabilities of computers to simulate human-like conversation that makes it easier to make use of LLM capabilities (Maslej and al. 2025), but on the other hand it will become much more relevant to dramatically increase individual skills of using human language that computers can serve purposes. Or, as OpenAI founder Andrej Karpathy claimed: *'The hottest programming language in 2023 is plain English'* (Karpathy 2023). Respectively, users must reflect, understand and articulate their thoughts in a way that may not be necessary when accomplishing a typical task using computers today.

The new interface paradigm, exemplified by AI-driven chatbots such as those developed by (OpenAI 2022), enable forms of communication that mirrors techniques of human dialogue than ever before. This fundamental shift necessitates a deeper exploration of how principles from Speech Act Theory can inform the development and learning of more effective prompting strategies.

1.2 Purpose and Audience

This paper is intended primarily for users of AI chatbots who seek to improve skills for various practical applications but may not possess deeper expertise in neither prompting techniques nor linguistics. By drawing insights from Discourse Analysis (Brown und Yule 1983) and Speech Act Theory (Austin 1962) (Searle, Expression and Meaning: Studies in the Theory of Speech Acts 1979), the paper aims to use an established framework for establishing the very principles of Prompt Engineering from a linguistic perspective. The overarching goal lies in supporting chatbot users in moving beyond isolated, one-shot prompts toward sequential prompt-completion tuples that in aggregation reflect the turn-taking nature of meaningful dialogue between humans (Holtel 2024).

To this end, the paper first introduces key aspects of Speech Act Theory, emphasizing parts most relevant to the practice of prompt crafting within conversational AI systems.

It then proposes six recurring prompt-completion patterns directly derived from speech acts that compile to a pattern language in vain of (Alexander 1979). This framework is intended to guide both the learning and teaching of prompt engineering, offering a practical methodology for designing effective, context-sensitive interactions with large language models.

2 Understanding Human Conversation

This paper first takes a look at formal and functional approaches towards understanding human conversation by means of three theories in the realm of human discourse analysis. All grasp the linguistic structure of language and pursue human patterns typically. Three dedicated approaches seem to be especially helpful in shedding light into the dialogical character of prompt crafting as a meaningful way to interact with a computer in human language.

2.1 Cooperative Principles

(Grice 1975) suggested that effective and meaningful conversation between humans mainly relies on an implicit agreement between speakers to cooperate by following a set of conversational rules. He identifies four 'maxims' that guide this cooperation: quantity (provide the right amount of information), quality (speak truthfully and with evidence), relation (be relevant), and manner (be clear and orderly). His claim is that these maxims help ensure that communication remains coherent and purposeful. In case speakers deliberately flout these rules—such as being vague, off-topic, or ironic—this creates implicatures, which listeners can only interpret based on their own assumptions and context available.

2.2 Relevance

(Sperber and Wilson 1986) proposed that human cognition is geared toward maximizing relevance, which they define as a balance between cognitive effects and processing effort. According to their theory, communication is driven by two principles: First, humans naturally attend to the most relevant information, and second, any act of communication conveys an implicit promise of relevance. This would mean speakers aim to provide information that yields worthwhile insights with minimal mental effort for the listener. Such relevance is achieved when an utterance produces meaningful effects, such as introducing new knowledge or correction of misconceptions—while demanding low cognitive resources. Unlike (Grice 1975), who introduces a normative set of rules how cooperative communication should occur, (Sperber and Wilson 1986) offer a cognitively grounded model explaining why and how individuals interpret messages as they do. This accounts for the comprehension of indirect speech, metaphors, and implicatures through the audience's inference of the speaker's intention to be relevant.

2.3 Speech Acts

Speech Act Theory, initialized by (Austin 1962) and further elaborated by (Searle, Speech Acts: An Essay in the Philosophy of Language 1969, Searle, Expression and Meaning: Studies in the Theory of Speech Acts 1979), moved beyond analyzing literal meanings of words. They focused on the intentions behind them and the pragmatic functions they serve in communication. The central insight has been that speaking is not merely about conveying information but about *encouraging dedicated actions* through language. Searle calls them performative acts (such as making a promise, issuing a request, giving a warning, or offering an apology) which actively shape social interactions and realities. In this sense, utterances like *"I promise to arrive on time"* or *"I apologize for my behavior"* are not just statements; they commit the speaker or attempt to repair social bonds. Speech Act Theory emphasizes that understanding language requires lot of attention to context, speaker intention, and the effect of utterances on listeners.

All three approaches could help to improve prompt engineering in its own regard. For the rest of this paper, the author takes speech acts as a prime example how to match insights from discourse theories upon prompt engineering.

2.4 Applying Speech Acts to Prompt Crafting

While prompt engineering laid the technical foundation for providing a framework for introducing capabilities of natural human language into the human computer interaction realm, speech acts explain how language functions as a performative tool in conversations between humans. (Austin 1962) introduced the concept of Speech Acts that describe and explain the way humans talk with each other. He therefore distinguished three such acts, namely locutionary, illocutionary, and perlocutionary.

A locutionary act refers to the basic act of uttering a meaningful sentence. The illocutionary act pertains to the speaker's intent behind the utterance (e.g., making a promise or giving an order), while the perlocutionary act concerns the effect the utterance has on the listener, such as persuading or frightening them. Austin's classifications underscored the performative nature of language—speech is not merely descriptive but even action-driven. Building on Austin's framework, philosopher John (J. Searle 1969) further refined this theory by introducing five broad categories of illocutionary acts: *Assertives* convey information or describe the world (e.g., *"The sky is blue"*); *Directives* attempt to get the listener to do something (e.g., *"Please close the window!"*); *Commissives* commit the speaker to a future action (e.g., *"I promise to call you"*); *Expressives* convey the speaker's emotional state (e.g., *"I apologize for being late"*); and *Declaratives* change the state of affairs through speech (e.g., *"I now pronounce you husband and wife"*). These different ways to talk are very natural for humans in mutual communication, structuring all their interactions smoothly and enabling rich social coordination. The speech acts likely considered most relevant to human-machine interaction today are:

- Assertives – When an AI states or describes the world, committing to a proposition's truth like *"Your order was delivered today at 14:32."*
- Directives – When a user issues a command to a virtual assistant, such a user saying, *"Set an alarm for 7 AM!"*

- Commissives – When an AI agent confirms an action, like a booking system responding, *"Your flight is scheduled for 10 AM."*
- Expressives – When an AI generates empathetic responses, such as a chatbot saying, *"I'm sorry you're experiencing issues ..."*

Back in mid-1980s computer scientists (Winograd and Flores 1986) applied speech acts to human-machine interaction while arguing that computers can engage in communicative acts based on predefined linguistic rules. But only today, AI-driven chatbot systems inform chatbot development, voice assistants, and conversational AI, because they produce interactions that are highly contextually relevant and effective.

Since the sudden increase of AI-chatbot capabilities, we can now consider embracing all possible speech acts used in human-to-human interaction to the realm of human-to-computer interaction.

We see more evidence that chatbots can achieve the quality of human interaction. (Chen, Li and Ye 2024) e.g. evaluated the suitability of AI-generated conversations, specifically from ChatGPT, for use by comparing them to human-written dialogues across multiple pragmatic features. The results demonstrate that chatbots performed on par with humans replies in most aspects of pragmatic competence.

This paper is a contribution to making available the full spectrum of Speech Act Theory to human-machine interaction. This could lead to more natural, context-aware, and effective communication between a user and a dedicated chatbot by conducting turn-taking chat sessions while closing the gap between computational logic, natural human habits and our norms of conversation.

It is notable that chatbots are not entities that qualify for contributing to speech acts on the same level as humans, which would especially mean conscious understanding and believe what they assert. As (Rosen and Dale 2024) demonstrated while large language models like ChatGPT can generate coherent and contextually appropriate replies, they lack illocutionary intent—a purposeful, goal-directed use of language—resulting in measurably lower semantic divergence compared to human responses. (Jian 2024) found that while LLMs show some superficial alignment with human pragmatic reasoning in structured tasks, they fall short of reliably modeling the context-sensitive, goal-directed behavior expected of human speakers. Nevertheless, (Williams and Bayne 2024) consider chatbots as valuable 'proxy-asserters' that provide speech acts on behalf of someone else—in the case of chatbots e.g. those that engineered the technical system or those contributing their own assertions to the training corpus of an LLM.

3 Six Speech Acts-Inspired Prompting Crafting Pattern

The performative act of a human-computer chat is defined by its dialogical nature that unfolds as a sequence of prompt-completion tuples, where a user prompt and system response (called completion) not only exchanges information but create an action that incrementally shapes the direction, context, and mutual understanding of the interaction (Muktadir 2023) (Schulhoff 2024) .

From an informational point of view this discourse between the human and the chatbot can be interpreted as the cognitive act of thriving to a 'cone of uncertainty' aiming to decrease individual uncertainty (emotional or cognitive) for a given issue at the beginning of the chat (Holtel 2024). Plausibly, uncertainty is at a maximum at the beginning of the chat (typically it is the intention to start a chat at all) and decreases toward the end of a turn-taking dialogue with the chatbot. It is notable to understand the only the user will end the chat because a chatbot will ever create a completion—a chatbot will ever have that last word.

Following patterns formats and structures according to (Alexander 1979) here they are ordered according to the natural flow of conversation after launching a new chatbot session: **CommonGround** (i.e. *'Start by revealing what you know and do not know to unlock richer chatbot conversations.'*), **ScopeControl** (i.e. *'Anchor your prompts with context to guide the chatbot toward focused, coherent answers.'*), **PreciseWording** (i.e. *'Use clear, specific language to shape meaningful and accurate chatbot responses.'*), **RealmRefinement** (i.e. *'Refine and expand your prompts to steer the chatbot toward deeper, more relevant insights'*), **ValidatedInformation** (i.e.*'Actively verify chatbot replies to build trust and deepen your understanding'*), and **AffirmativeEnd** (i.e. *'Close the chat with a clear signal to affirm understanding and cognitive closure.'*).

3.1 Common Ground

A chatbot user should openly acknowledge expertise and uncertainty about a topic to set up a foundation for meaningful, multi-turn interactions that facilitate clarification, guidance, and deeper exploration.

Context. Before a human-computer chat interaction begins a user holds a degree of knowledge and uncertainty about a specific topic (e.g., *"What are the ethical implications of automated weapons?, "Is Berlin the capital of Germany?"*). Typically, a user lacks world knowledge about a topic s/he may be interested in to learn or to elaborate about or is seeking clarification, guidance, or detailed explanations.

Problem. How can a user steer the chatbot that it provides increasingly valuable completions from the very beginning of a chat towards the end of the chat?

Forces.

- Expectation Management: While the user anticipates a helpful reply, s/he may find it difficult to clearly express degree of knowledge or uncertainty early on or at all in the conversation.
- Vague Understanding: The user may struggle to clearly express what s/he does and does not know.
- Cognitive Biases: Humans tend to seek out information that supports existing beliefs (e.g. availability heuristic: relying on readily available examples rather than a comprehensive analysis)
- Context Criticality: A chatbot needs a strong initial frame reference to deliver meaningful responses.

Solution. The user should start conversations by clearly acknowledging knowledge and uncertainty to the chatbot through *Assertives* or *Expressives* that nurture the establishment of common knowledge in communication (Clark and Brennan 1991) Table 1.

Table 1. Examples.

Speech Acts	*Weak Prompt*	*Strong Prompt*
Assertives/ Expressives	*"Climate change is a complicated matter."*	*"I've read a bit about climate change, but I'm uncertain about how it specifically affects weather patterns in Europe."*
Assertives/ Expressives	*"Quantum computing seems to be a game changer."*	*"I've superficial knowledge about quantum computing, but I do not really understand how qubits differ from classical bits or why that matters."*
Assertives/ Expressives	*"GDPR are bad regulations."*	*"Coming across GDPR regulations a few times, I'm unclear on what specific rights it grants to individuals in the EU."*

Results. Explicitly stating the degree of knowledge early in chat sessions led to richer, multi-turn interactions, with chatbots providing more contextualized and exploratory responses. This helps align system replies with users' informational needs and fosters dialogical depth.

3.2 Scope Control

A user should provide relevant background information and define the scope of their inquiry to ensure the chatbot replies are aligned with their expectations.

Context. Once a chatbot session begins, each further prompt and each further completion add up to more data and information that builds and reframes the reference of what becomes relevant for a meaningful chat.

Problem. What can a user do that a chatbot becomes not distracted from the line of thinking and ongoing thoughts? How can s/he ensure that each further completion remains relevant and does not derail from the session topics at all?

Forces.

- Novice Curse: If chatbot users are novices, they are hardly capable of qualifying preliminary or final completions which will end up in questionable results with weak or no quality assurance at all.
- Quality of Context: Without rich context, chatbots may provide overly broad or unrelated responses. If context (either introduced as preload to the chat or provided by the chatbot itself proves wrong or the chat derails, this will decrease quality of results.

- Conversational Coherence: Clearly defined and confirmed context improves overall coherence in chatbot responses. If coherence breaks early in the chat session without being corrected, then it will be more likely that dialogical coherence breaks towards the end.

Solution. The user should use *Representatives* and *Directives* to set up, enhance, or even correct completions introduced by the chatbot for the issue under consideration Table 2.

Table 2. Examples.

Speech Act	*Weak Prompt*	*Strong Prompt*
Representative	*"Yoga practice improves health."*	*"Since I started practicing yoga regularly, I've noticed improvements in my flexibility, stress levels, and overall well-being."*
Directive	*"Help with gardening."*	*"I need advice on growing tomatoes in a small urban garden."*

Results. The chat discourse becomes more coherent and relevant, especially when users set clear a context using *Representatives* and *Directives*. If the user determines that the chatbot is too narrow-minded in considering specific content, this can lead to insufficient outcomes.

3.3 Precise Wording

To obtain a valuable conclusive completion, a chatbot user applies a rich vocabular and smart text phrasing in a way that s/he minimizes ambiguity and enhances interactivity.

Context. The chatbot user is doing a turn-taking chat session with a chatbot while either introducing more information and context or reacting on the chatbot's requests.

Problem. How can the user guarantee that the chatbot really understands and processs the replies s/he provides to the chat session?

Forces.

- Ambiguity vs. Precision: Vague questions and non-specific thoughts lead to generic responses with less value.
- Inquiry Overload: Very complex prompts are poised to confuse processing of its data in a meaningful way. Prompt chaining instead may increase cognitive load on the user to facilitate the dialogue.
- Interactivity: Well-formulated inquiries keep interactions engaging and motivated.

- Politeness: Being polite to a chatbot increases performance (Yin, et al. 2024).

Solution. The user should use structured, clear, and incremental completions that accumulate in decreasing uncertainty and increasing accuracy of responses over the course of the chat. *Directives* are best for strict control while *Expressives* help nurture a natural conversation flow Table 3.

Table 3. Examples.

Speech Act	*Weak Prompts*	*Strong Prompts*
Directives	*"Tell me everything about art!"*	*"Compare Impressionism and Expressionism based on their artistic techniques."*
Directives	*"Explain rocket and plane."*	*"Would you mind explaining the key differences between a rocket and a plane?"*
Expressives	*"You might want to just talk politics?"*	*"You might want tell me about the political process of opinion making?"*

Results. When users apply this pattern with rich vocabulary and clear intent, the chatbot responses become significantly more relevant, structured, and aligned with user expectations. Conversely, chatbot performance deteriorates if wording is too precise that there is no room for getting insights beyond a very narrow point of view.

3.4 Realm Refinement

Users should iteratively refine their inquiries or expand the discussion by requesting elaboration, clarification, or broader context to ensure more precise and relevant responses.

Context. As the session progresses, the user needs to refine questions or expand the discussion based on prior responses.

Problem. How can the user guide the chatbot to provide better answers toward the end of the session?

Forces.

- Context Drift: As the session evolves, earlier responses may become misaligned with the user's intent, requiring refined prompts to maintain relevance.
- Cognitive Load: Breaking complex inquiries into smaller, iterative refinements helps users manage mental effort across multi-turn interactions.

- Emerging Curiosity & Uncertainty: New insights often trigger follow-up questions, prompting users to elaborate or shift focus for deeper exploration.

Solution. The chatbot user should exploit especially precise *Expressives* or dedicated *Directives* that drive conversation forward and refine inquiries Table 4.

Table 4. Examples.

Speech Act	*Weak Prompts*	*Strong Prompts*
Directives	*"What are some practical examples of cognitive bias in everyday decision-making?"*	*"Provide three practical examples of the 'paradox of choice' bias!"*
Expressives	*"Abstract art remains a mystery."*	*"I've always been drawn to abstract art because its emotional depth strikes me."*

Results. By applying precise Directives and intentional Expressives, users guide the chatbot to generate richer, more targeted responses that better align with their evolving goals. With non-precise and weak-intentional refinements, conversations often stall with generic or misaligned answers.

3.5 Validated Information

Users should confirm the accuracy and usefulness of chatbot responses by verifying facts to reflect and opinionate their understanding or concerns.

Context. The user wants to be sure that he has received correct, meaningful and useful information from turn-taking talks with a chatbot.

Problem. How can the user verify the validity of chatbot responses?

Forces.

- False Fluency Risk: Chatbots may present incorrect or speculative information in a confident tone, making it hard to detect inaccuracies without user verification.
- Overreliance on System Authority: Users may place excessive trust in the chatbot's output, especially when it sounds authoritative, reducing their critical engagement.
- Ambiguity of Truth in Complex Topics: In areas lacking clear-cut answers, users must actively engage to distinguish between established facts, interpretations, and opinions.

Solution. The user should use *Directives* and *Expressives* to force the chatbot to validate its responses Table 5.

Table 5. Examples.

Speech Act	*Weak Prompts*	*Strong Prompts*
Directives/ Expressives	*"Tell me about the Pythagorean theorem."*	*"So, the Pythagorean theorem only applies to right-angled triangles, correct?"*
Directives/ Expressives	*"Explain math concepts."*	*"It's frustrating when math concepts are introduced without practical examples."*

Results. When users apply this pattern by explicitly questioning facts or expressing their understanding, chatbot responses become more precise, transparent, and aligned with user expectations. In contrast, if users fail to challenge or verify responses, they risk accepting plausible sounding but incorrect information, which can lead to misunderstanding and poor decision-making.

3.6 Affirmative End

Users often leave chatbot sessions open-ended without signaling closure, which can lead to confusion or wasted effort. Structured endings reduce uncertainty, conserve mental energy, and help transition purposefully to new tasks.

Context. Every session must end sometime. But the only way to end a chat session is top stop replying to a completion. There is no intuitive way to decide why or how to end a session.

Problem. How can the chatbot user close a session in a structured and meaningful way that marks a conclusive end of the current conversation and his state of mind?

Forces.

- No Stop Trigger: A chatbot will reply to any prompt given—it will never end a chat by itself.
- Definition of Done (Sutherland, et al. 2019): If there is no reminder when a chat session is ending then there is no understanding when or how to stop.
- Fading Intention: If an initial purpose has been weak or unclear, this might lead to an unguided and meaningless chitchat with a chatbot without results.
- Undirected Workload: If trial-and-error drives chat progress, this consumes high amounts of mental energy and time.

Solution. The chatbot user should use *Expressives* to close conversations as an affirmation that the line of thought has systematically reduced subjective uncertainty or the original need of information or explanation to an acceptable degree Table 6.

Table 6. Examples.

Speech Act	*Weak Prompts*	*Strong Prompts*
Expressives	*none at all*	*"I now understand the basics of microbiology. Thanks!" "Gotcha!"*
Expressives	*none at all*	*"That's all I needed." "You made my day!" "Appreciated."*

Results. When users deliberately affirm the end of a chat using strong *Expressives*, they experience greater clarity and satisfaction, reinforcing their learning path or resolution of open topics. In contrast, vague or absent closures lead to lingering uncertainty or the temptation to reengage with the chatbot without a real purpose and waste of time. Structured endings help users recognize cognitive completion and conserve attention for future tasks.

4 Conclusion and Final Remarks

This paper argues that prompt engineering should be shifted from a directive paradigm to a dialogic one. Each prompt is treated as a speech act, by which the practice is reframed as intentional, social, and context-sensitive rather than mere instruction giving. To operate this shift, a pattern language grounded in speech-act theory is proposed so that intent is conveyed, context is managed, and expectations are aligned across turns.

Interaction is shifted from telling a model what to do toward co-construction of shared understanding, and principles from conversational design—grounding, repair, and accountable turn-taking—are echoed. Improvements in task performance and transparency about why exchanges succeed, or fail are thereby enabled.

Limitations are acknowledged, including assumptions of cooperative settings and added overhead in time and tooling. Future work is suggested to develop metrics linking speech-act–aware prompting to reliability and satisfaction, or to extend the pattern language to multimodal and multi-agent contexts.

By recasting prompts as speech acts, prompting can be transformed into a principled, conversational craft that is effective, intelligible, and humane.

Acknowledgments. I am deeply grateful to John Searle, who passed away during the writing of this paper. His seminal work at the intersection of the philosophy of language and linguistics laid important foundations for our quest to contemporary approaches to prompt engineering. I expect his insights will remain invaluable in helping us understand, inform, and shape humanity's evolving relationships with talking machines in the years to come.

Disclosure of Interests.. The author has no competing interests to declare that are relevant to the content of this article.

References

Alexander, Christopher: The Timeless Way of Building. Oxford, UK: Oxford University Press. (1979)

Austin, J. L.: How to Do Things with Words. 2nd. Harvard University Press. (1962)
Brown, Gillian, and George Yule: Discourse Analysis. Cambridge, MA: Cambridge University Press. (1983)
Card, S.K.: The Psychology of Human-Computer Interaction. CRC Press, Boca Raton (1983)
Card, S.K.: The Psychology of Human-Computer Interaction. CRC Press, Boca Raton (2018). https://doi.org/10.1201/9780203736166
Chen, X., Li, J., Ye, Y.: A feasibility study for the application of AI-generated conversations in pragmatic analysis. J. Pragmat. **223**(1), 14–30 (2024). https://doi.org/10.1016/j.pragma.2024.01.003
Clark, Herbert H., and Susan E. Brennan: Ground in communication. In Perspectives on Socially Shared Cognition, by Laruen Resnick, B. Levine and M. Teasley, Stephanie John, pp. 13 American Psychological Association. (1991)
Englbart, Douglas C.: Augmenting Human Intellect: A Conceptual Framework. Washington. (1962)
Foucault, M.: Archaeology of Knowledge. Routledge, London (1969)
Foucault, M.: Archaeology of Knowledge. Routledge, London (2002)
Grice, H.P.: Logic and conversation. In: The Logic in Grammar, by Donald Davidson, pp. 64–75. Dickenson Pub. Co., Encino, CA (1975)
Harris, Zellig S.: Discourse Analysis (Reprint). 81. (1952)
Harris, Zellig S.: Discourse Analysis (Reprint). 81. (2023)
Holtel, S.: Phrasebooks can teach us ChatGPT: decoding prompt crafting as function allocation. In: Proceedings of the 29th European Conference on Pattern Languages of Programs, People, and Practices. Irsee: ACM, pp. 1–9 (2024)
Jian, M.: Analysing the Communicative Effectiveness of Large Language Models under the Rational Speech Act Framework. Master Thesis, Edingburgh (2024)
Karpathy, Andrew: The hottest new programming languaga is English. twitter. (2023) https://twitter.com/karpathy/status/1617979122625712128.
Maslej, N., et al.: Artificial Intelligence Index Report 2025. Stanfard University, Stanford, MT (2025) https://arxiv.org/abs/2504.07139
Muktadir, Golam Md: A Brief History of Prompt: Leveraging Language Models. (Through Advanced Prompting). arXiv (Cornell University). Accessed 14 Feb 2024. doi:https://doi.org/10.48550/arXiv.2310.04438. (2023)
Nielsen, Jacob: AI Is First New UI Paradigm in 60 Years. May 19. Accessed 29 Jan 2023. https://www.uxtigers.com/post/ai-new-ui-paradigm. (2023)
Norman, D.: The Design of Everyday Things. Basic Books, New York (1988)
OpenAI: Introducing ChatGPT. (2022) https://openai.com/blog/chatgpt
Rosen, Z.P., Dale, R.: LLMs Don't do things with Words but their lack of illocution can inform. In: Proceedings of the 46th Annual Conference of the Cognitive Science Society (2024)
Sahoo, Pranab, Ayush Kumar Singh, Sripama Saha, Vinija Jain, Samrat Mondal, and Aman Chadha: Systematic Survey of Prompt Engineering in Large Language Models: Techniques and Applications. .(2025) arXiv 12. doi:https://doi.org/10.48550/arXiv.2402.07927
Schegloff Emanuel, A.: Sequence Organization in Interaction: volume 1: a primer in conversation analysis. In: A Primer in Conversation Analysis. 1st. Los Angeles. Cambridge University Press (2007)
Schulhoff, Sander: The Prompt Report: A Systematic Survey of Prompting Techniques. (2024) arXiv. doi:https://doi.org/10.48550/arXiv.2406.06608
Searle, John: Expression and Meaning: Studies in the Theory of Speech Acts. Reprint. Cambridge, MS: Cambridge University Press.—. 1969. Speech Acts: An Essay in the Philosophy of Language. Vol. New Ed. Cambridge: Cambridge University Press. (1979)
Sperber, D., Wilson, D.: Relevance: Communication and Cognition. Blackwell Publishers, Oxford, UK (1986)

Sutherland, J., Coplien, J.O., den Hollander, M., Ramos, C., et al.: A Scrum Book: the Spirit of the Game. Pragmatic Bookshelf (2019)

White, Jules, et al.: A Prompt Pattern Catalog to Enhance Prompt Engineering with ChatGPT. (2023) arXiv. doi:https://doi.org/10.48550/arXiv.2302.11382.

Williams, Iwan, and Tim Bayne: Chatting with bots: AI, speech acts, and the edge of assertion. Inquiry 1–24. (2024) doi:https://doi.org/10.1080/0020174X.2024.2434874.

Winograd, T., Flores, F.: Understanding Computers and Cognition: a New Foundation for Design. Ablex, Norwood, NJ (1986)

Yin, Ziqi, Hao Wang, Kaito Horio, Daisuke Kawahara, and Satoshi Sekine: Should We Respect LLMs? A Cross-Lingual Study on the Influence of Prompt Politeness on LLM Performance. (2024).arXiv. doi:https://doi.org/10.48550/arXiv.2402.14531.

Crafting Conversational Prompt Patterns: A Structured Approach to GenAI Prompt Engineering

Adrian Schuckart(✉)

Munich, Germany
adrian.schuckart@gmail.com

Abstract. Effective GenAI interactions depend on well-structured prompts, yet many users struggle to articulate their intent, leading to inconsistent and shallow outputs. This paper introduces Conversational Prompt Patterns, a framework for refining GenAI generated responses through structured, iterative dialogue. It defines three core patterns: the *Automation Pattern* for efficiency and standardization, the *Argumentation Pattern* for critical thinking and exploration and the *Amplification Pattern* for expanding and enriching ideas. By establishing a Conversational Prompt Pattern Language, this work provides a scalable methodology to enhance GenAI reliability, reduce uncertainty and improve user engagement. These patterns empower users to move beyond static queries, unlocking GenAI's potential as a collaborative reasoning and ideation partner.

Keywords: GenAI · Prompt Engineering · Conversational Approach · Prompt Pattern · Pattern Language · Human-AI Interaction · Conversational AI

1 Setting the Scene

As Generative AI (GenAI) continues to evolve, its integration into professional environments has shifted from experimental curiosity to a fundamental driver of efficiency and innovation. While early adopters explored its capabilities as a novel technology, bigger organizations now seek structured approaches to harness its full potential. Previous discussions have outlined the need for skill development in Prompt Engineering, emphasizing that workforce adoption requires more than static prompt libraries or purely technical explanations [1, 2]. Instead, what is needed is an approach that mirrors how humans naturally interact, with prompts evolving dynamically in a conversational structure.

The challenge organizations face is not just how to implement GenAI, but how to interact with it effectively. Research indicates that prompt structure directly influences GenAI's ability to generate relevant, high-quality responses [3, 4]. Yet, many users engage with GenAI in a rigid, static manner, treating it as a one-shot query system rather than an interactive dialogue partner. This often results in incomplete outputs, hallucinated responses, or a lack of actionable insights. A more structured, iterative approach, where

T. Plummer et al. (Eds.): EuroPLoP 2025, LNCS 16494, pp. 132–151, 2026.
https://doi.org/10.1007/978-3-032-19157-1_8

prompts are refined step by step, can reduce uncertainty, improve response quality and align GenAI generated insights with user needs.

Further developments in GenAI technology reinforce this narrative. Companies like DeepSeek [5] and OpenAI have introduced features as reasoning models that implicitly acknowledge the widespread difficulty users face in formulating tasks and questions in a way that GenAI can effectively interpret. OpenAI states that reasoning models think before they answer, producing a long internal chain of thought before responding to the user. Reasoning models excel in complex problem solving, coding, scientific reasoning, and multi-step planning for agentic workflows [6]. DeepSeek's cost-efficient reasoning model optimizes how GenAI processes user inputs but does not fundamentally change the fact that unclear prompts lead to unreliable outputs. Similarly, OpenAI's release of the 'Deep Research' tool suggests that even advanced users struggle to structure complex queries, requiring GenAI-driven interpretation and synthesis to bridge the gap.

The introduction of tools designed to generate structured insights from minimal input confirms that GenAI companies are increasingly shifting the burden of clarity from the user to the model, a workaround rather than a long-term solution [7]. To address the formulating problem of users, this paper introduces the concept of Conversational Prompt Patterns, a framework for designing prompts that progressively transition from broad to specific, ensuring that GenAI generated content becomes relevant, accurate and tailored to evolving needs.

These three prompt types of *Automation*, *Argumentation* and *Amplification Prompt Patterns*, form the core of a self-developed pattern language proposed in this paper. Each represents a recurring structure observed in practical GenAI usage and has been formalized to help users shape effective multi-turn interactions. It builds upon the principles established in previous research [8] on Prompt Engineering by defining three core prompt modes:

- *Automation Prompt Pattern* - These prompts guide GenAI to produce structured business deliverables like reports, summaries, or emails by refining outputs step by step, ensuring consistency, clarity, and scalability across repetitive tasks.
- *Argumentation Prompt Pattern* - These prompts encourage critical thinking, facilitating the structured exploration of multiple perspectives, counterarguments and reasoned conclusions.
- *Amplification Prompt Pattern* - These prompts are used to enhance, elaborate and enrich ideas, transforming a basic concept into a fully developed output through iterative refinement.

This pattern paper is intended for intermediate users of GenAI, particularly those who have moved beyond initial experimentation and are now seeking structured, repeatable, and adaptive ways to interact with language models. It speaks to professionals who use GenAI tools such as ChatGPT in their daily work as consultants, analysts, instructional designers, educators and innovation leads as well as those who have experienced the limitations of static prompts or generic libraries. Rather than offering a technical or purely academic lens, the paper introduces a practical, conversational framework that supports deeper reasoning, scalable ideation, and workflow integration. It will be especially useful to those who want to refine their prompt engineering skills and adopt a pattern-based approach that aligns with the evolving nature of human-AI collaboration.

This paper expands on the importance of conversational prompting, showing how prompt sequences that reduce ambiguity over time can help users unlock GenAI's real decision-support potential. By demonstrating how *Automation, Argumentation* and *Amplification* patterns operate within an interactive structure, this work provides a scalable and adaptable methodology that organizations, educators and GenAI practitioners can use to refine their GenAI interactions. Understanding how to guide GenAI responses effectively is no longer an experimental advantage, it is a necessity for ensuring that organizations maximize efficiency, encourage innovation and integrate GenAI seamlessly into decision-making processes. The Conversational Prompt Pattern Language presented in this paper offers a practical framework for achieving this goal, reinforcing the idea that interacting with GenAI should be an evolving conversation, not a single command.

2 Towards a Conversational Approach

The ability of GenAI to assist in professional and creative domains hinges not only on model capability but also on how users interact with it. While GenAI have demonstrated impressive performance in various fields, their effectiveness is often constrained by human interaction skills, particularly in how tasks are framed and structured. Studies indicate that GenAI can outsmart professionals in their profession. GenAI can diagnose diseases better than a medical doctor who uses GenAI for diagnoses. Professionals fail to fully utilize GenAI when they are not provided with proper guidance on how to integrate it into their workflows. This limitation is not rooted in the technology itself but in the human capacity to articulate precise instructions and refine GenAI outputs iteratively [9].

Understanding how to interact with GenAI effectively is a relatively new cognitive challenge, like the adoption of spreadsheets in the 1960s. Just as early spreadsheet users had to learn new paradigms of data organization and calculation in the way they communicate with a machine, today's users must develop a structured approach to prompting GenAI systems and relearn how they communicate with a machine [10]. This shift requires not just technical knowledge of GenAI capabilities but also a conceptual understanding of how structured dialogue affects GenAI generated responses.

Historically, user interaction with digital systems has been shaped by paradigm shifts. One such example is the introduction of the computer mouse in 1968 by Douglas Engelbart, which fundamentally changed how users engaged with digital environments. This innovation introduced "tactile immediacy", allowing users to manipulate digital elements with a sense of direct control [11]. GenAI, on the other hand, introduces a different form of engagement "vocal presence" where interaction occurs through text-based dialogue, creating the illusion of conversing with an intelligent entity. Unlike the immediacy of tactile input, this conversational dynamic requires deliberate structuring of interactions to achieve high-quality outputs [12].

GenAI as a general-purpose technology exhibits a unique pattern of economic impact. Some technologies create "mushroom-like" growth, characterized by rapid, temporary expansion driven by short-lived factors like speculative investments or one-off productivity spikes [13]. Many enterprise software solutions, for instance, generate temporary efficiency gains but fail to scale beyond their initial applications. GenAI, however, follow a "yeast-like" growth model, fostering gradual but sustained improvements across multiple domains by consistently enhancing workflows, knowledge management and automation [14]. The key to unlocking this potential is not the technology itself, but how users integrate it into structured interactions.

Despite GenAI's potential to outperform human capabilities in specific areas, it operates fundamentally differently. Consider the case of Stephen Wiltshire, an artist with an exceptional memory who can recreate entire cityscapes from a single viewing [15]. While this ability is extraordinary in humans, it would be trivial for a GenAI model if it could store and retrieve exact visual information. However, GenAI do not store data in a literal sense. Instead, they rely on lossy compression, meaning they retain semantic relationships rather than exact knowledge. This introduces hallucinations, the tendency of GenAI to generate plausible but incorrect information due to the probabilistic nature of its knowledge retrieval process [16]. This phenomenon is not unique to GenAI, similar issues have been observed in compression-based errors in scanned documents [17]. The challenge for users, therefore, is to interact with GenAI in a way that reduces information loss and maintains contextual accuracy.

This issue of hallucinations is not a new challenge in digital systems. Historically, lossy compression errors have caused real-world problems, such as incorrect numerical values in scanned documents [18]. The problem arises when GenAI attempts to reconstruct meaning from incomplete or ambiguous data, resulting in hallucinated outputs that may appear highly confident but lack factual grounding. Unlike previous digital errors that were detectable through verification, GenAI hallucinations often go unnoticed, as the responses can be linguistically fluent and contextually plausible [19]. This makes critical evaluation of GenAI generated content an essential skill for users.

Unlike traditional software, where explicit programming or direct manipulation determines outcomes, GenAI require structured dialogue and iterative refinement. Achieving high-quality responses does not depend on coding skills but rather on domain expertise and the ability to craft effective prompts [20]. Many existing GenAI training programs simplify prompt engineering into a formulaic structure, suggesting that clear instructions, context and formatting are sufficient for effective interactions [21]. However, real-world usage of GenAI requires a more dynamic approach, where prompts evolve in response to GenAI generated outputs rather than being predefined one-time commands [22].

AI interactions follow a conversational cycle. Users begin with an initial query, often through direct text input, document uploads or structured data insertion. GenAI then generates a completion based on a combination of general world knowledge (pre-trained data), conversational memory (context from the ongoing session) and external inputs (if available). The user evaluates the response and provides further refinement, often engaging in multiple iterations before achieving the desired output. This process is not dissimilar to iterative problem-solving in human collaboration, where each turn builds upon previous exchanges [23].

However, GenAI introduce unique challenges due to their internal mechanics. GenAI responses are influenced by earlier turns in the conversation, but the way attention mechanisms prioritize information can lead to unpredictable shifts in focus. A single change in phrasing can disproportionately affect the GenAI's response, a phenomenon akin to the butterfly effect, where small causes create large and unintended consequences [24]. Moreover, GenAI models exhibit short-term memory constraints, often described as a "goldfish memory" problem, where prior conversations are not retained across different sessions unless explicitly reintroduced by the user [25]. This necessitates manual reinforcement of key details to maintain logical consistency in longer interactions.

Given these constraints, users require structured approaches to interact with GenAI effectively. Conversational Prompt Patterns provide a framework for guiding GenAI from broad initial queries to refined, high-precision outputs, addressing the challenges posed by human-GenAI dialogue dynamics. The next sections outline three distinct patterns, *Automation*, *Argumentation* and *Amplification*, each designed to address specific interaction challenges and improve the quality of GenAI generated responses.

3 Patterns

3.1 Mining of the Patterns

The patterns described in this paper emerged from digital upskilling initiatives at PricewaterhouseCoopers GmbH WPG in Germany, complemented by the author's independent consulting practice. They draw on practical experience in designing and delivering GenAI training and in advising professionals on conversational prompting strategies [8]. Work in this area began in early 2021, before the public release of GPT-3 [26], and incorporated lessons from supporting thousands of employees as they experimented with prompt formulation and iterative refinement. These efforts build on earlier digital transformation curricula launched in 2018 [27] and have since been informed by the evolving adoption lifecycle of digital skills [28], where prompt engineering and GenAI fluency are becoming core capabilities. The patterns were tested and refined in the course of these training programs, ensuring they represent practices validated in organizational settings across a wide range of use cases.

3.2 Introduction to the Patterns

Prompting GenAI is not a one-step activity but a dynamic, conversational process. High-quality results emerge through structured interactions that refine the model's output across multiple turns. The patterns introduced in this section, *Automation*, *Argumentation* and *Amplification* capture recurring strategies used by intermediate users to guide LLMs more effectively. Each pattern addresses a different need: *Automation* structures and standardizes outputs for consistency, *Argumentation* supports open-ended exploration and critical reasoning, and *Amplification* expands initial ideas into more elaborate, actionable outcomes. Rather than prescribing perfect prompts, these patterns provide flexible frameworks for reducing uncertainty and improving user-AI collaboration. The following sections explore each pattern in more detail.

3.3 *Automation Prompt Pattern* - Efficiency and Standardization

In many organizational contexts, the value of GenAI lies in its ability to streamline routine, repetitive, and document-heavy tasks. Yet while technology holds potential for boosting efficiency, its actual impact is often limited by how users engage with it. A common assumption is that one well-phrased prompt will produce a usable result. In practice, however, GenAI performs best when guided through a structured sequence of refinements, especially when consistency, clarity and formatting are critical [29]. The *Automation Prompt Pattern* addresses this challenge by providing a framework for progressively refining AI-generated content, rather than relying on a single prompt. It is particularly well-suited to workflows where standardization and repeatability are essential, such as meeting summaries, report generation, customer communication, or internal documentation. Through incremental guidance, the user collaborates with the AI to produce outputs that are not only more precise and polished but also scalable across teams and use cases. The pattern shows how a conversational prompt sequence can be used to improve clarity, reduce post-editing effort, and align GenAI outputs with professional expectations.

Context:
In corporate environments, repetitive tasks such as summarization, report generation, and structured document processing are essential parts of daily workflows. Employees often turn to GenAI to automate these tasks in order to save time and reduce manual effort. However, many struggle to articulate their needs in a structured way, which frequently results in inconsistent and unreliable outputs. This challenge is particularly pressing in areas like business reporting, customer service, and data extraction, where results must be consistent, scalable, and easily adjustable.

Problem:
While GenAI tools often just automate repetitive workflows, users often struggle to frame their queries effectively, leading to:

- Overly generic outputs that lack the specificity needed for practical use.
- Inconsistent structure across GenAI responses, requiring additional manual refinement.
- Loss of contextual complexity of the problem solved when multiple prompts are needed to complete a task.

These issues arise because GenAI do not inherently understand business structures or formatting needs unless explicitly guided. Users may assume that a single prompt is sufficient when an iterative, conversational approach produces more reliable results.

Forces:
Several forces influence the effectiveness of an *Automation Prompt Pattern*: Crafting Conversational Prompt Patterns: A Structured Approach to GenAI Prompt Engineering

1. Standardization vs. Adaptability: GenAI must generate responses that follow a consistent format while remaining adaptable to different user needs and variations in task requirements [30].

2. Efficiency vs. Accuracy: A highly efficient process should minimize user input, but without sacrificing output precision [31].
3. Contextual Dependence vs. Conversational Drift: GenAI builds on prior messages, which create opportunities for continuity and nuance. Without clear prompts it might drift away from the original intent [32].
4. User Expectation vs. GenAI Capabilities: Users expect immediate, polished outputs, while GenAI perform best when guided through iterative refinement [33].

Solution:
An *Automation Prompt Pattern* structures GenAI interactions as an ordered sequence of prompts and completions. Instead of issuing a single instruction, the user guides GenAI through a structured conversation to refine results.

Step-by-Step Framework:

1. General Request - GenAI generates a high-level summary
2. Add Structural Constraints - GenAI refines the output to meet business formatting expectations.
3. Target a Specific Audience - GenAI tailors the response to stakeholder-specific concerns.
4. Refine for Clarity and Impact - GenAI removes unnecessary complexity.
5. Final Validation and Optimization - GenAI produces a concise, polished version of the output.

This process ensures precision and consistency while leveraging the GenAI's ability to refine responses dynamically.

Consequences:
Applying the *Automation Prompt Pattern* leads to outcomes that explicitly resolve the forces at play:

- Standardization vs. Adaptability: Outputs converge on a consistent, reusable structure (sections, fields, tone), while still adaptable for audience and domain-specific variation.
- Efficiency vs. Accuracy: Iterative refinement minimizes user effort while steadily improving precision, producing polished deliverables with fewer edits.
- Contextual Dependence vs. Conversational Drift: The ordered conversational sequence anchors the AI, reducing drift while maintaining continuity across turns.
- User Expectation vs. GenAI Capabilities: Users learn that quality emerges from guided iteration, managing expectations and building trust in the process.

Follow-on Effects:

- Outputs become reusable templates that can be standardized across teams.
- New users onboard faster, as the conversational structure teaches them how to prompt effectively.
- Review processes become more objective, since each refinement step serves as a quality checkpoint.

Liabilities / Trade-Offs:

- The process requires more conversational turns, which may increase time or token costs.
- Over-standardization may reduce nuance or creativity in outputs.
- Longer conversations risk accumulating "context debt", requiring recap prompts to keep alignment.

Results
By following an *Automation Prompt Pattern*, users achieve:

- Scalable and standardized outputs, addressing the need for consistency while adapting to varied use cases.
- Improved clarity and precision, balancing efficiency with the accuracy required for business contexts.
- Anchored conversations that stay on track, reducing drift while maintaining contextual continuity.
- Professional, ready-to-use deliverables, meeting user expectations through iterative refinement, not one-shot prompting.

Example:
Scenario: Automating Meeting Summaries

1. General Request

User "Summarize today's team meeting notes."
AI: "The team discussed project deadlines, budget updates and client feedback."

2. Add Structural Constraints

User: "Structure this as a meeting minutes document."
AI: (Formats content into sections: Agenda, Key Decisions, Action Items.)

3. Target a Specific Audience

User: "Make it suitable for an email summary to executives."
AI: "Subject: Key Takeaways from Today's Meeting: Budget, Deadlines, and Client Strategy."

4. Refine for Clarity and Impact

User: "Refine action items into clear, assigned tasks with deadlines."
AI: "1. John to finalize budget proposal by Friday. 2. Lisa to draft client response by Wednesday"

5. Final Validation and Optimization

User "Shorten to three sentences while keeping all key details."
AI: (Generates a final, concise version.)

3.4 *Argumentation Prompt Pattern* - Critical Thinking and Debate

Large language models are increasingly used not only for completing tasks, but also for supporting complex reasoning, strategic reflection and ethical analysis. However, many users unintentionally limit the potential of GenAI by asking narrow, binary or prematurely closed questions. When the interaction lacks space for exploration, the model often responds with overly generalized answers that miss the depth and nuance needed for decision-making or critical thinking [34]. The *Argumentation Prompt Pattern* responds to this challenge by providing a framework for iterative, open-ended inquiry. Rather than seeking immediate answers, this pattern helps users structure a conversation that starts with broad "how might" questions, explores multiple perspectives, surfaces trade-offs, and gradually refines toward a well-considered conclusion. It transforms the interaction into a collaborative reasoning process, allowing GenAI to act more like a thinking partner than a static answer machine. This pattern is especially useful in consulting, strategy development, policy discussions, education, and innovation, where divergent thinking and structured synthesis lead to better outcomes. The sections that follow outline how to use this pattern to guide GenAI through progressive layers of argumentation and insight refinement, ultimately supporting more thoughtful and defensible results.

Context:
In decision-making, research, consulting, and innovation, GenAI is often used to analyze complex problems, explore alternative approaches, and support strategic thinking. These domains demand flexible reasoning, perspective-taking, and iterative development of ideas, which makes interactions with GenAI particularly challenging.

Problem:
When users ask GenAI to evaluate complex topics, they often face three major issues:

- Narrow Framing: Users ask questions in a yes/no or pro/con format, leading to limited, one-dimensional answers.
- Lack of Exploration: GenAI defaults to general statements instead of generating creative, divergent perspectives.
- Premature Conclusions: Users accept first-level responses, without guiding GenAI to expand, refine and challenge its reasoning.
- These challenges prevent GenAI from reaching its full potential as a tool for structured reasoning and creative problem-solving.

Forces:
Several competing forces impact how effectively an *Argumentation Prompt Pattern* works:

1. Exploration vs. Conclusion: GenAI must strike a balance between open-ended exploration and delivering a clear, convergent recommendation [35].
2. Breadth vs. Depth: GenAI responses need to navigate between covering a broad range of perspectives and delving deeply into selected aspects [36].
3. Divergence vs. Refinement: GenAI can generate many ideas, but users must guide it toward structured, actionable insights [37].

Solution:
An *Argumentation Prompt Pattern* should start broadly, encourage creative exploration, then progressively refine toward a meaningful conclusion.
Step-by-Step Framework:

1. Open Exploration - GenAI generates several broad possibilities.
2. Divergent Thinking - GenAI expands on less obvious approaches.
3. Constraints and Trade-offs - GenAI challenges its own ideas, uncovering risks.
4. Refinement and Prioritization - GenAI narrows down the ideas to workable solutions.
5. Actionable Insights - GenAI delivers a structured, strategic recommendation.

Consequences:
Applying the *Argumentation Prompt Pattern* helps balance the forces in reasoning-focused GenAI interactions:

- Exploration vs. Conclusion: The conversation stays open long enough to surface new ideas, but the structured sequence ensures it converges on a defensible recommendation.
- Breadth vs. Depth: GenAI begins with a wide survey of possibilities, then progressively deepens the analysis in areas most relevant to the user.
- Divergence vs. Refinement: Idea generation and counterarguments create diversity, while guided prioritization prevents the process from becoming unfocused.

Follow-on Effects:

- Users gain richer insights than from one-shot answers, making GenAI feel like a thinking partner.
- The pattern builds trust in reasoning outputs, since risks and trade-offs are explicitly considered.
- It supports structured decision-making, giving users outputs they can defend in professional contexts (e.g., consulting, education, policy).

Liabilities / Trade-Offs:

- Take more interaction turns, which may frustrate users seeking quick answers.
- Without careful guidance, exploration may drift into irrelevant tangents.
- The iterative process can expose biases or uncertainties in GenAI's reasoning that requires extra user oversight.

Results:
By applying an *Argumentation Prompt Pattern*, users can:

- Broader exploration of possibilities, balancing open-ended inquiry with the need to reach a clear, defensible conclusion.
- Balanced breadth and depth of insights, covering diverse perspectives while probing deeply into the most relevant ones.

- Structured synthesis of ideas, moving from divergent thinking to refined, actionable strategies.
- Defensible, well-reasoned recommendations, meeting user expectations for trustworthy outcomes by guiding GenAI through iterative argumentation rather than one-shot answers.

Example:
Scenario: GenAI in Hiring Decisions

1. Open Exploration

User: "How might GenAI improve fairness in hiring?"
AI: "GenAI could remove names from resumes, analyze skills objectively, and suggest diverse candidates."

2. Divergent Thinking

User: "How might fairness be improved in unconventional ways?"
AI: "Using GenAI to predict career growth potential rather than past job history; dynamic, bias-checking algorithms in real time."

3. Constraints and Trade-offs

User: "How might these ideas create unintended consequences?"
AI: "GenAI predictions may reinforce systemic biases if training data is flawed; anonymization may ignore cultural context."

4. Refinement and Prioritization

User: "Which approaches might be easiest to implement for HR teams?"
AI: "Bias-checking algorithms can be integrated with existing hiring software; resume anonymization is also feasible."

5. Actionable Insights

User: "How might HR teams implement bias-checking while ensuring transparency?"
AI: "By providing employees access to GenAI's decision metrics, creating audit trails, and allowing human oversight."

3.5 *Amplification Prompt Pattern* - Idea Expansion and Enrichment

One of the most overlooked opportunities in working with GenAI is its potential to act not just as a generator of ideas, but as a co-creator, a thought partner that helps evolve raw input into refined, well-developed, and actionable concepts. In creative and strategic contexts, users often begin with an abstract notion or fragment of an idea. Yet without structure, such interactions tend to result in generic, inflated, or disconnected outputs that do not deliver meaningful innovation [38]. The *Amplification Prompt Pattern* responds to this by treating the interaction as a shared creative process. Rather than relying on GenAI to merely expand or elaborate, this pattern frames the conversation as a collaborative back-and-forth, where both user and AI take turns building on, reshaping, and enriching each other's contributions. Through this interplay, ideas gain clarity, originality, and structure. Unlike the *Automation Pattern* (focused on efficient refinement) or the *Argumentation Pattern* (oriented around critical exploration), *Amplification* is about evolving an idea together, balancing imaginative divergence with practical convergence. It is particularly useful in brainstorming, innovation, strategy, and creative content development, where progress emerges not from a single perspective, but through mutual ideation.

Context:
In creative work, early-stage ideas are often fuzzy and underdeveloped. Users may have a concept or direction in mind but struggle to articulate or expand it fully. While GenAI can support these situations, it is often treated as a one-way tool, used only to generate more content without meaningful interaction.

Problem:
Users often expect GenAI to independently produce breakthrough ideas. However:

- Outputs may remain vague, conventional, or overly verbose.
- Original intent can get diluted through unstructured expansion.
- Without mutual shaping, responses can drift or lack strategic coherence.

What is missing is a shared process of co-creation, where the user does not just prompt but responds, redirects, and builds alongside the AI, amplifying both inputs into something greater.

Forces:
Several tensions shape the *Amplification Prompt Pattern*:

1. Creativity vs. Focus: The interaction should spark new ideas without losing sight of the core concept or purpose [39].
2. User Initiative vs. AI Momentum: Users must contribute actively and not overly defer to GenAI's suggestions, which can feel polished but may lack depth or direction [40].
3. Originality vs. Relevance: Generating novel concepts must be balanced with ensuring they are feasible, aligned to context and valuable to the user's goals [41]. Crafting Conversational Prompt Patterns: A Structured Approach to GenAI Prompt Engineering
4. Exploration vs. Convergence: The goal is not endless ideation, but evolving toward something specific, refined, and ready for action [42].

Solution:
An *Amplification Prompt Pattern* organizes the interaction as a mutual ideation loop. The user proposes a seed, the AI expands or reshapes it, and the user in turn challenges, specifies, or redirects the response. This cycle continues until the idea reaches a well-structured and usable form.

Step-by-Step Framework:

1. Seed the Initial Idea - The user introduces a rough concept, and GenAI responds with a basic expansion to set the foundation.
2. Expand with Additional Dimensions - GenAI adds relevant channels, audiences or formats and the user responds by adding focus or context to the expansion.

3. Refine the Concept with Specifics - The user sharpens the direction based on GenAI's additions, prompting the AI to suggest concrete tactics or content elements.
4. Enhance with Unique or Unconventional Angles - Both parties push the idea further by exploring creative twists, differentiators or storytelling elements.
5. Finalize the Concept into an Actionable Plan - The user prompts GenAI to structure all the developed elements into a cohesive, executable roadmap with clear phases, milestones, and messaging.

Consequences:

- Creativity vs. Focus: Ideas evolve with structure, avoiding both aimless wandering and premature narrowing.
- User Initiative vs. AI Momentum: Users remain active contributors, steering the process so that GenAI's expansions are guided and meaningful.
- Originality vs. Relevance: Novel twists are balanced with alignment to context and user goals, producing outcomes that are imaginative and useful.
- Exploration vs. Convergence: The process begins with divergence but converges toward a well-structured, actionable plan.

Follow-on Effects:

- Early-stage concepts become mature and executable, not just expanded text.
- Users experience deeper creative engagement, as they shape ideas interactively rather than passively consuming suggestions.
- The pattern fosters a true sense of co-creation, positioning GenAI as a partner in ideation rather than a tool for output.

Liabilities / Trade-Offs:

- The iterative process may require more time and effort than "one-shot ideation."
- Without user discipline, the dialogue can spiral into over-elaboration.
- Stronger user involvement is required, passive users may fail to reap the benefits.

Results:
By applying an *Amplification Prompt Pattern*, users can:

- Focused creativity, balancing imaginative divergence with the need to stay aligned to the core concept or purpose.
- Active user-driven collaboration, ensuring users guide and shape the process instead of deferring to AI momentum.
- Original yet relevant outcomes, encouraging novelty while keeping results feasible, contextual, and strategically aligned.
- Convergent innovation, moving from broad exploration to refined, actionable plans that avoid endless ideation.

Example:
Scenario: Creating a Unique Podcast Concept

1. Seed the Initial Idea

User: "Suggest an idea for a GenAI-themed podcast."
AI: "A show exploring the future of GenAI in everyday life."

2. Expand with Additional Dimensions

User: "Let's make it stand out. What would make it more original?"
AI: "Focus on real-world failures and unexpected uses instead of standard interviews."
User: "That's good. Could we add an audience participation layer?"

3. Refine the Concept with Specifics

AI: "Allow listeners to submit questions, which are answered live using GenAI."
User: "Let's deepen that. How can we weave in a narrative or story element?"

4. Enhance with Unique or Unconventional Angles

AI: "Each episode could follow a fictional case, like a detective solving crimes using GenAI."
User: "Perfect. Can you outline a launch plan and messaging strategy?"

5. Finalize the Concept into an Actionable Plan

AI: "Here's a promotional roadmap with audience segments and episode themes."
User: "Great. Prioritize these steps for a three-month rollout."
AI: "Adjusted roadmap: Phase 1 – teaser campaign and pilot episode in month one; Phase 2 - audience participation features in month two; Phase 3 - full narrative arc by month three." Crafting Conversational Prompt Patterns: A Structured Approach to GenAI Prompt Engineering

3.6 Comparing the Patters

While each pattern addresses a different challenge in GenAI prompting, together they form a complementary pattern language. Table 1 summarizes their core goals, conversational flows, user/AI roles, and contexts of use.

Together, these patterns illustrate complementary modes of human–AI interaction. While each addresses a distinct need, efficiency, reasoning, or creativity, they are not isolated. In practice, users may move fluidly between them: an *Automation* sequence can evolve into *Argumentation* exploration, or *Amplification* can benefit from *Automation* structuring. The pattern language thus supports both specialization and transition, giving practitioners a flexible repertoire for shaping GenAI conversations.

Table 1. Comparing the Patterns.

Pattern	Goal	Flow	User Role	AI Role	Typical Context
Automation	Efficiency & standardization	Linear refinement	Defines constraints, validates outputs	Produces consistent, structured deliverables	Reports, summaries, documentation
Argumentation	Critical thinking & decision-making	Divergence to convergence	Asks probing questions, challenges outputs	Surfaces perspectives, trade-offs	Strategy, consulting, policy
Amplification	Creative co-creation	Iterative loop	Actively builds, redirects, enriches	Expands, twists, enhances user ideas	Innovation, brainstorming, content creation

4 Discussion

The introduction of Conversational Prompt Patterns provides a structured methodology for guiding GenAI interactions, ensuring that users can iteratively refine outputs rather than relying on single-shot prompts. While these patterns help mitigate common issues in human-AI interactions, their effectiveness remains limited by the user's ability to structure and engage in iterative dialogue with GenAI. Despite their structured nature, the patterns do not inherently resolve the challenges of human cognitive biases, GenAI's inherent limitations and the evolving nature of GenAI-based interactions.

The *Automation Prompt Pattern* is particularly effective in corporate, operational and process-driven environments, where efficiency and standardization are critical. By breaking down complex tasks into structured steps, this pattern reduces cognitive load and ensures consistency in GenAI generated outputs. However, its rigid structure risks prioritizing efficiency over adaptability, potentially limiting the GenAI's ability to handle nuanced or dynamic problem-solving tasks. Moreover, automation through structured prompting assumes that users can effectively define step-by-step refinements, yet many users may lack the skill to identify necessary adjustments, leading to formulaic outputs that require human intervention to remain contextually relevant.

The *Argumentation Prompt Pattern* is valuable in consulting, policy analysis and education, where structured reasoning and debate are essential. By treating GenAI as an exploratory reasoning tool rather than a static responder, this pattern enables a more nuanced discussion of trade-offs, competing perspectives and complex decision-making processes. However, the pattern's reliance on open-ended questioning can introduce new challenges. While "How might" questions foster creative exploration, they also risk generating broad or unfocused responses if the user does not skillfully guide GenAI toward a structured synthesis of insights. This limitation mirrors the challenges of human debate, without convergence toward a well-defined outcome, the conversation may remain exploratory without yielding actionable conclusions. Furthermore, since GenAI does not inherently challenge assumptions or assess validity, users must remain critical of the reasoning structure to avoid reinforcing biased or misleading arguments.

The *Amplification Prompt Pattern* is designed to expand and enrich ideas, making it ideal for creative work, product development and strategic innovation. Unlike the *Automation* and *Argumentation Patterns*, which focus on efficiency and structured debate, the *Amplification Pattern* prioritizes ideation, iteration and elaboration. By treating GenAI as a dynamic brainstorming partner, users can progressively build upon an initial concept, unlocking more refined and innovative outputs. However, this pattern assumes that expansion always leads to improvement, which is not always the case. Excessive elaboration may introduce complexity without clarity, making it difficult to extract practical insights from over-expanded ideas. Additionally, because GenAI models generate content based on probabilistic associations rather than true creative reasoning, amplification may produce content that feels original but lacks substantive novelty. Without user intervention to prune and refine ideas, GenAI-driven expansion may lead to content inflation rather than meaningful innovation.

Beyond the individual limitations of these patterns, GenAI themselves present inherent constraints that users must actively manage. GenAI's lossy compression of information introduces the risk of hallucinations, information loss and misinterpretation, meaning that even well-structured patterns cannot eliminate inconsistencies. The goldfish memory analogy highlights the challenge of maintaining coherence across longer GenAI interactions, making it essential for users to reintroduce key information periodically. Additionally, unlike past innovations such as the graphical user interface, which introduced tactile immediacy, GenAI rely solely on text-based interactions, requiring users to develop an understanding of structured dialogue as an interaction paradigm rather than intuitive, hands-on manipulation. While Conversational Prompt Patterns provide essential scaffolding for GenAI interaction, they do not replace the need for GenAI literacy, critical thinking, or domain expertise. Their effectiveness depends on users' ability to internalize structured interaction methods, actively manage GenAI unpredictability and critically evaluate generated content. Moreover, while these patterns provide a framework for systematic GenAI adoption, they do not guarantee organizational integration, as companies may still struggle with training gaps, resistance to new interaction models and the misalignment of GenAI capabilities with business needs.

In conclusion, Conversational Prompt Patterns represent a significant advancement in GenAI interaction design, but they should not be viewed as static solutions. Instead, they function as adaptable frameworks that require continuous refinement, expert oversight and integration into broader GenAI literacy initiatives. Their success depends not only on how well they structure GenAI responses but also on how effectively users and organizations adapt to this new paradigm of human-AI collaboration.

5 Conclusion

This paper has introduced Conversational Prompt Patterns as a structured approach to improving interactions with GenAI, addressing the limitations users face when formulating prompts. By distinguishing between *Automation*, *Argumentation* and *Amplification*

Prompt Patterns, this paper provides a framework that enhances GenAI engagement through iterative refinement, structured dialogue and strategic expansion. While these patterns offer a method to reduce uncertainty, standardize outputs and refine reasoning, they are not a definitive solution to all challenges in human-AI interaction. The effectiveness of these patterns still depends on the user's ability to critically evaluate GenAI generated responses, recognize hallucinations and iteratively refine inputs to improve output quality. Despite the structured methodology provided in this work, broader challenges remain. GenAI systems continue to struggle with context retention, lossy compression of knowledge and hallucinations, which means that even the most refined prompting strategies cannot fully eliminate inconsistencies. The goldfish memory problem, where GenAI loses prior conversation details unless explicitly reinforced, highlights the need for users to actively manage GenAI memory limitations. Additionally, as GenAI evolve, it is unclear how improvements in GenAI retrieval mechanisms and adaptive learning will impact the necessity for structured prompt engineering. The butterfly effect in AI responses, where minor phrasing variations can cause significant changes in output, further emphasizes the importance of structured interaction models that help stabilize response quality.

As GenAI continues to develop, the role of prompt engineering may shift significantly. Advances in adaptive memory, real-time contextual awareness and multimodal GenAI models may reduce the burden on users to structure prompts manually. However, the need for strategic, human-led refinement will likely persist, particularly in fields requiring high levels of precision, such as legal, financial and medical applications. Future research should explore how GenAI itself can assist in shaping better prompts, potentially integrating GenAI-assisted meta-prompting techniques, where AI guides users in structuring their inputs dynamically. Additionally, cross-disciplinary insights from cognitive science, human-computer interaction and organizational behavior will be critical in refining how humans engage with GenAI. Lessons from historical technology adoption cycles, such as the shift from command-line interfaces to graphical user interfaces, suggest that GenAI may eventually incorporate more intuitive interaction paradigms, reducing the reliance on manually structured prompting. However, until such advancements materialize, Conversational Prompt Patterns remain a necessary bridge, helping users extract more meaningful and reliable insights from GenAI. In conclusion, while Conversational Prompt Patterns provide a structured methodology for interacting with GenAI, their long-term relevance will depend on the evolution of GenAI models, user adoption of structured interaction methods and the continued refinement of human-AI collaboration strategies. Organizations, educators and GenAI practitioners must not only develop technical proficiency in GenAI tools but also cultivate a deeper understanding of how structured conversations influence GenAI outputs. Future research should investigate how GenAI interfaces can better support iterative dialogue, ensuring that users and GenAI systems work symbiotically to achieve high-quality, contextually relevant outcomes.

Disclosure of Interests. The author is employed at PricewaterhouseCoopers GmbH WPG, Germany, where he holds the role of Head of Prompt Engineering at Assurance based in Munich and has been involved in developing and delivering training programs related to Generative AI. In addition, the author is partly self-employed, providing independent research and consulting on

AI-related topics. While this paper was self-published by the author, it reflects personal research conducted in the context of academic discussion at EuroPLoP. The author has no financial or non-financial interests that are directly relevant to the submitted work. Parts of this paper were prepared with the assistance of large language models (LLMs), including ChatGPT, which were used to support drafting and refinement of the text.

References

1. Holtel, S., Böse, I.: Problem-based effectual action fuels digital mindsets. In: EuroPLoP '22: Proceedings of the 27th European Conference on Pattern Languages of Programs, pp. 1–12. ACM, New York (2023). https://doi.org/10.1145/3551902.3551979
2. White, J., et al.: A Prompt Pattern Catalog to Enhance Prompt Engineering with ChatGPT. arXiv preprint arXiv:2302.11382 [cs.SE] (2023). https://doi.org/10.48550/arXiv.2302.11382
3. Enhancing learners' critical thinking skills with AI-assisted technology.: https://www.cambridge.org/elt/blog/2023/03/30/enhancing-learners-critical-thinking-skills-with-ai-assisted-technology/, Accessed 16 Jun /06/16
4. Huang, L., et al.: A Survey on Hallucination in Large Language Models: Principles, Taxonomy, Challenges, and Open Questions. arXiv preprint arXiv:2311.05232 [cs.CL] (2024). https://doi.org/10.48550/arXiv.2311.05232
5. DeepSeek-AI, Guo, D., Yang, D., Zhang, H., Song, J., Zhang, R., et al.: DeepSeek-R1: Incentivizing Reasoning Capability in LLMs via Reinforcement Learning. arXiv preprint arXiv:2501.12948 [cs.CL] (2025)
6. Learning to reason with LLMs.: https://openai.com/index/learning-to-reason-with-llms/, Accessed 16 Jun 2025
7. Karnatak, N., Baranes, A., Marchant, R., Zeng, H., Butler, T., Olson, K.: Expanding the Generative AI Design Space through Structured Prompting and Multimodal Interfaces. arXiv preprint arXiv:2504.14320 [cs.HC] (2025)
8. Schuckart, A.: GenAI and prompt engineering: a progressive framework for empowering the workforce. In: EuroPLoP '24: Proceedings of the 29th European Conference on Pattern Languages of Programs, People, and Practices, pp. 1–8. ACM, New York (2024). https://doi.org/10.1145/3698322.3698348
9. A.I. Chatbots Defeated Doctors At Diagnosing Illness.: https://www.nytimes.com/2024/11/17/health/chatgpt-ai-doctors-diagnosis.html/, Accessed 16 Jun 2025
10. Raković, L., Sakal, M., Pavlicevic, V.: Spreadsheets – How it started. International Scientific Journal of Management Information Systems. **9**(4), 9–14 (2014)
11. Douglas Engelbart's 1968. Demo: Transforming Human-Computer Interaction, https://www.interactiondesignhistory.com/Fall2024/silicon-age/mid-century-innovations/douglas-engelbarts-1968-demo-transforming-human-computer-interaction/, Accessed 16 Jun 2025
12. What Are Conversational Experiences? An Introductory Guide.: https://rasa.com/blog/conversational-experiences/, Accessed 16 Jun 2025
13. How efficient growth can fuel enduring value creation in software.: https://www.mckinsey.com/industries/technology-media-and-telecommunications/our-insights/how-efficient-growth-can-fuel-enduring-value-creation-in-software/, Accessed 16 Jun 2025
14. The impact of generative AI as a general-purpose technology.: https://mitsloan.mit.edu/ideas-made-to-matter/impact-generative-ai-a-general-purpose-technology/, Accessed 16 Jun 2025
15. See This Incredible Artist Draw a Whole City From Memory.: https://www.nationalgeographic.com/science/article/autism-artist-stephen-wiltshire-cities-genius/, Accessed 16 Jun 2025

16. Gilbert, H., Sandborn, M., Schmidt, D.C., Spencer-Smith, J., White, J.: Semantic Compression With Large Language Models. arXiv preprint arXiv:2304.12512 [cs.AI] (2023). https://doi.org/10.48550/arXiv.2304.12512
17. An Overview of AI Hallucinations with RAG and Knowledge Graphs.: https://www.digitalocean.com/community/conceptual-articles/ai-hallucinations-with-rag-and-knowledge-graphs/, Accessed 16 Jun 2025
18. Kriesel, D.: Traue keinem Scan, den du nicht selbst gefälscht hast. Mitteilungen der Deutschen Mathematiker-Vereinigung 22(1), 30–34 (2014). doi:https://doi.org/10.1515/dmvm-2014-0015
19. When AI Gets It Wrong.: Addressing AI Hallucinations and Bias, https://mitsloanedtech.mit.edu/ai/basics/addressing-ai-hallucinations-and-bias/, Accessed 16 Jun 2025
20. The AI.: Job That Pays Up to $335K—and You Don't Need a Computer Engineering Background, https://time.com/6272103/ai-prompt-engineer-job/, Accessed 16 Jun 2025
21. Best practices for prompt engineering with the OpenAI API.: https://help.openai.com/en/articles/6654000-best-practices-for-prompt-engineering-with-the-openai-api/, Accessed 16 Jun 2025
22. Generative AI. Prompt Engineering, https://umdearborn.edu/digital-education/generative-ai-um-dearborn/generative-ai-prompt-engineering/, Accessed 16 Jun 2025
23. The Art of Iteration Prompting: Mastering AI Through Deliberate Refinement, https://www.edendigital.io/iteration-prompting/, Accessed 16 Jun 2025
24. Butterfly Effect & Hallucination.: https://www.libra-tw.org/butterfly-effect-hallucination/, Accessed 16 Jun 2025
25. AI chatbots need to be much better at remembering things: Have scientists just cracked their terrible memory problem?, https://www.livescience.com/technology/artificial-intelligence/ai-chatbots-chatgpt-bad-at-remembering-things-have-scientists-just-cracked-their-terrible-memory-problem/, Accessed 16 Jun 2025
26. Schuckart, A.: Introduction to work with GenAI. In: EuroPLoP '23: Proceedings of the 28th European Conference on Pattern Languages of Programs, pp. 1–16. ACM, New York (2024). https://doi.org/10.1145/3628034.3628042
27. Holtel, S., Kowalcyzk, M., Paegle, L.: A myriad of S-curves towards digital mastery: How to spark and nurture digital upskilling at Enterprise level. In: EuroPLoP '21: Proceedings of the 26th European Conference on Pattern Languages of Programs, pp. 1–10. ACM, New York (2022). https://doi.org/10.1145/3489449.3489993
28. Holtel, S., Kowalcyzk, M., Paegle, L.: Beating paths through the digital jungle: How companies master digital culture change. In: EuroPLoP '20: Proceedings of the European Conference on Pattern Languages of Programs 2020, pp. 1–11. ACM, New York (2020). https://doi.org/10.1145/3424771.3424797
29. Generative AI. in Operations, https://www.mckinsey.com/capabilities/operations/our-insights/generative-ai-in-operations/, Accessed 16 Jun 2025
30. Weisz, J.D., He, J., Muller, M., Hoefer, G., Miles, R., Geyer, W.: Design principles for Generative AI applications. In: CHI '24: Proceedings of the 2024 CHI Conference on Human Factors in Computing Systems, pp. 1–22. ACM, New York (2024). https://doi.org/10.1145/3613904.3642466
31. Balancing Efficiency and Accuracy.: https://fastercapital.com/content/Balancing-Efficiency-and-Accuracy.html/, Accessed 16 Jun 2025
32. Context Drift.: Why AI Loses Coherence Over Time and How to Fix It, https://coascendence.com/2025/03/10/context-drift-why-ai-loses-coherence-over-time-and-how-to-fix-it/, Accessed 16 Jun 2025
33. Prompt Engineering.: The Catalyst for GenAI Adoption, https://community.intel.com/t5/Blogs/Thought-Leadership/Big-Ideas/Prompt-Engineering-The-Catalyst-for-GenAI-Adoption/post/1635845/, Accessed 16 Jun 2025

34. Park, S., Subramonyam, H., Kulkarni, C.: Thinking Assistants: LLM-Based Conversational Assistants that Help Users Think By Asking rather than Answering. arXiv preprint arXiv:2312.06024 [cs.HC] (2024). https://doi.org/10.48550/arXiv.2312.06024
35. Holstein, J., Diener, M., Spitzer, P.: From Consumption to Collaboration: Measuring Interaction Patterns to Augment Human Cognition in Open-Ended Tasks. arXiv preprint arXiv:2504.02780 [cs.HC] (2025)
36. Wang, S., Tong, Y., Zhang, H., Li, D., Zhang, X., Chen, T.: BPO: Towards Balanced Preference Optimization between Knowledge Breadth and Depth in Alignment. arXiv preprint arXiv:2411.10914 [cs.CL] (2025)
37. Bansal, P.: Prompt engineering importance and applicability with Generative AI. J. Comput. Commun. **12**, 14–23 (2024). https://doi.org/10.4236/jcc.2024.1210002
38. How Generative AI. Can Augment Human Creativity, https://hbr.org/2023/07/how-generative-ai-can-augment-human-creativity/, Accessed 16 Jun 2025
39. Managing the Creative Frontier of Generative AI: The Novelty-Usefulness Tradeoff, https://cmr.berkeley.edu/2023/07/managing-the-creative-frontier-of-generative-ai-the-novelty-usefulness-tradeoff/, Accessed 16 Jun 2025
40. Vorvoreanu, M., Passi, S., Dhanorkar, S., Heger, A., Walker, K.: Fostering appropriate reliance on GenAI: Lessons learned from early research. Microsoft Technical Report MSR-TR-2025-4. Microsoft Corporation (2025)
41. Ensuring Quality And Relevance In AI-Generated Content.: https://elearningindustry.com/ensuring-quality-and-relevance-in-ai-generated-content/, Accessed 16 Jun 2025
42. Chiu, Y.-H., Chen, C.-C.: Elevating and Sharpening Convergent Thinking: The Potential of Generative AI for Creative Professionals. SSRN preprint (2024). https://ssrn.com/abstract=4911494

Design Patterns for Dealing with Run-Time Errors in Business Processes

Daniel Lübke(✉), Maximilian Nixdorf, and Elias Baalmann

Digital Solution Architecture GmbH, Hanover, Germany
daniel.luebke@digital-solution-architecture.com
https://www.digital-solution-architecture.com

Abstract. Implementing error-resilient business processing is a critical aspect of modern digitization initiatives, particularly when processes are automated using workflow engines. Automated business processes, modeled using Business Process Model and Notation (BPMN) or other modeling languages, must be designed to handle errors effectively to ensure reliability, maintainability, and robustness. Error situations can arise due to various reasons, such as system failures, data inconsistencies, external service disruptions, or business rule violations. The choice of an appropriate error-handling strategy depends on multiple factors, including the type of error, the operational context, and the required quality attributes such as availability, consistency, and fault tolerance. This paper presents eight distinct design patterns for handling errors in both analytical and executable business process modeling. These patterns provide structured approaches to error resolution, recovery, and mitigation, enabling organizations to build resilient workflows that minimize disruptions and ensure seamless execution. By applying these patterns, organizations can enhance their ability to recover from failures, maintain business continuity, and improve overall process reliability. The presented design patterns serve as a guideline for business analysts, process designers, and software engineers in developing robust business processes that are both adaptable and fault-tolerant. This work contributes to the field of business process management (BPM) by offering practical strategies that bridge the gap between theoretical process modeling and real-world execution challenges.

Keywords: business process · design pattern · process pattern · BPMN · error handling · compensation

1 Introduction and Motivation

Automating and executing business processes is an important area of practice when digitizing business processes. Business processes that are modeled as executable business processes are also known as workflows. These are later executed in a process engine. Today's most commonly used modeling language for these tasks is BPMN.

T. Plummer et al. (Eds.): EuroPLoP 2025, LNCS 16494, pp. 152–187, 2026.
https://doi.org/10.1007/978-3-032-19157-1_9

Especially when automating business processes, questions about error handling arise: A workflow should not just be stuck somewhere or abort without anyone noticing. This makes error handling important and automatic error handling a necessity when hundreds of process instances are started daily in digitized environments.

Errors can arise from different sources, which might profit from different error handling strategies:

Internal Implementation Defects: When automating an executable business process, implementation errors can be made. From wrong data mappings to unwanted dead-locks or live-locks many types of defects might be introduced by the process implementers. Like with any other software artefact, defects will propagate into production before they are found. If a process instance fails due to such errors, workflow engines allow to deal with these errors better than traditional programming languages.

External Dependency: Other software systems or business partners might not be available, respond in time, or respond differently than expected. This may lead to errors and the question arises how to proceed in these cases.

Wrong or Unexpected User Input: Users may input wrong data, which either has not been fully validated or which can only be validated later on in the process.

Business Errors: Other business-related errors like inconsistent data or the need to conduct the business process slightly out of its specification may arise during execution and begs the question how to deal with the arising error conditions.

This paper presents patterns for addressing errors with different error handling strategies. The following stakeholder groups can profit from knowing and applying these patterns:

Process Analysts: who design processes together with business representatives, can rely on a pattern language, which allows for easier communication and structured decision making.

Process Implementers: (and Software Developers), who implement automated business processes, can better understand and possibly re-use templates in their tools, which allows for easier communication and shorter development times.

The remainder of this paper is structured as follows: After presenting related work in Sect. 2, we will explain the mining process in Sect. 3. Section 4 presents an overview of the patterns found and how they are organized before Sect. 5 describes and explains all patterns before the paper concludes and gives an outlook to possible future work.

2 Related Work

The probably best known pattern collection in the business process domain is the "Workflow Patterns" collection by van der Aalst et al. [16]. However, these patterns describe "only" structures used to judge the power of modeling languages and assess the features of workflow engines but are no design patterns that help modelers to decide how to design business processes by detailing problems, contexts, forces, and consequences.

Because public repositories like those hosted on GitHub (and previously Sourceforge) allow researchers to access a huge number of projects and contained artefacts easily, some research is concerned with pattern mining such repositories: For example, Surian et al. mined collaboration patterns [15] and Hartel et al. [4] have analyzed models created with the Eclipse Modeling Framework (EMF) and compiled a list of usage patterns (and error patterns).

These models can also be used for mining design patterns. For example, the collection of Approval Process Patterns [7,9] has been mined from BPMN process models publicly available on GitHub.

Most of the patterns presented in this paper can be applied to both analytical as well as executable business processes (also called workflows): They are not merely syntactic but each of the patterns will describe desired behavior in a given business context. Other existing pattern collections on the business level have been gathered in the "Content" category of patterns identified by a literature survey by Fellmann et al. [2].

3 Pattern Mining Method

Implementing executable business processes in digitization projects is one of the main topics of the authors' worklifes. From this experience initial pattern ideas were derived and known uses in our projects as well as from publicly available sources like GitHub were gathered. Ideas that gained three or more known uses were further refined into patterns that are presented in this paper.

Two projects, which will be mentioned frequently in the known uses sections, are:

Land Registry Platform "Terravis": Terravis [6] is a large scale process integration platform that allows land registries, notaries, banks, and others to efficiently conduct business processes fully digitally. It uses Informatica ActiveVOS as its workflow engine. Terravis is very open about its development challenges [1] and as such is a good candidate to be able to describe known uses with more details.

Credit Card Provider: We are involved in multiple software projects at a credit card provider. All processes are automated using the Camunda workflow engine. Unfortunately, we are not allowed to give concrete names and details.

Some of the design patterns are mined also from functionality of different business process management systems (BPMS): For example, Camunda, SpiffWorkflow, and ActiveVOS are shown as known uses or examples as part of the pattern descriptions.

When describing the patterns, we use BPMN for the solution sketches. Although the patterns do not require the use of BPMN, BPMN is an easy to use and widespread notation that makes it a good choice.

BPMN defines Activities as a super class of tasks (atomic activity), sub-processes (set of other activities), and call activities (re-usable sub-processes). While for visual clarity we use tasks in our diagrams, we talk about activities. In general, errors might also arise from sub-processes. Also, reactions to errors might be complex and thus the error handling might be organized in a sub-process.

4 Introduction to the Patterns

4.1 Patterns Overview

This paper presents eight patterns as shown in Table 1. These patterns are concerned with how to handle run-time errors in business processes, especially executable business processes.

Whenever an error occurs, the simplest possible solution is to just abort the running process instance. This pattern is called *Abort Process*. However, this will not reach the goals of the process instance. For trying to repair a process instance and resume it, other design patterns are presented. If an automated part of the process instance fails, e.g., because of unexpected data, the task can be delegated to a user (*Delegate Step to User*).

If it is likely that a run-time error does not only cause problems in the current step, the whole process can be moved to a user. This allows to skip automated parts, which will likely fail due to the same problems and the user, who is more flexible, can finish the process instance. This pattern is called *Further Manual Processing*.

In case of errors that are due to wrong inputs or decisions prior in a process, the process can jump back to a safe checkpoint so that mistakes can be corrected (*Return to Last Checkpoint*).

If a common user is likely to not handle the problem, e.g., because it is a technical problem, the task can instead be referred to technical support staff (*Escalate to Technical Support*).

When an error is due to inconsistent inputs it can be efficient to let a user correct the inconsistent data before continuing the process (*Correction by User*).

For errors that are likely only temporary, an activity can be retried (*Retry*). In contrast, for persistent errors it might be useful to use a different activity (*Substitution Activity*).

4.2 Implementation Effort and Cost per Error

The following discussion, supported by Fig. 1 positions the error handling patterns along two dimensions: *implementation effort* and *cost per error*. This argument does not account for indirect factors such as opportunity costs or reputational damage that might result from choosing one pattern over another. It is

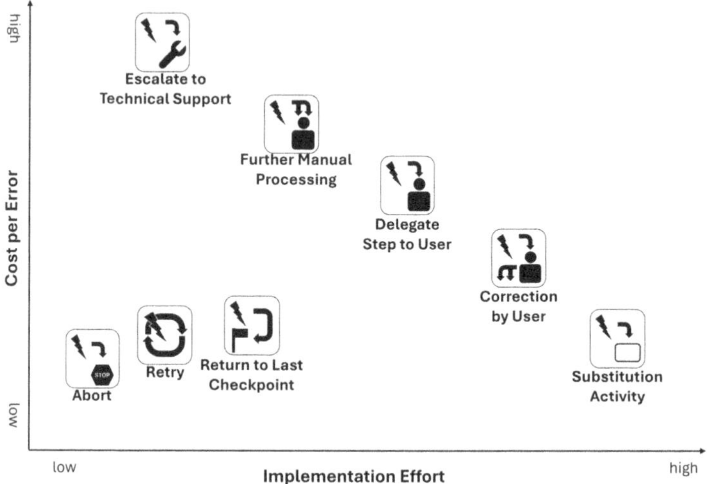

Fig. 1. Implementation Effort and Cost per Error

also necessarily a generalization. In practice, specific contexts—such as the technology stack in use or the skills and structure of the team—may significantly influence both implementation effort and cost per error.

Implementation Effort.

- **Abort Process** is generally straightforward to implement: the error is caught and the process is terminated without further consideration.
- **Retry** is often supported natively by process engines, requiring little more than configuration. Additional effort may be necessary to ensure idempotency to make the environment safe for retries.
- **Escalate to Technical Support** is the default fallback after retries in engines such as Camunda 7. Custom tooling, such as automated alerts in communication platforms, may be added, but is not strictly necessary.
- **Return to Last Checkpoint** is also commonly supported by engines, requiring only configuration. However, it demands more design effort to determine where checkpoints should be placed within the process.
- **Further Manual Processing** can be challenging if no manual process exists. In many cases, however, a manual process predates automation, so implementation is often limited to creating a handover from the automated process to the legacy manual one.
- **Delegate Step to User** requires machine-supported handover of work to a user integrated in the actual process. This is simple if the error case is narrowly defined, but more general incidents can require substantial implementation effort.

- **Correction by User** is similar in complexity to *Delegate Step to User*, but can demand more effort since the user must be given options to decide how the process should proceed after correcting data.
- **Substitution Activity** is typically the most demanding to implement. The required effort depends on the type of activity being replaced, but designing an alternative implementation that is independent from the primary one often involves substantial additional work. Careful consideration is needed to define which failure modes should be covered.

Cost per Error. Abort Process, Retry, and Return to Last Checkpoint are generally inexpensive at runtime.

- **Abort Process** incurs no direct runtime cost, though it may have business implications.
- **Retry** can generate additional cost depending on the resource consumption of the retried activity.
- **Return to Last Checkpoint** may cost more than a retry because multiple activities may be re-executed.

For the remaining patterns, cost per error is largely determined by human involvement. There is an inverse relationship between the implementation effort invested before execution and the cost per error at runtime: more proactive automation reduces per-error cost, while reliance on manual intervention increases it.

- **Substitution Activity** automates error resolution, usually without human involvement. While invoking an alternative automated service may be slightly more expensive than the primary activity, no further runtime cost is generated.
- **Correction by User** is typically a lightweight task: the system guides the user to correct erroneous data, often limited to updating one or two fields. This does not require special expertise and is relatively inexpensive.
- **Delegate Step to User** is more costly, as the user must complete the full activity.
- **Further Manual Processing** raises the cost further, since the user must carry out the remainder of the process.
- **Escalate to Technical Support** is usually the most expensive option, requiring personnel with both technical and domain expertise to analyze and correct the issue.

Summary. In general, the patterns *Abort Process*, *Retry*, and *Return to Last Checkpoint* form a cluster with low implementation effort and low cost per error. They are technical solutions that can resolve certain errors efficiently, but they also have a high probability of not leading to the desired business outcome. This is why further forces must be considered when deciding which pattern to apply in a specific context.

4.3 Process Direction and Error Handling Type

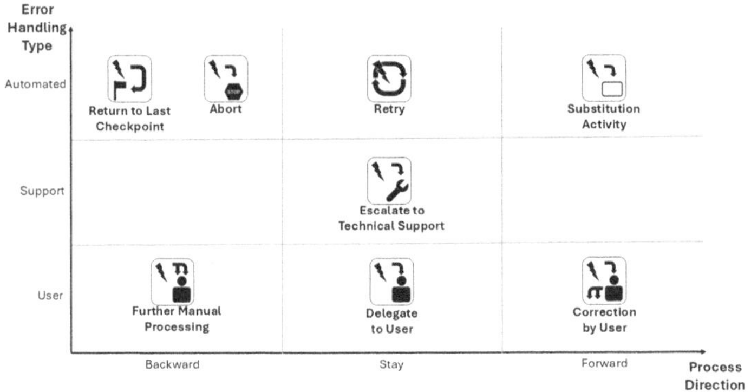

Fig. 2. Process Direction and Error Handling Type

Another option to group the patterns is illustrated in Fig. 2. In this depiction the patterns are ordered by the *process direction* on the x-axis and the *error handling type* on the y-axis. This is meant to emphasize that different error handling patterns require different participants. Based on this information an informed decision can be made to choose appropriate error handling patterns, depending on the available human or technical resources. The process direction has an impact on the error handling cost and the process requirements in terms of which data has to be persisted, and thus can help to choose the appropriate solution for a given error.

Process Direction. The process direction describes how the error handling solution impacts the process flow. *Stay* indicates that the error handling happens more or less at the same process step, for example when using the *Retry* pattern. Here the same activity gets retried multiple times and the process itself stays on the same step until the problem is solved or escalated. *Backward* indicates one or multiple step/s back in the process - e.g. when using the *Return to Last Checkpoint* pattern. When using the backward-direction-patterns, data may have to be rolled back to a previous state, and thus this data still has to be available at the time when the error occurs. In similar fashion, *forward* indicates the opposite: one or multiple step/s ahead in the process.

Error Handling Type. The error handling type focuses on the actor that performs the error handling, be it either human or software-driven. *Automated* describes a software-driven approach that is performed without human interaction - this can range from low (*Retry*) to medium implementation effort (e.g. *Substituation Activity*). *Support* indicates a technical solution that has to be handled by an engineer or developer, since it requires a non-standard solution. *User* on the other hand means that the problem can be handled in a pre-defined way, by either the customer itself or a dedicated member of the support staff.

Summary. Overall, this way of ordering the patterns can help to make an educated decision regarding which error patterns could be used, when decisions have to be made based on available resources. For fully automated systems the *Retry pattern* can be a reliable choice to handle certain errors like server outages. If a large team of support staff is available, the patterns in the lower row could be considered as the preferred options. It is important to keep in mind however, that this alone is not enough to make a final decision which pattern should be used, as this decision also depends on the underlying context and possible process constraints.

4.4 Icons for the Design Patterns

All patterns have an icon that can be used in design work. The icons are styled the same way as icons from another process-related pattern collections called "Approval Patterns" [7–9] so that during design work on business processes these icons can be combined easily. Especially, all icons are square and feature a line border with rounded edges. To distinguish the icons in this pattern collection from the Approval Patterns icons, all error handling patterns feature a lightning strike in the top left corner.

From an error a need for a reaction emerges that is symbolized by an arrow pointing from the lightning strike to an action or role at the bottom. If a (business) user needs to perform an activity, a symbolized person is used in the icon and a wrench symbolizes technical support. Other symbols are used depending on specialized solutions of a design pattern, e.g., a stop sign for cancelling a process.

Table 1. Patterns Presented in This Paper

	Pattern	Problem/Solution
	Abort Process (Section 5.1)	**Problem:** How to handle a process that encounters a non-recoverable error? **Solution:** Terminate the process instance safely after an error is encountered.
	Delegate Step to User (Section 5.2)	**Problem:** How can the process continue after an error that requires further analysis and/or human interaction, because it is not solvable through the automated process, where the exact same result is required? **Solution:** The failing activity in question will be analyzed and solved through human interaction, resulting in the same outcome as if the failing activity would have succeeded. The pattern is shown in Fig. 5
	Further Manual Processing (Section 5.3)	**Problem:** How can the process be successfully completed when an exception arises that the modeled process cannot handle or resolve? **Solution:** Reroute the process to a manual or legacy workflow to handle scenarios that the modeled process cannot address, allowing completion despite its limitations.
	Escalate to Technical Support (Section 5.4)	**Problem:** How can the state of the process and the surrounding system be repaired after an unexpected error at run-time? **Solution:** *Delegate the resolution of errors to technical support, who can troubleshoot and resolve issues in the system or with external services, allowing the process to continue.*
	Retry (Section 5.5)	**Problem:** How can the business process instance proceed when an activity cannot be completed temporarily? **Solution:** The error-prone activity gets retried a specified amount of times.
	Return to Last Checkpoint (Section 5.6)	**Problem:** How can a process handle an error so that participants in the process can still reach the desired process outcome? **Solution:** In case of an error jump back to a previous activity in the process, which was in a stable and consistent state.
	Correction by User (Section 5.7)	**Problem:** How can the process be completed successfully without having to restart the whole process? **Solution:** Allow a user to correct the data and determine whether the process should proceed.
	Substitution Activity (Section 5.8)	**Problem:** How can the process instance progress without interruption in case of errors? **Solution:** Call a Substitution Activity in error cases that offers rougly the same functionality but is usually inferior to the primary activity (e.g., with regards to performance, data quality, costs).

5 Pattern Descriptions

In this main section of this paper all design patterns are presented in detail.

The pattern descriptions follow a standard design pattern template, e.g., as outlined by Wellhausen & Fießer [17]:

Context: The context describes the circumstance under which a design pattern is applicable.

Problem: The problem for which this design pattern offers a solution.
Forces: Quality attributes and other factors that are influencing whether to apply this design pattern or not.
Solution: A description of the solution with a BPMN sketch for the process structure.
Consequences: A description of which quality atttributes are improved ("benefits") and which quality attributes are getting worse ("liabilities") if this design pattern is used.
Example: An example illustrating how a design pattern works.
Related Patterns: References to alternative or complementing design patterns from this or other pattern collections.
Known Uses: Known uses in which projects this design pattern has been applied.

5.1 Pattern: Abort Process 

Context

The organization has a (possibly automated) business process in place that may encounter errors at run-time; for example due to errors in called services or due to mistakes in its implementation.

Problem

How to handle a process that encounters a non-recoverable error?

Forces

- **Manual Effort:** When users or technical support staff needs to intervene in otherwise automated processes, this requires manual effort that incurs costs and probably lengthen process cycle times.
- **Process Efficiency:** Processes can use resources differently, require more resources, and/or reach a better or worse outcome depending on how errors can be handled and compensated for.
- **End-User Friendliness:** Business Process are designed to deliver a desired outcome for process stakeholders. How much (more) effort must be invested in error cases and whether the desired process outcome is reached at all.
- **Data Quality:** Data can be inconsistent due to errors and data quality can be less if certain parts of the process instance have not been executed as expected.
- **Risk of Subsequent Errors:** The guarantees that a business process – even in error cases - gurantees functional correctness for any results, which are delivered.
- **Availability:** The availability of an offered business process to its users and stakeholders.

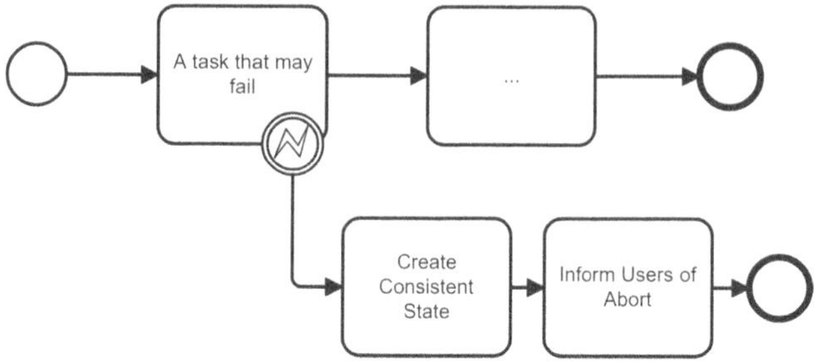

Fig. 3. Solution Sketch for Abort Process

Solution

Terminate the process instance safely after an error is encountered.

Figure 3 shows the design idea behind this pattern: "A task that may fail" is being executed. If it fails, an error is caught with BPMN's error boundary event. This will lead the process instance to its exception flow. To safely terminate the process instance, the process instance and its environment is made consistent again. Afterwards, all users are informed who need to know that the process instance was terminated. After this step, the process instance is completed.

Example

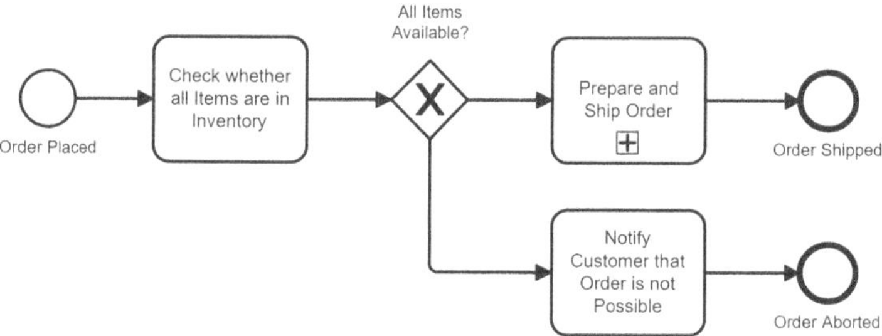

Fig. 4. Order Process Using the Abort Process Pattern

One example for applying this design pattern is shown in Fig. 4: After the customer has placed an order, the inventory is checked. If not enough items are in stock, the order is cancelled and the corresponding order process is terminated.

Consequences

Benefits

- **Manual Effort:** No manual effort is required for working around or fixing error conditions because no activities are performed in error cases.
- **Risk of Subsequent Errors:** The process does not proceed without required data returned from failing activities and as such guarantees an all or nothing semantics.

Liabilities

- **Process Efficiency:** The business process does not reach it goals in any error cases, even if they would be recoverable. The end result for business process users are not achieved if an error occurs.
- **End-User Friendliness:** End-users does not reach their goals in error cases and must start the business process all over again.
- **Availability:** The business process is not available if a service or required stakeholders are not available.

Tips and Tricks

When implementing this pattern, make sure that the process is completed in a consistent state. If changes are done that must be undone, use (BPMN) transactions or consider to use *Compensating Transactions* [3].

If the process may have active parallel branches when an error occurs, make sure to really terminate the whole process instance, i.e., all active branches. For example, use BPMN's terminate end event or group the parallel branches into a subprocess to which error boundary event is attached.

If the termination of the process instance has impact on the process initiator or any other user or system involved in the process (e.g., a customer) make sure to make necessary notifications.

If the process instance is triggered by another software system, consider replying with useful information so that the caller can analyze the problems, e.g., by using the Error Report pattern [18].

Related Patterns

- This pattern can be a possible action by the technical support staff in the *Escalate to Technical Support* pattern.
- This pattern can be combined with the *Compensating Transaction* pattern [3].
- This pattern can be added after unsuccessful *Retry* or *Substitution Activity* patterns.

Known Uses

- Both the BPEL[1] and BPMN 2.0[2] specifications define that unhandled runtime errors lead to the termination of a process instance. In addition, BPEL allows to define a so called termination handler to clean up the process.
- The Swiss land registry platform Terravis [1] terminates purely technical helper processes in case of errors. It also uses this pattern during process initilization: If necessary process data cannot be fetched and/or evaluated at process start (e.g., because a land registry system is not available), the process is terminated and an exception is returned to the process initiator.
- Processes from GitHub [11] use this pattern

[1] http://docs.oasis-open.org/wsbpel/2.0/OS/wsbpel-v2.0-OS.html#_Toc164738527.
[2] https://www.omg.org/spec/BPMN/2.0/PDF.

5.2 Pattern: Delegate Step to User

Context

The organization has an automated business process in place that may encounter errors at run-time which can not always be resolved automatically and may require user interaction to solve them, e.g. the update of a address that cannot be resolved, either by the end-user or by a designated employee for that task.

Problem

How can the process continue after an error that requires further analysis and/or human interaction, because it is not solvable through the automated process, where the exact same result is required?

Forces

- **Manual Effort:** The amount of work done by process participants varies due to the number of tasks and the type of tasks assigned to them. Depending on error handling the amount of work can increase and be distributed differently.
- **Implementation Effort:** The amount of work for process designers and possibly software engineers to implement the solution.
- **Process Efficiency:** Processes should deliver value for their stakeholders. The required amount of work influences the efficiency for reaching the goals. In the best case, error handling should not impact efficiency negatively.
- **End-User Friendliness:** Process Participants – especially Process Initiators – want to achieve their goals easily and do not want to be exposed to the complexity of end-to-end processes. Error handling should ideally be transparent to them.
- **Data Quality:** Business Processes rely on data. Executable business processes even more so [10]. Decisions are based on available data. Thus, data quality will enhance decisions and bad data quality will reduce the quality of the overall process result or might even lead to mistakes and errors.
- **Functional Correctness:** Business Processes should achieve their goals and this requires to make decisions and perform tasks correctly. Error situations might impede the ability to do this.
- **Availability:** Business Processes should be available in as many situations as possible. Error situations might reduce the availabilty of functionality for the organization.

Solution

The failing activity in question will be analyzed and solved through human interaction, resulting in the same outcome as if the failing activity would have succeeded. The pattern is shown in Fig. 5

The erroneous activity or task that is forwarded to the user in order to be addressed - BPMN engines support this through human tasks, specific tasks that

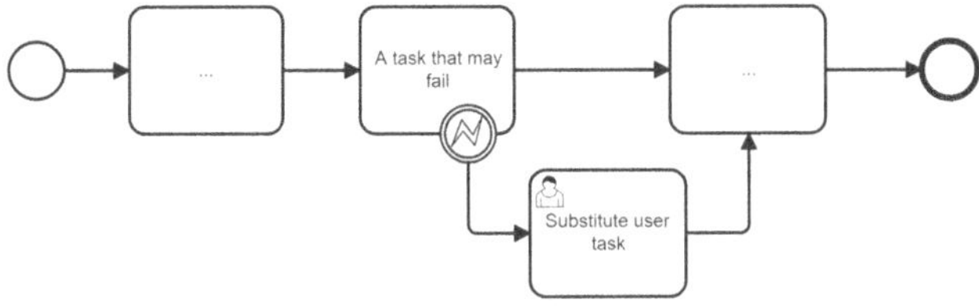

Fig. 5. Solution Sketch Delegate Step to User

require human interaction for completion. These are depicted by the symbol of a person. This solution can consist of non-standard steps outside the regular process (e.g., sending information in a signed document via physical mail that would normally be sent digitally).

Example

The example shown in Fig. 6 depicts a payment process. The end-user enters their payment information and the process continues to validate the given information before further processing the payment. This validation may fail because the data in question may not be requested automatically. Should this occur, a task for manual verification is created for a support-member.

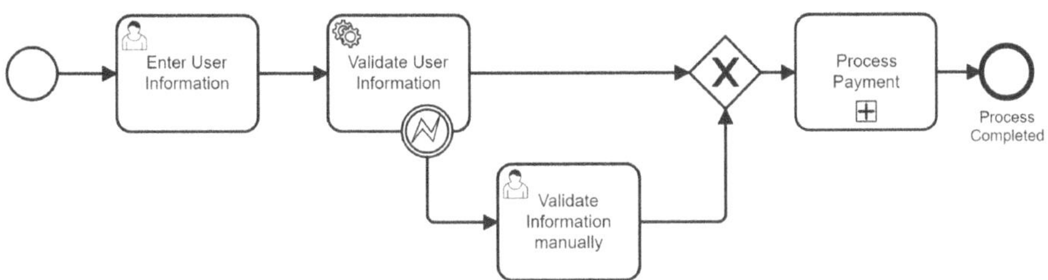

Fig. 6. Example Delegate Step to User

Consequences

Benefits

- **End-User Friendliness:** Depending on the solution the end user has no additional effort but there could be a delay depending on the solution of the error.
- **Data Quality:** Assuming the correctness of the solution implemented via human interaction the data quality remains as good as during the automation.
- **Functional Correctness:** Assuming the correctness of the solution implemented via human interaction the functional correctness remains as good as the solution of the substituted step. Because of the human factor the is a small possibility for an error.

Liabilities

- **Manual Effort:** Varying human effort depending on the solution.
- **Implementation Effort:** Depending on the task at hand the implementation effort for a solution with the exact same outcome can range from negligible to extensive.
- **Process Efficiency:** The process may be slowed down significantly, including potential impact on following activities/tasks.
- **Availability:** The process in question will not be available during manual error solving. Depending on the difficulty of the solution this can take quite some time.

Tips and Tricks

Make sure the outcome of the substitute user activity is exactly the same as the expected result from the substituted activity. Keep in mind that this may also require changes to process variables.

Related Patterns

- This pattern may be used as a follow-up pattern to the *Retry* pattern.
- This pattern may in some cases be very similar to the *Escalate to Technical Support* pattern.
- This pattern is similar to the *Further Manual Processing* pattern, with the difference that it must be possible to continue the process after intervention.

Known Uses

- A credit card company uses this pattern, when – during mandated customer data actualizations – addresses cannot be validated. This may happen, e.g., if the customer has diplomatic status. The validation for these cases is being done by customer service agents.
- The same credit card company uses this pattern when certain thresholds are not met safely or validations cannot be completed via services during their application and card onboarding process.

5.3 Pattern: Further Manual Processing

Context

During process execution, scenarios arise that were either unforeseen during the modeling phase or were intentionally left out due to their complexity or low likelihood of occurrence.

Problem

How can the process be successfully completed when an exception arises that the modeled process cannot handle or resolve?

Forces

- **Manual Effort:** The amount of work done by process participants varies due to the number of tasks and the type of tasks assigned to them. Depending on error handling the amount of work can increase and be distributed differently.
- **Implementation Effort:** The amount of work for process designers and possibly software engineers to implement the solution.
- **Process Efficiency:** Processes should deliver value for their stakeholders. The required amount of work influences the efficiency for reaching the goals. In the best case, error handling should not impact efficiency negatively.
- **End-User Friendliness:** Process Participants – especially Process Initiators – want to achieve their goals easily and do not want to be exposed to the complexity of end-to-end processes. Error handling should ideally be transparent to them.
- **Data Quality:** Business Processes rely on data. Executable business processes even more so [10]. Decisions are based on available data. Thus, data quality will enhance decisions and bad data quality will reduce the quality of the overall process result or might even lead to mistakes and errors.
- **Functional Correctness:** Business Processes should achieve their goals and this requires to make decisions and perform tasks correctly. Error situations might impede the ability to do this.
- **Availability:** Business Processes should be available in as many situations as possible. Error situations might reduce the availabilty of functionality for the organization.

Solution

Reroute the process to a manual or legacy workflow to handle scenarios that the modeled process cannot address, allowing completion despite its limitations.

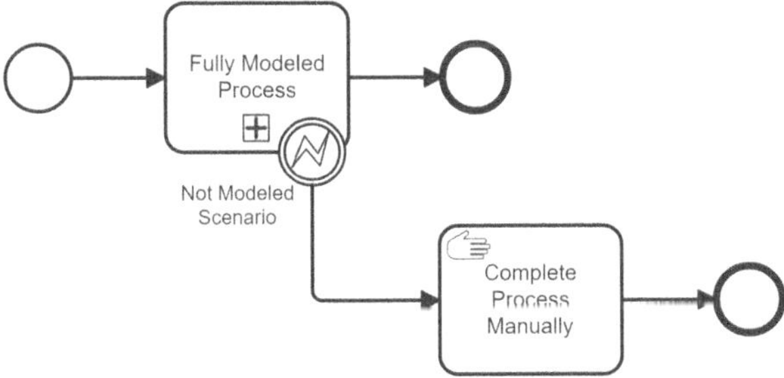

Fig. 7. Solution Sketch for Further Manual Processing

This approach ensures that exceptions are managed without halting the overall process, maintaining continuity and customer satisfaction. While manual workflows are less efficient and more error-prone than automated processes, they provide a practical fallback for handling edge cases or unexpected complexities. Over time, insights gained from manual handling can inform enhancements to the process model, gradually reducing reliance on these fallback mechanisms (Fig. 7).

Example

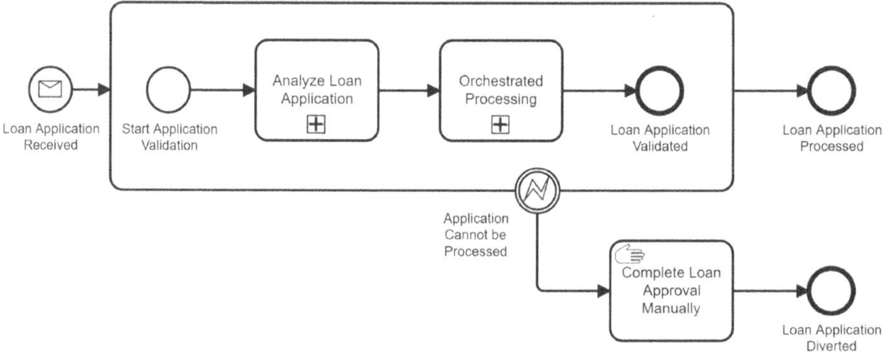

Fig. 8. A Loan Application Process Using Further Manual Processing

An example for the *Further Manual Processing* design pattern is shown in Fig. 8: A loan is analyzed and further processed after the customer has placed a request. If for whatever reason an error occurs, the process instance is handled completely manually.

Consequences

Benefits

- **Implementation Effort:** By falling back to a manual process in special cases, the automation effort can be focused on the main paths of a process improving time to market.
- **End-User Friendliness:** The end user can expect correct behaviour of the process even in special cases that have not been automated or even fully modeled yet.
- **Availability:** The process can stay available even in scenarios that have not been implemented in detail.
- **Functional Correctness:** The agents can ensure that the process is completed correctly even after an error occurred.

Liabilities

- **Manual Effort:** In cases of errors, manual effort is required.
- **Data Quality:** Since the process is not completed normally, data quality can suffer, because some tasks might have to be skipped.
- **Process Efficiency:** For scenarios where further manual processing is required, there will no automation that could improve the efficiency.

Tips & Tricks

If automated processing is terminated and the process control is passed on to a user, the user should be able to see the exact current process context, changes that have been successfully made, and the steps that need to be done because they either failed or could not be executed. Manual processing is made easier if the current process state is as transparent as possible.

Related Patterns

- This pattern is a generalization of the *Delegate Step to User* pattern. In contrast to fixing one step the whole process is done manually instead.
- This pattern can be combined with the *Retry* and *Substition Activity* patterns to ensure manual processing is only performed after other options are exhausted.

Known Uses

- A Swiss company in the financial sector employs this pattern for the customer onboarding process. Whenever the application is to complex (foreign heritage, unclear fraud status, ...) the mainly manual legacy onboarding process is used rather than the automated process.

5.4 Pattern: Escalate to Technical Support

Context

The organization has an automated business process in place that may encounter errors at run-time; either due to errors in called services or due to mistakes in its implementation.

Problem

How can the state of the process and the surrounding system be repaired after an unexpected error at run-time?

Forces

- **Manual Effort:** The amount of work done by process participants varies due to the number of tasks and the type of tasks assigned to them. Depending on error handling the amount of work can increase and be distributed differently.
- **Implementation Effort:** The amount of work for process designers and possibly software engineers to implement the solution.
- **Process Efficiency:** Processes should deliver value for their stakeholders. The required amount of work influences the efficiency for reaching the goals. In the best case, error handling should not impact efficiency negatively.

- **End-User Friendliness:** Process Participants – especially Process Initiators – want to achieve their goals easily and do not want to be exposed to the complexity of end-to-end processes. Error handling should ideally be transparent to them.
- **Data Quality:** Business Processes rely on data. Executable business processes even more so [10]. Decisions are based on available data. Thus, data quality will enhance decisions and bad data quality will reduce the quality of the overall process result or might even lead to mistakes and errors.
- **Functional Correctness:** Business Processes should achieve their goals and this requires to make decisions and perform tasks correctly. Error situations might impede the ability to do this.
- **Availability:** Business Processes should be available in as many situations as possible. Error situations might reduce the availabilty of functionality for the organization.

Solution

Delegate the resolution of errors to technical support, who can troubleshoot and resolve issues in the system or with external services, allowing the process to continue.

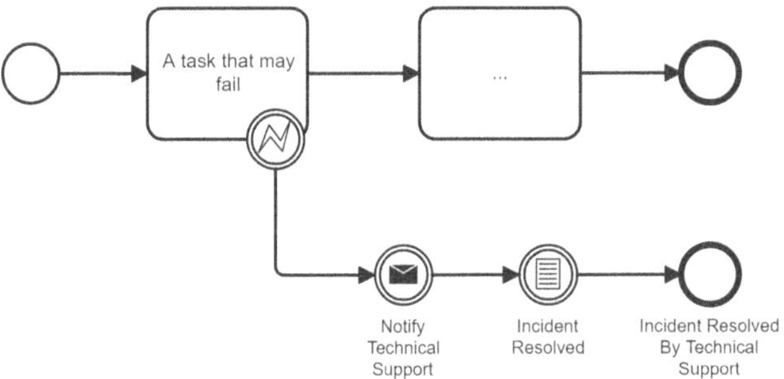

Fig. 9. Solution Sketch for Escalate to Technical Support

To inform technical support a ticket is created that includes error information. Technical support can then analyze further using all tools that are available (admin cockpit, logs, ...). Often fixing the issue includes modifying the process instance in the orchestration platform and modifying state in related systems or even deploying a new version of the process or a related system. When a consistent state is reached again, the process is continued (Fig. 9).

Example

A service task fails because of some unexpected behavior. In Fig. 10 a state was reached that is invalid in the system. The screenshot shows how a tool (here Camunda 7) could help notify technical support and even support in analysis by providing information about the error and the process state. Technical support

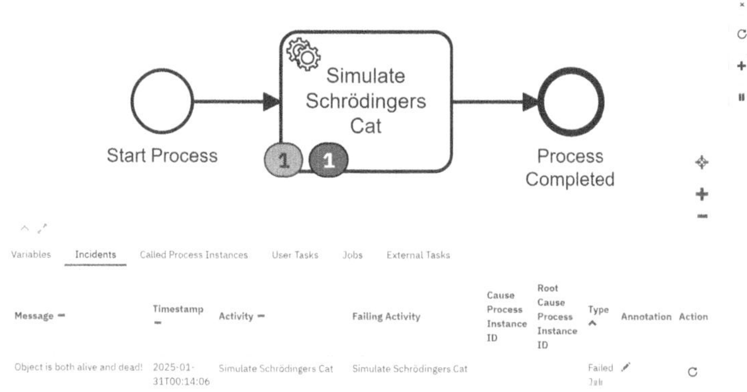

Fig. 10. Camunda Cockpit Enabling Incident Handling for Technical Staff

could now decide to fall back to *Abort Process* which Camunda Cockpit even has a dedicated button for. Or they could try to do fix the state some other way (maybe just kill the cat?) to allow the process to continue.

Consequences

Benefits

- **Implementation Effort:** While not defined in the BPMN specification, incidents are supported by process platforms as the default for not automatically recoverable errors.
- **End-User Friendliness:** The technical support is taking over responsibility for the process, ideally acting transparent to the user.
- **Data Quality:** Any inconsistencies in data introduced by the error can be manually repaired by technical support.
- **Functional Correctness:** Technical support can ensure the correct outcome of the process and even plan improvements to the process to prevent errors in the future.
- **Availability:** Unless technical support is not available, errors can be resolved in a timely manner, minimizing impact on process availability.

Liabilities

- **Manual Effort:** To repair a process manual effort of well-trained personal is required to ensure a consistent state is reached and the process can continue.
- **Process Efficiency:** Establishing a consistent state can be expensive, because it can involve multiple people working on various components.

Tips and Tricks

When this pattern is implemented it is important to set up alerting to notify the appropriate support staff promptly. Consider the tradeoff between the manual effort of regularly fixing errors in the system and the implementation effort to prevent the need for manual intervention. Consider that manually fixing the state in a complex process manually can be error-prone.

Related Patterns

- This pattern can be combined with the *Return to Last Checkpoint* pattern to allow technical support to efficiently restart the process.
- This pattern can be combined with the *Retry* pattern to be the last resort.
- *Abort Process* can be an outcome of this pattern.

Known Uses

- Many Business Process Management Systems (BPMS) (e.g., ActiveVOS[3], Camunda[4], SpiffWorkflow[5]) support suspending process instances when encoutering run-time errors and send notifications. People with enough priviledges may repair and resume the process.
- The Swiss land registry platform Terravis [1] uses this pattern for all main processes so that processes, which have proceeded to the land registry or notary can be completed successfully.
- A credit card company uses this pattern in the backoffice processing of credit card applications: When an error is encountered, the development team is responsible to repair the process instance so that the process can be processed further.

The screenshot in Fig. 11 shows how Informatica ActiveVOS displays processes from the Terravis platform [1] when they have been suspended due to an error.

5.5 Pattern: Retry 

Context
The organization has an automated business process in place that may encounter errors at run-time, mainly due to network/connection issues causing for example notifications or payments to fail.

Problem
How can the business process instance proceed when an activity cannot be completed temporarily?

[3] https://docs.informatica.com/process-automation/informatica-activevos/9-2-5/designer/process-exception-management/suspending-a-process-on-uncaught-faults/making-all-processes-eligible-for-suspension-on-uncaught-faults.html.
[4] https://docs.camunda.io/docs/components/concepts/incidents/.
[5] https://spiff-arena.readthedocs.io/en/stable/explanation/process_error_handling.html#process-error-handling.

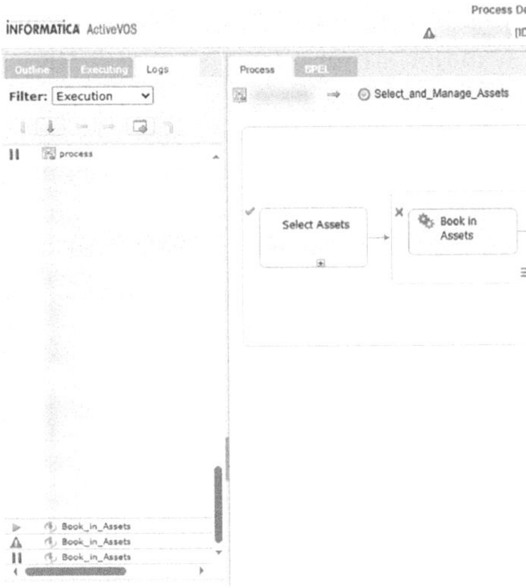

Fig. 11. Informatica ActiveVOS with a Process from Terravis suspended due to a Service Fault

Forces

- **Manual Effort:** The amount of work done by process participants varies due to the number of tasks and the type of tasks assigned to them. Depending on error handling the amount of work can increase and be distributed differently.
- **Implementation Effort:** The amount of work for process designers and possibly software engineers to implement the solution.
- **Process Efficiency:** Processes should deliver value for their stakeholders. The required amount of work influences the efficiency for reaching the goals. In the best case, error handling should not impact efficiency negatively.
- **End-User Friendliness:** Process Participants – especially Process Initiators – want to achieve their goals easily and do not want to be exposed to the complexity of end-to-end processes. Error handling should ideally be transparent to them.
- **Data Quality:** Business Processes rely on data. Executable business processes even more so [10]. Decisions are based on available data. Thus, data quality will enhance decisions and bad data quality will reduce the quality of the overall process result or might even lead to mistakes and errors.
- **Functional Correctness:** Business Processes should achieve their goals and this requires to make decisions and perform tasks correctly. Error situations might impede the ability to do this.
- **Availability:** Business Processes should be available in as many situations as possible. Error situations might reduce the availabilty of functionality for the organization.

- **System Load:** Depending on the cause of the underlying problem, the retry pattern can cause a major strain on the system if the error causes multiple processes to fail at the same time.
- **Cascading Error Potential:** Each error causes an additional execution and can cause additional errors capped by the maximum number of retries. Should a large amount of processes fail, this can put additional strain on the system which in turn can cause other services/activities to fail due to high system load.

Solution

The error-prone activity gets retried a specified amount of times.

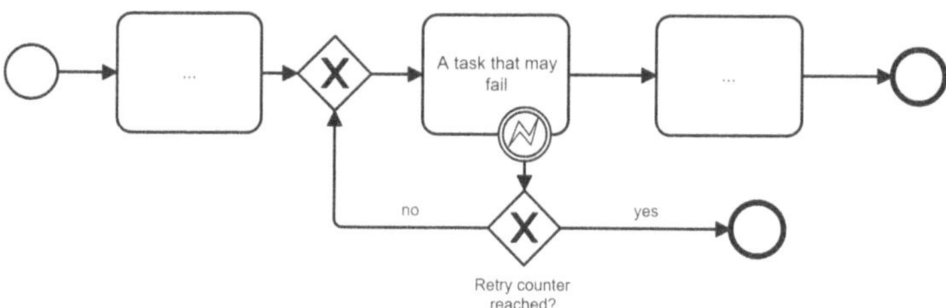

Fig. 12. Solution Sketch for Retry

Figure 12 shows the Retry pattern. The error-prone activity or task (e.g. a notification to an external partner) gets retried multiple times when an error occurs. Since the most likely reason for this error is a temporary network issue, there is a high likelyhood that the activity/task can be completed succesfully after one or more retries.

Example

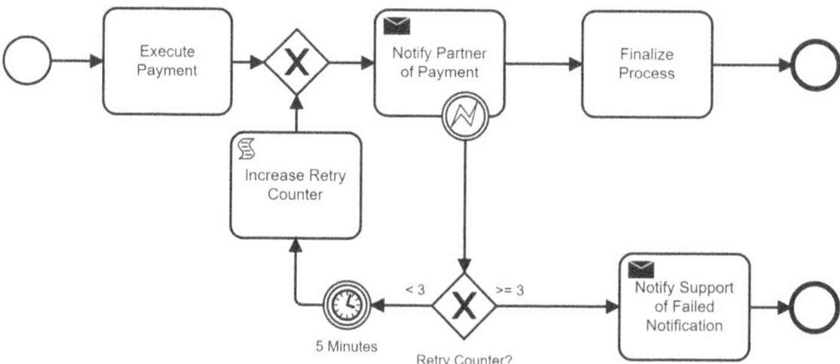

Fig. 13. Example Scenario for Retry

Figure 13 shows an example for the Retry pattern. After execution of a payment the recipient of the payment gets notified. During this notification a network error can occur. The transmission of the notification is repeated 3 times, each after a delay of 5 min. Should these retries fail as well, a support member is notified about the failed notification.

Consequences

Benefits

- **Manual Effort:** No manual support necessary.
- **Implementation Effort:** The implementation effort for a repeated execution of an activity or task is low.
- **End-User Friendliness:** The end user may notice a small delay depending on the retry interval time, but in most cases no delay will be noticed.
- **Data Quality:** The Data Quality stays the same since the same activity is simply retried.
- **Functional Correctness:** If successful, the correctness of the failed task/activity remains the same.
- **Process Efficiency:** Retrying a task/activity causes additional load on the system but will, if successful, guarantee the same process outcome.

Liabilities

Availability: The process will stay available while not all retries have been exhausted. Once none are left the process will no longer be available.
System Load: Retrying a task/activity causes additional load on the system.
Cascading Error Potential: Longer network outages may cause a cascade of errors and can seriously impact the stability of a system if left unchecked.

Tips and Tricks

When implementing this pattern make sure to set the retry-interval according to cause of the problem. There needs to be ample time for the problem to get solved - e.g. allow a server to restart, thus allowing the activity to correctly send the request in question.

Remember to limit the amount of retries to a realistic amount - if a problem does not solve itself after a set amount of times it will probably require further analysis and further retries may cause stress on the system.

Make sure that the failing/retried activity is idempotent. It should only perform its actions once, even when the same request gets received multiple times. For database operations this could for example be solved by using transactions.

Related Patterns

- This pattern can be used as a step before using a number of different patterns. Should the retry pattern fail, another pattern may be used to resolve the issue:
  - *Abort* pattern
  - *Escalate to Technical Support* pattern
  - *Compensating Transaction* pattern [3,12]
  - *Further Manual Processing* pattern

- The *Circuit Breaker* pattern can be used to reduce retry attempts when it detects a complete partner system failure that would result in a series of failed retries.

Known Uses

- The Swiss land registry platform Terravis [1] uses this pattern when sending registrations to the land registry. This activity may fail due to temporary connectivity issues on the land registry side which may be resolved quickly, resulting in a successful retry after a few minutes.
- When trying to reach Credit Card customers by phone, call center agents retry the calls several times depending on the business case until the customer is deemed not reachable.
- The Microsoft Azure Troubleshooting Resources[6] list the *Retry* pattern as a solution to temporary outages of network resources.
- The workflow engine ActiveVOS allows to configuratively define retries on service tasks.

5.6 Pattern: Return to Last Checkpoint 

Context

A business process, perhaps an executable one, is being performed and an activity may fail at run-time, e.g., because products or data or external dependencies are not available.

Problem

How can a process handle an error so that participants in the process can still reach the desired process outcome?

Forces

- **Manual Effort:** The amount of work done by process participants varies due to the number of tasks and the type of tasks assigned to them. Depending on error handling the amount of work can increase and be distributed differently.
- **Implementation Effort:** The amount of work for process designers and possibly software engineers to implement the solution.
- **Process Efficiency:** Processes should deliver value for their stakeholders. The required amount of work influences the efficiency for reaching the goals. In the best case, error handling should not impact efficiency negatively.
- **End-User Friendliness:** Process Participants – especially Process Initiators – want to achieve their goals easily and do not want to be exposed to the complexity of end-to-end processes. Error handling should ideally be transparent to them.

[6] https://learn.microsoft.com/en-us/azure/architecture/patterns/retry.

- **Data Quality:** Business Processes rely on data. Executable business processes even more so [10]. Decisions are based on available data. Thus, data quality will enhance decisions and bad data quality will reduce the quality of the overall process result or might even lead to mistakes and errors.
- **Functional Correctness:** Business Processes should achieve their goals and this requires to make decisions and perform tasks correctly. Error situations might impede the ability to do this.
- **Availability:** Business Processes should be available in as many situations as possible. Error situations might reduce the availabilty of functionality for the organization.

Solution

In case of an error jump back to a previous activity in the process, which was in a stable and consistent state.

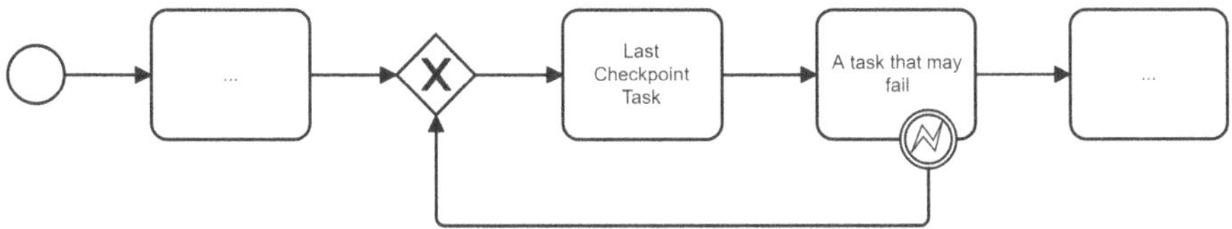

Fig. 14. Solution Sketch for Return to Last Checkpoint

Typically, business processes can be divided into different parts, which reach certain intermediate milestones. These milestones have a consistent state but have not yet reached the final process goal. If an error occurs, this design pattern proposes to jump back to the latest safe point, called a checkpoint, so that tasks and decisions can be re-taken so that the process can continue successfully (Fig. 14).

Example

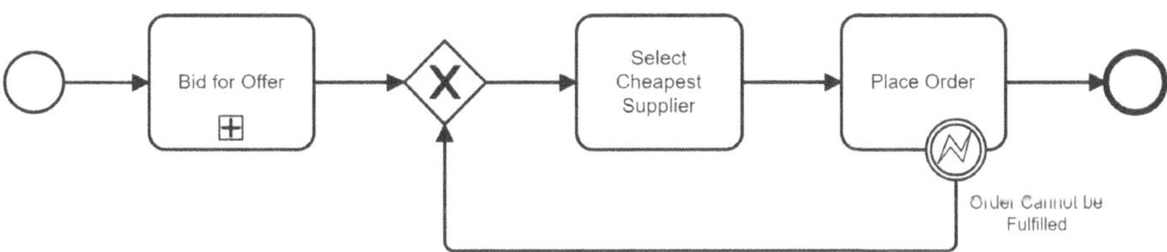

Fig. 15. Supplier Selection Process Using Return to Last Checkpoint Design Pattern

A business owner can order supplies via a B2B ordering platform. After submitting and validating the order, the process will identify the cheapest supplier that can deliver in time. If the supplier cannot fulfil the order, the process jumps back to the provider selection (Fig. 15).

Consequences

Benefits

- **Functional Correctness:** The process does not proceed in cases of error but returns a last known safe state where (typically) a user will make changes so that the process can execute further.
- **End-User Friendliness:** End-users may modify data. The end user experience is influenced about how they are advised when a process jumps back to the last checkpoint.

Liabilities

- **Manual Effort:** No manual effort is required for working around or fixing error conditions because no activities are performed in error cases.
- **Process Efficiency:** The business process does not reach it goals in any error cases, even if they would be recoverable. THe end result for business process users are not achieved if an error occurs.
- **Availability:** The business process is not available if a service or required stakeholders are not available.

Tips and Tricks

Some process engines offer support for this pattern. For example, Activitii & Camunda 7 and all of their forks will jump back to the last transaction checkpoint, which is either defined by task types (e.g., user tasks) or manual Asynchronous Continuations. This is oftentimes quite handy but it is not possible to have a checkpoint before another user task because the user task will be a technically enforced checkpoint.

In most cases the checkpoint will be a user task. The user should be informed about what error occurred and possibly what to do differently.

It is very likely that the activities executed since the last checkpoint must be undone. Consider using BPMN transactions or *Compensating Transactions* [3].

Related Patterns

- This pattern may result in similar behavior like *Delegate Step to User* when the checkpoint is a user task.
- This pattern may be performed by technical support in the *Escalate to Technical Support* pattern.
- When the checkpoint is a user task that allows to re-submit the same request, users can trigger the *Retry* pattern.

Known Uses

- The Camunda 7 workflow engine uses Asynchronous Continuations to manage fallbacks to last "save points" in cases of errors[7][8]

[7] https://docs.camunda.io/docs/components/best-practices/development/understanding-transaction-handling-c7/.

[8] https://www.digital-solution-architecture.com/blog/2023-08-24/Asynchronous-Continuations-in-Camunda-7.php.

- Terravis [1] uses this in a position keeping booking process that when an instructed booking fails, the process returns to the data entry task so that agents can change the data according to the error message.

5.7 Pattern: Correction by User 

Context

A business process, is executed and am activity may fail at run-time, e.g., because the activity cannot proceed with the current state of data.

Problem

How can the process be completed successfully without having to restart the whole process?

Forces

- **Manual Effort:** The amount of work done by process participants varies due to the number of tasks and the type of tasks assigned to them. Depending on error handling the amount of work can increase and be distributed differently.
- **Implementation Effort:** The amount of work for process designers and possibly software engineers to implement the solution.
- **Process Efficiency:** Processes should deliver value for their stakeholders. The required amount of work influences the efficiency for reaching the goals. In the best case, error handling should not impact efficiency negatively.
- **End-User Friendliness:** Process Participants – especially Process Initiators – want to achieve their goals easily and do not want to be exposed to the complexity of end-to-end processes. Error handling should ideally be transparent to them.
- **Data Quality:** Business Processes rely on data. Executable business processes even more so [10]. Decisions are based on available data. Thus, data quality will enhance decisions and bad data quality will reduce the quality of the overall process result or might even lead to mistakes and errors.
- **Functional Correctness:** Business Processes should achieve their goals and this requires to make decisions and perform tasks correctly. Error situations might impede the ability to do this.
- **Availability:** Business Processes should be available in as many situations as possible. Error situations might reduce the availabilty of functionality for the organization.

Solution

Allow a user to correct the data and determine whether the process should proceed.

Figure 16 illustrates the approach: when an error occurs, a user intervenes to correct the invalid data. The user then decides whether to continue the process

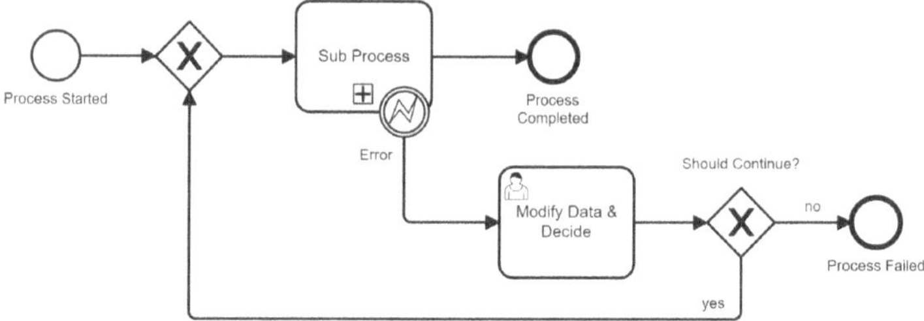

Fig. 16. Solution Sketch for Correction by User

with the corrected data or to terminate it. If the process continues, the previously failing activity is retried with the updated data. There can be multiple iterations of corrections until the data is finally accepted or the process terminated.

Example

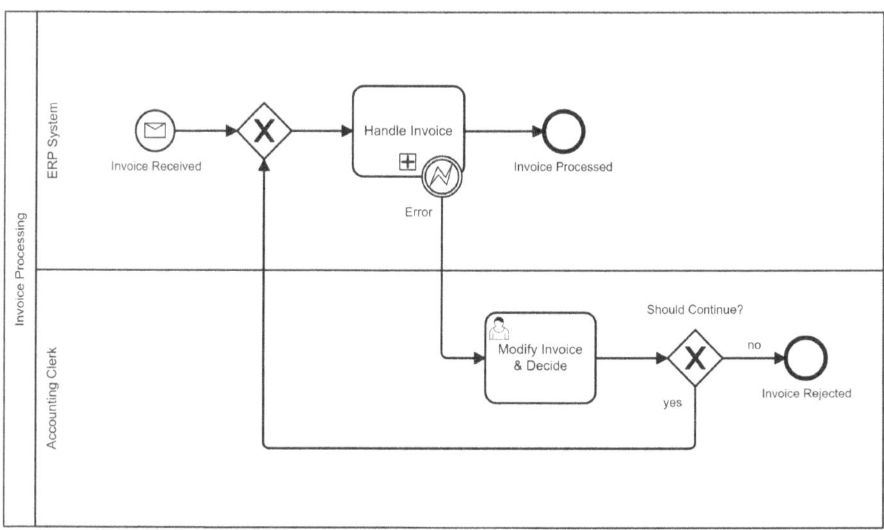

Fig. 17. Invoice Processing Using the Correction by User Pattern

Example 1. Invoice Processing

Figure 17 shows an invoice handling process. A company receives invoices from suppliers, which are automatically processed by an ERP system. The system checks each invoice for errors, such as missing purchase order numbers, incorrect amounts, or mismatched supplier details. If an invoice contains errors, the automated process cannot continue, as it may lead to incorrect payments or accounting inconsistencies. When an error is detected, a user (e.g., an accounting clerk) is assigned a task to review and correct the invoice data. The clerk can correct the data (e.g., update the purchase order reference, adjust tax calculations) and resume processing or reject the invoice if the issue cannot be resolved. Once the issue is addressed, the process continues from the point of failure or is terminated if necessary.

Consequences

Benefits

- **Implementation Effort:** By allowing the manual intervention, special data constellations can be ignored during implementation, reducing the initial effort.
- **Process Efficiency:** While the manual intervention does take some time, most of the process can be executed as normal.
- **End-User Friendliness:** Allowing the user to correct the data rather than having to do the full data entry again is beneficial.
- **Availability:** Unless the process has to be aborted, it stays available even when errors occur.

Liabilities

- **Manual Effort:** To correct the data manual intervention is necessary.
- **Data Quality:** Potentially guessing is involved when the data is corrected, this can lead to incorrect data.
- **Functional Correctness:** A human element is introduced in the process which can be error-prone.

Tips and Tricks

- Provide users with **clear and detailed error information** to help them quickly understand the issue, make informed decisions, and modify the data efficiently.
- **Monitor recurring errors**—if certain data patterns frequently cause the same issues and require the same corrections, consider automating their handling to improve efficiency.
- **Log all changes** to maintain a precise history of modifications, ensuring traceability and enabling restoration of the correct state in case of manual errors.

Related Patterns

- This pattern uses the *Retry* pattern in case the user decides to continue the process.
- This pattern builds on the *Return To Last Checkpoint* pattern by not returning all the way but allowing intermediate intervention.
- *Abort Process* can be an outcome of this pattern.

Known Uses

- In a Swiss financial institute, invoices are corrected using this pattern because not all suppliers use the correct rounding rules
- If you apply for grants for energy efficiency in Germany, you have to sent an application. If information is missing in this application you are asked to supply the missing information after submission.

5.8 Pattern: Substitution Activity 

Also known as: Alternative Activity, Replacement Activity

Context

A business process, perhaps an executable one, is being performed and an activity may fail at run-time, e.g., because another party or service is not responding or cannot perform the necessary activity.

Problem

How can the process instance progress without interruption in case of errors?

Forces

- **Manual Effort:** The amount of work done by process participants varies due to the number of tasks and the type of tasks assigned to them. Depending on error handling the amount of work can increase and be distributed differently.
- **Implementation Effort:** The amount of work for process designers and possibly software engineers to implement the solution.
- **Process Efficiency:** Processes should deliver value for their stakeholders. The required amount of work influences the efficiency for reaching the goals. In the best case, error handling should not impact efficiency negatively.
- **End-User Friendliness:** Process Participants – especially Process Initiators – want to achieve their goals easily and do not want to be exposed to the complexity of end-to-end processes. Error handling should ideally be transparent to them.
- **Data Quality:** Business Processes rely on data. Executable business processes even more so [10]. Decisions are based on available data. Thus, data quality will enhance decisions and bad data quality will reduce the quality of the overall process result or might even lead to mistakes and errors.
- **Functional Correctness:** Business Processes should achieve their goals and this requires to make decisions and perform tasks correctly. Error situations might impede the ability to do this.
- **Availability:** Business Processes should be available in as many situations as possible. Error situations might reduce the availabilty of functionality for the organization.

Solution

Call a Substitution Activity in error cases that offers rougly the same functionality but is usually inferior to the primary activity (e.g., with regards to performance, data quality, costs).

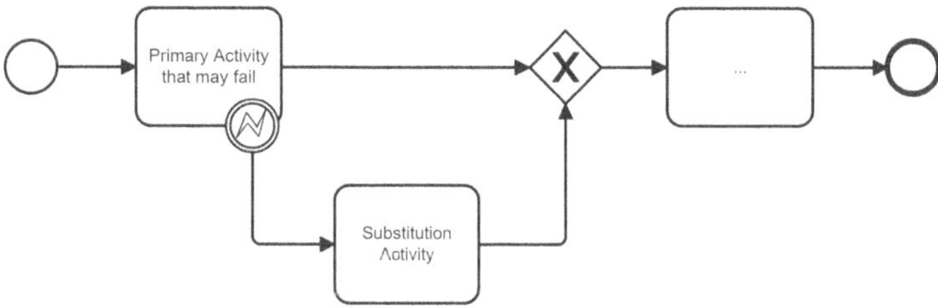

Fig. 18. Solution Sketch for Substitution Activity

The solution idea is sketched in Fig. 18: The primary activity is usually performed because it offers the best quality characteristics for the process. For example, it might be quicker or the returned data might be more acurate.

If this primary activity cannot be completed successfully, a substitution activity is performed that allows the process instance to proceed. The returned data might be not as acurate or the execution might be slower or more costly but the process instance can proceed normally.

Example

A business process is designed that will plan the resources for courier transports for the next day. Depending on the weather forecast, more car drivers or more bike drivers will be commissioned. Each morning, the planning process starts by getting a weather forecast from a commercial forecaster, because the data is more acurate and the time resolution is higher. Sometimes the provider is unavailable. In this case, a default allocation of cars and bikes is used instead.

Consequences

Benefits

- **Manual Effort:** If an automated activity is used as a substitution activity, no additional manual effort is created.
- **End-User Friendliness:** If an automated activity is used as a substitution activity, the end-user does not see a difference in cases of errors in the primary activity.
- **Functional Correctness:** If the substitution activity can provide the same level of functional correctness, then the functional correctness of the whole process remains the same.
- **Availability:** The availability of the business process is increased: It fails only if both the primary and the substitution activity are failing.

Liabilities

- **Implementation Effort:** Implementing a substitution activity adds more work for process desginers and possibly software engineers.
- **Process Efficiency:** In case of invoking the substitution activity, the process duration is negatively impacted. In addition, the primary and the substituation activity do not provide the same quality (e.g., the substitution activity is more expensive) thereby negatively impacting process efficiency.
- **Data Quality:** The substitution activity usually is inferior to the primary activity and thus might deliver older or more coarse-grained data – although this is dependent on the concrete details of the substituation activity.

Tips & Tricks

When using this pattern, you still need to define an error handling strategy if the substituion activity fails. Possibly, you have multiple replacement activity candidates that can be tried in sequence, e.g., multiple service provider.

If service costs are negligible and performance is of high concern, consider always calling the substitution activity in parallel and use its results if the primary activity fails.

Another option to speed up the invocation of the replacement activity is to use the *Circuit Breaker* pattern [13] if it is a service call, e.g., a BPMN service task, so that the primary activity fails immediately, if the service is unavailable.

Related Patterns

In case of failure any Process Error Pattern can be applied to handle failures when performing the replacement activity.

Using the *Circuit Breaker* pattern [13] is possible for both the primary activity as well as the substitution activity – in case they are automated. Applying it to the former, it will reduce the time to call the substitution service when the primary service is unavailable.

Known Uses

- German energy providers will estimate client's electricity, gas, and water usage in case the client did not send meter values back in time[9] or the meter was broken[10].
- In US[11] and Australian[12] jurisdictions filed cases must be personally served to the defendants. If this cannot be done, e.g., because a defendant is avoiding to be served, alternative delivery methods are allowed.

[9] https://www.merkur.de/leben/wohnen/wann-duerfen-anbieter-stromverbrauch-schaetzen-zr-12837276.html.

[10] https://www.verivox.de/strom/ratgeber/bei-defektem-zaehler-kein-kostenloser-strom-schaetzung-erforderlich-1000717/.

[11] https://www.merriam-webster.com/legal/substituted%20service.

[12] https://www.lexology.com/library/detail.aspx?g=47db0641-14fd-4099-8bc4-84a724b19fa0.

6 Conclusions and Outlook

This paper presented eight design patterns that give guidance on how to handle errors in different ways when designing business processes – especially if they are executable. These design patterns help process analysts and process implementers to make better informed decisions and to choose between different possible solutions.

To improve usefulness and usability of the design patterns, future research could implement the patterns into existing process modeling tools. Such tool support could either guide the process designer by an internal decision tree or offer process fragments and skeletons, which can be incorporated into process models. Such an approach reduces development time when automating business processes, e.g., by adding this tooling into a modeler for executable BPMN. This could be accomplished by using reusable fragments. Feasible approaches for accomplishing such a composition have been presented by Schumm et al. [14] and Laue & Kirchner [5]. However, as a prerequisite research into optimal BPMN modeling of the different patterns is required because BPMN is powerful but offers many possibilities to express the same semantics.

Overall, this paper presented the first set of patterns for dealing with error conditions in business processes and can serve as a foundation for further research while already offering help for process implementers. Especially, we would like to encourage the community of people involved in business process modelling or execution to use these patterns, give feedback, and also to suggest new design patterns!

Acknowledgements. We want to thank Mary Carol for being our shepherd. We also like to thank Olaf Zimmermann for his detailed feedback to the patterns and the contents and structure of this paper.

We want to also thank the participants of the writers' workshop at the EuroPLoP conference for their input and helpful discussion.

References

1. Berli, W., Lübke, D., Möckli, W.: Terravis – large scale business process integration between public and private partners. In: Plödereder, E., Grunske, L., Schneider, E., Ull, D. (eds.) Lecture Notes in Informatics (LNI), Proceedings INFORMATIK 2014. vol. P-232, pp. 1075–1090. Gesellschaft für Informatik e.V., Gesellschaft für Informatik e.V. (2014)
2. Fellmann, M., Koschmider, A., Laue, R., Schoknecht, A., Vetter, A.: Business process model patterns: state-of-the-art, research classification and taxonomy. Bus. Process. Manag. J. **25**(5), 972–994 (2019)
3. Gray, J., et al.: The transaction concept: virtues and limitations. In: VLDB. **81**, 144–154 (1981)
4. Härtel, J., Heinz, M., Lämmel, R.: EMF patterns of usage on GitHub. In: Pierantonio, A., Trujillo, S. (eds.) ECMFA 2018. LNCS, vol. 10890, pp. 216–234. Springer, Cham (2018). https://doi.org/10.1007/978-3-319-92997-2_14

5. Laue, R., Kirchner, K.: Patterns for discussing and modelling variability in business processes. In: Proceedings of the 23rd European Conference on Pattern Languages of Programs (2018)
6. Lübke, D.: Using metric time lines for identifying architecture shortcomings in process execution architectures. In: 2015 IEEE/ACM 2nd International Workshop on Software Architecture and Metrics (SAM), pp. 55–58. IEEE (2015)
7. Lübke, D.: Design patterns for approval processes. In: Proceedings of the 28th European Conference on Pattern Languages of Programs (2023). https://doi.org/10.1145/3628034.3628035
8. Lübke, D.: Even more design patterns for approval processes. In: Proceedings of the 30th European Conference on Pattern Languages of Programs (2024)
9. Lübke, D.: Further design patterns for approval processes. In: Proceedings of the 29th European Conference on Pattern Languages of Programs, People, and Practices. EuroPLoP '24, Association for Computing Machinery, New York, NY, USA (2024). https://doi.org/10.1145/3698322.3698339
10. Lübke, D., Unger, T., Wutke, D.: Analysis of data-flow complexity and architectural implications. In: Lübke, D., Pautasso, C. (eds.) Empirical Studies on the Development of Executable Business Processes, pp. 59–80. Springer (2019)
11. Lübke, D., Wutke, D.: Analysis of prevalent BPMN layout choices on GitHub. In: Proceedings of the 13th Central European Workshop on Services and their Composition (ZEUS 2021) (2021)
12. Microsoft: Compensating transaction pattern. https://learn.microsoft.com/en-us/azure/architecture/patterns/compensating-transaction. Accessed 30 May 2025
13. Nygard, M.: Release It. The Pragmatic Bookshelf (2017)
14. Schumm, D., Karastoyanova, D., Leymann, F., Strauch, S.: Fragmento: advanced process fragment library. In: Pokorny, J., et al. (eds.) Information Systems Development, pp. 659–670. Springer, New York, New York, NY (2011)
15. Surian, D., Lo, D., Lim, E.P.: Mining collaboration patterns from a large developer network. In: 2010 17th Working Conference on Reverse Engineering, pp. 269–273. IEEE (2010)
16. van der Aalst, W., ter Hofstede, A., Kiepuszewski, B., Barros, A.: Workflow patterns. Distrib. Parallel Databases **14**(3), 5–51 (2003)
17. Wellhausen, T., Fiesser, A.: How to write a pattern? A rough guide for first-time pattern authors. In: Proceedings of the 16th European Conference on Pattern Languages of Programs. EuroPLoP '11, Association for Computing Machinery, New York, NY, USA (2011). https://doi.org/10.1145/2396716.2396721
18. Zimmermann, O., Stocker, M., Lübke, D., Zdun, U., Pautasso, C.: Patterns for API design-simplifying integration with loosely coupled message exchanges (2022)

Patterns as Distinctions

Michael Weiss[1(✉)]

Carleton University, Ottawa, Ontario K1S 5B6, Canada
michael_weiss@carleton.ca

Abstract. This essay explores the relationship between design, patterns, and form. It defines design as the act of making distinctions. Patterns capture proven solutions to recurring design problems within a given context. By applying patterns successively, form emerges as an adaptive response to design challenges. Each time a pattern is applied, it introduces distinctions at different levels: between problem and solution, form and context, or centers in general. The act of distinction creates a "boundary between two sides," which Spencer Brown calls a "form." The paper has three goals: 1. Develop the concept of patterns as distinctions by applying Spencer Brown's calculus of form. 2. Define a practical language for reasoning about pattern sequences. 3. Offer an initial exploration of distinctions as a framework for understanding Alexander's 15 properties. The audience for this paper includes anyone interested in pattern theory as well as patterns authors.

Keywords: Design · Patterns · Distinction · Laws of Form · ChatGPT

1 Introduction

The word *design* traces back to the Latin *designare*, which translates to "to mark," "to indicate" or "to designate."[1] Design is a gradual, piecemeal process [2]. It starts with a vague notion (an initial sketch or prototype) and proceeds by making distinctions ("marks") in both the context and the thing that is being designed, negotiating constraints (context) and choosing features (thing) [15]. Its goal is to create things that are meaningful to users in their context.

Patterns capture proven solutions to common design problems in a given context [6]. By applying patterns successively, form emerges as an intentional and adaptive response to design challenges. Each time a pattern is applied, it introduces distinctions at different levels: between problem and solution; between form and context; or between centers in general.

In Spencer Brown's calculus of form, making a distinction is the act of drawing a boundary that separates a space into two parts [18]. For example, when we draw a circle on an empty sheet of paper, we create a boundary between the inside of the circle and its outside. This distinction is not a negation, but a *differentiation*. This act creates what Spencer Brown calls a "form."

[1] https://en.wiktionary.org/wiki/designo#Latin

T. Plummer et al. (Eds.): EuroPLoP 2025, LNCS 16494, pp. 188–217, 2026.
https://doi.org/10.1007/978-3-032-19157-1_10

The paper has three goals. The first goal is to develop the concept of patterns as distinctions by applying the calculus of form [18]. Central to this effort is Spencer Brown's idea of form, which combines both the notions of wholeness and differentiation. The second goal is to define a practical language for reasoning about pattern sequences. Its intent is to be able to experiment with pattern sequences within ChatGPT. The third goal is to offer an initial exploration of distinctions as a framework for understanding Alexander's 15 properties.

The contributions of the paper are both theoretical (representations of patterns, pattern sequences, and properties using the calculus of form) and practical (prompts for reasoning about pattern sequences). Its audience includes anyone interested in pattern theory (it discusses pattern representation, pattern sequences, and properties) as well as patterns authors (its lessons may help them write better patterns and pattern languages).

The paper is organized as follows. Section 2 reviews related work on design, patterns, and distinctions. Section 3 introduces a formal representation of patterns as distinctions. Section 4 discusses how pattern sequences, building on the representation of individual patterns, can be represented using distinctions. Section 5 explores the link between properties and distinctions. Finally, Section 6 summarizes the findings and discusses future work.

2 Related work

2.1 Design and form

Design is about the creation of form [1]. In *Notes on the Synthesis of Form*, Alexander writes about the structure of design problems [1, p. 15]:

> "(E)very design problem begins with an effort to achieve fitness between two entities: the form in question and its context. The form is the solution to the problem; the context defines the problem."

In other words, solving a design problem consists of finding a form that fits a given context. Finding this form involves a process of adaptation between the form and the context. While *Notes on the Synthesis of Form* presents adaptation as a structured process of problem decomposition and fitness, in *The Nature of Order*, Alexander later shifts to a generative approach, where form emerges through a process of "unfolding" that is inspired by nature [4].

Although good design must ultimately "fit" its context, the designer also plays an active and even decisive role in framing what that context is. In other words, designers do not respond passively to a single, fixed "context." Rather, they define the boundary of the problem, choose which elements or constraints matter, and thereby shape what "fitness" will mean in practice. Alexander uses the example of designing a kettle to make this point [1, p. 17]. If a designer reframes the problem from "making a kettle" to heating water, the designer may decide that using an electric immersion coil is a more effective way.

This means that there is no single boundary between problem and context. There can be different boundaries. The designer's changing the definition of the problem, in turn, redefines what is considered the context. In the case of the kettle, reframing the problem to heating water, changes the design constraints from considerations like the size of a stove's heating elements to the location of electrical outlets, or portability needs for an immersion coil.

2.2 Patterns and form

Patterns are solutions to problems in a context. In *A Pattern Language*, Alexander offers the following definition of patterns [6, p. 10]:

> "Each pattern describes a problem which occurs over and over again in our environment, and then describes the core of the solution to that problem, in such a way that you can use this solution a million times over, without ever doing it the same way twice."

As noted by Kohls [12], this definition contains two essential properties of patterns. A pattern is both a solution to a problem in a context, and it describes the form of the solution, which can then, like a blueprint, be applied over and over without repeating itself. Kohls uses the analogy of a path to illustrate this idea ("no two hikes along a path will be the same") [12].

Patterns have a dual nature. They are both a thing and a rule for creating that thing. They are both product and process [6, p. 247]:

> "The pattern is, in short, at the same time a thing ... and the rule which tells us how to create that thing, and when we must create it. It is both a process and a thing; both a description of a thing which is alive, and a description of the process which will generate that thing."

In *The Timeless Way of Building*, Alexander describes a pattern as a "morphological law, which establishes a set of relationships in space" [2, p. 90]:

> "$X \to r(A, B, ...)$, which means: Within a context of type X, the parts A, B, ... are related by the relationship r."

Morphology, literally the science of form, in biology is the study of the size, shape, and structure of organisms and the relationships of their parts.[2]

Each pattern is itself a network of relationships among other patterns, which are themselves networks of relationships among patterns [2, p. 90]:

> "For though each pattern is itself apparently composed of smaller things which look like parts, of course, when we look closely at them, we see that these apparent "parts" are patterns too."

Form and patterns are, thus, deeply linked. Not only is the outcome of applying a pattern a form, but so is a network of patterns in a pattern language.

---

[2] https://www.britannica.com/science/morphology-biology

George Spencer Brown (also Spencer-Brown) was a somewhat enigmatic figure. A British mathematician, engineer, philosopher, and poet, he is best known for his book *Laws of Form* [18], which introduces the calculus of form. This book starts out as a simplification of Boolean algebra, reducing it to one operator, but adds the concepts of self-referentiality and time. His work has influenced cyberneticists like von Foerster and Varela, and sociologists like Luhmann and Baecker.

Fig. 1. Soapbox: Spencer Brown

2.3 Form and distinction

For Spencer Brown [18, p. 1] (see the soapbox in Fig. 1 for more on this author), form is both distinction and unity (wholeness):

> "We take as given the idea of distinction and the idea of indication, and that we cannot make an indication without drawing a distinction. We take, therefore, the form of distinction for the form."

Calling out something means to distinguish it from what it is not. The inside of an object only exists in relation to its outside. Both sides of a distinction—inside and outside—require one another. Through this, distinction creates unity. This is what Spencer Brown means, when he declares [18, p. 1]:

> "Distinction is the perfect continence."

The word *continence* (self-restraint) derives from Latin *continere* – "to hold together," "to connect," but also "to hold in position," or "to restrain."[3] Distinction implies connection between the two sides of a distinction. Distinction is not about keeping things apart, but about holding them together in a form.

Note that we are now dealing with two concepts of form [10]. Spencer Brown's form as distinction and Alexander's form as *gestalt* operate at different levels of abstraction.[4] The former provides the logic of differentiation that enables design, while the latter describes the outcome of this process.

Form *as distinction* works as a generative principle that guides the design process. It establishes the differentiations that structure how a designer approaches a problem and develops solutions. This form as distinction serves as a blueprint: a set of distinctions that must be drawn and maintained throughout.

Form *as gestalt*, by contrast, refers to the emergent pattern that arises when these distinctions are implemented and stabilized in a concrete artifact. Alexander's "quality without a name" [2] describes this outcome: a coherent whole that results when the underlying distinctions have been properly embodied.

[3] https://en.wiktionary.org/wiki/contineo#Latin

[4] Gestalt is German for "form" or "unified whole" [14]. This meaning is reflected in the core tenet of Gestalt theory that the whole is greater than the sum of its parts.

2.4 Direct precursors

To my knowledge there are four precursors to this paper. One is a passing reference by Alexander to Spencer Brown's work when he discusses how contrast (one of his 15 properties of wholeness) is used in nature [3, p. 247]:[5]

> "The nearest thing I know to a general explanation of its [contrast's] appearance in the world is the one given by Spencer Brown. His beautiful account of all mathematics arising from the contrast (distinction) between nothing and something tries to show how all structure and form, at the most elementary level, come from contrast."

The second one is Iba's paper on the role of contrast in patterns [11]. He notes that a pattern typically contains a contrast between a problematic and a desired state that results from applying the solution. This contrast is not just a comparison between these states, but motivates the reader to aspire the positive consequences of the pattern and avoid its negative consequences.

Iba cites Alexander's observation that contrast, instead of separating opposites, connects them, and contributes to creating wholeness [3, p. 202]:

> "The contrast, instead of separating things, brings them together."

This conclusion is in line with Spencer Brown's view of distinction that distinction creates unity between the things that are distinguished.

The third is a somewhat oblique statement in *The Timeless Way of Building* that I came across while researching whether Alexander had himself used the concept of distinction as an operation. Indeed, there is this tantalizing observation on how patterns drive the differentiation process [2, p. 273]:

> "Each pattern is an operator which differentiates space: that is, it creates distinctions where no distinction was before."

There is an echo of Spencer Brown in this statement. However, this is the only place that I could find where Alexander refers to distinctions in this way. Alexander also does not elaborate on how those distinctions work. While this observation piques our imagination, it requires the operationalization of distinctions that Spencer Brown's calculus offers to develop it further.

The fourth is Tsigkas's book [20] on architecture as a continuous differentiation process through the lens of systems theory. This book explores the use of Spencer-Brownian distinctions between patterns of a pattern language. It proposes the mark as a representation of connections between patterns. However, the discussion remains at an abstract level, and the book does not provide sufficiently concrete guidance on how to reason about the distinction between patterns or chaining patterns in pattern sequences using distinctions.

---

[5] I discovered this fact through a short passage in Quillien's *Delight's Muse* [17, p. 39].

3 Conceptualizing patterns as distinctions

3.1 Calculus of form

Let a rotated L-shaped symbol (the "mark") represent a distinction [18]:

$$\rceil$$

This symbol is a shorthand for a boundary that separates the space into two regions: inside and outside. The distinction should not be read as a negation of the inside, but a differentiation from the outside. The two sides of the distinction are the spaces, states, or contents that are distinguished by the distinction.

$$\overline{\text{inside}}\rceil\ \text{outside}$$

Another way to visualize a distinction is by using circles. We draw a circle to indicate the boundary and label the inside and outside of the circle:

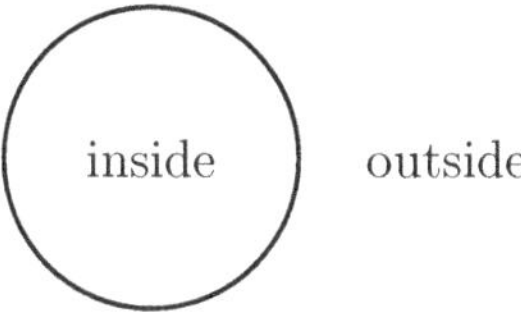

With this sketch of the calculus of form, let us turn to patterns.

3.2 Applying the calculus to patterns

Let us start with two observations from the previous section. The first concerns the nature of patterns. A pattern is a solution to a problem in a context. This solution provides a way of resolving the forces at play in the problem. We can express the interaction between problem and solution through a distinction:

$$\overline{\text{Solution}}\rceil\ \text{Problem}$$

This states that the solution is a response to the problem. The problem, in turn, constrains the alternatives that can be considered as solutions.

We can define the distinction between the problem and the solution by considering the forces present before and after the solution is applied. An effective solution resolves the underlying forces in the problem. This makes the states before and after applying the solution distinct. Analyzing the forces and consequences of a pattern gives us a means of operationalizing this distinction.

The distinction between problem and solution forms the core of a pattern. However, the solution is also applied within a context ("a solution to a problem *in* a context"). Decisions on how to frame the problem and how to approach the solution are constrained by the context. This can be represented by another boundary, one that separates form (as gestalt) from context:

$$\overline{\overline{\text{Solution}}\ \text{Problem}}\ \text{Context}$$

As we noted earlier, this boundary is not given, but negotiated by the designer. The designer decides how the context is defined and what aspects of this context they want to focus on in their design. This is quite intuitive, when we consider that initially the problem is not well-understood, and it only becomes clarified as the designer learns from attempting to solve the problem.

The second observation concerns the design process. Design evolves through an incremental process of unfolding. At each stage, a pattern is selected in response to the current context and applied to the design. When a pattern is applied, it creates a resulting context. This resulting context, in turn, becomes the starting point for the next pattern in the unfolding process.

To capture this, we can write:

$$\text{Resulting Context} = \overline{\overline{\text{Solution}}\ \text{Problem}}\ \text{Context}$$

The resulting context is not just a label. While the solution captured by a pattern addresses the problem, it may lead to new problems, in turn. The resulting context captures the new situation after the solution has been applied. It includes any unresolved forces that result from the solution. Resolving a problem is like carefully removing a block in the game of Jenga. This shifts the weight and stress patterns throughout the structure and creates new points of instability.

3.3 Design evolution and re-entry

One aspect of design that we did not consider so far is that solutions are rarely ever static. Rather, a solution only remains a solution as long as it maintains the balance that solves the problem. Otherwise, the distinction between problem and solution will erode, causing the problem to re-emerge. The distinction between problem and solution must, thus, be continuously sustained or reiterated.

This notion of reiterating the distinction between problem and solution can be expressed through a re-entry operation. A *re-entry* is a form of self-reference that allows a distinction to be crossed and subsequently re-entered [18].This operation is shown as a hook. The following expression states that the distinction between problem and solution should be applied recursively:

$$\underline{\overline{\overline{\text{Solution}}\ \text{Problem}}}\ \text{Context}$$

The circular symbol of the ouroboros (a serpent devouring its own tail) shown in Fig. 2 is a metaphor for this process. If the head represents the problem, the tail represents the solution. The serpent biting its tail represents the distinction between problem and solution. While solving the problem initially, the solution already contains a new variation of the problem that surfaces with time.

Fig. 2. The ouroboros as a metaphor for re-entry (Wikimedia Commons)

This consideration does not only apply to problem and solution, but also to the distinction between context and the solution to the problem. The context may change, requiring the designer to reconsider the balance between problem and context. In analogy to the first re-entry, we can represent the recursive distinction between context and problem through a second re-entry:

The idea of recursively revisiting the distinctions of problem, solution, and context aligns with Alexander's notion of organic growth and repair [5, p. 67f]:

> "Any living system must repair itself constantly in order to maintain its balance and coordination, its quality as a whole. In the case of an organism, it is only the constant repair, the adjustment of chemical fields, the replacement of cells, and the healing of damaged tissues, which maintain the basic morphology of the organism."

3.4 A worked example

Representation We will use the Stable Teams pattern from *A Scrum Book* [19] to illustrate the pattern representation. Table 1 shows short descriptions of the elements of this pattern. These were automatically extracted from the full pattern description using the prompts described in Appendix A.1.

Table 1. Elements of the Stable Teams pattern.

Element	
S_1	Keep teams stable and avoid shuffling people around between teams. Dedicate members to a single team.
P_1	Constantly shifting team members creates inefficiency, loss of predictability, and hinders team cohesion.
C_1	Teams are delivering products in a changing business landscape, under pressure to be efficient and predictable.
R_1	A stable, predictable, and cohesive team environment that fosters trust, improves velocity, and reduces long-term risk.

Without Stable Teams, organizations frequently reassign team members between projects, disrupting team cohesion and reducing productivity. When teams are unstable, efficiency drops due to continuous onboarding, shifting team dynamics, and loss of shared understanding.

Stable Teams structures work to fit the team, rather than changing teams to fit the work. The resulting work environment now exists as the *difference* between a stable, predictable team dynamic and its alternative—an unstable, ever-changing team. Abbreviating the elements from Table 1, we can write:

$$\text{Predictability} = \overline{\overline{\text{Keep teams stable}}\rceil\ \text{Shifting team members}}\rceil\ \text{High variance}$$

Table 2 shows the points of distinction between problem and solution. To identify these, the forces and consequences were extracted from the pattern description. The details of how this is done can be found in Appendix A.2. Then, consequences were matched up with the forces they resolve. For example, force F_1 (efficiency lost) corresponds to consequence C_1 (familiarity and trust). As a result of stable membership in teams (C_1), efficiency increases (F_1 resolved).

The analysis further shows that all forces have a counterpoint in the solution. However, not all consequences do. For example, consequence C_7 (reduced long-term risk from member loss) is not tied to a force. Rather, it is a benefit of using Stable Teams and helps teams deal with the risk of losing a team member, as explained in another pattern, Moderate Truck Number [19].

Design evolution Consider an organization that has adopted Stable Teams. Several factors could lead to the breakdown of team stability over time such as resource constraints, required critical expertise, political reasons, or growth. Driven by short-term needs, managers may start to move employees across teams, disrupting established collaboration structures.

To maintain the difference between a stable, high-performing team and an unstable, ever-changing team, organizations must keep team membership consistent. This could include policies that minimize unnecessary team changes,

Table 2. Problem-solution distinction.

Force		Consequence	
F_1	Efficiency lost when reshuffling teams	C_1	Familiarity and trust improve efficiency
F_2	Administrative overhead of tracking shifting people	C_2	Predictable capacity (velocity)
F_3	Risk of delays when adding/reassigning people (Brooks' Law)	C_2	Predictable capacity (velocity)
F_4	Multitasking inefficiency from distributing people across teams	C_6	Flexible work assignment at team level
F_5	Changing requirements exacerbate instability	C_5	Cross-training and capability building
F_6	Short-lived teams discourage investment in processes and relationships	C_3	Stable teams invest in improvements
F_7	Freezing requirements blocks learning	C_4	Pride, cohesion, and engagement grow

cultural norms that emphasize long-term team cohesion, or self-selecting teams that form around shared purpose and expertise. This can be expressed as:

$$\text{Predictability} = \overline{\underline{\text{Keep teams stable}|}\ \text{Shifting team members}|}\ \text{High variance}$$
$$\text{Policies, norms, and self-selection}$$

The label on the re-entry hook indicates the means (policies, norms, and self-selection) by which the pattern is maintained. This label is optional.

There may also be a need to grow the team. However, as a stable team grows too large, it becomes inefficient. Rather than starting a new team that must build cohesion from anew, Mitosis [19] suggests splitting a large team into two smaller teams. This allows the new teams to retain the culture and knowledge of the original team. It requires a sequence of Stable Teams and Mitosis.

4 Reasoning about pattern sequences

4.1 Pattern sequences

A pattern sequence is a series of patterns, in which the context of each pattern is informed by the solution of the preceding pattern; that is, with the exception of this first pattern, which is applied to the initial context. A pattern language, by contrast, is a network of related patterns that contains many possible pattern sequences. Not all patterns in a pattern language are required to solve a specific problem. Rather, a pattern sequence is a path through a pattern language.

A pattern language defines the order in which the patterns can be applied. This order mirrors their morphological importance [2, p. 373]. Each pattern needs smaller, more specific patterns to *complete* them. It also depends on the larger, more general patterns that it itself completes. Alexander writes [2, p. 313]:

> "Each pattern sits at the center of a network of connections which connect it to certain other patterns that help to complete it."

For a particular design, a subset of patterns from the pattern language are chosen and organized by their proximity to each other. The patterns in a sequence are applied one by one, and each one refines the outcome of the previous pattern in the sequence. Alexander talks about "unfolding" the sequence of patterns [2, p. 365]. The idea behind unfolding is that a design starts with a whole that is incrementally differentiated with each step.

More formally, when patterns complete each other, the outcome of one pattern influences the conditions under which the next one is applied. When a pattern is applied in the resulting context (R) of another pattern, its context (C) is narrowed down to a specific situation, i.e., to a specific set of constraints [9]. The sequence proceeds from larger to smaller design decisions.

There can be different types of relationships between patterns in a sequence, as shown in Fig. 3: linear, forked, and merged [23]. In a linear relationship, a pattern builds on the previous pattern's resulting context. If pattern A is above pattern B in the pattern language, then A must be applied before B, for example, Sitting Room before Alcove (the sitting room contains an alcove) [2, p. 379].

In a forked relationship, two patterns are applied in the same resulting context of a third pattern. For example, Positive Outdoor Space and Wings of Light both follow Building Complex. These two patterns complement each other (placing a house on a lot determines which spaces form the garden) [2, p. 379]. In a pattern sequence, either of these patterns could be applied first, unless there is also a relationship between those patterns that determines their order.

In a merged relationship, two patterns are fused into the context of a third pattern. Alexander gives the example of Circulating Realms and Car House Connection, which are both above Main Entrance. Together, they create the framework for the entrance to the house [2, p. 379]. Again, the order of these patterns is not fixed, but they are should be applied closely to each other.

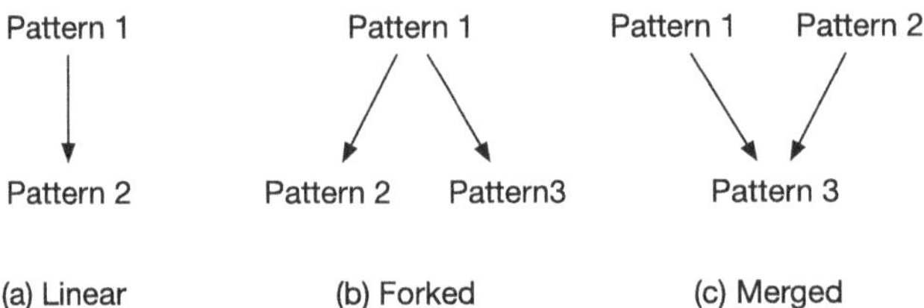

Fig. 3. Types of pattern relationships in a sequence.

Note that some authors have argued for a more expansive view of pattern sequences that includes alternatives and repetition [16]. There are potential advantages of doing so; it allows one sequence to represent multiple related paths through a pattern language. However, including alternatives and repetitions also blurs the line between pattern languages and sequences. This paper adopts the canonical view of pattern sequences as a single path through a language [2,9].

Linear A linear sequence of three patterns, in which each pattern builds on the previous pattern's resulting context, can be represented as:

$$R_1 = \overline{\overline{S_1}\rceil\, P_1}\rceil\, C_1$$

followed by

$$R_2 = \overline{\overline{S_2}\rceil\, P_2}\rceil\, R_1$$

and

$$R_3 = \overline{\overline{S_3}\rceil\, P_3}\rceil\, R_2$$

Forked When there is a fork between two patterns, a single resulting context (R_1) leads to multiple patterns, each solving a different problem in parallel:

$$R_1 = \overline{\overline{S_1}\rceil\, P_1}\rceil\, C_1$$

followed by

$$R_2 = \overline{\overline{S_2}\rceil\, P_2}\rceil\, R_1$$

and

$$R_3 = \overline{\overline{S_3}\rceil\, P_3}\rceil\, R_1$$

The order of the last two patterns in this sequence is not fixed, unless there is also a linear relationship between them.

Merged Multiple patterns can also feed into a single merged context:

$$R_1 = \overline{\overline{S_1}\rceil\, P_1}\rceil\, C_1$$

and

$$R_2 = \overline{\overline{S_2 \rceil}\, P_2 \rceil}\, C_2$$

followed by

$$R_3 = \overline{\overline{S_3 \rceil}\, P_3 \rceil}\, \overline{\overline{R_1 \rceil}\, \overline{R_2 \rceil} \rceil}$$

Again, the order in which the two patterns converging into the context of the third are applied is undetermined. The nested boundaries in the last expression represent the intersection of the resulting contexts. (You can convince yourself of that by creating a Venn diagram with circles representing R_1 and R_2.)

We can capture these definitions in the first prompt in Appendix A.4. It defines templates for each type of relationship (linear, fork, and merge).

4.2 A worked example

As an example, we will use patterns from *A Scrum Book* [19]. In particular, we will focus on the pattern language for highly-effective teams described in Chapter 4 of the book. Fig. 4 shows a subset of the patterns from this pattern language and their relationships, as reconstructed from the descriptions.

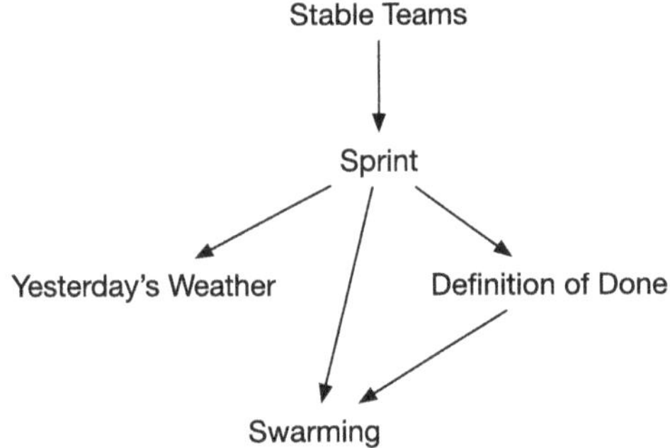

Fig. 4. Patterns from the pattern language of highly-effective teams.

Pattern representations The pattern representations were extracted from their respective descriptions and are shown in the tables below:

- Stable Teams (Table 1)
- Sprint (Table 3)
- Yesterday's Weather (Table 4)

- Definition of Done (Table 5)
- Swarming (Table 6)

The details of extracting the pattern representations can be found in Appendix A.1. The result for the Stable Teams pattern is:

Pattern: Stable Teams

R = ((S) P) C

Where:

S (Solution): Keep teams stable and avoid shuffling people around between teams. Dedicate members to a single team.
P (Problem): Constantly shifting team members creates inefficiency, loss of predictability, and hinders team cohesion.
C (Context): Teams are delivering products in a changing business landscape, under pressure to be efficient and predictable.
R (Resulting Context): A stable, predictable, and cohesive team environment that fosters trust, improves velocity, and reduces long-term risk.

Final representation:

R = ((Keep teams stable and avoid shuffling people around between teams) Constantly shifting team members creates inefficiency, loss of predictability, and hinders team cohesion) Teams are delivering products in a changing business landscape, under pressure to be efficient and predictable

Here we use a text-based syntax for the calculus of forms, Bricken's parens syntax [8]. It uses parentheses ( ) to represent the mark. Writing:

$$R = ((S)P)C$$

is equivalent to the following form in Spencer Brown's notation:

$$R = \overline{\overline{S\,}|\; P\,}|\; C$$

Pattern order The patterns within a sequence should respect the order from largest to smallest. This order can either be given in the pattern language or be inferred. To infer the order, we define larger and smaller patterns in terms of their spatial and temporal relationships [9]. Larger patterns either contain smaller patterns (spatial order) or precede them in time (temporal order).

Using the prompt from Appendix A.3, we obtain this order:

Table 3. Elements of the Sprint pattern.

Element	
S_2	Organize development into recurring, fixed-length, time-boxed intervals called Sprints.
P_2	Without a shared cadence, feedback is delayed, variance accumulates, and teams lose focus and predictability.
C_2	A development effort is underway, with a value stream and product backlog, operating under agile principles and business pressure to deliver regularly.
R_2	Teams work iteratively with clear rhythm, regular feedback, and measurable progress, enabling learning, adaptation, and improved predictability.

Table 4. Elements of the Yesterday's Weather pattern.

Element	
S_3	Use the number of estimation points completed in the last Sprint to forecast how many will be completed in the next Sprint.
P_3	Teams often overestimate their capacity due to ambition or external pressure, leading to disappointment, or unsustainable performance.
C_3	A team with historical performance data is beginning a new Sprint and must forecast its delivery realistically.
R_3	Teams make grounded, data-driven forecasts, reducing risk, managing expectations, and improving long-term predictability.

Table 5. Elements of the Definition of Done pattern.

Element	
S_4	All work must meet an agreed, objective Definition of Done created by the Scrum Team; if the work doesn't meet it, it is not done and cannot be delivered.
P_4	Without a shared definition of "done," team members and stakeholders have inconsistent expectations, leading to uneven quality and technical debt.
C_4	A Scrum Team is producing Product Backlog Items and needs to assess what work is complete and releasable, while maintaining quality and transparency.
R_4	The team delivers high-quality increments with fewer surprises, less technical debt, reliable forecasts, and shared understanding of completeness.

Table 6. Elements of the Swarming pattern.

Element	
S_5	Focus the team's maximum effort on one Product Backlog Item at a time, with one team member as Captain, and complete it before moving to the next item.
P_5	Working on too many items in parallel causes context switching, excessive work-in-progress, delays, lower quality, and inefficiencies in flow.
C_5	A Scrum Team is implementing work from the Sprint Backlog and must decide how to organize its efforts to maximize flow and meet the Sprint Goal.
R_5	The team moves toward continuous flow, accelerates delivery, improves quality, reduces technical debt, and cultivates shared ownership.

1. Stable Teams
2. Sprint
3. Definition of Done
4. Swarming
5. Yesterday's Weather

The result also includes a rationale. For example, for Swarming it says:

> Swarming (Collaboration strategy during a Sprint)
>
> Spatial: Happens within a Sprint on a single PBI.
>
> Depends on: Stable Teams (trust, cross-skill collaboration) and Definition of Done (shared end-state).
>
> Smaller in scope: A behavior pattern within Sprint execution.

Pattern sequences Finally, we explore potential pattern sequences. We first establish a template for representing pattern sequences. Then we prompt ChatGPT to suggest sequences that illustrate the three types of relationships between patterns (linear, forked, and merged). For the details see Appendix A.4.

The first pattern sequence is *linear*. It consists of Stable Teams, Sprint, and Yesterday's Weather. The result describes a way of "chaining" these patterns:

> Predictable Delivery Sequence (Linear)
>
> Pattern 1: Stable Teams
> R1 = ((S1)P1)C1
> Context: An organization with shifting staffing and unstable team composition.
> Solution: Keep teams stable to reduce variance and build trust.
>
> Pattern 2: Sprint
> R2 = ((S2)P2)R1
> Context: Stable teams need a rhythm for delivering increments.
> Solution: Organize work into fixed-length, recurring Sprints.
>
> Pattern 3: Yesterday's Weather
> R3 = ((S3)P3)R2
> Context: A team needs to forecast realistic capacity for its next Sprint.
> Solution: Use the last Sprint's completed work as a predictor of future capacity.

We can read this result as follows. The sequence starts with Stable Teams. It enables a predictable, cohesive team (R_1):

$$R_1 = \overline{\overline{S_1}\rceil\, P_1}\rceil\, C_1$$

Sprint depends on team stability. Its context C_2 subsumes the resulting context of Stable Teams R_1. Sprint enables a regular delivery cadence (R_2):

$$R_2 = \overline{\overline{S_2}\rceil\, P_2}\rceil\, R_1$$

Yesterdays's Weather requires a stable delivery schedule. It enables reliable forecasts and expectation management (R_3):

$$R_3 = \overline{\overline{S_3}\rceil\, P_3}\rceil\, R_2$$

The next sequence uses a *fork*. Here is the core of the response:

Quality and Flow Sequence (Fork)

Pattern 1: Sprint
R1 = ((S1)P1)C1
Context: Stable teams need cadence to deliver increments.
Solution: Establish fixed-length Sprints.

Pattern 2: Definition of Done
R2 = ((S2)P1)R1
Context: Within a Sprint, work completion is ambiguous.
Solution: Establish a shared Definition of Done.

Pattern 3: Swarming
R3 = ((S3)P1)R1
Context: Within the same Sprint, multitasking reduces throughput.
Solution: Swarm on one Product Backlog Item at a time.

The last sequence illustrates the use of a *merge*:

Reliable Increment Sequence (Merge)

Pattern 1: Definition of Done
R1 = ((S1)P1)C1
Context: Teams lack shared clarity about when work is complete.
Solution: Create a clear, testable Definition of Done.

Pattern 2: Swarming
R2 = ((S2)P2)C2
Context: Teams slow down by multitasking and splitting attention.
Solution: Focus the team on one item until Done.

Pattern 3: Yesterday's Weather
R3 = ((S3)P3)((R1)(R2))
Context: Forecasting depends on reliable, completed increments.
Solution: Use past velocity (based on Definition of Done + Swarming) to predict future capacity.

The relationships identified between the patterns align with the sequences implied by Fig. 4. Note that the pattern map was not supplied to ChatGPT.

5 Understanding properties through distinctions

Alexander identified 15 recurring properties of natural and human-created systems that help a system come alive, defined in Table 7. This section offers an initial exploration of the link between these properties and distinctions. Its goal is to understand Alexander's properties through the lens of distinctions.

5.1 Interlude on centers

The unity of a system results from the interaction and mutual support of a configuration of centers, and the properties—for this, we need to think of the properties as transformations—that bring them into being [7, p. 429]. The concept of a *center* was introduced in *Nature of Order* [3, p. 84]:

> "I use the word center to identify an organized zone of space—that is to say, a distinct set of points in space, which, because of its organization, because of its internal coherence, and because of its relation to its context, *exhibits centeredness*, forms a local zone of relative centeredness with respect to the other parts of space."

From this definition, we can identify three characteristics of centers:

1. Centers are recognizable and *distinct*.
2. Their distinctiveness (or centeredness) is *relative* to their context, which allows centers to have varying degrees of distinctiveness.

3. Centers need other centers to create unity.

Patterns can be thought of as centers that focus on specific aspects of the design of a system [7, p. 131]:

> "A pattern is a center, made up of centers at many levels of scale. Altogether, the centers that form a pattern take care of some recurring problem or opportunity in the life of the community."

Given an initial configuration of centers, they are then transformed by applying the properties (remember to think of them as transformations). Each property works to increase the unity of the system of centers [7, p. 431]. Depending on the property, centers are either added or removed in this process.

5.2 Interpretation of the properties

The first characteristic makes centers recognizable and distinct. This is what gives each center its identity. However, by the second characteristic, this distinctiveness is relative: a center obtains its identity only through its relationships to other centers. The third characteristic states that centers need other centers to create unity: centers mutually reinforce one another.

From this, we can conclude that to transform a center involves modifying the distinctions that define its relationships to other centers. Since properties transform configurations of centers, all properties must therefore *involve distinctions to some degree*. This conclusion is also justified by the language that Alexander uses to describe the properties in *Nature of Order* and elsewhere [3,4,7].

We propose that each of Alexander's 15 properties can be interpreted as a way of (primarily) sharpening, modulating, or blending distinctions:

- To sharpen a distinction means to strengthen it by separating centers.
- To modulate means to adjust a distinction to fit its context, i.e., to attune it to the nature of the relationship between these centers.
- To blend distinctions is the same as folding them back into the whole.

Note that these are not strict categories, but dimensions. Properties are multidimensional. However, one of these dimensions usually dominates. That is where the properties have been placed in the following.

Our interpretation of the properties is informed by several previous interpretations. Quillien's *Delight's Muse* [17] offers an introduction to the *Nature of Order* books. Kohls' thesis [13] provides an in-depth analysis of the properties and examples from various fields. Waguespack represents choices in information system design as centers and maps properties to design principles [21]. He also presents examples of these principles from agile software development [22].

Properties that sharpen distinctions These properties sharpen distinctions by separating centers from one another.

Table 7. Definitions of Alexander's properties from [3, p. 239–242].

Property	Definition
Levels of scale	A strong center is made stronger partly by smaller strong centers contained in it, and partly by its larger strong centers that contain it.
Strong centers	A strong center requires a special field-like effect, created by other centers, as a primary source of its strength.
Boundaries	The field-like effect of a center is strengthened by the creation of a ring-like center, made of smaller centers which surround and intensify the first. The boundary also unites the center with the centers beyond it, thus strengthening it further.
Alternating repetition	Centers are strengthened when they repeat, by the insertion of other centers between the repeating ones.
Positive space	A given center must draw its strength, in part, from the strength of other centers immediately adjacent to it in space.
Good shape	The strength of a given center depends on its actual shape, and the way this effect requires that even the shape, its boundary, and the space around it are made up of strong centers.
Local symmetries	The intensity of a given center is increased by the extent to which other smaller centers which it contains are themselves arranged in locally symmetrical groups.
Deep interlock and ambiguity	The intensity of a given center can be increased when it is attached to nearby strong centers, through a third set of strong centers that ambiguously belong to both.
Contrast	A center is strengthened by the sharpness of the distinction between its character and the character of surrounding centers.
Gradients	A center is strengthened by a graded series of different-sized centers which then "point" to the new center and intensify its field effect.
Roughness	The field effect of a given center draws its strength, necessarily, from irregularities in the sizes, shapes, and arrangements of other nearby centers.
Echoes	The strength of a given center depends on similarities of angle and orientation and systems of centers forming characteristic angles thus forming larger centers, among the centers it contains.
Void	The intensity of every center depends on the existence of a still place—an empty center—somewhere in its field.
Simplicity and inner calm	The strength of a center depends on its simplicity—on the process of reducing the number of different centers which exist in it, while increasing the strength of these centers to make them weigh more.
Not-separateness	The life and strength is merged smoothly—sometimes even indistinguishable—with the centers that form its surroundings.

CONTRAST is the prototypical example. Its description explicitly refers to the distinction between the characteristics of a center and those of its surrounding centers. Contrast enhances the coherence of an emerging center [7, p. 432] and provides it with identity [22]. This can apply to people (e.g., team members) or to things (e.g., concepts). Examples include the definition of roles in a team and the creation of shared understanding [22]. We can write:

$$\overline{\text{center}\,}\big|\ \text{centers with different characteristics}$$

BOUNDARIES strengthen a weak center by surrounding it with a boundary [7, p. 432]. The boundary consists itself of smaller centers. A boundary does not exclude, but connects inside and outside of the boundary. For example, a sprint is bounded by sprint planning and sprint review [22]. This mirrors Spencer Brown's notion that a (boundary-creating) distinction does not separate the two sides of the distinction, but instead unites them, as we saw in Section 2.3:

center ring-like center

ALTERNATING REPETITION combines two systems of centers interwoven in a repeating pattern, as in melody and countermelody. The centers in one system highlight those in the other by creating contrast. For example, a daily scrum establishes a rhythm within a sprint, enabling adjustments to the product backlog when priorities or requirements change [22]. This can be expressed by making two distinctions: one between systems, and another between repetitions. The second distinction feeds back into the first distinction through a re-entry hook:

centers in system 1 centers in system 2

LEVELS OF SCALE make a given center stronger by introducing smaller centers within or adjacent to it [7, p. 432]. These levels must be sufficiently distinct to separate larger centers from smaller ones, yet they must still be connected. For example, consider product and sprint backlogs. Both consist of backlog items, but at different scopes: product and sprint [22]. This property also contains elements of modulation: transitions between levels should be smooth. Thus,

larger centers smaller centers

Properties that modulate distinctions Properties in this group modulate distinctions by adjusting to fit their context.

ROUGHNESS means that a pattern can be applied in countless ways, never exactly the same, each time shaped by local circumstances. This property refines our understanding of distinctions. Distinctions are contingent on the criteria used to make them. These criteria are not static (compare the example of the teapot in Section 2.1). The re-entry conveys that a pattern must be adapted to the environment and the designer's goals every time it is applied:

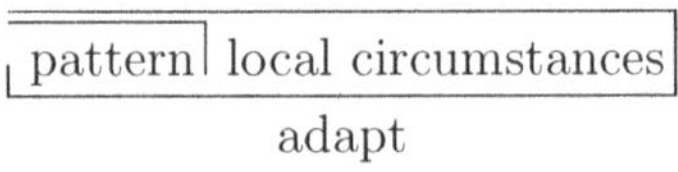

A perhaps less obvious example is that of STRONG CENTERS. The strength of a strong center comes from its relation to other centers in its field. It must be tuned to those centers, so that it is in balance with them. To come into place, strong centers need other centers from which they can be differentiated. Strong centers are often nested within a hierarchy of such centers. In Scrum, the product owner, as maintainer of the product vision, is a strong center [22]. The development team is another strong center that supports this center. Thus,

$$\overline{\overline{\overline{\overline{\text{strong center}}\!\rceil\ \text{other center } 1}\!\rceil\ \ldots}\!\rceil\ \text{other center } n}\!\rceil$$

POSITIVE SPACE transforms latent centers into centers of their own [4, p. 69]. These latent centers are found in the spaces between other centers. Each new center draws its strength from the other centers around it. An example of a latent center is a potential product or feature set. It comes to life through existing centers that include development team (resources), product owner (vision), product backlog (needs), and stakeholders (feedback) [22]. We write:

$$\overline{\text{existing centers}}\!\rceil\ \text{new centers}$$

DEEP INTERLOCK AND AMBIGUITY intensify the connection between the opposing sides of a boundary. Both sides share the boundary [4, p. 78]. The boundary is the site of interlock. It is ambiguous to which side the boundary belongs. An example of deep interlock is the concept of a single team per value stream in Scrum. In this case, the opposing sides are sprints, and the shared boundary is the team (expanded from [22]). The following form contains two re-entries, one from the first, the other from the second center. This signifies a process of mutual adjustment between centers and boundary. We write:

$$\overline{\text{center } 1}\!\rceil_{\lrcorner}\ \overline{\text{boundary}}\!\rceil_{\llcorner}\ \overline{\text{center } 2}\!\rceil$$

LOCAL SYMMETRIES create coherence by grouping smaller centers into a larger whole [3, p. 188]. These smaller centers share similar features, which contribute to the unity of the larger structure [13]. In Scrum, local symmetries help structure related elements, such as backlog items, into consistent groups [22]. An example is a product increment: it groups together related backlog items that should be completed during a sprint. We can capture this insight as:

$$\overline{\text{center}}\!\rceil\ \text{groups of centers with similar characteristics}$$

ECHOES are recurring centers that are structurally similar [4, p. 78]. Their resemblance contributes to the unity of the whole. Echoes share characteristics, but differ in some dimensions such as scale. In Scrum, the product vision is a strong center. Product roadmap, product backlog, and sprint goals echo this vision [19]. They are centers that echo the initial center. Another example of echoes are consistently applied practices like backlog planning [22]. Thus,

center echo of the center

GRADIENTS introduce a gradual transition of smaller centers toward or away from a given center [4, p. 78]. These centers are similar, but their properties vary according to the gradient. While there is contrast between the smaller centers, this contrast is more gradual than suggested by CONTRAST. [13]. The transition zooming in from product vision to product backlog and individual product backlog items or zooming back out, is an example of gradients [22]. We write:[6]

center smallest other center 1 ... largest other center n

Properties that blend distinctions These properties blend distinctions by folding them back into the whole.

THE VOID removes unnecessary centers. It creates a large, homogeneous structure that promotes the growth of smaller centers at its edge [4, p. 74]. The contrast between the quiet of the void and the intricacies of the surrounding smaller centers enables future distinctions. An example is a culture that prioritizes fixing defects over enhancements [19]. This discipline creates a void—pausing new development to reduce complexity and avoid costly rework later. We use a re-entry to symbolize the idea of a void as a "generator" of future distinctions:

smaller centers future distinctions

GOOD SHAPE results from the coherence of the centers that make up the shape and its boundary. The distinctions of the parts are subordinate to the gestalt of the whole. The goal is to make the overall shape "more distinct, more recognizable" [7, p. 435]. For example, in a stable team, no single member dominates, which fosters cohesive relationships. Team consistency allows its members to develop stronger working relationships and a collective identity [19]. Each member is a center within the whole; the team acts as one. Therefore,

coherent centers boundary

[6] This form describes a gradient toward a given center. A gradient can also point away from the center. In this case, "smallest" and "largest" need be switched.

SIMPLICITY AND INNER CALM remove complexity. Simplicity is achieved by keeping only what is essential. In a well-designed system, distinctions are reduced to only those that serve a purpose. This translates to agile practices like time-boxing and focusing on stakeholder value, which allow teams to concentrate on essential features, avoid unnecessary complexity, and reduce waste [19]. To achieve simplicty, non-essential centers need to be removed:[7]

$$\overline{\text{non-essential center}}\rceil = \overline{\ \rceil}\rceil =$$

NOT-SEPARATENESS removes distinctions between centers [4, p. 79]. Its intent is to unify. Centers and their contexts merge into one whole. This property works by creating bridges across boundaries that are considered too sharp [7]. It is typically applied toward the end of designing a system. Maintaining the balance between the autonomy of sprint teams and the overall product vision and priorities is an example of non-separateness [22]. Similarly to DEEP INTERLOCK AND AMBIGUITY, we use re-entries to represent the linking of centers:

$$\underline{\overline{\text{center}}\rceil\ \overline{\text{surrounding centers}}\rceil}$$

6 Conclusion

6.1 Findings

This paper introduced the idea that patterns create *distinctions*. This idea builds on Spencer Brown's calculus of form and Krippendorff's theory of design. Spencer Brown reduces the creative act to a single fundamental operation: the distinction [18]. For Krippendorff, design is a circular process in which designers make distinctions in both context and what is being designed [15].

For Spencer Brown, a distinction is not just a separation, but also the foundation of *form*. Form emerges from the act of drawing a distinction, which creates a boundary between two states—inside and outside, marked and unmarked. This is the most fundamental act of cognition and design: in marking a difference, we simultaneously create structure. Design, then, is not only about solving problems but about the construction of form through successive distinctions.

The idea of creation through distinction aligns well with Alexander's concept of "unfolding," introduced in *Nature of Order* [4]. For Alexander, form as gestalt does not arise from the designer's imposition but through an adaptive process of unfolding, where each step builds on the wholeness of what came before. Patterns contribute to this process: by drawing distinctions, they help resolve tensions in a given context and, in doing so, give rise to new structures.

[7] We replace the non-essential centers with an empty mark, which then gets cancelled.

The paper introduced the concept of patterns as distinctions, and proposed a representation of patterns based on the calculus of form. This perspective allows us to interpret patterns as operators that generate form, and ensure coherence and adaptation within an evolving design. The calculus of form offers a formal system for describing how forms emerge from distinctions.

Representing patterns as distinctions lends itself to representing pattern sequences as a sequence of successive distinctions. Patterns are organized into sequences based on how the outcome of one pattern enables or conditions the next. Different types of relationships—linear, forked, and merged—are illustrated using Scrum patterns. The paper then showed how the representation of sequences enabled reasoning about pattern sequences using ChatGPT.

The paper also interpreted properties through the lens of distinctions. The properties were grouped according to whether they sharpen, modulate, or blend distinctions. For each property we created a representation in terms of distinctions. We also presented an example of applying these representations to unfold a simple geometric structure into a richer, more coherent form.

Finally, ChatGPT is a useful platform for experimenting with pattern representations. It can extract structured representations from textual pattern descriptions, and apply rules to construct pattern sequences from the representations of individual patterns. Automating these tasks enables researchers to conduct experiments at scale, while maintaining consistency.

6.2 Limitations

As with any approach, ours has some limitations. One is the high level of abstraction of the pattern representation. Another limitation is the difficulty of turning the representation into a practical tool for pattern authors. The paper tries to address this issue by operationalizing the representation using ChatGPT.

6.3 Future work

A lot of the work presented in this paper is still preliminary. There are many areas for future work. This section is organized by research goal.

Conceptualizing patterns as distinctions

- Study larger pattern collections to help refine the representation.
- Identify sources of pattern instability in their environment.

Reasoning about pattern sequences

- Explore how pattern languages can be merged using the representation.
- Define quality criteria for evaluating patterns and pattern sequences.

Link between properties and distinctions

- Explore the link between patterns and properties on the basis of distinctions.
- Examine how the forms for representing properties can be combined.

Acknowledgments. I would like to sincerely thank my shepherd, Rebecca Wirfs-Brock for her amazing feedback. It has pushed the ideas proposed in the paper much further, especially their application to Alexander's 15 properties. I also thank the participants in the writers' workshop at EuroPLoP: Adrian Schuckart, Elias Baalmann, Felix Mahr, Joe Yoder, Maximilian Nixdorf, Michael Krisper, and Steve Holtel.

ChatGPT was used for brainstorming and to experiment with the pattern representation. DeepL Write was used to make the writing more succint. Where the article relied on AI tools for assistance, the outputs were verified for accuracy, validity, and appropriateness. The author acknowledges the potential of language models for bias, errors, and gaps in knowledge.

Disclosure of Interests. The author has no competing interests to declare that are relevant to the content of this article.

A Prompts

This section describe the prompts used to represent patterns and to reason about pattern sequences. It is grouped into three sections:

- Extracting pattern representations
- Identifying points of distinction between problem and solution
- Inferring the order of patterns
- Reasoning about pattern sequences

After comparing different models for this purpose, including the recently introduced reasoning models, we selected ChatGPT 4o. This model produced the most consistent results. It also does not have usage quota and is thus more suitable for repeated experiments. To ensure that previous ChatGPT interactions do not affect the outcome, I turned off memories under the settings.

A.1 Extracting pattern representations

The following prompt describes the process of mapping from pattern descriptions to representations. It first defines what we mean by a pattern. Then it specifies the text-based syntax for the calculus of form, the parens notation [8]. It also describes the structure of a pattern that follows the Alexandrian format.

You are an expert on pattern languages. Help me extract the elements of a pattern and produce the following pattern representation.

Definitions:
1. Let a pattern (with Christopher Alexander) be defined as a solution to a recurring problem within a specific context.
2. Let a mark in Spencer Brown's calculus of form be represented as ( ) by applying William Bricken's parens notation.
3. Let a pattern with solution S, problem P, context C, and resulting context R be represented in the parens notation as follows:
R = ((S) P) C
4. Patterns are described using the Alexandrian format:
###
Name: noun phrase that captures the essence of the solution
Context: situation in which the problem occurs
Problem: succinct statement of the problem
Forces: elaboration on what makes the problem challenging
Solution: succinct statement of the solution
Resulting context: situation that results from applying the solution
###

Steps:
1. When I give you a pattern description, represent this pattern in the form:
R = ((S) P) C
2. Only output these elements: S, P, C, and R.
3. Use plain, clear language, but be concise.

To create a representation for a specific pattern, use this prompt, attaching a file with the pattern description or including the pattern description:

Represent the [PATTERN] pattern.

A.2 Points of distinction between problem and solution

This prompt identifies the points of distinction between problem and solution:

Identify the points of distinction between problem and solution.

Steps:
1. Identify the forces underlying the problem.
2. Identify the consequences of applying the solution.

3. Number the forces (F1, F2, ...) and consequences (C1, C2, ...).
4. Identify corresponding forces and consequences.

Output a table with corresponding forces and consequences as well as a rationale.
Identify forces and consequences that do not have a match. These need to be resolved by other patterns.

A.3 Inferring the order of patterns

The following prompt infers the order of the patterns:

Order the patterns from larger to smaller patterns, where larger patterns either include smaller patterns (spatial order) or come before them (temporal order). Provide a rationale.

A.4 Reasoning about pattern sequences

This prompt defines the types of relationships in a pattern sequence:

Create pattern sequences from given patterns.

Definitions:

A pattern sequence represents a specific path through a pattern language. It is built on the idea that patterns need other patterns to complete them. A sequence defines the order in which patterns should be applied.

If a pattern is represented by R = ((S)P)C, a linear sequence of three patterns can be represented as:

Pattern 1: R1 = ((S1)P1)C1
Pattern 2 completes R1: R2 = ((S2)P2)R1
Pattern 3 completes R2: R3 = ((S3)P2)R2

When two patterns build on the same context of a third pattern, from which they are forked, this can be represented as:

Pattern 1: R1 = ((S1)P1)C1
Pattern 2 completes R1: R2 = ((S2)P1)R1

Pattern 3 completes R1: R3 = ((S3)P1)R1

Multiple patterns can also feed into a single merged context:

Pattern 1: R1 = ((S1)P1)C1
Pattern 2: R2 = ((S2)P2)C2
Patterns 3 completes R1 and R2: R3 = ((S3)P3)((R1)(R2))

Note: In the calculus of forms, ((R1)(R2)) represents the intersection of the resulting contexts.

Requirements:
- Identify potential sequences of 3 or more patterns
- Preserve the order of the patterns: larger pattern should precede smaller patterns
- Identify their relationships (linear, fork, or merge)
- Define relationships between pattern pairs as: linear, fork, or merge
- Name each sequence based on its supported action
- Provide each the parens representation for each pattern
- Describe the context of each pattern

Steps:
1. I provide patterns
2. You suggest sequences with names and relationships

Wait for me to provide you with a list of patterns.

This prompt generates pattern sequences from a set of given patterns:

Suggest pattern sequences with these patterns:

[PATTERNS]

Steps:
1. Include examples of each type of relationship.
2. Check that all sequences preserve the order of the patterns and correct the order if necessary.

References

1. Alexander, C.: Notes on the Synthesis of Form. Harvard University Press (1964)
2. Alexander, C.: The Timeless Way of Building. Oxford University Press (1979)
3. Alexander, C.: The Nature of Order: The Phenomenon of Life. Oxford University Press (2002)
4. Alexander, C.: The Nature of Order: The Process of Creating Life. The Center for Environmental Structure (2002)
5. Alexander, C., Angel, S., Silverstein, M., Ishikawa, S., Abrams, D.: The Oregon Experiment. Oxford University Press (1975)
6. Alexander, C., Ishikawa, S., Silverstein, M.: A Pattern Language: Towns, Buildings. Oxford University Press, Construction (1977)
7. Alexander, C., Neis, H., Moore Alexander, M.: The Battle for the Life and Beauty of the Earth: A Struggle between two World-Systems. Oxford University Press (2012)
8. Bricken, W.: Distinction is sufficient. Tech. rep, Iconic Math (2017)
9. Buschmann, F., Henney, K., Schmidt, D.C.: Pattern Oriented Software Architecture: On Patterns and Pattern Languages, vol. 5. Wiley (2007)
10. Groll, S.: Forms of design some considerations for a macro theoretical perspective in design. Journal of Engineering Design pp. 1–18 (2025)
11. Iba, T.: Contrast within a pattern: Capturing a gap between problematic and good consequences. In: Conference on Pattern Languages of Programs (PLoP). pp. 1–6 (2021)
12. Kohls, C.: The structure of patterns. In: Conference on Pattern Languages of Programs (PLoP). pp. 1–10 (2010)
13. Kohls, C.: The theories of design patterns and their practical implications exemplified for e-learning patterns. Ph.D. thesis, Katholische Universität Eichstätt-Ingolstadt (2013)
14. Kohls, C., Scheiter, K.: The relation between design patterns and schema theory. In: Conference on Pattern Languages of Programs (PLoP). pp. 1–16 (2008)
15. Krippendorff, K.: On the essential contexts of artifacts or on the proposition that "design is making sense (of things)". Design Issues **5**(2), 9–39 (1989)
16. Manns, M.L., Yoder, J.W.: Sequences & scenarios for fearless change. In: Conference on Pattern Languages of Programs (PLoP). pp. 1–14 (2020)
17. Quillien, J.: Delight's Muse on Christopher Alexander's The Nature of Order: A Summary and Personal Interpretation. Lulu.com (2008)
18. Spencer Brown, G.: Laws of Form. Allen and Unwin (1969)
19. Sutherland, J., Coplien, J.: A Scrum Book: The Spirit of the Game. Pragmatic Bookshelf (2019)
20. Tsigkas, A.: Between Theory and Practice in Architectural Design. Routledge (2025)
21. Waguespack, L.: Hammers, nails, windows, doors and teaching great design. Information Systems Education Journal **6**(45), 3–18 (2008)
22. Waguespack, L., Schiano, W.: Scrum project architecture and thriving systems theory. In: 2012 45th Hawaii International Conference on System Sciences. pp. 4943–4951. IEEE (2012)
23. Washizaki, H., Kubo, A., Takasu, A., Fukazawa, Y.: Relation analysis among patterns on software development process. In: International Conference on Product Focused Software Process Improvement (PROFES). pp. 299–313. Springer (2005)

Be Clear! Guiding Autistic Students in Higher Education Projects

Michel Koolwaaij and Tineke Jacobs(✉)

HAN University of Applied Sciences, Ruitenberglaan 26,
6826 CC Arnhem, The Netherlands
tineke.jacobs@han.nl
http://www.han.nl

Abstract. This paper aims at providing action perspectives for teachers in higher education who supervise project groups that might include autistic students. Autistic students often experience problems with group work, as working in teams appeals to (non-verbal) communication, social-emotional reciprocity, and social relationships. For non-autistic fellow students and non-autistic teachers, it is hard to understand these problems. Because the teacher is responsible for creating a context in which optimal learning for all students takes place, they need to be aware of the most common problems and pitfalls, and have possibilities to cope with them. Starting with the concepts of Double empathy problem and Normalizing power, a context is created for many of the problems autistic and non-autistics face in their interactions. Then nine patterns are presented, which help teachers to guide autistic students not only to survive group work, but even to thrive. These patterns vary from observing the need for (extra) help students to work together, to setting and maintaining the stage for the team for working together smoothly, to patterns for dealing with individual problems of autistics in the team.

Keywords: Autism · Autistics · Group work · Students · Guiding · Higher Education · Project work · Project Groups · Neuro-divergence

1 Introduction

To become a good professional, software engineering students in higher education need to become familiar with project work. That is why a lot of assignments in universities of applied sciences consist of working together in projects [16,17]. For students, this is challenging. They need to find a balance between working together *and* and performing individually. If they only focus on their individual learning outcomes, they will fail the learning outcomes of working together. However, if they only focus on working together, they will not be able to prove that they are up to becoming a good professional individually. For autistic students, this is even more challenging: according to the DSM5[1], they have difficul-

[1] DSM stands for Diagnostic and Statistical Manual of Mental Disorders. It is a reference book on mental health and brain-related conditions and disorders. The American Psychiatric Association (APA) is responsible for the writing, editing, reviewing and publishing of this book.

T. Plummer et al. (Eds.): EuroPLoP 2025, LNCS 16494, pp. 218–253, 2026.
https://doi.org/10.1007/978-3-032-19157-1_11

ties with (non-verbal) communication, social-emotional reciprocity, and social relationships. These are the main ingredients of working in group projects. In addition, they benefit from working with clear assignments and in clear contexts. By definition, projects do not offer this clarity.

For teachers who have to guide this, this is a big challenge too: to begin with, it is not always clear whether there is an autistic participant (diagnosed or not) in the group. This could imply that problems only surface at a later stage. As a teacher, you want to prevent problems as much as possible, but you also want to know what to do if problems do occur. Your goal is for the group to function as a whole as well and as quickly as possible. Otherwise, the individuals cannot demonstrate their competence.

1.1 Autistics? Students with Autism? Some Remarks on Our Use of Language in This Paper

In this paper we do not differentiate between diagnosed and non-diagnosed autistics. Although the terms *neurotypical* and *neurodivergent* are used frequently to describe non-autistic and autistic people, we will not use these terms in the patterns we present as neurodivergence includes autism, but autism is not the same as neurodivergence. When we speak of autistics, we mean persons with characteristics associated with autism. When we speak of autism we mean characteristics of autism. Sometimes we use the term allistic for non-autistic people. With this disclaimer we also want to indicate that a teacher never makes a diagnosis. Teachers are 'just' sometimes confronted with behavior that is either unexpected to them, or they feel it is difficult for them to respond adequately.

1.2 Target Group

This paper aims at teachers guiding project groups, although we do not rule out the possibility that students can also take advantage of the paper. If you ever feel that your usual interventions in a project group do not work out well, and you find yourself back more than once in one or more of the following situations, this paper might be useful to you.

- You notice that a student never actually asks questions, while at the same time he does not seem to be *in control*.
- You notice that a student is constantly asking questions about what you consider unimportant details, thereby monopolizing conversations and preventing the group from moving forward.
- You notice that a student panics for reasons you do not understand. They suddenly stop performing and run away from the group.
- You notice that a student is not producing, although you sense or even observe they are clever enough to perform.
- You hear yourself say: "Read it again, it is clearly written." You then see the student read and continue to read without significant change.

- You hear yourself say: "Good question, but that is irrelevant for now", either because you think it does not help the group at the moment or because you feel the need to move on.
- You notice that one student complains about the rest: "They chose the wrong solutions too quickly, much more research is needed".
- You notice that the rest of the group complains to one student with texts like: "Ask for help more often before you do the wrong things".
- You hear yourself repeatedly think things about specific students like: "Come on", "Just keep going", "Don't be so dramatic", "Get used to it".
- You see students who are exhausted significantly sooner than others.

Note that these characterizations in it self are not unique to autistics. Non-autistics could of course also exhibit these behaviors. The point is that we observed that teachers who feel stuck while guiding groups often experience the same problems, but do not always think of the possibility that autism might play a role. In pattern OBSERVE AND COUNT TILL THREE (Chap. 7) we shall elaborate further on this topic.

1.3 Zooming In: Why Group Work Is Extra Difficult for Autistics

Autistics can experience context and environment differently than non-autistics. For example, as a result of a different sensitivity to stimuli, and/or problems with interpreting non-verbal communication. This can lead to texts and situations having multiple meanings or being perceived differently than they were intended. In addition:

- Most people have an incomplete or incorrect picture of autism.
- People with autism often experience that explaining their limitations does not lead to understanding or support.
- People with autism are used to staying away from challenging situations to avoid overstimulation or misunderstandings.
- People with autism often have bad experiences with social contacts.
- People without autism often react negatively and dismissively to people with autism.

For autistic students, this means that they have to deal with (much) more ambiguity in projects than other students. Ambiguity that distracts from the actual intended learning path. Nevertheless, they too will have to learn to perform in projects as it will be regularly asked of them in professional practice.

Sometimes groups benefit from autistics without a word being said about it. When they actively and early clarify matters and succeed in doing so in a good way, everyone benefits. But often things get stuck, for the whole group, or for the autistic student. The group finds questions for clarification difficult to handle and pushes them (and thus also the autistic teammate) aside, or the autistic teammate remains silent, understanding less and less *why things are the way they are* until joining in is no longer possible.

1.4 Incidence of Autistics in Higher Education

According to statistics, in Dutch higher education approximately 2% of students are diagnosed with autism, while 0.2% have characteristics but do not have a formal diagnosis [7]. Probably due to the fact that autistic students tend to enroll more in STEM[2] studies [2], numbers in our university in the computer science department show a considerably higher percentage: approximately 10% (non-diagnosed students excluded)[3].

1.5 Two Starting Remarks: The Double Empathy Problem and Normalising Power

Before starting with describing patterns, two starting remarks need to be made. They eliminate two common fallacies and really help to be more understanding and supportive for autistics.

Everyone working with autism should be familiar with the ***Double Empathy Problem*** [13,19]. The Double Empathy Problem refers to the difficulty both neurodivergent and neurotypical individuals face in understanding each other's perspectives and experiences. It challenges the idea that only neurodivergent people struggle with empathy, highlighting that communication issues arise on both sides. The concept suggests that misunderstandings occur due to different social and cognitive frameworks rather than a lack of empathy. Essentially, it emphasizes that empathy difficulties are mutual, not one-sided.

Another structural mechanism that also deserves attention is the concept of ***Normalising Power***, as described by Michel Foucault [12]. While the Double Empathy Problem highlights mutual misunderstanding, normalising power explains why this misunderstanding so often leads to judgment or pressure to conform—especially for autistic students.

Normalising power refers to the subtle, often invisible way in which social norms are enforced. It does not work through explicit rules or punishments, but through expectations about what is considered *normal* behaviour, communication, and emotional expression. These norms are typically shaped by neurotypical perspectives and can unintentionally marginalise those who do not naturally fit them.

1.6 Outline of This Paper

Before diving into the patterns, this paper presents an overview of related work (Sect. 2), followed by a methodology chapter which explains the characteristics of the projects in our university and how we observed the patterns (Sect. 3). The next chapter provides a summary of the patterns (Sect. 4) and explains the coherence between the nine patterns that follow. The first three patterns are about

[2] Science, Technology, Engineering and Mathematics.

[3] This percentage is based on the internal HBO-ICT database; provided to us by oral conversation with colleagues from the study coaches department.

creating an autism friendly environment. AN INCLUSIVE KICK-OFF (Sect. 5) helps students to start with their projects even if the teacher is absent. LET'S GET IT CLEAR (Sect. 6) helps them to clarify everything that is unclear in the beginning of the project. Having done the above, the fourth pattern, OBSERVE AND COUNT TILL THREE (Sect. 7) aims at detecting if remarkable behavior of one or more students might be due to a lack of substantive baggage, or autism. LET'S COME TOGETHER (Sect. 8) helps any team to proceed in times that students start to complain about each other. The patterns IGNITION (Sect. 9) GET LOOSE (Sect. 10), POWER SUPPLY (Sect. 11), WHEN THINGS GET HEATED. OR TURN INTO ICE (Sect. 12) and LET THEM SHOW IT (Sect. 13), help the teacher deal with special situations concerning individual autistics in the group they are guiding. In the final Sect. 14, we draw conclusions and give some pointers to future Work.

2 Related Work

2.1 Related Patterns

This pattern paper is the third one in a series on guiding [16] and grading [15] higher education students within group work. The paper on guiding, Supporting ICT-Students to Make the Most out of Their Projects, provides a context for this paper as it describes a general guiding process for student groups. This paper fills in a blank: what to do if the guiding gets stuck because of difficult student's behavior as experienced by the teacher? The paper on grading, Grading individual students in ICT project confidently, can be read separately.

As far as we know, autism-related patterns are not yet described in the pattern community. Of course, many of the pedagogical patterns described by Joseph Bergin and the pedagogical patterns editorial board [3] could be applied, as they certainly help teachers to improve their approaches. We do not rule out that this may lead to better communication, and everybody (autistics and non-autistics) will benefit from that. But, this is not the same as helping teachers who get stuck with guiding autistics. Of course, this book also contains patterns for guiding team work in education. However these patterns are not focused on higher education and projects, some of the patterns (e.g. the ones about feedback and grading) can be applied very well. The same counts for project work in higher education. Some of the patterns can certainly be helpful, but they do not address specific higher education problems.

2.2 Other Sources

About Autism. Recently, knowledge about autism and autistics is becoming more and more the focus of attention due to increasing incidence [2], and to the fact that equal access to curriculum by all students in education has become a focal point in educational policies worldwide. For example, the Universal Design for Learning (UDL) framework [6] has even become part of the American Higher Education Opportunity Act. Due to these facts a wide range of practical books about autism in education have seen the light lately. Many of them provide introductions to autism in general [9, 22], and the vast majority focus on students in primary and secondary education [9]. Sometimes the books are aimed at helping parents, sometimes at autistic children and sometimes at their teachers. Of course, some of the advice authors provide for younger kids may apply to grown-ups as well (e.g. use clear and unambiguous language), but the context in higher education is often too different. Fortunately, many autistics make it to higher education. A body of research on higher education for autistic students is developing. For instance, we found some articles in which the higher education experiences of autistic adults are described, including suggestions on making these experiences more 'autism-friendly' [18, 21, 25, 27]. But we did not find any on practical suggestions for teachers in the classroom, let alone on guiding project teams with autistics. In the context of UDL we found one book aimed at higher education [5], but it's focus is not specifically on autism-related issues. In general, the available publications seldom help with dealing with preparations for working in ambiguous contexts, and that is exactly the case in higher education.

About Project Work in Higher Education. Currently the body of knowledge on the subject of didactics of guiding project groups in higher education is not being replenished very actively. A -Dutch- book with the (translated) title Project-based Education in Higher Professional Education - The Teacher as Project Developer and Project Supervisor [26] provides a good starting point on the topic, but is, of course, not accessible for many. Fleming [11] could be a good starting point for those who want to get a first glance at organizing a project for students. When focusing on learning through teaming Toth and Sousa [23] provide practical insights. Dohn and Wagner [8] compared the way two projects were guided and the impact on motivation and students' perceptions of the learning outcomes. Oudtshoorn and Hay [20] and Burdett [4] also focus on the perceptions of students performing in the projects, but with a slightly different angle: do students think project work is worth the effort when it comes to learning and what works? A literature study on best practices of managing dynamics in group projects [10] gives some pointers for teachers. All in all practical advice on this theme appears to be rather a rare find.

3 Characteristics of the Projects in Our University and How We Observed the Patterns

The patterns were observed during 10 years, in several learning units of both the embedded software development and the software engineering study programs at the HAN University of Applied Sciences in the Netherlands, which has a 25-year tradition in project-related student courses. For the analysis, we relied on our own experiences as teachers and on informal interviews with colleagues. Furthermore, co-author Michel is an autistic teacher himself who contributed to research on autism for 5 years as a lecturer-researcher with the Research Center in Flourishing with Autism (School of Social Studies), HAN University of Applied Sciences.

In the following, we specify the context for the projects in our university in the department of ICT. Students gain 15 ECTS[4], which equals 420 h of work for every project. They do at least one group project per year during the first three years of their 4-year study. Groups in year two consist of 4 to 6 students. In year three, the project is aimed at getting used to the concept of interdependence, so then group size is 20–25. The projects are not designed to build up on each other, but they share a common structure, so students will profit from earlier experiences. The key characteristics are:

- The duration of the project is between 8 and 10 weeks, in which the students exclusively work on the project.
- The project is preceded by 8 weeks of courses on the main subjects that will be addressed in the project.
- The final individual grade for every student is a function of a group and an individual grade. This is done so that students are challenged to be a team player, rather than solely focus on their own performance.
- Before the start of the project the course teachers put together the groups in consultation. Personal and professional characteristics of each individual are taken into account, and they assess how successfully these students might be working together as a team. Usually, the teachers try to distribute autistic students evenly across the groups.
- It is not a rule that the course teachers are the project teachers as well. So, the teachers do not always know (all) the students they will be guiding.
- The only prerequisite for participating in the project is that the student followed the previous courses. They do not need to pass the tests concerning the course subjects. Therefore capacities within the project teams may vary.
- Each group is assigned at least two teachers, who share the responsibility for guiding the group towards reaching the described learning outcomes. For this task they receive approximately 60 h altogether.
- The guiding team have at least weekly contacts in which they share observations, and decide on their focus points during their guidance with the project groups.
- Teachers guide 2 to 15 groups per project period.
- Learning outcomes and assessment criteria are transparent beforehand and are about the content of the assignment, working together and personal learning goals every student has to work on.

[4] ECTS stands for The European Credit Transfer and Accumulation System (ECTS). This system helps European higher educational institutions to translate academic credit marks between institutions. A full time student gets 60 ECTS per year.

- In all projects the scrum ceremonies Daily Stand Up, Retrospective and Sprint Review are applied in one way or an other. Sometimes Sprint planning meetings are held.
- At the start of the project a reference book is provided to the students and teachers in which the frameworks and expectations for project work and the guiding and grading process are described.
- Every diagnosed autistic student who has registered has a special 'study coach' who is available for 10–30 h per year (dependent on the need) to help them overcome general problems related to studying. To compare: for every allistic student this is 2,5 h per year.

4 Our Patterns: An Overview

4.1 Summary of the Patterns

A quick overview of all nine patterns is given in Table 1. Here you see the problem and main solution for every pattern. The full descriptions follow as of Sect. 5.

Our patterns help teachers to guide groups with autistics in them. Although every student can benefit from the patterns, autistic or not, some of the patterns show how working in a project group impacts autistics extra. In only three patterns the forces are solely autism-related: LET'S COME TOGETHER, GET LOOSE and WHEN THINGS GET HEATED.OR TURN INTO ICE.

In fact, OBSERVE AND COUNT TILL THREE is the central pattern. Teachers should apply this continuously, if they want to make their guiding as inclusive as possible. It helps them to catch signals and act accordingly using whichever pattern seems to be appropriate for the situation. As the patterns have their context in project work, for some of them there is an expected 'order of appearance' in time: AN INCLUSIVE KICK-OFF is the pattern you start with when the team have to get to know each other. This is followed by LET'S GET IT CLEAR which is about clarifying the fuzzy project context as much as possible. As the project gets into gear the patterns LET'S COME TOGETHER (focused on overcoming annoyances in the team) and IGNITION (to be applied if a student does not start working) and POWER SUPPLY (for students who tend to get worn out during a full day of project work) could be helpful. If you feel that your questions too often fall on deaf ears GET LOOSE (about having inviting conversations) is the pattern you should use. At the end of the project, if students get stuck writing a summary, LET THEM SHOW IT might be the way to go. Last but not least we described a pattern that could be used 'in case of emergency', if a student is getting a melt down. This is WHEN THINGS GET HEATED. OR TURN INTO ICE. In Fig. 1 these relationships are depicted.

Table 1. Problems and Solutions

Pattern	Problem	Solution
AN INCLUSIVE KICK-OFF	How can students get to know each other safely without a teacher, including autistic students?	Send a written, structured, safe introduction task beforehand and have students record the outcomes.
LET'S GET IT CLEAR	How can you avoid confusion about the project process, especially for autistic students?	Make expectations and language around instructions explicit in a reference book and actively use it.
OBSERVE AND COUNT TILL THREE	How do you recognize autism-related behavior that looks like lack of motivation or competence?	Take action after three observations and explore with the student what support is needed.
LET'S COME TOGETHER	How can you turn tensions and irritations into better collaboration?	Share observations, prepare the conversation with the autistic student, and facilitate open dialogue.
IGNITION	How do you get an autistic student started on an unclear task in the early phase?	Be present during task division, check for understanding, and help them to chunk the work while relating to what they already know.
Get Loose	How do you help a student who is stuck but does not ask for help?	Ask concrete, bounded questions and help the student formulate their help request.
Power Supply	How can autistic students preserve their energy throughout the day?	Help the team structure their days with regularity, predictability, and opportunities for rest or withdrawal, so that is a good balance between work and breaks, and group and individual work.
WHEN THINGS GET HEATED. OR TURN INTO ICE	How do you stay connected with a student who explodes or freezes under stress?	Acknowledge their experience, co-create coping options, and involve the whole team without taking sides or placing blame
LET THEM SHOW IT	How do you support a student who performed well but can not write it down?	Help them focus on the things they would do different or exactly the same in their future career.

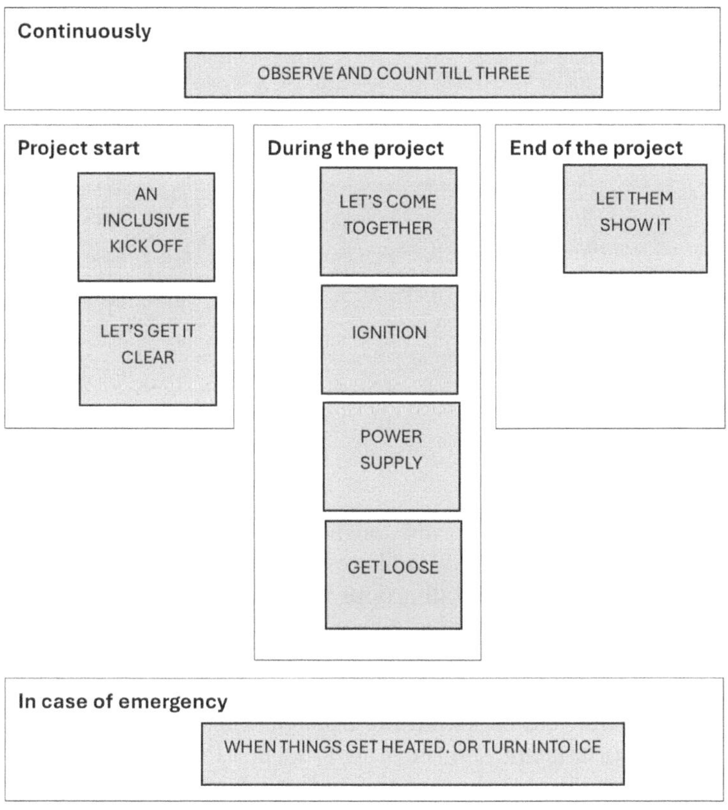

Fig. 1. Relationships between the patterns

4.2 The Pattern Format

The basic pattern format as explained by Tim Wellhausen and Andreas Fießer [28] will be used to describe the patterns. Therefore, every pattern consists of a context, forces, problem, solution, and a consequences section. In the context section, we give several examples of possible autistic behavior which lead to the problem. We realize that we do not strictly follow Wellhausen and Fießer in doing so, but we think this helps teachers to connect to their specific situations more easily. If relevant in the forces section, we differentiate between autism-related forces and forces due to other factors. This is due to the fact that many forces caused by autism-related problems, cannot be simply solved by one specific solution. Nevertheless, it is possible for teachers to cope with them. Although it is common use in the pattern community to choose titles closely related to the solution, we decided on titles that emphasize the process and/or the problem because it is difficult to relate to a solution if the problem is not yet clear. We think this enhances the usability of the paper for readers new in the field of working with autistics.

5 An Inclusive Kick-Off

5.1 Context

At the start of a project, students are assigned to a group and get an assignment. Also, a reference book is made available to them. The teacher has many groups to guide and is not able to join all groups in person for a kick-off. The teacher does not know how well the students know each other. What they do know is that there might be an autistic student in the group. If so, getting to know each other can be difficult. Typical behavior could be: The autistic student remains silent, stares into the void or withdraws from the conversation. A gap develops between the autistic student and the other students. Perhaps the other students try to unsuccessfully involve the autistic student. Or perhaps the other students find each other and exclude the autistic student based on their behavior.

5.2 Problem

How does a teacher allow a new group of students to get to know each other in the absence of a teacher, in a way that also enables potential autistic people to connect?

5.3 Forces

Autism Related

- **People with autism often have bad experiences with social contacts.** They are often reacted to negatively. For example, when they ask a lot of questions or when they act in a socially unexpected way.
- **In addition to the unfamiliarity with the group members, an autistic student probably is also uncertain about other aspects**: Where do we have to work? Do I know it there? Are there (too) many stimuli there? Will our teachers be of any help for me when push comes to shove?
- **Switching in unexpected situations sometimes makes autistics 'close down'**.

<u>Due to other factors</u>

- **Students prefer to dive into the content of the project immediately**, especially at the beginning of a project. They think getting to know the team mates should happen, but it should not take too long. So they tend to kick off with only exchanging names, telephone numbers and starting a Whatsapp-group.
- **A leader-figure will not stand up in every team**, however every team's development would benefit from it, according to Belbin [24]. If there is no natural leader, conversation does not easily get going.

5.4 Solution

- **The teacher takes the lead by making the introduction a formal moment with instructions.** They explain that they can not be present at that moment, but that this does not prevent the students from starting with their project. By doing so, the team knows the teacher shows their active involvement.
- **The teacher makes sure there is a quiet space available for the students to meet.** This prevents sensory overload, and also shows the teacher is involved
- **The teacher sends an agenda some time before the meeting**. They express their expectation that all students prepare for the meeting and that the team takes notes so that the teacher and the team can refer back to them. An example agenda includes:
  - ***Scope of the meeting, which is limited to the introduction***. Delving into the assignment or other subjects are planned for another moment. Let them know when you expect them to do that.
  - ***An instruction about the way to get to know each other***. For example: In turns, everyone tells their name, age, hobbies. In the 2nd round, everyone answers the question 'What are my qualities?'. In the 3rd round, everyone answers the question "What do I probably need help with?". And in the 4th round, everyone answers the question "What would I like to learn during this project?". In a fifth round, they can say what else they want their group members to know about them.
  - ***An item named Any Questions?***, for everything else that came up and seems to be important to ask.
  - ***An item named Agreements for Working Together***. This will include group agreements, and if deemed necessary, tailored ones for individuals. The only prerequisite you give is that they are derived from the former agenda items, and fit into the framework of the reference book.

5.5 Consequences

Benefits

- Because the teacher appears to be actively involved with the team, although not present in person, the team learns that they have to be independent, but that the teacher will also be actively involved in the upcoming process in his absence.

Liabilities

- There is little room for spontaneity. This can come across as academic and artificial.
- It is possible that important information is not shared because it is not mentioned as a question in the instruction.
- If students do not prepare, this can lead to irritation and the beginning of distrust.

6 Let's Get It Clear

6.1 Context

Many students struggle with distinguishing between main and secondary issues. Autistics are even worse at it. At the start of a project, ambiguity is all over the place by definition. A reference book is available. The teacher wants to direct the attention to the intended learning path as quickly as possible.

6.2 Problem

How does the teacher help the students to clarify everything that is unclear during the first fuzzy phase of the project?

6.3 Forces

Autism Related

- **In oral explanations or answers to questions, different words are used than in the written assignments/explanations.** Different words provide new information and possibly cause confusion.
- **Fellow students often have their own translation of the assignment.** This is very logical to them and may (but certainly not always) correspond with the intention of the teacher, but causes confusion for the autistic student. In the old days this was called 'lack of theory of mind' [1]. Nowadays we know this is due to a different way of experiencing information.
- **It is not always clear when students *must* follow an instruction, and when instructions are indeed suggestions.** This is caused by the fact that, in order not to sound too directive, teachers often use texts such as: "You could use this approach", "It might be a good idea to do..."

Due to Other Factors

- **Teachers suffer from "the curse of expertise"** [14]. They do not always realize well enough which knowledge and skills they take for granted based on their previous experiences.
- **Students do not, or hardly, read the reference book**, which means that they often do other things than intended.
- **Teachers hardly, or never, read the reference book**, which means that they often deviate in their guidance from what is described in the reference book.

6.4 Solution

Actively Work with a Well-Structured Reference Book for Expressing Expectations. Distinguish between different phases in the project. For example: if the project includes a phase in which the assignment must first be analyzed, clearly separate this from the phase in which a result must be delivered. Indicate how long each phase will approximately take.

In Fig. 2, the activities during guiding are depicted, including the most likely order. However, depending on the situation, a different order and/or repetition of steps might be a good idea. Any way, focus points during these activities should be:

- ***Be aware of the language you use***. In the reference book as well as in spoken words. For example, do you want students to follow a school instruction or make a choice themselves? Tell them. Make sure that you only provide uncertainty in the areas where you want the student to discover or choose for themselves. The formulated learning outcomes provide context: that is where the uncertainty may (must) be. The rest must be as stable as possible.

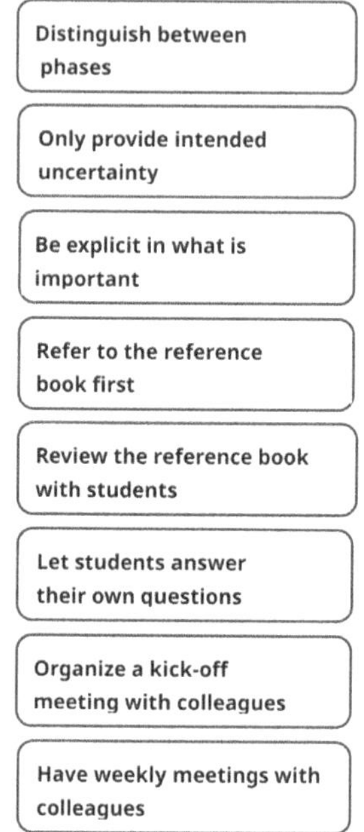

Fig. 2. Possible solution steps to make things clear

- ***Be explicit in your guidance about the elements that will be important in the summative assessment at the end of the project***. Of course, students can read that in the reference book, but it is difficult for them to translate the abstractly formulated learning outcomes into what actually happens in their project. For example, you can say: if you continue doing this, you will definitely see that reflected in your grades.
- ***If the students ask questions about the process, always refer to the reference book first***. Can the answer be found there? No? Correct any ambiguities immediately and make a new version available. Communicate this to all people (students as well as colleagues) involved.
- ***If students continue to have doubts about what is in the reference book: review it together with the students***. This will help you to find out where the student's ambiguity comes from and to remove it immediately. Students also learn that they can solve many questions without the teacher's intervention.
- ***If students continue to ask similar questions about subsequent passages, encourage the student to formulate an answer to you themselves***. They are in higher education, so at some point students should be able to do these kinds of translations themselves.
- ***Organize a kick-off meeting with colleagues*** in which you review the study guide so that you reduce the chance that they will give different instructions.

- ***Have weekly meetings with colleagues*** in which you speak of current problems, help each other out, answer questions on the basis of the reference book, and/or decide updates in the reference book need to be made.

6.5 Consequences

Benefits

- Students greatly appreciate the diminishing lack of ambiguity/vagueness and will express this in evaluations.
- Not only the autistic student gets on track faster, his group members also benefit from less delay due to confusion.
- Teachers develop a common understanding of guiding towards the learning outcomes which benefits students as well as teachers during the current project period, and the next.

Liabilities

- More clarity can lead to unintended instruction, which causes students to stop thinking for themselves.
- Encouraging questions can lead to an overload of questions.

7 Observe and Count Till Three

7.1 Context

When the project proceeds, the teacher gets to know the students better. They know that people are different, and so are students. There can be less ambitious, (less) smart, (too) self-assured, diligent, and lazy students in every group. You know that autistics are often wrongly seen as difficult. For example, because they ask (too) many questions, do not ask questions at all, make the same mistakes over and over, leave for or work from home suddenly, or do not get started on given assignments. Behavior that can just as easily be exhibited by chance factors, less smart or lazy students.

7.2 Problem

How can a teacher recognize a well-intentioned autistic student, stuck due to unintended ambiguity, so that they will be effective in offering all students an appropriate learning experience?

7.3 Forces

Autism Related

- **Non verbal signals from autistics are often misinterpreted by people without autism**, mostly negatively.
- **Autistic people often have no idea they are misinterpreted** and other people have negative impressions of them.
- **Not starting (or continuing) a task by autistics is often the result of not knowing the purpose or meaning of the task**. Other people may wrongfully think it is due to incompetence or lazyness.
- **Autistic people avoid asking questions frequently**, because they will feel they are a burden when they do so. This is even the case when they are lost.
- **Sometimes people with autism keep trying instead of asking for better instructions**, because they rather doubt their own abilities than the instructions.
- **Sharing their autism diagnosis with other people can backfires regularly**, so loads of autistic people will not tell anyone and try to mask all symptoms.

Due to Other Factors

- **Teachers are always happy to share their expertise.** So they like it when students ask questions. Even if it would be a better idea not to answer them.
- **As a teacher, you have an idea of the expected course of the learning path for the students**. That gives you something to hold on to: you know what to do and when. This could make you insensitive to individual student's needs.
- **Teachers try to avoid an imbalance in time spent guiding every individual student.** Of course they want to take everyone seriously, and go the extra mile if necessary. But they are afraid that an imbalance will backfire when the grades have to be set.

7.4 Solution

Actively check from the beginning if you sense frustration, be it with yourself or with the students. If so, make use of the 1,2,3-rule: 1 time is a coincidence, 2 times is noteworthy and 3 times it is a pattern.

Find out about the cause of the frustration and then act. Frustrations could be one of the situations described in Sect. 1.2 (Target group). For instance, does the student from your point of view ask too few or too many questions? Does the student panic or complain for no obvious reason? Is the student clearly underachieving?

Concerning counting: mind that every observation counts. They need not be exactly the same observations. It also does not matter when you make your observations. They can be made during your visits to the team, before and afterwards. It could even be an observation a colleague told you about. To act means finding out what the background of the student in question is and what they need to start performing. You could:

- ***Check in the minutes of the kick-off meeting if the students shared their needs for working together***. If they did so, you will sometimes see the autistic student referring to their autism.
- ***Check with the university whether the student has a diagnosis and if it is known which special needs apply for this student***.
- ***Tactfully check with the student in question***. Share your factual observations, for example: "I see you repeatedly doing this. Are you aware of it?" or: "Have you heard someone else say that to you in the past?". If so, there are two options:
  - *The student is able to formulate how this has been resolved in the past.* If so: check if you think this could work (is it do-able, realistic?) and make clear agreements, using the 5xW-1xH acronym: what, why, where when, who and how. Check during your next visits if the desired behavior appeared to be effective.
  - *If the student cannot think of different options for action, do not hesitate to suggest one or more you think that might help.* Stress that you too do not know if it will work, but going on with the current unhelpful activities surely will not work. Ask the student to try and to be willing to fail. Stress that may be difficult, but it is far better than doing nothing. Also stress that you do not mind it going wrong. Again, make clear agreements about which actions the student is going to take (5xW 1xH). Complement with agreements about the number of attempts and the moment at which the student reports to you again if it does not work.

As many autistics are inherently bound to agreements, you are pretty sure that if the student reports back, they are the good-willing, but lost one. **If the student does not report back, your first hunch should be that the agreement was not clear enough**. Check that actively with the student. If it was indeed unclear: do not blame the student, but make a new better one and check again after a while. **Do not hesitate to spend more time on the autistic student in the beginning**; this will pay off and level out in the course of the project. The sooner the autism-related problems are cleared up, the sooner the team as a whole will get on track.

7.5 Consequences

Benefits

- A clear agreement creates a way of working that could become a routine for the student to maintain and in later instances fall back to.
- If fellow students know the agreements, they can also help each other sticking to it.

Liabilities

- Someone may feel awkward or unsafe because you take them aside.
- In case the student is indeed unmotivated or not suited to understand the tasks, time is lost the teacher could have spend at other students.

8 Let's Come Together

8.1 Context

The group of students has been working on the assignment for a few weeks now. Their progress is comparable to other groups. However, as a supervising teacher, you notice tensions. This manifests itself in several ways. The autistic student can complain to you about the other students not complying with agreements or having different interpretations of the assignments. Or their fellow students come to complain to you because the autistic student is overly critical or does not accept decisions. Perhaps the autistic student suddenly takes on all tasks, or does nothing at all. A team meeting in which the tensions are discussed and solved is necessary.

8.2 Problem

How does the teacher ensure that students use annoyances to improve the team?

8.3 Forces

Autism Related

- **People with autism often stick to agreements** because they want to do well.
- **Many people with autism have the experience that the world is black and white**. An assignment is just as it is and therefore they want to stick to it exactly. They are not suspicious of possible shades of grey.
- **Some people with autism want all the control when they notice that others are not complying with agreements.**
- **Some people with autism drop out when they notice that others are not complying with the agreement.**
- **Non-autistics often connect more easily among themselves** because they have less difficulty understanding subtle hints and non-verbal communication.
- **People with autism often have problems with understanding specific social contexts**. In almost every situation there are unwritten social rules that apply, with a chance of being unknown to someone autistic.
- **Students with autism often have the experience of being excluded or bullied.**
- **Students with autism often have the experience of not being able to trust other people.**
- **More often than you would think a team acts according to implicit plans**. New insights can lead to a new method or planning that deviates from existing agreements. This can be completely logical for all students, as a result of which the new plan stays implicit.
- **For teachers is hard to distinguish between the team acting well according to the new insights, and the autistic group member who does not notice the change**. This implies that an individual need for help is not always detected by the teacher.

8.4 Solution

Have a group discussion, including the autistic student. Ask what they expect from it and adjust expectations if possible. You could:

- ***Indicate that the group process is being disrupted and that your goal is to solve it for everyone.*** Nobody likes to complain.
- ***Tell them what behavior you see in the autistic student, but also indicate the effect on the group and ask for the reason.*** Ask questions like "what happened according to you" and "what did you intend to accomplish?".
- ***As soon as you know the reason of the observed behavior, indicate that it is in everyone's interest to discuss this together***.

- ***Explain to the autistic student how group members could experience the discussion***. The autistic student may not foresee defensive (negative) remarks, resistance or questions.
- ***If necessary, help with choosing the words to describe the problem or to respond to reactions.*** A structured method for giving feedback could be very helpful.
- ***Be present at the group discussion, but let the autistic student do the talking***.
- ***Be alert for miscommunication, talking loudly, talking quickly or talking softly or very slowly***. If this happens, jump in and help.
- ***Make agreements about which group member will do what, might complaints arise again.*** Plan a meeting during which the agreements will be evaluated.
- ***In case of difference in interpretations, let the students explain to each other how they interpret the task or situation.*** Probably they will understand the differences and come to a decision everyone agrees to. If not they can ask the product owner or client to decide.
- ***Stay neutral in the process and keep amplifying your neutrality.*** You are not here to blame or pick sides, but to coach the students towards understanding each other.

8.5 Consequences

Benefits

- Growing understanding for each other's actions.
- The behavior is adjusted to each other and does not escalate (further).

Liabilities

- The autistic student will probably feel misunderstood and alone against the others, including the teacher. If there is any sign of you taking sides, blame the autistic student or assume intentions, it can escalate further.

9 Ignition

9.1 Context

One of the first things when starting with a new project is finding out and framing the actual assignment with a product owner or client. This requires various actions, and the team divides the work. After a short period, it appears that everyone has made at least some progress, except for the autistic student. They may have all kinds of excuses, but has not even started yet.

9.2 Problem

How does the teacher get the autistic student to start with the tasks assigned to them?

9.3 Forces

Autism Related

- **People with autism often have problems with executive functions.** Think of planning and organizing, but also simply starting a task. Every bit of doubt contributes to this.
- **If someone does not start a task, it is quickly thought that this person is stupid or lazy.**
- **People often continue at a high pace on their own train of thought, without checking whether others can still follow.**
- **People with autism need switching time to make connections between verbal communication, non-verbal communication and the context.** If the context is also unclear, they quickly fall behind and do not catch up during the meeting.
- **Autistic people have often trained themselves to repeat words or give socially desirable answers, without knowing exactly what is meant.** Their experience is that this leads to fewer problems in the short term than if they ask further questions. In this way, they give the impression that they understand what they have to do, and will therefore also take action.

Due to other factors

- **When students are not (yet) sure of the situation, or themselves, their tendency is to formulate vaguely.** They think this prevents them from making mistakes. For example they formulate tasks like: "Will you make sure that ... is done or arranged?".
- **For teachers it is logical that the project ties in with the student's prior knowledge. For students this is much less logical.** They see a new assignment. For example, in the preceding courses, students have learned to specify requirements and interview stakeholders. But now they have a short description of the client's wishes. To them it is not evident that they have to interview the client and specify requirements themselves.

- **Students often present themselves better than they are.** They may not know exactly what they have done, but they sense that doing something is better than doing nothing. In addition, doing something may lead to something good, and if not, you have at least shown commitment.

9.4 Solution

Help the Student with Chunking Tasks. This is the process of cutting task in subtasks. Thereby:

- ***Make sure that you, as a teacher, are present during the discussion where the division of tasks is discussed.***
- **Explicitly link to the knowledge students have previously acquired.** For example in previous projects or courses.
- ***During the discussion, ask for each task whether everyone understands what the purpose is.*** Have someone else explain it each time. Pay attention to the attitude of the students who are listening. An inquiring or agreeing attitude speaks for itself. If the student is neutral or absent, ask whether the student can explain it again in different words.
- ***Ask whether the task suits the student in question.*** Proceed with questions like: "What will be your first step?", "What will you deliver?" and "What do you think you will enjoy the most about this task?"
- ***If student thinks the task is not enjoyable or to difficult, do not immediately give the task to someone else.*** Maybe the student needs the practice to become better or tedious tasks need to be distributed.
- ***If you cannot be present, ask each participant individually the next time you are with the group what they are going to do.*** Have them explain it as specifically as possible. If it turns out that it was not clear, call everyone together again.

9.5 Consequences

Benefits

- By doing this together, students not only have a concrete image of their own role or task, but also of that of others, and can more easily help each other if something goes wrong with the other.
- The autistic student gains (more) self-confidence because he or she performs just as well as the rest.
- The autistic student will become better in figuring out the first and next steps of tasks, what is a benefit for the rest of his life.

Liabilities

- Doing this can take a lot of time.
- Sometimes someone gets sick or requirements change, so tasks change or are redistributed. This often means the process starts all over again.

10 Get Loose

10.1 Context

The autistic student has been working on a task for a long time. When you check the work, you conclude that the student has been walking in circles for days without making any progress. The team reports that they tried to help, but that they mainly got yes/no, or other very short sentence answers. They seem to have given up on it.

10.2 Problem

How do you ensure that you help the student get back on track by means of a conversation that invites them to ask a question again next time?

10.3 Forces

<u>Autism Related</u>

- Language is often very complicated for people with autism. It is very hard to ask appropriate questions when you have no idea what the connection is between the subject and the words.
- **Where people without autism often listen to their feelings, people with autism often respond based on experience.** This makes it difficult for them to form an image of something they have not yet experienced and hard to formulate questions the other person understands.
- **Autistic people often take words literally.** Alternative meaning through context or non-verbal communication can easily be missed. In these cases the autistic person is sure to be on the right track, so feels no need to ask questions.
- **People without autism can respond seemingly aggressive to questions.** This can either be defensive ("So you think I am doing it wrong?") or offensive ("If you still do not get it, pay attention").

- **Asking a good question for help is difficult for everyone, but even more difficult for people with autism** because of the communication barrier.
- **Both non-verbal and verbal signals from someone with autism are often not picked up by people without autism**. So maybe the autistic student did ask for help (multiple times), but nobody noticed.
- **People with autism can lose self-confidence and/or self-esteem if they notice that they are the only one who can not do something.** Many people do not like to admit they are the only one who does not understand; the effect of normalizing power comes in here.

10.4 Solution

- **Change the way you ask your questions:**
  - **Ask very specific questions**, such as: "Which outcome did you expect?" and "What outcome did you get?".
  - **Avoid open why- and how-questions**. Instead of "How did you do this?" ask, for example: "What steps did you take?" Or: "Will you finish everything on time?" Instead of: "How are you doing?"
  - **Keep away from questions that refer to the student instead of the problem**. For example, instead of asking "What do you want to do next?" ask "What is the best next step to solve the problem?".
  - **Verify when you suspect that the student is giving socially desirable answers**. This can be a very direct question like "Did you just give me a socially desirable answer?" or "Did you really think this through?'. Always use boolean questions in these situations.
  - **Give the student time to process the information**. Wait calmly for the answer.
  - **Ask your questions one by one**. Do not ask the next question if the previous one has not yet been answered. Otherwise the autistic student will likely only answer the last question asked or get a sensory overload.
- **As soon as you have found the question for help, offer help**. Otherwise you only achieved the student experiencing lots of energy loss with no result.
- **Even though it is sometimes easier and faster if you do an action yourself, this does not help the student**. Not only do you want the student to be able to do it themselves, the student can also feel very stupid because of this.
- **When explaining, always use who, what, where, when and how**. In this case, do not explain why, because very often this does not match completely in a logical sense. For autistiscs this can lead to doubt ("I must have misunderstood") or frustration ("this cannot be, you are obviously wrong").
- **When demonstrating something: attune your senses to each other**. For example, say out loud what you are doing, for example: "I am now typing www.han.nl in the web browser".

10.5 Consequences

Benefits

- The student with autism gains more self-confidence as he or she experiences more independent success.
- The other students see that the autistic student is getting going again and will start to see him or her as a full-fledged group member.
- As a teacher, you will be seen as helpful.

Liabilities

- Students may become dependent on you, or may think that they are dependent on you.

11 Power Supply

11.1 Context

A group assignment at school means that you have to work together with others in a busy, social work environment. All students lose energy during the day, but the autistic student often loses it much faster. One can notice this, for example, because they suddenly have difficulties expressing themselves, start complaining about fatigue, become hyperactive and noisy, or suffer from dizziness or other fatigue problems. The autistic are less productive earlier in the day than their non-autistic peers.

11.2 Problem

How does a teacher ensure that students with autism also reach the end of the day productively?

11.3 Forces

Autism Related

- **People with autism often have an abnormal stimulus processing.** This means that, compared to other people, they are more sensitive to some stimuli and less sensitive to others. For example, the commotion from a classroom further down the hall can cause a lot of stimuli. Or sunlight coming in through the windows. There is also often a lot of movement from fellow students and teachers walking back and forth, getting things out of their bags, etc. This consumes energy.
- **The student with autism has to be much more alert to communication and misunderstandings.** In addition to processing all the aforementioned stimuli, this consumes energy too.
- **All forms of change and unpredictability** can cost an autistic person a lot of energy.
- **People with autism can become hyperfocused once busy with a task.** As a result, they forget to rest, eat and/or drink. Which is exhausting in the end.
- **It is frustrating for students with autism when they are suddenly no longer able to perform at the level that they know they can achieve at other times.**

11.4 Solution

Help the Group to Build in as Much Routines as Possible. For example, by scheduling the scrum ceremonies and breaks at the same time every day. But also think of:

- ***Give the group clarity in advance about when you expect something***, for example about when you will come by and what your agenda items will be. They can prepare, which reduces uncertainty.
- ***Accept, or facilitate, that the student with autism occasionally withdraws from the team.*** For example to a quiet space to work alone for an hour, or to take a walk.
- ***Allow devices or methods which help to reduce sensory overload***, such as noise-canceling headphones or sunglasses during designated types of work or times of the day. Stress that using them all day could prevent the team form working together, so a balance has to be found.
- ***Discuss with the group that they remind each other at fixed times to take a break.***
- ***Always ensure sufficient processing time for thc student with autism, for questions and conversations.*** One way to achieve this is by stimulating other people to accept 'awkward' silences by counting to 10 slowly. This is helpful for them as well.

11.5 Consequences

Benefits

- Autistic students will last almost as long every day as other students.
- Autistic students will perform equal in the afternoons compared to the mornings.
- Other students will learn to accept differences and adjust their behavior.

Liabilities

- Students who take a break by walking away from the workplace are more prone to coming back later than agreed on. They is also an extra chance of to coming back overexcited as they might experience unexpected things on the way. Both can, of course, lead to hassle; undoing the effect of the break.

12 When Things Get Heated. Or Turn Into Ice

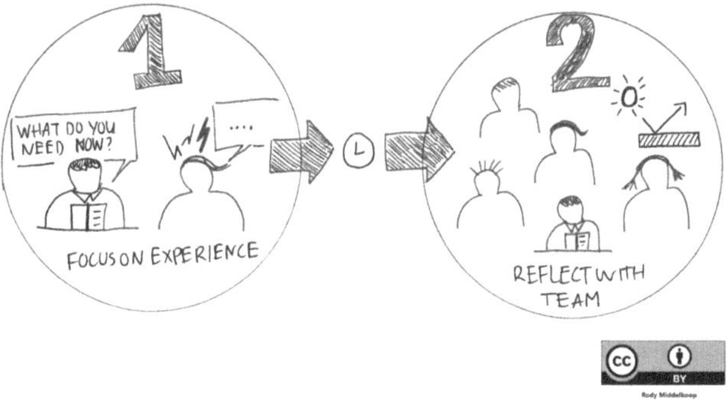

12.1 Context

Suddenly, things get out of hand. Maybe the student gets very emotional out of nowhere, crying, walking away angry, or talking with a very loud voice. You could also detect the student freezing for no apparent reason or see no intention to participate. It is almost impossible to avoid situations in every project that are overwhelming to autistic people. Think of sudden changes, a noisy environment, very fast discussions without any processing time. The autistic student quickly becomes overstimulated, resulting in behavior that is perceived as inappropriate by others. Fellow students tend to think "Get used to it" and that is also your prime thought. When you ask the autistic what is going on, the reaction you get is not helpful at all. Maybe the student stays silent, answers in one-syllable sentences, or gives a very long answer that sounds like a bad excuse. Often, everything you do makes it worse. The student gets angry more frequently, clashes with other students, starts withdrawing and in the end even fails the project.

12.2 Problem

How do you ensure that the autistic student feels understood, while panicking, even if you do not understand it yourself or cannot change the circumstances?

12.3 Forces

Autism Related

- **Different challenges. Unfair reactions** Each student has his or her own challenges. One has a part-time job that takes up a lot of time, another suffers from migraine attacks and a third has a lot of travel time to get to school. In many cases, students and teachers are good at taking the challenges of others into account. Students with autism often have quite different challenges. For example, they have difficulty with change, with the hustle and bustle or with long meetings and therefore need longer switching time, more rest periods and more support.
- Not all students put 100% into school. For autistic students it can feel very unfair when others get away with such behavior, when they themselves get punished for things related to their autism (for instance sensory overload, not having enough information to understand an assignment or rapid loss of energy).
- **Persons without autism often struggle to imagine autistic sensory difficulties.** They easily play it down: "Just neglect it, that is what I also do".
- **Persons without autism can easily relate to common inconveniences.** Things may feel very unfair for autistic people when other peoples minor inconveniences are taken seriously and their own major problems (for instance exclusion or sensory overload) are not.
- **Persons without autism often struggle to recognize and understand autism.** Therefore their first impression is not always a positive one. It takes time to change that.
- **Different coping mechanisms.** Some autistics will mask and act like everything is good. Others will shutdown, walk away or try to make other people aware of their problems.
- **Autism is pervasive.** You can not turn it off or get used to it. You can learn to deal with it. This requires understanding from others.
- **The quickest way to deal with problems that you do not experience, but someone else does, seems to be downplaying the problem**: "Don't be so difficult".

12.4 Solution

Ask the student what they need right now and accept the answer by any means. Even if you do not think this way of coping is appropriate or helpful. When the student is in a position to reflect on the situation again, talk to them. This could be (much) later than the situation occurred:

- ***Let the student explain what they experience***. What is their perspective and how does it make them feel? Do not interrupt and do not judge.
- ***Try to empathize or at least sympathize***. Chances are you cannot relate to the problem, but never tell the student that it is no problem or should not be a problem. It can make him feel stupid or not worthy. Instead say something like "I cannot relate to this, but it sounds very painful (or frustrating or difficult) for you".
- ***Ask them if they dealt with this before and in what situation***. If so, how did they cope with this. What was the result?
- ***When the result was good, suggest to do the same thing now***. If the result was not good or they has never dealt with it, ask if they can think of possible options how to deal with it.
- ***Sometimes the student has no, or no realistic, answer to your question.*** In that case make them think of alternatives. Give it time. Maybe the next day they have better options.
- ***Sometimes there is no way to take away the problem. If so, then explain that you understand it is a problem, but nothing can be done now.*** Let the student choose how to deal with it. Maybe the student can participate and take an extra long break afterwards? Or maybe the student will not participate but get the information another way. Be flexible and do not be shy about unusual solutions.
- ***Reflect on the situation with the whole group.*** Which situations escalate more easily? How to de-escalate? The autistic student probably knows best. Does he simply need cool down time? Does he need comforting words? Something else? Most of the times knowing how not to escalate is enough. Keep calm whatever happens, and do not take it personal.

12.5 Consequences

Benefits

- Teacher and student, and also student and group, develop a better bond, making it increasingly easier for the student to accept 'the impossible' when necessary and thus be able to return to work more quickly.

Liabilities

- If you go too far in always facilitating the autistic student to the detriment of the group members, they will feel disadvantaged.

13 Let Them Show It

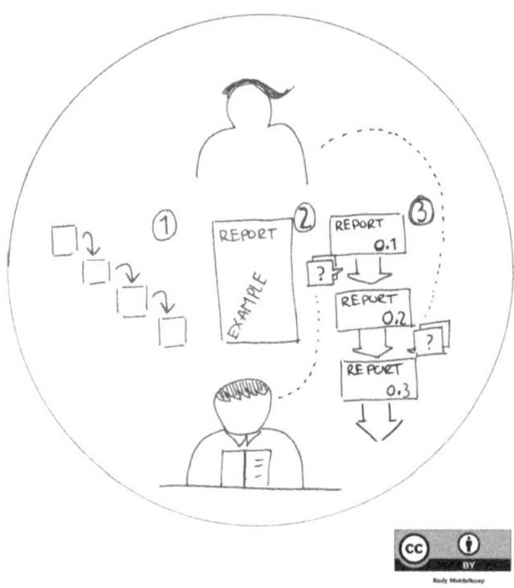

13.1 Context

In order to be able to grade students at the end of the project [15], it is customary for students to provide a summary of their most important activities in the project. Linked to this, they show that they have achieved the required level and what they have learned. This is often done in the form of a report, but an extensive oral assessment could also be possible. This report must be written, or the assessment must be carefully prepared. However, you notice that the autistic student does not start on it, or works on it all day without results. If you point out to the student that this is really important, because otherwise he will not pass, despite the fact that you have seen him do very good things in the project, a counterproductive effect occurs. If you ask why the student does not write anything, you get answers such as "I do not know what to write" or "This takes me too much time". You worry that the student will not fail unjustly, because: no summary, no final grade.

13.2 Problem

How do you stimulate an autistic student to come up with a summary in a reasonable amount of time that is in line with their performance during the project?

13.3 Forces

<u>Autism Related</u>

- **People with autism often have difficulty organizing a large amount of information in their heads.**

- **Many of the cognitive load of the autistic student already goes to carrying out the assignment and working together with group members.** Writing a report adds ambiguity and complexity to that.
- **For people with autism it is often very difficult to get an image of something they have not yet experienced and very easy to recall events from memory.**
- **People with autism are generally better at recognizing patterns than at making connections.** Due to hyperfocus or problems with central coherence, they are often so concentrated or goal-oriented that side effects such as reactions escape them. Or they see it as a separate event. But, when noticing the same result over and over, they are often quick to recognize the pattern from memory.

Due to Other Factors

- **In the eyes of students, the summary is often something that is not related to their assignment or project.** They think it is 'something that has to be done for school'.
- **If a template for the summary is available, students will fill in the template instead of summarizing their own performance.** This, of course, prevents the student from learning.
- **For the average student it is more fun to add something extra to your project result than to reflect on their learning.**

13.4 Solution

Let them change their focus from writing a report 'for school' to writing a text they would want to use themselves when doing a next project. You could:

- ***Provide a (written) explanation in which the purpose of the summary (learning) and the connection to the work carried out and the summary are described.***
- ***Avoid vague texts*** such as "Write what you have done and learned" or "It is for the teacher to be able to assess your work". It is better to take a top-down approach. "What good results from this project do you want to enjoy in your next projects as well? What happened that led to these results? Write down the situation, the results and what happened so you can do the same next project". Same with bad results, except then the question is "what can you do next time so it will go better".
- ***Provide various examples of good reports.***
- ***Have students make a first version in which they write down (based on memory) what they have done.***
- ***You can ask them specific questions about this first version***, such as "What result did you expect and what result did you actually get?", "What is your explanation for this difference?". They can then add the answers to these questions to the text.

- ***Have the student do this themselves for the second version***. Provide feedback on this and ask the following specific questions. For example: "What knowledge do you have after you have completed this task that you did not have before?" Or "On what points do you think this version is better than the former one?". Repeat this until the student can do it independently.

13.5 Consequences

Benefits

- Once autistic students can independently write a good report, their self-confidence grows and tension and uncertainty decrease. As a result, they perform better in the group assignment.
- In subsequent group assignments, writing reports is no longer a big problem.

14 Conclusions and Further Work

Guiding students in group projects can be complex. Teachers have expectations on how students behave, on their knowledge, and on their skills. When students do not meet those expectations, it is tempting to blame the student's intelligence or attitude. That may be true sometimes, but the cause could just as well be a lack of clarity or mutual misunderstanding.

The latter is very often the case when dealing with autistic students. The diagnosis of autism is mainly based on these difficulties. Even when autistic students manage to participate successfully, they generally have to work harder to overcome those problems than other students. The good news is that this gives teachers the opportunity to really make a difference. With some adjustments, they can guide these students in learning their own strengths and weaknesses, while at the same time becoming more confident in working with other people.

This paper gives higher education teachers the tools to do just that. Building upon existing knowledge about autism, it fills a knowledge gap by providing directly applicable patterns. The majority of the available literature seldom offers concrete solutions. It only describes the challenges of autistic students and general teaching strategies. A regularly offered advice is, for example, to be clear. Every teacher tries to be clear, so what does it mean actually? This paper clarifies it. Our solutions are based upon common guidelines for working in groups, supporting autistic people, and dealing with differences in perception. We hope it helps reduce the double empathy problem, starting from the non-autistic side. If students would read this paper, which we suggested in the first chapter, the gap could become even smaller.

Apart from autistic students, other groups of students could benefit from teachers applying these patterns. Think of students with ADHD (Attention Deficit Hyperactivity Disorder), hearing problems, grown up in a different country with different habits etc. Although they all experience different struggles, the solutions tend to be very similar: be clear. Even better news is that the patterns actually work for everyone, because who would complain about clear instructions?

Therefore, we can safely say that applying these patterns will benefit all. So try them, practice them, and share them. Maybe at first you will find it hard, outside of your comfort zone. But when you see a student shine, where at first you thought it impossible, you realize that it was worth every effort.

Working on a paper always includes thinking across its boundaries. Our goal was to provide guidelines on how to support autistic students in higher education. However, it might be interesting to investigate how non-STEM teachers might benefit from these patterns, or to what extent they are applicable to autistic people working in IT. Furthermore, some possibilities for new patterns emerged during writing: - What consists of a good reference book and how could you keep it up to date during a project? This closely connects to the LET'S GET IT CLEAR-pattern. - The solution to the pattern GET LOOSE, Change the way you ask questions, in fact, is a parent pattern. It's children could be worked out in patterns on their own.

Acknowledgments. Many thanks to:

– Our shepherd Diego Moreira da Rosa, Computing professor at the Federal Institute of Rio Grande do Sul (IFRS), who helped us improve our paper in the early stages.

– Rody Middelkoop, our much valued colleague at the HAN University of Applied Sciences, who has the incredible talent to draw what we think, while sharpening our thoughts at the same time.

– Judith Hovius, a treasured colleague at the Research Center in Flourishing with Autism, whose deep philosophical insight into human behavior has profoundly shaped our thinking about interaction between autistic and non-autistic people, especially in an educational environment.

– Joost Kraaijeveld for helping out with the images in the last days before the final version.

– Workshop G at EuroPlop 2025: Marc Schmidt, Mary Tedeschi, Diethelm Bienhaus, Petr Pícha, Premek Brada and Sridevi Ayloo.

Disclosure of Interests. The authors have no competing interests to declare that are relevant to the content of this article.

References

1. Apperly, I., Butterfill, S.: Do humans have two systems to track beliefs and belief-like states. Psychol. Rev. **116**(4), 953–970 (2009). https://doi.org/10.1037/a0016923. PMID 19839692
2. Bakker, T., Krabbendam, L., Bhulai, S., Begeer, S.: Background and enrollment characteristics of students with autism in higher education. Res. Autism Spectrum Disorders **67**, 101424 (2019). https://doi.org/10.1016/j.rasd.2019.101424, https://www.sciencedirect.com/science/article/pii/S1750946719301126
3. Bergin, J., et al.: Pedagogical patterns: advice for educators. Joseph Bergin Software Tools (2012)

4. Burdett, J.: Making groups work: university students' perceptions. Int. Electron. J. **4**(3), 177–191 (2003)
5. Burgstahler, S.E., Cory, R.C.: Universal Design in Higher Education: From Principles to Practice. Harvard Education Press (2010)
6. CAST: Universal design for learning guidelines version 3.0 (2024). https://udlguidelines.cast.org
7. CBS: Afgestudeerden in het hoger onderwijs (2023). https://www.cbs.nl/nl-nl/longread/rapportages/2023/afgestudeerden-in-het-hoger-onderwijs/2-afgestudeerden-in-het-hoger-onderwijs-in-studiejaar-2020-21
8. Dohn, H., Wagner, K.D.: Strategies and methods of teaching in contemporary higher education with reference to project work. Innovations Educ. Train. Int. **36**(4), 285–291 (1999). https://doi.org/10.1080/1355800990360404
9. Droney, C., Verbiest, A.: The eveyday autism handbook for schools- 60+ essntial guides to staff. Jessica kingsley Publishers (2022)
10. Fittipaldi, D.: Managing the dynamics of group projects in higher education: best practices suggested by empirical research. Univ. J. Educ. Res. **8**(5), 1778–1796 (2020)
11. Fleming, D.S.: A Teacher's Guide to Project-Based Learning. AEL Inc, Charleston, WV (2000)
12. Foucault, M.: Discipline and Punish: The Birth of the Prison. Pantheon Books (1977). originally published in 1975 as *Surveiller et punir*
13. Heasman, B., Gillespie, A.: Perspective-taking is two-sided: misunderstandings between people with and without autism involve both Partiesm. J. Autism Dev. Disord. **49**(10), 4050–4062 (2019)
14. Hinds, P.: The curse of expertise: the effects of expertise and debiasing methods on prediction of novice performance. J. Exp. Psychol. Appl. **5**(2), 205–221 (1999). https://doi.org/10.1037/1076-898X.5.2.205
15. Jacobs, T.: Grading individual students in software engineering projects confidently. In: Proceedings of the 29th European Conference on Pattern Languages of Programs, People, and Practices. EuroPLoP '24, New York, NY, USA.Association for Computing Machinery (2024). https://doi.org/10.1145/3698322.3698330
16. Jacobs, T., Van Heesch, U.: Supporting ICT-students to make the most out of their projects. In: Proceedings of the 27th European Conference on Pattern Languages of Programs. EuroPLop '22, Association for Computing Machinery, New York, NY, USA (2023). https://doi.org/10.1145/3551902.3551972, https://doi.org/10.1145/3551902.3551972
17. Jazayeri, M.: Combining mastery learning with project-based learning in a first programming course: an experience report. In: 2015 IEEE/ACM 37th IEEE International Conference on Software Engineering, vol. 2, pp. 315–318 (2015). https://doi.org/10.1109/ICSE.2015.163
18. MacLeod, A., Allan, J., Lewis, A., Robertson, C.: 'here i come again': the cost of success for higher education students diagnosed with autism. Int. J. Incl. Educ. **22**(6), 683–697 (2018)
19. Milton, D.: On the ontological status of autism: the 'double empathy problem. Disabil. Soc. **27**(6), 883–887 (2012)
20. Oudtshoorn, G., Hay, D.: Group work in higher education: a mismanaged evil or a potential good? South African J. Higher Educ. **18** (2004). https://doi.org/10.4314/sajhe.v18i2.25459
21. Sarrett, J.C.: Autism and accommodations in higher education: insights from the autism community. J. Autism Dev. Disord. **48**, 679–693 (2018)

22. Stuurman, S.: De kanarie in de schoolbanken- Een gids voor autisme-inclusief onderwijs. Amsterdam University Press (2024)
23. Toth, M.D., Sousa, D.A.: The power of student teams-Achieving social, emotional and cognitive learning in every classroom through academic education. Learning Sciences International (2019)
24. Tuckman, B.: Developmental sequence in small groups. Psychol. Bull. **63**(6), 384–399 (1965)
25. Van Hees, V., Moyson, T., Roeyers, H.: Higher education experiences of students with autism spectrum disorder: challenges, benefits and support needs. J. Autism Dev. Disord. **45**, 1673–1688 (2015)
26. Van Holten, M., Van Vliet, R.: Projectonderwijs in het HB)-De docent als projectontwikkelaar en projectbegeleider. Bohn Stafleu van Loghum (2009)
27. Waisman, T., Simmons, M.: Autism spectrum disorder and the implications for higher education. J. Educ. Thought (JET)/Revue de la Pensée Éducative **51**(3), 317–338 (2018)
28. Wellhausen, T., Fießer, A.: How to write a pattern? a rough guide for first-time pattern authors. In: Proceedings of the 16th European Conference on Pattern Languages of Programs, pp. 1–9 (2011)

A Pattern Collection for Generating Accessible Teaching Materials for Blind and Visually Impaired Students in Computer Science and Electrical Engineering

Diethelm Bienhaus(✉) and Michael Kreutzer

Technische Hochschule Mittelhessen, University of Applied Sciences, Giessen, Germany
{diethelm.bienhaus,michael.kreutzer}@mni.thm.dehttps://mni.thm.de

Abstract. Graphical representations such as circuit schematics, Karnaugh–Veitch (KV) maps, or Unied Modeling Language (UML) diagrams are widely used in computer science and engineering education. However, these visual formats are often inaccessible to blind and visually impaired (BVI) students, since they rely on visual perception for conveying both structure and semantics. Existing accessibility guidelines (e.g., WCAG) provide little support for subject-specific materials, leaving educators without actionable workflows for producing equivalent alternatives.

We contribute a collection of five pedagogical design patterns that enable accessible representations of diagrams, graphics, and numerical data in Science, Technology, Engineering, and Mathematics (STEM) teaching. The patterns address (1) transformable text-first authoring, (2) accessible diagram generation via textual modeling, (3) tactile and haptic rendering workflows, (4) audio-based representations of time-series and quantitative plots, and (5) human-in-the-loop generation of explanatory descriptions. Each pattern is derived from classroom practice, supplemented by tool recommendations and implementation examples.

Together, the collection provides a structured methodology for producing multi-modal STEM learning materials that are usable with screen readers, Braille displays, tactile printers, or sonification tools. While developed in the context of computer engineering education, the patterns generalize to other domains that rely on diagrammatic reasoning.

Keywords: accessibility · blind and visually impaired (BVI) · accessible teaching materials · STEM education · assistive technologies · artificial intelligence

T. Plummer et al. (Eds.): EuroPLoP 2025, LNCS 16494, pp. 254–279, 2026.
https://doi.org/10.1007/978-3-032-19157-1_12

Nomenclature

AI	articial intelligence
BVI	blind and visually impaired
MDS	Multimodal Diagrammatic System
HTML	Hypertext Markup Language
KV	Karnaugh Veitch
OOP	Object-Oriented Programming
STEM	Science, Technology, Engineering, and Mathematics
TML	textual modeling language
UML	Unied Modeling Language
UN-CRPD	United Nations Convention on the Rights of Persons with Disabilities
WHO	World Health Organization
WYSIWYG	What You See Is What You Get
XMI	XML Metadata Interchange

1 Introduction

Four years ago, we welcomed a blind student in the first-semester programming course, where object-oriented programming in Java is taught. In this course, class diagrams are used as graphical representations of classes and their relationships, and are typically developed manually on the blackboard.

This traditional teaching approach, which relies heavily on blackboard drawings, proved unsuitable for the blind student. This situation motivated the development of alternative solutions to ensure that course materials are accessible to blind and visually impaired learners.

In the following year, another blind student began studying computer science and enrolled in the course Technical Informatics. This course introduces electronic and logic circuits, which are first designed on the blackboard and then implemented and tested using simulation tools. KV maps, which provide a structured method for simplifying Boolean functions to minimal logical expressions, are also an essential part of the curriculum.

Here too, the challenge was evident: neither blackboard drawings nor graphical circuit diagrams, KV maps, or visual simulation tools are accessible to blind and visually impaired students.

In collaboration with colleagues and the students themselves, solutions were developed over the past few years that enabled blind students to access course materials containing graphical content in a barrier-free way. In addition, purely text-based collaboration methods were introduced, allowing blind, visually impaired, and sighted students to work together inclusively.

This paper presents these experiences – along with insights from other institutions and organizations – in the form of pedagogical patterns. The aim is to demonstrate that with freely available software tools and relatively little effort, effective solutions can be created to support the inclusion of blind and visually impaired learners.

2 Blind and Visually Impaired (BVI) Students in STEM

Science, Technology, Engineering, and Mathematics (STEM) disciplines are inherently visual. Fields such as computer science, electrical engineering, mathematics, and physics frequently rely on diagrams, schematics, graphs, charts, and other visual representations to convey complex concepts effectively. While these visual tools are valuable for sighted learners, they create significant barriers for students who are blind or have severe visual impairments. Limited access to visual information can hinder participation, comprehension, and achievement, thereby reducing educational and professional opportunities in STEM programs and careers [15,30].

Globally, individuals with visual impairments represent a substantial and growing population. The World Health Organization (WHO) reports that more than 2.2 billion people live with some form of vision impairment, including 43 million who are blind [32]. Despite international mandates for inclusive education, such as the United Nations Convention on the Rights of Persons with Disabilities (UN-CRPD) [29], students with visual disabilities remain underrepresented in STEM disciplines [28]. Key barriers include inaccessible instructional materials, limited availability of assistive technologies, insufficient educator training, and inconsistent institutional support [26].

Traditional STEM education depends heavily on blackboard drawings, printed diagrams, laboratory equipment, and digital visualizations. Graphical representations such as UML class diagrams, electronic circuit schematics, KV maps, molecular models, and data plots often lack standardized text-based equivalents. Although screen readers and refreshable Braille displays enable access to textual information, these tools cannot automatically interpret or convey the semantic content of images or diagrams [27]. As a result, blind and visually impaired students frequently rely on verbal descriptions from instructors or peers, which may be incomplete or difficult to comprehend without spatial context.

To address these challenges, researchers and educators have developed a range of accessibility strategies. Text-based approaches—for example, PlantUML for software diagrams [22], or netlist representations for electronic circuit design [3]—encode visual information in structured textual formats readable by screen readers. Tactile methods, including embossed graphics, swell paper, and 3D printing, create raised structures that can be explored through touch, enabling spatial understanding [13,19]. Multimodal systems combine auditory, haptic, and kinesthetic feedback to convey complex information dynamically, such as through sonification of graphs or interactive tactile displays [4,33]. Universal Design for Learning (UDL) further emphasizes creating materials accessible to all learners, reducing the need for individual adaptations [6].

Despite these advances, significant gaps remain. Many STEM courses continue to rely on inaccessible materials, and educators may lack the training or resources to implement inclusive practices effectively [26,28]. Moreover, tactile and multi-modal solutions often require specialized equipment and may not scale well in typical classroom settings. Addressing these issues requires coordinated efforts among institutions, educators, and technology developers to integrate accessible teaching tools into standard curricula.

The inclusion of blind and visually impaired students in STEM is not only a matter of equity but also a driver of innovation. Designing educational environments that accommodate diverse sensory modalities fosters more flexible, creative approaches to teaching and learning that benefit all students [4,13]. Continued research, collaboration, and policy support are critical to ensuring that visually impaired learners can participate fully and succeed in the increasingly technology-driven world of STEM.

3 Used Terms

Blindness and visual impairment are two related but distinct conditions. Blindness is a complete or nearly complete loss of vision, while visual impairment refers to a decreased ability to see, even with correction.[1]

Visually Impaired. "The term 'visually impaired' is used to indicate blind plus partially sighted people together." (Glossary of terms and acronyms in common use by the European Blind Union.)

Graphic. A graphic is a broad, general term for any visual representation of information, ideas, or data with the purpose of information and communication.

Diagram. A diagram is a type of graphic that illustrates e.g., the relationships or functions of a system, process, or concept. A diagram is an illustration following formal rules, commonly used in a technical domain. Examples from electronics and computer science are Circuit diagrams, State Charts, Flow Charts or UML (Unified Modeling Language) diagrams.

Drawing. A drawing is a manually or digitally created depiction representing e.g., objects, scenes, or ideas. Examples are technical drawings like blueprints or freehand sketches. Drawings do not follow a formal specification.

4 Pattern Collection

Core of Content provides a general approach. The three patterns Accessibility of Diagrams and Accessibility of Graphics introduce specialized solutions for different types of graphically represented teaching content. Graphics with Generated Explanation can be applied to gain accessibility of different types of graphics. Sonification of Time Series shows how time series can be made accessible to BVI people. Figure 1 illustrates the relationships between the five patterns.

[1] https://lifeafterblindness.com/understanding-the-differences-between-blindness-and-visual-impairment/.

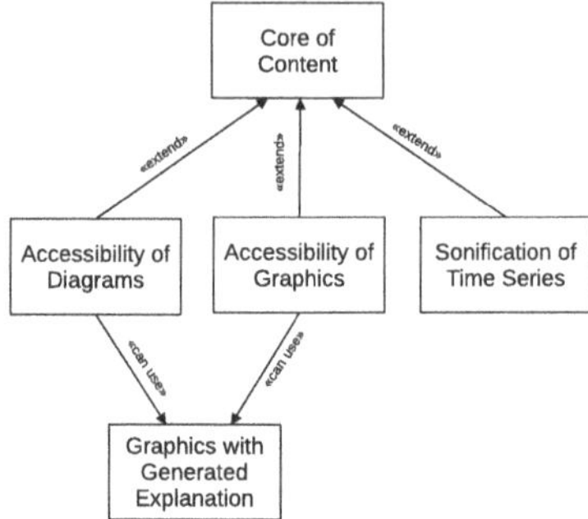

Fig. 1. Pattern relationships

Pattern 1: Core of Content

Context

Visually appealing course materials are a goal for many educators and are appreciated by students.

Graphically designed course materials are appealing for sighted people. Graphics support the content to be taught.

What You See Is What You Get (WYSIWYG) tools such as Word or PowerPoint make it very easy to place graphics almost anywhere.

Problem

Graphics are usually not accessible for the visually impaired. Text within graphics cannot be extracted by assistive tools.

Solution

Extract the core content of teaching materials and represent it in a multi-directionally transformable format.

First, eliminate all purely decorative graphics. Analyze whether and what information is conveyed by typographic layout. Identify the graphics that carry the content to be taught.

This paper distinguishes between diagrams and graphics. In case of diagrams that adhere to a formal specification, such specifications typically define formats for textual representation. These structured formats enable systematic interpretation, transformation, and accessibility enhancement through computational means. Pattern Accessibility of Diagrams presents solutions to gain accessibility for this type of diagrams.

By contrast, graphics such as photographs, freehand drawings, and various other illustrative visualizations do not follow a formal specification. As a result, there is no underlying metamodel that can be leveraged to interpret or describe their content programmatically. To make such unstructured graphics accessible—particularly for BVI students haptic solutions are a promising approach. Tactile representations provide a means of conveying the structural and spatial properties of these graphics in a non-visual form, as introduced in pattern Accessibility of Graphics .

Use simple, plain-text formats with minimal formatting whenever possible. Plain text is easy to process with screen readers, Braille displays, and text-to-speech tools, making it more accessible for BVI students. Markdown is a particularly suitable format. It offers basic yet effective formatting options and can be easily converted into various output formats such as HTML or PDF. However, purely textual materials may not be engaging for sighted students. They are accustomed to visually rich course materials, such as textbooks, handouts, and slide decks that follow well-designed layouts. To address this, rendering tools can be used to convert the core content into visually appealing formats. By generating PDFs or web-based HTML documents, course materials can be presented in a way that meets the expectations of sighted learners—without compromising accessibility.

Examples

Figure 2 shows an example of a graphic that is used only for decoration. Such graphics do not carry any content. If they are to be used for visual reasons, the graphic should be labeled as purely decorative in the text-only version of the course materials.

Fig. 2. Solely decorative image

Figure 3 shows an example where two small pictures are freely positioned on a slide. They illustrate the explanatory text left of them. However, they contribute to the content. Arrows point to the words "Dog" and "Human". The arrows shall visualize the relationships "generalization" and "specialization" between classes in object-oriented programming.

The words "Dog" and "Human" can be found by assisting tools. The arrows and the content of the small pictures are not accessible. Intended was an additional visualization of the concepts which are described in the text on the left side. It would be better to use diagrams whose structure is specified and which can be represented textually as introduced in the pattern Accessibility of Diagrams .

The author of the following slide (Fig. 4) has inserted a table as an image on the slide. Arrows point to areas of the image and link explanations to the actual elements of the table.

The table is not accessible for the visually impaired. Explanations are extracted as text by assistive systems. The assignments and the table cannot be extracted. It is better to insert the table as a textual table. Explanations should also be assigned to the contents of the table as text.

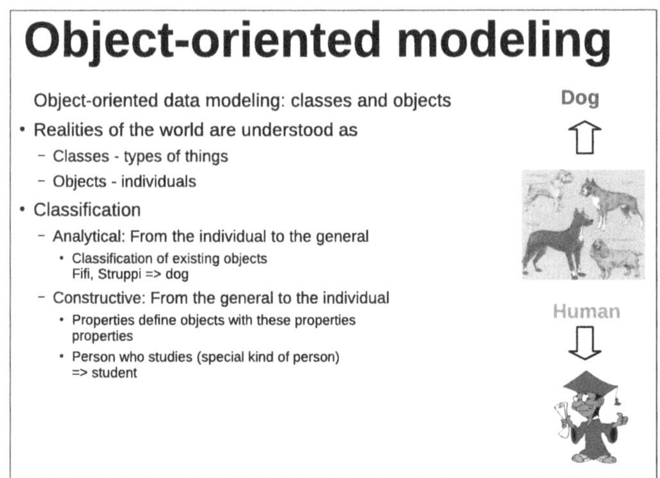

Fig. 3. Pictures and tool-accessible text placed freehand on a slide

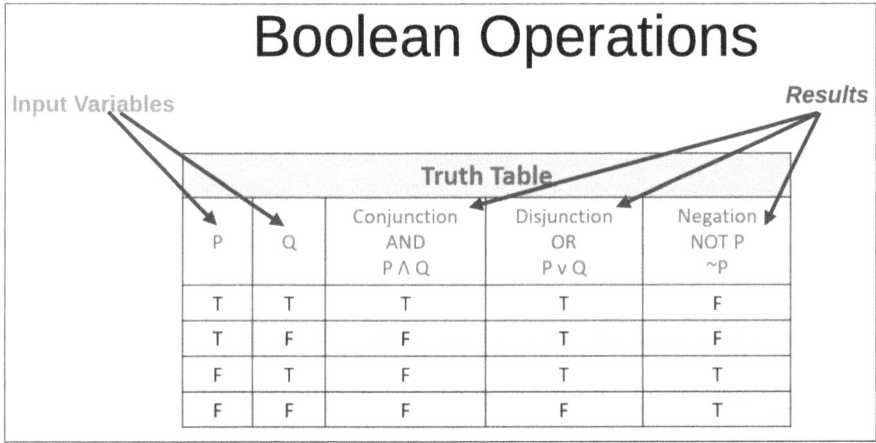

P	Q	Conjunction AND P ∧ Q	Disjunction OR P ∨ Q	Negation NOT P ~P
T	T	T	T	F
T	F	F	T	F
F	T	F	T	T
F	F	F	F	T

Fig. 4. Table included as an image and mixed with textual information on a slide (image source: www.onlinemathlearning.com/)

Markdown is designed to use a minimal set of tags. Hence, it is easier to parse when access is done via text-to-speech or is read on a Braille display. Tools like Pandoc[2] can convert markdown text in a variety of formats like PDF, Hypertext Markup Language (HTML) and office formats. As a result, it is possible to provide the clean text with the content for BVI students and to give the others rendered outputs (e.g., PDF).

[2] https://pandoc.org/.

Listing 1.1 shows the Markdown text which is rendered into the slide shown in Fig. 4 using Pandoc.

```
# Boolean Operations
Operation: Conjunction
Operation name: AND
Input Variables: P, Q
Operation formula: $P \land Q$

Truth table:
| P | Q | P AND Q |
|---|---|-----|
| 0 | 0 | 0   |
| 0 | 1 | 0   |
| 1 | 0 | 0   |
| 1 | 1 | 1   |
```

Listing 1.1. Markdown of the slide in Fig 4

This markdown is then converted into a slide in PDF using Pandoc with a user defined LaTeX Beamer template accomplishing the CI specifications of the university (Fig. 5).

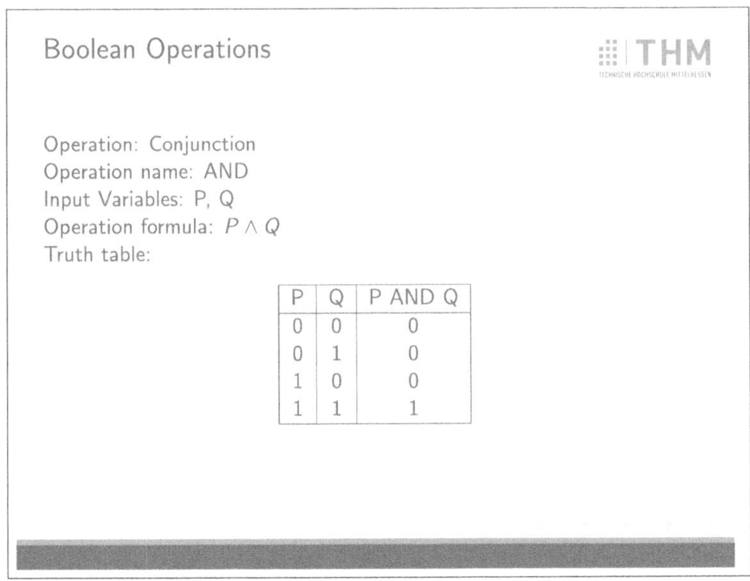

Fig. 5. Slide generated from markdown text

The slides have the usual layout for sighted students. The markdown text is provided for the visually impaired and is easily accessible for them using assistive technologies.

Consequences

+ Textual descriptions of graphics make them accessible for BVI learners
+ Various output channels such as Braille displays or text-to-speech can be used by BVI learners
+ Authors are encouraged to focus on the core content of the teaching materials
+ pure text based representations are independent from proprietary office tools and incompatibility problems can be avoided

- The creation of teaching materials takes longer
- Tool chains must be set up to generate teaching materials for sighted people
- Changes and corrections are more time-consuming during creation because the tool chain for generating teaching materials for sighted people must be triggered again and again
- Free manual placement of graphics on slides and other teaching materials is not possible
- Inserting content such as tables as screen shots from textbooks or websites should be avoided, but this leads to more work because the content has to be rewritten in text form
- Graphic design options such as placing arrows over graphics to visualize relationships are limited

Related Work

Prior research has demonstrated that single-source authoring can enable accessible learning materials for BVI students in STEM. The *PreTeXt* project illustrates how semantically structured source files can be transformed into multiple accessible outputs, including web, EPUB, and Braille, while maintaining consistency across modalities [2].

Complementary studies on lightweight markup (e.g., R Markdown) show that such workflows reduce authoring overhead and generate accessible HTML and PDF outputs that integrate well with screen readers [25].

For mathematical content, web-based outputs can rely on MathJax together with the Speech Rule Engine to provide adaptable accessibility features such as structural navigation and speech rendering, making them effective for non-visual exploration [7].

When PDF is required, LaTeX-based tool chains can embed tagged formulae to improve screen-reader access; however, these retrofits remain more fragile than web-first alternatives [1].

Pattern 2: Accessibility of Diagrams

Context

Diagrams are an important form of representation, especially in technical disciplines. They are used for communication between people and for documentation. Such diagrams are usually precisely specified.

In computer science, UML diagrams are widely used. There are specifications for UML. Formats are defined for the data exchange of UML models. Some software tools support code generation or reverse engineering.

In the first two semesters, it is mainly class diagrams that are taught.

Class diagrams primarily show the elements within classes and the relationships between classes as two-dimensional visual graphics.

Problem

Graphical representations of diagrams are not accessible to BVI learners.

Solution

Analyze which concepts are represented by the diagram and find a textual representation for them. Implicit information as expressed by the spatial arrangement of diagram elements can be made tangible with haptic interface devices.

Most software modeling tools use a textual storage format. These formats are often not designed for humans but are used for data exchange. One example is XML Metadata Interchange (XMI)[3] for the exchange of UML models. Model elements are represented textually as XML structures .

There are tools that use a simple textual representation that is easier for humans to read. UML4ALL, PlantUML and Mermaid are examples of such text based UML tools. These tools generate diagrams from the textual description for visual users. BVI learners can have the textual description read aloud using text-to-speech, use screen readers or read on Braille lines.

A two-dimensional graphic is perceived by sighted people by "jumping" between the spatially arranged elements with the eye. BVI learners have sequential, one-dimensional access to the textual description. In order not to increase the cognitive load unnecessarily, information on relationships between elements should be provided near to the description of the elements. The spatial arrangement of elements in a diagram often contains implicit information such as grouping or proximity of content. Such information can be made haptically accessible to BVI learners. Examples include 2D Braille displays or structured surfaces (Swell Touch Paper, 3D printing).

[3] https://www.omg.org/spec/XMI/.

Examples

Listing 1.2 is an example of a textual description following these recommendations and 6 shows the generated UML class diagram.

```
@startuml
class Person {
  + firstname: String
  + surname: String
}
class Student {
  + matriculationNumber: int
  + degreeProgram: String
}
Person ^-- Student
class Lecturer {
  + title: String
  + department: String
}
Person ^-- Lecturer
class Book {
  + title: String
  + ISBN: String
}
Student "1" o-- "n" Book
@enduml
```

Listing 1.2. PlantUML source code

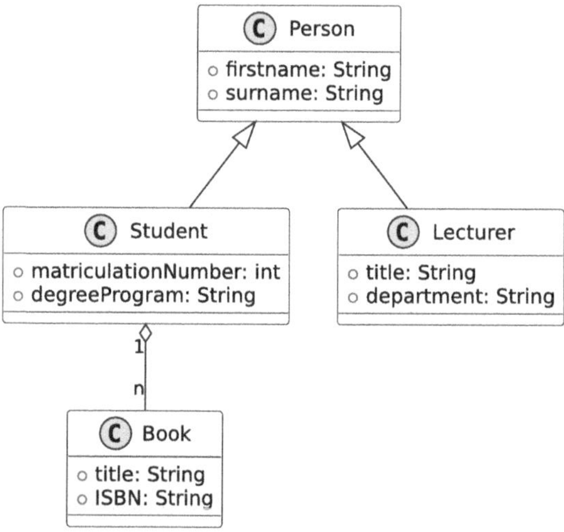

Fig. 6. Generated UML Class Diagram

Consequences

+ Multi-modal accessibility is achieved by making textual explanations of diagrams accessible using assistive technology.
+ Haptic devices can make information available that is contained in the spatial arrangement of elements in diagrams.
+ Textual descriptions of diagrams can be used in part to generate code.

- A new, purely text-based representation must be learned for the creation of teaching materials.
- Changes and corrections are often more time-consuming, as the graphic representation must be re-rendered after changes are made.
- Text-based exchange formats such as XMI are designed to be easily processed by software - but not primarily for human readability.

Related Work

In [9] a Multimodal Diagrammatic System (MDS) facilitates the perception of graphical information for BVI students by integrating multiple sensory modalities: visual, auditory, and haptic. The system generates an auditory representation of diagrams by means of programmatically generated sine wave tones. Simultaneously, haptic feedback is delivered via a vibration motor, triggered when a user's finger contacts specific x-y screen coordinates corresponding to points, lines, or curves.

In [17] the author present a project which makes the content of UML diagrams accessible for BVI students. In that project, a user interface for Windows was developed using the standard components of Microsoft Windows so that it is compatible with screen readers. This allows experienced users to use their usual screen reader. In addition, alternative interfaces such as spatial sound or a force feedback joystick are used to display spatial information on the diagram.

In [31] a solution is presented that allows visually impaired people easy access to class diagrams. It utilizes existing accessibility tools of current mobile devices. A physically tactile grid is attached over a tablet so that a tactile navigation is possible. By using Apple software, navigation can be carried out with the native VoiceOver solution, which is well known among visually impaired people. The authors developed a user interface which arranges classes in a grid. Detailed information is displayed in a separate area, which can be navigated using the VoiceOver system. In studies, the authors have compared their solution with the textual modeling language (TML) PlantUML. Across several studies, the authors found that their solution is often better suited to new users, as it significantly lowers the learning curve compared to PlantUML.

PATTERN 3: ACCESSIBILITY OF GRAPHICS

Context

Graphics constitute a fundamental modality of visual representation for sighted individuals. They are deeply integrated into everyday life, appearing in various forms such as city maps, architectural floor plans, and numerous types of instructional illustrations.

In educational contexts, graphical representations are extensively employed in teaching materials at both school and university levels. These include diagrams, sketches, and technical drawings, which are often created using software tools or produced as freehand illustrations.

Problem

However, non-textual content, such as images, maps, charts, and diagrams, remains largely inaccessible to BVI students. This inaccessibility presents a significant barrier to information acquisition and equal participation in educational and professional environments.

Solution

Provide textual, tactile, or auditory access to information represented visually in graphics.

In HTML files the so called "alt text" (alternative text) can give an additional text-based descriptions of visual details of an image. Originally intended to give some information if the HTML page is not loaded properly. Such descriptions are useful to provide accessible information for people who are visually impaired. This approach can be applied in other formats, too.

Important authoritative regulatory and guideline documents for "alt-text" are W3C: "Web Content Accessibility Guidelines (WCAG)"[4], W3C WAI: "Resources on Alternative Text for Images"[5], W3C WAI: "Understanding Guideline 1.1: Text Alternatives"[6], and UN-CRPD: "The Convention on the Rights of Persons with Disabilities" [7]

To make graphics perceivable through touch, they must be converted into raised, tangible structures. Color gradients present a significant challenge in this context. Instead, black-and-white graphics composed of lines, contours, and strokes are generally more suitable for tactile representation.

For more complex graphics that include areas beyond simple contours, the first step is to identify the edges of shapes. Many software tools begin this process by converting images into grayscale. Edge detection filters are then applied to extract outlines and essential details. Once the graphic is sufficiently simplified, it can be transformed into a tactile format using raised structures.

[4] https://www.w3.org/TR/WCAG21/.

[5] https://www.w3.org/WAI/alt/.

[6] https://www.w3.org/WAI/WCAG22/Understanding/text-alternatives.

[7] https://social.desa.un.org/issues/disability/crpd/convention-on-the-rights-of-persons-with-disabilities-crpd.

Additional information about a graphic can be embedded as metadata. Assistive technologies such as 2D Braille displays can then present this information as text or audio output.

Emerging articial intelligence (AI) technologies are increasingly capable of interpreting and describing graphics. These advancements offer promising solutions for making visual content more accessible to BVI students.

One solution for creating raised structures on paper is the use of Swell Touch Paper. This special paper can be printed on using standard printers or written on with a pen. When heat is applied, the printed areas expand, forming raised contours that are easily perceivable by touch.

3D printers have also gained popularity as a tool for producing tactile graphics. They allow for the creation of detailed contours and textures. Educational materials printed in this way are durable and can be reused over extended periods.

Electronic tactile displays, such as 2D Braille displays, provide dynamic tactile feedback. These devices can render static or even animated graphics in real time. They work by precisely raising and lowering an array of pins to create touchable images and patterns.

Examples

An alternative text for Fig. 6 is generated using a web-site that supports generating alt-text by means of AI[8] devices. The generated alt-text:

> UML class diagram showing Person superclass with subclasses Student and Lecturer; Student linked to multiple Books with attributes like title and ISBN.

Class members were unfortunately suppressed by this tool.

Prompt for chatGPT: "write a alt-text for a html web site describing this diagram". Answer:

> UML class diagram showing four classes and their attributes. The classes are Person (attributes: firstname, surname), Student (matriculationNumber, degreeProgram), Lecturer (title, department), and Book (title, ISBN). Student and Lecturer both inherit from Person. There is an association from Person to Book indicating that one person can be linked to many books (1 to n).

This description contains the details of the class diagram.

PunktBilder is a software developed at the centre for blind persons (BliZ) at THM. The *PunktBilder* software is used to create tactile images for BVI students at THM. Images are displayed in *PunktBilder* (Figs. 7, 8) and can control 2D Braille displays.

Consequences

+ Multi-modal accessibility is achieved by making textual explanations of graphics accessible using assistive technology.
+ Generative AI can take over the creation of textual descriptions of graphics for authors.

---

[8] https://barrierefreies.design/werkzeuge/ki-generator-alternativer-text-von-bildern.

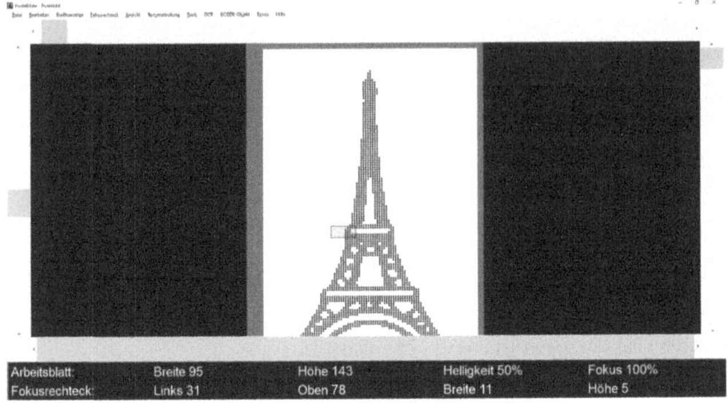

Fig. 7. Screenshot from the *PunktBilder* application (Source: THM/BliZ)

Fig. 8. Dot pattern for the logo of the THM (left), converted with *PunktBilder* for a 2D Braille display (right) (Source: THM / BliZ)

+ The use of 'alt text' in HTML documents better fulfills regulatory requirements for accessibility.

- The manual creation of textual descriptions of graphics is time-consuming, and consideration must be given to which aspects and content of a graphic are significant.
- The automatic generation of textual descriptions Generative AI should be checked by authors for content accuracy.
- Devices for the production of tactile output formats such as 3D printers or thermal printers are expensive and complex to use.
- Devices for dynamically changeable tactile outputs are expensive and require special software to control them.

Related Work

Non-profit organizations like *ProBlind*[9] are actively working to improve access to graphics for blind and visually impaired individuals. As part of a global community initiative, they are developing a free online database of tactile graphics,

[9] https://www.problind.org/en/.

accessible worldwide. They have developed a tool chain to convert graphics into tactile graphics, as shown in Fig. 9.

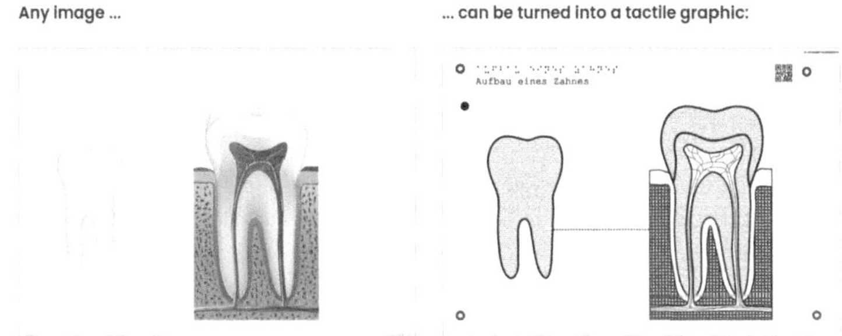

Fig. 9. Generation of tactile graphics (Screenshot from `www.problind.org`)

Many other schools for the blind and organizations that support the blind and visually impaired provide libraries of graphics that can be printed as tactile graphics.

In [21] the accessibility challenges faced by visually impaired people in interpreting graphical data, such as images and maps, is addressed. Their solution introduces the concept of a tactile gist as a simplified, touch-based representation of essential visual information. Based on experiments with VIP participants, the study establishes new design rules for 2D tactile representations using two mediums: thermo-formed paper and a force-feedback tablet called F2T.

In [12] this Force-Feedback Tablet (F2T) is introduced. The F2T's architecture is based on a flat thumb-stick mounted on a 2D actuated support, enabling force feedback effects on user's finger.

In [10] the challenge of accessibility of maps is addressed. The authors pointed out, that mobility and orientation are major challenges for visually impaired individuals. Primarily because verbal descriptions and GPS systems do not effectively convey spatial layouts. Unlike sighted individuals who rely on visual perception or maps, visually impaired people face limited access to geographical maps, which significantly impacts their mobility. The authors review various accessible interactive map solutions developed for visually impaired users, including a range of prototypes such as 3D-printed maps and devices with dynamically actuated structures.

Pattern 4: Sonification of Time Series

Context
Time series are widely used in science and engineering. Examples are the results of experiments, laboratory analyses or simulation results. Such data is usually represented as a sequence of tuples (time | value). To analyze and interpret such results, they are displayed visually as graphs.

Problem
Graphical representations of time series are not accessible for BVI students and people in general. A sequential output of the data on Braille lines or by means of text-to-speech is not well suited to represent and convey the time based aspect of the data.

Solution
Provide sonifications of time series.
Sonification is the use of non-speech audio to convey information. For a time series $x(t)$, data points can be mapped to sound parameters: amplitude, rate of change, loudness or stereo position etc. BVI students can listen as time unfolds, effectively hearing the trend.

Advanced sonification techniques comprise spatial audio (3D audio, auralization), where time or value is represented by left-right panning for added dimensionality.

Examples
Highcharts[10], in collaboration with the Sonification Lab at the Georgia Institute of Technology, has developed a free tool that enables the exploration of time series as charts and their sonification, employing sound as a medium for data visualization.

The charging of a capacitor is covered in STEM courses for several reasons: it illustrates central concepts important in many disciplines, such as the creation of differential equations or the modeling and simulation of technical systems.

Figure 12 shows a typical circuit for charging a capacitor via a resistor. The time constant τ is calculated from the product of the capacitance C and the resistance value R: $\tau = R * C$. The charging curve is described by the following formula:

$$U(t) = U_0 * (1 - e^{-\frac{t}{\tau}})$$

Listing 1.3 shows the first 20 entries of a time series of charging a capacitor via a resistor($\delta t = 0.1$, $\tau = 2$).

[10] https://www.highcharts.com/.

```
t,U
0,0
0.1,0.48770575499286
0.2,0.951625819640405
0.3,1.39292023574942
0.4,1.81269246922018
0.5,2.21199216928595
0.6,2.59181779318282
0.7,2.95311910281287
0.8,3.29679953964361
0.9,3.62371848378227
1,3.93469340287367
1.1,4.23050189619513
1.2,4.51188363905974
1.3,4.77954223238984
1.4,5.03414696208591
1.5,5.27633447258985
1.6,5.50671035882778
1.7,5.72585068051273
1.8,5.93430340259401
```

Listing 1.3. time series of charging a capacitor

This time series was imported and Highcharts generated the chart shown in Fig. 10. On top of the page, there are the buttons for playing the sound: Play, Stop and Loop.

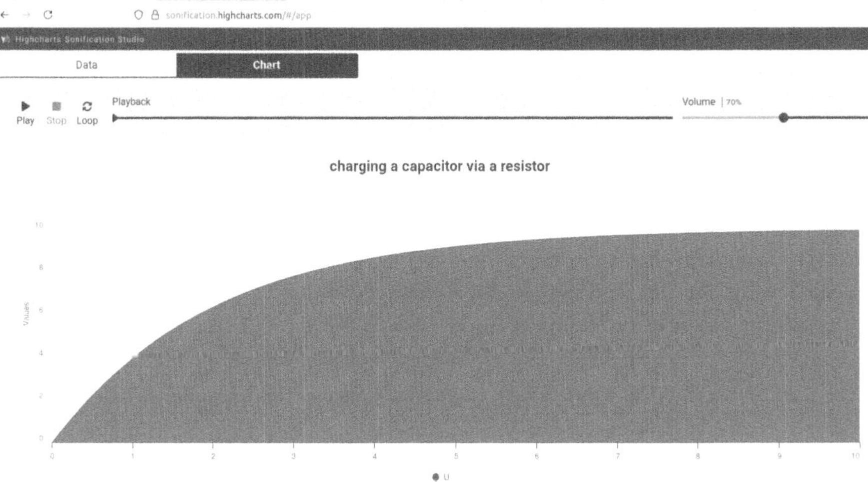

Fig. 10. Screenshot from the sonification web site

Consequences

+ Time series usually contain the temporal progression of signals; sonification allows the dimension of time to be experienced intuitively.
+ Some tools allow the playback speed to be adjusted or zoomed in on specific points in time.
+ Web-based solutions are easy to use for sonification and are usually easily accessible.

- Understanding and correctly interpreting audible time series requires experience and training, among other things.
- Devices for spatial audio reproduction are more expensive than normal headphones.
- Sonification software usually needs to be installed, and training in the use of the software is necessary.

Related Work
In [23] Physical-computing Streaming Sensor data Toolkit (PSST) is introduced. This toolkit enables BVI developers to create accessible representations of real-time sensor data. PSST allows users to filter, highlight, and transform time series of raw or computed sensor values into different output formats including tonal sonification, non-speech audio, speech, and SVG files for tactile displays.

in [5] SonoUno is presented. It is a sonification software for astronomical data presented on a table (txt or csv files). Goal of the project is enabling accessibility to scientific data, from the Earth or with instruments on board of satellites. Such data is available in databases such as Simbad, NASA, ESA, among others.

The study presented in [18] tested the hypothesis that musical sonification can serve as an effective alternative to visualizing time-series data when visual representation is unavailable or not accessible especially for BVI people. The authors developed a time-series sonification method that can translate both univariate and multi-variate time series into a musical format.

In [8] a study examining the educational outcomes of BVI children aged 0 to 8 learning sonification concepts is presented. BVI children face significant barriers to participating in Science, Technology, Engineering, and Mathematics (STEM) education and careers, which have traditionally depended on visually based information. The authors had developed an app "Sonoplanet" for the sonification in an educational context.

Pattern 5: Graphics with Generated Explanation

Context

Graphics are an important way of presenting information for sighted people. Images are frequently used in electronic media such as websites and online platforms. In teaching, images are often used in web-based materials to convey content. Other digital resources - such as lecture notes, exercise sheets and presentation slides - also tend to contain a variety of images, graphics and illustrations.

Problem

Although electronic media can be made accessible to blind and visually impaired users through the use of assistive technologies, this does not usually work for the graphic components embedded in these media. As a result, the information conveyed by visual representations often remains inaccessible to people with visual impairments.

Solution

Augment visually represented information with a generated and verified textual description.

In HTML files the so called "alt text" (alternative text) can give an additional text-based descriptions of visual details of an image. Originally this "alt text" is intended to give some information if the HTML page is not loaded properly. Such descriptions are useful to provide accessible information for people who are visually impaired. This approach can be applied to other formats, too.

Additional information about a graphic can be embedded as metadata. Assistive technologies such as 2D Braille displays can then present this information as text or text-to-speech tool can produce audio output.

Emerging artificial intelligence technologies are increasingly capable of interpreting and describing graphics. These advancements offer promising solutions for making visual content more accessible to blind and visually impaired individuals.

Examples

Figure 3 illustrates the problem of mixing text which can be found by assisting tools within a picture. e.g., a text-to-speech tool will say"Dog" without a contextual relation. A solution would be a picture in a pixel image format and additional the picture describing text. Artificial intelligence tools can generate such texts. Generated texts should be checked by the authors.

Figure 11 shows a .png picture from a programming teaching slide illustrating the concept of Instantiation. The arrow follows the UML specification.

Fig. 11. Visualization of the concept of instantiation in object-oriented programming

Here a generated description of this picture (chatGPT):

> This image is a visual metaphor for the Object-Oriented Programming (OOP) concept of instantiation.
>
> Description:
>
> - At the top of the image, there's a gray box labeled "Dog", which represents a class in OOP.
>
> - Below it, there is a picture of different dog breeds (e.g., Boxer, Cocker Spaniel, etc.).
>
> - A dashed arrow labeled <<instantiate>> points from the dog images to the class "Dog", indicating that these individual dogs are instances (objects) of the class.

Simulation of electronic circuits is an important topic in technical electronics and technical informatics. Figure 12 shows a screenshot of a circuit and a simulation result using the simulation tool LT-Spice.

An AI-generated description of this figure can be improved if the context is given in the prompt: "explain this figure in the context of technical electronics"

Answer from chatGPT:

> This figure illustrates the behavior of a simple RC (Resistor-Capacitor) charging circuit, commonly studied in technical electronics to understand transient response in linear time-invariant systems.
>
> Left Side: Circuit Diagram

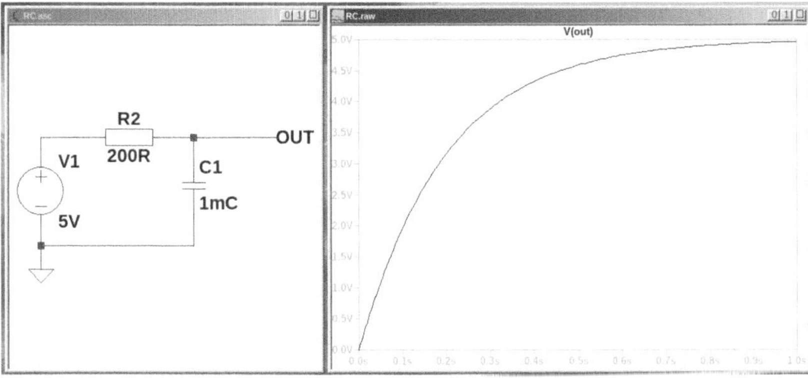

Fig. 12. Screenshot of Circuit and Timeline Graph

The left side of the figure shows the schematic diagram of an RC circuit. It consists of:

- A DC voltage source $V_1 = 5\,\mathrm{V}$
- A resistor $R_2 = 200\,\Omega$
- A capacitor $C_1 = 1\,\mathrm{mF}$

The resistor and capacitor are connected in series, and the voltage across the capacitor (marked as `OUT`) is observed over time. This configuration is typically used to study the charging process of a capacitor.

Right Side: Voltage-Time Plot

The right side of the figure displays the simulation output: a voltage-time plot of V_{out}, the voltage across the capacitor, from $t = 0$ to $t = 1$ second.

The voltage exhibits an exponential rise, which is characteristic of a capacitor charging through a resistor. The governing equation is:

$$V(t) = V_{\mathrm{source}} \cdot \left(1 - e^{-t/RC}\right)$$

where:

- $V_{\mathrm{source}} = 5\,\mathrm{V}$
- $R = 200\,\Omega$
- $C = 1\,\mathrm{mF}$
- $\tau = RC = 0.2\,\mathrm{s}$ is the time constant

At approximately $t = \tau$, the capacitor reaches about 63% of its final value. The graph confirms that the capacitor voltage asymptotically approaches 5V, with the majority of charging occurring within the first second.

...

It serves as a fundamental demonstration of key concepts including time constants, exponential behavior, and transient analysis in electrical circuits.

Consequences

+ The use of ‘alt text’ in HTML documents ensures that regulatory requirements for accessibility are better met.
+ Generative AI can be used by authors to create textual descriptions.
+ Generative AI tools can be integrated into your own applications. For example, a Python script can be used to add excellent"alt text" to entire folders full of images.
+ The generated explanation is not only helpful for blind and visually impaired people to gain access to the illustration. Sighted students can also benefit from this description.

– Automatically generated descriptions should be checked by authors to ensure that the content is correct.

Related Work
The generation of explanatory text for graphics has been studied from both automated and human-centered perspectives. Evaluations of automatic image captioning systems show that while machine-generated descriptions can provide basic accessibility, their quality often lacks accuracy and specificity, highlighting the need for human editorial review [20]. Complementary research on alternative text creation documents the roles and processes through which authors, editors, and reviewers collaboratively ensure reliable descriptions, emphasizing that “alt text” production is a socio-technical practice rather than a purely technical task [11]. In addition, user studies with blind and visually impaired participants underline that effective descriptions must focus on data content, task relevance, and structural clarity rather than only surface-level visual features [14]. Together, these findings support our approach of combining automated captioning with human-in-the-loop validation to ensure pedagogically useful and trustworthy explanations of graphics.

5 Conclusion and Future Work

This pattern collection presents simple solutions that make it easier for blind and visually impaired people to access graphically represented technical content with little effort.

The proposed solutions – PlantUML or YAML formats for UML class diagrams, simplified LTspice netlists for electronic circuits, Java-based templates for logic circuits, and structured Markdown for KV maps – were derived from four years of practical experience with blind students in programming and technical informatics courses.

Structured interviews confirmed that these approaches are comprehensible, practical, and pedagogically effective, significantly lowering accessibility barriers and fostering inclusion in mixed-ability classrooms. Notably, the extracted textual content has proven valuable not only to visually impaired learners but also to sighted students, who appreciate the concise and well-structured representations. Our approach helps to create easy accessible course content using open source tools, ensuring equitable participation for blind, visually impaired, and sighted students alike.

Building on this foundation, future work will explore the integration of generative artificial intelligence (AI) to further enhance accessibility. Our current work includes the automated generation of textual descriptions for graphical content and the creation of audio podcasts from course materials and textbooks to enable multi-modal access for a broader range of learners.

Generative AI for accessible content production has recently gained significant attention as a promising strategy for reducing educational barriers. Research demonstrates that large language models and image-to-text systems can automatically generate alternative text, audio descriptions, or multi-modal summaries, thereby supporting blind and visually impaired learners in STEM and other fields [16,24].

Upcoming research will therefore expand the existing pattern collection with new solutions leveraging AI-driven methods, investigate hybrid approaches that combine text-based formats with haptic or auditory feedback. Findings will be used to extend this pattern collection.

Acknowledgements. Many thanks to my shepherd Ralf Laue for the really helpful comments and hints. And many thanks to the members of our workshop at EuroPLoP 2025: Tineke Jacobs, Marc Schmidt, Mary Tedeschi, Daniel Pinho, Petr Pícha, Filipe Correia and Premek Brada.

References

1. Armano, T., Capietto, A., Coriasco, S., Murru, N., Ruighi, A., Taranto, E.: An automatized method based on latex for the realization of accessible pdf documents containing formulae. In: Computers Helping People with Special Needs (ICCHP 2018), Part II. Lecture Notes in Computer Science, vol. 10896, pp. 583–589. Springer (2018). https://doi.org/10.1007/978-3-319-94277-3_91
2. Austin, D., Beezer, R., Cantino, M., Kolesnikov, A., Maneki, A., Sorge, V.: Pretext as authoring format for accessible alternative media. In: Computers Helping People with Special Needs (ICCHP 2024), Part I. Lecture Notes in Computer Science, vol. 14750, pp. 184–191. Springer (2024). https://doi.org/10.1007/978-3-031-62846-7_22
3. Bienhaus, D., Kreutzer, M., von Zabiensky, F.: Accessible representations of visual artifacts in technical informatics education. In: Proceedings of the International Conference on Computers Helping People with Special Needs (ICCHP) (2023)
4. Brock, A.M., Jouffrais, C.: Interactive audio-tactile maps for visually impaired people. In: Proceedings of the 17th International Conference on Human-Computer Interaction, pp. 17–28 (2015). https://doi.org/10.1145/2850440.2850441
5. Casado, J., García, B., Gandhi, P., Díaz-Merced, W.: A new approach to sonification of astrophysical data: the user centred design of sonouno. Am. J. Astronomy Astrophy. **9**(4), 42 (2021). https://doi.org/10.11648/j.ajaa.20210904.11

6. CAST: Universal design for learning guidelines version 2.2 (2018). http://udlguidelines.cast.org
7. Cervone, D., Sorge, V.: Adaptable accessibility features for mathematics on the web. In: Proceedings of the 16th Web for All Conference (W4A '19), pp. 17:1–17:4. ACM (2019). https://doi.org/10.1145/3315002.3317567
8. Damsma, P.: Hearing a circle: an exploratory study of accessible sonification for young children with blindness and low vision. Br. J. Vis. Impair. **43**(3), 597–616 (2025). https://doi.org/10.1177/02646196241253534
9. Doore, S.A., Dimmel, J.K., Kaplan, T., Guenther, B.A., Giudice, N.A.: Multimodality as universality: designing inclusive accessibility to graphical information. Front. Educ. **8** (2023). https://doi.org/10.3389/feduc.2023.1071759
10. Ducasse, J., Brock, A.M., Jouffrais, C.: accessible interactive maps for visually impaired users. In: Pissaloux, E., Velázquez, R. (eds.) Mobility of Visually Impaired People, pp. 537–584. Springer, Cham (2018). https://doi.org/10.1007/978-3-319-54446-5_17
11. Edwards, W., Wu, A., Stangl, A., Bigham, J.P.: How the alt text gets made: roles and processes of alternative text creation. ACM Trans. Comput. Hum. Int. **30**(3), 1–37 (2023). https://doi.org/10.1145/3577008
12. Gay, S., Pissaloux, E., Romeo, K., TRUONG, N.T.: F2t: a novel force-feedback haptic architecture delivering 2d data to visually impaired people. IEEE Access **PP**, 1–1 (2021). https://doi.org/10.1109/ACCESS.2021.3091441
13. Giudice, N.A., Legge, G.E.: Blind navigation and the role of technology. IEEE Trans. Neural Syst. Rehabil. Eng. **26**(6), 1203–1215 (2018)
14. Jung, C., Mehta, S., Kulkarni, A., Zhao, Y., Kim, Y.S.: Communicating visualizations without visuals: investigation of visualization alternative text for people with visual impairments. arXiv preprint arXiv:2108.00141 (2021). https://arxiv.org/abs/2108.00141
15. Kamei, T., et al.: Barriers and supports for students with visual impairments in stem. J. Visual Impair. Blindness **115**(2), 97–109 (2021)
16. Karamolegkou, A., et al.: Evaluating multimodal language models as visual assistants for visually impaired users. In: Che, W., Nabende, J., Shutova, E., Pilehvar, M.T. (eds.) Proceedings of the 63rd Annual Meeting of the Association for Computational Linguistics, vol. 1, pp. 25949–25982. Association for Computational Linguistics, Vienna (2025). https://doi.org/10.18653/v1/2025.acl-long.1260
17. King, A.: Re-presenting visual content for blind people. Phd thesis, University of Manchester (2007). https://www.alasdairking.me.uk/research/PhD.htm
18. Last, M., Usyskin Gorelik, A.: Listen to the sound of data. In: Baughman, A.K., Gao, J., Pan, J.-Y., Petrushin, V.A. (eds.) Multimedia Data Mining and Analytics, pp. 419–446. Springer, Cham (2015). https://doi.org/10.1007/978-3-319-14998-1_19
19. Lazar, J., et al.: Swell paper and tactile graphics for blind learners: a review. Br. J. Vis. Impair. **35**(3), 219–233 (2017)
20. Leotta, F., et al.: Evaluating the effectiveness of automatic image captioning for web accessibility. Univ. Access Inf. Soc. (2023). https://doi.org/10.1007/s10209-023-00999-3
21. Pissaloux, E., et al.: A new approach to assist virtual image accessibility for visually impaired people. In: Antona, M., Stephanidis, C. (eds.) Universal Access in Human-Computer Interaction. User and Context Diversity. pp. 251–261. Springer International Publishing, Cham (2022)
22. PlantUML: Open source tool for UML diagrams (2023). https://plantuml.com

23. Potluri, V., et al.: PSST: enabling blind or visually impaired developers to author sonifications of streaming sensor data. In: ACM UIST (2022). https://doi.org/10.1145/3526113.3545700, https://www.microsoft.com/en-us/research/publication/psst-enabling-blind-or-visually-impaired-developers-to-author-sonifications-of-streaming-sensor-data/
24. Schauer, S., Simbeck, K., Schüssler, L.: Generating accessibility: Using ai to improve higher education for the visually impaired. In: du Boulay, B., Mascio, T.D., Tovar, E., Meinel, C. (eds.) Proceedings of the 17th International Conference on Computer Supported Education - Volume 1: CSEDU. vol. 1, pp. 15–25. SciTePress, Porto (2025). https://doi.org/10.5220/0013136300003932
25. Seo, J., McCurry, S.: Latex is not easy: creating accessible scientific documents with r markdown. J. Technol. Persons Disabil. **7**, 157–171 (2019). https://scholarworks.calstate.edu/concern/publications/v118rj164
26. Smith, D., Kelly, S.: Barriers to participation for students with visual impairments in STEM. J. Blindness Innov. Res. **7**(2) (2017)
27. Stefik, A., et al.: Accessible multifaceted graphics for blind students. In: Proceedings of the 12th International ACM SIGACCESS Conference, pp. 47–54 (2007). https://doi.org/10.1109/ICPC.2007.42
28. Supalo, C.A., Kennedy, S.H.: Using adaptive technologies to teach chemistry to students who are blind or visually impaired. J. Chemic. Educ. **89**(1), 28–32 (2012). https://doi.org/10.14448/jsesd.05.0004
29. United Nations: convention on the rights of persons with disabilities (2006). https://www.un.org/development/desa/disabilities/convention-on-the-rights-of-persons-with-disabilities.html
30. Wentz, B., Lazar, J., Stein, M.: Accessibility of web-based STEM education for students with disabilities. ACM Trans. Accessible Comput. **5**(3), 1–27 (2014)
31. Wildhaber, F., Salloum, N., Gygli, M., Kennel, A.: Self-directed creation and editing of uml class diagrams on mobile devices for visually impaired people. In: IEEE Tenth International Model-Driven Requirements Engineering (MoDRE) (2020). https://doi.org/10.1109/MODRE51215.2020.00012
32. World Health Organization: world report on vision (2021). https://www.who.int/publications/i/item/world-report-on-vision
33. Zhao, H., et al.: Designing interactive sonification for the blind. In: CHI '08 Extended Abstracts on Human Factors in Computing Systems, pp. 3249–3254 (2008). https://doi.org/10.1145/1352782.1352786

Patterns for Teaching Agile with Student Projects – Team and Project Setup

Daniel Pinho[1,2], Petr Pícha[3(✉)], Filipe F. Correia[1,2], and Přemek Brada[3]

[1] Faculty of Engineering, University of Porto, Porto, Portugal
{daniel.pinho,filipe.correia}@fe.up.pt
[2] INESC TEC, Porto, Portugal
[3] University of West Bohemia in Pilsen, Pilsen, Czechia
{ppicha,brada}@kiv.zcu.cz

Abstract. Higher education courses teaching about agile software development (ASD) have increased in commonality as the ideas behind the Agile Manifesto became more commonplace in the industry. However, a lot of the literature on how ASD is applied in the classroom does not provide much actionable advice, focusing on frameworks or even moving beyond the software development area into teaching in an agile way. We, therefore, showcase early work on a pattern language that focuses on teaching ASD practices to university students, which stems from our own experiences as educators in higher education contexts. We present five patterns, specifically focused on team and project setup phase: CAPPING TEAM SIZE, SMALLER PROJECT SCOPE, BUSINESS NON-CRITICAL PROJECT, SELF-ASSEMBLING TEAMS, and TEAM CHOOSES TOPIC as a starting point for developing the overall pattern language.

Keywords: Agile Software Development · Higher Education · Patterns · Student Team Projects

1 Introduction

As the principles behind the Agile Manifesto [2] grew in popularity in the software industry, higher education courses on agile software development (ASD) have become more and more common [14]. A wide variety of literature on how Agile is found in the classroom does not provide directly actionable advice, focusing on frameworks [18], exploring team dynamics [17], and even moving beyond the software development area [13] into teaching in an agile way.

In this paper, we present the first steps towards a pattern language focused on courses teaching ASD practices to university students, showcasing a subset of patterns in the language. These patterns come from our own experiences as educators at the University of Porto and the University of West Bohemia in Pilsen, working with students in bachelor's and master's software engineering courses.

T. Plummer et al. (Eds.): EuroPLoP 2025, LNCS 16494, pp. 280–306, 2026.
https://doi.org/10.1007/978-3-032-19157-1_13

Our working definition of "agile courses" (and similar) within the context of this and following papers on the pattern language covers all higher education software engineering courses that include teaching the principles and/or practices of agile development, from general adaptability of the process to change to specifics, like sprint retrospectives, stand-ups, backlog refinement, and so on. We see learning Agile in this sense as a valuable outcome for the students, not only because agile methodologies are prevalent in practice, but also as the ability to adopt one's process to fit current circumstances while keeping on the path to set goals is a good skill to have in general. As such, proper guidance for teachers on how to facilitate this learning is a worthwhile effort and sorely needed.

The patterns in this work target an audience of university professors and teachers who either teach project-based software engineering courses with agile elements (or a whole process) looking to improve or validate their approach, or are building a similar course looking for guidance and support. We chose this target audience for the patterns because they, the educators, are the ones who have the most control over the students' working environment and, as such, can take action directly in an impactful way.

However, the specific patterns described in this paper are not strictly Agile-related and can be used in any course with collaborative student projects. This is due to these patterns dealing with the stage of setting up the teams, gathering project topics and assigning them. Agile practices are not in strong effect in this phase but it is a necessary ground work for further patterns in our proposed language, which will be the focus of future work.

The remainder of this work is structured as follows. Section 2 explores related work and background for this paper. Section 3 introduces the pattern language, describes its sources 3.1, the template used 3.2 and the common context for all the patterns within 3.3. Section 4 then showcases the five patterns we are presenting: CAPPING TEAM SIZE (4.1) sets a boundary on the student project team. SMALLER PROJECT SCOPE (4.2) discusses how large in scope should projects be to maintain reachable learning objectives. BUSINESS NON-CRITICAL PROJECT (4.3) advises customers (internal and/or external) to propose project topics that are not business-critical but still bring value. SELF-ASSEMBLING TEAMS (4.4) argues for giving students the freedom to form their own teams. TEAM CHOOSES TOPIC (4.5) advocates that students have a say in the topics they work on to increase their buy-in. Finally, in Sect. 5 we draw our conclusions from this work and propose future research.

2 Related Work

We found a lack of existing literature on teaching agile practices and processes with projects that would present guidance in an actionable manner, in pattern form or otherwise. The following presents some examples of the closest related work we found and how it differs from our goals.

As a basis, Sutherland and Coplien [16] gives a good overview of what we want the students to learn in general, but is not specific to teaching via student projects.

Jacobs [8] has done work on patterns for teachers to support software engineering students in their projects. Though it does includes some advice on agile practices (like retrospectives, daily stand-ups and product delivery meetings with the customer), Agile is not its central focus.

They further focused on specifically on the category of patterns for grading student team projects [9]. Their results are both more narrow, on the category level, and more general, in the sense of not focusing on Agile, than ours.

Köppe [10], and subsequently de Cortie et al. [4] have published a two-part work on learning patterns for group assignments. Though very valuable and providing overall guidance, the patterns are written from the students' perspective and do not focus on agile projects.

Tamayo Avila et al. [18] performed literature reviews and a correlational study to propose an enhancement for a pre-existing framework for fostering student learning and performance with agile practices. It is, however, more narrowly focused on improving internal team cohesion, rather than the overall guide on teaching through student projects that we aim for.

Sæter et al. [17] performed a case study to explore team dynamics in agile student teams and how gender composition affects teamwork. We were not able to find a more general study of similar kind absent the gender aspect.

López-Alcarria et al. [13] performed a systematic literature review to analyse how agile methods can support education for sustainable development. They found that agile principles and methods overlap with education for sustainable development competencies, and note that educators can establish parallels between agile contexts in the industry and the classroom. However, they do not provide substantially detailed and actionable guidance.

Other sources focus on applying agile methodologies to teaching and course design activities themselves [7], provide experience reports and case studies on teaching Agile [6], or teaching agile principles and practices via lab courses [15] or other means [11]. None of which is directly applicable or conducive to our goals.

Our work in this and subsequent papers is part of a wider efforts with other authors and the community at large to catalogue, evolve and maintain patterns related to teaching software engineering in higher education courses with student projects. The results of this work are kept in an online, publicly accessible, text-based repository[1] and open to contributions.

3 Pattern Language Overview

The entire pattern language is focused specifically on agile software project execution practices in the context of student team projects in higher education. In other words, it strives to provide comprehensive guidance for teachers on how to set up and run collaborative student project courses to simultaneously provide the opportunity for students for a hands-on experience with agile practices whilst also keeping the projects manageable from both the teams' and staff perspective.

[1] https://github.com/ReliSA/STePSEnHECs-PaCt.

As a result, not all patterns in the language are strictly agile in nature or tie back to its principles directly. To serve as a blueprint for courses, the language necessarily covers even methodology-agnostic activities, and connective tissue and grounding aspects. This is especially true for the specific patterns described in this paper, dealing with team and project setup. The agile practices the overall language does cover are the ones that need to be tailored to our context from typical form in industry practice. We do not intend to cover aspects of agile projects that can be applied equally in educational environment as in practice, as there is ample material on general agile guidance already in existence.

The patterns were mined from our experiences as teachers and educators involved in software engineering higher education courses, with complementary information gathered from the literature. We discussed the processes we employ when preparing and teaching our courses and documented the practices where we identified similarities between our approaches. We also confirmed the wider-spread usage of the patterns by surveying some of our colleagues running similar courses in their institutions. As the starting point were specifically the courses we teach ourselves (see 3.1), alternative solutions and even different permutations of the whole language are almost certain to exist. However, we cannot fully confirm them as patterns with enough observations and thus do not include them in our language at this time.

Although we were able to mine twenty distinct patterns so far, we present only five in fully described form in this paper. The full set can be found captured in patlet form in Appendix A, organized in several categories, and will be explored further in future work. We did this to describe our gathered knowledge more thoroughly and gradually.

Figure 1 shows the entire current state of our pattern language, organized roughly into categories on the top level by *Project stage*. This paper focuses on the *Team and Project Setup* (i.e., *Preparation*) stage, which ends by pairing teams with assigned topics. In the *Execution* stage, the patterns deal mainly with *Process Tailoring* (super-category) overseen by *Guidance* and split by measure of *Agility* into those close to industry use (or beyond; *Team Autonomy*) and those with *Reduced Agility* for educational purposes. The *Evaluation* stage deals with patterns related to *Grading*. The position of individual patterns within categories is a result of their mutual relations and readability of the figure, rather than any further meaning.

3.1 Source Courses

The main sources of the patterns themselves and their known uses are the courses we teach at our respective institutions. Among the authors of this paper, we have decades-worth of experience teaching agile practices in particular and software engineering in general. Here we will describe the basic fact of our courses with links to provide the reader with more information in case of interest.

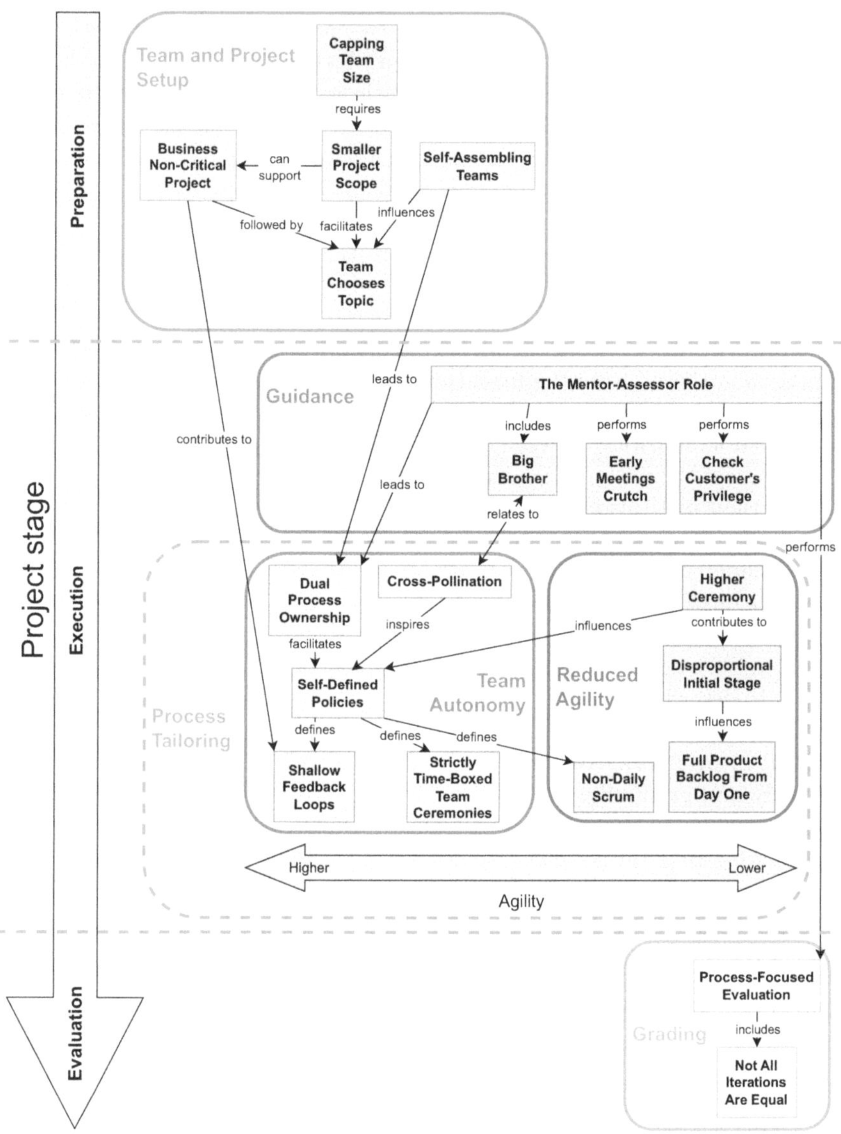

Fig. 1. Current state of the pattern language.

Software Engineering (ES). Software Engineering[2] (ES) is a course taught at the University of Porto in the spring semester of second year of the Informatics Engineering and Computation Bachelor's degree programme. Students form teams of 4–6 members working on a software project developing a Flut-

[2] https://sigarra.up.pt/feup/en/UCURR_GERAL.FICHA_UC_VIEW?pv_ocorrencia_id=541882.

ter app on a topic of their choice (usually within a larger theme chosen by the staff). The project's Scrum-based process is divided into two-week Sprints, plus a longer Sprint 0. Weekly lectures are mostly dedicated to teaching agile practices and methods (Unified Process, eXtreme Programming, Scrum, etc.) while also going into topics such as requirements engineering and a bit of UML. Weekly lab classes are dedicated to working on the projects.

Large Scale Software Development (DS). Large Scale Software Development[3] (DS) is a course at University of Porto for the fall semester of first year of the Master's degree studies. Each class has a project for an external customer (or with the staff working as the customer), and all teams work on the same implementation (using Large Scale Scrum). The teams consist of 5–6 students using two-week Sprints with an introductory Sprint 0. Weekly lectures are focused on scaled agile practices, while the weekly lab classes are dedicated to project work and team synchronization.

Advanced Software Engineering (ASWI). Advanced Software Engineering[4] (ASWI) is a course thought at the University of West Bohemia in Pilsen in the second semester of Master's studies. The projects within the course mostly run on a custom process model[5] developed over the year. It is a mash of base Rational Unified Process (RUP) [12] structure infused with some agile practices, similar to Disciplined Agile Delivery (DAD) [1]. The project topics are gathered and screened beforehand by the staff from internal and external customers. After assigning the projects, the teams consisting of 3–7 members (with the average of 4) run through the whole project from requirements analysis all the way to release. The iterations range from 1–3 weeks in length (based on the teams' choices). The lectures cover the entirety of software development process, its practices, foremost process models and methodologies with a focus shifting more towards agile ones through the years. Lab classes exist only in the first weeks to help teams jump onto the process and kick start the projects. Afterwards, there are only mentor consults/evaluation reviews between individual teams and their mentor after each iteration.

Team Software Project (TSP). Team Software Project[6] (TSP) is a year long course (officially split into TSP1 and TSP2, one per semester) taught at the University of West Bohemia in Pilsen. It covers the second and third semesters of Master's studies and its first half runs in parallel to ASWI. Though the course

[3] https://sigarra.up.pt/feup/en/UCURR_GERAL.FICHA_UC_VIEW?pv_ocorrencia_id=540677.

[4] https://portal.zcu.cz/portal/studium/prohlizeni.html?pc_lang=en, search Courses with Course abbreviation ASWI.

[5] https://shorturl.at/FHCHw (in Czech).

[6] https://portal.zcu.cz/portal/studium/prohlizeni.html?pc_lang=en, search Courses with Course abbreviation TSP.

can be taken separately, it most usually serves as an extension of ASWI, both in terms of man-hours and timeline. For students only enrolled into TSP, it only covers basic project milestones and artifacts, leaving most of the process choices to the team. The progress is checked by a process mentor supporting the teams on the practices and processes, as oppose to domain mentors helping with specific technologies. There are no lectures and all the time spent in the course is meant for working on the projects, concluding with presentations at the end of each semester.

Other Courses. We have gathered further source courses by surveying our colleagues from other institutions and the wider community. The reported comparable courses include:

- ***Team Project (TP)***[7] course taught at Babeș-Bolyai University Cluj-Napoca,
- ***Software Construction (SC)***[8] course from the University of Applied Sciences and Arts Northwestern Switzerland,
- and ***System Engineering (SE)*** course formerly taught at the Free University of Bozen-Bolzano.

3.2 Pattern Template

The pattern description follows a format with explicitly defined sections. It is a slightly modified version of the template devised by Wellhausen and Fießer [20] with each pattern having the following:

- **Name** of the pattern
- **Context** – a situation and circumstances in which the pattern is applied (on top of the ones common to all patterns in the language, see 3.3)
- **Problem** – statement of the problem, which the pattern aims to address
- **Forces** – the forces causing or complicating the problem that need to be balanced by the solution
- **Solution** – the resolution to the pattern's problem, balancing the forces (a succinct statement in bold, followed by deeper explanation)
- **Implementation** – (optional) expands on the specifics or variations of applying the solution
- **Consequences** – the resulting circumstances of the solution application, either benefits (signalled with a +) and liabilities (signalled with a −)
- **Related Patterns** – other patterns from the language with identified relation to the current one
- **Examples/Known Uses** – particular forms of solutions applied either in source courses (see 3.1) or gathered from elsewhere

[7] https://www.cs.ubbcluj.ro/files/curricula/2025/syllabus/IE_sem5_MLE5012_en_dsuciu_2025_9414.pdf.
[8] https://www.fhnw.ch/plattformen/swc/.

We decided to use a section-based format as it facilitates the reader's comprehension of the pattern contents, facilitating skimming when necessary. This format has also facilitated collaboration between us, the authors, particularly regarding organising our thoughts.

3.3 Common Context

The following common context applies not only to the five patterns described in this paper, but to every pattern in the pattern language:

> You are running or planning to establish a university course on software engineering with collaborative student projects and including some aspects or the entire process of agile development. The goal being to provide learning by experience of agile principles and practices as well as general project management skills. No prior knowledge or experience of the students in these domains is assumed[9].

4 Patterns

Figure 2 showcases the relationships between the patterns discussed in this paper, i.e. all from the Team and Project category.

Table 1 includes the patlets of each pattern discussed in the paper. These are short descriptions for each pattern, outlining the problem they are addressing and showcasing the respective solution. They are then described in full using the template from 3.2.

4.1 Pattern: Capping Team Size

Context. Within the common context (see 3.3), we are setting up the course. The parameters of the projects must be specified, put in the syllabus, communicated to the students enrolling. They are also mutually influential with the rest of the course design.

Problem. How to best set up the student team size to maximize product and educational efficiency?

Forces

- Bigger teams are harder to manage, especially for the inexperienced students, who are either learning or just learned (theoretically) the project management skills.
- Agile, specifically, is even harder to grasp, as it is more a mindset than a rigid methodology.

[9] In cases the course is preceded by others that teach some of these skills, the patterns should be modified accordingly.

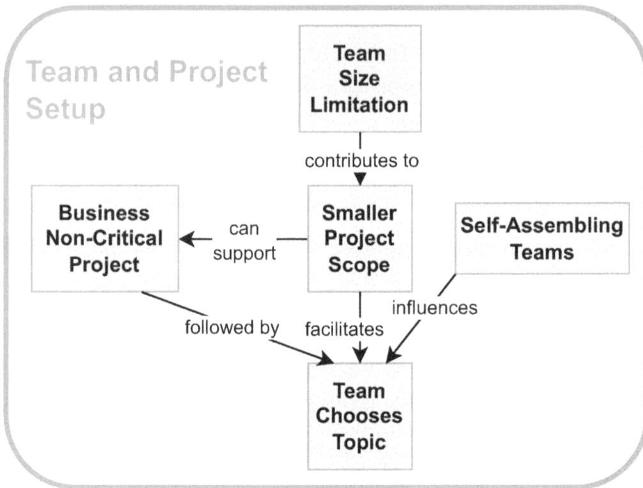

Fig. 2. Identified relationships between patterns in the Team and Project Setup category.

Table 1. Patlets for each pattern in the Team and Project Setup category.

Pattern	Problem	Solution
Capping Team Size	How to best set up the student team size to maximize product and educational efficiency?	Put a reasonable upper limit on team size
Smaller Project Scope	How to efficiently teach the practices given the limited capacity of the course?	Assign smaller, worthwhile projects accounting for the educational activities within and the team's capacity
Business Non-Critical Project	How not to risk relationship between teachers and customers inherent in students working on core business?	Accept projects that are not on the customer's critical path or essential for their operations
Self-Assembling Teams	How to assemble teams quickly and minimize the initial social and inter-personal hurdles?	Allow teams to self-assemble to create a sense of ownership and freedom of choice
Team Chooses Topic	How to pair up the teams with the project topics?	Curate a selection of project topics, but account for the teams' preferences when assigning them

- Bigger teams leave open the risk of some members coasting or hiding their minimal contributions.
- On the other hand, a team that's too small (and thus, its capacity) reduces the space they have in the project to sufficiently experience and learn project management practices.
- Rigidly enforced team size might lead to incomplete teams and lone students given the variable number of students enrolled into the course each year.
- Course-specific parameters like class size and learning objectives might play a role.

Solution. Have an upper and lower limit on (preferred) team size and set the upper boundary low enough.

Excluding specific exceptions[10], the lower limit on team size is apparently two members, as a sole student cannot really be considered a team. Though not ideal, the mechanism of avoiding two-member teams might not be available.

The upper limit is much more within the teacher's discretion. The general advice for team size in industry (cap at 8–10 members [16]), might prove too challenging for novice students in terms of team management practices they are just learning. The ideal seems to be an average team size of around four to six students, but may vary on the course parameters, like class size and learning objectives.

Consequences

+ Team is still manageable in size for novices while providing ample space to experience and learn project management practices.
+ Starting small is in line with agile principles and applying it to team size itself provides further opportunity to showcase this approach to the students.
+ The flexible team size and teacher's final say in forming them (see Self-Assembling Teams, 4.4) negates the possibility of individual students being left out of the teams.
– The smaller team size necessarily limits the scope of the projects the teams can handle, leading to Smaller Project Scope (4.2).
– Enforcing the limits or reforming Self-Assembling Teams 4.4) to even out the team sizes more or to fit differently estimated project topics might still breed some resentment and frustration among the students right from the start of their projects.

[10] Students in distance learning mode are sometimes impossible to align on schedule and group to teams. Foreign exchange students cannot always be grouped neither together nor with local students as they might leave in the middle of the project, for example. Legislation or university policy might demand a student must be allowed to take the course even if (for whatever reason) they cannot be placed in any team.

Related Patterns

- The pattern contributes to the need for Smaller Project Scope (4.2) as the team's limited size clearly leads to its reduced capacity to work on the project[11].

Examples/Known Uses

- ***ES*** – Depending on the number of students in a class group (around 25 students), team size is set to four or five students (in exceptional cases, six students) to have four or five teams of students.
- ***DS*** – Class groups (of 20–26 students) are divided into four or five teams of 4–6 students of the same size.
- ***ASWI*** – The team size is set to two to five students, with the most common being four.
- ***TSP*** – Due to the course running for two semesters, the default team size is set a bit higher to three to seven members, with two-person teams being the (purely circumstantial) exception and the most frequent team size being again four students.
- ***TP*** uses team size of 8–10 people.
- ***SC*** uses teams of maximum 3 students.

4.2 Pattern: Smaller Project Scope

Context. On top of the common context (see 3.3), after deciding on the Capping Team Size (4.1), another course aspect to consider is the scope of the projects the student teams will be working on.

Problem. How to efficiently provide students with practical education on the process and practices while creating a worthwhile product given the limited time the students have as dictated among others by the credit volume of the course?

Forces

- The students do not work full time on the project, juggling it with their responsibilities from other parts of the course (lectures, exams; plus the overall spent time limitation on the course per the number of credits gained from passing), other courses, personal lives and, potentially, part-time jobs. Depending on how many credits the course is worth they may have more time, but there is no exclusivity on the students' end.

[11] The direction of this relation is education context-specific, as team size is often part of the course design and/or syllabus or a decision by the staff based on available manpower, course objectives and other factors. In industry, in contrast, the project scope would dictate the team size necessary for its completion.

- Agile processes combine several moving parts, including ceremonies, practices, and principles, to name a few. Hands-on experience with these helps students see how everything fits, leading to better comprehension and a sense of being more than just theoretical stuff they need to recite for the exam.
- Students should have something to work towards, and a project with a clear goal is a good way to keep them engaged. Even better if they can see a real-world benefit to a customer who validates their effort and results, rather than "yet another" artificial (purely) educational assignment which will only end up in a drawer forever.
- Students may be hardwired from other courses that all that matters for the project is the quality of the end result, automatically ignoring the "whys and hows" to reach it reliably.

Solution. Assign smaller projects to students that can be of value while accounting for the team's size, the expected engagement from the course, and the educational activities within the project.

When we, as educators, want to teach students about the mechanisms behind the processes they are working on, we should focus their attention at the mechanisms themselves. However, it is easy for students to not see the forest for the trees depending on their previous experiences in other courses, where the project's end result was all that mattered.

As such, in order to shift the students attention, educators can propose topics that are *smaller* in scope but that still make for a coherent and well-thought out project.

With this, students should not be working fully at capacity, giving them room for agile ceremonies, other tasks (such as the ones that may be present for evaluation purposes but that do not advance development), and also giving them slack time. In a course where each student should have 80 h of development time, they should be working on a 60-hour project.

This can be achieved, in the case of an externally-proposed topic, by giving students room to negotiate scaling down the scope of the topic. On the other hand, if the students are proposing their own topic, they can start small, having room to grow with the guidance of their professor.

Consequences

+ Having projects that are smaller in scope helps students to maintain a sustainable pace, helping them remain aligned with agile principles. The sustainable pace assists in students not scrambling to get things done at the last minute, which together with a reduced workload gives students the room to be intentional about their actions and really take in the reasons behind what they are doing in the course of their projects.
+ Smaller projects are also more easily and accurately grasped mentally. This can spark creativity, when students are given a choice to come up with their own project topics, or help assess the topics assigned or up for selection.

– A reduced project scope can backfire and steer students the wrong way, downplaying what they need to work on for the project and resulting in poorer time management, which in turn leads the team to work at an unsustainable pace.

Related Patterns

- The need for smaller project scope is partially driven by the CAPPING TEAM SIZE (4.1) as the aggregate team capacity puts a limitation on the scope from the start[12].
- These smaller projects can also facilitate TEAM CHOOSES TOPIC (4.5). In case of a self-suggested topic by the team, it can spring forth creativity – creating "something that does one thing very well". In case of picking from pre-prepared topic selection, it can at least help students in comprehending and assessing the complexity and overall effort needed for the project. In either case, it enables them to make a better informed decision.
- The smaller scope also supports the BUSINESS NON-CRITICAL PROJECT (4.3) topic, as the customers rarely have proposals that are small enough for the courses, yet very important or business critical.

Examples/Known Uses

- ***ES*** – Teams are encouraged to keep their project topics simple with an easy-to-implement minimum viable product, with the option to grow in scope as the semester progresses and the team implements their initial view of the project. Students are expected to work around 60–75 man-hours per team member during the semester, with the project's scope being adjusted to the team's size.
- ***ASWI, TSP*** – Customers are informed by the course staff prior to topic submissions on the estimated scope of the projects, taking into account the administrative overhead the students have to apply in the projects (HIGHER CEREMONY, see Appendix A). They are also encouraged to submit topics that can be easily scaled up or down based on the specific project context (i.e., the varying number of team members). The topics are subsequently screened by the course staff in this regard to the best of their ability. The mentors are also ready to assist the teams to resolve a situation where the fact that the topic is significantly more/less complex than originally estimated is discovered during the project's execution. In terms of concrete targeted scope in man-hours (mh), the courses differ:
  - ASWI – 60–80 mh per team member,
  - TSP – 80–100 mh per student, per semester,

[12] The note on this relation from CAPPING TEAM SIZE (4.1) applies here.

Thus, if we imagine a case of team of four members who are all enrolled in both subjects, the total expected scope is 880–1120mh. On average, around a third of the time, however, is spent on ceremonies, overhead, and other activities needed more for learning than the product itself.
- ***TP*** uses teams of 8–10 students with the expected 50 h spent per student per semester.
- In ***SC*** teams of 3 students work on a small, approx. 4K LOC, application.

4.3 Pattern: Business Non-Critical Project

Context. In addition to the common context (see 3.3), through Capping Team Size (4.1) and Smaller Project Scope (4.2), we now need a mechanism for coming up with the actual project topics to assign to teams.

Problem. How to minimize the risks inherent in students working on parts of the customer's core business?

Forces

- Students need a topic to work on, and industry-oriented ones have their unique interesting factors, such as opportunities to interact with external customers and the potential to use new or different technologies.
- Companies and other organisations may be willing to collaborate with student projects seeking free manpower or to start relationships that may lead to future hiring. However, this goal often takes second place when faced with the daily work and demands of the business, sometimes resulting in limited availability.
- The students, as well as the course staff, cannot guarantee the extent and quality of the products the teams deliver as the product is at best a co-equal, often even secondary, goal next to practical education in processes and practices.
- In case of IT customer, their product release schedules may not align with course's needs.
- Customers may further hesitate to take part in student projects due to risk of inexperienced students with no legal responsibility unintentionally interfering with business critical assets, leaking trade secrets and other confidential data.
- Potential failure or overall bad experience with the projects may jeopardize the working relationship between the teaching staff and the customers, either internal (colleagues) or external (industry partners).
- The risk of failure in something crucial increases stress in all parties involved, but especially the students due to their lack of experience.

Solution. Accept projects that are not on the customer's critical path or essential for their operations.

Rather then customer's business products themselves, these may include nice-to-have utilities, research tools, quality of life software for non-IT customers, etc.

When outside organisations decide to assume the customer role, they are giving students the opportunity to get a taste of "the real world", with them being able to form connections with practitioners and learn more about how different organisations operate, all in addition to practising agile methods and learning through iterative delivery.

Giving customers an opening to propose project topics that fall outside of their main products and features can give them this opportunity to build bridges with the university and the people who will be entering the workforce in the future, while minimising the inherent risk that comes with student projects—where the quality of the end result can vary to the point that there may not be much there at all.

Consequences

+ The non-criticality of projects enables students and educators to be connected to outside organisations, while reducing any risks that come from the variable quality of student projects. These opportunities can help kickstart the students' future careers, as they come into the workforce with connections and a world-view that is closer to the practitioners' reality.
+ If customers' expectation is lowered and not critically dependent on the projects' results, the room for disappointment shirks, yet there is still space to be pleasantly surprised.
+ Non-critical topics reduce stress from consequences of a potential failure.
– Companies may not be interested in proposing topics that are not useful for them; as they would be taking on the role of a customer, the availability required of them to be in meetings and work with the students may not be worth it for them.

Related Patterns

- Having companies propose project topics that are not their main, critical path can actually produce ideas with a Smaller Project Scope (4.2).
- These customer-proposed topics can be a source of curated projects students can choose from in Team Chooses Topic (4.5).
- Due to the non-critical nature of the projects and their time constraints, the students might not have the access to the end users of the developed software (i.e., the customer's customers), or at least their fully representative sample, or the time to gain it. This may contribute to the deployment of the Shallow Feedback Loops (see Appendix A).

Examples/Known Uses

- ***DS, ASWI, TSP*** – When gathering topics for projects prior to their publishing to the student teams to for expressing interest, the customers are advised by the course staff to not submit any business critical topics, as the results as their quality cannot be properly guaranteed. This results in mostly nice-to-have applications, extensions, integrations, etc. being proposed by the external customers and supporting software for research projects larger in scope than individual thesis topics being submitted by internal customers.
- In ***TP***, the project topics are often proposed by industry specialists but have limited significance and serve primarily for educational purposes.

4.4 Pattern: Self-Assembling Teams

Context. Within the common context (see 3.3), new students enrol into our course. The semester has either just begun or is close to it. The actual work on the projects should start in the near future.

Problem. How to assemble the teams from the individual students quickly and in a way that minimizes the initial social and inter-personal hurdles?

Forces

- Teams need to be formed relatively quickly for the work on the projects to start.
- Being forced to cooperate with newly acquainted or unfitting team members (on personal or professional level) can lead to resentment, tension and frustration in the team.
- Some, but not all, students formed interpersonal relationships in their previous studies or personal lives and have a pallet of (soft and hard) skills each that can be complementary or contrary to each other, none of which the course staff is necessarily aware of.
- Trying to assemble the "perfect" teams puts a lot of pressure and effort on the course staff in the setup stage, especially if the number of students is high. Furthermore, the underlying data for such an effort might be missing or unreliable.
- The teams need to meet certain general (e.g., Capping Team Size, see 4.1) or course-specific criteria.
- A completely hands-off approach to team formation can lead to breaking the aforementioned criteria, delays, or leave some students out in the cold.

Solution. Allow and encourage the students to form the teams on their own at the very beginning of the course or (if possible) even before.

After all, self-organizing teams (in terms of internal roles and structure) are one of the staples of Agile and boosting this up to the level of team assembly itself helps strengthens this principle in the minds of the students.

Make them aware of any criteria that need to be met and give them a near enough deadline to "register" their team composition and put a approval/vetting process in place to review the teams formed. After the deadline has passed, resolve any cases where full teams were not formed – such as incomplete teams or isolated students without a team – using accessible knowledge and your best judgment.

Consequences

+ Teams form quicker when students leverage their interpersonal relationships and prior experience with each other, compared to if the staff needed to learn about them first.
+ Joining a team voluntarily, as opposed to getting stuck in one by a decree from authority, is one less frustration students need to deal with navigating the already tricky realm of team dynamics and collaboration.
+ Self-assembled teams can feel higher measure of ownership and autonomy of their team and the project as a whole.
+ Lower time and effort investment on the staff side, and requirements for prior knowledge on individual students skills, experience and personalities.
+ Due to the vetting process, any and all criteria for the teams are still met, or at the very least, their exceptions are monitored and regulated by the course staff.
+ The chance of a lone student without a team needing to work on a solo project is dramatically lowered.
– Teams self-assembled based on pre-existing friendships while ignoring skill sets may cause issues.
– Some resentment can still arise in those teams forced to accept lone students, or those formed entirely from such individuals.
– Even voluntarily formed teams may face issues in team dynamics and cooperation, which still needs mediation and other actions from the course staff.

Related Patterns

- The pattern influences the Team Chooses Topic (4.5) of the project topic (or at least the expressed preferences) as all team members need to sign-off on, or at least concede to, the collective decision.
- After assembling into teams, the students should also agree on their individual roles and take partial ownership of the details of their process, which they share with the mentor (staff member), who sets the more coarse outline of the process. Thus, taking part in Dual Process Ownership (see Appendix A).

Examples/Known Uses

- ***ES, DS*** – Students in the same lab class self-assemble in teams depending on the team size defined by the teachers during the first lab class. When teams deviate from the expected size (either when a team has too many students or there are students without a team), the teacher intervenes and facilitates team assembly with the students.
- ***ASWI*** – Students are told to form the teams of the expected size on their own at the very beginning of the term and given at most two weeks to do so. As part of their registration they also assign the team lead (or at least a contact person), express their preferences for project topics (see TEAM CHOOSES TOPIC, 4.5) and provide their team profile in regards experience with different technologies. The course staff vet the team registrations and make any changes as necessary. Any students unassigned to any team by the deadline (if any) are either assigned to as existing team or grouped together to new teams. Either is done based on the target team size, technical experience compatibility, preferred topics and other criteria.
- ***TSP*** – The process is broadly similar to the one used in ASWI. Only it starts several months before the term starts and it is supported by a custom web application for team registrations and searching for teammates. If the team is at least partially enrolled in both courses, TSP version is followed.
- In ***TP*** project teams used to be formed randomly or based on various other criteria, but participants' motivation was negatively affected. Now, they use self-assembling teams following exactly this pattern.
- ***SC*** uses an online sign-up sheet for students to form teams.
- In ***SE***, students are free to form the teams on their own.

4.5 Pattern: TEAM CHOOSES TOPIC

Context. We are in the common context (see 3.3). We have the students grouped into teams. We also have the curated list of feasible topics satisfying all the criteria for the projects. In other words, SMALLER PROJECT SCOPE (4.2), BUSINESS NON-CRITICAL PROJECT (4.3) and SELF-ASSEMBLING TEAMS (4.4), or their valid equivalents, have already been applied.

Problem. The best situation is a team working on a project their are enthusiastic about and qualified for. How to find the best fit when assigning the assembled teams to the gathered project topics?

Forces

- Having all students work on topics that are consistent in terms of difficulty helps with evaluation, enabling comparable evaluation criteria.
- The topics the students work on should be adequate for the course, in terms of scope, complexity, number of features, and tech stack.

- Feeling motivated helps students bring out their best work, but extrinsic motivation (such as that fuelled by a good grade) is not enough; intrinsic motivation [5] (related to personal development and attachment to the work in progress) is paramount in a software project [3].
- The staff is not equipped to judge the teams' preferences, confidence, ambitions and experiences with different technologies without adequate information.

Solution. Curate the selection of project topics, but take into account the preferences of team members when assigning them.
The project topics available to students should be managed by the professors, enabling different topics to be consistent in terms of scope, technology, and complexity.

There might be a discrepancy in pace of teams forming due to pre-existing relationships between students, or lack there of. To give all teams a level play field, with the opportunity for them to go through the team forming process [19], the task of choosing a project topic ought to not be immediate. Teams should have time (depending on the course calendar, two or three weeks at the course's beginning or even before its start) to assess their options and make the choice they feel is best.

Regardless of the origin of the project topics, students should have a say on which topic they will be working on during the semester.

Implementation. The following are alternative ways of applying the general solution in a still generic-enough way:

- Let students come up with their own project topics. With adequate guidance on the professor's part, students can come up with a topic they are invested in and that also meets the course's learning objectives.
- Let students bring topics from their own contacts gained through previous studies, participation in research, personal relationships with people in the industry, or jobs they might already have.
- Prepare a pool of topics and let students pick from it. These topics can be proposed internally, by the professors, or externally, by outside organisations and customers. This can give the professors more control over the consistency between different topics, while giving students agency on their work.

Any mixture of all of the above is obviously also possible, e.g., have a prepared pool of topics as a default, but allow (or even encourage) students to bring or come up with their own proposals.

Consequences

+ Being able to have a say in what they will work on helps with students' sense of ownership, commitment and buy-in.

- Giving the teams a choice about their topics requires some care. In an instance where students propose their topics, they may end up with contrasts between teams, with some topics being more complex or wider in scope than others. This can make it harder to evaluate the students' work due to the different playing fields.
- If the description of a topic is too surface-level, short or vague, it can lead to mismatch between expectations and reality in either direction on the students' or teachers' part. For example, the topic can appear easy to students and turn up to be overly challenging for their experience level. Or the topic (no matter its source) can be assessed as complex enough by the staff when its significant portion can be easily addressed by a free, third-party solution, thus drastically cutting the effort needed for the overall product.

Related Patterns

- Giving teams a choice over the topics can be made easier by ensuring a Smaller Project Scope (4.2), as students can better understand the point of the project and what they will be doing on them, as well as compare between different topics, if these are small.
- The history team members have with each other (if any) can influence how the team chooses their topic. For instance, if students had the opportunity to form Self-Assembling Teams (4.4) and chose colleagues they are already friendly with or had worked with previously, they will have a stronger familiarity and team identity compared to other teams where the students are not really familiar with each other. That can lead to a more confident and appropriate topic choice or an idea for their own project.
- Apart from the above, the pattern obviously follows the collection of Business Non-Critical Project (4.3) topics.

Examples/Known Uses

- ***ES*** – The course's teachers select a common, broad theme for the project topics. In previous years, student apps have been related to student life, and more recently to the UN's Sustainable Development Goals[13]. Students then choose a specific topic within these broader themes and receive feedback from their teachers throughout the process.
- ***ASWI, TSP*** – A "call for topics" is sent out to both the industrial partners and internal organizational units of the university by the course staff well in advance (i.e., before the semester in which the course is taught starts). The gathered topics are screened for complexity, estimated scope (Smaller Project Scope, see 4.2), educational value, technology, business criticality (Business Non-Critical Project, see 4.3), etc. The students are also allowed to bring their own topic proposals, but a customer from outside the

[13] https://sdgs.un.org/goals.

team needs to be defined. The resulting set is published to the students and the teams can express their preferences. The staff then assigns the projects mainly on these, outside of collisions in preferences or a stark mismatch of the topic and team's profile (technology experience, etc.).
- In ***TP***, the project teams pick a topic proposed by industry specialists or they define the project topic themselves, while project's difficulty is assessed by and instructor to remain consistent across teams. Project topics are not imposed, as this would decrease motivation for implementing the project.
- In ***SE***, students were free to choose their own topic.

5 Conclusions and Future Work

In this paper we presented the beginnings of a pattern language that focuses on ASD practices in higher education context, with five patterns for team and project setup forming an initial subset: Capping Team Size (4.1), which advised composing even smaller teams than is usual in industry; Smaller Project Scope (4.2), which focused on how smaller projects can help students learning the different moving parts in the process; Business Non-Critical Project (4.3), which discussed how external customers can reduce the risks that come with student projects while maintaining the benefits students get when working with real-world customers; Self-Assembling Teams (4.4), which endorsed students' freedom to form the teams to boost cooperation; and Team Chooses Topic (4.5), which dived into the benefits of letting students be involved in choosing the topics they work on. The rest of the patterns proposed for the language are captured in patlet form in Appendix A.

We recognize that some, if not all, of the patterns may be applicable in contexts outside of ours, e.g., non-agile courses, projects shorter than a semester, even industry in some cases. However, given we observed these patterns in a specific context (see 3.1 and 3.3), we make no definite proclamations regarding their wider applicability.

We further argue that the application of the solutions is more beneficial to agile courses than others. As the agile mindset is more challenging to teach and/or learn than a rigidly prescribed methodology, the students benefit from learning on smaller teams to manage, necessarily related to smaller project scopes, less critical assignments with less stress of failure and the option to choose their teammates as well as the topic they feel comfortable with.

In the future we plan to expand this budding pattern language with more patterns, fully describing the rest of our mined set (see Appendix A) and potentially capturing more, diving into the relationships between them, exploring the different practices employed by educators, and learning more about how students can learn about ASD in a university environment.

Acknowledgements. The authors would like to thank the shepherd of this paper, Tineke Jacobs, as well as Workshop Group G at EuroPLoP '25, for their work, valuable feedback and overall help in improving the patterns and their presentation.

Further thanks to Dan-Mircea Suciu, Eduardo Guerra and Martin Kropp for providing additional known uses for the individual patterns.

A Pattern Language Patlets

This appendix includes the patlets for all patterns for the language, grouped by their categories.

A.1 Category: Team and Project Setup

Capping Team Size

Problem: How to best set up the student team size to maximize product and educational efficiency?
Solution: Put a reasonable upper limit on team size.

Smaller Project Scope

Problem: How to efficiently teach the practices given the limited capacity of the course?
Solution: Assign smaller, worthwhile projects accounting for the educational activities within and the team's capacity.

Business Non-Critical Project

Problem: How not to risk relationship between teachers and customers inherent in students working on core business?
Solution: Accept projects that are not on the customer's critical path or essential for their operations.

Self-Assembling Teams

Problem: How to assemble teams quickly and minimize the initial social and inter-personal hurdles?
Solution: Allow teams to self-assemble to create a sense of ownership and freedom of choice.

Team Chooses Topic

Problem: How to pair up the teams with the project topics?
Solution: Curate a selection of project topics, but account for the teams' preferences when assigning them.

A.2 Category: Guidance

The Mentor-Assessor Role

Problem: How to perform both guiding the team and grading their performance, which both require deep insight into inner team dynamics, practice applications and communication (internally and externally), while saving on manpower and scheduling difficulties?

Solution: Have a single person embody both the mentor and the assessor role.

Big Brother

Problem: How to grant the mentor/assessor access to detailed information of inner workings of the team, to get the full picture for evaluation and insight for mentoring?

Solution: Unless this conflicts with information sensitivity on customer's side make even internal team notes/communications freely accessible to the mentor/assessor.

Early Meetings Crutch

Problem: How to facilitate hands on learning for good practices that are hard to explain otherwise?

Solution: In early team meetings, let the mentor be a fly on the wall and subsequently give team a constructive feedback on their conduct, structure and communication skills.

Check Customer's Privilege

Problem: How to mitigate the customer's (especially IT-industrial ones) tendency to "take over" the project and play roles that the team should learn by doing, e.g., requirements analyst, architect and project manager?

Solution: Inform and enforce the role the customer should stick to, including "playing dumb", and help the team in situation when customer oversteps.

A.3 Category: Process Tailoring Reduced Agility

Higher Ceremony

Problem: How can we reliably verify the students have tried out and learned all the standard practices, even those that would not be call for producing hard evidence (paper trail) in industry due to the projects' smaller scale?

Solution: Explain this dilemma and the educational reasons for the level of ceremony to the students openly and clearly. Set the process to necessitate the taught practices and tools to a sufficient but not extremely overwhelming degree.

Disproportional Initial Stage

Problem: How to ease the burden on new student teams who struggle to balance preparation and execution when thrown directly into iterative development cycles?

Solution: Allocate enough time at the beginning of the project to allow teams to establish a shared understanding, set up tools, and practice agile fundamentals without the pressure of immediate delivery.

Full Product Backlog from Day One

Problem: How to help the teams who may be lost in terms of what to work on first at the point they do their first team planning?

Solution: Push and help the teams to define a set of features/user stories to work on throughout the project, having a general idea of what will be worked on at which time.

Non-Daily Scrum

Problem: How to resolve the need to showcase the usefulness of stand-ups with the potential impracticability of their daily performance due to time constraints or conflicting schedules, which could lead to skipped or poorly attended meetings that undermine team alignment?

Solution: Introduce a cadence for stand-ups that matches the team's capacity and work rhythm, such as (bi-)weekly, while maintaining the focus on frequent updates and collaboration.

A.4 Category: Process Tailoring Team Autonomy

Dual Process Ownership

Problem: How to help inexperienced students with potentially the most challenging and simultaneously most educationally potent role of Scrum Master (or equivalent)?

Solution: Use a mentor, an experienced staff member, as a crutch to help oversee, tailor and adhere to the team's process. Simultaneously, have an internal process owner (an individual or the whole team, their choice), as the mentor cannot be present all the time.

Self-Defined Policies

Problem: How to device detailed team policies (on code, notations, roles, tools, planning strategies, etc.) without rigidly imposing them, risking dismissal, resentment and blockers to learning through experimentation?

Solution: Define just as much of the process as necessary (for comparisons and manageability on the course level) and give students free reign over the rest. Also, be prepared to bend or change even the process structure you do have if they come with a justified case for it and explicitly encourage such ideas.

Strictly Time-Boxed Team Ceremonies

Problem: How to help focus meetings, so people, especially inexperienced students, do not wonder off from the topic at hand wasting everyone's time?
Solution: Leverage limited class time to have hard time constraints on routine meetings with specific purpose (e.g. Sprint Review and Sprint Planning).

Shallow Feedback Loops

Problem: How to ensure timely feedback on the product increments that the teams provide when a non-business critical nature of the project and unavailability of end users may cause delays?
Solution: Ask customers to act as proxy users who provide feedback on their behalf.

Cross-Pollination

Problem: How to provide students with the advice/experience they might be more receptive to than the one from a perceived prescriptive authority (a teacher)?
Solution: Allow teams to learn and draw inspiration from each other through opening internal team data and mentor evaluations to the whole class, casual contact between members of different teams, and/or organized experience exchange events.

A.5 Category: Grading

Process-Focused Evaluation

Problem: How to properly assess the quality of work and learning outcomes in a course of this nature?
Solution: Base the larger part of students' evaluation on the handling the process and practices, attitude and problem solving during project management, not the product and its quality.

Not All Iterations Are Equal

Problem: How to account for the learning curve at the start of the project and the necessary ceremonies that might exist at the end of it (due to the educational context) in the evaluation process?
Solution: Put less weight in evaluation on the temporal extremes of the project takong their specific context into account.

References

1. Ambler, S.W., Lines, M.: Disciplined Agile Delivery: A Practitioner's Guide to Agile Software Delivery in the Enterprise. IBM Press (2012)
2. Beck, K., et al.: Manifesto for agile software development (2001). https://www.agilemanifesto.org/
3. Beecham, S., Baddoo, N., Hall, T., Robinson, H., Sharp, H.: Motivation in software engineering: a systematic literature review. Inf. Softw. Technol. **50**(9–10), 860–878 (2008). https://doi.org/10.1016/j.infsof.2007.09.004
4. de Cortie, T., Bosma, G., Broeckhuijsen, R., Köppe, C.: Learning patterns for group assignments-part 2. In: Proceedings of the 20th Pattern Languages of Programs conference, PLoP, vol. 13 (2013)
5. Deci, E.L., Ryan, R.M.: Self-determination theory. In: Lange, P.A.M.V., Kruglanski, A.W., Higgins, E.T. (eds.) Handbook of Theories of Social Psychology, vol. 1. SAGE Publications Inc. (2012). https://doi.org/10.4135/9781483346243.n302
6. Devedžić, V., et al.: Teaching agile software development: a case study. IEEE Trans. Educ. **54**(2), 273–278 (2010)
7. Fernanda, S., Manuel, S., Germania, R., Samanta, C., Danilo, J., Patricio, A.: Agile methodologies applied in teaching-learning process in engineering: a case of study. In: 2018 IEEE Global Engineering Education Conference (EDUCON), pp. 1201–1207. IEEE (2018)
8. Jacobs, T.: Supporting ICT-students to make the most out of their projects. In: Proceedings of the 27th European Conference on Pattern Languages of Programs, EuroPLop 2022. Association for Computing Machinery, New York (2023). https://doi.org/10.1145/3551902.3551972
9. Jacobs, T.: Grading individual students in software engineering projects confidently. In: Proceedings of the 29th European Conference on Pattern Languages of Programs, People, and Practices, EuroPLoP 2024. Association for Computing Machinery, New York (2024). https://doi.org/10.1145/3698322.3698330
10. Köppe, C.: Learning patterns for group assignments: part 1. In: Proceedings of the 19th Conference on Pattern Languages of Programs, pp. 1–12 (2012)
11. Kropp, M., Meier, A., Mateescu, M., Zahn, C.: Teaching and learning agile collaboration. In: 2014 IEEE 27th Conference on Software Engineering Education and Training (CSEE&T), pp. 139–148. IEEE (2014)
12. Kruchten, P.: The Rational Unified Process: An Introduction. Addison-Wesley Professional (2004)
13. López-Alcarria, A., Olivares-Vicente, A., Poza-Vilches, F.: A systematic review of the use of agile methodologies in education to foster sustainability competencies. Sustainability **11**(10), 2915 (2019). https://doi.org/10.3390/su11102915
14. Rico, D.F., Sayani, H.H.: Use of agile methods in software engineering education. In: 2009 Agile Conference, pp. 174–179. IEEE (2009). https://doi.org/10.1109/AGILE.2009.13
15. Schroeder, A., Klarl, A., Mayer, P., Kroiß, C.: Teaching agile software development through lab courses. In: Proceedings of the 2012 IEEE Global Engineering Education Conference (EDUCON), pp. 1–10. IEEE (2012)
16. Sutherland, J., Coplien, J.O.: A Scrum Book: The Spirit of the Game. Pragmatic Bookshelf (2019)

17. Sæter, G.E., Stray, V., Almås, S., Lindsjørn, Y.: The role of team composition in agile software development education: a gendered perspective. In: Šmite, D., Guerra, E., Wang, X., Marchesi, M., Gregory, P. (eds.) Agile Processes in Software Engineering and Extreme Programming, vol. 512, pp. 179–195. Springer, Cham (2024). https://doi.org/10.1007/978-3-031-61154-4_12
18. Tamayo Avila, D., Van Petegem, W., Snoeck, M.: Improving teamwork in agile software engineering education: the ASEST+ framework. IEEE Trans. Educ. **65**(1), 18–29 (2022). https://doi.org/10.1109/TE.2021.3084095
19. Tuckman, B.W., Jensen, M.A.C.: Stages of small-group development revisited. Group Organ. Stud. **2**(4), 419–427 (1977). https://doi.org/10.1177/105960117700200404, http://journals.sagepub.com/doi/10.1177/105960117700200404
20. Wellhausen, T., Fießer, A.: How to write a pattern? A rough guide for first-time pattern authors. In: Proceedings of the 16th European Conference on Pattern Languages of Programs, pp. 1–9 (2011)

Patterns for Classifying Notional Machines

Anja Bertels(✉)

Cologne University of Applied Sciences (TH Köln), Gummersbach, Germany
anja.bertels@th-koeln.de

Abstract. Notional Machines are conceptual models that help students understand abstract programming concepts. This paper presents three patterns that can be used to classify different types of Notional Machines in computing education: visual representation, tangibility, and analogy. The first pattern describes how Notional Machines can be visualized through either handmade or machine-generated representations. The second pattern investigates the role of tangible artifacts as an interactive representation of programming and computing concepts. Finally, the third pattern explores the use of analogies to map complex programming concepts to familiar real-world phenomena. This paper is intended to provide a framework for instructors to effectively incorporate Notional Machines into their teaching practices.

Keywords: Computing Education · Notional Machines · Misconceptions

1 Introduction

The main objective of Computing Education Research as a discipline is to understand and improve how computing concepts are taught and learned. Ongoing research aims to improve teaching practice through various measures, such as live coding, peer instruction, or visualization tools [21]. High dropout rates in programming courses are a recurring issue that motivates investigating this area [25].

One of the challenges students face when learning to program is understanding abstract concepts. They do not understand the properties of their program and do not know how to control it [9]. A general problem identified with learning is the "education of attention", meaning what to attend to and what to ignore, since not all available information is relevant all the time [1].

To reason about a program's behaviour, students must develop a mental model, an internal representation of how the system works [2]. When these mental models are flawed or incomplete, misconceptions can arise. Misconceptions can be defined as errors in conceptual understanding and are often resistant to change when they result from an incorrect mental model [24].

Misconceptions about programming can be addressed through the use of Notional Machines. A Notional Machine is a pedagogic device that provides

T. Plummer et al. (Eds.): EuroPLoP 2025, LNCS 16494, pp. 307–326, 2026.
https://doi.org/10.1007/978-3-032-19157-1_14

Fig. 1. Popular Notional Machine for storing and assigning variables (AI generated using Google Gemini 2.5; September 30, 2025)

an abstraction of the physical machine to help understand certain aspects or concepts of programming. The Notional Machine simplifies a real concept, for example by describing a variable as a box that stores a value (see Fig. 1), and therefore does not need to accurately describe every detail of the real machine. Nevertheless, it is important that the chosen abstraction is complete and consistent. Completeness in this context means all observable behaviour of the real machine must be explainable within its defined scope by the Notional Machine. Consistency means that reasoning within the Notional Machine must correctly predict the behaviour of the real machine. [5].

1.1 Research Background

In Computing Education Research, Notional Machines are recognized as a signature pedagogy [10]. In a literature review on Learning Theories in Computing Education Research from 2022, Szabo et al. [29] identified them as the most popular learning theory. In an ITiCSE Working Group Report from 2020, Fincher et al. [10] defined the term "Notional Machine" to provide a holistic characterization including a pedagogical purpose, a generic function to draw attention to something, a specific focus within programs or computing, and a representation that highlights specific aspects of the focus.

Most work using Notional Machines tracks changes in students' attitude or performance after an intervention, or observes difficulties, successes, and overall understanding of students [10]. The literature evaluating the pedagogical effectiveness of Notional Machines and their impact on students is still limited. Results of interventions using Notional Machines mostly suggest that explicit reference to a Notional Machine helps comprehension, while its absence leads to misconceptions [8,18,22]. One aspect that has been widely explored in this context is the visualization of Notional Machines through software systems, such as Novis, UUhistle and Jeliot [4,23,28]. There is some disagreement in the literature about the relationship between a Notional Machine and its visualization. Using the characteristics defined by Fincher et al. [10], the visualization is defined as part of the Notional Machine. Dickson et al. [8] on the other hand argue that "A notional machine and a visualization usually relate closely, but a notional machine may have multiple possible visualizations, and a visualization may be useful for multiple notional machines", describing the two as distinct, yet related, entities.

While the adoption in the research community is undeniable, the Cambridge Handbook of Computing Education Research states: "Despite some noticeable treatment in the literature, notional machines do not feature prominently in curricula or texts for computing courses" [12]. In fact, educators mostly use Notional Machines without realizing it. They intuitively explain concepts through analogies or sketching and create Notional Machines ad hoc [4]. This approach can be successful, and students may adapt the representations used, but it is likely that these ad hoc Notional Machines are inconsistent or incorrect. For example, sketching out a code trace on paper has been correlated with higher scores on code reading problems, but sketches are not always consistent with the correct execution of the Notional Machine [16]. If little attention is paid to the use of Notional Machines, students may also come up with their own incorrect models [27]. It has been found that explicit teaching of a Notional Machine is a promising approach and that a clear view of the relationship between the mental model, the Notional Machine, and its visualization has positive effects [8].

Much of the research about Notional Machines deals with the application for novices. However, advanced learners or even experts can also benefit from the use of Notional Machines [11]. By adding or omitting details, Notional Machines can be adjusted for different audiences [10]. Instructors are not limited to using only one Notional Machine. They often draw on a diverse collection of Notional Machines that focus on different concepts or aspects of a concept. Another option is the gradual expansion of Notional Machines to include new concepts [10].

Since most usage is unstructured, categorizations are necessary to highlight distinctions and provide an overview for educators. The development of different categorizations and distinctions has mostly built on top of each other, with the origin lying in the Dagstuhl Seminar 19281 [16], titled "Notional Machines and Programming Language Semantics in Education". Du Boulay, who coined the term "Notional Machine", contributed a presentation called "Notional Machines and Research from the 1970s and 1980s". He talked about influential work, difficulties of learning programming and Notional Machines. In addition, he divided Notional Machines into stories and (machine generated) representations as two overarching categories. A breakout group was formed with the goal of categorizing Notional Machines and their representation in order to develop a better understanding of the characteristics of Notional Machines. In this group, Fincher et al. [11] identified three areas in which a Notional Machine might play a role: The programming environment, the programming language, and the task of programming itself. Interestingly, the categorizations mentioned cover different dimensions: While du Boulay in his presentation distinguishes Notional Machines by their abstraction, the breakout group focuses on the areas of interest. Those areas of interest have been adapted to a model commonly used to classify misconceptions. Following this, a Notional Machine can focus on the *programming language*, the *machine*, and the *interaction* between the two [10].

When designing Notional Machines, specifying the focus area is not sufficient. More importantly, there has to be a distinction between *how* instead of *what*. In the natural sciences, there are two ways to create a model, called *Aris-*

totelian and *Galilean*. The Aristotelian model omits aspects of the system that are irrelevant to the model and is therefore a simplification. The Galilean model, on the other hand, includes aspects that are not part of the system in order to make the model more comprehensible [26]. This provides another distinction that focuses specifically on the conceptual design of Notional Machines. The Working Group that emerged from the Dagstuhl Seminar 19281 presented their results in three thematic groups, extending du Boulay's categorization. They distinguish between machine-generated representations, such as program visualization tools, hand-made representations, and analogies. This categorization focuses on the representation of Notional Machines as well as the conceptual design. Of course, these dimensions are orthogonal and a Notional Machine that uses an analogy also has a representation that could be machine-generated or hand-made. The authors conclude that putting Notional Machines in categories is hard and there are many gray areas between the identified categories [10].

1.2 Research Aim

The main aim of this paper is to develop a classification specifically focusing on the relevant distinctions to apply Notional Machines and ultimately answer the question "What types of Notional Machines are there and which is the right one for this specific context?". This classification can help either creating or choosing suitable Notional Machines. The groundwork is the grouping from Fincher et al. that classifies Notional Machines as having a handmade representation, a machine-generated representation, or being an analogy [10].

To achieve this, the following three objectives are specified:

- Create an overview of different types of Notional Machines to increase awareness about their existence
- Clearly distinguish the different types of Notional Machines to help educators correctly apply them
- Clarify the contexts suitable for the different types of Notional Machines

In the context of education, patterns can be helpful guidelines for instructors to determine the appropriate level of abstraction and the most suitable representation for their specific context [3]. Thus, we can assume the pattern format to assist educators in comprehending the relevance of Notional Machines in the field of Computer Science through its efficiency and ease-of-use. Notional Machines can be categorized into different patterns to aid educators in their selection and design of teaching tools. The pattern format was previously endorsed at Dagstuhl Seminar, where the Breakout Group focusing on "Categorizing Notional Machines and their Representation or Visualization" conducted an introduction to pattern languages [16]. However, the pattern approach did not seem to be further pursued, although it remains promising.

Research suggests two main areas of interest for instructors: The appropriate level of abstraction and the representation of the Notional Machine. When creating a model from a system, aspects that are not relevant are either omitted or new aspects that are not part of the system are included [10]. What exactly can and should be omitted or included is contextual and determines how well suited a Notional Machine is. Omitting aspects also prevents an overload of unnecessary information, as the correct and consistent Notional Machine will hold exactly the right amount of detail [8]. Once the level of abstraction is chosen, a Notional Machine must have a representation in order to be used. The representation draws attention to certain aspects of the focus [10]. The representation, like the level of abstraction, depends on the context. For some student groups or levels of prior knowledge, the concept has to be more abstract than for others. Similarly, different types of representations can be suitable for different groups of students.

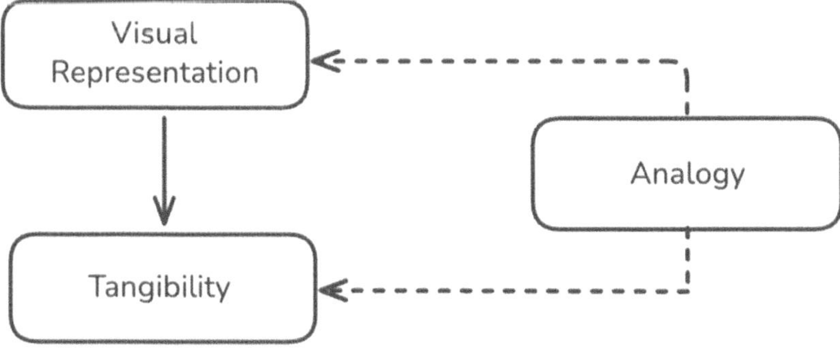

Fig. 2. The three patterns presented in this paper

To address the research objectives taking into account the main areas of interest, in this paper, three patterns are presented to classify Notional Machines. Both handmade and machine-generated representations are classified under the overarching pattern *Visual Representation*. Despite their evident differences in form and the range of possibilities they offer, these two forms of representation exhibit significant overlap, making them suitable for similar applications. Furthermore, the *Tangibility* pattern expands the categorization to encompass physical, three dimensional objects. In related literature, Notional Machines represented in a tangible way are summarized as handmade representations or not mentioned at all. Here, a deliberate distinction is made because tangible representations can offer specific aspects of the context that are highly relevant for the application. The value of tangible representations in certain conceptual contexts can surpass that of other forms of representation. A presentation by Colleen Lewis at the Dagstuhl Seminar focused on a pedagogical approach known as concrete-to-representational-to-abstract, wherein the transition from three-dimensional to two-dimensional to abstracted representations of Notional Machines is strongly advocated [16]. Using this approach, the concrete Notional Machine can be related to the pattern *Tangibility*, while the representational Notional Machine corresponds to the pattern *Visual Representation*. The third pattern presented in this paper, *Analogy*, corresponds to the same category defined by Fincher et al. This category prioritizes the context of a Notional Machine over its representation, which makes it orthogonal to the other patterns. In summary, the three patterns shown in Fig. 2 deal with the visualization and abstraction of a Notional Machine to help instructors choose the most suitable Notional Machine for their specific context (Fig. 3).

The patterns will be described using the following format:

- **Name:** The pattern name helps to refer to the patterns using the core of the solution.
- **Context:** The situation in which the pattern can be applied.
- **Problem:** The specific main challenge that arises from the context.
- **Forces:** The competing concerns and constraints that make the problem hard to solve and have to be balanced within the pattern.
- **Solution:** The core of the pattern and approach to solve the main problem while balancing the forces.
- **Consequences:** The benefits and liabilities of applying the proposed solution.
- **Known Uses:** Concrete examples of the pattern in use.

2 Visual Representation

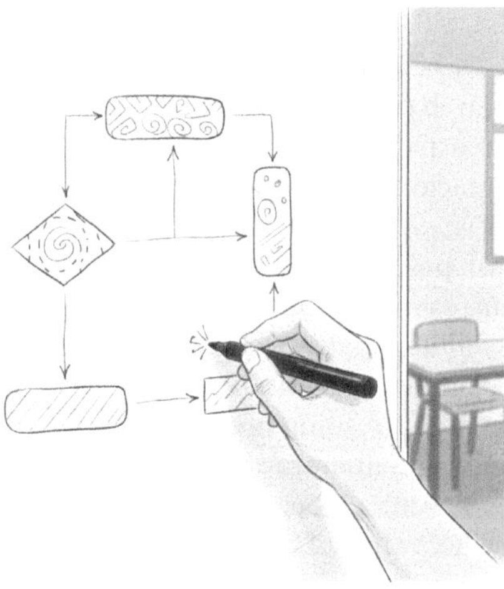

Fig. 3. Stylized representation of *Visual Representation* (AI generated using Google Gemini 2.5; September 30, 2025)

2.1 Context

Instructors want to convey abstract programming concepts. The concepts are novel and part of an unfamiliar domain for students. Various aspects of the concept are similar, with small but important distinctions.

2.2 Problem

Understanding abstract concepts is difficult for novices due to their unfamiliarity and the lack of visibility of programming in the "real world". The different components and their interrelatedness are difficult to grasp. Students confuse concepts and cannot effectively process verbal explanations with a high information density. They need to understand what actually happens.

How can abstract programming concepts be represented to help novices overcome confusion and difficulties in processing explanations?

2.3 Forces

- **Abstraction:** It is a prevalent challenge to choose the right scope. On the one hand, the abstract nature of concepts makes them difficult to understand. On the other hand, this abstraction is necessary to form an accurate understanding. The level of abstraction inherent in the concept should be accurately reflected.
- **Clarity vs. Complexity:** The concept must be presented clearly and accurately, avoiding any potential for ambiguity. The primary goal should be to ensure student understanding. As complexity increases, this task becomes more difficult and students struggle to recall all the pertinent aspects. The integration of concepts with existing knowledge can enhance comprehensibility, but may constrain the complexity and precision of the subject matter in terms of details.
- **Misconceptions:** Various factors may contribute to the development of misconceptions. It is possible that students have divergent interpretations of the same concept, resulting in the development of different mental models. Such ambiguity should be avoided. The potential for erroneous interpretation should be reduced. Different prior knowledge from students can contribute to challenges in comprehension of fundamental concepts. Especially edge cases can be difficult to understand.
- **Functionality:** The concept has to be presented in a way that is easy to understand for students, but at the same time it has to be accurate and must not lack correctness. From a pedagogical perspective, the representation must be usable for educational purposes and content accuracy.
- **Engagement:** The effective presentation of content is crucial for capturing students' attention, and it is imperative to employ engaging and interesting methods to achieve this objective. Engagement enhances students' interest in programming concepts and can have positive effects on learning overall. Clarity and Accuracy are connected with Engagement, and it is a challenge to balance all aspects, especially when they conflict with each other.

2.4 Solution

Provide learners with handmade or machine-generated visual representations.

Notional Machines can have two-dimensional visual representations that are conceived as an abstraction from a particular concept. Relevant details can be clearly displayed and complexity can be adjusted through adding or removing details from the visualization. Furthermore, a visual representation functions as a common ground for discourse and illustration of conceptual understanding, thereby facilitating the identification of misconceptions. Visualizations enhance engagement and serve as a functional tool for the transfer and application of knowledge. Concepts can be integrated by using animations, step-by-step visualizations, or overlaying information. The specific representation used depends on the concept, its corresponding misconceptions, and the educator's objectives.

Visual representations should be designed carefully to highlight the key aspects of Notional Machines. This representation can facilitate the comprehension of complex concepts, rendering them more concrete and accessible. These artifacts also serve as catalysts for reflection and discussion. The visual representation of a Notional Machine can also facilitate the establishment of a valid mental model [19].

Machine-generated representations should be designed so that it is possible to create animated visualizations and show dynamic changes or process states. They enable users to transition between different states. Although machine-generated representations can also be three-dimensional, they are still viewed on a two-dimensional screen. This important distinction implies limitations as well as benefits as opposed to truly three-dimensional representations.

Handmade representations can be visualized ad hoc and are more readily reproduced by learners, for instance, through the act of sketching in an evaluative context. These tools have the capacity to facilitate the establishment of cognitive connections, thereby enhancing the ability to retrieve specific components of conceptual machines and the theoretical frameworks they encompass. They can exist on paper, whiteboards, or other physical or digital surfaces where spontaneous drawing and annotation are possible. Handmade representations can be used to interact with or respond to individual questions.

The employment of visual representations in the teaching process can be achieved through a variety of methods, including the focus on edge cases, the creation of specific use cases, or the addressing of individual questions posed by learners. Additionally, visual representations of Notional Machines can be used to create cognitive conflict if learners hold invalid mental models.

2.5 Consequences

Benefits

- Learners' ability to remember and recall content is improved by the presence of a visual representation [7].
- A visual representation is a practical tool for individual explanations, as the visual aspect can focus on the most challenging part for the target group or this aspect can be visually enhanced.

- The understandability is improved by the use of a visual aid.
- The teaching of changes in a concept is facilitated by the use of a visual representation when changes are visually highlighted.
- Visual representations can be reused and refined in an iterative manner.

Liabilities

- The creation of a visual representation of a Notional Machine necessitates the allocation of materials, time, and financial resources by educators.
- Machine-generated visual representations may encounter availability issues due to software versioning conflicts or technology constraints.
- The process of familiarizing oneself with a machine-generated visual representation, whether through a designated tool or other means, can often be a time-consuming endeavor.
- The fabrication of handmade visual representations is often accompanied by a heightened propensity for errors, attributable to the capacity for ad hoc modification by any individual.

2.6 Known Uses

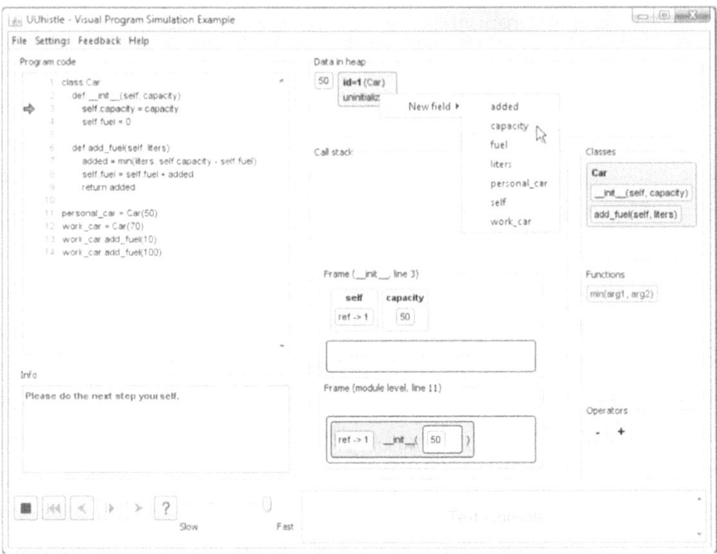

Fig. 4. Screenshot from the execution of a visual program simulation exercise in UUhistle. Note: This reference includes [28]

- **IDE Debugger:** Modern IDEs provide debuggers that visually show the current state of variables, the call stack, and the execution path of a program step-by-step. This teaches students how the program's state changes over time and helps them trace control flow to find errors.
- **UUhistle:** UUhistle is a software simulator that provides dynamic visual representations to explain the execution of Python programs, often showing the memory model and variable bindings, see Fig. 4. The focus lies on on teaching operational semantics.

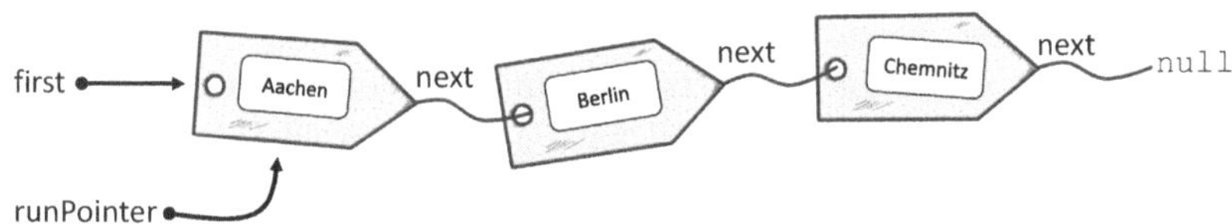

Fig. 5. Example illustration with city names as data. [20]

- **Linked List Drawing:** Sketches of linked lists are used to explain the static structure of the data type, illustrating concepts such as nodes, references, and null terminations, see Fig. 5. These drawings help students visualize the relationship between data elements and how the structure is maintained in memory. To create a more dynamic representation, this example can also be visualized on a whiteboard, using a magnet as the runPointer reference (Fig. 7).

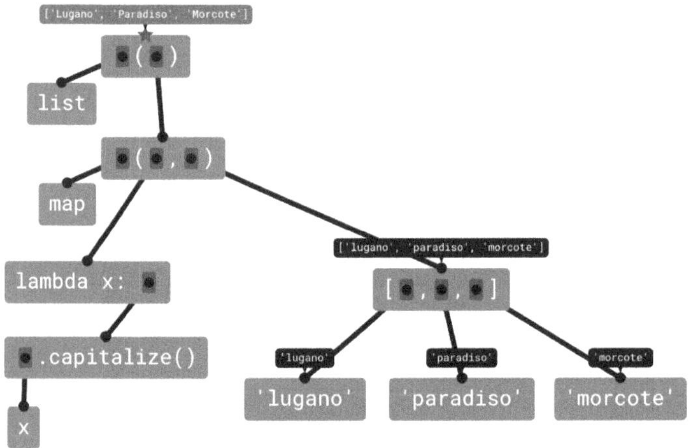

Fig. 6. Screenshot from the Activity Sequence example in Python

- **ExpressionTutor**[1]: ExpressionTutor is an online tool that visually guides students through the evaluation of complex arithmetic and logical expressions. It highlights sub-expressions according to the rules of operator precedence and associativity, teaching the fixed mechanical rules of evaluation, see Fig. 6.

3 Tangibility

Fig. 7. Stylized representation of *Tangibility* (AI generated using Google Gemini 2.5; September 30, 2025)

3.1 Context

The concept to be conveyed encompasses processes, states, or algorithms that remain hidden when they are simply observed from an outside perspective. Verbal or visual explanations are highly complex in order to fully cover all aspects of the concept.

3.2 Problem

The abstract nature of programming concepts poses a significant challenge. Learners encounter significant challenges in grasping the hidden processes represented with Notional Machines, which impedes both the clarity of understanding and the efficacy of error identification.

How can the abstract and hidden processes within a Notional Machine be represented to improve a learner's conceptual understanding?

[1] https://expressiontutor.org/, last accessed September 30, 2025.

3.3 Forces

- **Correctness vs. Simplicity:** Constructs such as assignments, loops, and function calls are executed "behind the scenes" and are not visible to learners. It is imperative that the behaviour and underlying mechanics are accurately reflected. However, distilling the concept down to its fundamental components can facilitate student comprehension. An elevated level of detail has been demonstrated to increase the cognitive load experienced by the reader.
- **Knowledge Construction vs. Ease of Use:** In order to comprehend processes and states, static representations are inadequate. Constructing knowledge through engagement and exploration is a much more sustainable approach. Engagement through interaction has been demonstrated to increase motivation and allow learners to develop a deeper understanding. However, the absence of clues or guidance can further support misconceptions and lead to incorrect and error-prone mental models. Edge cases are of particular concern. When learning new concepts, the employment of readily available and user-friendly instructional tools is crucial to minimize the time and effort required to set up the learning environment as well as to reduce frustration.
- **Constraints vs. Freedom:** Learners should be able to explore and experiment with the concept freely, without being overly constrained by representational limitations. Conversely, a representation is inherently constrained due to its nature as a model of the actual concept. Another constraint that may impede the desired conceptual freedom is economic efficiency.

3.4 Solution

Provide a tangible representation of the Notional Machine that allows learners to interact with it.

Students adopt the role of the executing machine and interact with the concept to comprehend its behaviour. The Notional Machine can be represented by a physical object, model, interactive device, or tools, thereby enabling learners to directly influence and even manipulate the Notional Machine. This enhances interaction and facilitates comprehension of imperceptible processes and states by rendering them physical and accessible. Tearing something apart and reassembling it can help to explore ideas as well as remembering the process.

The students actively participate in experiencing what is happening "behind the scenes", while the instructors can use the tangible representation to show and remove operations. Depending on the Notional Machine, the object can be 3D printed or constructed. Furthermore, the incorporation of everyday objects is a viable option. It is imperative that learners have the opportunity to engage with the object and observe it from multiple perspectives when applying the pattern, as this is the distinguishing factor compared to other types of representation. To some extent, learners take on the role of the computer by physically interacting with a tangible representation.

3.5 Consequences

Benefits

- Manipulation of a physical model activates additional senses and strengthens embodied cognition.
- Interacting with a tangible model facilitates active learning [14].
- The hidden processes and states of the Notional Machine become visible and understandable.
- Tangible representations can reduce cognitive load by transference of abstract information from the mind to the material realm. Learners can focus on the physical representation [17].
- The use of tangible objects in learning environments fosters collaboration and discussion. They enhance engagement and foster collaboration among students, motivating them to investigate and discuss various scenarios or use cases [14].
- Tangible models are engaging and motivating for learners [14].

Liabilities

- The creation of a physical model requires additional time, effort, and resources.
- A tangible object is limited in representing all aspects of a Notional Machine, particularly in the case of more complex processes or concepts.
- It is imperative that learners demonstrate the ability to transfer their understanding of the tangible object to abstract programming concepts and, ultimately, the source code.
- A tangible representation limits the number of users that can access it concurrently. In a course with multiple students, it is not feasible for all students to experience the tangible object in the same way at the same time because experiencing it includes touching and interacting with it.

3.6 Known Uses

- **Bubble Sort with Legos:** To visualize the process of bubble sort, each Lego brick represents a data element, and the learners arrange the bricks according to the result of the comparison and swap process of the algorithm, see Fig. 8.
- **Software Architecture models:** 3D printed objects can be used to build physical models of software architectures, representing components, connections, and the flow of data between them.
- **Variable as a Box**[2]: A variable is represented as a physical box with a label that represents the variable name. The box can contain different values. To represent type safety, boxes with different shapes or colors can represent different data types (Fig. 9).

[2] https://notionalmachines.github.io/nms/VariableAsBox.html, last accessed May 6, 2025.

Fig. 8. Initial state of the tangible model that teaches the Bubble Sort algorithm [6]

4 Analogy

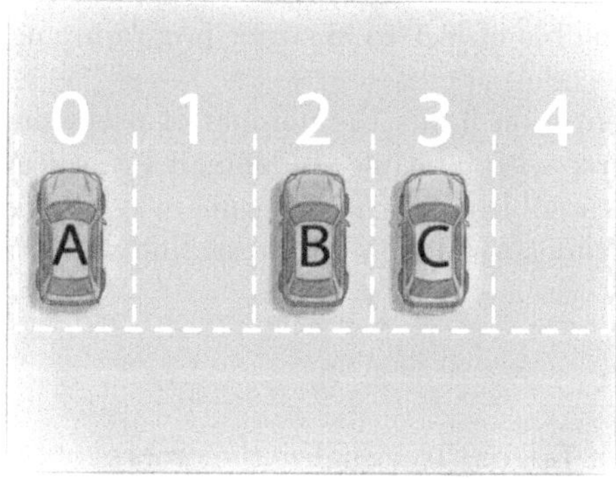

Fig. 9. Stylized representation of *Analogy* (AI generated using Google Gemini 2.5; September 30, 2025)

4.1 Context

An unfamiliar concept is introduced. It is part of a domain that is completely new to learners. The concept under discussion is one that may be characterized as formal, incorporating abstract elements, terminology, and elucidations. Strengthening transfer competencies in learners may be necessary.

4.2 Problem

There is a lack of real-world equivalence of what happens when code is executed. The unfamiliarity of the domain increases the challenge faced by learners as they attempt to comprehend the novel programming concept. Retention becomes harder with each concept, especially in the case of transformative threshold concepts.

How can instruction bridge the gap between the unfamiliar, abstract nature of code execution and the real world to improve learners' comprehension of programming concepts?

4.3 Forces

- **Abstraction vs. Concreteness:** The integration of concepts with learner's existing knowledge fosters enhanced relatability and comprehension, thereby suggesting an additional abstraction from the already abstract concept. Simultaneously, the representation must accurately reflect the core functionality and behaviour of the concept, while avoiding oversimplification or misrepresentation of key details.
- **Familiarity vs. Novelty:** The introduction of a new domain should be related to existing knowledge, providing a solid foundation and facilitating the retention of the new concept. Demonstrating the relationship between novel domains and existing knowledge or experiences can also foster engagement. Identifying domains that are readily relatable to learners' daily lives or other areas of knowledge can pose significant challenges, particularly when learners possess diverse cultural and demographic backgrounds. Furthermore, establishing common ground among learners with varying levels of prior knowledge can pose a significant challenge. In instances where the domain is entirely novel, it has the potential to induce confusion when familiar domains are employed. The introduction of novel perspectives increases curiosity.
- **Engagement vs. Cognitive Load:** The concept should be presented in a manner that is both engaging and captivating, thereby capturing the learner's attention and fostering further exploration. However, it is imperative to refrain from introducing additional complexity or cognitive overhead to achieve this objective. It is important to consider the cognitive load to ensure that learners can comprehend the relationship and are not overwhelmed or frustrated.

4.4 Solution

Introduce the new programming concept by drawing an analogy to a familiar real-world domain or concept that learners can relate to.

Every analogy consists of two domains: the source domain and the target domain. The source domain comprises knowledge that is familiar to the learner, while the target domain signifies the domain of the programming concept [13].

In order to identify an appropriate analogy, educators must first establish a foundation of understanding regarding the existing familiarity of learners with different domains.

The analogy must be precise enough to represent the characteristics of the corresponding programming concept while being flexible enough to cover a variety of scenarios. This aligns with the theory of constructivism, a theoretical framework that posits that individuals construct their own understanding of the world through the active process of constructing their own knowledge. The establishment of parallels between the source and target domains also supports knowledge transfer competencies.

4.5 Consequences

Benefits

- Analogies can function as mnemonic devices, facilitating the formation of mental connections.
- The employment of an analogy facilitates comprehension of abstract concepts.
- Constructivism posits that familiarity with concepts enhances comprehension.
- The utilization of analogies has been demonstrated to facilitate the competency of transferring knowledge, a pivotal skill in the field [15].

Liabilities

- Every analogy has limits that educators must be aware of, as failure to do so can result in the propagation of erroneous knowledge.
- Analogies have the potential to redirect the emphasis of a Notional Machine, potentially resulting in the oversight or simplification of certain characteristics.
- If the Analogy is not chosen appropriately, it can support incorrect implications and lead to confusion.
- The source domain that is most suitable for creating analogies is impacted by individual differences. A variety of factors, including cultural differences, prior knowledge, and personal interests, have the potential to influence the outcome.

4.6 Known Uses

- **Decorator Pattern as Subway Sandwich:** The Decorator Pattern can be explained through the analogy of a subway sandwich, where additional "layers" of functionality are added to the "base". The "decorated" sandwich is not returned to the customer until the very last step is completed.
- **Linked List as Music Playlist:** A Linked List can be explained using the analogy of a music playlist, where each node represents a song and the references between nodes represent the order of the playlist.

- **Array as Parking Lot**[3]: An Array can be explained using the analogy of a parking lot, where each index represents a parking spot and the values represent the cars parked in those spots.
- **Washing Machine as CPU Pipelining:** This analogy illustrates how multiple steps of a process can be overlapped. In a single-stage process, waiting for the whole load to finish is necessary before starting the next. With pipelining, much like starting the next load of wash while the first is drying, the CPU starts executing the next instruction before the previous one has completely finished all its execution stages.
- **Network Protocols as Conversation:** This analogy highlights that communication on a network is more than a simple one-way transmission; it is a structured exchange. Just as people follow rules (like listening, taking turns, and confirming understanding) to have a successful conversation, network devices follow protocols that define the syntax, semantics, and synchronization of communication. This analogy makes abstract concepts like handshaking, error checking, and layered communication more concrete by relating them to everyday social interactions.

5 Discussion and Future Work

The three patterns described in this paper are all effective strategies to support the teaching of Notional Machines in programming education. Notional Machines are of significant value to educators, as they serve as a foundational approach and signature pedagogy in the instruction of programming skills to students. The utilization of visual representations, tangible models, and analogies can facilitate the comprehension and engagement of learners with abstract concepts. The diversity in the representation and preparation of Notional Machines that is presented in these patterns has great potential for effective use in teaching. However, no representation is fully intuitive, and students still need to be taught syntax and implementation details. Although the three patterns presented are distinct and specific in their context statements, the problems they solve are similar. This phenomenon can be traced back to the fundamental challenge of teaching complex and abstract concepts.

While visual representations are relatively widespread, the specification of tangible, physical objects in particular could open up a new perspective. The utilization of analogies and metaphors has been employed in the context of novice education; nevertheless, their implementation in the realm of higher-curricular programming concepts remains underrepresented. The specific application contexts and their constraints offer further potential for exploration.

An alternative perspective on this issue is the combination of the patterns. In essence, the patterns delineated in this paper can function as foundational elements for a more diverse and holistic approach to programming education.

[3] https://notionalmachines.github.io/nms/ArrayAsRowOfParkingSpaces.html, last accessed May 7, 2025.

To illustrate, tangible representations have the capacity to incorporate an analogy. The integration of tangible objects with machine-generated representations is another subject that merits further exploration. The patterns could also be used sequentially, guiding learners through the learning process, as indicated in the concrete-to-representational-to-abstract approach by Colleen Lewis [16]. The utilization of multiple Notional Machines is a strategy employed to direct attention toward disparate aspects. Alternatively, the expansion of a singular Notional Machine over time, accompanied by the introduction of novel concepts, has been observed [10].

Future work should focus on the systematic expansion of the pattern set to fully map the spectrum of representational forms for Notional Machines. New patterns and sub-patterns need to be incorporated for under-investigated forms, such as role-playing. Furthermore, empirical validation of the patterns presented here is crucial. This step is necessary to statistically substantiate and reinforce their pedagogical efficacy within computing education.

6 Conclusion

In summary, the three patterns *Visual Representation*, *Tangibility*, and *Analogy* offer valuable approaches to representing and designing Notional Machines in order to teach programming concepts in a more accessible and understandable way.

A more thorough examination of the specific frameworks underlying these diverse patterns is warranted. The establishment of a concrete distinction, in conjunction with the formulation of guidelines for educators to assist them in implementing the various patterns in their teaching, has the potential to serve as a foundation for more effective and engaging programming education. Furthermore, the potential for combinations and integrations of the patterns identified in this study offers a promising avenue for future research endeavors.

Acknowledgments. I am very grateful for the valuable feedback of my shepherd Waheedullah Sulaiman Khail. His expertise greatly contributed to the improvement of this paper and elevated the overall quality of this work. I would like to thank my Workshop Group at EuroPLoP 2025 for their feedback and the interesting discussions that helped refine the patterns: Aliaksandr Birukou, Cesare Pautasso, Christian Kohls, Dan Zhu, Marius Nißlmüller, Simon Schulte.

Disclosure of Interests. The author has no competing interests to declare that are relevant to the content of this article.

References

1. Adolph, K.E., Kretch, K.S.: Gibson's theory of perceptual learning. Int. Encyclopedia Soc. Behav. Sci. **10**, 127–134 (2015)
2. Ben-Ari, M.: Constructivism in computer science education. ACM Sigcse Bull. **30**(1), 257–261 (1998)

3. Bergin, J., et al.: Pedagogical patterns: advice for educators. Joseph Bergin Software Tools (2012)
4. Berry, M., Kölling, M.: The state of play: a notional machine for learning programming. In: Proceedings of the 2014 Conference on Innovation & Technology in Computer Science Education, pp. 21–26 (2014)
5. Berry, M., Kölling, M.: Novis: A notional machine implementation for teaching introductory programming. In: 2016 International Conference on Learning and Teaching in Computing and Engineering (LaTICE), pp. 54–59. IEEE (2016)
6. Bertels, A., Deimel, D.: Improving coding workshops: a pattern collection. In: Proceedings of the 29th European Conference on Pattern Languages of Programs, People, and Practices. EuroPLoP '24, Association for Computing Machinery, New York (2024). https://doi.org/10.1145/3698322.3698323
7. Clark, J.M., Paivio, A.: Dual coding theory and education. Educ. Psychol. Rev. **3**(3), 149–210 (1991)
8. Dickson, P.E., Brown, N.C., Becker, B.A.: Engage against the machine: rise of the notional machines as effective pedagogical devices. In: Proceedings of the 2020 ACM Conference on Innovation and Technology in Computer Science Education, pp. 159–165 (2020)
9. Du Boulay, B.: Some difficulties of learning to program. In: Studying the Novice Programmer, pp. 283–299. Psychology Press (2013)
10. Fincher, S., et al.: Notional machines in computing education: the education of attention. In: Proceedings of the Working Group Reports on Innovation and Technology in Computer Science Education, pp. 21–50. ITiCSE-WGR '20, Association for Computing Machinery, New York (2020). https://doi.org/10.1145/3437800.3439202
11. Fincher, S., et al.: Capturing and characterising notional machines. In: Proceedings of the 2020 ACM Conference on Innovation and Technology in Computer Science Education, pp. 502–503 (2020)
12. Fincher, S.A., Robins, A.V.: The Cambridge handbook of computing education research. Cambridge University Press (2019)
13. Forišek, M., Steinová, M.: Metaphors and analogies for teaching algorithms. In: Proceedings of the 43rd ACM technical symposium on Computer Science Education, pp. 15–20 (2012)
14. Fraser, D.S., et al.: Literature review in learning with tangible technologies. NESTA Futurelab Report **12** (2004)
15. Gick, M.L., Holyoak, K.J.: Analogical problem solving. Cogn. Psychol. **12**(3), 306–355 (1980)
16. Guzdial, M., Krishnamurthi, S., Sorva, J., Vahrenhold, J.: Notional machines and programming language semantics in education: report from dagstuhl seminar 19281. No. 7 in dagstuhl reports, schloss dagstuhl - leibniz-zentrum für informatik, Germany (2019). 10.4230/DagRep.9.7.1, dagstuhl Seminar 19281 : Notional Machines and Programming Language Semantics in Education ; Conference date: 07-07-2019 Through 12-07-2019
17. Hollan, J., Hutchins, E., Kirsh, D.: Distributed cognition: toward a new foundation for human-computer interaction research. ACM Trans. Comput. Hum. Interaction (TOCHI) **7**(2), 174–196 (2000)
18. Johnson, F., McQuistin, S., O'Donnell, J.: Analysis of student misconceptions using python as an introductory programming language. In: Proceedings of the 4th Conference on Computing Education Practice, pp. 1–4 (2020)
19. Juha, S.: Notional machines and introductory programming education. ACM Trans. Comput. Educ **13**(2), 1–31 (2013)

20. Kohls, C., Dobrynin, A.: Programmieren lernen mit Kotlin: Grundlagen. Carl Hanser Verlag GmbH Co KG, Objektorientierung und fortgeschrittene Konzepte (2023)
21. Luxton-Reilly, A., et al.: Introductory programming: a systematic literature review. In: Proceedings Companion of the 23rd Annual ACM Conference on Innovation and Technology in Computer Science Education, pp. 55–106 (2018)
22. Ma, L., Ferguson, J., Roper, M., Wood, M.: Investigating and improving the models of programming concepts held by novice programmers. Comput. Sci. Educ. **21**(1), 57–80 (2011)
23. Moreno, A., Myller, N., Ben-Ari, M., Sutinen, E.: Program animation in jeliot 3. ACM SIGCSE Bull. **36**(3), 265–265 (2004)
24. Qian, Y., Lehman, J.: Students' misconceptions and other difficulties in introductory programming: a literature review. ACM Trans. Comput. Educ. (TOCE) **18**(1), 1–24 (2017)
25. Robins, A., Rountree, J., Rountree, N.: Learning and teaching programming: a review and discussion. Comput. Sci. Educ. **13**(2), 137–172 (2003)
26. Roman, F., Stephan, H., Zalta Edward, N., et al.: Models in science. EN Zalta, The Stanford encyclopedia of philosophy (2012)
27. Sorva, J.: Students' understandings of storing objects. In: Proceedings of the Seventh Baltic Sea Conference on Computing Education Research-vol. 88, pp. 127–135 (2007)
28. Sorva, J., Sirkiä, T.: Uuhistle: a software tool for visual program simulation. In: Proceedings of the 10th Koli Calling International Conference on Computing Education Research, pp. 49–54. Koli Calling '10, Association for Computing Machinery, New York (2010). https://doi.org/10.1145/1930464.1930471
29. Szabo, C., Sheard, J.: Learning theories use and relationships in computing education research. ACM Trans. Comput. Educ. **23**(1), 1–34 (2022)

Patterns for Hybrid Meeting Situations

Simon Schulte[(✉)] and Christian Kohls

Cologne University of Applied Sciences (TH Köln), Steinmüllerallee 1, 51643 Gummersbach, Germany
{simon_ludwig.schulte,christian.kohls}@th-koeln.de

Abstract. This paper describes patterns for hybrid meeting situations Central room mic and loudspeaker, Cover points of interest with cameras and Getting closer. A hybrid meeting situation refers to any context where some participants are co-located and others join remotely in a meeting. The patterns try to improve the inclusivity and effectiveness of such hybrid meetings, especially for online participants, by addressing common communication and technical challenges. The target group is anyone who uses hybrid meetings as part of their work.

Keywords: hybrid meetings · hybrid · patterns · meeting technology · conference systems

1 Introduction

Due to the COVID-19 pandemic and the lockdown that followed, there has been a rapid increase in virtual meetings. As a result, online conferencing tools such as Microsoft Teams, Zoom and others have become very popular. [1] But even after the COVID-19 pandemic, not all companies are returning to work exclusively on site. The results of a survey by Randstad [2], in which 630 human resource managers from companies in Germany were asked about the availability of home office in their company, show that 66% of the companies offer the option of working from home.

This situation results in an increase in hybrid meeting situations. Hybrid meetings combine in-person and online participation by allowing people to interact simultaneously in a physical space and via digital platforms such as Zoom or Microsoft Teams [5]. They can thus be classified as a subform of hybrid collaboration, as physical and digital spaces are linked synchronously [6].

Well-organized and effectively facilitated hybrid meetings offer the combined benefits of in-person interaction and virtual participation. However, it's important to note that communication dynamics differ significantly in these settings. For example, remote participants may feel excluded from informal conversations or struggle to contribute effectively due to technical limitations. [1] Also, it can be difficult for virtual attendees to follow conversations if there are multiple speakers, background noise, or if the speaker is not easily identifiable due to

T. Plummer et al. (Eds.): EuroPLoP 2025, LNCS 16494, pp. 327–336, 2026.
https://doi.org/10.1007/978-3-032-19157-1_15

camera placement or microphone issues [4]. Virtual attendees may also be overlooked when trying to participate, leading to reduced engagement. Technical difficulties, such as poor audiovisual equipment, can further hinder participation and understanding [1,3]. For online participants, it may also be difficult to follow on site interactions with equipment such as whiteboards [3].

The three patterns described in this paper Central room mic and loudspeaker, Cover points of interest with cameras and Getting closer address these problems. These patterns were identified from our own observations. To describe the patterns, the following format is used which includes: Name, Context (with on-site/online subcontexts for hybrid settings), Problem, Forces, Solution, Tips for Implementation, Consequences and Examples.

- **Name** A short, memorable title that captures the essence of the pattern.
- **Context** The situations or environments where the pattern applies. In this case, the context is further separated into an on-site context and an online context, as this paper describes patterns for hybrid meeting situations.
  - **Context on-site** The context specialized for on-site participants.
  - **Context online** The context specialized for online participants.
- **Problem** A description of the problem the pattern addresses.
- **Forces** Describe what makes the problem a problem and what makes it hard to solve.
- **Solution** Describes how to solve the problem.
- **Tips for Implementation** In addition to the solution, it can help to implement the solution.
- **Consequences** Describes what implications, both positive and negative, will the solution have when it is implemented.
- **Examples** Shows in which cases the solution is already implemented and working.

2 Central Room Mic and Loudspeaker

2.1 Context

A group of people convene in a conference room for a hybrid meeting. The meeting is held, via a video conferencing platform. Examples of this are Zoom, Microsoft Teams or Cisco Webex.

Context On-Site. In a typical scenario (especially in a large meeting), on-site participants might each use their own laptop to connect to remote participants. The device setup can vary in the amount of laptops, multiple personal laptops with microphones/speakers may be in use.

Context Online. Online Participants use their laptop to join the meeting and be seen by the build-in webcam of their laptop. Some of the participants use the build-in microphone and loudspeaker of their laptop, while others use an additional headset.

2.2 Problem

Remote participants struggle to hear clearly when many people speak in a large room, due to inconsistent audio pickup and background noise.

2.3 Forces

- Constantly muting/unmuting disrupts the flow of conversation.
- People often forget to mute, introducing background noise.
- In a large room with dispersed speakers, maintaining uniformly clear audio is technically challenging.
- If all on-site attendees use individual microphones or laptops, echoes and feedback can occur.
- In large meetings, several people often speak one after the other or even simultaneously.

2.4 Solution

Use a central room microphone with loudspeaker for the people participating on site, which can record and play back 360° sound.

2.5 Tips for Implementation

The microphone should be placed at the same distance as possible from all people present in the room. This minimizes excessive volume differences between the online participants.

2.6 Consequences

- Participants on site do not have to manually control their microphone and can therefore concentrate more on the meeting.
- Participants on site can no longer forget to mute or unmute themselves.
- There can no longer be any feedback noises, as the microphone does not pick up the sound output via the speakers.
- People sitting further away from the microphone may be quieter than people sitting closer to the microphone.
- Each person participating on site can do without the microphone and loudspeaker function of their own laptop. Instead, all participants can speak freely without having to manually control a microphone.

2.7 Examples

There are several out-of-the-box conference systems that use this pattern. One example would be a portable conference system from Jabra (see Fig. 1). The conference system also offers the advantage that it does not have to be permanently installed in a room, but can be flexibly integrated into different meeting situations (see Fig. 2).

Fig. 1. Portable conference system from Jabra.

Fig. 2. Portable conference system from Jabra in a meeting room.

3 Cover Points of Interest with Cameras

3.1 Context

Employees of a company have a meeting together. The meeting takes place in a hybrid form, via a video conferencing platform. Examples of this are Zoom, Microsoft Teams or Cisco Webex.

Context On-Site. On site, the group uses a CENTRAL ROOM MIC AND LOUDSPEAKER for audio. In addition, each person has their laptop in front of them to join the meeting, so that every on-site participant is visible to the online participants via their webcam. They also see the face of each person who has joined the meeting with their webcam and can clearly hear what everybody says.

Context Online. Online participants use their laptop to join the meeting and be seen by the build-in webcam of their laptop. Also, some of the participants use the build-in microphone and loudspeaker of their laptop, while some use an additional headset. They also see the face of each person who has joined the meeting with their webcam and can clearly hear what everybody says.

3.2 Problem

Online participants need to see the entire room to be aware of events that take place in all the areas.

3.3 Forces

- People tend to focus less on remote participants.
- On-site participants are more involved in the meeting.
- Remote participants and on-site participants should perceive non-verbal signals in a similar way.
- Important non-verbal signals such as body language, sideways glances or reactions of other participants may not be accessible to all people.
- Standard webcams or permanently installed cameras often only record the speaker or part of the room.
- Remote participants should not feel isolated and unable to respond to subtle social cues.
- Even low latency times in the transmission prevent direct, smooth interaction.

3.4 Solution

Install multiple cameras to cover all relevant areas of the meeting room. Ensure that not only the active speaker but also key focal points (e.g. presentation screens, whiteboards, or any area of interest) are visible to remote participants, providing several angles of view.

3.5 Tips for Implementation

Furniture in a conference room is often aligned to a specific point. This could be a television or a screen, for example. In this case, it is advisable to point one of the cameras from this point towards the plenum. This can give the impression that the participants on site are looking at the people connected online.

3.6 Consequences

- Online participants can better follow what is happening in the conference room.
- People connected online are more likely to have an outside view of what is happening on site.
- People attending on site do no longer need their laptop to participate in the meeting.
- On-site participants cannot be seen in close-up via the room cameras.
- Online participants cannot easily see who is speaking on site.
- High acquisition costs for several cameras to cover all angles.
- Multiple installed cameras can lead to confusion for online participants, as they always have to identify the right angle.
- Multiple cameras must be used to avoid blind spots.
- Only one person on site needs to have a laptop to bring everyone on site into the meeting.

3.7 Examples

Any number of cameras can be used to cover the points of interest. However, at least one camera should cover the plenum on site so that the participants can actually do without their laptops. Figure 3 shows a scenario at Cologne University of Applied Sciences in which the conference table is aligned with a centrally placed monitor, on which the online participants and the digitally shared content can be seen. The monitor is therefore a point of interest for the on-site participants. It is therefore advisable to place the camera filming the plenary session centrally below or above the monitor (see Fig. 4). The monitor itself does not need to be captured by a camera in the scenario shown, as it is a digital medium that can be mirrored in the virtual meeting room.

Fig. 3. Conference table with a room microphone and loudspeaker centrally aligned to a monitor with camera.

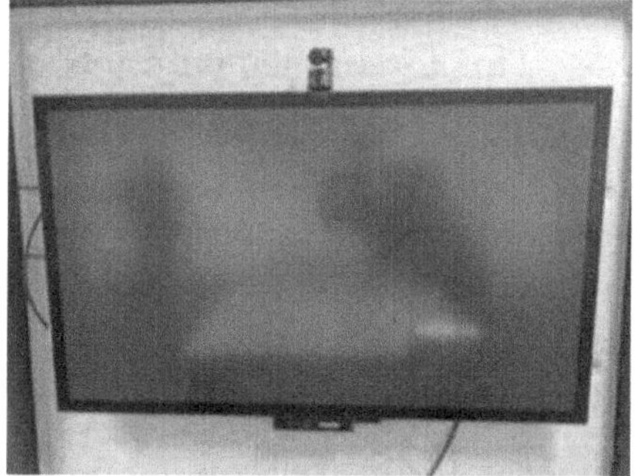

Fig. 4. Monitor with camera.

4 Getting Closer

4.1 Context

Employees of a company have a meeting together. The meeting takes place in a hybrid form, via a video conferencing platform. Examples of this are Zoom, Microsoft Teams or Cisco Webex.

Context On-Site. Some of the employees sit together in a conference room. They use a room microphone and a room loudspeaker together. In addition, the meeting is recorded on site by room cameras. On site, only a few participants use their laptop to join the meeting with their built-in webcam.

Context Online. Online participants use their laptop to join the meeting and be seen by the build-in webcam of their laptop. Also, some of the participants use the build-in microphone and loudspeaker of their laptop, while some use an additional headset. They also see the conference room, the people and all the points of interest through different camera angles, from cameras that are installed in the conference room. They also can clearly hear what everybody says.

4.2 Problem

More than one room camera leads to confusion for online participants, as they always have to identify the right angle and select the view in the conference software for a full-screen view. If only one room camera is installed, there are blind spots in the room where important objects for the meeting may be, such as whiteboards or flipcharts. Also, people on site are visible to online participants from a more outside view, which means that the meeting is getting more impersonal.

4.3 Forces

- Standard cameras have limited viewing angles and cannot cover the entire room.
- Wide-angle cameras can cause distortion.
- Several cameras must be used to avoid blind spots.
- Multiple camera angles can be confusing for online participants.
- Permanently installed cameras cannot react to spontaneously changing seating arrangements.
- Furniture, pillars or participants can block camera lines of sight.

4.4 Solution

Place a 360° camera with an integrated 360° microphone and speaker at the center of the on-site participants. This setup allows online attendees to see the entire room and hear voices from a center point, creating a more immersive experience that simulates being in the room. The 360° audio ensures all voices are picked up evenly.

4.5 Tips for Implementation

The camera should be placed the same distance away from all participants. It is also a good idea to place it in the center of the area where the meeting is taking place.

4.6 Consequences

- Close-up visibility of on-site participants is limited compared to individual webcams.
- 360° cameras cannot capture all social nuances.
- In order to be able to place the camera in the center of the room and at the same time equally far away from all participants, the room may have to be rearranged.
- Remote participants gain a more immersive view of the meeting, since they can observe the entire room from a single panoramic perspective.
- The need for multiple fixed cameras is reduced, simplifying setup and lowering the risk of blind spots.

4.7 Examples

The company *Owl Lab* uses the features described in this pattern for its *Meeting Owl* conference system (see Fig. 5). This conference system has a 360° camera and also includes a speaker an a room microphone. The system can also recognize who is speaking to focus the view on that person. The conference system also offers the advantage that it does not have to be permanently installed in a room, but can be flexibly integrated into different meeting situations (see Fig. 5 and 6).

Fig. 5. 360° camera with integrated microphone and loudspeaker in a meeting situation.

Fig. 6. 360° camera with integrated microphone and loudspeaker in a meeting situation.

5 Discussion

The proposed solutions are not the only possible approaches. A central microphone reduces coordination effort, while providing each participant with an individual microphone ensures more even voice pickup but adds logistical complexity. Multiple fixed cameras create comprehensive coverage, yet they risk overwhelming remote participants with too many viewing angles. A 360° system reduces blind spots and simplifies setup but offers limited close-up detail and may require rearranging the room layout. Organizations must balance inclusivity, technical complexity, and cost. For small teams, simple central solutions may suffice, whereas large conferences may benefit from combined or more sophisticated systems. At the same time, technical improvements alone do not guarantee equitable participation. Effective facilitation, moderation of turn-taking, and active involvement of remote participants remain essential.

6 Conclusion

The three patterns presented CENTRAL ROOM MIC AND LOUDSPEAKER, COVER POINTS OF INTEREST WITH CAMERAS and GETTING CLOSER address recurring challenges in hybrid meetings by improving audio clarity and visual inclusion. Each pattern can generate value on its own, but their combined application strengthens the effect. CENTRAL ROOM MIC AND LOUDSPEAKER and COVER POINTS OF INTEREST WITH CAMERAS can be implemented independently, as they target different dimensions of inclusion. They can also be applied together to create a more immersive experience. GETTING CLOSER builds upon the first two by integrating both audio and video into a single 360° system. In this way, it represents an evolution of the previous patterns, unifying their separate approaches. These patterns illustrate how technology can reduce typical barriers to hybrid meetings. Future work may extend the pattern set by different aspects, such as the integration of collaborative tools.

Acknowledgments. This work is supported through the InnoFaktur project by the European Regional Development Fund under grant NRW-EFRE-20500002.InnoFaktur. Special thanks to Apostolos Zarras for providing feedback as a shepherd. The constant feedback and exchanges have helped a lot to iterate the paper and to improve it. We would also like to thank the participants of the "Writers Workshop" for their feedback. A big thanks also goes to all of our colleagues for providing useful ideas, insights and feedback.

References

1. Ellis, R., Goodacre, T., Mortensen, N., Oeppen, R.S., Brennan, P.A.: Application of human factors at hybrid meetings: facilitating productivity and inclusivity. Br. J. Oral Maxillofac. Surg. **60**(6), 740–745 (2022)

2. Randstad. Wird in Ihrem Unternehmen Remote-Arbeit angeboten? . In Statista. Zugriff am 17. Februar 2025, von (2024). https://de.statista.com/statistik/daten/studie/1479023/umfrage/angebot-von-remote-work-in-unternehmen-in-deutschland/
3. Owl Labs. Mit welchen Problemen sind Sie bei der Teilnahme an hybriden Meetings konfrontiert? . In Statista. Zugriff am 17. Februar 2025, von (2024). https://de.statista.com/statistik/daten/studie/1557415/umfrage/umfrage-unter-beschaeftigten-probleme-bei-hybriden-meetings/
4. Enser, M., Moriceau, J., Abily, J., et al.: Background noise lowers the performance of Anaesthesiology residents' clinical reasoning when measured by script concordance: a randomised crossover volunteer study. Eur. J. Anaesthesiol. **34**, 464–470 (2017)
5. Saatçi, B., Rädle, R., Rintel, S., O'Hara, K., Nylandsted Klokmose, C.: Hybrid Meetings in the Modern Workplace: Stories of Success and Failure. In: Nakanishi, H., Egi, H., Chounta, IA., Takada, H., Ichimura, S., Hoppe, U. (eds) Collaboration Technologies and Social Computing. CRIWG+CollabTech 2019. Lecture Notes in Computer Science, vol 11677. Springer, Cham (2019). https://doi.org/10.1007/978-3-030-28011-6_4
6. Neumayr, T., Saatci, B., Rintel, S., Klokmose, C. N., Augstein, M.: What was hybrid? A systematic review of hybrid collaboration and meetings research. arXiv preprint arXiv:2111.06172 (2021)

Dark Patterns for Unethical Computer Science

Cesare Pautasso(✉)

Software Institute (USI), Lugano, Switzerland
c.pautasso@ieee.org

Abstract. As computer science changes people's lives and reprograms their world, its ethical implications should not be underestimated. In this paper we present eight dark patterns, which reflect how computer scientists focusing on simply doing their jobs, in specific situations, may blissfully ignore or willfully disregard the significant impact of their wonderful artificial machines on the ethical principles of goodness, truth and fairness. In other words, computer science is not neutral, as its applications and the design of information technology – implicitly or explicitly – reflect the ethical values of their makers. The dark patterns of forgetful mentalist, reverse improver, real virtuality escapist and willful ignorant disregard the ethical principle of truth. The principle of fairness is violated by the faceless assistant and reckless maintainer dark patterns, while the addiction peddler and autonomous killer dark patterns show a fundamental lack of concern towards the goodness principle. In writing this paper, our goal is to ensure the avoidance of these dark patterns in the future by raising awareness about them.

1 Introduction

Computer science has made a significant impact everywhere. The shift from atoms to bits has affected both our daily life and work [95]. Digital technology is the pervasive foundation of global connectivity, ubiquitous computing, and big data. As human-computer interaction get more and more seamless and artificial intelligence more and more intelligent, we are striding towards not only a more efficient economy but a more creative and interconnected society. The ultimate development level of human potential and freedom is within reach.

While there are many existing professional code of ethics [4], standards [1,5] and value-driven design methods [6], the dark patterns presented in this paper explicitly embody the precise and concrete disregard for specific ethical values. While it is hard to disagree with the importance of a value-driven, ethics-centered design processes [12], the question ultimately remains open concerning what, exactly, are the ethical values driving the design: people over profits (or viceversa?), sustainability over unlimited growth (or short term greed over long term investments?), truth over lies (or fiction over facts?), honor over treachery (or loyalty over ambition?), compassion over cruelty (or egoism over empathy?), and so on.

T. Plummer et al. (Eds.): EuroPLoP 2025, LNCS 16494, pp. 337–362, 2026.
https://doi.org/10.1007/978-3-032-19157-1_16

Unlike patterns (which help to identify and constructively resolve a trade-off among conflicting forces) or anti-patterns (which capture design mistakes and the corresponding corrective refactorings), dark pattern emphasize the negative consequences that are obtained when introducing the described harmful solutions [22]. The only way to avoid the negative consequences of a dark pattern is to avoid introducing it in the first place. This is the main reason for writing this paper – far from teaching how to achieve the harmful, untruthful, or unfair goals behind each pattern – we aim to raise awareness and ensure the avoidance of dark patterns in the future.

We do not aim to criticize computer scientists who are simply doing their jobs[1] and may be often face the difficult choice between keeping it or refusing to implement harmful or ethically questionable features. Instead we contribute to an ongoing discussion [3,6,7,9–11] on their responsibility [2] by taking a personal stand on what ethical values and principles [8] computer science should promote and the role computer scientists can play in this process.

The dark patters are documented by describing their context, problem, solution, consequences, and known uses. We also include an explicit discussion highlighting the ethical violation that occur when employing the pattern. We provide the reader with contexts in which computer scientists might determine to introduce the dark patterns, and then we attempt to refute them – following an existentialist path – by helping readers to freely realize where they can draw the line that they should not cross.

The rest of this paper is organized as follows: we first introduce related work on dark patterns and describe the methodology at the foundation of these patterns. Then, we describe the eight dark patterns, grouped according to the three ethical principles [8] of truth, fairness and goodness (Table 1), before we draw some conclusions and suggest directions for future research or practical applications.

2 Related Work

Dark patterns (or deceptive patterns [15]) have been studied in the context of user interface design [22], where dark user interface patterns consist of deceptive user interface designs intended to mislead or manipulate users into actions they might not otherwise take. The problem of such dark patterns is that they work exactly as intended [27] and often "appear to violate laws restricting the use of unfair and deceptive practices in trade" [21]. Dark patterns are also found within game design: they are "used intentionally by a game creator to cause negative experiences for players that are against their best interests and happen without their consent" [26]. An exploratory study on the dark side of Edge and Cloud computing has been presented in [25], focusing on unsustainable practices.

[1] One could argue that ethical considerations *are* part of professionally doing the job. Still, computer scientists love to tinker and joyfully build things just because they can. As a result, they often implement project requirements just like requested by product owners without considering nor challenging their harmful consequences.

Dark patterns have emerged from the confluence of deceptive retail practices with psychological nudges [24] under the pressure of growth hacking: aggressively driving product adoption to achieve market dominance [23]. In the age of artificial intelligence, hyper-dark patterns are "deceptive designs that heavily rely on the algorithmic manipulation of information gathered about individuals, which through personalisation manipulate users to unintended actions" [19]. A benchmark for detecting in large language models (LLMs) dark patterns such as Brand Bias, User Retention, Sycophancy, Anthropomorphization, Harmful Generation, and Sneaking has recently been published in [20].

A recent, systematic, ontological organization of dark patterns gathered from the academic literature, user interface design practice and legal/regulatory sources can be found in [16]. The main mechanisms identified are: sneaking [13], obstruction/forced action [18], interface interference [14], and social engineering [17]. Few of these papers include an analytical and essential presentation of the dark patterns, as they tend to cover superficial phenomenological aspects or discuss how users may circumvent and the legal system may prevent, control or mitigate the impact of such practices.

In this paper we include a broader set of dark patterns, which are orthogonal from user interface or game design issues as we focus on harmful computer science applications (e.g., Addiction Peddler, Autonomous Killer), epistemological consequences (Forgetful Mentalist, Willful Ignorant, Real Virtuality Escapist), or the unfair impact of rapid technological evolution (Faceless Assistant, Reckless Maintainer, Reverse Improver).

3 Methodology and Disclaimer

The patterns in this paper have been personally gathered and named by the author following pattern mining methodologies (e.g., [94,96]) which involved an extensive analysis of scientific and practitioners literature related to each pattern. Starting from concrete real-world instances of specific malicious practices, we extracted the underlying problem, distilled the essence of the corresponding solution and unfolded implications and consequences, particularly focusing on the impact of the solution on the ethical principles of truth, fairness and goodness [8]. We filtered the dark pattern candidates using the principle of restraint, which limits the scope of applicability of ethical considerations to serious matters, in which it is important, justified and relevant to decide between good and evil. We attempted to develop a rational ethical argument and provided elements for the reader to make their own decision on where to individually draw the line.

While all patterns are supported by known uses found in real world products and current events, we intentionally chose not to include specific product or company references. There are unfortunately too many to choose from. Our goal is to raise awareness about the dark patterns but not to highlight or apportion blame to specific instances.

By casting the patterns included in this paper as dark patterns, we make a very personal value judgment on some computer science aspects and practices that – in our view – have – in some circumstances – harmful impacts on individual people or an entire society. According to a diametrically opposite set of values, the same set of patterns might be considered as "normal" design patterns which can be generously introduced to, for example, increase financial revenue and maximize shareholder value.

4 Truth

Do not lie.
Do not make promises you intend not to keep [8].

There is a wide gap between bits of information and their intended relationship with reality. Computer scientists know how to process, communicate, and store large amounts of bits. Some computer scientists specialize in keeping bits secure, private and confidential. They can detect tampering and protect the channel from data loss. But, are such bits truthful? Can the information they carry be trusted? There is no easy way to add a true/false meta-bit, which can help us distinguish lies from the truth. Garbage in, garbage out.

The Willful Ignorant dark pattern suggests that ignorance – willfully ignoring truthful information – provides the illusion of quickly solving any problem in the short term. The Reverse Improver makes promises that will not be kept since it is hard for computer scientists not to keep from "improving" our software. The Real Virtuality Escapist breaks contact with true reality, which – thanks to the incredible progress of illusionary technology – has become more and more indistinguishable from a mirage. The Forgetful Mentalist provides confusing and unreliable guarantees about the preservation or the deletion of information.

Dark Pattern 1—Willful Ignorant

Context:

Powerful sensors have been deployed everywhere and deliver precise and accurate data measurements which are processed through analytics pipelines to produce valuable information, insightful knowledge and ultimate wisdom. Critical problems have been detected and are being monitored in real time.

Problem: *How to rapidly solve problems in a simple way?*

Solution:

Ignoring flashing warning indicators will not make the problem go away, but what if we stopped the sensors, dropped the databases and spared the intense computational effort of running those complex data analytics pipelines?

Table 1. Overview of the 8 Dark Patterns for Unethical Computer Science

Category DARK PATTERN *Problem* Solution.
Truth
1. WILLFUL IGNORANT *How to rapidly solve problems in a simple way?* Stop worrying about warning signs.
2. REVERSE IMPROVER *How to take advantage of softwareâĂŹs ease of change?* Unavoidable software updates undo user improvements.
3. REAL VIRTUALITY ESCAPIST *How to improve reality?* Make illusions indistinguishable from reality.
4. FORGETFUL MENTALIST *How to control our digital footprints?* Deleting really means hiding, until it doesnâĂŹt.
Fairness
5. FACELESS ASSISTANT *How to scale user support services to help a very high number of users?* Let users help one another. Replace human helpers with bots.
6. RECKLESS MAINTAINER *How to keep quickly innovating?* Carelessly break backwards compatibility.
Goodness
7. ADDICTION PEDDLER *How to drive engagement and increase returning users?* Make the app become a habit.
8. AUTONOMOUS KILLER *How to win the next war?* Let machines fight humans by themselves.

If stopping all measurements seems too radical, what if we simply adjusted their output to fit the expectations of who is in charge of assessing the magnitude of the problem?

Consequences:

The problematic measurements are no longer problematic because they disappeared. As any toddler knows: out of sight, out of mind. Ignorance is bliss [32,33]. Also, if you did not observe an event, it didn't actually happen in the first place [36].

However, is it easier to manage: what can be measured [30], what cannot be measured [34], or what is intentionally not measured? Reality has a way to make itself known in unexpected ways.

Ethical Violation:

Truthful messengers should not be blamed. Killing a carrier of bad news will ensure only fake good news is delivered henceforth, or even no news at all, after running out of messengers.

Drawing the line:

While sensing has a cost, we have reached a point – like never before – when it is possible to feed into computers incredible amounts of sensor data about the real world. This includes both the ability to observe natural phenomena, as well as to track people's movements, interactions or even their health. What is the justification for building such panopticon[2], if it does not give the rightful impulse towards actually solving problems and improving people's lives?

Known Uses:

Sharpies are a powerful tool to *correct* data visualizations.

While it is clear that the more people are tested, the more cases of contagion can be detected, it is hard to believe that a pandemic's exponential spread could be safely contained by simply stopping administering tests [35].

Emissions are carefully adjusted depending on whether a vehicle undergoes environmental compliance testing or be driven around real world streets [28].

There is no climate change crisis if the institutions tasked with carefully studying the planet's climate history and predicting its evolution are de-funded and shuttered [38].

Bias present in machine learning models often faithfully reflects the bias in the training data, which is a reflection of the state of reality at the time it was sampled [39]. Why blame the model as opposed to trying to improve the training set, or even better, the reality from which it was taken?

Willful ignorance: the decision to remain unaware of the impact of our decisions on others has been shown to promote selfishness and restrain altruism [37].

[2] Literally, seeing everything. Architecturally, a building designed to compel its inhabitants to behave as thought they are always under surveillance of an all-seeing eye [31]. In computer science, a metaphor for big data technology [29].

Dark Pattern 2—REVERSE IMPROVER

Context:

Software is easy to change. Software is meant to be changed [40]. The only software which does not change is unused or useless software [41,44].

Problem: *How to exploit software's ease of change?*

Solution:

For convenience, turn software downloads into subscriptions that will automatically fetch and silently install any updated releases.

Remove the need for locally installing software: deliver it "as a service" from the cloud instead [43].

Ship hundreds of updates every second.

Now you are ready to take advantage of how easy is it to change software.

Consequences:

Users will get used to seamlessly access the latest (and of course, greatest) version of the software.

Users who rarely use an app may get confused as the app logo and icon changed since the last time they installed it.

Users who frequently use an app will get confused as the features they rely on have changed, or they may have entirely disappeared.

Users may be unpleasantly surprised or disappointed when they find out that the improved release lacks previous features they started to rely on[3].

Ethical Violation:

Any user interface design decision is a promise made to users that a feature will be present in the software and accessible in a specific way. This promise is broken when an update of the software removes a valuable feature, or changes the way users can access it, reducing its accessibility [46] by breaking habits and voiding the time and effort spent into learning how to use the feature according to the old user interface design.

Valuable free features may not always disappear but instead they get taken hostage as users must pay a ransom to continue being able to access them.

Because of the need to apply security patches, users are encouraged – for their own sake – to accept all future updates. Breaking this trust has negative consequences on the vendor's reputation but also makes it less likely that truly beneficial security updates are applied in the future [45].

[3] See ADDICTION PEDDLER.

Drawing the line:

Is software continuously being improved towards perfection? What about so-called reverse improvements, which take away from users to give back to the software vendors?

Known Uses:

Enshittification is a popular business model [42] where users are first attracted to a software application with "unlimited forever" deals that are too good to be true. Then captive users with no alternative left are exploited as the terms and the corresponding software application features inexorably degrade.

The initial software release protects users privacy by storing data on their local device only and allowing anonymous access. It simply does not track users, not even with crash reporting telemetry. The software is later silently updated so that all user information is replicated without encryption to the cloud and every user click or keystroke is logged for analysis. Later, users notice something has changed when they are required to create an account so their identity can be authenticated when accessing their own local applications.

One day users discover that all of their colorful images display as black and white because their painting application vendor has mismanaged contract renewal negotiations with the organization owning the color palette used in the images.

Dark Pattern 3—Real Virtuality Escapist

Context:

Human-Computer Interaction devices offer the possibility of augmenting or replacing the source of human sensory input. Reality can be disappointing, or simply boring [53].

Thanks to computer science, representation and computation have been granted ontological power: reality exists because it can be represented and computed [48].

Problem: *How to improve reality?*

Solution:

The human body can take virtual reality only up to a certain physiological limit [55]. It has been a clear goal of technology to stretch such limit thanks to better illusions: visual, acoustic, kinetic, tactile, haptic, vestibular, and even olfactory and gustatory sensation simulations can fool the human senses.

It is getting harder and harder to notice the difference between reality and virtual reality. Introducing "real virtuality", a virtual reality that is so immersive that cannot be distinguished from reality.

Therefore, to improve reality, we only have to improve our perception of it.

Consequences:

Thanks to their improved perception of reality, people can dream with their eyes open [49]. They can travel without moving and make impossible experiences. They can see the future. They can relive the past. They can risk their lives without any danger. They can get attached to virtual places [52].

Indulging in escapism can lead to depression, anxiety, aggression, loneliness, and lower self-control. These can reinforce the real-life hardships triggering the need to escape, resulting in a vicious cycle [50].

Ethical Violation:

Where is the point in which virtual reality turns into real virtuality? Are people subjected to a new reality without being aware of the fact that they are immersed in a simulation [47]. Or do people willfully submit to their improved real virtuality, become attached to it and no longer wish to return back to the original one?

Drawing the line:

There are many useful applications of virtual and augmented reality, from entertainment, education and training, as well as remote presence with reduction of travel and the corresponding emissions. However, the real virtuality escapists lost touch with our original reality. They now live in their own dream universe, where we may not be invited.

Known Uses:

Self-indulgent escapism lets people get distracted from stressful situations. Despite the fleeting feelings of enjoyment and euphoria, e.g., when winning a game or exploring a virtual world, this kind of escapism has been demonstrated to be a "rather ineffective and unhealthy coping strategy to deal with negative life circumstances" [53]. Additionally, it takes away or prevents developing the problem solving competence needed to cope with the situation.

Humans are animals who are "congenitally indisposed to accept reality as it is. [...] Seeing what is not there lies at the foundation of all human culture" [54].

As more and more human to human interactions are mediated through screens, many lonely people have begun to bond with friendly artificial intelligence chatbots.

Dramatically reducing the cost of expensive intermediation services provided by mediums and removing the requirement to hold séances under the right conditions, nowadays anyone can hold conversations with the voices of dead people through their smart phone [51].

Dark Pattern 4—FORGETFUL MENTALIST

Context:

Bits are stored forever, in theory. In practice, it takes energy to beat entropy: an effort is needed both to remember and to forget.

Every person's interactions with the digital world leaves a trace. It is not clear who gets to own and therefore see and control the persistence of such traces.

Problem: *How to control our digital footprints?*

Solution:

Deleting information by default only hides it. Because deletion is such a harsh step, the unwanted bits that were carefully arranged are actually hidden from view but still preserved, just in case, so they can be undeleted.

To prevent data loss, use redundancy to store multiple independent copies of any information which should be preserved. A sufficiently high number of replicas will most likely escape outside your private sphere of control, making it difficult to ensure the information is really deleted everywhere, once it becomes necessary to rapidly and reliably doing so.

Consequences:

Store everything in the cloud so if you lose your device the data is still there [62]. Even in the cloud, no strong practical guarantees are made that any information is preserved in the long term, or erased in the short term. It takes a leap of faith to believe that every cloud service provider diligently removes every copy, scrubbing every disk within each data center.

Digital information does not fade out like the colors of a black and white picture from hundreds of years ago. It may break down as some pixels are no longer readable from the degraded physical media, or simply disappear into an error message as the software used to display it gives up while attempting to open an incompatible, ancient representation format[4].

Ethical Violation:

Is it truly deleted or really just not visible? Can we trust a recycle bin claiming to be empty?

Although – in some regions – people have a right to be forgotten [59], it is no longer possible to keep one's past skeletons hidden away in their closets, thanks to digital storage records, everyone will be held accountable to what they said, did (and thought) precisely anytime during their lifetime. There is no forgiving forgetfulness in a digital world.

Human memory works differently: forgetting keeps us sane [60].

There is money to be made to suppress past mistakes that no longer define us. There is an established industry offering data preservation guarantees with secure backup and disaster recovery. There is also an emerging industry offering data erasure and cleanup of hard to remove stains. Ransomware gangs not only hold data hostage [63] but could also blackmail threatening to reveal digital trash residues.

---

[4] See Reckless Maintainer.

Drawing the line:

We built wonderful long-term data storage and preservation systems, but we cripple them because of data retention and disposal policies [61], which determine information should be preserved for a limited time only [57].

We entrust our devices to both remember and forget our personal information. The convenience and reliability of off-device Cloud backups have led to a general acceptance of such information being leaked outside of our control [58]. However, the removal of information should never be implemented as simply removing our ability to access it, while transferring ownership and control to someone else instead.

Known Uses:

Archaeologists have been able to detect the presence of ancient civilizations and decode their signs traced on clay tablet fragments. What kind of digital traces are we sending into the future as bit rot [56] attacks our collective memory?

Social media posts are shared by everyone and will never be forgotten, that is, until the collective attention span drifts towards the next viral post.

An entire generation who grew up posting on social media is now applying for their first jobs hoping that time-limited data retention policies will prevent their future employers from browsing through their colorful history [64].

5 Fairness

Under equal conditions, treat people equally [8].

In a fair world, those in need should get help. Successful scalability to handle billions of users cannot be claimed if users are left to their own devices to fend for themselves, resolve issues, share workarounds, or handed over to polite but incompetent bots, wasting their time until they can find someone other than a Faceless Assistant.

Moving fast is great, but breaking things carelessly, disregarding those affected – as Reckless Maintainers do – is not fair. The rapid and unstoppable progress of technological evolution should not expect everyone to just to keep up or give up and simply go unaccounted for.

Dark Pattern 5—Faceless Assistant

Context:

Users depend on freely available commodity services. Service providers prioritize investing in service engineering and scalable delivery infrastructure. It is inefficient and time-consuming to find and train qualified support personnel [66].

Problem: *How to scale user support services to help a very high number of users?*

Solution:

There are multiple solutions that can be combined:

- Introduce a high degree of automation, through chat bots, voice assistants and automatic email replies.
- Let users help themselves [70] by poring over documentation, frequently asked questions lists [67], or even the open source code itself.
- Let users help one another by granting them access to self-moderating semi-official discussion forums.
- Introduce musical waiting queues on busy call center lines which insist in redirecting callers to the above automated self-service solutions. Keep callers waiting for a minimum amount of time, even if there are free operators.
- To improve throughput, introduce a hard time limit on support calls where operators are disconnected automatically with no obvious way for users to resume the conversation.
- Restrict the payout authority of call center operators and require customer to escalate claims to management to obtain more redress [65].
- If the user problem is due to a bug, blame the user and their input, never admit there is an issue that needs to be fixed or thank the user for reporting it [68].

Consequences:

While high quality information technology services with user friendly interfaces may work really well and most users may not ever need to ask for help, there are always exceptions and as the user population grows, they can become rather frequent.

Automated bots may deal successfully with common cases, while fail to understand how to solve uncommon or particularly difficult issues. Human operators take over and always deal with the edge cases. Human operators along the support request escalation stack are overwhelmed as they only receive the hard cases of increasingly frustrated users that could not receive automated assistance.

User frustration grows, service provider reputation suffers. Users may switch to paid service providers, assuming that these are available in the same market and that they provide some guarantees about a human-powered support experience.

Increasingle frustrated users, on the other hand, may confuse human operators with bots, and ask them to speak with a human, even if this is already the case. This often happens when operators follow a predefined script and do not appear to listen carefully to the user describing their specific problem.

As services quality degrades[5], however, users start to realize that "you get what you pay for" also applies to their helpdesk experience.

[5] See REVERSE IMPROVER.

Ethical Violation:

Users should not be led to believe they can rely on a free service which will simply be unable to help them when problems arise. Users who need help are in a weak position. They may be unable to access critical information (e.g., medical data, job interview schedules) in a timely manner. Especially if the source of the problem lies within the responsibility of the service provider (e.g., an account has been improperly locked out by some incorrect automated check), users should receive the help they desperately need without delay.

Drawing the line:

Maximizing the number of users does not entail only making sure a system has been provisioned sufficient capacity to handle the load, but also making sure the users *can be supported* in case they need help. The faceless assistant crosses the line by misleading users to expect help without having allocated sufficient capacity for it.

Known Uses:

Any major service provider makes it hard to contact human operators, redirecting support requests through automated channels.

GetHuman.com is trusted by hundreds of millions of customers worldwide to resolve their customer service problems and get in touch with hard-to-reach companies.

Digital transformation initiatives have morphed many passenger assistance call centers into chat bots, which may or may no longer be connected to human operators [69]. In case of travel disruptions, stranded users are placed into long queues leading up to a single person offering assistance in terms of the opportunity to scan a QR code, which – assuming a compatible[6] and sufficiently charged mobile device is available – when scanned, will give remote access to the aforementioned chat bot.

"They randomly locked my account after I moved years worth of irreplaceable photos to the Cloud. The account was suspended without warning, reason, or any legitimate recourse. I've submitted the compliance form many times, and each time I get an automated response that leads nowhere. No human contact. Just canned emails and silence."

Dark Pattern 6—Reckless Maintainer

Context:

Progress is unstoppable. Internet penetration is always at an all time high.

[6] See Reckless Maintainer.

Technological transitions take time: the future is already here, just not evenly distributed [72].

Perfect is the enemy of good enough. Shipping early helps to gain traction, get feedback and start learning from failures.

Problem: *How to keep quickly innovating?*

Solution:

Assume every user of your product is like you, the developer creating and updating it.

Backwards compatibility is not worth worrying about. Keep building on the bleeding edge and simply ignore whatever falls off the side of the rapidly advancing wave.

Ignore accessibility requirements: it does not matter if anyone who does not have the eyesight and the dexterity of a 25-year-old software engineer will not be able to navigate user interface designs where, for example, critical information should be displayed with a light gray color on white background using a tiny font size.

Discount the necessary performance: bundle heavyweight software frameworks, include sub-pixel resolution textures, deliver high-K video multimedia, assume infra-millisecond ping times. After all, everyone using the application enjoys an optical ultra-wide broadband Internet connection.

Consequences:

Users lacking digital skills, connectivity or sufficiently capable and up-to-date devices, as well as users who cannot afford to keep upgrading their digital devices – by definition – do not exist as part of the considered user population for a given software application. This greatly simplifies the design and reduces the development and quality assurance costs of the application itself, which now targets a narrow user group. No fallback options are provided to bridge across the introduced digital divide.

Keeping compatibility is expensive, but can help establish the necessary stability to build a technological foundation, a platform towards which developers will flock [73]. After such platform is established, the captured users can be periodically swindled by breaking backwards compatibility and forcing unwanted upgrades on them[7].

Ethical Violation:

Hard to reach users do not economically justify the investment required to make them part of the network. Unreachable users therefore remain so as reaching them would unfairly consume the value extracted from the users that have already been reached. This assumes that the missed opportunities and potential benefits for the disconnected users do not count.

Is Internet access a human right? [74] Should universal service requirements be applied across the entire technology stack [75] and not only at the electricity and communication network layers? While technology should "provide the means

[7] See Reverse Improver.

to help improving the human condition" [71], there is a significant harm and suffering inflicted on so-called digital immigrants – born before the invention of the Internet – as more and more information technology is designed under the assumption of a pervasively widespread, high level of digital literacy.

Drawing the Line:

The reckless maintainer acts as a digital divider. It is not enough to perform a simplistic cost/benefit analysis, disregarding to account for externalities, such as the life changing impact of being cut off from the network, the impossibility to access critical public services, emergency warning systems or reputable news sources. "Information systems should be accessible to avoid the indignities of information illiteracy and deprivation" [7].

Known Uses:

The new app can only run on the latest release of some operating system which requires very specific hardware that is unfortunately not yet available in your region.

Please update your browser to access the e-banking site. Please buy a new phone which can run the operating system required by the updated browser to fetch the public administration certificate.

This app is no longer supported. To view this content, a new and improved app is available to download from the app store. Once you download and sign in to the new app, all content you bought will be immediately accessible. If you are on the latest release, your collections will be transferred automatically. If you are not on the latest release, please follow these few easy steps. Your personal documents need to be re-imported to read them in the new app.

Make sure everyone should undergo strict security checks when registering their user account. An email and password are not enough: ask for a post address in the real world (who doesn't have a home anyway?) and a valid phone number (who doesn't have a phone nowadays?). Regularly force a password reset which requires to revalidate all of the above credentials.

6 Goodness

Do unto others whatever you would like them to do to you.

Who benefits from a software application? The user, whose requirements are satisfied, and/or the computer scientist, who elicits the requirements, designs, implements, tests and delivers a good solution? While there are many cases in which both developers profit and users prosper, the following dark patterns are present when this balance is broken – as in the case of the ADDICTION PEDDLER, where capturing more and more users trumps delivering value to them.

The principle of goodness and its implication on preserving human life is also in stark conflict with the AUTONOMOUS KILLER, a dark pattern which delegates to a machine not only the harmful act of killing but also life-or-death decision making while selecting and seeking targets.

Dark Pattern 7—Addiction Peddler

Context:

After installing and trying out new apps, only a few users open them for a second time.

Problem: *How to drive engagement and increase returning users?*

Solution:

To make the app grow on users and inevitably become part of their digital habits [79] use a combination of the following strategies:

- Driven by curiosity, users should be surprised as they discover something unexpected. Keep scrolling: there is something amazing just around the corner.
- Driven by notifications, users should be periodically reminded about the app. You got mail! A new message just arrived. What is it about? Who sent it?
- Driven by routine, users should be rewarded for coming back regularly. Inform users of everything they missed when they were away. Celebrate their return [80]. Keep those daily streak counters going up and up. Steadily build a habit.
- Driven by friends, users should cultivate a connection to their community. Everyone needs to belong. Sharing is caring. Some special features require multiple users to join forces.
- Driven by goals, users should be challenged and given a clear path towards achievement so they can precisely track their progress along the way [76].
- Driven by variable rewards, users actions should lead to an unpredictable effect. It looks like an app, but there is a slot machine inside [81].
- Driven by fear of missing out (FOMO), users should worry all the time whether something important has come up.

Consequences:

Users feel compelled to reopen the app again and again. Engagement metrics go through the roof. The app becomes indispensable.

Users keep binging more and more out of an infinite firehose, never fully satisfied but also never really given a chance to close the tap.

Users have difficulties keeping their concentration. Their attention flow is continuously interrupted [84]. Audible chimes, vibrating buzzes, light flashes: apps keep pinging their users relentlessly.

Users consciously or unconsciously make room in their daily schedule for some quality time with their app. Anything else comes after.

Users naturally seek social approval and embrace reciprocity [83]. Their interactions are however mediated by the app, which gets full control over who gets to like whom.

Users who enjoy ticking off tasks do not always realize the app has become their boss.

Given the vast array of stimulants embedded in the app, users may face sleep deprivation [78]. Nevertheless, as they wake up in the morning, they will dive right back into checking their app for all the things they missed while they were asleep.

Ethical Violation:

Weaknesses of the human psyche are exploited so that the time and attention dedicated to the app trumps everything else. Potentially useful apps are designed to become distractions, hindering users cognitive performance. Users are encouraged to follow their impulses, losing both their irreplaceable time and their freedom of choice as their agency is hijacked [77]. Eventually, users health begins to suffer as they find themselves unable to stop.

Drawing the line:

Returning users should keep opening their app because of its value proposition and benefits, not because they have been cunningly manipulated to do so [85]. The design of highly engaging user experiences should be done carefully to benefit users, not against their interests.

Known Uses:

Internet addiction [86] – an umbrella term which includes excessive use of mobile phones to access social media, online shopping or auctions, multiplayer games – is considered as a major public health threat in some countries.

"During the past 10 years, use of the internet and video games has become one of the most common leisure activities for children and adolescents." [82].

Dark Pattern 8—AUTONOMOUS KILLER

Context:

Remotely controlled drones can rapidly reach and deliver lethal payloads anywhere in the battlefield, on the ground, in the air and even under water. They are susceptible to electronic jamming and radio interference, which limits the maximum distance from which they can be remotely controlled.

Problem: *How to win the next war?*

Solution:

Let machines fight humans by themselves.

More powerful hardware and more lightweight artificial intelligence make it technologically inevitable for machines to become fully autonomous. This way, they not only control their low-level locomotion but can determine how to optimally achieve goals, coordinate among a swarm, seek, identify enemy targets and swiftly destroy them.

Consequences:

Removing the humans from the decision making loop only helps to increase both efficiency and scalability of existing semi-autonomous weapon systems. Given a machine's perfect vision capabilities, it would also contribute to decrease or prevent friendly fire incidents [90]. There is also no way that such killing machines would make mistakes, show mercy, defect or refuse to carry out war crimes.

Assuming the above are achieved, the expected human casualties for those controlling the autonomous weapons would be greatly reduced and therefore resorting to what appears to be low-risk and radiation-free wars would occur more easily and frequently [91].

What could possibly go wrong?

Ethical Violation:

Can the responsibility for inflicting death and destruction be ever delegated to an artificial intelligence algorithm? Machines cannot be held accountable [93], they have no conscience, but are getting more and more agency. How far can we stretch the "direct link" that should be kept between the intention of human operators and the machine carrying out their commands?

What if one army is about to be overwhelmed by a more powerful attacker? Can autonomous weapons help the defenders turn the tide and re-establish the battlefield balance? They might, but – in the next wave – autonomous weapons will be used against them. Another one of those endless arms races has just started. "The idea that human security will be enhanced by an unregulated arms race in autonomous weapons is, at best, wishful thinking" [92].

The use of autonomous weapons is abhorrent to the "principles of humanity and the dictates of public conscience", first established in the Hague Convention of 1899 [88].

Drawing the Line:

Machines fighting it out among themselves is one thing. Swarms of slaughterbots autonomously seeking out and destroying defenseless human beings is another.

Known Uses:

Even if low-tech anti-personnel mines are prohibited since 1997, they continue to strike even long after the war in which they have been deployed is over.

"The technical capability for a system to find a human being and kill them is much easier than to develop a self-driving car" that should guarantee the safety of its passengers [87].

"Machines that have the power and discretion to take human lives without human control are politically unacceptable, morally repugnant and should be banned by international law" [89].

7 Conclusion

In this paper we have introduced eight dark patterns which are enabled and empowered by unique aspects of computer science theory and practice. They involve ethical failures such as encouraging addiction, exploiting customers, breaking promises, misleading people, extracting obscene profits, promoting falsehoods, disregarding truth, or skirting accountability.

Most of the dark patterns collected in this paper are related to how computer science exposes the challenging relationship between information and truth and how it perturbs the tension between stability and change. Willful Ignorants first built a panopticon, then look away horrified at what they saw, wishing it would all go away. Reverse Improvers keep changing just because they can, slowly but surely redirecting benefits away from users. Real Virtuality Escapists lose touch with the shadows on the cave walls as they build their own virtual caves. Forgetful Mentalists discard information we wish to preserve and keep information we wish to destroy.

Automation also amplifies existing system efficiencies and inefficiencies. It can also enhance equality and – as described in two dark patterns – boost unfairness. Faceless Assistants are unable or unwilling to truly help users in need of assistance. Reckless Maintainers disregard whoever lost access when moving fast and breaking things.

The last two dark patterns focus on some questionable relationships between humans and computers, which range from unhealthy dependencies – Addiction Peddlers increase engagement with software applications by exploiting habit-forming psychological triggers – to utterly destructive ones in the case of Autonomous Killers.

Without a baseline of core values – a very personal choice – one cannot argue why a dark pattern is indeed dark. According to a diametrically opposite set of values, these same patterns collected in this paper can be used without any hesitation, for example, to make user engagement metrics go through the roof, maximize shareholder value creation, escape from reality, or exterminate the enemy.

8 Future Work

In this paper we focused on identifying and discussing ethical concerns and implications for each dark pattern, whose awareness should lead to their avoidance. More work is needed to support ethical computer scientists in their quest to avoid or mitigate these malicious practices – while keeping their jobs.

An orthogonal study could focus the legal aspects concerning each dark pattern identified in this paper. What is legal and what is ethical not always fully align, depending on the particular geographical region or historical time period. Also, legislation tends to react to technological advances as it takes time before people become fully aware of what has become possible and what the ethical implications are.

Acknowledgements. The author is grateful for the generous feedback of the shepherd and the EuroPLoP workshop participants. The structure of this paper is inspired from the ethical principles of goodness, fairness and truth, as defined by Betrand Meyer in [8].

References

A Ethics

1. Bohr, B.: How to turn ethical values into system requirements: lessons learned from adopting a new IEEE standard in the business world. IEEE Softw. **42**(1), 9–16 (2024). https://doi.org/10.1109/MS.2024.3472928
2. Elish, M.C.: Moral crumple zones: cautionary tales in human-robot interaction (pre-print). Engaging Sci. Technol. Soc. (2019). https://doi.org/10.2139/ssrn.2757236
3. Friedman, B., Hendry, D.G.: Value Sensitive Design: Shaping Technology with Moral Imagination. MIT Press (2019). ISBN: 978-0-262-03953-6. https://dl.acm.org/doi/book/10.5555/3360147
4. Gotterbarn, D., Miller, K., Rogerson, S.: Computer society and ACM approve software engineering code of ethics. Computer **32**(10), 84–88 (1999). https://doi.org/10.1109/MC.1999.796142
5. IEEE standard model process for addressing ethical concerns during system design. In: IEEE Std 7000-2021, pp. 1–82 (2021). https://doi.org/10.1109/IEEESTD.2021.9536679
6. Kapferer, S., Zimmermann, O., Stocker, M.: Value-driven analysis and design: applying domain-driven practices in ethical software engineering. In: Proceeding of the 29th European Conference on Pattern Languages of Programs, People, and Practices (EuroPLoP) (2024). https://doi.org/10.1145/3698322.3698332
7. Mason, R.O.: Four ethical issues of the information age. MIS Q. **10**(1), 5–12 (1986). ISSN: 0276-7783. https://doi.org/10.2307/248873
8. Meyer, B.: Rational Ethics. In: Informatics in the Future, pp. 49–64. Springer, Cham (2017). https://doi.org/10.1007/978-3-319-55735-9_5
9. Rost, J., Glass, R.L.: The Dark Side of Software Engineering: Evil on Computing Projects. Wiley (2011). https://ieeexplore.ieee.org/book/6381796
10. Schlossberger, E.: Engineering codes of ethics and the duty to set a moral precedent. Sci. Eng. Ethics **22**(5), 1333–1344 (2016). https://doi.org/10.1007/s11948-015-9708-3
11. Wiener, N.: Some moral and technical consequences of automation. Science **131**(3410 1960), 1355–1358. https://doi.org/10.4324/9781315259697-3
12. Zimmermann, O., Stocker, M., Kapferer, S.: Bringing ethical values into agile software engineering. In: Smart Ethics in the Digital World: Proceedings of the 21th International Conference on the Ethical and Social Impacts of ICT (ETHICOMP), pp. 90–93 (2024)

B Dark Patterns

13. Becher, S.I., Benoliel, U.: Sneak in contracts. Georgia Law Rev. **55**, 657 (2020). https://digitalcommons.law.uga.edu/glr/vol55/iss2/4
14. Benbunan-Fich, R.: The ethics of online research with unsuspecting users: from A/B testing to C/D experimentation. Res. Ethics **13**(3–4), 200–218 (2017). https://doi.org/10.1177/1747016116680664
15. Brignull, H., Leiser, M., Santos, C., Doshi, K.: Deceptive Patterns (2025). https://www.deceptive.design
16. Gray, C.M., Santos, C.T., Bielova, N., Mildner, T.: An ontology of dark patterns knowledge: Foundations, definitions, and a pathway for shared knowledge-building. In: Proceedings of the CHI Conference on Human Factors in Computing Systems, pp. 1–22 (2024). https://doi.org/10.1145/3613904.364243
17. Irani, L.C., Silberman, M.S.: Turkopticon: interrupting worker invisibility in amazon mechanical Turk. In: Proceeding of the SIGCHI Conference on Human Factors in Computing Systems (CHI), pp. 611–620. ACM (2013). ISBN: 9781450318990. https://doi.org/10.1145/2470654.2470742
18. Keren, H.: I Am Altering the Deal. Pray I Don't Alter It Any Further. Jotwell: J. Things We Like, 1 (2020)
19. Kitkowska, A.: The AI-empowered dark patterns. In: Handbook of Service Experience, pp. 257–270. Edward Elgar Publishing (2025)
20. Kran, E., Nguyen, H.M., Kundu, A., Jawhar, S., Park, J., Jurewicz, M.M.: DarkBench: benchmarking dark patterns in large language models. In: Proceeding of the 13th International Conference on Learning Representations (ICLR) (2025)
21. Luguri, J., Strahilevitz, L.J.: Shining a light on dark patterns. J. Legal Anal. **13**(1), 43–109 (2021)
22. Mathur, A., Kshirsagar, M., Mayer, J.: What makes a dark pattern... dark? Design attributes, normative considerations, and measurement methods. In: Proceeding of the Conference on Human Factors in Computing Systems (CHI). ACM (2021). ISBN: 9781450380966. https://doi.org/10.1145/3411764.3445610
23. Narayanan, A., Mathur, A., Chetty, M., Kshirsagar, M.: Dark patterns: past, present, and future: the evolution of tricky user interfaces. Queue **18**(2), 67–92 (2020). ISSN: 1542-7730. https://doi.org/10.1145/3400899.3400901
24. Thaler, R.H., Sunstein, C.R.: Nudge. Penguin (2021)
25. Toczé, K., Madon, M., Garcia, M., Lago, P.: The dark side of cloud and edge computing: an exploratory study. In: Proceeding of the 8th Workshop on Computing within Limits (LIMITS) (2022)
26. Zagal, J.P., Björk, S., Lewis, C.: Dark patterns in the design of games. In: Proceedings of 8th International Conference on the Foundations of Digital Games (FDG), pp. 39–46 (2013). http://fdg2013.org/program/papers/paper06_zagal_etal.pdf
27. Zuboff, S.: The age of surveillance capitalism: the Fight for a Human Future at the New Frontier of Power. PublicAffairs (2018). ISBN: 978-1-61039-569-4. https://dl.acm.org/doi/book/10.5555/3350443

C Willful Ignorant

28. Bovens, L.: The ethics of Dieselgate. Midwest studies in philosophy (2016)
29. Buschauer, R.: Datavisions—On panoptica, oligoptica, and (big) data. In: The International Review of Information Ethics **24**, 5–14 (2016). https://doi.org/10.29173/irie147

30. Drucker, P.F.: Management: Tasks, Responsibilities, Practices. Truman Talley Books (1986)
31. Galič, M., Timan, T., Koops, B.-J.: Bentham, Deleuze and beyond: an overview of surveillance theories from the panopticon to participation. Philos. Technol. **30**, 9–37 (2017). https://doi.org/10.1007/s13347-016-0219-1
32. Gray, T.: Ode on a Distant Prospect of Eton College, 1742
33. Lilla, M.: Ignorance and Bliss: On Wanting Not to Know. Farrar, Straus and Giroux, New York (2024)
34. Ridgway, V.F.: Dysfunctional consequences of performance measurements. Adm. Sci. Quart. **1**(2), 240–247 (1956)
35. Santos, S., et al.: The SARS-CoV-2 test scale-up in the USA: an analysis of the number of tests produced and used over time and their modelled impact on the COVID-19 pandemic. Lancet Public Health **10**(1), e47–e57 (2025)
36. Steinberg, A.M.: Can a falling tree make a noise in two forests at the same time? In: Causality and Locality in Modern Physics: Proceedings of a Symposium in Honour of Jean-Pierre Vigier, pp. 431–440. Springer, Dordrecht (1998). https://doi.org/10.1007/978-94-017-0990-3_51
37. Vu, L., Soraperra, I., Leib, M., van der Weele, J., Shalvi, S.: Ignorance by choice: a meta-analytic review of the underlying motives of willful ignorance and its consequences. Psychol. Bull. **149**(9–10), 611 (2023). https://doi.org/10.1037/bul0000398
38. Witze, A., Garisto, D., Tollefson, J.: Five climate and space projects on trump's chopping block. Nature **640**, 865 (2025)
39. Zhioua, S., Binkyte, R., Ouni, A., Ktata, F.B.: On the origins of sampling bias: implications on fairness measurement and mitigation. arXiv preprint arXiv:2503.17956 (2025)

D Reverse Improver

40. Beck, K.: Extreme Programming Explained: Embrace Change. Addison-Wesley Professional (2000). https://dl.acm.org/doi/abs/10.5555/318762
41. Brooks, F.P., Bullet, N.S.: Essence and accidents of software engineering. IEEE Comput. **20**(4), 10–19 (1987)
42. Doctorow, C.: Enshittification' is coming for absolutely everything. Finan. Times (2024). https://www.ft.com/content/6fb1602d-a08b-4a8c-bac0-047b7d64aba5
43. Drobnjakovic, K.: Building a deploy system that works at 40000 feet. In: Proceedings of the 4th International Workshop on Release Engineering (RELENG), p. 16. ACM (2016). ISBN: 9781450343992. https://doi.org/10.1145/2993274.2993275
44. Parnas, D.L.: Software aging. In: Proceedings of the 16th International Conference on Software Engineering (ICSE). Sorrento, Italy, pp. 279–287 (1994). https://doi.org/10.5555/257734.257788
45. Vaniea, K.E., Rader, E., Wash, R.: Betrayed by updates: how negative experiences affect future security. In: Proceedings of the SIGCHI Conference on Human Factors in Computing Systems (CHI '14). Toronto, Ontario, Canada, pp. 2671–2674. ACM (2014). ISBN: 9781450324731. https://doi.org/10.1145/2556288.2557275
46. Wentz, B., Lazar, J.: Exploring the impact of inaccessible redesign and updates. In: Designing Around People, pp. 3–12. Springer, Cham (2016). https://doi.org/10.1007/978-3-319-29498-8_1

E Real Virtuality Escapist

47. Bostrom, N.: Are we living in a computer simulation? In: Philos. Quart. **53**(211), 243–255 (2003). ISSN: 0031-8094. https://doi.org/10.1111/1467-9213.00309
48. Calleja. Digital games and escapism. Games Culture **5**(4), 335–353 (2010)
49. Carr, M., et al.: Dream engineering: simulating worlds through sensory stimulation. Conscious. Cogn. **83**, 102955 (2020). https://doi.org/10.1016/j.concog.2020.102955
50. Han, D.-I.D., Bergs, Y., Moorhouse, N.: Virtual reality consumer experience escapes: preparing for the metaverse. Virtual Real. **26**(4), 1443–1458 (2022). https://doi.org/10.1007/s10055-022-00641-7
51. Jiménez-Alonso, B., Brescó de Luna, I.: Griefbots. A new way of communicating with the dead? Integr. Psychol. Behav. Sci. **57**(2), 466–481 (2023). https://doi.org/10.1007/s12124-022-09679-3
52. Pal, D., Arpnikanondt, C.: The sweet escape to metaverse: exploring escapism, anxiety, and virtual place attachment. Comput. Hum. Behav. **150**, 107998 (2024). https://doi.org/10.1016/j.chb.2023.107998
53. Panova, T., Lleras, A.: Avoidance or boredom: negative mental health outcomes associated with use of Information and Communication Technologies depend on users' motivations. Comput. Hum. Behav. **58**, 249–258 (2016). https://doi.org/10.1016/j.chb.2015.12.062
54. Tuan, Y.-F.: Escapism. John Hopkins University Press (1998)
55. Witte, C., Gierszewski, S., Chouinard-Thuly, L.: Virtual is the new reality. Current Zool.-Spec. Issue Comput. Anim. Virt. Real. Anim. Behav. Res. **63**, 1–4 (2017). https://doi.org/10.1093/cz/zow119

F Forgetful Mentalis

56. Baker, M., Keeton, K., Martin, S.: Why traditional storage systems don't help us save stuff forever. In: Proceedings of the 1st IEEE Workshop on Hot Topics in System Dependability, pp. 2005–120 (2005)
57. Blanchette, J.-F., Johnson, D.G.: Data retention and the panoptic society: the social benefits of forgetfulness. Inf. Soc. **18**(1), 33–45 (2002)
58. Farkas, T., Hronyecz, E.: The risks and danger of smart devices exposing personal information: dark side of convenience. In: Proceedings of the 22nd Jubilee International Symposium on Intelligent Systems and Informatics (SISY), pp. 39–44. IEEE (2024). https://doi.org/10.1109/SISY62279.2024.10737613
59. Ghezzi, A., Pereira, Â., Vesnic-Alujevic, L. (eds.): The Ethics of Memory in a Digital Age: Interrogating the Right to be Forgotten. Springer, London (2014). https://doi.org/10.1057/9781137428455
60. Gravitz, L.: The Importance of Forgetting. Nature **571**, S12–S14 (2019)
61. Jones, A.: Lessons not learned on data disposal. Digit. Investig. **6**(1–2), 3–7 (2009)
62. Khan, M.T., Hyun, M., Kanich, C., Ur, B.: Forgotten but not gone: identifying the need for longitudinal data management in cloud storage. In: Proceedings of the Conference on Human Factors in Computing Systems (CHI). Montreal QC, Canada, pp. 1–12. ACM (2018). ISBN: 9781450356206. https://doi.org/10.1145/3173574.3174117
63. McIntosh, T., et al.: Ransomware reloaded: re-examining its trend, research and mitigation in the era of data exfiltration. ACM Comput. Surv. **57**(1), 1–40 (2024). https://doi.org/10.1145/3691340
64. Peaco, B.: Assessment of Job Applicants Facebook Profile: A Case Study by the Hiring Manager. Ph.D. thesis. Northcentral University (2017)

G Faceless Assistant

65. Dukes, A., Zhu, Y.: Why customer service frustrates consumers: using a tiered organizational structure to exploit hassle costs. Mark. Sci. **38**(3), 500–515 (2019). https://doi.org/10.1287/mksc.2019.1149
66. Hardalov, M., Koychev, I., Nakov, P.: Towards automated customer support. In: Agre, G., van Genabith, J., Declerck, T. (eds.) AIMSA 2018. LNCS (LNAI), vol. 11089, pp. 48–59. Springer, Cham (2018). https://doi.org/10.1007/978-3-319-99344-7_5
67. Sneiders, E.: Automated FAQ answering with question-specific knowledge representation for web self-service'. In: Proceedings of the 2nd Conference on Human System Interactions, pp. 298–305 (2009). https://doi.org/10.1109/HSI.2009.5090996
68. Xu, T., et al.: Do not blame users for misconfigurations. In: Proceedings of the Twenty-Fourth ACM Symposium on Operating Systems Principles (SOSP). Farmington, Pennsylvania, pp. 244–259. ACM (2013). ISBN: 9781450323888. https://doi.org/10.1145/2517349.2522727
69. Zaharia, S.E., Pietreanu, C.V.: Challenges in airport digital transformation. Transp. Res. Procedia **35**, 90–99 (2018). https://doi.org/10.1016/j.trpro.2018.12.016
70. Zaza, S., Junglas, I., Armstrong, D.J.: Who needs the help desk? Tackling one's own technological problem via self IT service. Inf. Organ. **31**(3), 100367 (2021). https://doi.org/10.1016/j.infoandorg.2021.100367. ISSN: 1471-7727

H Reckless Maintainer

71. Cerf, V.G.: Internet Access Is Not a Human Right. New York Times (2012)
72. Chatterton, T., Newmarch, G.: The future is already here: it's just not very evenly distributed. Interactions **24**(2), 42–45 (2017). https://doi.org/10.1145/3041215
73. Cusumano, M.A.: Platforms versus products: observations from the literature and history. In: History and Strategy, vol. 29, pp. 35–67. Emerald Group Publishing Limited (2012). https://doi.org/10.1108/S0742-3322(2012)0000029006
74. Mathiesen, K.: The human right to Internet access: a philosophical defense. Int. Rev. Inf. Ethics **18**, 9–22 (2012). https://doi.org/10.29173/irie299
75. van Dijk, J.: The Deepening Divide: Inequality in the Information Society. Sage (2005). ISBN: 1-4129-0402-1. https://doi.org/10.4135/9781452229812

I Addiction Peddler

76. Andrade, F.R.H., Mizoguchi, R., Isotani, S.: The bright and dark sides of gamification. In: Micarelli, A., Stamper, J., Panourgia, K. (eds.) ITS 2016. LNCS, vol. 9684, pp. 176–186. Springer, Cham (2016). https://doi.org/10.1007/978-3-319-39583-8_17 ISBN: 978-3-319-39583-8
77. Bosker, B.: The Binge Breaker. Tristan Harris believes silicon valley is addicting us to our phones. he's determined to make it stop. Atlantic **318**(4), 56–63 (2016). https://www.theatlantic.com/magazine/archive/2016/11/the-binge-breaker/501122/

78. Dresp-Langley, B., Hutt, A.: Digital addiction and sleep. Int. J. Environ. Res. Public Health **19**(11), 6910 (2022). https://doi.org/10.3390/ijerph19116910
79. Eyal, N.: Hooked: How to Build Habit-Forming Products. Penguin (2014)
80. Govender, T., Arnedo-Moreno, J.: A survey on gamification elements in mobile language-learning applications. In: Proceedings of the 8th International Conference on Technological Ecosystems for Enhancing Multiculturality, pp. 669–676 (2020)
81. Harrigan, K.A., Collins, K., Dixon, M.J., Fugelsang, J.: Addictive gameplay: what casual game designers can learn from slot machine research. In: Proceedings of the International Academic Conference on the Future of Game Design and Technology (Futureplay). Vancouver, British Columbia, Canada, pp. 127–133. ACM (2010). ISBN: 9781450302357. https://doi.org/10.1145/1920778.1920796
82. Olsen, M., André, F., Delfin, C., Håkansson, A., Claesdotter-Knutsson, E.: Children and adolescent's self-reported gaming habits-an exploratory, cross-sectional study of gaming among 9–15-year-old school children. Emerg. Trends Drugs Addictions Health **4**, 100058 (2024). https://doi.org/10.1016/j.etdah.2023.100058
83. Singh, V.K., Mani, A., Pentland, A.: Social persuasion in online and physical networks. Proc. IEEE **102**(12), 1903–1910 (2014)
84. Stothart, C., Mitchum, A., Yehnert, C.: The attentional cost of receiving a cell phone notification. J. Exp. Psychol. Hum. Percept. Perform. **41**(4), 893 (2015). https://doi.org/10.1037/xhp0000100
85. Witte, J.: Consumer manipulation–a definition, classification and future research agenda. J. Inf. Commun. Ethics Soc. **23**(1), 14–31 (2025)
86. Young, K.S.: Caught in the Net: How to Recognize the Signs of Internet Addiction—And a Winning Strategy for Recovery. 1st. Wiley, USA (1998). ISBN: 0471191590. https://dl.acm.org/doi/abs/10.5555/522189

J Autonomous Killer

87. Adam, D.: Lethal AI weapons are here: how can we control them? Nature **629**, 521–523 (2024)
88. Eyffinger, A.: The 1899 Hague Peace Conference: The Parliament of Man, the Federation of the World. Martinus Nijhoff Publishers (1999)
89. Guterres, A.: Video Message to the informal consultations on lethal autonomous weapon systems. SG/SM/22643. UN (2025). https://press.un.org/en/2025/sgsm22643.doc.htm
90. Hawley, J.K.: Patriot wars: automation and the Patriot air and missile defense system. Ethical Autonomy Series - Voices from the Field (2017)
91. Leveringhaus, A.: Ethics and Autonomous Weapons. Springer (2016). https://doi.org/10.1057/978-1-137-52361-7
92. Russell, S., Aguirre, A., Conn, A., Tegmark, M.: Why You Should Fear "Slaughterbots"—a Response". IEEE Spectrum (2018). https://spectrum.ieee.org/why-you-should-fear-slaughterbots-a-response
93. Sparrow, R.: Why machines cannot be moral. AI Soc. **36**, 685–693 (2021). https://doi.org/10.1007/s00146-020-01132-6

K Other References

94. Hanmer, R.: Pattern mining patterns. In: Proceedings of the 19th Conference on Pattern Languages of Programs (PLoP), p. 23 (2012)
95. Negroponte, N.: Being digital. Vintage (2015). ISBN: 978-0-679-76290-4. https://dl.acm.org/doi/book/10.5555/546722
96. Sasabe, A., Kaneko, T., Takahashi, K., Iba, T.: Pattern mining patterns: a search for the seeds of patterns. In: Proceedimgs of the 23rd Conference on Pattern Languages of Programs (PLoP), pp. 1–16 (2016)

How scientific conferences work.

A brief introduction covering main conference elements, content selection, ratings and predatory conferences in computer science and beyond

Aliaksandr Birukou(✉)

Springer Nature, Heidelberg, Europaplatz 3, 69115 Heidelberg, Germany
birukou@gmail.com

Abstract. This manuscript describes scientific conferences, how they are organized, the role of various parties involved, and introduces the main processes related to content selection and publication. It is aimed mainly at people starting their career in science, such as Master or PhD students, but can also be used by industry professionals attending scientific conferences. Conference organizers might also find it useful, especially if they organize their first conference.

Keywords: scientific conferences · conference proceedings · scientific events · workshops · program committee · peer review.

1 Introduction

Scientific conferences play a major role in the discussion and dissemination of scientific results. They also provide researchers with great networking opportunities. In areas like computer science, engineering, and, to a certain extent, materials science, mathematics [25,8], they also produce formal and peer-reviewed publication of research results known as conference proceedings.

The purpose of this paper is to provide an introduction to the world of scientific conferences. While other authors [37] published books about conferences, they covered only specific aspects (e.g., organization, presentation). During the course of my work (more recently in publishing at Springer Nature, but previously as a researcher at several universities) I interacted with many researchers from different fields and countries and community or commercial organizers of scientific conferences. However, all of them needed to start somewhere and answer the questions such as:

- What is a scientific conference?
- How does it work?
- Does it always have conference proceedings?
- What is the role of the program committee?
- How to create a functional program committee?
- How does peer review take place?

T. Plummer et al. (Eds.): EuroPLoP 2025, LNCS 16494, pp. 363–381, 2026.
https://doi.org/10.1007/978-3-032-19157-1_17

- What are workshops?
- How to pick up a good conference?
- What are predatory conferences and how to avoid them?

Upcoming sections should help the reader to address these and similar questions by introducing the main elements of scientific conferences, looking at some more advanced conference elements, and covering several topics related to the research evaluation and publication ethics. While my experience is mostly based on computer science conferences of different subfields and sizes, I have basic knowledge about conferences in other disciplines and tried to distill "main" versus "advanced" (often more relevant for computer science or which occur only at some conferences) elements. The idea is that the readers less familiar with the conferences can start with Section 2, while those who have basic knowledge can also read Sections 3 and 4.

2 Main elements of the conference

A scientific (academic) conference is a venue for researchers to present and discuss their recent research work. It can also be called a symposium, congress, workshop, colloquium, forum, seminar, summit, convention. This list is not exhaustive, but I would like to distinguish events discussing research from other form of gatherings which might include researchers: hackathons, meetups, unconferences, roundtables, retreats. Normally, conferences leave traces, increasing their impact beyond direct participants. Depending on the community, such traces can include (more or less in the increasing the amount of information available): conference program, "word-of-mouth" communication about the talks, a book of abstracts (for instance, for most of medical and life science conferences), or published proceedings containing the novel results presented at the conference (similarly to journal articles or books in some disciplines). Some conferences put presentations, videos of the talks, and other artifacts online on the website or in a repository. Unfortunately, many of conference websites do not survive beyond a couple of years, and therefore publishers play an important role in digital preservation of conference results for the conferences publishing proceedings. The subsequent subsections introduce the conference identification and then describe how the research content is selected for the conference program and conference proceedings, where applicable.

2.1 Identifying conferences

Nowadays, each conference has a website, a distinctive *conference name* (e.g., International Semantic Web Conference), often it has an *acronym* (e.g., ISWC), *dates* and *location* of the current edition (e.g., November 2-6, 2025, Nara, Japan). Conferences are linked in series, for instance, ISWC 2025 is the 24th edition in the ISWC *conference series*. A series might only contain one conference, though, as some conferences exhaust their topic in one edition, while other conferences repeat over the years reflecting the progress of research on their topic. Interestingly enough, while the first international conference of chemistry, the Karlsruhe Congress, held on 3-5 September 1860 did not have a website, we know a lot about the topics discussed and participants [11]. Despite its significance, there was no successor conference in the series. The topic of conference series and its evolution was extensively discussed in the Crossref/Datacite group on Persistent Identifiers (PIDs) for Conferences [12] which run through 2016-2020. The group concluded that in many cases, despite renaming, splits, or mergers, the series of conference events have a common identity which is captured by conference series.

2.2 Conference lifecycle

A "basic" conference lifecycles involves stages before the conference, such as planning the location, defining the conference team, topics, the process for selection of contributions and budgets; during the conference, e.g., registration of participants, conference schedule, coffee breaks; and after the conferences, for instance, sharing the photos of the event, organizing proceedings [39]. A more detailed definition is available in [36] (Section 3.1).

2.3 Call for papers

A typical Call for Papers (CfP) lists topics and types of papers the conference invites authors to submit. It also mentions the organizers and, in some cases, the program committee. It also lists the important deadlines, explains the peer review process, links instructions for authors and paper templates. The CfP also contains the information about how to submit: via a submission system or e-mail. It usually also lists ethical rules and disclosures. In the context of scientific conferences the novelty of results presented is one of the most important factors, distinguishing them, for instance, from some industry or professional gatherings. Therefore, the majority of the conferences that publish proceedings would not accept papers submitted or published elsewhere. Other factors influencing the selection of conference presentations or papers include: statistical significance of the numbers, maturity or suitability of the methods, increment with respect to the state of the art tools. Conferences also might expect certain impact of the results, varying from regional to top international.

TIP: Due to the variety of the acceptance criteria it is recommented to browse programs, presentations and proceedings of previous conference editions to understand which ones are important to the conference.

While after the COVID-19 pandemic online or hybrid conferences became normal, usually it is still expected that one of the authors presents the paper at the conference (in person or online). Finally, the CfP often includes information about whether and where conference proceedings will be published and indexed.

2.4 Conference governance

Each conference is different, and in this section I try to cover the main committees involved in organizing and running the conference.

Conferences are usually organized by the academic community, with several researchers prominent in the conference field forming a *steering committee*. Such a committee can be formal or informal, and its members change or remain stable over years. There are also private companies or academic societies organizing conferences, but in this case they would also rely on academics for defining the scientific program. The steering committee is responsible for selecting the location and organizers of the next conferences and defines its future topics and policies.

Organizing committee The steering committee appoints a *general chair*, responsible for the overall organization of the conference edition. The general chair appoints the *organization committee* of a conference focused on the overall setup of the conference beyond its content. The organization committee includes a *local chair* and a team of *local organizers* responsible for the logistics of the event: where it takes place, securing the necessary rooms, arranging the coffee breaks, lunches, social events, and making sure the venue has appropriate technical facilities for the presentations.

Program Committee The program committee (PC) of a conference issues a *call for papers* and is responsible for organizing a *peer review process*. This includes defining types of papers the reviewers will evaluate (e.g., abstract only, full, short, poster, demo papers), criteria for accepting papers, type of peer review (single-/double-blind, open, etc., as explained later in 2.5), a schedule for the review tasks and deadlines (including authors' rebuttals, if applicable), and how conflicting opinions of the reviewers will be handled [2]. The PC members also review conflict of interest or publication misconduct cases, act as ambassadors for the conferences by inviting potential authors and endorse the conference to authors and readers. The PC contains various roles, main ones are:

- One or several *program chairs*, normally appointed by the general chair(s) are responsible for defining the topics of the conference program and organizing the peer review. They also select keynote speakers. Program chairs appoint dozens (or hundreds, depending on the conference size) of
- *program committee members* who peer review papers in small or medium-sized conferences or invite *additional reviewers* to do this in larger conferences. Some conferences have *senior PC members* who supervise more junior PC members.

You can find more information about Program Committee in Section 3.

2.5 Peer review

The main goal of the peer review process is to select a suitable number of papers that meet quality criteria and topics listed in the call for papers of the conference. While there are projects [5] studying peer review, in the following I shall list the most common types used by conferences nowadays.

A *single blind* or single anonymous peer review process is where only the reviewers are anonymous to the authors, while the author names are known to the reviewers. A *double blind* or double anonymous peer review process is where both the author and the reviewers are anonymous, i.e., reviewers do not know whose paper they review and authors do not know the reviewers. An *open* peer review is where the reviews and reviewers' names are published next to the paper, while *transparent* is where only reviews, but not the reviewers' names are published.

A basic conference peer review process is shown in Figure 1[1]. Authors submit a paper, the PC selects several reviewers who then provide their reviews (also known as review reports) by a certain deadline, after which the PC selects papers for the conference. The authors then do their best to implement the reviewers' comments and submit a *camera ready*, i.e., the final version, which is then published in the conference proceedings. Unlike the journal peer review, in the conference peer review there is usually no revision, i.e., the paper is accepted or rejected as it is. This is because conferences have tight timelines, since the dates of a conference are fixed and influence important milestones for submitting reviews and the final versions. However, some conferences introduce more stages, such as *bidding*, where reviewers check submitted papers and express preferences about which ones they would like to review. This stage might be automated using tools such as the Toronto Paper Matching System [6]. Another optional stage is *rebuttal*, during which the authors might reply to reviewers' comments by clarifying aspects in the paper which were misunderstood by the reviewers.

It is worth mentioning that reviewers are usually researchers who have expertise in the conference field. They normally act as volunteers, e.g., are not paid. There are experiments on paying peer reviewers, see, for instance [38], but no big changes as of now. Some journals have in-house editors, i.e. ex researchers who are paid to select papers for the journal, but I am not aware of similar roles for conferences. Overall, most researchers feel that reviewing is a community service which is an essential part of academic job and it looks good in one's CV.

TIP: If you would like to start reviewing it is worth checking if your community / conference provides any trainings for reviewers. There are also a number of free courses for peer reviewers. Another common way to start is to ask your supervisor to delegate you one or several reviews and ask them to read your report and suggest improvements before you submit it. For bigger conferences it is advisable to get involved in the workshop program committees, which might be easier, and then progress to the main PC as you built up your record as a reviewer.

[1] Inspired by http://www.cs.ucsb.edu/~ebelding/courses/284/papers/ReviewingPapersStudentGuide.html

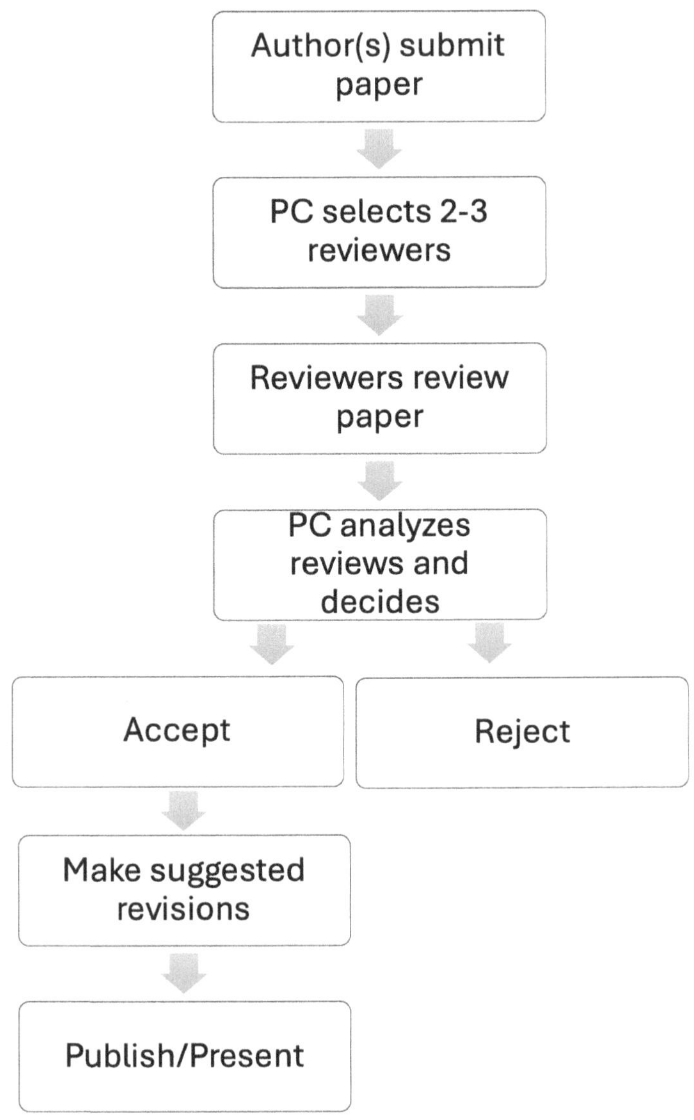

Fig. 1. Conference peer review process

A *review report* includes the recommendation (accept/reject/boarderline), confidence of the reviewer in the topic (novice/medium/expert) and detailed feedback on the paper, including the assessment of the novelty, significance (if applicable), relation to existing literature, and suggested improvements. Some conference use lightweight informal reviews, others complex forms with many criteria. Earlier we showed [13] that many criteria can be reduced to three main ones: 'soundness', 'contribution' and 'innovation'.

Some communities or conference setup allow for more focus on providing feedback to the authors rather than selecting a reasonable number of papers for the conference program. *PLoP (Pattern Languages of Programs, People and Practices) series uses *shepherding* [14], which is the process of a *shepherd* (often a PC member) working with an author (*sheep*) over several iterations of their paper providing constructive comments. Other conferences might use a shepherding-like process for borderline papers. This involves several revisions.

If the conference does not publish proceedings, the review can be done on abstracts (or extended abstracts of several pages) and there is no need to submit a camera-ready.

3 Advanced conference elements

3.1 Submission systems

To help the program committee to implement the peer review process and make it more efficient, a *submission system*, also known as a conference management system is normally used. It is a tool which enables online submission and peer review of papers. Its main functions include: keeping track of submitted abstracts and papers; managing the selection of reviewers and papers assigned to them; monitoring the status of reviews, ratings and comments; providing reports on the peer review process, paper selection, etc; collecting licenses to publish/copyright forms. More advanced systems would also help with checks for plagiarism or duplicate submission, creation of the conference schedule, proceedings preparation, conference registration, hotel booking, transfer to the venue, and payment of the registration fee. It is worth mentioning that previously a lot of conferences used e-mail submissions (and I personally have not experienced submissions via snail mail), but this is increasingly rare nowadays. Also, while a conference submission system seems similar to a journal submission system, the former ones have specific conference functions. Since 2011 I have seen at least three attempts to implement "the common (journals/conferences) submission system" which all failed. Still, I would not exclude such attempts being successful in the future with *special issues* (also called *collections*) gaining popularity. They have similar characteristics as conferences: clear deadline for the final version, all articles submitted appear together online, etc.

TIP: always check what timezone the deadline is in. For instance, many conferences would use "Anywhere on Earth" time zone which means noon of the following day in Germany or Italy, while other conferences might specify midnight in China or USA as the deadline.

Mario Malicki in 2017 [15] analyzed the mentions of submission systems in the prefaces of Lecture Notes in Computer Science (LNCS), the major book series publishing conference proceedings. In such prefaces the conference organizers provide additional information about the conference, peer review, etc. The main systems used were: EasyChair (66%), Microsoft Conference Management Toolkit (CMT) (4%), PRIMORIS (3%), Online Conference Service (OCS, later EquinOCS) (2%), EDAS (1%).

3.2 Conference proceedings

2

While many researchers would be familiar with *books* and *journals* publishing research results, there are also *conference proceedings*. In fact, Crossref, a non-profit open digital infrastructure organization for the global scholarly research community which assigns Digital Object Identifiers (DOI) to published content, supports three distinct content types: books, journals, conference proceedings.

Conference proceedings constitute a formal archive of the papers that add up to the scientific body of knowledge. Proceedings are not a book of abstracts. Papers in conference proceedings contain original/primary research results[3], published as full or short papers. Proceedings are rather common in computer science, where more than 60% of original research results appear in conferences [10], some areas of engineering, but also in materials science, mathematics and become more common in other disciplines. The main publishers of proceedings are Institute of Electrical and Electronics Engineers (IEEE), Springer Nature, SPIE (the international society for optics and photonics), the Association for Computing Machinery (ACM)[4]. Main types of proceedings are:

- *pre-proceedings*, which are ready in time for the conference. I am not sure who started this practice, but in the late 20th century it was common for main conference publishers (IEEE, Springer, ACM) to provide proceedings before the conference in the print form, which then moved to the electronic form in the 21st century;
- *post-proceedings*, which are done after the conference, and some conferences prefer to introduce one more round of revisions, thus creating proceedings of revised selected papers.

Some conferences, e.g., VLDB since 1976 or ECML PKDD since 2013 [7] have a journal track, i.e., proceedings published in a journal. It can be a dedicated

[2] This section reuses my previous work [8].

[3] this term defines new research results, i.e. novel knowledge produced during research and added to the scientific body of knowledge. It is different from the research that entirely based on a summary, review, or synthesis of earlier publications on the subject of research.

[4] This is based on analysing Scopus, Web of Science and Dimensions databases. I am planning to include statistics in the future version of this manuscript.

proceedings journal (for one[5] or many[6] conferences) or a special issue in a regular journal[7]. Even a more common practice is to do a special issue with a selection of best extended papers from the conference, where authors can add additional findings and provide better explanations. The practice, while common in computer science, can be deemed inappropriate in other disciplines, because the main result already appeared in the conference proceedings.

While I started the section outlining books, proceedings and journals as distinct types, in reality many conference proceedings are published as books or journals. See [8] for a discussion on the topic.

Why proceedings are so important in computer science? Authors of primary research in computer science often favor conference proceedings over journals because the format helps them get their work out to the global community faster. In fact, conferences are pivotal to the entire research lifecycle in this field, with the commissioning process, ongoing exchange of ideas, and publishing schedules closely tied to large international events. When I analyzed primary research in computer science in Scopus[8] for 2012-2016 I found that 63% of original research results are published in conference proceedings, with only 37% published in journals, similar numbers were reported by Meho [10].

In a viewpoint published in Communications of ACM [9], Lance Fortnow explains that computer science emerged in the 1950s as a new field. It was easier to start from scratch in terms of how research was communicated, and the conference system therefore developed as a vehicle for the rapid dissemination of research papers through conference proceedings, fast reviews, and community get-togethers. It was natural that publishers and societies then started publishing the resulting conference proceedings, and that these are recognized as valuable contributions to the field. In 2013, for example, the ACM Distinguished Service Award was given to Gerhard Goos, Juris Hartmanis, and Jan van Leeuwen, the founding editors of the Lecture Notes in Computer Science (LNCS) series.

3.3 Workshops

I mentioned several names used for academic events in the previous section. While this document will not cover all of them, it is useful to have a closer look at workshops and poster session.

Workshops may come in various forms, but several features are common and make them different from conferences or other academic events. First, workshops are usually more focused [16]. For instance, while a conference covers a broad

[5] Proceedings of the VLDB Endowment `https://dl.acm.org/journal/pvldb`

[6] Procedia Computer Science. https://www.sciencedirect.com/journal/procedia-computer-science

[7] `https://www.vldb.org/dblp/db/journals/tods/tods1.html`

[8] Scopus is an abstracting and citation database indexing research literature including conference proceedings, journals and selected books.

topic (for instance, the 34th International Joint Conference on Artificial Intelligence, IJCAI 2025), a workshop's scope would be a narrow subtopic of such a topic (for instance, the 2nd International Workshop on Large Language Models for Financial Services, FinLLM 2025). Second, the workshop usually has an order of magnitude fewer participants than a conference. The latter may not apply to standalone workshops, which could attract a large number of participants just for the event. If workshops are co-located with a conference, normally there are multiple parallel workshops, and the audience naturally splits along the various subtopics.

The workshop program can contain one or several keynotes and short or long research talks, making it similar to a mini-conference (it has fewer participants and lasts fewer days). Often, a workshop might have a goal beyond presenting papers and discussing them. For instance, the participants might agree to write a book as the result of the workshop, or work on a joint paper, manifesto, a roadmap. If the workshop has proceedings, they can be standalone or workshop papers can be included in main conference proceedings.

Workshops take place as standalone events or often are co-located with a conference on a broader topic, like in the example of IJCAI and FinLLM. In the latter case, normally a conference issues a call for workshops, where researchers can propose a workshop on a specific topic.

3.4 Poster sessions

A poster session allows participants to present results of their research in a visual format (poster). A purpose of a poster [17] is "to outline a piece of work in a form that is easily assimilated and stimulates interest and discussion." Poster sessions usually last a couple of hours and allow poster authors to present their ideas or results to the session participants. Poster sessions usually have a separate process for submission and peer review of the contributions. They are either requested as a short paper or an extended abstract and thus lower the barriers for the participants. This allows to present less mature research, not fully developed ideas, and also enables participation of researchers from industry, who might not be willing to write full papers. Some conferences use poster sessions for giving more time to authors of regular papers to discuss their work, outside of the rigid slot dedicated to their presentations. If the poster session has proceedings, they can be standalone or posters (usually short papers describing posters) can be included in main conference proceedings.

3.5 Other conference sessions

A conference might also have tracks (also called sessions or special sessions) dedicated to specific topics or types of research. An example of topic-driven session was "Automated Verification of Embedded Control Software" special session at the 11th International Symposium On Leveraging Applications of Formal Methods, Verification and Validation (ISoLA 2022). An example of "type-driven" session was "Applied Data Science Track" at the European Conference on Machine Learning and Principles and Practice of Knowledge Discovery in Databases - ECML PKDD 2025. Also, many conferences host an *industry track* inviting contributions tested in the industry context or developed in cooperation with industry participants.

Such tracks might be chosen during general conference submission or run independently with its own PC, CfP and submission process. They might also have different acceptance criteria than the main conference.

3.6 How to create a functional program committee?

Various PC roles Some conferences recruit PC members only by invitation, while others allow them to apply to serve in the PC. Depending on the format, the conference can also have *track chairs*, playing the role of the program chairs for a specific track; *workshop chair*, selecting workshops for the conference; *tutorial chair*, organizing the tutorial (long lectures on advanced topics, often with practical exercises); *poster/demo chairs* organizing poster/demo sessions; *award chairs* selecting papers for specific awards (e.g., best paper of the conference or retrospective awards to the papers which proved to have significant impact on the community); *industry track chairs*, selecting innovative applications in industry; *publicity chair*, responsible for the promotion of the conference; *finance or sponsorship chair*, responsible for the budget and finding sponsors; *proceedings chair*, who prepares the conference proceedings and sends them to the publisher. ExOrdo, published a blog post describing various conference roles [1].

As discussed above, tracks could be called (special) sessions and therefore such (special) session/track chair should not be confused with the *session chair* role at the conference. The latter is normally an experienced participant who moderates specific conference session in the program.

Factors to consider in building of the program committee. In this subsection I will share some best practices for building a functioning program committee[9].

- *Expertise of the PC members* must match some of the conference topics to enable meaningful selection of papers and their peer review (if applicable). If someone's publication record is stellar in security, it does not mean they can assess papers in the field of human-computer interaction. For bigger conferences, there are tools like *bidding* or automated systems (see Section 2.5) that match the specific expertise of members with the topics of the paper.
- *Geographical spread* should match the authorship and readership of the conference. The diversity of the reviewers helps to represent various scientific schools and methods used in the conference field.

[9] a reader familiar with scientific journals, might recognize many parallels with best practices for building journal editorial boards.

- *Seniority.* There are extreme examples of conferences that only involve doctors of sciences[10] in the PC. However, a good mix of experienced and more junior PC members normally provides a good balance for timely selection of papers. PhD students should get some guidelines and supervision when doing their first reviews, even though there is no clear evidence that training works [3].
- *Succession planning.* The right balance between continuing members of conference committees and new members helps to grow the conference community and its expertise. The steering committee in cooperation with the program committee can help achieve this.

TIP: to become a part of the program committee you would normally need to get actively involved in reviewing papers, and after several successful conferences put yourself forward to other available roles.

4 Research evaluation and ethics

This section introduces conference ratings and their use in research evaluation. It then proceeds with discussing predatory conferences.

4.1 Conference ratings

11

As I mentioned earlier, conferences play an important role in several research fields, such as computer science, where more than 60% of the research results are published in conference proceedings [10]. The authors of this study also identified several problems related to evaluating impact of conference proceedings: first, rankings such as Google Scholar and Microsoft Academic miss or underestimate some conferences due to the young age of the conference or the unreliable size, which forces researchers to look for new methods of ranking conferences. Secondly, the authors showed that Scopus' CiteScore is an effective method of evaluating computer science conferences. Thirdly, the CiteScore shows that conference papers also have a high impact, as do articles in leading computer science journals. Research [26] showed that a small number of elite conferences have higher average citations rate than elite journals. The authors of [27] looked at the bibliometrics of conferences and concluded: conferences are more popular than journals; about 78% of publications reflecting the most relevant research are published in conference proceedings; publications in journals are cited more than those in conferences (57% vs. 43%, respectively); the distribution of publications in conferences vs journals is country-dependent. While

[10] the next level after PhD, only existing in some countries, see `https://en.wikipedia.org/wiki/Doctor_of_Science`

[11] This section uses a lot of material previously published by myself and co-authors in [25]

there is a range of metrics for evaluating journals, e.g, Impact Factor, SCImago Journal Rank (SJR), there is no common metric for evaluating conferences [28].

The first attempts to create conference rankings appeared in Computer Science. The most frequently used rankings, based on the experience of the authors, are the Computing Research and Education Association of Australasia, CORE and ERA Ranking [29], Qualis (2012), China Computer Federation (CCF) ranking (2012), MSAR (2014), and GII-GRIN-SCIE (2014). The CORE Conference Ranking [30] provides evaluation of major computer science conferences. Decisions are made by academic committees based on data requested as part of the submission process. ERA Ranking (2010) was created in the framework of Excellence in Research in Australia (ERA). It incorporates data from a previous ranking attempt by CORE. Qualis [31] has been published by the Brazilian ministry of education and uses the H-index (strictly speaking, H-index percentiles) as a performance measure for conferences. The latest edition was released in 2021. The fifth edition of the list of journals and conferences recommended by the CCF [32] was released in 2022 and assigns A (highest), B, C (lowest) ranks to conferences in each CS subarea. Interestingly, the release mentions that "the influence of journals and conferences is not directly related to the influence of a single paper published there. Therefore, it is not recommended to use this list as a basis for academic evaluation" – in line with the Declaration on Research Assessment (DORA)'s principles [33]. In other words, DORA principles suggest that one should not look at the A/B/C label of the conference where research is published, but look at the research itself. This is because (sorry, it is an important result which I know anecdotally but do not have a citation) using a label assigned based on some criteria (like quality of the papers and impact of authors involved) when used as the new criteria is dangerous. The label might disconnect from the criteria which led to its creation and can be misused, e.g., by predatory actors. Currently, I see that while some universities mandate rating/ranking-based policies for research evaluation, others are trying to get away from this and assess selected best research contributions of the researchers, departments, or universities.

MSAR [12] was the Microsoft Academic's field rankings for conferences. It was similar to the h-index and calculated the number of publications by an author and the distribution of citations to the publications. Field ranking only calculated publications and citations within a specific field and shows the impact of the scholar or journal within that specific field. GII-GRIN-SCIE conference rating [13] is an attempt to develop a unified rating of computer science conferences led by GII (Group of Italian Professors of Computer Engineering), GRIN (Group of Italian Professors of Computer Science), and SCIE (Spanish Computer-Science Society), see [34]. The latest version ranks all conferences in four tiers (top notch, very high quality, good, and work in progress) based on the CORE, Qualis and MSAR rankings and it was released in 2021. Last but not the least, there is

[12] Was available at `https://academic.microsoft.com/home` till end of 2021

[13] Available at `http://gii-grin-scie-rating.scie.es/` (date accessed 2025/05/03.

also Google Scholar Top publications [35] tool which lists both conferences and journals in the same ranking.

In [25] we proposed a metric for the conferences indexed in Scopus and used bibliometrics methods to compare it with the most frequently used computer science conference ranking, CORE. The results showed that some conference proceedings in computer science, engineering, material science, physics and astronomy, and mathematics are comparable with top journals in those disciplines.

4.2 Predatory conferences

In the beginning of the 21st century, with publications moving online, increasing number of researchers, and Open Access gaining popularity the research community faced the development of predatory publishing. Grudniewicz et al. [18] defined predatory journals and publishers as "entities that prioritize self-interest at the expense of scholarship and are characterized by false or misleading information, deviation from best editorial and publication practices, a lack of transparency, and/or the use of aggressive and indiscriminate solicitation practices.". Unfortunately, conferences also were targeted by such malevolent entities. As early as in 2005, a group of MIT students noticed the phenomenon and created an automated generator SciGen of nonsence (also called fake) papers. They then used it to submit several fake papers and organize a session at the World Multiconference on Systemics, Cybernetics and Informatics (WMSCI) [19]. The tool is available online and was used by several researchers to generate more than a hundred fake papers, successfully published at several conference and later retracted. The phenomenon continues with Generative Artificial Intelligence (Gen AI) technologies, such as ChatGPT used for creating papers [20]. However, the discussion of the use of such paper generators is out of scope for this paper, so in the following I shall focus on highlighting characteristics of predatory conferences.

Predatory conferences share the following characteristics

- Their main goal is to get researchers' money via registration or publication fees, as opposed to legitimate conferences' goal of enabling exchange and dissemination of novel research ideas.
- Peer review is non-existing or very superficial with short deadlines, prioritizing profit over research integrity. In one example, researchers got only one review for another! paper and while they asked the conference to withdraw their paper, the organizers published it anyway.
- Conferences may list a fake program committee with some (or even all) of the members not being aware of being PC members.
- Such conferences often use unsolicited mailing to attract submissions or engage in tricks like inviting authors to present their paper without review.
- Sometimes the conference does not take place or has much less participants that a legitimate conference would do (the latter still normally assume each paper should be presented at the conference, in-person or virtually, depending on the conference format.

- Such conferences might use names of existing conferences or for well-known bi-annual conferences can put an edition "in-between" years where the "real" conference takes place.
- Often it is not clear from the conference website if the conference took place in the past or published proceedings (if applicable).
- In my experience, many predatory conferences emphasize indexing [in Scopus or Web of Science], thus attracting authors whose research evaluation policies require indexed publications. A lot of such conferences were removed later from indexing services [21].

Many practices mentioned in Section 2.4 in relation to building program committees might seem obvious, but they are still often neglected by predatory conferences and help researchers distinguish predatory conferences from the legitimate ones. In addition, predatory conferences adapt and become more sophisticated than simply copying the name and acronym of legitimate ones.

I would like to mention that while the organizers of fake/predatory conferences aim at authors' money, the decision of authors to participate is more controversial. I had the pleasure of co-organizing a panel with representatives of Scopus, Web of Science, eLIBRARY.RU[14], and the Russian Association of Science Editors and Publishers (RASEP) at the ScienceOnline 2019 conference, which reviewed the conference spikes in certain series and publishers. The panel participants concluded that while questionable conference proceedings were removed from indexing databases, many papers could have been of decent quality and could sustain rigorous peer review if submitted to "non-fake" conferences [23]. This is because not all authors are submitting because of the "publish or perish" pressure and may be tempted to go for a predatory conference. Some of them are not aware of the predatory conference phenomenon, or inexperienced in choosing publication venue (either being in the beginning of their research career or moving from another research field). Such authors might submit regular paper to the predatory conference.

TIP: If you are not familiar with conferences in a specific topic it is advisable to ask colleagues (or your supervisor, for MS/PhD students) to make sure the conference you selected is a legitimate one.

This shows that education about predatory/fake conferences is important. Think. Check. Attend. is an example of initiatives aimed at educating researchers about fake or predatory conferences [24]. Norddeutscher Rundfunk and Westdeutscher Rundfunk broadcasting companies created a documentary (in German, but it also has English subtitles) about fake science, describing also fake conferences [22].

5 Conclusion and future work

This paper introduced basics of scientific conferences and also covered a number of advanced topics. I hope it provides a good introduction to the world of scien-

[14] the biggest abstracting and indexing service in Russia also indexing content from several other countries

tific conferences. Future work includes adding more examples, practical tips and advanced topics (e.g., attending conference, writing a good paper) and making it a short book for those starting in international research.

Acknowledgments. This paper is a write-up of various author workshops, lectures and courses about how publishing works, and presentations at academic and publishing conferences and meetings. A lot of concepts are defined based on my conversations with researchers and conference organizers or come from various projects and workgroups on conference linked open data, conference persistent identifiers, best practices for organizing international conferences. The list of people who contributed to creating this body of knowledge is vast. Still, I shall try to mention the main ones and apologize in advance in case I forgot some. Alexander N. Dudin invited me to the first scientific conference I attended in 2003 in Gomel, Belarus. Fausto Giunchiglia, whose "Research Methodology" course at the University of Trento in 2004 covered conferences. Paolo Giorgini and Enrico Blanzieri, my supervisors, who encouraged my conference travels during the PhD. Fabio Casati and Vincenzo D'Andrea, who introduced me to different viewpoints and conference attendance strategies during my Postdoc time at Trento. Fabio gets special thanks for making any travel/meal together a fun experience. Gloria Origgi, for introducing me to the [very different] world of conferences in philosophy. Florian Daniel, for explaining the social aspects of conference attendance and providing clear strategies for PhD students attending conferences. Imrich Chlamtac, and the conference department of European Alliance for Innovation, for introducing me to commercial and organizational aspects of running conferences. Attila Nagy and Petros Stratis, who showed me how information technology helps to run conferences. Alfred Hofmann, for convincing me to join Lecture Notes in Computer Science (LNCS) team and tremendous support over 8 years. Anna Kramer, Christine Reiss, and the whole LNCS team for sharing this journey with me and their help along the way. Ronan Nugent, Ralf Gerstner, Beverley Ford, Wayne Wheeler for teaching me various aspects of attending conferences, now from the publisher side, and (also to Celine Chang, Mio Sugino, Jorge Nakahara) for attending multiple conferences together. Asdaa Kotani, Ran Schweitzer and Frans Lettenström, for organizing many author workshops, where I could teach hundreds of researchers about various aspects of publishing, including conferences. Jeffrey Robbens and Chris Bendall, for helping with the preparation for such workshops. Anurag Acharya and Miriam Kessler (for the initial inspiration) and Volha Bryl, Kai Eckert, Markus Kaindl, Andrey Gromyko, Henning Schoenenberger, Volker Böing, Frank Holzwarth, Mario Malički, Markus Richter, Gabi Schäfer, Stephen Cornelius, Viktoria Dobisch, Jacqueline Lenz, and Ute Vriesinga for introducing conference identifiers in Springer internal systems and SpringerLink. Judy Salk, Heiko Paulheim, Jörg-Rüdiger Sack, Marcel R. Ackermann, Geoffrey Bilder, Martin Fenner and Steve Scott for various projects related to conference identifiers and catalogs. Alice Meadows, for encouraging me to write a Scholarly Kitchen blog post about conference proceedings, Olga Kirillova, for organizing its translation into Russian, and Ran Dang - in Chinese. Dmitry Kochetkov, Anna Ermolayeva, Konstantin Samouylov for helping me to pursue research on conferences at Peoples' Friendship University. My lovely wife, Volha Bryl, and the father-in-law, Andrey Bril, for reading and commenting on the preliminary versions of this paper. Last but not least, the shepherding of Cesare Pautasso for EuroPLoP 2025 made this paper way better, so I would like to thank him for his dedication, comments and very constructive approach. Special thanks go also to the participants of EuroPLoP 2025 Workshop H, who provided insightful comments about the paper and a lot of ideas for future extensions: Anja Bertels, Christian Kohls, Marius Nisslmüller, Simon Schulte, Dan Zhu.

Disclosure of Interests. I work at Springer Nature, which is one of major publishers of scientific conferences. However, the paper does not promote my employer or its conferences.

References

1. Brian Campbell. Who sits on a conference organising committee? `https://www.exordo.com/blog/whos-sits-on-a-conference-organizing-committee/`, last accessed 2025/03/08
2. Kulamer et al. Recommended Practices to Ensure Technical Conference Content Quality. Presented by Gordon MacPherson at the 4th World Conference on Research Integrity Rio De Janeiro, Brazil, June 2, 2015.
3. Hesselberg J-O, Dalsbø TK, Stromme H, Svege I, Fretheim A. Reviewer training for improving grant and journal peer review. Cochrane Database of Systematic Reviews 2023, Issue 11. Art. No.: MR000056. DOI: 10.1002/14651858.MR000056.pub2.
4. Sarabipour, S., Khan, A., Seah, Y.F.S. et al. Changing scientific meetings for the better. Nat Hum Behav 5, 296–300 (2021). https://doi.org/10.1038/s41562-021-01067-y
5. Squazzoni, F. et al. Unlock ways to share data on peer review. Nature **578**, 512-514 (2020). DOI: 10.1038/d41586-020-00500-y
6. Charlin, L. and Zemel, R. The Toronto Paper Matching System: An automated paper-reviewer assignment system. (2013). `https://www.cs.utoronto.ca/~lcharlin/papers/tpms.pdf`, last accessed 2025/03/09
7. Greene, D., Bringmann, B., Fromont, E. *et al.* Introduction to the special issue for the ECML PKDD 2018 journal track. *Data Min Knowl Disc* 32, 1177–1178 (2018). https://doi.org/10.1007/s10618-018-0586-6
8. Birukou, A. Everything* You Ever Wanted to Know about Conference Proceedings But Were Afraid to Ask. The Scholarly Kitchen. (2020) https://scholarlykitchen.sspnet.org/2020/01/30/guest-post-everything-you-ever-wanted-to-know-about-conference-proceedings-but-were-afraid-to-ask/, last accesses 2025/03/09
9. Lance Fortnow. 2009. ViewpointTime for computer science to grow up. Commun. ACM 52, 8 (August 2009), 33–35. https://doi.org/10.1145/1536616.1536631
10. Lokman I. Meho, Using Scopus's CiteScore for assessing the quality of computer science conferences, Journal of Informetrics, **13**(1), 419-433 (2019). https://doi.org/10.1016/j.joi.2019.02.006.
11. Wikipedia. Karlsruhe Congress. `https://en.wikipedia.org/wiki/Karlsruhe_Congress`, last accessed 2025/05/01
12. PIDs for Conferences & Projects `https://www.crossref.org/working-groups/conferences-projects/`, last accessed 2025/05/01
13. Elize Brezis, Aliaksandr Birukou. Arbitrariness in the peer review process. Scientometrics **123**, 393–411 (2020). `https://doi.org/10.1007/s11192-020-03348-1`
14. Harrison, N. B. (1999). The language of shepherding. Pattern languages of program design, 5, 507-530.

15. M. Malicki and A. Birukou. Creating a dataset of peer review in computer science conferences published by Springer. https://www.slideshare.net/slideshow/creating-a-dataset-of-peer-review-in-computer-science-conferences-published-by-springer/71110491#22, last accessed 2025/05/12
16. Gautam Kamath https://kamathematics.wordpress.com/2023/08/08/principles-for-planning-an-academic-workshop/, last accessed 2025/05/02
17. Society for Industrial and Applied Mathematics. Guidelines for Meeting Participants. https://www.siam.org/conferences-events/about-siam-conferences-and-events/conference-guidelines/guidelines-for-meeting-participants/, last accessed 2025/05/02
18. Grudniewicz et al. Predatory journals: no definition, no defence. Nature **576**, 210-212 (2019). https://doi.org/10.1038/d41586-019-03759-y
19. Adam Conner-Simons. How three MIT students fooled the world of scientific journals. https://news.mit.edu/2015/how-three-mit-students-fooled-scientific-journals-0414, last accessed 2025/09/30
20. Haider et al. (2024). GPT-fabricated scientific papers on Google Scholar: Key features, spread, and implications for preempting evidence manipulation. Harvard Kennedy School (HKS) Misinformation Review. https://doi.org/10.37016/mr-2020-156
21. JournalsInsights. (Updated) Scopus Discontinued Journals 2025 https://journalsinsights.com/scopus-discontinued-list, last accessed 2025/05/03
22. NDR/WDR. Exclusiv im Ersten: Fake Science - Die Lügenmacher (Documentary in German with English subtitles) https://www.ardmediathek.de/video/dokumentation-und-reportage/exclusiv-im-ersten-fake-science-die-luegenmacher-englut/das-erste/Y3JpZDovL2Rhc2Vyc3RlLmRlL3JlcG9ydGFnZSBfIGRva3VtZW50YXRpb24gaW0gZXJzdGVuL2U1ODIzNWJkLWU2MzQtNDExNC05ZjgwLTNlMDQ0YTJmZWExMw, last accessed 2025/05/03
23. RETRACTED On the Conference about the Conference! Round Table "Scientific conferences as the essential means of communication: development challenges". Science Editor and Publisher. 2019;4(3-4):223-234. (In Russ.) https://doi.org/10.24069/2542-0267-2019-3-4-223-234
24. Think. Check. Attend. https://thinkcheckattend.org/, last accessed 2025/05/03
25. Kochetkov, D., Birukou, A., Ermolayeva, A. (2022). The Importance of Conference Proceedings in Research Evaluation: A Methodology for Assessing Conference Impact. In: Vishnevskiy, V.M., Samouylov, K.E., Kozyrev, D.V. (eds) Distributed Computer and Communication Networks. DCCN 2021. Communications in Computer and Information Science, vol 1552. Springer, Cham. https://doi.org/10.1007/978-3-030-97110-6_28
26. Vrettas, G., Sanderson, M.: Conferences versus journals in computer science. J. Am. Soc. Inf. Sci. 66(12), 2674–2684 (2015)
27. Franceschet, M.: The role of conference publications in CS. Commun. ACM 53(12), 129–132 (2010)
28. Almendra, V.S., Enăchescu, D., Enăchescu, C.: Ranking computer science conferences using self-organizing maps with dynamic node splitting. Scientometrics 102(1), 267–283 (2014). https://doi.org/10.1007/s11192-014-1436-y
29. Butler, L.: ICT assessment: moving beyond journal outputs. Scientometrics 74(1), 39–55 (2008). https://doi.org/10.1007/s11192-008-0102-7
30. CORE Rankings Portal. https://www.core.edu.au/conference-portal, last accessed 2025/05/03

31. QUALIS CONFERNCIAS (2016). https://qualis.ic.ufmt.br/, last accessed 2025/05/03
32. List of International Academic Conferences and Journals Recommended by the Chinese Computer Federation (CCF), 2022 Edition. https://www.ccf.org.cn/Academic_Evaluation/By_category/, last accessed 2025/05/03
33. San Francisco Declaration on Research Assessment. https://sfdora.org/read/, last accessed 2025/05/03
34. Cabitza, F., Locoro, A.: Exploiting the collective knowledge of communities of experts. In: KMIS, pp. 159–167 (2015)
35. Google Scholar conference ranking. https://scholar.google.com/citations?view_op=top_venues&hl=en, last accessed 2025/05/03
36. Franken, J., Birukou, A., Eckert, K., Fahl, W., Hauschke, C., and Lange, C. (2022). Persistent Identification for Conferences. Data Science Journal, 21(1), 11. DOI: 10.5334/dsj-2022-011
37. Burford, J., Henderson, E.: Making Sense of Academic Conferences. Routledge, 2023.
38. Else H.: Publishers trial paying peer reviewers — what did they find? Nature, 2025. DOI: 10.1038/d41586-025-00968-6
39. Birukou, A., Pautasso, C., Weiss, M. (2025). Towards a Pattern Language for Academic Conferences. Report of the EuroPLoP 2025 focus group. In EuroPLoP 2025 proceedings [this volume]. https://doi.org/10.1007/978-3-032-19157-1_20

Design Patterns for Creating Engaging eHealth Applications for People with Parkinson's

Marius Nißlmüller[1](✉) and René Reiners[2]

[1] Fraunhofer FIT, Sankt Augustin, Germany
marius.nisslmueller@fit.fraunhofer.de
[2] RWTH Aachen University, Aachen, Germany
rene.reiners@rwth-aachen.de

Abstract. With eHealth applications rising in popularity, revenue, and use, more disease-specific apps are being developed. In the context of chronic Parkinson's disease (PD), which is after Alzheimer's, one of the most common neurodegenerative diseases, eHealth apps can significantly benefit People with Parkinson's (PwP). Through sensors, medication tracking, medical tests, or symptom diaries, the patients can collect data on which doctors can fine-tune their treatment plans, improving the patient's quality of life. This paper proposes five design patterns, focusing on increasing user engagement in such an eHealth application for PwP. The patterns try to carefully suggest using gamification and nudging elements to fulfill the three basic needs of the self-determination theory (SDT), which are essential for fostering an intrinsic motivation to use an application. The design patterns are based on user research with PwP, family members, medical personnel, and related work studies. They were evaluated through iterative user tests with usability experts, PwP, and family members.

Keywords: eHealth · user engagement · Parkinson's disease · design patterns

1 Introduction

Idiopathic Parkinson's disease (PD) is one of the most common neurodegenerative diseases, affecting 2-3 % of people older than 65 years [24]. As it is currently a non-curable condition, treatment therapies focus on controlling the symptoms but do not stop the neurodegeneration and increasing disability of the disease [6]. It is commonly associated with tremors in the hands or legs, but the symptoms can also include muscle rigidity, slow and reduced movement, and postural instability [6]. Mental and physical comorbidities, like anemia or arterial diseases, are also common, especially with elderly patients [32]. People with Parkinson's (PwP) can usually be categorized into two Personas, as one group is open and outspoken about their disease (Fig. 10), while the other group feels embarrassment and fears stigmatisation (Fig. 9).

T. Plummer et al. (Eds.): EuroPLoP 2025, LNCS 16494, pp. 382–404, 2026.
https://doi.org/10.1007/978-3-032-19157-1_18

The attending doctor must fine-tune treatments because each patient's disease progression is unique [5]. Nevertheless, a neurologist cannot accompany their patients every day. In today's reality, neurologists in Germany only see each PD patient once every three months for a short consultation [12]. During these consultations, the doctor tries to evaluate the patient's condition through verbal reports by the patient and accompanying family members. If there is enough time, a nurse will perform standardized tests to measure the current state for a more objective comparison. However, this only provides a snapshot of the health status at the time of the consultation. Some events and details relevant to improved treatment can be forgotten by the patient, like when they felt good or bad, and how severe some symptoms were.

Depending on the physical state of the patient, electronic Health (eHealth) applications can help to solve this challenge of accessing more frequent and robust data about a patient's health and condition. These applications, installed on mobile phones or other portable devices, are a companion in the patient's daily life. They can use sensors to track and measure data, allow user input, such as symptom reporting, or educate about the disease and its treatment. Regardless, such an application is only the technical foundation for data collection. To receive data, frequent use by the patients is necessary – provided that the medical treatment approach is right. This requires a particular motivation, e.g., filling out weekly questionnaires and reporting health and symptom changes. Thus, eHealth applications must foster high levels of user engagement to realize their full potential. In other words, the success of these applications greatly depends on how actively users interact with them. Therefore, it is essential to design eHealth applications that are engaging and user-friendly so that people are more likely to use them consistently and derive maximum benefits from them.

This paper proposes design patterns on how to increase user engagement in a mobile eHealth application for PwP, on the example of the publicly funded ParkProReakt project, which developed and evaluated such an app as part of a clinical trial [34]. Specific engagement patterns for such Parkinson's apps are necessary, since it is a non-curable condition and therefore influences the motivation and usage approach. While other eHealth apps can promise betterment or improvement of an illness as a reward for frequent use, applications for PwP can only accompany, help deal with the symptoms, and collect data for professionals to personalize the therapy. This might result in an improved quality of life, but not in a permanent relief. The engagement approach must thus be different from eHealth apps in general.

ParkProReakt aims to create a new holistic method of care that proactively recognizes a change in the patient's symptoms instead of reacting to it. Thus, it provides more information for the caregivers on improving the treatment and the patient's quality of life. For this, the app combines motor tests and a cognitive questionnaire, which the PwP would typically complete during their quarterly appointment with their neurologist (Fig. 1a). Additionally, non-scientific surveys allow the users to log their movement behavior and other symptoms in the app, as well as document falls and occurrences of "freezing", a state in which the patient's movement is like being "frozen" and almost unable to move at all (Fig. 1b).

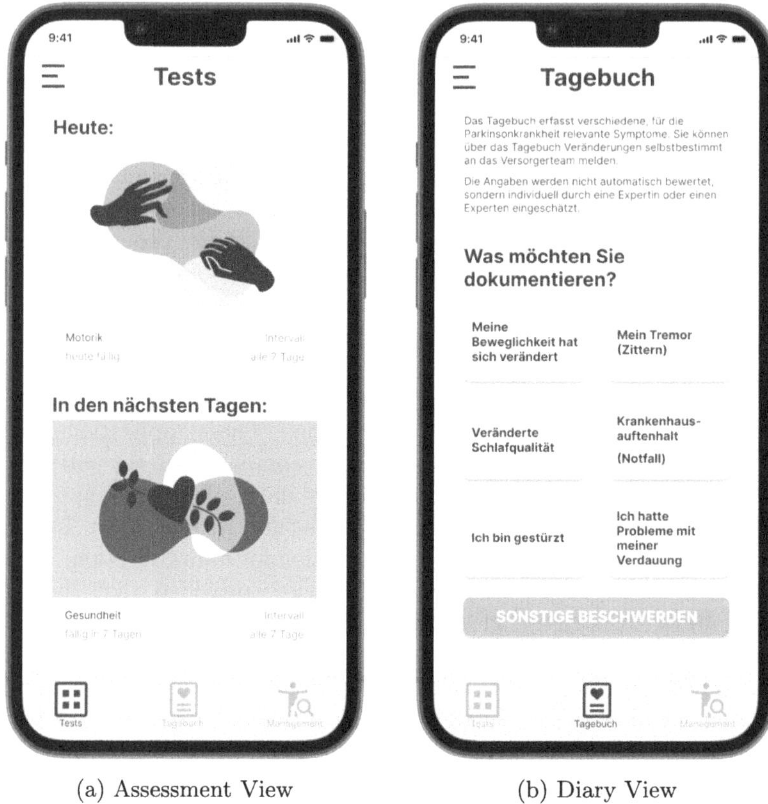

(a) Assessment View (b) Diary View

Fig. 1. Start View of Assessments and Diary.

The data gathered by the app is accessible to doctors and caregivers only. A web platform notifies the caregivers if a patient's health status is trending downwards or if the data suggests a deterioration. It then suggests looking into it and contacting the patient. However, the doctor can also use the data collected during the quarterly consultation visits to analyze why and when the disease worsened and to adjust medication. Both use cases can benefit the patient by enabling the caregivers to fine-tune treatment. However, the design of the web platform is not part of this paper.

While the patterns described in this paper are based on this specific PD application, they are generalized so that they can be applied to all commercial or non-commercial systems, given that the app falls into the context described by the first pattern. This is primarily the context of being an application that connects PwP and caregivers or healthcare professionals. If this is not the case and an application is developed only to be used by the PwP, not all patterns, such as the medical tests on demand, are recommended. But other patterns, like the digital symptom and well-being diary or the personal goals, can be applied without such a connection.

2 Related Work

Existing approaches for PD-related eHealth applications try to leverage user engagement techniques to improve patient engagement and treatment plan adherence [1,9,13]. Those examples are presented in the following section, while the theory behind user engagement – namely, gamification and nudging – is explained in the next section.

Digital applications in the health domain promise to gather more health data and provide more regular and personalized treatment/therapy than analog meetings. A review analysis of 234 eHealth apps concluded that if such an app "is simple and intuitive to use, provides instructions to better manage a condition, and shares data with designated individuals" [19], it is considered valuable and therefore it is appreciated by its users. For PD, we already see various eHealth approaches targeting different areas of the disease and its medical association.

One approach is using wearables to measure movement symptoms like tremors. The Motor Fluctuations Monitor for Parkinson's Disease (MM4PD) demonstrates how a smartwatch accelerometer and gyroscope can measure and classify resting tremor severity [25]. Combined with information about a patient's medication, the MM4PD system captures data correlating with clinicians' analog ratings and provides insight into the medicine's effect patterns. Continuous measuring, achievable only by wearables and not by short doctor visits, provides the necessary advantage, as the authors confirmed with a pilot study under controlled conditions, followed by a longitudinal patient and control study.

More recently, the cloudUPDRS project demonstrated an eHealth application to measure UPDRS scores as a certified medical device in the UK [31]. Using the accelerometer and touch screen, the app can perform "hand and leg tremor measurements, as well as gait and bradykinesia assessments using finger tapping" [31]. From interviews with 22, surveys with 166, and audience panels with 16 patients and carers, essential factors for developing an application for PwP were identified. The results generally acknowledge that an eHealth app has transformative potential, especially for involving the patient directly in the care and therapy.

The ParkProTrain project developed a therapy application that supports PwP to perform activating exercises in their home environment [29]. ParkProTrain aims to support the custom workout plan, a follow-up to a stationary treatment at a Parkinson's facility. The tablet app shows the personalized workout plan, instruction videos for each exercise, and a calendar to view the successful training days. After each exercise, the users are asked to rate the tasks, providing feedback to the therapist. To achieve frequent use of the app and the workouts, the app was developed using a user-centered design approach, cooperating with usability experts, physiotherapists, and PwP. For motivation, patients can choose workouts different from those recommended in their workout plan, giving them a sense of autonomy. In addition, frequent app activity is rewarded with badges and trophies, which are gamification elements and will be addressed in detail in the next section. A nine-month-long longitudinal study to analyse the influence of the training app is described as the next step by Schmeier et al. [29], but the results are not yet published.

A similar approach is the 9zest training app, which underwent a single-cohort pilot study [16]. The app also includes exercises for PwP to perform at home and adapts exercises based on self-reported attributes. If a user reports problems or accidents during a workout, an algorithm adapts the training plan for the next iteration and reduces the difficulty or variation. The authors also cite intrinsic and extrinsic barriers of PwP, which come with the non-motor symptoms of PD, such as depression and fatigue, as well as low outcome expectation, lack of time, and fear of falling, that might prevent patients from using such an app. 9zest tries to circumvent this by including "behavior change techniques, including prompts/cues, goal setting, graded tasks, and performance feedback" [16].

But to generalize the best practice applications, the realm of specific eHealth or especially Parkinson's Disease-related patterns is scarce. Research is ongoing, and projects like the "Design Patterns for Mental Health"[1] are a beginning, but were created with mental health applications in mind, so some ideas or even patterns might apply to other diseases but lack verification. However, they remain on a top-level approach and sometimes lack examples or illustrations. There remains a need for patterns describing the development of PD-related eHealth applications.

3 User Engagement Theory

High user engagement can relate to more frequent or intense use of a system and, therefore, higher impact, data collection, and/or revenue. Developers can use specific techniques and approaches to increase this engagement and influence users' decision-making.

That is why, based on the conclusion of the previous research about eHealth applications for PD, the following subsections present two methods commonly used to address user engagement in this domain. One is gamification, which uses game design elements to motivate. The other is nudging, which works more subconsciously or concealed than gamification by changing how choices are presented. While gamification also takes advantage of human behaviour, nudging does so without being visible. Both methods have been applied in general and in eHealth applications specifically, and they can thus be used to develop design recommendations in this thesis.

3.1 Gamification

In the context of this paper, gamification will be defined as "the use of game design elements in non-game contexts" [11]. Applications are said to be "gamified" as soon as elements, typically known from games, appear in a non-game

[1] https://designpatternsformentalhealth.org/ (accessed on 11.08.2025).

context, like a web forum, social media sites, or an eHealth application. Such elements can include tangible elements like achievements and progress bars, and more abstract elements like challenges or quests, narrative, and feedback [26]. Using gamification, developers and designers aim to increase engagement with the underlying system [11].

Research suggests that there is a potential to enrich eHealth applications with gamification elements by facilitating patient self-management [20]. The article cites the following elements for use in a health context:

1. Badges
2. Leaderboards
3. Points and Levels
4. Challenges and Quests
5. Social Engagement Loops and Onboarding

A successful approach to gamification can also lead to the desired behavior by forming habits by reinforcing a reward response and leading to satisfying outcomes for the users [26]. Another goal is to create an intrinsic motivation that leads users to perform actions because of the pleasure they give and the attraction they feel towards it. To maintain intrinsic motivation, particular psychological needs have to be fulfilled [4,27]. These are the three basic needs of the self-determination theory (SDT) [28] that can be defined as [23]:

Autonomy - Feeling agency, acting in accordance with one's goals and values.
Competence - Feeling able and effective.
Relatedness - Feeling connected to others, a sense of belonging.

However, the use of gamification does not constantly improve engagement but also has the potential to cause addiction, undesired behavior, or off-task behavior [3]. Depending on the gamification scenario and environment, these negative traits can influence the core service offering and deter users from the application's original purpose. According to the authors, these risks can be mitigated if the gamification design considers possible risks and monitors the interactions after a release.

3.2 Nudging

Thaler and Sunstein coined the concept of nudging in their book "Nudge: Improving Decisions about Health, Wealth, and Happiness" [33]. The book defines a nudge as "any aspect of the choice architecture that alters people's behavior in a predictable way without forbidding any options or significantly changing their economic incentives. To count as a mere nudge, the intervention must be cheap and easy to avoid. Nudges are not mandates. Putting fruit [in a grocery store] at eye level [hoping that people then choose fruit over unhealthy alternatives] counts as a nudge. Banning junk food does not" [14].

Nudging is used, e.g., by policymakers to promote decisions either by indirect means, like warning labels on cigarette boxes to discourage smoking, or direct interventions, like making an opt-out system for organ donation, relying on the tendency that people stick to a status quo [30].

In the context of this paper, nudges are a possible design recommendation to increase user engagement since such concepts were already tested in other eHealth applications, e.g., diabetes management [15]. The nudges can be implemented as "information displays, auditory alerts, visualizations, gamification rewards, recommends actions, and so on" [10]. Thus, ensuring that the nudges are personalized to the behavior is essential since they may become distracting and too frequent, leading to the user ignoring them or rejecting the eHealth application [10].

Nevertheless, nudging is criticized because of its subconscious influence on people. Concerns are raised that nudges undermine the autonomy of people or that nudges prevent broader reforms because they do not address underlying causes for problems (e.g., "Why don't people voluntarily become organ donors?") [8,17,30].

Another risk lies in accidentally creating a so-called dark pattern, which can be defined as "tricks used in websites and apps that make you do things that you didn't mean to, like buying or signing up for something" [18]. Dark patterns are usually created by the designer's intent and abuse the knowledge of the power that nudges and need fulfillment have. They subvert the user's intent to benefit from the service. However, by trying to align with the SDT needs, defined in Subsect. 3.1, and the above definition of nudges, a strong focus on the user's autonomy could prevent a dark pattern from forming.

4 Methodology

This work followed the Design Research Methodology (DRM), which was created "to support a more rigorous approach for design research to become more effective and efficient" [7]. The application scheme can be seen in Fig. 2.

Through the related work, the research classification generated an understanding of initial goals, problems, objectives, relevant topics, and current research and design gaps. Already existing solutions to facilitate user engagement in mobile eHealth environments were also in focus. These solutions included approaches to incorporating user engagement elements in such applications, which were subsequently gathered and structured to get an overview of the status quo.

Following this, a descriptive study identified the participating actors, followed by user research in the form of interviews, which represented the typical user groups of the eHealth application as personas (see Fig. 9 and Fig. 10). Interview participants were recruited from a local support group and consisted of six PwP with varying degrees of age and severity of the disease, four family members, and one neurologist. The semi-structured interviews helped us understand their respective motivations and needs, preferences, and challenges regarding user engagement. The interviews' evaluation aimed to learn if and to what degree PwP have to be motivated to perform the tests and diary logging, how

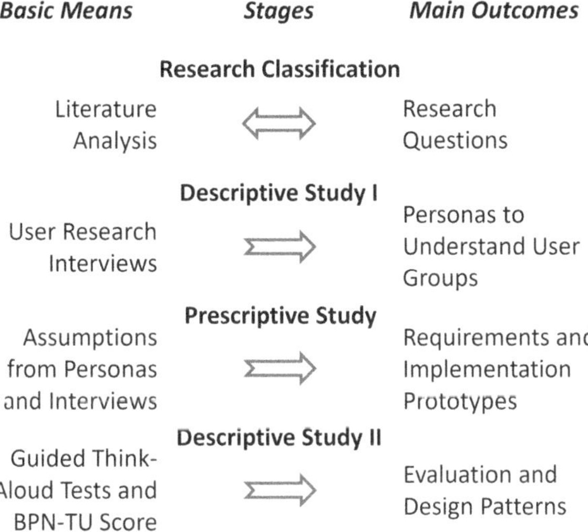

Fig. 2. Research Agenda.

exactly caregivers benefit from the increased data availability, and whether we can turn that benefit into another motivator for the patients. Another goal of the interviews was to get an insight into how user engagement in the mobile application might deteriorate over time. The stakeholder interviews were recorded for a thematic analysis to identify common themes and barriers to user engagement among the stakeholders. A problem understanding was developed from this stage, and prerequisites were derived to develop the patterns. This process used a human-centered approach, following the insights gathered from interviews and the respective analysis.

In the prescriptive study, the gathered assumptions were synthesized into requirements to increase user engagement of PwP in the application. The structure for the requirements was that of a user story for a software epic. This means that each requirement represented a larger feature and followed the format of [22]:

```
As a <type of user>, I want <goal> so that <reason>.
```

Acceptance criteria supplemented each requirement to define the scope and expectations of the user story. The requirements are available in Appendix A.3. Based on those requirements, an initial example selection of suitable user engagement elements and options was developed from gamification and nudging. The requirements were summarized and evaluated, focusing on the special demographic that are PwP, represented as personas, and the concrete usage scenario of mobile eHealth applications. The requirements were implemented in the mid-/high-fidelity prototype of the ParkProReakt application. Visualizing the created requirements in this prototype, according to established design guidelines for this specific application, allowed for a realistic usage scenario. Additional design guidelines for PwP and older people in general were also respected.

The prototypes were evaluated with an iterative testing process in the second descriptive study. In the first iteration, think-aloud tests were carried out with certified usability engineers to refine the designs and gather feedback on the implementation and concepts from the scientific usability perspective. The results from this round of tests provided valuable input for improving the prototypes before starting a second iteration of tests. For the second iteration, PwP and family members were approached. An example of how the improved prototype looked can be seen for the assessment view in Fig. 3a and for the diary entry view in Fig. 3b. Compared to Fig. 1a, the improved Fig. 3a features a button to view historical test data and signals to the user which assessment has been completed by showing a checkmark and a grey overlay. Figure 3b is an entirely new screen, which enables the user to view their past diary entries from Fig. 1b.

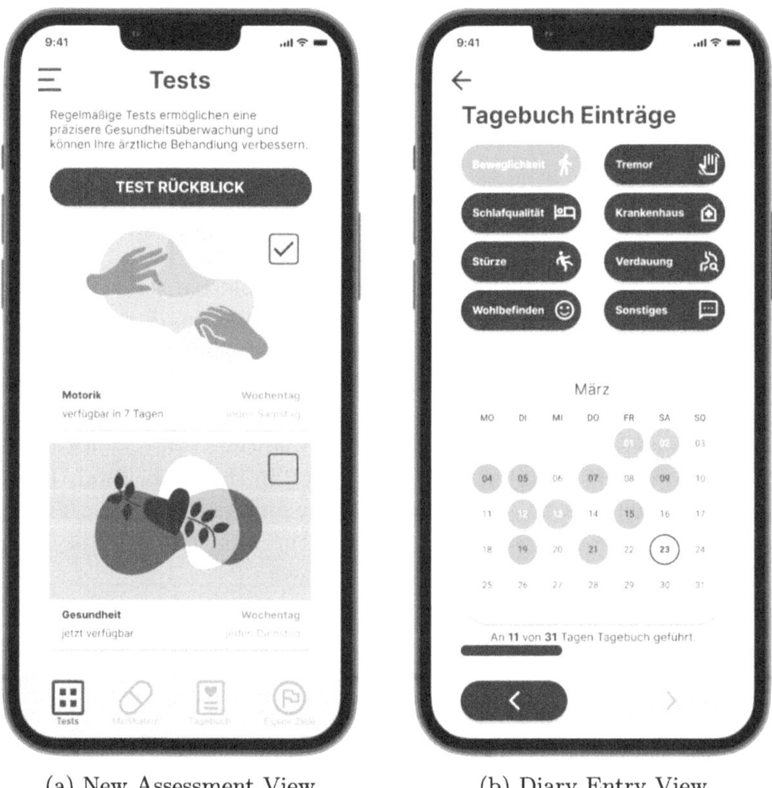

(a) New Assessment View

(b) Diary Entry View

Fig. 3. Start View of Assessments and Diary.

In addition to the tests of the prototype, the participants of both evaluation test rounds filled out a questionnaire to gather comparable feedback on the perceived impact and engagement delivered by the new elements. The 12-item Basic Psychological Need Satisfaction for Technology Use Scale (BPN-TU) was used for this questionnaire, which was recently developed and validated [21]. The BPN-TU measures fulfillment of the SDT's basic psychological needs for autonomy, competence, and relatedness using a Likert scale. Fulfilling these needs can trigger an intrinsic motivation, which attracts users to the application. For each statement in the questionnaire, the participants can respond if they strongly disagree, disagree, neither disagree nor agree, agree, or strongly agree. The BPN-TU results were used to evaluate the effectiveness of the design elements for user engagement by determining whether the improvements met the basic needs.

While the results from experts, PwP, and their family members who participated in the tests provided insight into whether the application, including the requirements, is need-fulfilling, it was also of interest whether the improved application rates are better than the original. For this, the BPN-TU was sent out to various PwP using the current application. This group used the original application for varying amounts of time and was asked to rate their experience. The results of this baseline evaluation were compared with the prototype evaluation to see if the version implementing the requirements achieves a higher need fulfillment than the original application. As can be seen in Table 2, the version with the implemented requirements showed a 47% improvement in basic psychological need satisfaction compared to the baseline application.

Based on the evaluated requirements and the previous user research, the five design patterns for engaging eHealth apps for PwP were developed, bundled into one collective pattern, which prioritizes and orders the other patterns. The patterns are therefore refined requirements, generalized with qualitative data from the literature and user research, and fine-tuned with the quantitative results of the user study. They rely on common elements and aspects observed and validated in different eHealth apps, but are contextualized through knowledge gained from the research on the ParkProReakt project. Since the patterns described in this paper are meant for a higher-level view of the problem, the pattern structure of context, problem, solution, and illustration by [2] will be applied, supplemented by a discussion.

5 Design Patterns

Our user research revealed that PwP show considerable motivation to try new therapy approaches, such as an eHealth application, but they always have specific requirements in mind. These requirements, supported by needs for autonomy, competence, and relatedness, have to be fulfilled to keep the PwP as active app users.

Therefore, five feature-related recommendations were formulated as design patterns. Each design pattern is related to a requirement, which was derived from analysing interviews with PwP. Each requirement, therefore, contained traces of context, problem, and solution of a pattern. The patterns with the basic SDT-need(s) it targets, and an exemplary list of possible gamification elements can be seen in Table 1.

The problems of the patterns are solved by describing a model solution, which includes user engagement elements. Connecting the design recommendations to features and requirements was chosen to make them specific enough to be effortlessly applied. Although the development was based on the ParkProReakt application, other existing eHealth applications for PD include one or more of these features and can thus be improved by the design pattern's solution. However, the patterns are still in an early and immature form and provide an initial contribution towards increasing user engagement. The five patterns are bundled in the overarching pattern "Mandatory and Optional Features of a Parkinson's Disease eHealth Application", which describes the context of PD applications and in what order and priority the five specific patterns should be implemented.

5.1 Mandatory and Optional Features of a Parkinson's Disease eHealth Application

Context: Mobile health applications for PwP in Hoehn & Yahr stage 1-4, and without a cognition-impairing disease or comprehension and communication difficulties, can provide caregivers with more data about the well-being of the patients, making it possible to adjust their therapy. Such applications can also help patients in their daily lives and improve how they deal with and live with the disease.

Problem: If an eHealth application does not fulfill the needs and requirements of its users, they can be deterred from using the application. If, for example, exercises in a training app are not adapted to the skill level of the user, a lack of competence is created if the training is either too easy or too hard. And if the medical tasks designed by the caregivers are too strict and narrow, e.g., limiting the possibilities too much, the autonomy of users is suffering. This can prevent PwP from using the application or reduce their engagement with it, since their basic needs of the self-determination theory are not fulfilled, and an intrinsic motivation to use the application is not created.

Solution: Therefore, the features of a PD eHealth application must strive to fulfill the basic needs to create an intrinsic motivation to use the app. This can be achieved by applying the following patterns to the included features:

1. Digital Symptom and Well-Being Diary
2. Digital Medical Assessments
3. Tracking of Personal Goals and Activities
4. Medication Reminder and Tracker
5. PD Newsfeed and Notes

Table 1. Overview of the 5 Patterns, the Targeted SDT-Needs, and Exemplary Gamification Elements.

Pattern	*Targeted SDT-Need*	Exemplary Gamification Elements
1. Digital Symptom and Well-Being Diary	*Autonomy*	Achievements, Goals, Progress Bars
2. Digital Medical Assessments	*Autonomy, Competence*	Achievements, Goals, Challenges, Time Pressure, Progress Bars, Performance Graphs, Rules, Feedback
3. Tracking of Personal Goals and Activities	*Autonomy, Competence*	Achievements, Goals, Challenges, Time Pressure, Progress Bars, Performance Graphs
4. Medication Reminder and Tracker	*Autonomy, Competence*	Feedback, Time Pressure, Rules, Purpose
5. PD Newsfeed and Notes	*Autonomy, Relatedness*	Access, Social Engagement, Social Discovery

1. Digital Symptom and Well-Being Diary

Context: Medical personnel adapt the medication and therapy of PwP based on reported symptoms and well-being. The more information a neurologist has about the patient, the better they can react.

Problem: At the quarterly appointments, patients can no longer remember exactly which symptom occurred on which day, which makes it difficult for the doctor to assess their health. Only a few patients keep a manual diary, because they often forget to do so. With a digital diary, a one-sided focus on negative symptoms can also put a strain on the patient's mental health.

Solution: Therefore, a symptom diary should be part of every eHealth application for PwP. It should allow for recording negative symptoms, positive aspects, and good days in the patient's life. This enables a holistic view of the patient's health and positively influences their mental health. To ensure that the diary entry is not forgotten, its added value should be clearly stated, and the previous use of the diary should be retrieved in an activity diagram. Reminders should point out a daily entry. This can help the doctor assess the patient's health better and give both them and the patient a comprehensive review of the patient's condition (Fig. 4).

Discussion: A well-documented diary of symptoms and mental well-being is crucial for PD therapy, since the complicated medication schedule comes with side effects and has to be fine-tuned to each patient. During the user study, multiple interviewees expressed forgetfulness about when and which specific symptoms occurred. They complained that even using an analog diary is not working for them because they lack reminders or prompts. The expected benefit from such a feature was twofold: On the one hand, it would ease the next doctor appointment because nothing would be forgotten, and the neurologist would have a better picture of the progression. On the other hand, the interviewees expressed their interest in tracking the course of their symptoms to assess their health. While all interviewees said they would like such a symptom review, it was also discussed that this might manipulate their feelings, worsening their mental health if they saw how often they have symptoms, and thus influencing their next symptom documentation. In addition to that, the interviewees were wondering why the diary in the analysed application only allows for documenting "negative" aspects/symptoms instead of also giving the option to track when they feel good: "Why should I only write down the negative things when I've been practicing for so long that I'm supposed to write down five things that were good every day?". As a result, this pattern solution recommends a holistic diary.

Fig. 4. Diagram of the Symptom Diary Design Pattern.

2. Digital Medical Assessments

Context: Health assessments in eHealth apps related to PD are important for capturing the patient's condition. The assessments are done to receive an uninfluenced snapshot of the health and usually evaluate a certain score or result.

Problem: The direct display of assessment results without a doctor's classification, medical assessment, and contextualization can lead to distorted results and impair the actual purpose of the assessment. Patients may adjust their behavior and focus on scoring high on the test instead of answering without bias and giving a realistic picture/snapshot of their health. Being confronted with worsening results due to the progressive nature of PD further risks demotivating the patient.

Solution: Therefore, eHealth applications for PwP that include medical assessments should hide the results/score from the patients and only make it available for medical personnel. Instead, a feedback mechanism should be implemented that tracks and displays the patient's general participation in the assessments. This can motivate the patient to take the assessments regularly without focusing on achieving a high score. The emphasis should be on participation and recording health progression rather than scoring high results. The medical assessment and contextualization of the results remain essential but should only occur in a personal consultation (Fig. 5).

Discussion: User study feedback was unanimous that while receiving an assessment result/score in the app is generally of interest, they would rather not see the score because of the risk of being demotivated by a downward trend. Further discussion around this topic from the interviews substantiated that showing an assessment result could undermine the assessment's purpose, which is to receive an objective and uninfluenced insight into the patient's health. If it were possible to view the result in the app, it might feel like a verdict and lead to frustration, or a "gaming" of the assessment, where people try to achieve a higher score by manipulating how the assessment is conducted or answering dishonestly. The interviewees preferred that the results stay with the doctors, who can evaluate and judge the results better and discuss the scores during the next appointment. This observation is more nuanced than the related work study, where it was argued that 87 % of respondents would prefer receiving direct assessment feedback by prioritizing the medical benefit of an unbiased assessment [31]. However, both the interviews and the study results show that receiving feedback of any kind, even with positive remarks or a thank you for participation, can replace the interest in receiving test results in the app. The pattern solution tries to satisfy these forces.

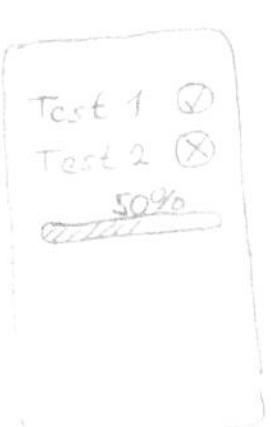

Fig. 5. Diagram of the Medical Tests on Demand Design Pattern.

3. Tracking of Personal Goals and Activities

Context: PwP have personal activities and goals, like regular exercises or a particular diet, which they set themselves or are recommended by their neurologist or psychotherapist.

Problem: Completing personal goals is sometimes forgotten because patients can lack motivation to complete tasks seen as tedious. This can lead to PwP not achieving individual therapy goals, worsening their health.

Solution: Therefore, PD-related health apps should provide a function that allows users to set their own goals, exercises, or tasks. It should be possible to track the completion of such goals, and the user should receive reminders to complete the tasks. Additionally, the possibility to review past activity and goal completion must allow users to keep track of their previous activity (Fig. 6).

Discussion: In addition to performing tests or documenting symptoms, the user study revealed the need for a reminder system and a companion for non-medical tasks. Since movement and a healthy lifestyle can benefit PwP, not everyone is motivated by the same things. For example, some said they have no problem doing daily yoga sessions but struggle to motivate themselves to go walking, while others thrive on a walk. If the app reminded them to, for example, go walking and showed them their past activity, it would motivate them more and give them another reason to use the app frequently. This customizability aspect also promotes the need for autonomy.

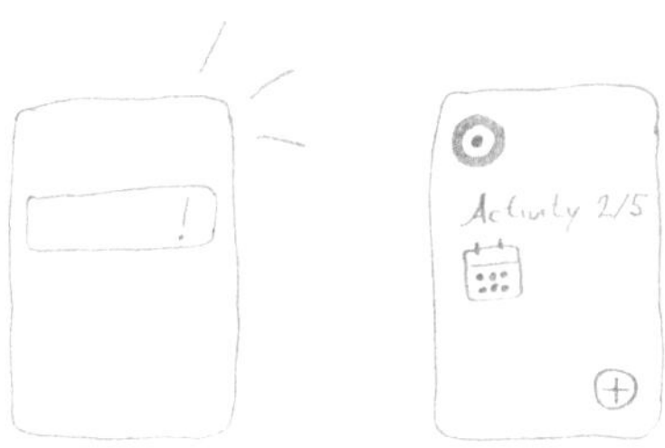

Fig. 6. Diagram of the Activity Design Pattern.

4. Medication Reminder and Tracker

Context: With early Parkinson's and a mild symptom picture, taking the medication at the right time might not be so important. There is often a certain flexibility regarding the time of intake or a prescription as needed. The patient usually pre-sorts the tablets into weekly or daily pillboxes to avoid the hassle of breaking open blisters and putting the tablets together several times a day. In the later stages of PD, medication intake is more extensive and has to be more precise. Adherence to the prescribed plan worsens over time, and only a subset of patients can follow it without mistakes in intake or dosage.

Problem: Taking a pill can be forgotten if an alarm or notification comes when the patient is nowhere near his pillbox, or the notification is closed before the pill is taken. Some PwP already use digital medication tracker apps, but since most are just a reminder, they cannot control whether a drug was taken.

Solution: Therefore, after reminding that it is time for a specific drug, the medication feature must ask again and try to verify that the patient has taken the medicine. This can be achieved by having each reminder be a multi-step dialog, guiding the user to get a glass of water, e.g., search for the right pill in the box, take the pill, and then follow related intake guidelines, such as a specific time interval before the next food intake. The app should also provide a function that allows PwP to save the exact time of medication intake to keep track of the relationship between intake time and symptoms (Fig. 7).

Discussion: The majority of interviewees in the user study reported that they were using pill boxes with compartments for each day of the week to organize their intake and to receive visual reminders to either take the medication if they see pills in the box or a confirmation that they already took it if the compartment is empty: "If the box is empty, its enough of a reminder for me.". However, knowing when they need to take medication differed between the interviews. While one group of PwP, especially with a previous professional medical background, e.g., working as a nurse, needs no reminder or alarm to take their medication since they have an internal feeling or clock, the other group of people was manually setting alarms on their phone to work as a medication reminder. Nevertheless, all interviewees confirmed that they would expect a medication plan in a PD-related app, regardless of their preference.

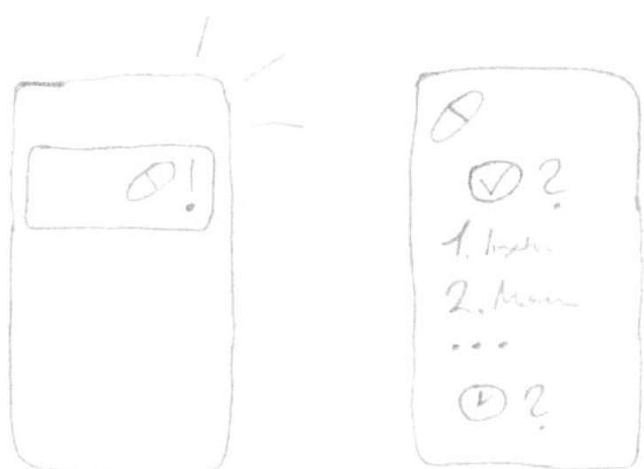

Fig. 7. Diagram of the Medication Design Pattern.

5. Parkinson's Disease Newsfeed and Notes

Context: For PwP, it is important to have access to up-to-date information and news about the disease. This includes news from support groups, new research findings, and contact options for other patient groups. Until now, PwP have often needed several apps to access this information.

Problem: The lack of a central platform that offers self-monitoring features and up-to-date information about Parkinson's means that PwP have to use multiple apps. This is cumbersome and impractical. In addition, there is a risk of missing relevant information if it cannot be loaded automatically.

Solution: Therefore, a Parkinson's app should offer up-to-date information and content about the disease. This app should automatically download news and information from support groups, new research findings, and contact opportunities with other patient groups. Alternatively, PwP should also have the option to enter this information manually to collect all relevant data in one place. PwP can find all the necessary information in one app by implementing such a solution. Entries similar to appointments and events should be treated like a calendar entry, for which the user is reminded when the date approaches (Fig. 8).

Discussion: Participants reported that information about Parkinson's disease is sometimes scattered across multiple apps or platforms, most of which are not designed to be accessible for PwP. Within a PD-related application, they desire a collection of contacts, news, and dates, such as information about their local support group. The interviews expressed the need to either enter the content manually or have it appear like a news feed. This connection aspect helps to achieve relatedness to others, one of the three basic needs.

Fig. 8. Diagram of the Newsfeed Design Pattern.

6 Conclusion and Future Work

This paper's outcome is a step toward a user-centered and comparable approach to designing eHealth applications for PwP, focusing on basic need fulfillment and increasing user engagement.

The proposed design patterns were used in the ParkProReakt project to develop a redesign of the application. They are still only a snapshot of how the requirements and demands of today's PwP can be implemented with an approach for more user engagement. As technology advances and the demographic of PwP alters to include more digital natives, the requirements and design patterns will have to change and adapt over time. Future users might want more gamification than proposed through these patterns, and thus, experts will need to revise and question their approaches regularly. More comprehensive user research with diverse caregivers and a quantitative study could further validate the results.

Concerning the need for relatedness to others, it still requires further research to investigate how eHealth applications can connect patients without negatively impacting their mental state by confronting them with extreme cases or revealing too much of their condition. A more extended observation is also necessary to rule out a potential novelty effect of such measures, as the design patterns can only be called truly successful if the user engagement remains sufficient over a more extended period.

Finally, it is also unclear how much motivation a user group such as patients requires through design, since they can be intrinsically motivated simply by their disease and the promise of an improved quality of life. As long as the app delivers on that promise, it might be enough to keep users engaged without requiring a more detailed focus on user engagement techniques.

Acknowledgments. This work was supported by the ParkProReakt consortium and Fraunhofer FIT. The ParkProReakt project was funded by the German Innovation Committee of the Joint Federal Committee (grant number 01NVF20019).

Disclosure of Interests. The authors have no competing interests to declare relevant to this article's content.

A Appendix

A.1 Personas

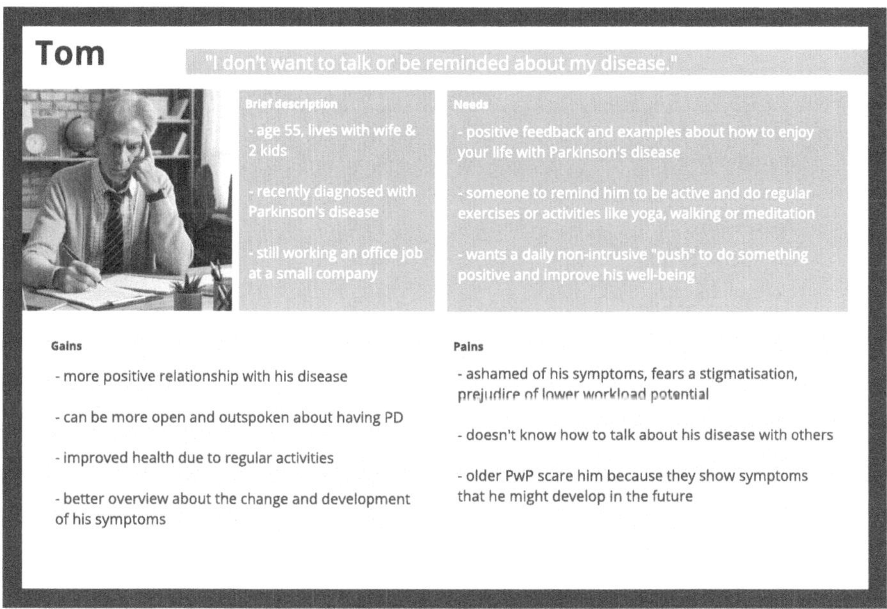

Fig. 9. Persona of a Suppressor.

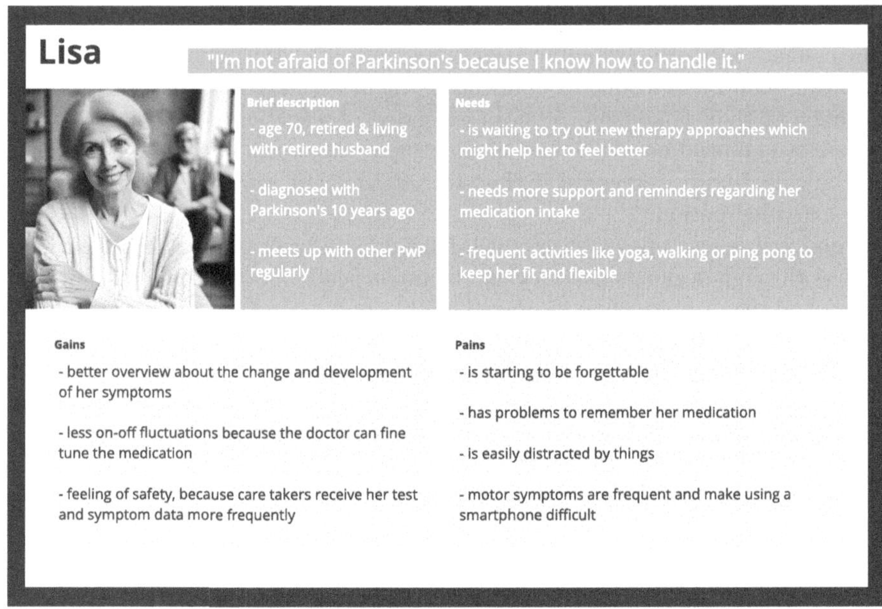

Fig. 10. Persona of a Recognizer.

A.2 BPN-TU Results

Table 2. Improvement in BPN-TU - Baseline Compared to PwP & Family

Question	Baseline	PwP & Family	Improvement
Autonomy 1	29	42	44 %
Autonomy 2	28	43	54 %
Autonomy 3	31	40	29 %
Autonomy	**88**	**125**	**42 %**
Competence 1	26	40	54 %
Competence 2	26	34	31 %
Competence 3	25	41	64 %
Competence	**77**	**115**	**49 %**
Relatedness to Others 1	22	33	50 %
Relatedness to Others 2	25	32	28 %
Relatedness to Others 3	20	35	75 %
Relatedness to Others	**67**	**100**	**49 %**
Relatedness to Technology 1	26	42	62 %
Relatedness to Technology 2	23	35	52 %
Relatedness to Technology 3	29	39	34 %
Relatedness to Technology	**78**	**116**	**49 %**
Total	**310**	**459**	**47 %**

A.3 Requirements

Requirement 1: Symptom Diary **As a** PwP, **I want** to be able to record both negative symptoms and positive aspects of my days, **so that** I can maintain a comprehensive diary that helps my doctor understand my condition in a holistic way and supports my health.

Acceptance Criteria:

1. The diary should allow entries for negative symptoms and positive aspects.
2. The diary should highlight its benefits to encourage daily use.
3. The application should display previous entries in an activity diagram.
4. There should be daily reminders to make a new entry.

Requirement 2: Feedback Mechanism for Test Participation **As a** PwP, **I want** the app to track and display my participation in health tests without showing scores, **so that** I can focus on consistent participation and monitoring health progression rather than competing for high scores.

Acceptance Criteria:

1. The app should track the frequency of test participation.
2. The app should display a feedback mechanism that emphasizes participation.
3. The test results should not display numerical scores or rankings.
4. The feedback on participation should be motivating and positively framed.

Requirement 3: Customizable Goals and Task Management **As a** PwP, **I want** to set my own health-related goals, exercises, or tasks in the app, **so that** I can track my progress and receive reminders to complete them, which helps me stay engaged and monitor my health activities over time.

Acceptance Criteria:

1. Users can set and customize their own goals, exercises, or tasks within the app.
2. The app allows to track the completion of these set goals.
3. Users receive reminders to complete their tasks or exercises.
4. The app provides a review feature for past activities and goal completions.

Requirement 4: Medication Reminder and Verification **As a** PwP, **I want** the medication reminder feature in the app to guide me through the process of taking my medication and verify its intake, **so that** I can ensure proper medication adherence and track the timing of my intake relative to my symptoms.

Acceptance Criteria:

1. The intake process should be a multi-step dialog.
2. The app should allow users to record the exact medication intake time.

Requirement 5: Information Hub **As a** PwP, **I want** the app to provide up-to-date information about Parkinson's disease, including news, research findings, and support group details, **so that** I can access all relevant and supportive content in one place, enhancing my knowledge and engagement with the community.

Acceptance Criteria:

1. The app should automatically download and update content related to Parkinson's disease.
2. Users should have the option to enter information manually.

References

1. Adlakha, S., Chhabra, D., Shukla, P.: Effectiveness of gamification for the rehabilitation of neurodegenerative disorders. Chaos, Solitons & Fractals **140**, 110192 (2020). https://doi.org/10.1016/j.chaos.2020.110192, https://www.sciencedirect.com/science/article/pii/S0960077920305889
2. Alexander, C., Ishikawa, S., Silverstein, M.: A Pattern Language: Towns, buildings, construction, Center for Environmental Structure series, vol. 2. Oxford Univ. Press, New York, NY, 41. print edn. (1978)
3. Andrade, F.R.H., Mizoguchi, R., Isotani, S.: The bright and dark sides of gamification. In: Micarelli, A., Stamper, J., Panourgia, K. (eds.) Intelligent Tutoring Systems, LNCS, vol. 9684, pp. 176–186. Springer International Publishing, Cham (2016). https://doi.org/10.1007/978-3-319-39583-8_17
4. Aparicio, A.F., Vela, F.L.G., Sánchez, J.L.G., Montes, J.L.I.: Analysis and application of gamification. In: Botella, F., Lozano, M., Gallud, J.A., Peñalver, A., Mashat, A. (eds.) Proceedings of the 13th International Conference on Interacción Persona-Ordenador - INTERACCION 2012, pp. 1–2. ACM Press, New York (2012). https://doi.org/10.1145/2379636.2379653
5. Armstrong, M.J., Okun, M.S.: Diagnosis and treatment of parkinson disease: a review. JAMA **323**(6), 548–560 (2020). https://doi.org/10.1001/jama.2019.22360
6. Balestrino, R., Schapira, A.H.V.: Parkinson disease. Euro. J. Neurol. **27**(1), 27–42 (2020). https://doi.org/10.1111/ene.14108, https://onlinelibrary.wiley.com/doi/10.1111/ene.14108
7. Blessing, L.T.M.: DRM, a Design Research Methodology. Springer, London Limited, London (2009). DOI: 10.1007/978-1-84882-587-1, https://www.researchgate.net/publication/235701003_DRM_a_Design_Research_Methodology
8. Congiu, L., Moscati, I.: A review of nudges: definitions, justifications, effectiveness. J. Eco. Surv. **36**(1), 188–213 (2022). https://doi.org/10.1111/joes.12453, https://onlinelibrary.wiley.com/doi/full/10.1111/joes.12453
9. Damaševičius, R., Maskeliūnas, R., Blažauskas, T.: Serious games and gamification in healthcare: a meta-review. Information **14**(2), 105 (2023). https://doi.org/10.3390/info14020105, https://www.mdpi.com/2078-2489/14/2/105
10. Davidson, E., Winter, J.S., Chiasson, M.: It-based regulation of personal health: nudging, mobile apps and data. J. Inform. Technol., 026839622211126 (2023). https://doi.org/10.1177/02683962221112678

11. Deterding, S., Sicart, M., Nacke, L., O'Hara, K., Dixon, D.: Gamification. using game-design elements in non-gaming contexts. In: Tan, D., Amershi, S., Begole, B., Kellogg, W.A., Tungare, M. (eds.) Proceedings of the 2011 annual conference extended abstracts on Human factors in computing systems - CHI EA 2011, p. 2425. ACM Press, New York (2011). https://doi.org/10.1145/1979742.1979575
12. Eggers, C., Wellach, I., Groppa, S., Strothjohann, M., Klucken, J.: Care of patients with parkinson's disease in germany: status quo and perspectives as reflected in the digital transition (Jun 2021)
13. Janssen Daalen, J.M., Schootemeijer, S., Richard, E., Darweesh, S.K.L., Bloem, B.R.: Lifestyle interventions for the prevention of parkinson disease: a recipe for action. Neurology **99**(7 Suppl 1), 42–51 (2022). https://doi.org/10.1212/WNL.0000000000200787
14. Kosters, M., van der Heijden, J.: From mechanism to virtue: evaluating nudge theory. Evaluation **21**(3), 276–291 (2015). https://doi.org/10.1177/1356389015590218
15. Kwan, Y.H., et al.: A systematic review of nudge theories and strategies used to influence adult health behaviour and outcome in diabetes management. Diabetes & Metabolism **46**(6), 450–460 (2020). https://doi.org/10.1016/j.diabet.2020.04.002, https://www.sciencedirect.com/science/article/pii/S1262363620300574
16. Landers, M., Ellis, T.: A mobile app specifically designed to facilitate exercise in parkinson disease: single-cohort pilot study on feasibility, safety, and signal of efficacy. JMIR mHealth and uHealth (2020). https://www.semanticscholar.org/paper/A-Mobile-App-Specifically-Designed-to-Facilitate-in-Landers-Ellis/2b1e1a77c3591e43b03b8186c9d891bcdda2e727
17. Marteau, T.M., Ogilvie, D., Roland, M., Suhrcke, M., Kelly, M.P.: Judging nudging: can nudging improve population health? BMJ (Clin. Res. ed.) **342**, d228 (2011). https://doi.org/10.1136/bmj.d228
18. Mathur, A., Kshirsagar, M., Mayer, J.: What makes a dark pattern... dark? In: Kitamura, Y. (ed.) Proceedings of the 2021 CHI Conference on Human Factors in Computing Systems. pp. 1–18. ACM Digital Library, Association for Computing Machinery, New York (2021). https://doi.org/10.1145/3411764.3445610
19. Mendiola, M.F., Kalnicki, M., Lindenauer, S.: Valuable features in mobile health apps for patients and consumers: content analysis of apps and user ratings. JMIR Mhealth Uhealth **3**(2), e40 (2015). https://doi.org/10.2196/mhealth.4283
20. Miller, A.S., Cafazzo, J.A., Seto, E.: A game plan: gamification design principles in mhealth applications for chronic disease management. Health Inform. J. **22**(2), 184–193 (2016). https://doi.org/10.1177/1460458214537511
21. Moradbakhti, L., Leichtmann, B., Mara, M.: Development and validation of a basic psychological needs scale for technology use. Psychol. Test Adapt. Developm. **5**(1), 26–45 (2024). https://doi.org/10.1027/2698-1866/a000062
22. Patton, J.: Finding the forest in the trees. In: Johnson, R. (ed.) Companion to the 20th annual ACM SIGPLAN Conference on Object-Oriented Programming, Systems, Languages, and Applications, pp. 266–274. ACM Conferences, ACM, New York (2005). https://doi.org/10.1145/1094855.1094961
23. Peters, D., Calvo, R.A., Ryan, R.M.: Designing for motivation, engagement and wellbeing in digital experience. Front. Psychol. **9**, 797 (2018). https://doi.org/10.3389/fpsyg.2018.00797
24. Poewe, W., et al.: Parkinson disease. Nat. Rev. Disease Primers **3**(1), 1–21 (2017). https://doi.org/10.1038/nrdp.2017.13, https://www.nature.com/articles/nrdp201713

25. Powers, R., et al.: Smartwatch inertial sensors continuously monitor real-world motor fluctuations in parkinson's disease. Sci. Trans. Med. **13**(579) (2021). https://doi.org/10.1126/scitranslmed.abd7865
26. Robson, K., Plangger, K., Kietzmann, J.H., McCarthy, I., Pitt, L.: Is it all a game? understanding the principles of gamification. Bus. Horizons **58**(4), 411–420 (2015). https://doi.org/10.1016/j.bushor.2015.03.006, https://www.sciencedirect.com/science/article/pii/S000768131500035X
27. Ryan, Deci: Intrinsic and extrinsic motivations: classic definitions and new directions. Contemporary Educ. Psycho. **25**(1), 54–67 (2000). https://doi.org/10.1006/ceps.1999.1020, https://www.sciencedirect.com/science/article/pii/S0361476X99910202
28. Ryan, R.M., Deci, E.L.: Self-determination theory and the facilitation of intrinsic motivation, social development, and well-being. Am. Psychol. **55**(1), 68–78 (2000). https://doi.org/10.1037//0003-066x.55.1.68
29. Schmeier, B., Hoffmann, A.K., Wollgast, J., Deck, R., Hauptmann, B., Schrader, A., Jochems, N.: Parkprotrain: design und entwicklung einer therapie-app zum training von parkinson-patienten. In: Alt, F. (ed.) Proceedings of Mensch und Computer 2019, pp. 789–793. ACM Digital Library. Association for Computing Machinery, New York (2019). https://doi.org/10.1145/3340764.3344909
30. Schmidt, A.T., Engelen, B.: The ethics of nudging: an overview. Philosophy Compass **15**(4), e12658 (2020). https://doi.org/10.1111/phc3.12658, https://compass.onlinelibrary.wiley.com/doi/full/10.1111/phc3.12658
31. Stamate, C., et al.: The cloudupdrs app: a medical device for the clinical assessment of parkinson's disease. Pervasive Mobile Comput. **43**, 146–166 (2018). https://doi.org/10.1016/j.pmcj.2017.12.005, https://www.sciencedirect.com/science/article/pii/S1574119217303607
32. Tenison, E., Henderson, E.J.: Multimorbidity and frailty: tackling complexity in parkinson's disease. J. Parkinsons Dis. **10**(s1), S85–S91 (2020). https://doi.org/10.3233/JPD-202105
33. Thaler, R.H., Sunstein, C.R.: Nudge: Improving decisions about health, wealth, and happiness. Penguin, New York, NY, rev. and expanded ed., with a new afterword and a new chapter edn. (2009)
34. Van Munster, M., et al.: ParkProReakt–evaluation of a proactive approach to healthcare in Parkinson's disease: a study protocol for a randomised controlled trial. BMJ Public Health **3**(2), e002265 (2025)

Pattern Creation for Hybrid Creative Spaces: A Conceptual Blending Approach

Dan Zhu(✉) and Christian Kohls

Cologne University of Applied Sciences, 50678 Cologne, Germany
{dan.zhu,christian.kohls}@th-koeln.de

Abstract. This paper introduces a conceptual blending method for creating patterns in hybrid creative spaces, offering a deductive, generative complement to traditional (inductive) pattern mining. Starting from validated physical and digital pattern languages—PL-CS and PL-CMI—the workflow (i) stages input patterns, (ii) aligns them via a generic schema (timespaceagentaction) to map correspondences, (iii) performs selective projection to compose a blended pattern, and (iv) completes and elaborates it through pattern-writing workshop. In a EuroPLoP workshop with seven experts, 13 blended patterns were produced, demonstrating novel yet legible solutions when designs demand cross-domain or re-contextualized use. Blended patterns remain traceable to their sources and evaluable in practice, yielding a shareable protocol for education and deployment. We outline implications for design education, tools and a blended pattern repository that links retrospective mining with prospective invention.

Keywords: Hybrid spaces · Creativity · Conceptual blending · Pattern language · Design method

1 Introduction

Design disciplines often confront the dual imperative of novelty and legibility: solutions must be sufficiently original to address emergent needs, yet grounded in shared practice to be understood and realized. In this process, structured creativity methods already play a central role. Design thinking foregrounds problem reframing, empathic research, and iterative prototyping [4,6]; TRIZ systematizes invention through patterns of contradiction and resolution [14]; and pattern languages codify reusable solutions to recurrent problems in many fields (e.g., software engineering, human-computer interaction) as well as the built environment [15]. Each of these contributes valuable lenses.

As one of the distinct approaches to guide the design process in architecture and spatial design, pattern language contains rules for how humans interact with built forms—it codifies practical solutions developed over millennia, which are appropriate for local customs, society and climate [18]. A canonical process

T. Plummer et al. (Eds.): EuroPLoP 2025, LNCS 16494, pp. 405–417, 2026.
https://doi.org/10.1007/978-3-032-19157-1_19

for creating pattern language comprises three sequential phases: pattern mining, pattern writing, and pattern symbolizing [13]. Among these, pattern mining from precedents, typological analysis, or casebased reasoning is the most research intensive because it seeks to surface meaningful structures, recurring relationships, and tacit expertise from a domain. However, pattern approach is often criticized more as a retrospective analysis tool than as a practical design method [7]. In architecture and spatial design, relying on patterns alone can make it difficult to generate genuinely new spatial logics when faced with unfamiliar norms, hybrid programs, or rapidly changing cultural and technological contexts. This paper argues that conceptual blending offers a principled, repeatable method for creating new design patterns rather than only discovering existing ones, thereby complementing and extending conventional patternbased methods.

Conceptual blending theory, originally from the field of cognitive linguistics, provides a useful model to describe how the human mind can integrate heterogeneous information in representations [10]. Conceptual blending connects input spaces, projects selectively to a blended space, and develops the emergent structure through *composition*, *completion*, and *elaboration* [8], a process that can then be evaluated against domain constraints in design practice. In contrast to unguided brainstorming, blending is structured by explicit mappings and by governing principles, which together support disciplined exploration. By combining design patterns with conceptual blending, we can "supercharge" the early generative phase: patterns provide pre-structured culturally tested knowledge as input spaces; blend is an "emergent structure", yielding meaning that did not exist as such in either of the input spaces independently [10]. The result is creativity grounded in rigor: designers innovate from structured inputs rather than from scratch.

The remainder of the paper situates the approach within related work, especially pattern language for creative spaces and computer mediated interactions, then details the blend-for-pattern workflow and its validity, and presents design cases that illustrate the creation of new patterns from known constituents. We conclude with a discussion of contributions, implications for design education, and directions for future research.

2 Pattern Language as a Lens on Human–Environment Interaction

Alexander's pattern language [1] positions the built environment as a structured conversation between recurring human activities and spatial configurations. Each pattern articulates a problemsolution pair linking situations, forces, and spatial roles (e.g., "Degrees of publicness", "Small public squares", or "Hierarchy of open space"). Overall, patterns describe how human purposes (dwelling, meeting, moving, learning) are mediated by built forms through recurring relations–thresholds, edges, centers, paths, transitions, and degrees of enclosure. This framing treats design not as the invention of isolated entities, but as the composition of interlocking patterns that stabilize desirable behaviors and experiences across scales—from the city and neighborhood to building, room, and furniture. Patterns are written around human actions and social situations ("where people stop and talk", "where play naturally occurs", "how entrances invite or repel"), emphasizing behavioral consequences of spatial structure [1,22].

While pattern languages supply a normative and compositional vocabulary, other research programs provide explanatory mechanisms for why patterns work. Roger Barker's *behavior settings* operate at a human scale, defining recurrent placetimeactivity units (e.g., a classroom lesson, a Saturday market) in which a stable fit between the physical milieu and a behavioral program organizes roles, sequences, and norms such that people entering the setting tend to enact its script [2]. James. J. Gibson introduces *affordances* to describe the action possibilities an environment offers to an organism in relation to its bodily capacities and skills [11]. Affordances are not conceived as subjective interpretations or intrinsic object properties but as *relational* features of the organismenvironment system that are directly perceivable and guide behavior. Drawing on Barker's behavior settings and Gibsonian affordances, spatial features are read as action possibilities that couple users to environments: surfaces afford sitting, a lounge affords relaxing and gathering, a playground affords playing and physical interactions. Taken together for design, behavior settings articulate the *patterned* social ecology to which those affordances are bound; patterns can thus be seen as curated collections of affordances arranged to sustain a desired behavior setting. This supports the pattern language emphasis on linking spatial features to typical acts, and this stance is subsequently adapted by works in the area of creative space.

"Creative space" refers to environments, such as workplaces and learning environments, intentionally shaped to foster ideation, experimentation, knowledge exchange, and learning [23]. Building on the pattern language approach, researchers have compiled inventories of spatial, social, and organizational features correlated with creative performance. These studies provide core claims on built form shapes interaction leading to creativity, through repeatable spatial relations. Among these, Thoring's work [21] has been known for its comprehensive inventory of creativity-supporting elements that can be read as a pattern language for creative spaces (PL-CS). The PL-CS includes 49 design patterns, which are expressed not only as forms but as spatial affordances for creative behavior [5] (e.g., "Invitation chair" for initiating conversations with encounters; "Semi-privacy" for oscillation between focus and serendipity).

Pattern thinking extends naturally from the built environment to computer-mediated interaction, where recurring problems and solution structures can likewise be articulated, composed, and reused. Schümmer and Lukosch propose A Pattern Language of Computer-Mediated Interaction (PL-CMI) that systematizes best practices for collaborative work and learning in digitally mediated contexts (e.g., base technologies, virtual objects, and interaction conventions) [20]. The language comprises 71 patterns that address how groups convene, coordinate, create, and reflect through software systems. Like architectural pattern languages, PL-CMI is action-centric: it links software structures to typical human activities. This can be seen as an extension of human-environment interaction from the physical to the digital world.

Both PL-CS and PL-CMI were built using an inductive approach to pattern mining, which generalizes patterns from systematic analysis of many concrete cases and authors' own expertise, thus providing a testable library of patterns [12,19]. Despite being rigorous and well suited to precedent-rich domains, this inductive approach is largely retrospective. It excels at articulating what already works and at systematizing best practices, but it is often inadequate when designs demand hybrid programs, cross-domain analogies, or radically recontextualized uses for which no solutions immediately exist. Design research shows that for "wicked" or unprecedented problems, *reframing* (creating new frames) is required beyond applying established solutions [6,17]. To address this gap, we propose *conceptual blending* as a complementary, creativity-forward pattern-mining method that creates new design patterns rather than only discovering existing ones.

3 Conceptual Blending as a Generative Method for Cross-Domain Pattern Creation

Conceptual Blending Theory (CBT), introduced by Gilles Fauconnier, is a cognitive framework that explains how the human mind combines different mental spaces to construct new meanings [8]. CBT describes how we cognitively structure and manipulate information dynamically during thought and communication and explicitly explains how individuals integrate elements from separate conceptual domains to generate novel ideas, insights, and patterns. This process underlies metaphors, creativity, problem-solving, and linguistic meaning construction. The CBT helps explain how new patterns can be formed unconsciously from existing knowledge structures.

Conceptual blending models the emergence of new meaning by mapping counterparts across input schematic "mental spaces", projecting selected elements into a novel blended space, and developing emergent structure through three operations: *composition*, *completion*, and *elaboration* [9]. Composition selects and combines elements projected from the inputs so that new relations become available in the blended space; completion fills the resulting scene with background frames, scripts, and world knowledge that the blend implicitly invites; and elaboration then "runs" this completed scene as a mental simulation to explore consequences over time and context, yielding further inferences. Together, these operations turn partial structures into a coherent, testable configuration that can be inspected, reasoned with, and refined. The conceptual blending model consists of four connected spaces: two *input spaces*, a *generic space* capturing the shared schematic structure, and the *blend space*, which can be "run" as a simulation while retaining links to its sources [9].

To demonstrate the process, we select one pattern from PL-CS and one from PL-CMI and apply them within the conceptual blending model (see Fig. 1). The rationale for this pairing is a similarity of *topology* (e.g., relational structure).

For example, "The bulletin board" from PL-CS facilitates the display of people's expertise and informal exchange of supplies [21]; as a physical-domain pattern, it presupposes a concrete artifact (e.g., a rectangular board) typically placed on public walls. By contrast, the "Feedback loop" from PL-CMI explains bidirectional communication—returning information about the result of a process or creative act [20]; as a digital-domain pattern, it emphasizes interactive function rather than fixed form (e.g., e-mail reply, comment threads, or contact buttons on web pages). Prior to cross-space mapping, we specify in the generic space their common relational structure: both are intended to make ongoing informal exchanges of expertise and resources visible and actionable. We interpret this as the affordance of *knowledge-share-ability*–artifacts that enable users to share knowledge.

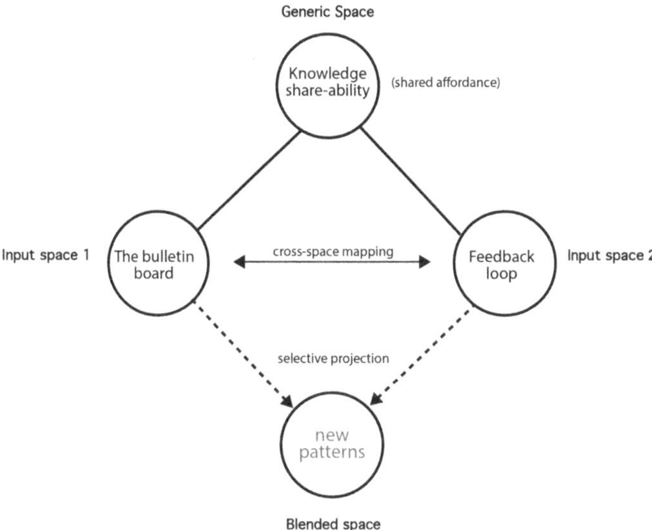

Fig. 1. Four mental spaces in conceptual blending model

In CBT terms, each input space typically is composed of a frame or specific elements, or both [9], providing the material for selective projection into the blended space. Figure 2 further explains the operations of composition, completion, and elaboration. The input space of "The bulletin board" includes the board and its context—the wall to which it is attached, the board's content (pinned pictures, ads, posters), and the users who read and post. Elements in one input space are then mapped to counterparts in the other using rules such as identity and analogy [8,16]: the physical wall maps to a window on a computer screen; physical content maps to digital content; static postings map to a continuous flow of information, and so on. From there, elements are selectively projected into a blended space, yielding a new combination: screen-on-wall, digital content, continuous flow of information, colleagues as audience/contributors.

Importantly, mapping is partial, selective, and purpose-driven–not all elements must align; only those relevant to the design purpose are blended, while inconsistencies are discarded. The blended space remains *webbed* to its inputs through these mappings, so that "real inferences can be computed in the inputs from the imaginary situation in the blended space" [9]. Within the blend, new logic and structure can emerge and be further completed and elaborated, for example, in a pattern-writing workshop that specifies context, problems, forces, solutions, etc.

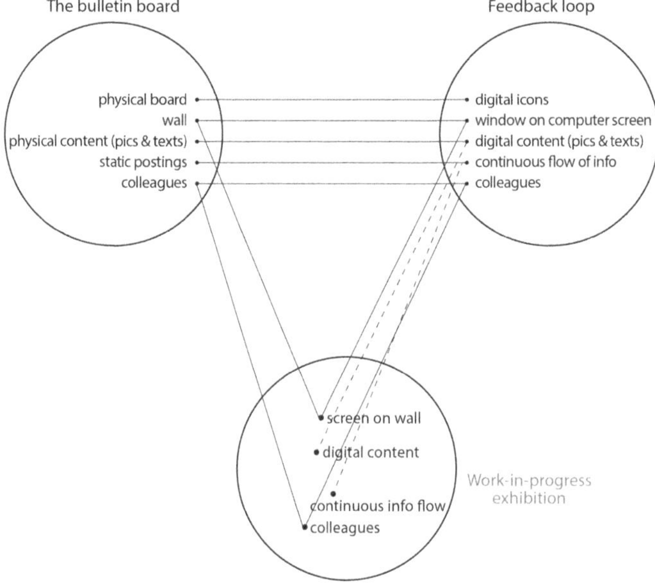

Fig. 2. Blended pattern "Work-in-progress exhibition"

The pattern-writing workshop took place at the 28th European Conference on Pattern Languages of Programs, People, and Practices (EuroPLoP). Participants included seven pattern experts from computer science, HCI, and e-learning. The workshop used conceptual blending as a structured process to guide participants in creating cross-domain patterns from selected, well-known patterns. It resulted in 13 new patterns [24], each documented in a modified Alexandrain pattern format: (1) a distinguishable name; (2) an intent; (3) affordances addressed; (4) a context statement; (5) a problem statement; (6) a force/scenario description; (7) a solution description; and (8) cross-links to the originating source-patterns.

4 Blended Patterns

Feedback from the workshop's pattern experts affirmed that the proposed method enables systematic, structured creation of blended patterns. Using the blend-for-pattern workflow, the team produced 13 blended patterns: "Market Display", "Speaker's Corner", "Indicate Buddies to Join and Watch", "Who's Here", "The Remote Four Eyes Principle", "Gift from a Stranger", "Work in Progress Exhibition", "Digital Info Board", "Changing Labels", "Table Related Sessions", "Open Inspection", "Workspace Window", and "Popup Collaboration". In what follows, we present six exemplary blended patterns.

4.1 Work-in-Progress Exhibition

This pattern facilitates the display of ongoing work to gather feedback and promote informal exchanges. It integrates the characteristics of two existing patterns to effectively increase the visibility of an individual's work progress and to receive feedback in time.

Intent. Facilitate the display of ongoing work to gather feedback and promote informal exchanges of expertise and supplies.

Affordance. Knowledge Share-ability

Context. Users are working on projects and need a way to showcase their progress, gather feedback, and exchange expertise and supplies with peers. A platform that combines visual display and interactive feedback mechanisms can enhance collaboration and improvement.

Problem. Work-in-progress often remains isolated until completion, missing opportunities for early feedback and informal exchanges that could enhance the outcome. There is a need for a platform that allows ongoing work to be visible and open to interaction.

Forces/Scenario. In a collaborative workspace, team members often work on individual parts of a larger project. However, without visibility into each other's progress, team members or collaborators feel isolated in their work processes, and opportunities for feedback and resource sharing are missed.

Solution. Set up a visual display area, such as bulletin boards, where ongoing projects can be showcased. Integrate interactive elements that allow peers to provide feedback and offer resources or expertise. This setup promotes visibility, feedback, and informal exchanges among team members.

Related Patterns. The Bulletin Board (PL-CS), Feedback Loop (PL-CMI)

4.2 Open Inspection

In this pattern, the open floor plan configuration offers an overall view of the space, and the visual information of any changes is largely available to space users. The users perceive and actively filter the spatial information, and only select certain forms of visual contact and social interaction to participate. This pattern offers users the possibility to observe and control which social interaction they might or might not participate in.

Intent. Enhance the quality of interactions and contributions in a communal space by combining the benefits of visual contact and social interaction with mechanisms to remove low-quality content and manage disruptive members.

Affordance. Ownership-ability

Context. You have established a communication space or community platform aimed at fostering collaboration and interaction. Now you aim to maintain high-quality contributions while promoting a collaborative atmosphere.

Problem. Members of the community engage to benefit from high-quality interactions and contributions. However, unfiltered open spaces can lead to a factory-like atmosphere and distractions, due to low-quality or disruptive content. There is a need for a balance between open interaction and quality control.

Forces/Scenario. In an open office setting, interactions among employees foster collaboration and creativity. However, some employees dominate conversations with irrelevant topics, reducing productivity or overall interaction quality. The flow of discussion and contributions of the employees is not properly managed or reviewed, therefore, the relevance and quality cannot be ensured.

Solution. Combine open-plan spaces with designated areas for focused work, and implement a moderation system. Simultaneously, establish a team of moderators who review and approve contributions to ensure that they meet quality standards before being shared with the broader team.

Related Patterns. Nested Open Plan (PL-CS), Quality Inspection (PL-CMI)

4.3 Popup Collaboration

In this pattern, the popup concept offers flexible setting of the space and tools, which are perceived by the users as opportunities to have encounters, and to initiate informal collaboration spontaneously.

Intent. Support users in establishing spontaneous collaboration through flexible temporary workspaces, and awareness of other users' activities.

Affordance. Flexibility

Context. Users are working in an environment where collaboration opportunities can arise unexpectedly. They need flexible spaces that can be quickly set up, and an awareness system to identify potential collaborators.

Problem. Although users may be working in proximity or on related tasks, they often miss opportunities to collaborate because they are unaware of each other's activities. Additionally, static workspaces do not support the dynamic nature of spontaneous collaboration, leading to inefficiencies and missed synergies.

Forces/Scenario. In a creative agency, designers and developers often need to collaborate on projects at short notice. Traditional meeting rooms are often booked, and open-plan areas can be noisy and distracting. Additionally, often people are not aware that they are available and working on related tasks, hindering spontaneous and effective collaborations.

Solution. Provide the furniture and tools to quickly transform every space into a collaborative space. This includes things such as foldable portable workstations that can be set up on demand to create temporary collaborative spaces. Pair this with a user awareness system that tracks and displays users' activities, making it easier to identify potential collaboration opportunities.

Related Patterns. The Popup (PL-CS), Spontaneous Collaboration (PL-CMI)

4.4 Digital Information Board

This pattern integrates the human-centric quality of a physical lounge and an online welcome page. It is useful in the environment where old and new members gather by providing shared and updated information, and fostering informal communication.

Intent. Create a casual and inviting space where new members of a group or community can be introduced and important information can be shared, facilitating informal interactions and community building.

Affordance. Human-centric-ability

Context. You have a community space where members gather, and you want to enhance the sense of community by making it easier for new members to be recognized and for important information to be disseminated. Traditional meeting spaces do not fully support these goals.

Problem. New members often struggle to integrate into established communities because they are not recognized or acknowledged. Important information may also be missed if not shared in an engaging and accessible way.

Forces/Scenario. In a co-working space, new members often feel lost and disconnected from the existing community. Important announcements and information are often overlooked. There is a lack of informal interaction spaces that promote casual meetings.

Solution. Install a Digital Information Board in a central lounge area furnished with sofas and lounge chairs. This board should display profiles of new members, community news, upcoming events, and other relevant information. The relaxed setting encourages members to gather, fosters informal interactions, and makes it easier for new members to be recognized.

Related Patterns. The Lounge (PL-CS), Welcome Area (PL-CMI)

4.5 Speaker's Corner

This pattern provides a visible and engaging place or platform for users to present their ideas and interests, which can be seen as opportunities for social interaction and matchmaking. This pattern helps users actively connect with like-minded peers and foster collaboration.

Intent. Facilitate finding and engaging with peers who have the most in common with the user through an elevated, visible platform that encourages active participation and interaction.

Affordance. Social-ability

Context. In large communities or teams, it is often challenging for individuals to find others with similar interests or expertise. Creating a visible and engaging space can help users connect with like-minded peers and foster active participation.

Problem. In large user communities, it is difficult for individuals to identify and engage with others who share their interests or expertise. This can lead to missed opportunities for collaboration and a lack of community cohesion.

Forces/Scenario. In a bustling co-working space, users find it difficult to locate and connect with others who share their interests. Or there is a lack of spontaneous collaboration and interaction among community members. The community feels fragmented and lacks cohesion.

Solution. Create an elevated platform (physically or virtually) where users can present their ideas, projects, and interests. Integrate a matchmaking system that identifies and highlights users with similar interests, encouraging active participation and engagement.

Related Patterns. High Seat (PL-CS), Birds of a Feather (PL-CMI)

4.6 Workspace Window

This pattern indicates a new function of sharing the creative environment with other users, enhancing inspiration and collaboration. It integrates emerging technologies to effectively share creative workspaces and to connect users remotely.

Intent. Provide a view into the creative environment of other users in a shared space, enhancing inspiration and collaboration by sharing both the area of focus and the historical or cultural context.

Affordance. Creative Label-ability

Context. Users work in a shared digital or physical space and benefit from seeing what parts of the environment other users are focusing on. Additionally, the historical or cultural context of the space can spark creativity and enhance collaborative efforts.

Problem. While users need to see what others are focusing on in a shared space, understanding the broader cultural or historical context can further inspire and guide their work. However, providing too much information can overwhelm users and inhabit independent creativity.

Forces/Scenario. Users miss opportunities to take inspiration from the historical or cultural context of their work environment. There is a need to balance awareness and independent creativity in a shared space. Users express a desire for more engagement and interaction with the context and focus areas of others, such as in a collaborative virtual workspace for urban planners, where team members often focus on different parts of a city model. By implementing the "Workspace Window" pattern, the application allows users to see which parts of the city model others are viewing, and provides historical and cultural context about those areas.

Solution. Provide a shared view into the workspace that includes indicators of where other users are focusing. Integrate historical or cultural context relevant to those areas, enhancing inspiration and collaboration. This approach encourages users to explore and interact with both the content and the context of the shared space.

Related Patterns. Genius Loci (PL-CS), Remote Field of Vision (PL-CMI).

5 Discussion and Conclusion

This paper makes two primary contributions. First, it formulates a blend-for-patterns workflow that treats patterns as *blendable* inputs aligned through a common schema (e.g., time, space, agency, and action), thereby enabling them to join forces in a blended space. The approach provides a deductive, generative complement to established pattern-mining practices. Second, it demonstrates the method through design cases showing how blended patterns bridge physical and digital pattern languages and provide insights for emergent hybrid creative spaces. Starting from validated inputs (PL-CS, PL-CMI), the method formalizes cross-domain mapping and selective projection to produce novel yet legible blended patterns, demonstrated through a structured workshop generated 13 new patterns.

Deductive creation must be paired with empirical refinement. Next steps include: (1) extending the method to additional design patterns and pattern languages (e.g., game design, e-learning); (2) developing tools for mapping and blending evaluation; and (3) building a repository where blended patterns, evidence, and refinements accumulate over time.

The broader significance of integrating the CBT with patterns is twofold. Epistemically, it ties creativity to explicit structured moves (mapping, composition, completion, elaboration) that can be taught, replicated, and critiqued. Practically, it equips practitioners and students with a shareable protocol to invent patterns that remain traceable to their sources. In doing so, it addresses longstanding questions in the creativity literature—whether and how computational or systematic frameworks can model and augment creative practice [3]—by offering a cognitively informed, productive, and traceable design procedure.

Acknowledgments. This contribution has been developed in the project PLan_CV. Within the funding programme FH-Personal, the project PLan_CV (reference number

03FHP109) is funded by the German Federal Ministry of Education and Research (BMBF) and Joint Science Conference (GWK).

Disclosure of Interests. The authors have no competing interests to declare that are relevant to the content of this article.

References

1. Alexander, C.: A Pattern Language: Towns, Buildings, Construction. Oxford uni-Versity Press (1977)
2. Barker, R.G.: Ecological Psychology. Stanford University Press, Stanford (1968)
3. Boden, M.A.: Computer models of creativity. AI Mag. **30**(3), 23 (2009)
4. Brown, T., et al.: Design thinking. Harv. Bus. Rev. **86**(6), 84 (2008)
5. Dan, Z., Christian, K.: Towards a pattern language for creative affordances. In: Proceedings of the 29th European Conference on Pattern Languages of Programs, People, and Practices, pp. 1–10 (2024)
6. Dorst, K., Cross, N.: Creativity in the design process: co-evolution of problem-solution. Des. Stud. **22**(5), 425–437 (2001)
7. Dovey, K.: The pattern language and its enemies. Des. Stud. **11**(1), 3–9 (1990)
8. Fauconnier, G., Turner, M.: Conceptual integration networks. Cogn. Sci. **22**(2), 133–187 (1998)
9. Fauconnier, G., Turner, M.: Conceptual blending, form and meaning. Recherches Commun. **19**, 57–86 (2003)
10. Forceville, C., et al.: Non-verbal and multimodal metaphor in a cognitivist framework: agendas for research. Multimodal Metaphor **2**, 19–35 (2009)
11. Gibson, J.J.: The theory of affordances:(1979). In: The People, Place, and Space Reader, pp. 56–60. Routledge (2014)
12. Hanmer, R.: Pattern mining patterns. In: Proceedings of the 19th Conference on Pattern Languages of Programs, p. 23. Citeseer (2012)
13. Iba, T., Isaku, T.: A pattern language for creating pattern languages: 364 patterns for pattern mining, writing, and symbolizing. In: Proceedings of the 23rd Conference on Pattern Languages of Programs, pp. 1–63 (2016)
14. Ilevbare, I.M., Probert, D., Phaal, R.: A review of triz, and its benefits and challenges in practice. Technovation **33**(2–3), 30–37 (2013)
15. Leitner, H.: Working with patterns: an introduction. Patterns Commoning 15–25 (2015)
16. Li, B., Zook, A., Davis, N., Riedl, M.O.: Goal-driven conceptual blending: a computational approach for creativity. In: Proceedings of the 2012 International Conference on Computational Creativity, Dublin, Ireland, pp. 3–16 (2012)
17. Rittel, H.W., Webber, M.M.: Dilemmas in a general theory of planning. Policy Sci. **4**(2), 155–169 (1973)
18. Salingaros, N.A.: The structure of pattern languages. ARQ: Archit. Res. Q. **4**(2), 149–162 (2000)
19. Sasabe, A., Kaneko, T., Takahashi, K., Iba, T.: Pattern mining patterns: a search for the seeds of patterns. In: Proceedings of the 23rd Conference on Pattern Languages of Programs, pp. 1–16 (2016)
20. Schummer, T., Lukosch, S.: Patterns for Computer-Mediated Interaction. Wiley (2013)

21. Thoring, K.: Designing creative space: a systemic view on workspace design and its impact on the creative process. Ph.D. thesis, Delft University of Technology (2019)
22. Whyte, W.H., et al.: The social life of small urban spaces, vol. 116. Conservation Foundation Washington, DC (1980)
23. Wierzbicki, A.P., Nakamori, Y.: Creative Space: Models of Creative Processes for the Knowledge Civilization Age, vol. 10. Springer (2005)
24. Zhu, D.: Hybrid creative spaces pattern workshop: a report on investigation of tacit themes and design requirements. In: Proceedings of the 28th European Conference on Pattern Languages of Programs, pp. 1–7 (2023)

Focus Group Reports

Towards a Pattern Language for Academic Conferences. Report of the EuroPLoP 2025 Focus Group

Aliaksandr Birukou[1](✉), Cesare Pautasso[2], and Michael Weiss[3]

[1] Springer Nature, Europaplatz 3, 69115 Heidelberg, Germany
birukou@gmail.com
[2] Software Institute (USI), Lugano, Switzerland
[3] Carleton University, Ottawa, ON, Canada

Abstract. This short paper reports on the focus group about academic conferences, organized at EuroPLoP 2025. It lists the methodology for running the focus group, discusses the results and suggests next steps towards the pattern language for academic conferences. The main findings suggest that the community and financial aspects are the most important for conference organizers, followed by the program.

Keywords: Conferences · Workshops · Conference Organizers · Academic Conferences · Patterns · Best Practices

1 Introduction

Scientific conferences play a major role in the discussion and dissemination of scientific results. They also provide researchers with great networking opportunities. In areas like computer science, engineering they also produce formal and peer-reviewed publication of research results known as conference proceedings [1].

However, best practices for organizing conferences are rarely formalized and often not always properly transmitted to the organizers of the new edition. Such transmission is ad-hoc, often only via word-of-mouth communication from the previous chair to the new chair. Sometimes such practices are at best summarized as instructions for the steering committee/organizers of the next edition. While there are similarities in organizing conferences, the best practices are usually not discussed/compared across the conferences, staying only in the community which created them.

Previous work on this topic includes several papers on patterns for organizing *PLoPs [2–4], and the literature on organizing conferences [5–7], but there are no comprehensive guidelines/best practices which explore diverse perspectives from different domains.

The goal of the focus group "Towards a Pattern Language for Academic Conferences" organized at the 30th European Conference on Pattern Languages of Programs, People, and Practices (EuroPLoP 2025) was to explore how best practices in organizing academic conferences can be captured and structured into a pattern language.

T. Plummer et al. (Eds.): EuroPLoP 2025, LNCS 16494, pp. 421–433, 2026.
https://doi.org/10.1007/978-3-032-19157-1_20

We aimed primarily at drawing from diverse participant experiences to identify recurring challenges and common solutions applied previously. While some new ideas about organizing conferences were also generated, this was not our main goal.

EuroPLoP is a European conference in "*PLoP" conference series which is held annually at Kloster Irsee, Germany and focuses on software patterns, pattern languages, and other applications of patterns (e.g., teaching, organizational processes). It adopts a writer's workshop format, where authors receive constructive feedback on pattern papers. The community has strong European presence, but international participation (USA, Japan, Latin America) is common. The retreat-like atmosphere fostering deep discussion and collaboration was ideal to get a diverse set of participants for the focus group. We hoped to get a "good enough" number of participants,[1] not too many, and not too few and enable them to share the stories and experiences, while the organizers could capture them on whiteboards and summarize for future pattern mining.

2 Session Structure

This section presents the methodology for running the focus group. The methodology was brainstormed by the organizers (Aliaksandr, Cesare, Michael) and was based on our experience of running focus groups and the goals we tried to achieve. It might incorporate elements of specific methodologies, but this was unconscious.

In particular, before the focus group we decided not to use any complicated conference lifecycle (such as the one introduced in [8], Sect. 3.1) which might prove difficult to introduce to diverse participants. Instead, we suggested to consider "basic" stages: before the conference, e.g., planning the location, defining the conference team; during the conference, e.g., registration of participants, conference schedule, coffee breaks; and after the conference, e.g., sharing the photos of the event, organizing proceedings.

We also considered several "viewpoints" on the conferences: those of organizers, participants and other.

The designed methodology seemed particular suitable for 1.5 hour format of the focus group, since it allowed us to spent minimum time on setting up the context and maximize the time for capturing experience of the participants.

2.1 Methodology

The focus group was structured as follows:

- Each participant introduced themselves and explained their interest in the conference topic.
- We introduced the basic conference lifecycle grouping actions before, during, and after the conference [7] and conference roles: organizers, participants, other.
- We suggested that the participants focus on the organizers' perspective and list problems and solutions. It was not necessary to have a pair, so people could list only problem or solution or both.

[1] We got 12 people with mixed background, see Sect. 2.1, which met our expectations.

- We grouped problems (blue color) and solutions (yellow color) while participants were adding them to several flip charts, and towards the end of the session several clusters emerged.
- The participant voted on the most important clusters of "problems & solutions". Each of them got 3 "votes" which they could apply to one or several clusters.
- We took photos of the flip charts and promised to include them in the report of the focus group.

2.2 Participants

We got roughly 12 (several people came later and attended partially) participants with diverse background ranging from junior researchers attending their first conferences to experienced academics, who attended many conferences. Roughly half of participants had experience in organizing academic or practitioners' conferences as well as conferences with participation from both industry and academia. Several participants served as chairs or co-chairs. The mix of participants' background suggested us the expansion of the initial "academic conferences" scope to include also industry/practitioner conferences' patterns and see if those solutions can apply in academic context.

3 Results of the Focus Group

This section introduces the results of the focus group captured at the event and summarized after the conference.

3.1 Problems and Solutions

As described above, we took photos of the flip charts, see Fig. 1. Blue notes listed problems, while the yellow ones represented solutions. Orange circles were the names of the clusters agreed by the participants.

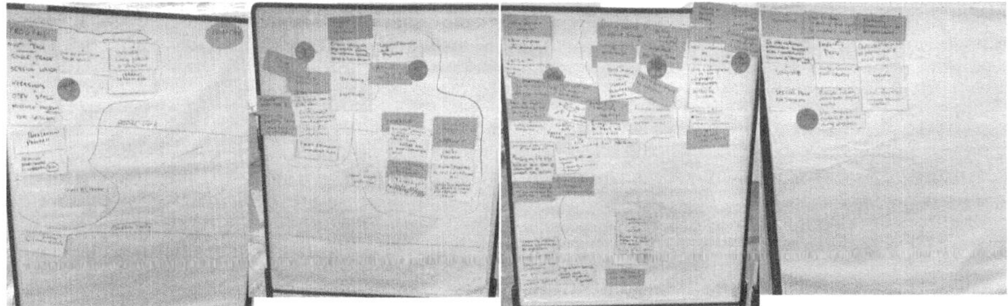

Fig. 1. Four flipcharts on which participants collected problems and solutions for conference organizers clustered into 7 clusters. See Appendix for bigger photos.

The subsections below list the clusters emerged during the focus group.

3.2 Program

This cluster only included solutions for creating a conference program. While not explicitly mentioned, the problems addressed were:

- *How to create an attractive and relevant conference program.*
- *Which types of sessions should the program offer and how to spread them across conference days.*
- *How to highlight relevant slots to conference participants online and on-site (offline).*
- *How to organize an efficient submission process for selecting conference contributions.*

Solutions were:

- *Type of program*: e.g., single track vs. multiple tracks.
- *Session length*: deciding how long each session should be.
- *Workshops*: planning and scheduling workshops at the conference.
- *Open space*: scheduling speakers, topics proposed by participants during the conference.
- *Multiple presentations per session:* have several related presentations at each conference session.
- *Paper program:* make the conference program available in an analog paper format.
- *Highlight what/where is happening (now): taking advantage what the digital version of the program can offer.*
- *Select my program:* make it possible for participants to mark the sessions/talks they would like to attend.
- *Ensuring peer review and publishing by hierarchy of editors:* make sure the organizers have enough qualified people to organize peer review and publication of proceedings [where applicable].
- *Clear and precise call for papers and instructions:* covering topics, manuscript formatting and length, as well as submissions and notification deadlines.
- *Transparent/timely feedback to submissions.*
- *(Flexible) Submission system:* a system for handling the selection (most often, peer review) of submitted papers.

3.3 Financial Aspects

This cluster included both problems and solutions related to conference budget, registration, sponsorship and other money-related aspects.

The problems listed by the participants included:

- *Changes in conference size:* as the conference grows bigger it might require different arrangements.
- *Estimate break-even:* how many participants (paid registrations) are required to cover the expences for organizing the conference.
- *Getting "true" numbers of previous years:* several participants mentioned that often conference only share marketing slogans like "big number of participants, great attendance" and it is hard to get real numbers to plan the next year edition.
- *Funding (who takes the risk/how to find):* this was perceived as fundamental for running a conference.
- *Financing (team, low-[income] attendees):* what is a viable ratio between free and paid registration?

The solutions proposed were:

- *[for Funding]*
  - *Corporate sponsorship*
  - *Local tourism grants: e.g., offered by several European cities, promoting tourism.*
  - *Expo hall.*
  - *Go to "small" cities/countries who will support the conference.*
  - *Check [local] laws to prevent problems.*
  - *Create & disseminate sponsorship plan.*
- *[for Financing]*
  - *Ensure having an organization owning the conference [finances]. Do not do it as a person!!*
  - *Transparency.*
  - *Draft budget.*

3.4 Logistics

This cluster included both problems and solutions addressing logistical aspects of organizing the conference, such as catering, registration, technical aspects of sessions, presentations.

The problems listed by the participants included:

- *Attendees with special needs (childcare, allergies).*
- *Catering.*
- *Ensure quality of online presentation.*
- *Infrastructure (Zoom accounts, cameras, microphones)*
- *Internet/ WiFi connectivity at the venue*

The solutions listed by the participants included:

- *Logistics resources and playbooks:* they help to pass the knowledge between organizers of different editions.
- *Name badges should include the name on both sides*
- *[for Catering]*
  - *Non-stop catering*
  - *Allergens [indicated next to food]*
  - *Special diets*
  - *Ensure food is good enough quality*
- *[for Quality of online presentation]*
  - *Stage manager ("Inspizient"): in theater, a stage manager is responsible for managing scenery and equipment for theatrical productions and other stage events. Similar solution applies in hybrid (online+offline) conference to increase the quality of online presentations.*

- *[for Infrastructure/Internet]*
  - *Online program.*
  - *Allow speakers to test laptop/slides/microphone.*
  - *Offer team assistance to speakers immediately before the session.*

3.5 Community

This cluster included both problems and solutions addressing the creation, curation, and expansion of the conference community.

The problems listed by the participants included:

- *Create a community:*
  - *Provide clear purpose + recommendation on who should attend.*
  - *Consider conference types [by number of participants]: 10–20/20–30/30–100/100–250/250–600/600–1200/1200+*
  - *Consider main activities, length, structure of the conference.*
  - *Celebrate [achievements, best papers, test of time awards].*
  - *Announce next edition (at the banquet, at the opening/closing session)..*
  - *Recruit next years' organizers at the current year' edition (or at least invite them to attend it).*
  - *Organize "conference retrospective" and gather feedback from participants. Then process them and turn into actions for future organizers.*
- *Start a new or continue the existing series?*
  - *If recurring conference, ensure succession plan for organizers.*
  - *Create a book of best practices/lessons learnt for further conference editions. A toolbox for organizers might include relevant spreadsheets, e-mail templates.*
- *How to support networking and participants' interaction?*
  - *Online community platforms.*
  - *Enough time for breaks and social events.*
  - *"Real" workshops, i.e. where participants do something together and not mini-conferences.*
  - *Maintain "past year" mailing list.*
- *How to get in touch with people as a new attendee?*
  - *Standing bar-like tables to connect easily.*
  - *Assign a "conference buddy" / Dinner with unknown friends.*
  - *Place name cards on lunch tables to shuffle participants.*
  - *Student tutor meeting.*
  - *Consider games, interactive sessions chaired by The Gamemaster which let people meet and informally introduce themselves.*

- *Inclusiveness* can be addressed by following solutions:
  - *Support visa invitations for the international attendees.*
  - *Scholarships or special price for students.*
  - *Live streaming and language translation (subtitles).*
- *How to draw industry participants to academic conferences* can be done by:
  - *Organizing an Industry Day.*
  - *Inviting speakers from industry.*
  - *Providing industry participants display booths.*
  - *Using companies' products or services during the conference.*
- *Marketing/communication to get attendees* can be solved as follows:
  - *Dedicated design team on graphics/visuals and social media.*
  - *Narratives [to target potential participants].*
  - *Testimonials from previous editions participants.*

3.6 Organizing Team

This cluster included problems and solutions for putting together an efficient team of organizers.

The problems listed were::

- *The committee has to ensure activity tracking for different stakeholders.*
- *Build a working committee/Assemble the right team.*
- *Getting things done, in particular, how to keep up with the deadlines?*

The solutions proposed included:

- *Trusted committee to take on tasks.*
- *Student volunteers.*
- *A pacemaker to remind about approaching task deadlines.*

3.7 Location

This cluster included solutions relevant to securing a good location. While not explicitly mentioned, the problem addressed was:

- *How to select an attractive location which meets financial constraints and can host enough participants?*

The proposed soultions included:

- *The conference can take place in the same location or move to the new one each year.*
- *In-house (university)* is an option, but one should consider if they have enough rooms and if the location is attractive enough.
- *Hotel* is another option, but one should take into account that one has to pay for the meeting rooms and might need to secure certain number of rooms for the participants.

- *How accessible is the location?*
- *Can attendees and speakers stay in the same location where the conference takes place?*
- *One can consider using meeting agencies, known venues and recommendations from the community* to select a good location.
- *Co-located smaller conferences/workshops* might make the conference more attractive.

3.8 Most Important Clusters

Results of voting:

- Financial aspects: 7
- Community: 7
- Program: 5
- Organizing team: 4
- Location: 3
- Logistics: 1

4 Discussion and Next Steps

The results show that the organizers of the conference should focus on the community and financial aspects, followed by the program. Organizers and location are also important, while logistics was perceived less important by the participants of the focus group.

In Sect. 3 we aimed at capturing the output of the participants with only minimum changes or explanations where we perceived they are required for readability and context. However, we also can summarize main findings, see a summary prepared by Microsoft Copilot (checked and modified by us) for the Location cluster.

When planning a conference, selecting the right location is crucial. The location can vary from year to year. Options include university venues, which may be cost-effective but require careful consideration of room availability and overall appeal, and hotels, which offer convenience but come with costs for meeting spaces and potential commitmen to block a certain number of rooms. Accessibility of the venue is key—both in terms of travel and whether attendees and speakers can stay onsite. To ensure a successful event, organizers might consult meeting agencies, rely on trusted venues, or seek recommendations from the community. Additionally, co-locating smaller workshops or conferences can enhance the event's attractiveness and value.

We also would like to have a closer look to the problem-solution imbalance. For instance, there were not explicit problems proposed for Program and Location. Is it because they are clear and do not require explicit statement, or unclear? We are planning to address this when writing patterns.

Reflecting on our expectations before the focus group and actual outcomes, the high importance of the financial aspects and low importance of logistics were unexpected. Ideally, we should repeat the exercise at several other conferences/workshops to include thoughts from more conference participants and organizers. However, not many conferences allow for focus group format.

We would like to further explore the top clusters and come up with several patterns representing the proposed solution. We might also consider organizing pattern mining workshops or focus groups dedicated to specific aspects, such as further exploring the conference participant's perspective.

Disclosure of Interests. Authors state that they have no competing interests.

Appendix. Bigger photos of flipcharts with problems and solutions.

(See Figs. 2, 3, 4 and 5)

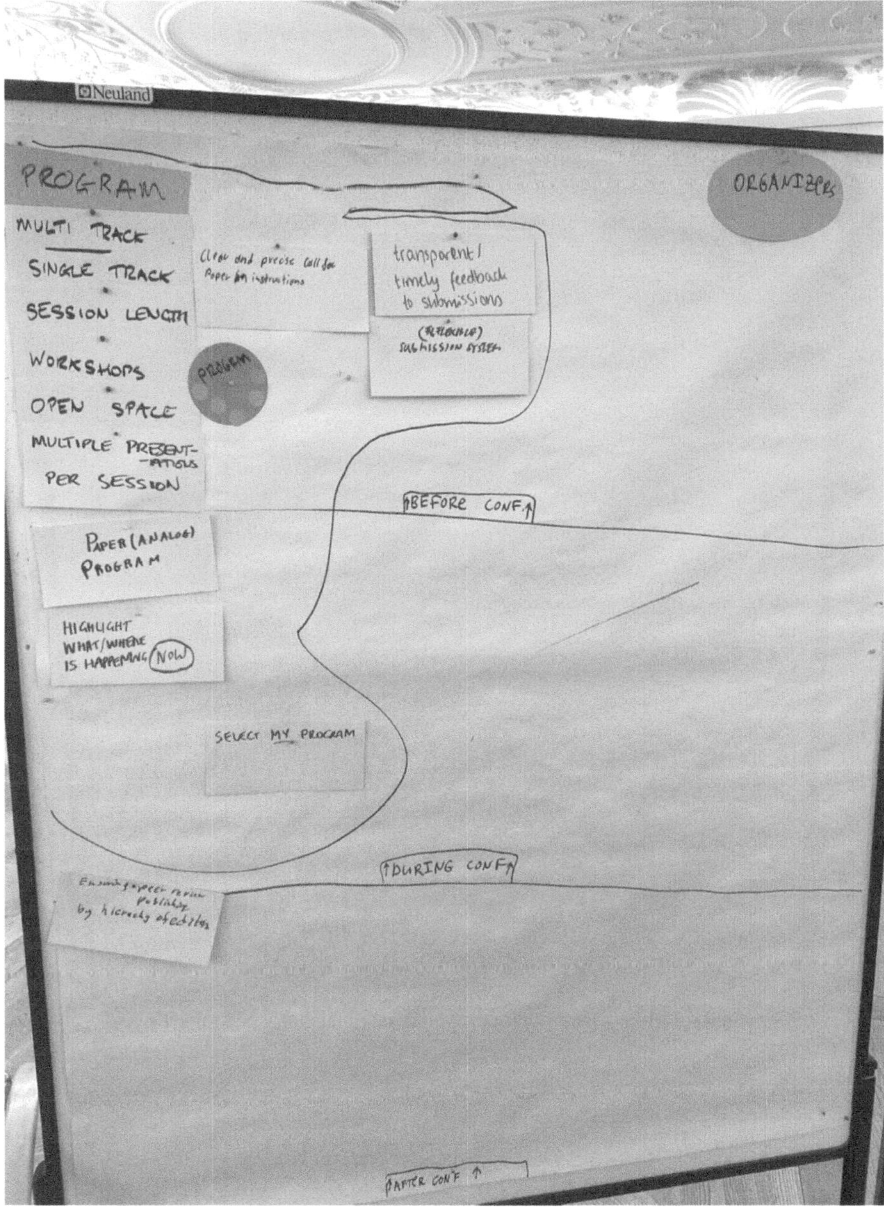

Fig. 2. Problems and solutions for conference1 organizers: Program cluster.

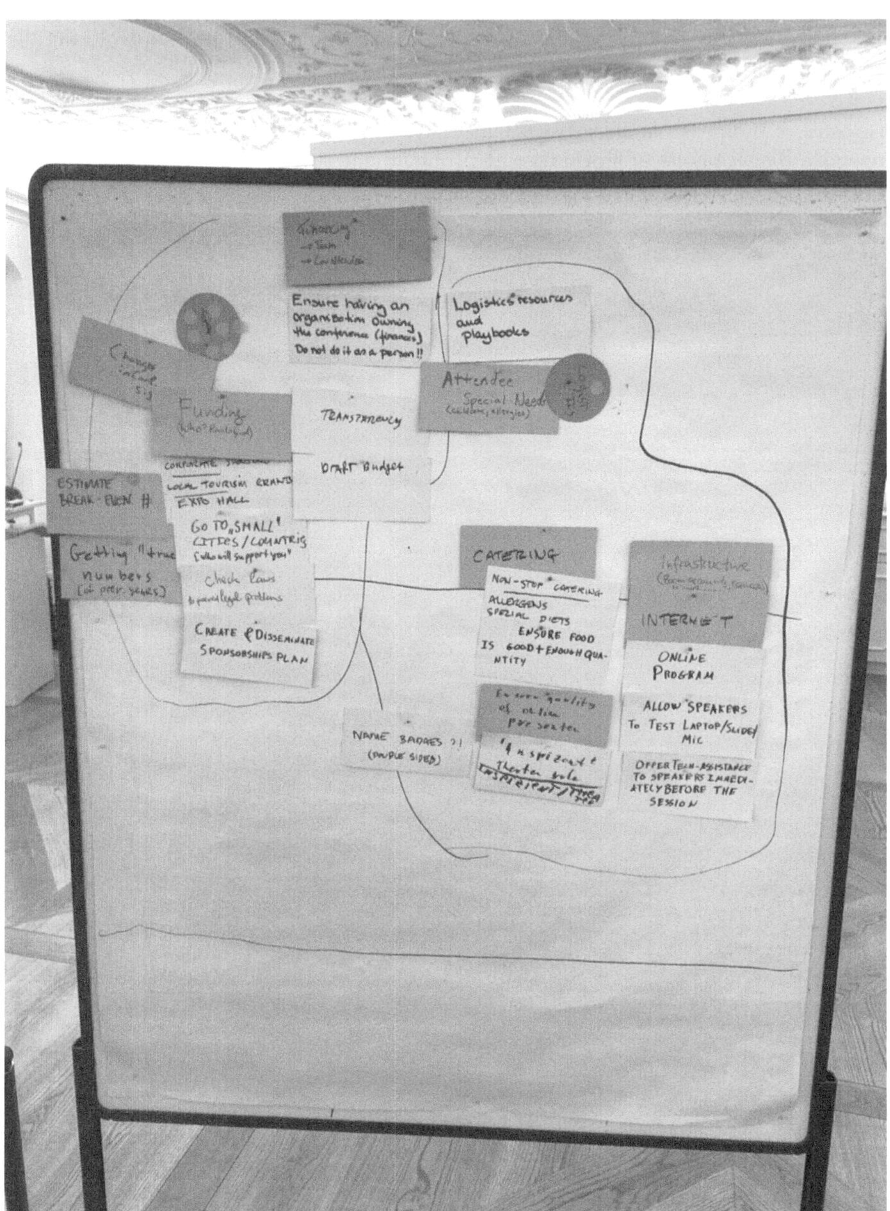

Fig. 3. Problems and solutions for conference organizers: Financial aspects and Logistics clusters.

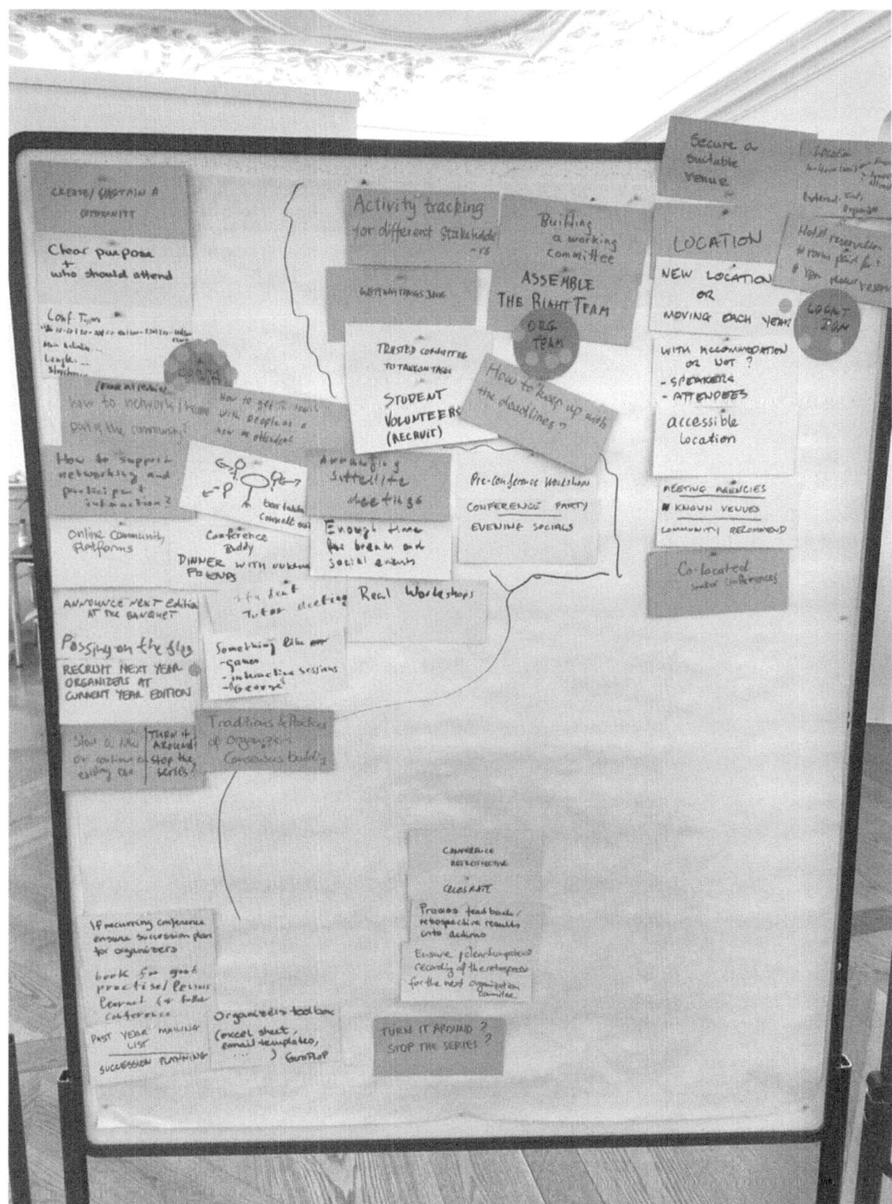

Fig. 4. Problems and solutions for conference organizers: Community, Organizing Team and Location clusters.

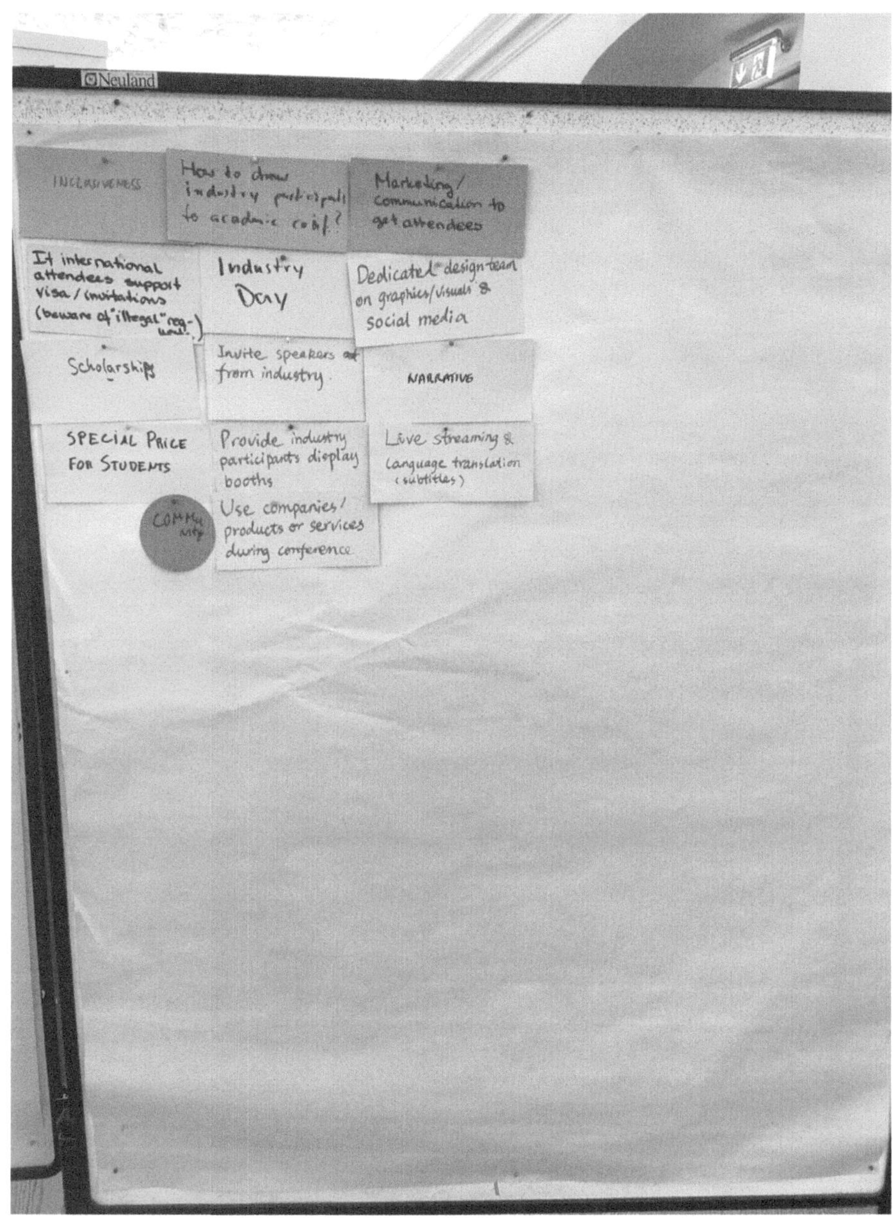

Fig. 5. Problems and solutions for conference organizers: Community cluster (continued).

References

1. Aliaksandr Birukou: How scientific conferences work. EuroPloP 2025 Part I, proceedings (2025)
2. Hvatum, L.B.: Patterns for organizing PLoP. In: Proceedings of the 17th Conference on Pattern Languages of Programs (PLOP '10), vol. 11, pp. 1–10. Association for Computing Machinery, New York, USA (2010). https://doi.org/10.1145/2493288.249329
3. Eto, K., Shibamura, S.: A pattern language for organizing events. In: Proceedings of the 1st Asian Conference on Pattern Languages of Programs (AsianPLoP '10), vol. 9, pp. 1–5. Association for Computing Machinery, New York, USA (2010). https://doi.org/10.1145/2371736.2371749
4. Akado, Y., Kogure, S., Sasabe, A., Hong, J.-H., Saruwatari, K., Iba, T.: Five patterns for designing pattern mining workshops. In: Proceedings of the 20th European Conference on Pattern Languages of Programs (EuroPLoP '15), vol. 9, pp. 1–13. Association for Computing Machinery, New York, USA (2015). https://doi.org/10.1145/2855321.2855331
5. Cathy Key: The Keynote Guide to Planning a Successful Conference. Keynote Networks Ltd. (2004), available at: https://spie.org/Documents/Students/Conference_guide.pdf
6. Kulamer, B., et al.: Recommended practices to ensure technical conference content quality. In: Originally Presented by Gordon MacPherson at the 4th World Conference on Research Integrity Rio De Janeiro, Brazil (2015)
7. Burford, J., Henderson, E.: Making Sense of Academic Conferences. Routledge, (2023)
8. Franken, J., Birukou, A., Eckert, K., Fahl, W., Hauschke, C., Lange, C.: Persistent identification for conferences. Data Sci. J. **21**, 11–11 (2022). https://doi.org/10.5334/dsj-2022-011

Exploring the Future of AI Learning through Music and Game Play

Mary Tedeschi[1(✉)], Joseph Corneli[2,5], Sergio Belich[3], Charles Jeffrey Danoff[4], Sridevi Ayloo[3], and Raymond Puzio[5]

[1] Pace University, New York, NY 10038, USA
mtedeschi@pace.edu
[2] Oxford Brookes University, Headington, Oxford OX3 0BP, UK
joseph.corneli@hyperreal.enterprises
[3] New York City College of Technology, Brooklyn, NY 11201, USA
{sbelich,sayloo}@citytech.cuny.edu
[4] Mr. Danoff's Teaching Laboratory, Chicago, IL 60613, USA
contact@mr.danoff.org
[5] Hyperreal Enterprises Ltd, G2 4JR, Glasgow, Scotland, UK

Abstract. We envisioned this focus group as more of a creative jam session than a traditional research activity. Laughter mixed with curiosity as participants imagined AI not as a tool, but as a bandmate offering melodies, suggesting rhythms, even challenging their musical instincts. Through spontaneous brainstorming and hands-on exercises, they explored how AI might co-create with artists. This playful experimentation echoed the spirit of the larger EuroPLoP conference, which centered on pattern recognition and collaborative learning fields where structure meets improvisation, and insight emerges from interaction. As AI is still scaling, there are "unknown unknowns" that need to be addressed as soon as possible. Our workshop explored these issues with AI-themed discussions (rather than being tied to any specific AI product). AI is frequently employed to grab attention, suggest innovation, or make something seem more advanced or futuristic than it may be. We wanted to engage participants in creative and critical thinking about such issues. The session concluded with a group reflection using the Project Action Review (PAR) technique, where participants reviewed personal insights and identified alternative research directions. Outcomes included the documentation of group reflections, a playful investigation of complex ideas, and the discovery of new connections among media, learning, and technology. We conducted a short pre- and post- survey, an analysis of which is included in our results.

Keywords: Artificial Intelligence · Expert Systems · Generative AI · Patterns · Project Action Review

1 Introduction

At EuroPLoP 2024, Mary Tedeschi led the "AI Future Envisioning with PLACARD" focus group in Germany, where three attendees participated in-person while others co-facilitated remotely. We used a futures studies technique and an interactive card game to

T. Plummer et al. (Eds.): EuroPLoP 2025, LNCS 16494, pp. 434–444, 2026.
https://doi.org/10.1007/978-3-032-19157-1_21

envision the future of AI, concluding the session with a co-created PAR that captured key learnings from the session. The workshop built on insights from six prior iterations of similar workshops in PLoP conferences [4]. In our previous focus group summary report, we identified as goals to "create 'dialogue' across [multiple] workshop interactions? What infrastructure would be needed to be able to make different sets of patterns and proto patterns (e.g., design prompts) interoperate?"

This year at EuroPLoP 2025, Mary and Sridevi Ayloo led a focus group onsite that experimented with a playful approach to the design and implementation of multiple interacting intelligent systems. We experimented with several simple rule-based systems, in which human workshop participants carried out the rules and reflected on the experience. Our overall aim was for the session to serve as a creative prompt; as such, the learning continued after the session was over. The workshop activities themselves broke down in the following sub-goals:

- **Framing**: To convey a sense of vibrant energy, to encourage participants to think in a creative way.
- **Interaction**: Building previous workshops, we wanted to experiment with media interactions. A session with a remote music teacher served both as an icebreaker and an experiment in remote-facilitated learning.
- **Game-play**: Last year we played a card game and explored AI making images in our paper. Inspired by the AI-supported card game Analogia [2, 3], we played Dixit in the focus group and used these ideas to explore AI making music.
- **Reflection**: We wanted to involve participants to build their capacity for reflection, and we used a structured methodology to achieve this.
- **Consolidation of learning**: We carried out a short survey to add to the body of knowledge we have been developing in the workshop series.
- **Implementation**: We demonstrated that a current AI tool could be brought into the mix, by creating a song based on participant contributions.

As a further research goal, we wanted to explore how AI can expand the human mind [13]; within the workshop itself, we did physical activities that were not directly using AI tools—but intended to prompt critical thinking about AI.

2 Workshop Activities

Mary Tedeschi introduced the session with a set of slides titled "Verve Sessions: Where AI Meets Music and Imagination." This was different from the original proposal name and flyer. The term "verve" was intentionally chosen to convey a sense of vibrant energy, enthusiasm, and creative spirit qualities we believed were essential for fostering a dynamic and memorable experience. Our introductory slides referred to "the vibrant spirit driving artistic and musical exploration". By invoking the idea of verve, we aimed to establish a tone of lively exploration and to distinguish our session as an engaging, imaginative space for discussing the intersection of AI, music, and learning. This framing helped set the stage for a focus group designed not only to inform but also to inspire. The outcomes envisioned included participants having fun and attendees learning how to play both the music and card games. The research goals of this experience were to explore how play-based learning, inspired by musical learning theory, can enhance the understanding and envisioning of future technologies like AI. By incorporating a technology-focused card game and a futures studies approach, the session aimed to demonstrate how interactive, playful environments can facilitate deeper, more creative thinking and engagement. The goal was to investigate how the process of co-creating future scenarios, through play and collaboration, supports learning and idea generation, while also making complex topics more accessible and memorable. This approach seeks to connect the theoretical foundations of musical learning—such as improvisation, exploration, and experiential knowledge—with the process of envisioning the future of AI. The experience was designed to connect to musical learning theory, emphasizing how people learn through play. Participants engaged in card games that further illustrated musical ideas, with opportunities to incorporate these games into music teaching. Ideas generated during the event were documented and captured in real-time in several artifacts, including a Project Action Review. This data is needed for PLoP 2025, which is following this event. The 5 participants were first-time PLoP attendees; they and the facilitators participated in all the activities, see Fig. 1. At the workshop, attendees had several suggestions about next steps for follow-up. First-time participants likely brought **unbiased, fresh viewpoints** unshaped by prior PLoP experiences or traditions. This aligns well with the **exploratory and imaginative nature** of futures envisioning work.

Fig. 1. - Facilitators and participants in the room.

2.1 Playful Engagement and Musical Exploration

Playful engagement refers to learning environments in which play (free or guided) forms a central mode of interaction — often emphasizing imagination, agency, intrinsic motivation, and creative exploration. In musical exploration, learners interact with sound, rhythm, improvisation, embodiment, and often collaboration [11]. Cris led this part of our session remotely from Brazil, guiding the five participants and the other facilitators. Her plan was to facilitate the group with guidance inspired by Música do Círculo [6], and by her own experience as a music educator, in active methodologies and consciousness expansion. The aim was to help the group feel more connected and creative, while encouraging them not only to think about patterns, but also to experience them in their own bodies.

The first step began with sounds such as a rhythmic pattern based on stepping-in-place, and a simple melody circulated around the circle. For example, participants would sing, "Lalalala, I'm Cris," followed by "Lalalala, I'm Mary," and so on, allowing everyone to remember each other's names while internalizing a shared rhythm. In the second step, an "arrow" gesture was introduced to call out specific individuals pointing to someone like Mary, who would then respond by saying her name.

The session then transitioned into a more playful and improvisational phase, initiated by a "wiggly arrow" gesture. This gesture signaled a shift in tone, prompting participants to respond with imaginative and evolved vocal expressions such as the spirited "Bipity boo, Mary." In the next step, another gesture was introduced to pass these transformed sounds around the circle, allowing participants to build on each other's contributions. Additional gestures were layered in, to help organize the sounds into distinct groupings, enhancing the sense of shared rhythm and creativity.

Fig. 2. - Online facilitation of an interactive musical exercise.

An additional component of the session (see Fig. 2) featured a musical interlude led by Cris, who introduced a special song rooted in Indigenous Brazilian traditions [9]. Brazil is home to approximately 305 Indigenous tribes, with a total Indigenous population of around 900,000 people. Cris demonstrated the song, and the group joined in seamlessly. The melody was easy to follow, encouraging full participation. (A participant from Brazil particularly liked this part.) The Indigenous Brazilian musical interlude is important because it brings cultural depth, emotional connection, and ethical reflection into a session focused on envisioning AI futures. It challenges dominant paradigms by honoring alternative worldviews, encourages inclusive participation, and reminds us that the future must be imagined with—not just for—diverse communities across the globe.

The experience culminated in a guided meditation, during which participants closed their eyes and engaged in a moment of collective stillness. In a short debrief, one of the facilitators in North America, Charlotte, remarked that it felt to her as though we were participating in a peaceful, synchronized movement that connected individuals across three continents, an evocative reminder of the power of music, gesture, and shared intention to transcend boundaries. For several participants, this segment felt spiritual and emotionally resonant.

We were not sure how many participants we would have, despite circulating a signup sheet in advance. Depending on the number of participants in the room, the group would have worked in either a single circle or multiple circles to ensure everyone was actively involved. It turned out we had a perfect number of people to use one circle for this workshop.

2.2 Dixit Card Game

Dixit is a creative, story-prompt card game designed by Jean-Louis Roubira and published in 2008 by Libellud [7]. The game consists of a deck of large, beautifully illustrated cards showing surreal, dreamlike scenes. It's usually played with 3–6 players.

A "storyteller" picks one card from their hand and gives a clue — a word, phrase, sound, or short story — that relates to the card. Other players choose cards from their hands that could also fit the clue. All cards are mixed and revealed, and players try to guess which card was the storytellers. Points are awarded based on correct or persuasive guesses. Unlike literal picture decks or flash cards, the illustrations are open-ended, which fosters deeper discussion. While Dixit is mainly a commercial game, it has been studied in psychology, education, and language learning.

Dixit was recommended by Cassandra Lee, MIT, in conversation, as we intended on using her Analogia Card Game instead or in addition to [4]. We introduced the Dixit [7] card game, in terms of its rules and scoring (with a slide "1 Minute How to Play"), and then played the game together. One participant knew the game previously. Everyone else was new to the game. Sridevi started the game as our first storyteller to give the participants an opportunity to understand the rules and learn how to play Dixit. After distributing the first round of six cards for each participant, Sridevi demonstrated how to play by selecting a card from the set of six cards in her hand and came up with a phrase for the selected card. She wrote the phrase on the flipchart so that all the participants knew what the phrase was. The participants, see Fig. 3., would then find a card from their set of six cards to match the phrase. Writing on a flipchart was not part of the original Dixit card game description. This step was used here to create active participation for first time Dixit card players, noting also that participants were from different countries/states/places where English need not be their first language.

During this phase, the remote co-facilitators played their own version of the game using the DixitWorld app [10]. Indeed, in our design of the in-person interactions, we drew some inspiration from this app. In the app, if a player is not available in real time, a chatbot takes the role of a player and performs the steps of selecting a phrase, after analyzing the image on the card.

The steps of writing the phrase and keeping the scores on the flipchart mirrored what we experienced with the app. We used paper disks on the floor to vote (in-person players would do this by pointing or by using tokens). In the workshop, we played a shortened version of the game (to 15 points rather than 30).

After completion of the game, we had a group discussion of Dixit in connection with AI research, and the future of music and AI (slide: "Dixit as a Window into AI Research"), with a design pattern orientation.

Fig. 3. - Online facilitation of interactive musical exercise.

2.3 Project Action Review

In the final session, we came together as one big group and had a discussion (see Fig. 4), looking for patterns across the two previous phases: music, games, and our discussion of the future of music with AI. Finally, we wrote up the findings, using the five questions of the Project Action Review [3]:

1. Review the intention: what do we expect to learn or make together?
2. Establish what is happening: what and how are we learning?
3. What are some different perspectives on what's happening?
4. What did we learn or change?
5. What else should we change going forward?

Procedurally, the online co-facilitators took notes on the discussion that was happening in the room; these were subsequently discussed in further online conversations when all co-facilitators reconvened to debrief.

In the PAR [4, 5], it was mentioned that Dixit is a model. Dixit models the challenge of giving a clue that is specific enough for some to guess, but vague enough to avoid being obvious to everyone. Other feedback came through in the PAR discussion, both about participants' experience of the session, including some "friction" that they experienced relative to the difference between their imagined idea of what the workshop would be about and what happened. This allowed us to reflect on the inevitability of interface friction in general. Participants also came up with creative suggestions to use AI to generate songs based on the workshop. We implemented this subsequently, by taking the Dixit clues and including some descriptive context about the EuroPLoP session as a prompt. We chose to use house and pop-jazz as the style to create new songs using Suno

Fig. 4. - The PAR was led by Joe and Charlie remotely

[12]. The song "Dixit Dreams" from Suno Model Version 3.5 provides a more abstract interpretative summary of the themes from the workshop:

[Verse]
Movie in the night I see
Sleepy fish floatin' free
Magic trick a silent show
Thinkin' deep nobody knows
[Prechorus]
Imagination is it real
Or just the way I feel
[Chorus]
Loneliness a painted card
Lonely is hard
Dixit dreams fall apart
Dixit dreams a work of art

We had previously encountered Suno in PLoP 2024, in the *Imagination Run Wild* session, "Deliver Your Patterns Through Song: A Hands-On Workshop on Creating Original Pattern Songs With Generative AI" [14].

3 Analysis / Survey Results

We gave the 5 participants a 5-question pre- and post-survey, with identical questions. They all answered everything. The survey, like other aspects of this workshop, was informative, rather than systematic. Our EuroPLoP 2025 focus group successfully achieved the hypothesized result of increasing participants' likelihood to use AI for patterns research. The 60% improvement in AI-patterns application intent and 40% improvement in general AI research adoption demonstrate a positive effectiveness of the session overall. Future sessions should maintain this application focus while strengthening foundational knowledge components.

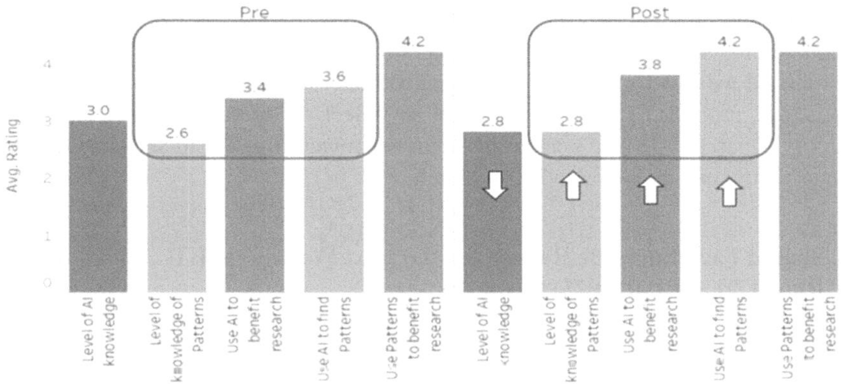

Fig. 5. – Average pre & post survey responses from surveys. The Likert scales for the level of knowledge questions were "1-No Knowledge" to "5-Expert" and the scale for the other questions were "1-Not at all" to "5-Extremely".

In Fig. 5 above, three questions surveyed increased slightly, and one decreased slightly in the post test. It's possible that as individuals learn more about the intricacies of AI, they become more aware of the limits of their own knowledge.

4 Discussion

Long before AI became today's buzzword, people were exploring computational intelligence under the name "expert systems". In computer labs filled with glowing CRT monitors, we experimented with VP-Expert [1], a standout tool of the late 1980s and early 1990s. It wasn't flashy, but it gave us a hands-on way to model expertise and for many of us, it was our first real taste of machine reasoning. According to Sylvia Friederich, "An inference engine [...] acts as the 'brain' of the system, simulating human-like reasoning." [8] In our 2025 EuroPLoP session, computers were used in a more incidental way: to bring co-facilitators from North and South America, and the UK, to our in-person breakout session in Germany. These co-facilitators acted as both experts and as remote peers.

4.1 Was this Effective?

Yes and no. While there were some positive outcomes, some technical aspects of the remote delivery of the music portion were challenging; participants asked why this portion was done remotely. We want to think more about this in the future: do we use an external expert (with some interface friction) or do we train someone with less expertise for local delivery? One possible relationship between Dixit and design patterns is that they both celebrate productive ambiguity, not too specific and not too vague. Indeed, images are always amenable to interpretation; in a social context discussing images, we must incorporate others' perspectives. We began with a guided music exercise led by a music teacher to explore human creativity and interpretation of sound. We then played the card game Dixit, which allowed us to experience ambiguous prompts, multiple interpretations, and group evaluation in a playful visual format. Only after these two activities did we experiment with AI-generated music, using themes from the previous exercises as prompts. This sequencing let us reflect on human-only and AI-assisted creativity separately before comparing them and made it easier to see shared design patterns across music, Dixit, and AI research.

4.2 Should Facilitators Be Remote for the Next Workshop (E.G., Imagination Run Wild at PLoP 2025)?

This remains an open question. Given the students' response to remote instruction—particularly in the music segment, it may be more effective to prioritize having all facilitators on-site.

4.3 What Are we Saying about AI? What Are we Proving?

We administered the same five questions to participants before and after the session. Pre-survey responses showed that most participants already had a baseline of knowledge of 3 ("Comfortable") on average. The post-survey revealed modest gains, but many responses remained unchanged. This suggests that while some learning took place, the intervention did not lead to significant shifts in understanding (which makes sense because we had not primarily intended to have the workshop be didactic in nature). During the session, students suggested turning the Dixit clues into a song, an imaginative idea we had not anticipated. Broadly, the evidence is that the main outcome is that attendees increased their confidence in thinking and talking about AI. Fostering this kind of creative element would require intentional planning in future iterations.

4.4 What about the Card Games?

Should we reconsider the choice of card game? Would offering multiple games simultaneously enhance engagement? These remain open possibilities. Games and play offer unique spaces for collaboration, collective creativity, and nuanced identity expression. In a world increasingly polarized by social media, we explored how intentionally designed games can encourage healthy and constructive dialogue.

5 Future Work

We are interested in exploring interactions between different card games and have planned a workshop on this theme for PLoP 2025. We have planned another workshop that explores the use of reflection methods for rapid pattern language creation. In our 2025 PLoP paper, we look at how contemporary Large Language Model-based AI tools can work directly in the pattern language format. One possible route for further work would be to combine all these features in a pattern-language generation computer game, using AI tools.

Acknowledgements. Apart from the organizers the focus group attracted 5 participants: Maximilian Nixdorf, Rita Peixoto, Marcelo Nunes, Phineas Speicher, Simon Furrer. We had 90 min to have an active session. We would like to express our gratitude to Pace University for funding this research. A special thank you to Dennis Dubbert from the Cologne Institute for Digital Ecosystems for his invaluable tech support and assistance with the focus group handout for the conference. We also appreciate Cassandra Lee for her insightful discussions and Sylvia Friedrich for sharing her expertise in writing an expert systems book. Thank you to Charlotte Pierce and Cris Viseu for their feedback on drafts of this paper. We used ChatGPT to create the first draft of the paper, namely by converting the workshop proposal into a narrative outline. This has since been thoroughly rewritten by us! Thanks to Richard Karcher for guidance and review of this paper. We also thank Shankar Ayloo for the photos.

Disclosure of Interests. There are no conflicting interests.

References

1. Friedrich, S., Gargano, M.: Expert Systems Design and Development Using Vp-Expert. John Wiley & Sons, New York, NY (1989)
2. Lee, C., Dimitrakopoulou, D., Roy, D.: Meeting at crossroads: an exploration of playful listening through a co-creative AI game. In: Proceedings of the Extended Abstracts of the CHI Conference on Human Factors in Computing Systems (CHI EA '25), vol. 392, pp. 1–11. Association for Computing Machinery, New York, NY, USA (2025). https://doi.org/10.1145/3706599.3719767
3. Chen, T., Lee, C., Mindel, J.R., Elhaouij, N., Picard, R.: Closer worlds: using generative AI to facilitate intimate conversations. In: Extended Abstracts of the 2023 CHI Conference on Human Factors in Computing Systems (CHI EA '23), vol. 68, pp. 1–15. Association for Computing Machinery, New York, NY, USA (2023). https://doi.org/10.1145/3544549.3585651
4. Tedeschi, M., Ricaurte, P., Ayloo, S., Corneli, J., Danoff, C.J., Belich, S.: AI future envisioning with PLACARD. In: Proceedings of the 29th European Conference on Pattern Languages of Programs, People, and Practices (EuroPLoP '24), vol. 36, pp. 1–7. Association for Computing Machinery, New York, NY, USA (2024) https://doi.org/10.1145/3698322.3698444
5. Corneli, J., Danoff, C.J., Pierce, C., Ricaurte, P., Macdonald, L.S.: Patterns of peeragogy. In: Proceedings of the 22nd Conference on Pattern Languages of Programs (PLoP '15), vol. 29, pp. 1–23. The Hillside Group, USA (2015) https://dl.acm.org/doi/abs/10.5555/3124497.3124531
6. LEADING MÚSICA DO CÍRCULO 2023.: https://www.musicadocirculo.com/leading-mdc-copy-1, Accessed 30 Sep 2025
7. Dixit.: https://www.libellud.com/en/our-games/dixit/, Accessed 30 Sep 2025
8. Friederich, S.: Interview by Mary Tedeschi, Expert Systems Design and Development Using VP-Expert, by interviewee with Gargano, M., John Wiley & Sons, p. 5–6 (1989)
9. Ohj ohj á Gorá roi roi agorá Cantiga de Gorá (Ikolen-Gavião).: https://www.cantosdafloresta.com.br/audios/ohj-ohj-gora/, Accessed 30 Sep 2025
10. Tempete Studio Dixit World (Version 1.0.4) Mobile application software: Apple App Store. https://apps.apple.com/us/app/dixit-world/id1340833766
11. Zachariou, A., Bonneville-Roussy, A., Hargreaves, D., et al.: Exploring the effects of a musical play intervention on young children's self-regulation and metacognition. Metacognition Learn. **18**, 983–1012 (2023). https://doi.org/10.1007/s11409-023-09342-1
12. Danoff, C.J..: Dixit Dreams, https://suno.com/song/8375ff9e-0471-46de-8b6b-544de1eecd98?sh=ZP6k57YxBuPdwIgY, Accessed 30 Sep 2025

13. Savage, N.: Can AI Expand the Human Mind? Communications of the ACM, 68(10), 12–14. (2025)https://doi.org/10.1145/3748644
14. Iba, T., et al.: Deliver your patterns through song!—a hands-on workshop on creating original pattern songs with generative AI. In: Proceedings of 31st Conference on Pattern Languages of Programs, People, and Practices, PLoP 2024. ACM, Skamania Lodge, Columbia River Gorge, WA, USA (2025). https://doi.org/10.64346/PLoP2024p18

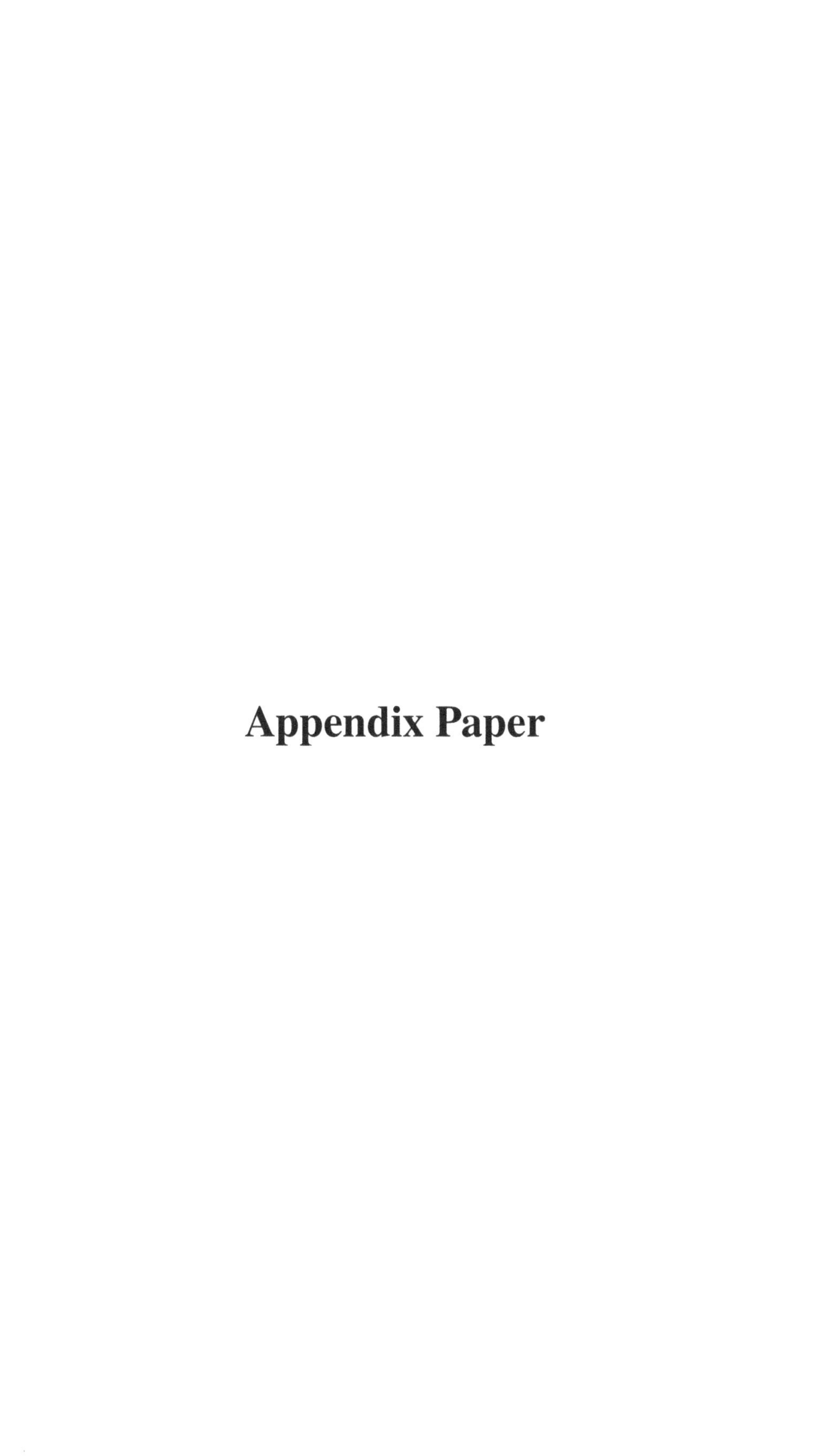

Appendix Paper

The Art of EuroPLoP 2025 A 30th Anniversary Retrospective

Fig. 1. Visual Emblem of the 30th Anniversary: The key artwork symbolizing EuroPLoP's enduring journey and the collaborative spirit of its community.

The European Conference on Pattern Languages of Programs (EuroPLoP) 2025 marked a significant milestone, celebrating its 30th anniversary. To commemorate this special occasion and capture the unique, collaborative atmosphere of the conference, we were delighted to host our long-time visual collaborator,

T. Plummer et al. (Eds.): EuroPLoP 2025, LNCS 16494, pp. 447–455, 2026.
https://doi.org/10.1007/978-3-032-19157-1

Sandy Linh Deimel, who has served as the designer of the conference logos and visual identity for many years (Fig. 1).

Mrs. Deimel attended EuroPLoP 2025 as an Artist-in-Residence, dedicated to creating a series of live drawings and visual summaries of the conference activities. Her work represents an artistic interpretation intended to capture the unique character and spirit of the events, meaning some renderings are closer to literal occurrences than others. These drawings uniquely utilize the pervasive, insider theme of the "sheep" and the "shepherd" to depict participants. This motif is drawn directly from the core EuroPLoP culture, where the paper review process, known as shepherding, designates authors as 'Sheep' and their dedicated mentors/reviewers as 'Shepherds'. By depicting participants as sheep, Mrs. Deimel not only rendered the activities in her distinct and charming style but also visually embodied this central cultural practice of collaborative improvement that defines the conference.

We extend our sincere gratitude to Sandy Linh Deimel for her creative presence and for providing these lasting visual records that capture the essence and special joy of our 30th-anniversary event.

The subsequent sections of this appendix present a curated selection of Ms. Deimel's live sketches, focusing particularly on the social gatherings, working groups, and celebratory anniversary activities that defined this memorable event.

A1. Copyright and Licensing Information

A.2 Welcoming and Introductory Session

The conference commences with the Welcoming and Introductory Session, a crucial gathering where participants are briefed on the event's structure, the philosophy of Pattern Languages, and the protocols of the Writers' Workshop format. This session also serves as the first opportunity for attendees to network and establish initial connections, setting a collaborative tone for the days ahead (Fig. 2).

Fig. 2. The Welcoming Session: Depiction of participants meeting and receiving the initial conference overview.

A3. The Writers' Workshops and Focus Groups

The Writers' Workshop is the central, high-value component of EuroPLoP. These intense but highly effective group discussion sessions are dedicated to providing constructive, in-depth feedback on submitted papers. Participants deeply value this focused collaboration, which is essential for authors to significantly improve their work with the guidance of their peers and mentors. A unique and integral aspect of this format is that authors attend their own workshop as 'flies on the wall', strictly listening and documenting the feedback without participating in the discussion of their paper. The drawings capture the focus and energy of these collaborative moments and the author's observational role.

A complementary set of daily activities are the Focus Groups. These sessions offer a chance for participants to prepare workshops for others, often serving as exploratory sessions to investigate new themes or domains that have not yet resulted in a publication. Brainstorming sessions are frequently employed to collectively discuss these areas and contribute shared experiences, paving the way for future publications. Additionally, some Focus Groups facilitate interactive learning experiences where participants can acquire and practice good practices within a specific domain (Fig. 3).

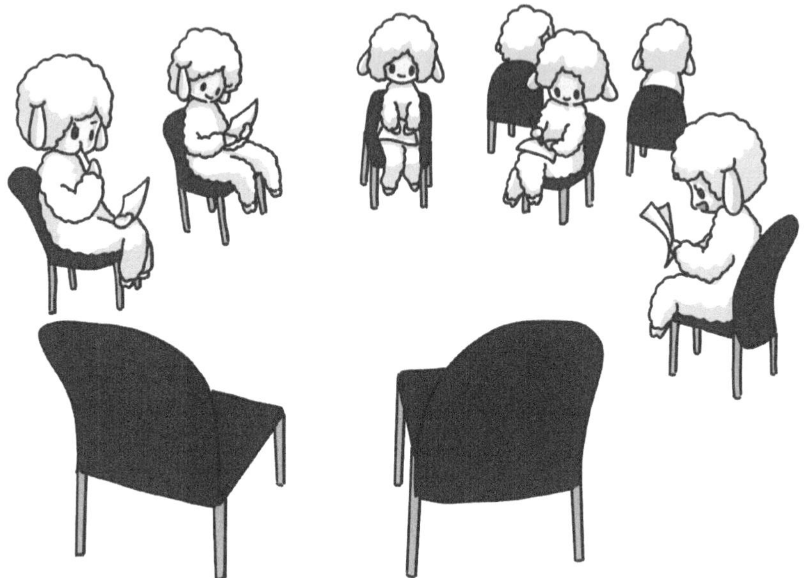

Fig. 3. The Writers' Workshop in action: Illustration of the intense, constructive discussion typical of the core conference activity.

A.4 Daily Social Sessions and Summaries

The EuroPLoP conference places high value on establishing strong personal bonds and an atmosphere of mutual trust, as these foundations are critical for the demanding feedback cycles in the Writers' Workshops. Two interwoven daily activities address both stress relief and academic knowledge exchange.

Daily social sessions are dedicated to stress relief and strengthening personal bonds among participants through relational building exercises. This daily ritual is vital, as the deeper personal connection and trust established here make the critical, in-depth feedback exchanged during the workshops significantly more bearable and constructive (Fig. 4).

The daily summaries are plenary sessions held at the close of each day where the entire conference gathers for vital knowledge exchange. Representatives from workshop groups share key insights and progress from their tracks, ensuring the whole community remains informed (Fig.5).

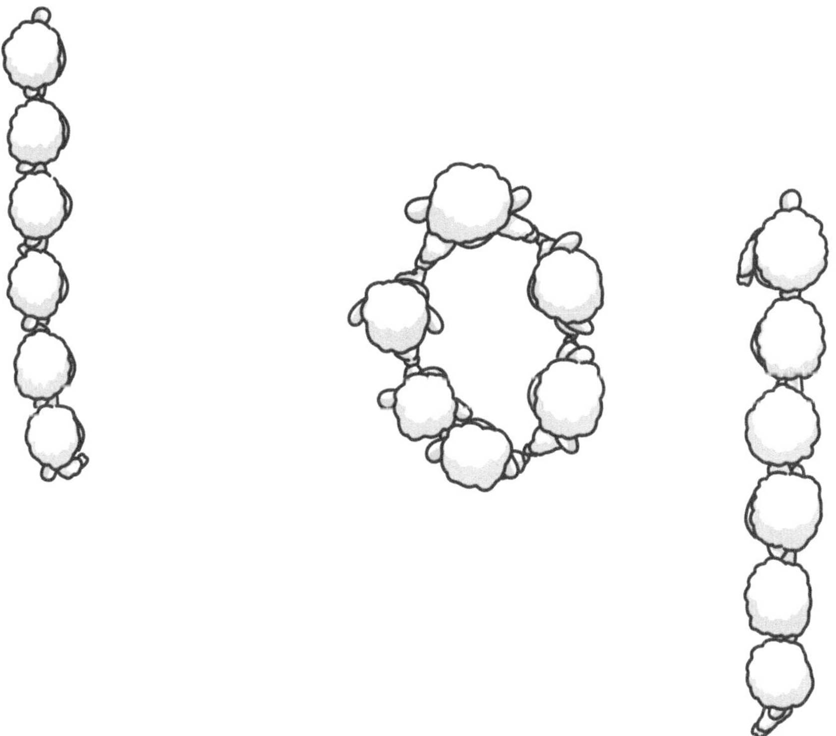

Fig. 4. Daily Social Session: Symbolic visualization of relational exercises, fostering stress relief and establishing the trust essential for critical Writers' Workshop feedback.

Fig. 5. Daily Summaries: Symbolic visualization of communal support, highlighting the group's active role in upholding and appreciating the presenter's contributions.

A.5 Evenings at EuroPLoP

After the intense intellectual demands of the day, EuroPLoP offers a wealth of recreational and social options, designed to encourage holistic participation and allow attendees to unwind in a manner of their choosing. Following dinner, the evening becomes participant-driven, with attendees naturally congregating in various spaces to build lasting connections.

Some opt for the informal socializing that occurs in the Keller (Cellar). This deeply anticipated setting fosters connection, where participants discuss the day's events, recap workshops, and explore intellectual or technical topics that deepen personal acquaintances and often leads to new ideas and future collaborations (Fig. 6).

Fig. 6. Informal Cellar Socializing: Highly anticipated evening gathering for drinks, relaxed discussion, and inspiring future collaborations.

Simultaneously, others engage in the recreational variety of activities aimed at mental decompression and recharging. The conference environment facilitates this through options like the sauna, or a fully equipped gaming room featuring competitive games such as table tennis, darts, pool, and kicker. These parallel activities ensure that everyone finds a comfortable outlet for relaxation and community bonding outside the academic focus (Fig. 7).

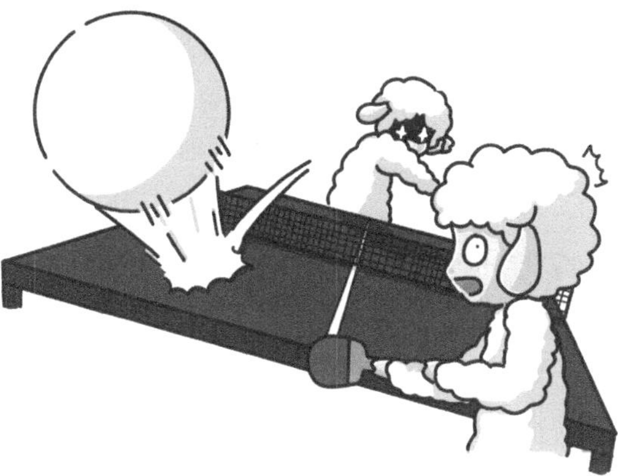

Fig. 7. Recreational Variety: Depiction of diverse evening recreational options, such as competitive table tennis, underscoring non-academic community bonding.

A.6 Special Single-Night Events

The conference schedule also features unique events held only once during the conference, offering distinctive breaks from the core activities. These single-night gatherings celebrate achievements and provide contrasting avenues for community bonding.

The Paint and Create offers a vital break from the intellectual intensity of the workshops. All participants gather one evening to engage in creative activities, providing a lighter, wholly non-academic outlet focused on co-creativity and shared enjoyment (Fig. 8).

In contrast to the creative session, the Banquet, typically held on the penultimate evening, is a formal gathering that celebrates the success of the intense collaborative work completed thus far. The evening serves as a dedicated opportunity to toast the community's successful work and collaboration, culminating in the presentation of various prizes to participants to recognize their special contributions, achievements, and unique service to the Pattern Languages community, most notably the prestigious Best Shepherd Award (Fig. 9).

Fig. 8. The Paint and Create event: View of the evening session, capturing the fun and co-creativity of the social interaction.

Fig. 9. The Banquet and Awards Ceremony: Illustration of the formal celebration, specifically capturing the moment of handing over the prestigious Best Shepherd Award.

A.7 The Closing Session: Celebrating Connections

The final ending session serves as the formal conclusion of the conference. It is a time for the entire community to gather, collectively relive the highlights of the past days, and offer final thanks to everyone who contributed to the event's success. A particularly emphasized part of this session is the celebration of the new professional and personal connections made. The artwork for this section visually encapsulates the true, lasting value of EuroPLoP - the cumulative network of relationships that participants build and carry with them (Fig. 10).

Fig. 10. The Closing Session: Metaphorical depiction of the conference's true value. A sheep covered with many threads of wool, symbolizing the cumulative wealth of new relations and connections gained at EuroPLoP that the participant can carry forward.

Author Index

T. Plummer et al. (Eds.): EuroPLoP 2025, LNCS 16494, p. 457, 2026.
https://doi.org/10.1007/978-3-032-19157-1

The manufacturer's authorised representative in the EU is Springer Nature Customer Service Centre GmbH, Europaplatz 3, 69115 Heidelberg, Germany. If you have any concerns regarding our products, please contact ProductSafety@springernature.com

Printed and bound by CPI Group (UK) Ltd, Croydon, CR0 4YY
07/07/2026
02160917-0015